SIXTH EDITION

AMERICAN BUSINESS VALUES

A GLOBAL PERSPECTIVE

Gerald F. Cavanagh, S.J.

Interim Dean

Charles T. Fisher III Chair of Business Ethics

Professor of Management

College of Business Administration

University of Detroit Mercy

Prentice Hall
Upper Saddle River, New Jersey

Library of Congress Cataloging-in-Publication Data

Cavanagh, Gerald F.
  American business values : a global perspective/Gerald F. Cavanagh, S.J.—6th ed.
    p. cm.
  Includes bibliographical references and index.
  ISBN-13: 978-0-13-607829-6 (alk. paper)
  ISBN-10: 0-13-607829-X (alk. paper)
  1. Business ethics—United States.   2. Industries—Social aspects—United States.   3. Social
responsibility of business—United States.   4. Free enterprise—United States.   I. Title.
HF5387.C379 2010
174'.40973—dc22

2008054696

Acquisitions Editor: Jennifer M. Collins
Editorial Director: Sally Yagan
Product Development Manager: Ashley Santora
Editorial Assistant: Elizabeth Davis
Editorial Project Manager: Claudia Fernandes
Marketing Manager: Nikki Jones
Marketing Assistant: Ian Gold
Permissions Project Manager: Charles Morris
Senior Managing Editor: Judy Leale
Production Manager: Wanda Rockwell
Creative Director: Jayne Conte
Cover Designer: Lisbeth Axell
Cover Illustration/Photo: Getty images, inc.
Full-Service Project Management: Integra Software Services Inc.
Printer/Binder: Bind-Rite/Command Web
Typeface: 10/12 Times

Credits and acknowledgments borrowed from other sources
and reproduced, with permission, in this textbook appear on
appropriate page within text.

Pearson Education Ltd., London
Pearson Education Singapore, Pte. Ltd
Pearson Education, Canada, Inc.
Pearson Education–Japan
Pearson Education Australia PTY, Limited

Pearson Education North Asia, Ltd., Hong Kong
Pearson Educación de Mexico, S.A. de C.V.
Pearson Education Malaysia, Pte. Ltd
Pearson Education Upper Saddle River,
  New Jersey

Prentice Hall
is an imprint of

www.pearsonhighered.com

10 9 8 7 6 5 4 3 2 1
ISBN-13: 978-0-13-607829-6
ISBN-10:   0-13-607829-X

CONTENTS

PREFACE

American Business Values: A Global Perspective, 6th ed., examines the ethics and values of businesspeople and business itself. A person's values have a pivotal influence on people's actions. Ethics and values influence leadership, innovation, product quality, on-the-job relationships, and government regulations. Moreover, work and business influence our personal goals, values, and life styles. American business values will be our primary focus. But we will also examine how those values affect people and business globally, and how American values are in turn being shaped by globalization.

The purpose of this book is to enable each person to:

- Understand how personal goals, values, and character mature, and how you can affect that development;
- Develop one's ability to make ethical judgments and to act ethically both within and outside the firm;
- Understand the strengths and weaknesses of the free market system;
- Gain insight on the environmental, social, political, and ethical issues that face us, and recognize the responsibilities of citizen, manager, and business firm;
- Grasp how one's character and integrity affect self, firm, family, and society.

A long-range view is required if business managers are to meet the needs of people in the global marketplace. This requires a plan that respects the needs of all stakeholders. Policies and plans that are effective for the firm require a consensus within that organization. That consensus builds on an understanding of the firm's mission and values. History and tradition also have a strong influence, so we will examine historical events that effect business.

Free markets around the world have been immensely successful in providing goods, services, and jobs to billions of people. Energetic and creative entrepreneurs, managers, and workers have made business effective. However, an ethical value is sometimes overlooked: the dignity of *each* individual person. Business actions and policies are ethical when they consider all who are touched by that decision—not only shareholders and managers, but also employees, customers, suppliers, neighbors, and community.

This sixth edition of *American Business Values: A Global Perspective* retains the best elements of the fifth, yet adds important new features. We investigate the changing values of industrialized peoples, especially Americans. Moreover, we also spotlight the way a firm's values influence a person's values, and the way that the values of the person can influence the organization. Chapter 1 examines Wall Street's strategies, outsourcing, advertising, the media, free market fundamentalism, financial and ethical bankruptcies, and restoring trust to business. Chapter 2 examines how we develop moral maturity, as well as the stress we face in life and at work. Chapter 3 provides models and skills that enable us to make ethical decisions, and shows how ethical behavior benefits the firm and how virtue can be developed. Chapters 4 and 5 probe the influential historical roots of American business. Chapter 6 investigates the limitations of the free market system, along with more cooperative alternatives. Chapter 7 examines personal values and beliefs and how they are influenced by the organization. Chapter 8 analyzes how values and ethics affect the performance of the firm. Chapter 9 studies the global market place, along with global climate change, sweatshops, micro loans, speculation, and global codes of conduct. Chapter 10 investigates sustainability, mission statements, spirituality at work, and business planning, and foresees shifts in future business values. Each chapter provides questions for discussion, additional readings, brief cases, and exercises that will help to clarify the issues.

This book is the result of research and enriching dialogue with businesspeople, scholars, and students. Charles Fornaciari was an immense help and support for the sixth edition. He rewrote three of the chapters, critiqued others, and did the index. Thanks to the University of Detroit Mercy and the faculty of the College of Business Administration for their support. Thanks also to editors Jennifer Collins Claudia Fernandes and Sadagoban Balaji of Prentice Hall for their help on this sixth edition.

Gerald F. Cavanagh, S.J.

Interim Dean
Charles T. Fisher III Chair of Business Ethics and
Professor of Management
College of Business Administration
University of Detroit Mercy
Detroit, Michigan

1

■ ■ ■

Free Markets Need
Ethical Norms

*Is it enough for Harvard to attract the brightest students, if we do not
excel in making them caring, active, enlightened citizens and civic
leaders?*

DEREK BOK, TWICE PRESIDENT, HARVARD UNIVERSITY

*The serious or complex problems we face cannot be solved by the
consciousness that created them.*

ALBERT EINSTEIN (1879–1955), NOBEL PRIZE–WINNING PHYSICIST

Entrepreneurs and business managers set the tone for our society. Their firms
provide the jobs, products, and services that we need. Innovative products and
services like Apple's iPhone, Google's search engine, and Toyota's Prius are now
part of our cultural landscape. Steve Jobs, Bill Gates, Larry Page, and Sergey Brin
are successful and highly rewarded businesspeople. Their goals, attitudes, and
activities heavily influence our personal goals and values. A businessperson's
values influence relationships with colleagues, customers, suppliers, and shareholders; affect the amount of leisure time the businessperson has; and ultimately
determine the person's success or failure. Business has more influence over most
of us than government or church and, in some cases, even more than our own
family; it is the dominant institution in our society. Businesspeople in most
nations are models for behavior, both good and bad. Because globalization is
extending free markets throughout the world, many other peoples are now being
pulled, often reluctantly, toward these same values. Let us examine the case of the
late Sam Walton and the company he founded, Wal-Mart.

Sam Walton has changed our purchasing habits and our values. Not only does Wal-Mart provide products, services, and jobs that we need, but its methods have an important influence on our lives. Wal-Mart is the largest, most successful, and profitable retailer in the world. Its business plan—low price, customer service, control of inventory—has become a model that is followed by business firms throughout the world. In the past, it has been listed as one of "America's Most Admired Companies."[1] The successes and limitations of Wal-Mart tell us much about the goals and values of business and businesspeople today.

THE SUCCESS OF WAL-MART

Sam Walton founded the first Wal-Mart store in 1962, the same year that Kmart and Target began. Walton heard about the new discount stores in the early 1960s, and copied winning strategies from around the world. Walton started with the principle "Give people high value, low prices and a warm welcome." Sam Walton visited each store and told his associates who work there, "I want you to promise that whenever you come within 10 feet of a customer, you will look him in the eye, greet him and ask if you can help him." Today, there are more than 1.9 million associates working at over 7,300 Wal-Mart stores and Sam's Clubs across 14 markets with over \$374 billion in annual revenue and almost \$12.88 billion in profits in its 2008 fiscal year.[2] Wal-Mart is the world's largest employer and retailer. Some estimate that more than one-tenth of U.S. productivity gains have come because of Wal-Mart's press for lower prices.

Wal-Mart has mastered information technology and global supply chain management, and this contributes to the success of their policy of "everyday low prices." Labor costs are also low, reflecting what Sam Walton said, "No matter how you slice it in the retail business, payroll is one of the most important parts of overhead, and overhead is one of the most crucial things you have to fight to maintain your profit margin."[3] These same skills enabled Wal-Mart to get emergency food, supplies, and equipment to the U.S. Gulf Coast after Hurricane Katrina struck in August 2005—much more quickly than the U.S. Government's Federal Emergency Management Agency was able to respond. Within two weeks of Katrina's landfall, Wal-Mart had reopened 111 of the 126 stores closed in preparation for the hurricane—even though 89 had sustained some form of storm-related damage.[4]

Most of Wal-Mart's stores have historically been in small towns, but now it is expanding to cities. This strategy has not been without its problems, however. Wal-Mart suffered a setback in the case of a proposed store in the Los Angeles suburb of Inglewood. The City Council rejected Wal-Mart's request for a building

---

[1] "America's Most Admired Companies: Recent Bad Press Hasn't Dimmed the Business World's Affection for Wal-Mart," *Fortune*, March 8, 2004, pp. 27–30.
[2] From Wal-Mart Web site: http://walmartstores.com/AboutUs/ and http://walmartstores.com/media/resources/r_2533.pdf, accessed May 6, 2008.
[3] Simon Head, "Inside the Leviathan," *New York Review of Books*, December 16, 2004.
[4] Ann Zimmerman and Valerie Bauerlein, "At Wal-Mart, Emergency Plan has a Big Payoff," *The Wall Street Journal*, September 12, 2005, p. B1.

permit. The firm then hired people to gather petitions to put the question on the ballot, but 60 percent of the voters rejected the proposal to put up the store and to exempt it from environmental review, traffic studies, and public hearings with regard to building the store. Likewise, in 2008 Chicago Mayor Richard Daley vetoed an application by the firm to open a store in the city's South Side. Today Wal-Mart has only one store within the Chicago city limits.[5] When it locates in a city, Wal-Mart provides much needed low-cost goods, jobs, and tax revenue and often uses a facility that had been abandoned. However, Wal-Mart acknowledges that it too often has been insensitive to local needs, and promises that it will do better in the future; critics say it still has a long way to go.[6]

When Wal-Mart comes to a new community, it has an immense advantage in its purchasing power and efficiency and thus forces many local retailers to close. Moreover, when setting up a new store, Wal-Mart generally obtains substantial local subsidies and tax breaks as the community builds new roads and water and sewer lines. In coming to a new town, Wal-Mart claims that it will add new jobs and new tax revenue. However, data show this is often not true. The local community ends up with much the same in taxes and jobs. In some locations, such as Cathedral City, California, Wal-Mart left the town when the tax breaks expired. This leaves the city with a hollowed out downtown, a large empty building, lost jobs, and huge shortfalls in tax revenues. A report found that Wal-Mart has collected more than $1 billion in state and local government subsidies during its decades-long expansion. The report finds some value in subsidizing inner-city sites, but questions the use of public money, when Wal-Mart's salaries and benefits force other retailers to reduce their own salaries and benefits in order to compete.[7]

In the wake of its success, Wal-Mart has also stirred backlash and criticism. Some of the complaints are that it pays full-time associates wages that are below the poverty level; it discriminates against women in pay and promotion; it relentlessly forces suppliers to cut prices; and when it opens a store it forces dozens of small mom-and-pop stores in the town's older downtown area out of business, thus gutting the downtown.

Wal-Mart's low wages have pressured supermarkets and other competitors to lower their own wages and benefits.[8] Wal-Mart's low wages also contribute to its 44 percent annual worker turnover. Over 70 lawsuits involving nearly 300,000 current and former employees have been brought against Wal-Mart in recent years alleging that the company engages in practices that denied employees breaks or forced them to work off the clock. To date, Wal-Mart has been assessed by juries or agreed to pay

---

[5] Monee Fields-White, "Wal-Mart Expansion Plans Hit Roadblock; Latest Blow to Retailer's Effort to Open a South Side Store Raises Questions about Its Future in Chicago," *Crain's Chicago Business*, March 24, 2008, p. 2.

[6] Robert McNatt, "Who Says Wal-Mart is Bad for Cities? Underserved Neighborhoods Welcome its Jobs, Low Prices and Tax Revenue," *BusinessWeek*, May 10, 2004; also Ann Zimmerman, "Defending Wal-Mart: CEO Scott Rebuts Critics of Pay Scales, Outlines Workplace Diversity Moves," *The New York Times*, October 6, 2004, p. B1.

[7] Barnaby J. Feder, "Wal-Mart's Expansion Aided by Many Taxpayer Subsidies," *The New York Times*, May 24, 2004, p. C7.

[8] For an account of a Wal-Mart associate trying to pay living expenses on her wage of $7 a day, see Barbara Ehrenreich, *Nickel and Dimed: On (Not) Getting By in America* (New York: Holt and Co., 2001).

more than $200 million to settle those claims.[9] Wal-Mart is sued roughly 12 times each day, making it the most sued institution in the United States, after the federal government. The lawsuits come from customers, employees, and almost every one of their other stakeholders.[10] While Wal-Mart's size explains some of the volume of law suits, they also indicate that many customers and associates feel exploited.

Wal-Mart shares much information on customer preferences with suppliers. It also demands the ability to influence the design of the product and how it is made, and that savings be passed along to Wal-Mart and its consumers. Generally, a supplier must sell to Wal-Mart, simply because it controls such a huge segment of the market. As a result, it dominates suppliers, also. As one supplier put it, the second worse thing a manufacturer can do is sign a contract with Wal-Mart; the worse thing is not to sign one.[11] Wal-Mart's unrelenting insistence that its suppliers lower their costs has coerced many firms to relocate their manufacturing to China, where wage rates are a small fraction of those in the United States.

Wal-Mart is currently the object of a class action law suit for sex discrimination by up to 1.6 million female associates. Plaintiffs analyzed the data that Wal-Mart was required to provide. The data show that, for example, while women make up 93 percent of the cashiers and 68 percent of the salespeople, they constitute only 14 percent of the managers and 36 percent of the assistant managers. Competitor stores have 57 percent women managers. On average, women receive their first promotion 4.4 years after joining Wal-Mart, while men receive their first promotion after only 2.9 years. Moreover, women's pay for the same job with the same seniority is substantially less. Wal-Mart argues that they have decentralized management, so decisions are made locally and should be settled locally; so a class action suit covering all of Wal-Mart is not appropriate. As of late 2007, the courts have continued to reject Wal-Mart's claims and are allowing the suit to proceed.[12]

For years Wal-Mart received intense scrutiny for its employee health-benefits policies. The benefits were often less than those of its competitors and critics argued that they were based on shifting the costs to employees and governmental agencies. In 2004 Wal-Mart said 23 percent of its associates were not eligible for health insurance, but that it did provide coverage for about 45 percent of its workers. An associate who did receive

[9] Jane M. Von Bergen, "Breaks at issue in Wal-Mart lawsuit; A Class Action for 186,000 Workers is Being Argued in a Philadelphia Courtroom. Plaintiffs Say They Were Denied Time to Eat or Rest," *The Philadelphia Enquirer*, September 26, 2006, p. D1; Steven Greenhouse, "Wal-Mart Settles U.S. Suit About Overtime," *The New York Times*, January 26, 2007, p. C1; Margaret Cronin Fisk and Lauren Coleman-Lochner, "Pressure on Wal-Mart Mounts with New Suit," *The International Herald Tribune*, May 30, 2007, p. 17; "Wal-Mart Workers Given Right to Class Action; 70 Lawsuits Maintain Retail Giant Failed to Pay for All Hours Worked," *The Toronto Star*, August 8, 2007, p. B4.

[10] O. C. Ferrell, "Business Ethics and Customer Stakeholders," *Academy of Management Executive*, 18, no. 2 (2004): 126–129.

[11] Jeffrey E. Garten, "Wal-Mart Gives Globalism a Bad Name," *BusinessWeek*, March 8, 2004, p. 24; Anthony Bianco and Wendy Zellner, "Is Wal-Mart Too Powerful?" *BusinessWeek*, October 6, 2003, pp. 100–110.

[12] "Wal-Mart Trial by Checkout: Facing a Giant Sex Discrimination Suit," *The Economist*, June 26, 2004; "No Way to Treat a Lady? As Sex Discrimination Suit Unfolds, Studies of Wal-Mart Practices Show a Big Gap in the Status of Men and Women," *BusinessWeek*, March 3, 2003; "Attention Wal-Mart Plaintiffs: Hurdles Ahead," *The New York Times*, June 27, 2004, p. BU5; "Class Action Bias Suit Against Wal-Mart Reaffirmed," *The New York Times*, December 12, 2007.

TABLE 1-1 Comparison of Wal-Mart's Sam's Club and Costco

	Wal-Mart's Sam's Club	Costco
Average hourly wage	$11.52	$17.00
Annual health cost per worker	$3,500	$5,735
Full-time workers covered by firm's health insurance	61%	98%
Part-time workers covered by firm's health insurance	11%	63%
Salary of CEO	$23,000,000	$350,000
Annual employee turnover	21%	6%
Number of stores	642	457
U.S. market share	40%	50%
Annual sales per store	$70,000,000	$121,000,000

The first two dollar figures are from Stanley Homes and Wendy Zellner, "The Costco Way: Higher Wages Mean Higher Profits," BusinessWeek, *April 12, 2004, pp. 76–77. The percentage figures are from 2007 and are reported in Michael Barbaro and Reed Abelson, "A Health Plan for Wal-Mart: Less Stinginess,"* New York Times, *November 13, 2007, pp. A1 & A27. The remaining are from each firm's 10K Reports.*

insurance was asked to pay 33 percent of its total cost, which was often characterized by critics as providing bare-bones coverage. That person paid an average of $150 per month for individual coverage and $264 per month for family insurance (not counting deductibles and other out of pocket expenses), while typically earning between $8 and $10 per hour and working between 32 and 40 hours per week (see Table 1-1).

Concurrently, a Georgia survey found that more than 10,000 children of Wal-Mart associates were in the state's health program for poor children, which cost taxpayers $10 million annually. A North Carolina hospital found that 31 percent of 1,900 patients who said they were Wal-Mart associates were on Medicaid, and another 10 percent of those patients had no insurance at all. Reacting to the fact that Wal-Mart was placing these costs on local governments, Maryland and California passed laws demanding that Wal-Mart provide better health coverage to their employees; 20 additional states are considering similar legislation. In comparison, critics pointed out that one of Wal-Mart's main competitors, Costco, paid the entire cost of insurance for 96 percent of its eligible workers.[13]

Wal-Mart began responding to these criticisms in 2005 by revising its insurance options. Since then it has reduced the period a part-time employee had to wait to be eligible to obtain insurance through Wal-Mart from two years to one—approximately half of those workers are now eligible to enroll in coverage. It made the process by which employees sign up for insurance simpler. It now offers a series of plans

[13] Reed Abelson, "States Are Battling Against Wal-Mart Over Health Care," *The New York Times*, November 1, 2004, p. 1, A13; Steven Greenhouse and Michael Barbaro, "Wal-Mart Memo Suggests Ways to Cut Employee Benefit Costs," *The New York Times*, October 26, 2005, p. C1.

designed to meet different employees' needs. Individual deductibles now are as low as $350 annually. Even policies comparable with those offered in the old system cost employees significantly less than they did in 2004. Related to this, Wal-Mart now offers almost 2,500 generic drug prescriptions to its employees at $4 per month. In 2007 Wal-Mart had over 100,000 more employees with health insurance than it did in 2004—with 48 percent of its workers now receiving Wal-Mart sponsored health care. While Wal-Mart has not yet caught up with Costco (which now charges its employees $200 per year for its better coverage), some critics are impressed that it has finally begun addressing its employee insurance concerns.[14]

Wal-Mart has also received much criticism for its environmental practices. Some of these concerns arise simply from Wal-Mart's sheer size—the number of miles its truck fleet drives, the amount of energy its stores consume (it is the largest private consumer of electricity in the United States), and the amount of garbage it produces daily is enormous—but part of the critique has been levied at the way the world's largest retailer manages its business practices. For example, Wal-Mart is a huge purchaser of goods made in China, which is relatively lax in environmental protection when compared with Western industrialized nations.[15] Likewise, Wal-Mart has also endured ongoing criticism for its hazardous waste disposal practices.

In late 2005 Wal-Mart announced that it was beginning to focus on improving sustainability practices in all areas of its business. Its programs range from working in consultation with various environmental groups, to building "sustainable value networks" comprised of employees, supplier, and environmentalists, to daily changes such as switching its outdoor signs to be run by more efficient light-emitting diodes (LEDS), to selling fair trade coffee, to selling more energy-efficient compact fluorescent light bulbs, and to using its size and leverage to require suppliers to produce products with more environmentally friendly packaging. The company plans to spend upwards of $500 million per year on finding ways to reduce its energy consumption. It says that by January 2008, it had sold 145 million energy-efficient light bulbs. Wal-Mart has partnered with the Clinton Climate Initiative (CCI) and the U.S. Conference of Mayors to provide energy-efficient building products at discounts of 5–70 percent to 1,100 cities.[16]

Wal-Mart now features a prominent "sustainability" link on its Web site (http://walmartstores.com/sustainability/), where it proclaims, "Wal-Mart's environmental goals are simple and straightforward: to be supplied 100 percent by renewable energy; to create zero waste; and to sell products that sustain our natural resources and the environment." As part of this process, Wal-Mart now issues a sustainability report that provides metrics of what it has achieved.

---

[14] Michael Barbaro and Reed Abelson, "A Health Plan for Wal-Mart: Less Stinginess," *The New York Times*, November 30, 2007, p. 1.

[15] These and other criticisms are contained in "Wal-Mart's New Greenwashing Report," by Sara Anderson, Institute for Policy Studies, November 20, 2007 at www.ips-dc.org, accessed February 6, 2008.

[16] Mindy Fetterman, "Wal-Mart Grows 'Green' Strategies; No. 1 Retailer Embraces Environment, but some say it's just 'Green-Washing'," *USA Today*, September 25, 2006, p. 1A; Marc Guenther, "Wal-Mart's Mixed 'Green' Bag," *Fortune*, November 16, 2007, http://money.cnn.com/2007/11/16/news/companies/walmart.fortune/index.htm; Michael Barbaro, "Wal-Mart Sets Agenda of Change: Chief Lays Out Environmental, Health and Ethical Goals," *The New York Times*, January 24, 2008, p. C3.

Wal-Mart has not entirely quieted its critics—some believe that many of its recent actions are simply attempts to turn attention away from the other controversies surrounding the company, while others note that its reports are vague in specific details. Other past critics applaud Wal-Mart for even stepping into the environmental arena because its presence is bound to heighten the conversation about the planet's environmental future.

In summary, Wal-Mart is very popular with consumers and investors. Wal-Mart has even been given credit for keeping inflation down, helping to improve the overall efficiency of the world's economy and helping the U.S. Gulf Coast recover after Hurricane Katrina. It shares much information with suppliers to help them design better products. In the last few years, as its reputation suffered, it began to contribute to community projects, improve employee benefits, and adopt environmentally friendly practices. Critics argue that Wal-Mart still provides low-wage jobs and few medical and retirement benefits; its low-cost strategy has forced competitors to cut back on what had previously been higher wages and benefits; and Wal-Mart and other low-cost retailers are responsible for gutting the downtown small shop areas of thousands of towns and cities. Low-cost goods are a notable benefit to consumers. Is this benefit worth the price of so many employees being paid such low wages with few, if any, health or retirement benefits? Does Wal-Mart take unfair advantage of its workers, suppliers, and communities? Are its recent healthcare and environmental initiatives enough to overcome these criticisms?

BUSINESS VALUES SHAPE PEOPLE

Wal-Mart and other firms have a strong **impact on our goals** and life styles. The values of businesspeople influence the way we treat colleagues and customers and the amount of family and leisure time we have. American business is often considered the archetype of business by people in other countries. English has become the language of commerce. The United States has the largest markets, and has a strong influence on global business and personal values. Yet attitudes and values do vary from country to country. We will here focus on American business values, so that American and other businesspeople may better understand their own goals and values.

The values and ethics of business and businesspeople provide a foundation. Whether one can trust a handshake without a contract, or how one will be treated as a worker, depends on managers' ethics and values. Business ethics and values have a profound influence on our lives, including new products, work-place design, relationships among colleagues at work, and government regulations. People's ethics and values hold together the fabric of a firm and a culture. Moreover, work and the business firm are so central to our lives that they in turn strongly influence our personal goals and life styles. In the last decade we saw in the headlines how the lack of ethics of some executives caused the collapse of dozens of firms, which resulted in the loss of hundreds of thousands of jobs, billions of dollars in savings and pensions, and widespread trust in business.

In this first chapter, we will explore ways in which values and ethics influence our lives and businesses. Later chapters will go into detail on how we develop moral maturity, make ethical choices, and the history behind the business values we hold

CEO	Chief executive officer of an organization
CFO	Chief financial officer of an organization
Common good	The well-being of all the members of the community; the good of the entire society taken as a whole
Conflict of interest	A situation in which a person may gain personal benefit from actions she or he may take based on obligations the person is entrusted to manage
Ethics	The principles of conduct governing an individual or a group, and the methods for applying them
Free market	An unregulated economic market operating by free competition of buyers and sellers
Goal	The result toward which effort is directed; the end to be pursued
Ideal	An ultimate goal that an individual or a society holds for itself; a standard of perfection
Ideology	A cluster of values integrated into a comprehensive, coherent, motivating statement of purpose
Market fundamentalism	All economic, social, and human interactions are contract-based and are measured by money
Moral	Dealing with or capable of distinguishing right from wrong
Norm	Criterion for distinguishing what is right from what is wrong, and what is correct from what is incorrect
Morality	The rightness or wrongness of principles, practices, and activities, along with the values and rules that govern them
Value	A lasting belief that a certain goal or mode of conduct is better than the opposite goal or conduct.

FIGURE 1-1   Business, Values, and Ethics Terms

today. For a definition of some terms that we will be using, see Figure 1-1. **Values** govern our personality and our actions. They undergird and direct the important decisions that each of us make. Whether we realize it or not, values profoundly influence our choices and our lives. To know one's values allows one to possess greater control over one's own actions and future.

A **value system** is at the foundation of personal and business decisions. Yet values become so much a part of us that we are generally unaware of their content and impact. An analogy might help. Consider the way we use a personal computer. As we learn to use the various programs, the procedure becomes habitual or automatic. Operating the computer—for word processing, accounting, inventory control, and other needs—becomes so much a part of us that we become explicitly aware of it only when we reflect on our actions, perhaps to teach another. Yet without knowing that procedure, it is impossible to accomplish the task. In a parallel fashion, to not understand our values prevents one from fully understanding one's own actions and the actions of others. In this chapter, we examine some business firms and current business practices, focusing on the values that undergird them.

Free enterprise values are familiar to each of us. For example, **freedom** is a foundation value of the economy—free markets, free movement of people, free entry into new business, freedom to take or leave a job. This freedom parallels the freedom that we cherish in political life—democracy. The enterprise system, stimulated by economic and political freedom, provides a multitude of benefits:

- An immense output of goods and services.
- New jobs that have been created.
- High standards of living available to many.
- Great rewards go to many, stemming from the skill, new ideas, inventions, and initiative of entrepreneurs.
- Encourages flexibility and innovation among people.
- Reinforces the value of personal freedom.

Yet in spite of these many successes of free markets, there exist serious problems, also. It is vital to be aware of and find the root causes of these difficulties, if we expect to improve our businesses and our lives. The unethical and even criminal actions of some business managers over the last decade sober our expectations and demand that we try to understand what happened so to make such actions less likely in the future.

Ethical and Financial Collapse

Ethical and legal business failures appear every day in newspapers and on TV. The long list of **executives that abused their power** and position, committed fraud, and attempted to gain unearned personal wealth has caused businesspeople and all Americans disappointment, embarrassment, and anger. Most American executives and firms have integrity. However, the list of those who do not is too long to ignore. The U.S. Department of Justice's Presidential Corporate Fraud Task Force reports there have been 1,236 corporate convictions between 2002 and 2007. This list includes at least 214 chief executive officers (CEOs), 53 chief financial officers (CFOs), and 128 vice presidents.[17] The following is a partial list of some of those errant business executives. John J. and Timothy Rigas, the founder and CFO of Adelphia, were both convicted of securities, wire, and bank fraud. At Enron, Chairman Kenneth Lay was convicted of 10 counts of fraud while CEO Jeffrey Skilling was convicted of 19 counts of fraud, conspiracy, and insider trading. Lay's indictment and conviction was later vacated because he died of a heart attack shortly after his conviction, while Skilling was sentenced to serve 24 years in prison and ordered to pay $45 million in restitution to the firm's shareholders. Andrew S. Fastow, the CFO, pled guilty to fraud and is also in prison.[18] Skilling and Fastow are two of more than 20 former Enron executives who have either pled guilty or been indicted. Scott D. Sullivan, CFO of WorldCom, pled guilty to accounting fraud and is now in prison while his boss, CEO Bernard Ebbers,

---

[17] Kate Plourd, "Quick: How Many CFOs Have Been Convicted?" *CFO.com*, July 18, 2007, http://cfo.com/article.cfm/9502734.

[18] Mimi Swartz with Sherron Watkins, *Power Failure: The Inside Story of the Collapse of Enron* (New York: Doubleday, 2003); Sarah Johnson, "What Skilling's Sentence Means," *CFO.com*, October 26, 2006, http://cfo.com/article.cfm/8070492; "Corporate Justice," *BusinessWeek*, December 18, 2006, p. 79.

was convicted of fraud and is serving 25 years.[19] Samuel D. Waksal, chief executive officer (CEO) of ImClone, pled guilty to securities fraud and insider trading and is serving seven years in prison. Martin L. Grass of Rite Aid is serving eight years for conspiracy and obstruction of justice. Michael Sears, CFO of Boeing, pled guilty to bribing an Air Force procurement officer with a $250,000 a year job, so that she would steer $23 billion in contracts to Boeing.[20] CEO Martha Stewart and her broker Peter Bacanovic were both convicted and went to jail for conspiracy and obstruction of justice over selling her shares of ImClone. We will discuss the case of Tyco and CEO Dennis Kozlowski below.

These are but a few of the more visible figures who have been involved in corporate crime in recent years. These privileged, well-educated people were more concerned with share price, growth, and their own power and wealth than with honesty and trustworthiness.[21] Some say that the above are but a few bad apples. Others say the lying and corruption are too widespread—they maintain that we have a more basic problem due to the structure of the corporation itself, because it is given vast power and limited liability under U.S. law.[22]

Taxes are necessary to provide the public services that benefit all of us. Taxes are the price we pay for civilization; one cannot have a civilized society without the funds to pay for it. Even though government is often inefficient, it does provide necessary services. And yet many people in the United States try to avoid their taxes. Wealthy people and business firms have the influence to place provisions in the tax code that exempt them from paying their fair share of taxes. That leaves working middle-class and poor Americans to pay the bill for public services and defense. Corporations have benefitted mightily from loopholes and **tax avoidance schemes**. A U.S. General Accounting Office investigation released in 2004 found that over 60 percent of U.S. corporations, doing $2.5 trillion of business, paid no federal tax during the boom years 1996–2000. Some 71 percent of foreign firms, having $750 billion of business in the United States, paid no U.S. taxes. The legislated U.S. corporate tax rate is 35 percent of profits. In the year 2000, among corporations with assets of at least $250 million, 45 percent paid no taxes, and another 35 percent paid less than 5 percent tax. By 2003 total tax revenue from corporations was 7.4 percent of federal tax receipts, the lowest rate since 1983 and the second lowest since 1934. In a parallel fashion, wealthy individuals hire advisors who use loopholes in the tax code so to pay little or no tax. Many object that it is not fair to give rich individuals and corporations special benefits to avoid their fair share of taxes.[23]

---

[19] Harry Maurer, "No Mercy for Ebbers," *BusinessWeek*, August 14, 2006, p. 25.

[20] Tim Weber, "Ex-Boeing Financial Chief Pleads Guilty to Felony: Conflict of Interest in Pentagon Dealings," *The New York Times*, November 16, 2004, p. C2.

[21] Thomas L. Carson, "Self-Interest and Business Ethics: Some Lessons of the Recent Corporate Scandals," *Journal of Business Ethics*, 43 (April 2003): 389–394.

[22] Ted Nace, *Gangs of America: The Rise of Corporate Power and the Disabling of Democracy* (San Francisco: Berrett-Koehler, 2003).

[23] See David Cay Johnson, *Perfectly Legal: The Covert Campaign to Rig Our Tax System to Benefit the Super Rich—and Cheat Everybody Else* (New York: Penguin, 2004); Mortimer Zuckerman, "An Intolerable Free Ride," *U.S. News and World Report*, May 17, 2004, p. 80; and John D. McKinnon, "Over 60 Percent of Corporations Didn't Pay Taxes," *The Wall Street Journal Online*, March 5, 2004.

Still another public scandal involves the **mutual fund industry**; it has been guilty of a variety of unfair practices, from misleading investors to illegally providing hedge funds and other large investors better prices and access. The funds also generated fees for themselves by overly trading stocks at the expense of long-term investors. This places an average individual investor somewhere between being a second class citizen and being a victim of a scam. Bank of America and Fleet Boston paid $675 million in penalties; mutual fund companies have been penalized $1.65 billion so far. However, this sum amounts to only 2 percent of their forecasted combined earnings, and no senior executives of the firms have been held liable.[24]

Wall Street and financial firms have been perhaps the most corrupt industry. Huge financial firm salaries and bonuses testify to the way they generated enormous fees for themselves, at the expense of their clients. The firms were involved in a **conflict of interest** between the investment bank activities and their own financial analysts. Bank analysts, who are supposed to produce unbiased assessments of firms for the bank's investors, were often pressured to provide glowing reports on a firm's financial future, so that their bank could obtain the lucrative merger and acquisition investment business from the analyzed firm, typically without investors knowing that the reports were skewed. Analysts and investment bankers turned investing into a game in which they always won and ordinary investors lost.

The investment firms also bribed CEOs with early shares of hot initial public offerings (IPOs), so that they would send them business. This fueled a vast transfer of wealth from ordinary investors to Wall Street bankers and their CEO clients. Merrill Lynch and CSFB agreed to pay $100 million to settle their cases. JPMorgan Chase, Morgan Stanley, Goldman Sachs, and Citigroup have all been involved in similar unfair activities.[25] Citigroup is the world's largest financial services company with 200 million customers in 100 countries and about 300,000 employees. It was ordered to close its private banking unit in Japan for a variety of violations of Japanese law, including money laundering. In the United States, it has agreed to pay $2.65 billion to settle a suit by WorldCom shareholders who maintained that Citigroup's support gave WorldCom credibility in spite of its fraud. It has also agreed to pay shareholders and creditors $2 billion and $1.66 billion, respectively, for its role in Enron's collapse. However, the settlements appear to have done little to change the culture of Wall Street.[26] Thus, it is not surprising that financial firms are deeply involved in the housing and credit crisis that enveloped the United States starting in 2007. As of mid-2008, U.S. federal prosecutors and the Federal Bureau of Investigation were conducting over 1,300 fraud and insider-trading investigations involving at least

---

[24] "America's Mutual Fund Scandal: A Big Legal Settlement Has More Bark Than Bite," *The Economist*, March 20, 2004, p. 83; Paula Dwyer, "Breach of Trust: The Mutual-Fund Scandal Was a Disaster Waiting to Happen, An Inside Look at How the Industry Manipulated Washington," *BusinessWeek*, December 15, 2003, pp. 98–108.

[25] "Senators Question Effectiveness of $1.4 Billion Settlement," *The New York Times*, May 8, 2003, p. C8.

[26] Eric Dash, "Citigroup Resolves Claims that It Helped Enron Deceive Investors," *New York Times*, March 27, 2008, p. C3; "Will It Matter: The Global Settlement," *BusinessWeek*, May 12, 2003, pp. 30–34, 114; "It's Cleanup Time at Citi: A New CEO Aims to Overhaul the Superbank's Culture," *The New York Times*, November 7, 2004, Sec. 3, p. 1; "Citi Starts to Settle," *BusinessWeek*, May 24, 2004, p. 52.

20 unnamed financial companies relating to their subprime mortgage lending practices with their both borrowers and investors.[27]

These scandals are not restricted to the United States. The European Union's major dairy provider, Italy's Parmalat, claimed to have $5.5 billion in a Bank of America account in the Cayman Islands that never existed; it is now in bankruptcy. Dutch Ahold, Japanese Snow Brand Milk Products, and others, including French, German, and Irish firms, have been involved in similar scandals.[28] These unethical and criminal activities are so widespread that many worry that they will undercut trust in business and the market system itself. Many thus ask: Are these high profile cases the beginning of an era marked by reduced ethics in business?

Americans were publicly warned earlier that the scandals were coming. Arthur Levitt, then chair of the U.S. Securities and Exchange Commission (SEC) saw the problem posed by "managed earnings" (falsification of accounting records to make earnings growth appear more consistent), and that auditing firms were approving such false reporting. He tried to implement new SEC regulations that would have prevented some of the scandals, but most of his proposals were rebuffed.[29] He ran into a powerful lobby of corporations, stock analysts, and institutional investors that derailed the proposed regulations. About a year after Levitt left the SEC, the Enron and WorldCom scandals broke and almost all of his proposals were enacted into the new legislation.[30] Likewise, former U.S. Federal Reserve Board member Edward Gramlich foresaw the current housing and credit crisis in the United States several years before it occurred. He wrote speeches, participated in policy debates, and wrote books such as Subprime Mortgages: America's Latest Boom and Bust, which tried to warn about the impending problems. Like Levitt at the SEC, Gramlich tried to proactively prevent the housing and credit crisis, but in the end he was unable to bring about those changes before the crisis happened.[31]

Without trust the market system would collapse. Hence it is essential that we understand why these scandals happened—for the sake of building a working and healthy market system, so to prevent them in the future. Let us examine the case of Dennis Kozlowski of Tyco.

Tyco and Dennis Kozlowski

Dennis Kozlowski majored in accounting and graduated from Seton Hall University in 1968. He joined Tyco in 1975. Kozlowski was quickly promoted; as

---

[27] Associated Press, "FBI Looking at more Mortgage Fraud Cases: Agency Taking Agents Off other Cases to Staff 'Tremendous Surge,'" *MSNBC*, April 16, 2008, http://www.msnbc.msn.com/id/24165427/; Amir Efrati, "Wall Street, Lenders Face Subprime Scrutiny," *The Wall Street Journal*, May 5, 2008, p. A4.

[28] "Parma Splat: What are the Lessons from the Scandal at Europe's Largest Dairy-Products Group," *The Economist*, January 17, 2004, pp. 59–61; and "The Year of Nasty Surprises: Suddenly the Continent is Awash in Accounting Scandals," *BusinessWeek*, March 10, 2003, pp. 48–49.

[29] On the fear, Kurt Eichenwald, "Could Capitalists Actually Bring Down Capitalism?" *The New York Times*, June 30, 2002, pp. 1 and 5; on the early ignored warning, Carol J. Loomis, "Lies, Damned Lies, and Managed Earnings: The Nation's Top Earnings Cop Has Put Corporate American on Notice: Quit Cooking the Books," *Fortune*, August 2, 1999, pp. 74–92.

[30] For his more recent reflections, see Arthur Levitt with Paula Dwyer, *Take on the Street: What Wall Street and Corporate America Don't Want You to Know* (New York: Pantheon, 2002).

[31] Michelle Maynard, "Being Right is Bittersweet for a Critic of Lenders," *The New York Times*, August 18, 2007, p. C1; Steven Pearlstein, "A Well-Grounded Economist," *Washington Post*, September 7, 2007, p. D1.

president of Tyco's Grinnell Fire Protection, Kozlowski cut salaries, but paid large bonuses to managers who produced improved earnings. He presented awards to the best performing managers and identified the worst performers at an annual company-wide banquet.

Kozlowski was made CEO of Tyco in 1992. For 27 years, Kozlowski was an effective and enterprising manager. Kozlowski lowered Tyco's U.S. taxes from 35 percent of income to 18.5 percent by moving headquarters to Bermuda. He also set up over 100 finance subsidiaries for sheltering interest, dividends, royalties, and other income; thus Tyco could brag that in 2001, while it had 65 percent of its revenue from the United States, only 29 percent of its taxable income came from the United States.[32] Tyco's revenues increased an average of 48 percent annually from 1997 to 2001 and its pretax operating margins averaged 22 percent. As a reward, Kozlowski's own compensation went from $9 million in 1997, to $67 million in 1998, then to $170 million in 1999; this made him the second highest paid CEO in the United States.

In 1995 Kozlowski moved Tyco's corporate headquarters from a small wooden building in Exeter, New Hampshire, to an expensive Manhattan office with spectacular views of Central Park. He also used Tyco funds to purchase a $16.8 million apartment for himself in Manhattan. Kozlowski's personal expenditures drew much attention: his $6,000 shower curtain for his apartment, the $110,000 hotel bill for a 13-day stay in London, and the $2 million birthday party for his new wife on the island of Sardinia—all charged as expenses to Tyco. He tried to avoid New York City's sales tax by shipping a $3.9 million painting destined for his New York apartment to New Hampshire, which has no sales tax. He divorced his wife of 29 years and in 2000 married the restaurant waitress for whom he threw the above party.

Kozlowski grew Tyco's revenues by means of acquisitions, but he and his associates often used numerous accounting schemes to inflate Tyco's earnings. One of the gimmicks involved firms about to be acquired. Before the acquisition, Kozlowski arranged to reduce revenues for the firm and also charged not-yet-due expenses; thus after the acquisition, Tyco could show artificially large revenues and lower expenses. From 1999 to 2001, Kozlowski acquired more than 700 companies, so that this scheme added much to the bottom line. Another trick shifted funds from one account to another; this inflated the company's profits by $186 million from 1999 to 2001, according to an internal Tyco report that was prepared for the Board of Directors after Kozlowski was arrested and forced to resign in 2002.[33]

Edward Breen took over as CEO of Tyco after Kozlowski left in 2002, but the wreckage of the actions of Kozlowski and his associates have haunted the firm for years afterwards. Kozlowski and his CFO, Mark Swartz, were convicted in 2005 on 22 larceny charges relating to misappropriation of $150 million in Tyco funds, sentenced for upwards of 25 years in jail time each, and ordered to pay a combined $240 million in fines and restitution. In late 2006 the former head of Tyco's tax department was sentenced to three years in prison for intentionally failing to report

---

[32] Anthonly Bianco, William Symonds, and Nanette Byrnes, "The Rise and Fall of Dennis Kozlowski: How Did He Become So Unhinged by Greed?" *BusinessWeek*, December 23, 2002, pp. 64–77.

[33] "Tyco Admits That It Used Various Accounting Tricks to Inflate Its Earnings," *The New York Times*, December 31, 2002, p. 1, C2; and Mark Maremont, "Finally, A CEO Faces a Jury: Kozlowski," *The Wall Street Journal*, September 25, 2003, pp. C1, C10.

$170 million in earnings on the firm's 1999 income tax return. In early 2007 a former Tyco executive vice president agreed to pay $2.7 million to the SEC to settle fraud charges regarding accounting tricks used to inflate operating income and cash flows at the company from 1997 to 2002. In 2007 Tyco agreed to pay $3 billion to settle shareholder claims arising from the actions of Kozlowski and his senior managers. This was followed shortly thereafter by accounting firm PriceWaterhouseCoopers's agreement to pay Tyco shareholders $225 million to settle a class-action lawsuit claims that it failed to uncover $5.8 billion in overstated earnings at the company from 1999 to 2002.[34] Finally, in mid-2007, Breen was able to move Tyco beyond dealing with Kozlowski-era-generated crises to split itself into three separate companies to finally correct what *BusinessWeek* called "a $40 billion empire constructed for all the wrong reasons—size without strategy, dealmaking without management."[35]

Kozlowski used Tyco funds for many personal expenses and illegally tried to avoid taxes. His actions for many years generated enormous amounts of shareholder wealth, but likewise, his actions also saddled Tyco with billions of dollars in lawsuits, penalties, and settlements and cost his shareholders untold sums of money. Which of Kozlowski's actions are those of a good CEO and which are not? From what you know, how would you evaluate his ethics? His moral maturity?

DEMAND FOR RESULTS

The press for greater efficiency, shedding businesses that are not profitable enough, and shifting operations overseas to obtain lower labor costs characterizes most businesses in the last decade. This has been done aggressively but perhaps legally by Wal-Mart, sometimes both legally and illegally at Tyco, and illegally by Enron, WorldCom, and Adelphia. In each of these instances, the impact on the people who are fired, outsourced, or lied to seems not to be an important or determining consideration for managers. Does this mark a shift in ethics and values over the period? Is this shift a benefit to citizens in the United States? Is it a benefit to citizens in other countries?

Shareholders Come First

The principal objective of Sam Walton at Wal-Mart, Dennis Kozlowski at Tyco, Jack Welch at General Electric (GE), and Bernard Ebbers at WorldCom was to increase **shareholder value**. Wall Street and investors demand this steady increase, and indeed force it on executives of publicly held firms as a goal. Wall Street analysts and the

---

[34] Mark Maremont, "Tyco Figures Will Be Jailed at Least 7 Years; Judge Orders Kozlowski, Swartz To Also Pay Back $240 Million; CEO's 'Kleptocratic Management,'" *The Wall Street Journal*, September 20, 2005, p. c1; Stephen Taub, "Former Tyco Tax Man Gets Three Years," *CFO.com*, November, http://cfo.com/article.cfm/8369609?f=search; Stephen Taub, "Ex-Tyco Finance Exec Settles SEC Charges," *CFO.com*, April 30, 2007, http://cfo.com/article.cfm/9101183?f=search; Katharine Webster, "Tyco paying $3 billion to settle lawsuit," *Boston.com*, May 15, 2007, http://www.boston.com/business/articles/2007/05/15/tyco_to_pay_3_billion_settlement/; Robert Weisman, "Auditor to Pay $225m, Settle Tyco Suit: Pact Ends Allegations that Hub office Failed to Spot Financial Abuse," *The Boston Globe*, July 7, 2007, p. B4.

[35] Brian Hindo, "Solving Tyco's Identity Crisis," *BusinessWeek*, February 14, 2008, p. 62.

demand that the share price move steadily upward exert an extraordinary pressure on executives, their policies, and their actions. Institutional investors—mutual funds, pension funds, and endowments—represent the interests of more than a hundred million Americans, and they, also, press for constantly increasing returns. However, focusing on increasing shareholder value as the primary purpose of the firm leads managers to neglect their responsibilities to other stakeholders: employees, customers, suppliers, and the community.

Making increased shareholder value the primary purpose of the firm leads to short-term goals, and a neglect of long-term investment in people, plant, and research and development which are essential to long-term growth and value creation.[36] Moreover, it elevates the role of shareholders above that of all the other stakeholders of the firm.[37] Jack Welch of GE and Al Dunlap of Sunbeam found that a way to keep shareholders happy was to lay off workers.

Outsourcing Products and Work

Historically, **layoffs**, significant deliberate reductions in the size of a company's workforce, were considered to be a last resort for a firm, to be used only when every other strategy had failed and the firm could not pay the wages. Executives now tell their workers that their firm does not have a responsibility for their employment but only for their "employability." They encourage workers to keep their skills fresh, so that they readily may move to a new job. But during the boom period, executives found that they could increase their share price by simply laying off workers to cut costs. These strategic layoffs have led to a breakdown of the traditional employment contract that gave an employer loyalty and good performance in return for the employer's promise of employment, career, and retirement security. Layoffs are often accompanied by **outsourcing** actions by firms. Firms layoff workers when the cost of labor is high (as in the United States) and then hire workers to do the same jobs in locations where the cost of labor is much lower—in overseas locations like India or China. While outsourcing and layoffs are separate actions, they have been used by many firms as complementary strategies.

Layoffs and outsourcing have several negative effects. First, lost jobs bring a loss of family income, and increased anxiety and health problems for the wage earner and for the entire family.[38] Social networks at work are destroyed, and marriages break up, triggered by the loss of a job and income.[39] Second, layoffs reduce loyalty to the firm. From the time of the first layoff, people in the firm feel less security and have less long-term commitment to the organization. Third, people who survive a layoff are expected to pick up the extra work. They are given "stretch goals" and are asked to "work smarter" with no new resources. The task requires more hours to accomplish, so

---

[36] Allan A. Kennedy, *The End of Shareholder Value: Corporations at the Crossroads* (Cambridge, MA: Perseus, 2000).

[37] Marjorie Kelly, *The Divine Right of Capital: Dethroning the Corporate Aristocracy* (San Francisco: Berrett-Koehler, 2003).

[38] Angelo J. Kinicki, Gregory E. Prussia, and Frances M. McKee-Ryan, "A Panel Study of Coping with Involuntary Job Loss," *Academy of Management Journal*, 43, no. 1 (2000): 90–100.

[39] Priti Pradhan Shah, "Network Destruction: The Structural Implications of Downsizing," *Academy of Management Journal*, 43, no. 1 (2000): 101–112.

often the person must work overtime at no extra pay. This then leaves less time for other human needs and interests, such as spouse, children, and recreation. Steve Kerr was GE's chief training officer and he called such additional demands on managers immoral, as in most cases the remaining workers are not provided the additional tools they need to do the job.[40]

On the other hand, the small number of firms that have a no layoff policy are doing well. Southwest Airlines has had such a policy for 30 years and financially is doing better than any other major airline. Southwest's president, James F. Parker, says, "We are willing to suffer some damage, even to our stock price, to protect the jobs of our people."[41] Also having a no layoff policy are S.C. Johnson, Pela, Federal Express, Lincoln Electric, and AFLAC. Executives at these firms argue that their no-layoff policy brings loyalty, higher productivity, and the motivation to suggest more efficient ways to do the work. Otherwise workers, fearing for their jobs, are afraid to make suggestions to improve their work. Moreover, these firms also have an edge in recruiting talented workers. When layoffs are necessary, responsible firms have a policy that provides training and helps laid off workers find another job. When Cisco Systems was forced to lay off 6,000 of its workers, the firm was innovative. If a laid-off worker agreed to work for a local nonprofit organization for a year, Cisco would provide one-third of their salary plus benefits and stock options, and that person would have priority to be rehired when business picked up.[42]

Using layoffs as a first solution to financial problems raises a question about the very purpose of the corporation. Should not executives be also responsible to workers, families, and the communities that share their risks? "Any reform package that fails to rebalance power by addressing the legitimate needs and rights of employees to monitor executive behavior and protect their human capital investments fails to complete the job."[43] Reform legislation has been designed to correct accounting and financial problems. But the social capital and the competitive advantage that workers provide a firm are not recognized in the U.S. legislation that has been enacted so far. Moreover, this legislation provided additional rules but has not affected the ethical climate within firms.

In the United States, we are narrowly focused on financial returns, and we measure that by increased wealth. However, **real wealth** is actually in **our resources: the people, the earth, and communities**. We have been so intent on increasing the amount of money in hand that we have destroyed much of our real wealth. In the name of increasing wealth or shareholder value, we destroy not only social capital in the loyalty of workers, but also natural capital when we strip mine, deplete forests and fisheries, or dump hazardous wastes, and communities in the way we design our cities and the self-centered manner in which many people live.[44]

---

[40] Interview with Steve Kerr, "Stretch Goals: The Dark Side of Asking for Miracles," *Fortune*, November 13, 1995, pp. 231–232.

[41] "Where Layoffs Are A Last Resort," *BusinessWeek*, October 8, 2001, p. 42.

[42] "Pink Slips with a Silver Lining," *BusinessWeek*, June 4, 2001.

[43] Thomas A. Kochan, "Addressing the Crisis in Confidence in Corporations: Root Causes, Victims, and Strategies for Reform," *Academy of Management Executive*, 16, no. 3 (2002): 140.

[44] David Korten, "The Difference Between Money and Wealth: How Out-of-Control Speculation is Destroying Real Wealth," *Business Ethics,* January, 1999, p. 4.

Competition in domestic and global markets is also a source of pressure for greater efficiencies. We witness the benefit of this at Wal-Mart, where "everyday low prices" enable us to purchase products at a considerable saving. These low prices are possible because Wal-Mart purchases products that are manufactured in low-wage countries. Global competition also stimulated the improved quality of the U.S.-made automobile. Two decades ago, Japanese manufacturers achieved major market share in the United States largely because of their better quality. Now Ford and GM have increased quality, offered warranties, and have narrowed the quality gap.

Market pressures have encouraged the outsourcing of jobs by U.S. firms. This outsourcing ranges from making garments, shoes, toys, and other labor-intensive products in sweatshops to highly trained people writing software for Microsoft in India. India has a surplus of well-educated young people. They speak English, and wage rates are a fraction of what they are in the United States.

Well-paying jobs are being lost and labor unions, which protect workers' rights, now have less influence in the United States. Moreover, many of the jobs that are being added are in the low-paying service sector, such as hospitality—workers in restaurants, motels, and taxi drivers. Furthermore, even a well-paying job is not as secure as it was two decades ago. In the United States, skilled and unskilled workers are on notice that they should develop their abilities and keep themselves flexible. Even though they are good workers, they can no longer count on their employer to keep them and provide for their retirement. Many technical jobs are also being sent overseas. Research and development activity and legal and accounting work are being outsourced by U.S. and European firms. However, such outsourcing of jobs presents another danger: Sending design jobs to China or India risks the loss of intellectual property. Often the developed country's technology is taken and used to compete against the firm itself.

On the other hand, a person in India or Kenya may need a job even more than does the U.S. citizen. On a larger scale, the future stability of the world depends on the prosperity of peoples in many poorer nations, and prosperity comes with having a job. One of the underlying causes of unrest and terrorism in Middle Eastern countries is the lack of jobs for the immense number of young, energetic males. The challenge is to encourage job and income growth that benefits both people in the United States and poorer peoples of the world.

For the sake of a healthy U.S. economy, incentives are called for—tax and otherwise—to keep many highly skilled jobs in the United States. Otherwise, American citizens will not be motivated to spend many years in graduate education, especially in the sciences and engineering, which is difficult and time consuming. Why spend five to seven years obtaining an advanced degree in a difficult field if there is little prospect of obtaining a job and a decent salary? A shortage of talented people with these credentials to do research work would further the downward economic spiral for the United States.

The above situation with all its difficulties has been summarized with stinging clarity by William Frederick, a business scholar and former dean of the University of Pittsburgh Graduate School of Business:

> Global free market capitalism is rampant, violating cultural borders as
> it has long done, repeating many of 19th century capitalism's worst
> excesses, at times exploiting Third World workers, raping the globe's

environments, stripping away ecological diversity, overworking the earth's fertile soils, amassing and hoarding and wielding mammoth fortunes, recruiting the West's armed might to secure existing markets and to open new ones, manipulating world financial institutions to promote market-centered economics, resisting full-scale, good-faith United States participation in regional and international environmental compacts and supporting various saber-rattling and saber-wielding policies of governments here and abroad. Clearly, one cannot treat business actions as if they are separated from today's major geopolitical struggles, because the actions taken by governments often mirror the interests of business.[45]

The above was written shortly before the attacks on the United States on September 11, 2001 and the bankruptcy of Enron that wiped out jobs and pensions for most of their 20,000 worldwide employees. The largest bankruptcy in U.S. history, WorldCom, was just a few months later. These, plus the many other fraud revelations that continue to this day, shock the nation and the world, and give additional weight to Frederick's warnings.

PURCHASING BEYOND OUR MEANS

Americans **consume much and save little**. We purchase fashionable clothes and autos, and go into debt to pay for it. We enjoy the convenience of our credit cards, but then are often unable to pay the amount due. Today the average American carries $9,000 in credit card debt.[46] Fifty-eight percent of American credit card–carrying households do not pay off their balances in full each month. The average credit debt in those households is now $17,000, and Americans collectively owe credit card companies $850 billion, a fourfold increase since 1990.[47] Consolidating credit card debt and using your home as collateral is a huge new industry, and is often described as one of the major factors of the housing and credit crisis that started in the United States in 2007. From 2001 to 2007, Americans shifted more than $350 billion in credit card debt into their mortgage or home equity payments.[48] When we hear radio ads for obtaining cash "even if you your credit is not perfect," we worry about the financial debacles and loss of homes that follow. Advertising and social pressure urge us to possess things and thus to demonstrate to others that we are a success. And we make our success clear to our neighbors by means of the goods we have: a larger house, a bigger car, and more expensive clothes. After the many products and services we buy, we have little to save. Yet savings are essential to a family and to the economy.

---

[45] William C. Frederick, "Notes for a Third Millennial Manifesto: Renewal and Redefinition in Business ethics," *Business Ethics Quarterly*, 10, no. 1 (2000): 156–157.

[46] J. Alex Tarquinio, "First, Self-Control. Then, Debt Control," *The New York Times*, March 29, 2008, p. C1.

[47] "Give Us Some Credit," *Albany Times Union*, May 6, 2008, http://www.timesunion.com/AspStories/story.asp?storyID=686360&category=OPINION&newsdate=5/6/2008.

[48] Christine Dugas, "Home-equity loans dry up; People in credit card jam look for other options," *USA Today*, September 6, 2007, p. 5B.

Savings are the life blood of the business system. Savings provide the funds for investment in new plant, research and development, and creativity. But our American propensity to use almost all of our discretionary income to purchase goods provides us minimal savings. Thus, in 2006 the savings rate of U.S. households fell to −1.0 percent of after-tax income, the lowest rate since the Great Depression. In other words, Americans now collectively either use their savings or borrow money to finance their current spending, and two-thirds of American families now admit to living paycheck to paycheck.[49] This also presents a problem for the future of families, because many do not have an adequate pension plan. Some have no pension funds at all. And, given takeovers and bankruptcies, those who do have a pension cannot always depend on it.

A lack of personal savings is also a long-term problem for business. Growth in productivity requires new investment. But new investment is limited by the amount of capital available. The lack of personal savings means that less capital is available for investment. But the problem lies not just with the inability or unwillingness of individuals to save. The U.S. federal government currently demands increasing amounts of capital, because of its large budget deficits. Thus, less money is available for private investment and this spawns an increase in interest rates. Borrowing thus becomes more expensive for business, individuals, and government. Because of the demand for capital and lack of savings in the United States, we must borrow more than two-thirds of the capital we need from abroad. If productivity in the United States declines because of a lack of capital at affordable interest rates, the entire economy will slow, thus threatening jobs and pensions. So note that large personal consumption, minimal personal savings, increased federal deficits, and larger personal and federal debt cause both short- and long-term problems for individuals and for the nation. Both personal and government behavior stems from short-sighted, self-interested values that might be characterized as an attitude of "look out for #1" and "let someone else worry about it."

Managing by the Numbers

In a large firm, it is difficult for top managers to know all the details of their products, markets, and employees. Given the greater distance from customers, new product ideas, production, and the public, executives find it difficult to monitor these areas. Thus, they turn to what they *can* understand—the control mechanism at their fingertips—"the numbers." Managers then rely on **financial measures** such as share price, return on equity, market share, total capitalization, and other numerical indices of success. Focusing on short-term measurable results can lead managers to reduce funding on activities that benefit the firm in the long term, such as **research and development, risk-taking, and training** programs.

In sum, short-term goals are a principal cause of fraud, lack of loyalty, lack of innovation, and short-sighted management. Managers, like all of us, are tempted to take the easy way out; they prefer short-term, measurable results so that their personal

---

[49] "Savings rate lowest since '30s Depression," *Toronto Star*, February 2, 2007, p. F2; John Pendygraft, "A Clean Break from Credit," December 28, 2007, *St. Petersburg Times*, p. 1D.

record looks good. Short-term, self-centered motives also breed unethical behavior. Note how the same shortsighted and self-centered values of managers can lead to both poor management and unethical behavior.

Lack of Trust in Business

Americans have little confidence in corporations or in corporate executives. On the one hand, this should not come as a surprise, given recent fraud and scandals. On the other hand, trust is essential for any institution and for that institution's leaders, especially in a democracy. When Americans are asked, not many institutions gain much support, but the low point to which corporations has fallen is notable. In one recent poll, just 11 percent of Americans expressed confidence in large corporations—a number far lower than their faith in the federal government (16%), small businesses (54%), and the U.S. military (67%).[50] Business cannot exist without trust, and such a low level of trust spells trouble for corporations and corporate executives.

Graduate business students' attitudes on some of these issues are shown in Table 1-2. Among these students only 31 percent now indicate that the real power in the

TABLE 1-2 Attitudes of Graduate Business Students on Business System and Power

	Percentage Agreeing*						
	1974	1981	1983	1988	1996	2004	2007
Business is overly concerned with profits and not enough with public responsibilities	75	70	51	66	69	60	81
Our foreign policy is based on narrow economic and power interests	70	75	54	53	38	64	84
Economic well-being is unjustly and unfairly distributed	80	34	34	42	38	51	66
The real power in the United States rests with							
a. The Congress	52	61	69	61	66	56	56
b. The giant corporations and financial institutions	81	88	87	89	88	79	100
c. The public	43	45	56	50	50	40	31

*Graduate business students from Wayne State University (1974), the University of Detroit (1981, 1983, 1988), and the University of Detroit Mercy (1996, 2004, 2007).

---

[50] John Harwood, "America's Economic Mood: Gloomy," *The Wall Street Journal*, August 2, 2007, http://online.wsj.com/article/SB118600572789185278.html.

country rests with the public and 100 percent agree that it rests with corporations and financial institutions. This indicates a significant feeling of **individual powerlessness**. Also noteworthy is the 66 percent who feel that "economic well-being is unjustly and unfairly distributed." This is the highest percentage that has felt this way since the "rebel" years of the early 1970s. Eighty-four percent feel that "U.S. foreign policy is based on narrow economic and power interests." This attitude is stronger than it has ever been. The extremely high percentage of business students who have consistently said that the real power in the United States rests with giant corporations and financial institutions is getting stronger in spite of the scandals and the resulting loss of confidence in business. They indicate corporate executives have the most power in the United States, and that it is being exercised for their own interests.

The countervailing power of democratic institutions appears to them to be not as strong. Cynicism is as apparent now as it was in the 1970s. These business students average 28 years of age, and most have worked at several full-time jobs. If these graduate business students are so disillusioned, the general population is even more critical. This cynicism is promoted by advertising. Advertising claims are often exaggerated and sometimes untrue. We have become accustomed to consumer products being glamorized beyond what is believable.

ADVERTISING AND MEDIA FORM VALUES

Abercrombie & Fitch (A&F), the clothing retailer, published racy magazines and catalogues. Its target audience was teenagers and young adults. The magazine included photos of nude and nearly nude young models. Its 2003 *Christmas Field Guide* featured the title "Group Sex" on its cover. To push its line of apparel, the *Guide* rarely pictured clothing, but used images of listless, barely clothed young people in an attempt to project an image of cutting-edge counterculture. Pro-family and feminist groups protested the *Guide*, and called for a boycott of A&F. In the wake of the protests, A&F withdrew the *Guide* in 2004. A&F sales have been dropping steadily for more than a decade.

The president of Citizens for Community Values placed an ad in the *Wall Street Journal* urging people to sell their A&F stock. When he learned that A&F had dropped the *Guide*, he said that it "doesn't change a thing . . . They have a track record of sexual exploitation and there are many different ways to continue that campaign." He and leaders of other groups have asked to meet with executives of A&F to discuss their advertising, but executives have refused. A&F judged that its magazine would give it a cutting-edge image, but found that "in terms of its racy content, it became harder and harder to outdo themselves, to provoke, to generate reaction, and to create the excitement of the past."[51] Is this another type of "race to the bottom" in order to obtain the attention of the potential purchaser? What does this tell us about sexually explicit advertising? Do such actions hurt the common good? Let us now examine the purpose of advertising.

Advertising is the **communication link** between retailer and consumer. Without advertising, the prospective purchaser is not aware of the price, quality, and

---

[51] David Carr and Tracie Bozhon, "Abercrombie & Fitch to End Its Racy Magazine," *The New York Times*, December 10, 2003, p. C1, C8.

availability of goods and services that might be of benefit. A free market requires a free flow of information, and some advertising provides information that is essential to consumers.

Looking at advertising from the consumer's viewpoint, the purpose of advertising is to provide information that will help that consumer to make or refuse to make a purchase decision. From the standpoint of the seller, the purpose of advertising is to convince people to purchase the product or service. As an example, one wonders why the consulting firm Accenture placed so much of its advertising budget into pictures of professional golfer Tiger Woods. Does golfing have anything to do with consulting? Is a prospective client of Accenture going to believe that there is a connection? Perhaps we are more gullible than we care to believe. The success of advertising is demonstrated by the fact that in the United States alone $149 billion was spent on it in 2007.[52]

Advertisers use a variety of approaches as they attempt to influence the purchasing decisions of consumers. Some advertising is informative and tasteful, and supports the values of individual responsibility, family, community, and sustainability. Note the British Petroleum (BP) and Royal Dutch Shell ads on how they are investing in renewable sources of power and clean air. GE advertises its commitment to wind and solar energy, "ecoimagination," and GE diesel and jet engines that use less fuel and produce less noise and pollution. Recall the Gallo TV ads that feature birthdays, weddings, baptisms, and other family-oriented activities. On the other hand, some advertising is self-oriented, sexist, and encourages antiwomen macho attitudes. Some ads are deceptive, crude, and demeaning. Many become suspicious and cynical about products that are thus advertised.

Children as Targets

Children have been targeted by advertisers. Many school lunch rooms are like fast-food courts lined with soft drink dispensers, all of which contribute to obesity among young people.[53] Moreover, 40 percent of U.S. teens get piped in TV news and ads in their classrooms. Also firms influence curricula by providing free materials; Exxon tells students that solar and wind energy is costly and unattainable, and the American Coal Foundation tells them that "the earth could benefit rather than be harmed from increased carbon dioxide."

By the age of two, children begin to ask for products by their brand name. Marketers want these children to nag their parents for their products, even though most requests will be denied. However, if parents deny 98 percent of the requests, the ad campaign pays off if the other 2 percent result in a purchase of the product. The average child sees 40,000 commercials, and receives 70 new toys each year. Children then want more and more things. Some parents report that they had to expand their home to hold the new toys. Marketers know that kids are now big business; in 1984 kids four to twelve years old spent $4.2 billion a year, but in 2004

---

[52] "2007 U.S. Advertising Expenditures Up Just 0.2%," *MediaBuyerPlanner*, March 26, 2008, http://www.mediabuyerplanner.com/2008/03/26/2007-us-advertising-expenditures-up-just-02/.

[53] Neil Buckley, "Health Lobby Aims to Burst School Soft-Drinks Bubble: School Boards Have Come to Rely on Income from Exclusive Sales Deals," *The Financial Times*, August 3, 2003, p. 12.

they spent $35 billion—much of it at stores designed just for them. They have developed a new vocabulary to describe kid marketing. Some examples: *Nag Factor* (or *Pester power*, *nudge factor*, *leverage*) refers to kids nagging parents to the point of purchase. *Shut-up toys* are toys costing $5 or less bought in desperation to pacify a child begging for something more expensive. *Viral marketing* pays cool kids to persuade peer kids to purchase a product.

Polls of parents show that 70 percent say kids are too focused on buying things, and 85 percent would like more limits on advertising to kids.[54] A few approve these techniques saying that they simply demonstrate the freedom and creativity of the market system. For example, Lucy Hughes, a vice president at Initiative Media, and co-creator of the Nag Factor, describes a recent study conducted by her firm:

> It was to help corporations help children nag their parents more effectively. Anywhere from 20% to 40% of purchases would not have occurred unless the child nagged their parents. . . . You can manipulate consumers into wanting and therefore buying, your products. It's a game. . . . The more insight you have about the consumer the more creative you can be in your communication strategies. So, if that takes a psychologist, yeah, we want one of those on staff. Somebody once asked me, "Lucy, is that ethical?" You're essentially manipulating these children. Well, yeah, is it ethical? I don't know. But our, our role at Initiative is to move products. And we know you move products with certain creative execution placed in certain type of media vehicle then we've done our job.[55]

Given the above, it is not difficult to see why many claim that such marketing takes advantage of uncritical children at an impressionable age and makes them victims of strategies designed to exploit them.

Marketers pay cool alpha boys to push products, and find "It" girls to host slumber parties, and then urge their friends to purchase products. Researcher Juliet Schor calls such marketers "predatory." These marketers' subtle message to children is that their meaning and self-worth comes from acquiring and owning. However, Schor's research shows that the more involved children become in the world of buying goods, the more likely they are to be depressed, be anxious, have a lower self-esteem, and have more psychosomatic complaints and poorer relationships with parents.[56]

Numerous other firms have self-centered advertising themes geared to children and their elders. Burger King claims, "Sometimes, you gotta break the rules." Neiman Marcus says, "Relax, no rules here." Bacardi Black Rum promises to take the drinker to a tipsy night where anything goes: "Some people embrace the

---

[54] Katy Kelly and Linda Kulman, "Kid Power: We All Want the Best for Our Children. But When They're Driving the Shopping Cart, How Much is Too Much?" *U.S. News and World Report*, September 13, 2004, pp. 47–31.

[55] Barak Goodman and Douglas Rushkoff, "The Persuaders," *Frontline* television series (Boston: WGBH, 2004), http://www.pbs.org/wgbh/pages/frontline/shows/persuaders/etc/script.html.

[56] Juliet B. Schor, *Born to Buy: The Commercialized Child and the New Consumer Culture* (New York: Scribner, 2004).

night because rules of the day do not apply." Do these ads of Burger King and Neiman Marcus promote, as one critic put it, "self-obsession, narcissism, and contempt for all rules"? Do they "strike at the sense of connectedness that any society needs to cohere and to care about its common problems and least fortunate members?"[57] These advertising strategies—albeit in many small ways—encourage materialism and self-centeredness and make it more difficult for us to develop common values in order to face our common problems.

Calvin Klein ran a series of ads in magazines and on buses with young teens posing in "what looks like opening scenes in a porn movie." In one ad, a girl is shown lying down with her skirt up, exposing her panties. In another shot from the crotch of a young curly headed boy, he gazes out sadly, as if looking for his next sexual relationship.[58] Sex is offered casually and as a commodity, but this is normal advertising copy for Calvin Klein. What effect does such advertising have on our values and morals?

Advertising Molds Values

Given the magnitude and pervasiveness of advertising, its effect on our values and the values of our children, it should concern us. However, it is difficult to clearly demonstrate that advertising affects our values. Advertisers do try to convince us that if we feel ill, unattractive, or unhappy, they have just the right product for us. Something we can buy can solve our problems. In order to sell, advertisers often intentionally appeal to lack of self-esteem, social status, and fear of ridicule.

Marketers have been accused of being creators of dissatisfaction. They present the handsome, immaculately dressed woman or man as an ideal to strive for; yet the ideal does not exist in the real world. Moreover, it can result in unattainable expectations and frustration, especially for the young and impressionable. Is it not shallow and dehumanizing to judge a person by the style of his or her clothes? Moreover, such an attitude sets one up to be disappointed when one discovers that money, possessions, and power do not bring happiness.

Advertising encourages consumption.[59] Marketing and advertising in its promotion of an affluent life style present Americans as materialistic, self-centered, and superficial. This picture is projected throughout the world, so it is not surprising that people in the Middle East, Asia, Africa, and Latin America see Americans as materialistic, selfish, and interested in themselves and not in others.

Marketing firms sell not only products, but political candidates as well. Advertising firms provide pictures of a political candidate in a 30-second TV ad in order to get us to vote for him or her. In place of seeing a statesman giving an explanation of a complex issue, we are subjected to carefully crafted images—with deftly chosen film footage and sound overlays. We are not introduced to a person, but rather presented an image, and are expected to vote on the basis of that image. Just as troubling, such

---

[57] John Leo, "Not Too Calvinist," *The Responsive Community*, Fall, 1995, pp. 12–14.

[58] "Not Too Calvinist," *Op. Cit.*

[59] Thomas Princen, Michael Maniates, and Ken Conca, eds., *Confronting Consumption* (Cambridge: MIT Press, 2003).

a strategy implies that complex issues are simple and easy to resolve, given a certain ideology. This is not only false but it implicitly denies that citizens need to be informed. It also undermines the patience to do the hard work that is required to vote intelligently in a democracy.

Advertisers tell us that they do not create values; they merely build on the values that they find already present. Successful advertising does appeal to our existing values. Nevertheless, advertising can reinforce and solidify childish, self-centered, and materialistic values latent in all of us. It does this especially among the less mature. In addition, advertising promotes brands, so it encourages people to choose Coke over juices, Fritos over vegetables, Porsches over people, fashionable clothes over art, and soap operas over reading. Along with its positive contributions of information, advertising also promotes shallowness, acquisitiveness, and egoism.

Advertisers also tell us that they do not influence our values. They say they are professionals, and they merely offer their skills without regard to the merits of a particular product or firm. However, morally this is an unacceptable position. Products, firms, and advertising strategies differ widely. Some products are worthwhile; others are trivial or even dangerous. Some firms treat customers and employees well; others do not. Some advertising campaigns are informative and humane, while others are manipulative and even deceptive.[60] Video games can be educational or violent and antisocial; but the number of "mature" games is increasing. One game, "Grand Theft Auto IV," sold 3.6 million copies the first day it went on sale in 2008. It casts the player as a gangster gunman with complete disregard for any laws.[61]

Television and films are major vehicles for advertising. TV advertising pays for programming and enables networks to be profitable. When a film gives a specific product a prominent place in that film, the film producer is usually paid. If you see a certain brand of beer or car in a film, you are more likely to purchase it. Columbia Broadcasting System (CBS) carried the 2004 Super Bowl. At halftime, Janet Jackson and Justin Timberlake sang. At the end of the song, Timberlake tore off Jackson's top, exposing her breast. The Super Bowl has an immense number of viewers—many of them children. Many people were shocked at the exposure. CBS and Viacom said that it was a surprise to them, and they did not approve the action. Yet prior to the halftime show, both had hyped the coming show as "shocking." The event set off Congressional hearings and a Federal Communications Commission (FCC) investigation. In the wake of threatened FCC and legislative sanctions, CBS and the other networks promised to clean up their programming. Such manipulative programming and advertising contributes to a distrust of business and to cynical people. Indeed a worldwide poll revealed that 45 percent of executives conceded that their corporations did not deserve the loyalty of their customers.[62]

---

[60] See Patrick E. Murphy and Gene R. Laczniak, *Marketing Ethics: Cases and Readings* (Lexington, MA: Lexington Books, 2006).

[61] Franklin Paul, " 'Grand Theft Auto' sales top $500 million: First week score one of the most lucrative entertainment events in history," MSNC.com, May 7, 2008, http://www.msnbc.msn.com/id/24502383/.

[62] "The Stat," *BusinessWeek*, March 8, 2004, p. 14.

WHY SOME FAIL

Let us return to the values of free enterprise. We have sketched above the competition, innovation, and growth, and also the short-term, self-centered, materialistic attitudes that free enterprise encourages. The intrusion of government results in inefficiencies and additional costs, and also discourages flexibility and creativity. The growth of a sense of personal entitlement encourages laziness, often expressed as "I have a right to an education or a job." Stemming from their own self-interest—primitive enterprise values—some feel that they should do the least amount of work for the best possible pay. These attitudes undermine business and a vibrant society.

A distinguishing feature of democratic capitalism and the entrepreneurial spirit is that individuals are encouraged to be the principal source of social and economic activities.[63] In fact, the past success of democratic capitalism in North America and Western Europe put those countries in a vulnerable position: They are envied by poorer peoples and criticized as exploitative. Moreover, parents who grow up in poverty do not know how to raise their children in affluence, and these children can become pampered and lazy. Both heavy-handed government and a personal sense of entitlement (or excessive self-interest) blunt the spirit of innovation and the attitudes that encourage the entrepreneur and business in general.

Self-Interest and Money

Business ideology holds that when individuals and firms pursue their own **self-interest**, market forces and the **"invisible hand"** bring about the most efficient use of resources and result in the greatest satisfaction of peoples' needs. According to this ideology of self-interest, the best that Intel can do for society is to provide quality chips at a low price and, in so doing, provide a good return to shareholders. This is Intel's contribution to society. If Intel fails in this, it is a failure as a business firm.

The ideology of self-interest has worked well for generations in the United States. And on many counts, it is still working well. It is justified by economic theory and blessed by the Protestant Ethic, which we will examine in Chapter 4. Individuals and businesses pursuing their own self-interest have brought goods and services, jobs, family income, and wealth to Western Europe, Japan, the United States, and now China, India, and other nations. Acquisitiveness coupled with creativity has made these economies successful. The ideology of self-interest acknowledges that people tend to be selfish. Capitalism, or free enterprise, builds on this self-centered motivation and guides it to work for the benefit of the entire society.

Many claim that economic goals—that is, increasing productivity, personal income, gross national product, and the availability of more and better goods and services—are the most important goals of our society. As U.S. President Calvin Coolidge put it just before the Great Depression of the 1930s, "The business of

---

[63] Michael Novak, "Toward a Theology of the Corporation," in *Business and Society: Dimensions of Conflict and the Corporation*, ed. P. Sethi and C. Falbe (Lexington: Lexington Books, 1887), pp. 1–20; see also Novak's, *The Spirit of Democratic Capitalism* (New York: Simon and Schuster, 1982).

America is business." One of the most valuable features of the free market is the potential for creating jobs. In a noteworthy case, Mohammad Yunus and his vision of micro-lending has provided work and income for 60,000,000 poor, illiterate women in developing countries, as we will see in Chapter 9. Most jobs are created by entrepreneurs who are creative, plan for the long term, and take risks.[64]

On the other hand, self-interest as a personal motivation has its negative aspects, and can even become pathological. Note this graphic description of how this motivation can be perverted:

> Bald, disrespectful and single-minded aggressiveness that is understood to be destructive in other circumstances has become celebrated in corporate trenches as "competitiveness". Angry egocentric lust for power that would qualify as tyranny in politics has been elevated to "strategic mastery" and "leadership" in business. And a runaway greed has been sanctioned as "wealth creation," making heroes out of billionaire workaholics.[65]

Is this an accurate description of those aggressive, competitive business managers, or is it one-sided and biased?

Two major problems spawned by business and industrialization are sweatshops and pollution. We will discuss both issues in later chapters, but for now note that exploitative workplaces and trashing the environment reduce costs, and so are promoted by short-term self-interest. It is in the short-term best interest of a firm to use cheap child labor and not to pay for the safe disposal of toxic waste, even though these actions injure people and society. The pursuit of self-interest generates these problems, so one can hardly expect that same motive to bring a solution. Thus, we must find more complete goals and values in order to have decent workplaces and a livable environment. To narrow the purpose of the firm to making a profit for shareholders is short-sighted. Kenneth Mason, when president of Quaker Oats, said that making a profit is no more the purpose of a corporation than getting enough to eat is the purpose of life. Getting enough to eat is a requirement of life. Life's purpose is broader and more challenging. Similar is the case with business and profit.

Moreover, an exclusive focus on self-interest can breed self-righteousness in pursuing narrow goals that result in indifference to consequences. These attitudes are described flippantly as "**creative greed**." Consider the values and tactics of men we will examine later: Conrad Black of Hollinger International and Jack Welch of GE. Each of these men looked to short-term self-interest, and their actions injured many other people. Critics note that our society idolizes men who are aggressive in their greed; it rewards them with money, power, and status, and thus reinforces selfishness and narrowness of vision.

---

[64] For examples, see Jim Collins, *Good To Great: Why Some Companies Make the Leap and Others Don't* (New York: HarperCollins, 2001).
[65] John Dalla Costa, *The Ethical Imperative: Why Moral Leadership Is Good Business* (Reading, MA: Addison-Wesley, 1998), p. 37.

Some corporate CEOs perceive MBA graduates as self-centered and not to be trusted. James Burke, a Harvard MBA who was CEO of Johnson & Johnson (J&J), says,

> In my business I'd as soon take a python to bed with me as hire a (Harvard MBA). He'd suck my brains, memorize my Rolodex and use my telephone to find some other guy who'd pay him twice the money . . . The problem begins with the selection process. If you lean heavily on test scores, you necessarily end up with people who are very adept at quantification. And human nature being what it is, people who are good at numbers tend to put a lot of faith in numbers. Which means that kids are coming out of business schools with less and less language skills, less and less people skills, and more and more to unlearn. The really important decisions don't have anything to do with quantification, as everyone figures out—eventually.[66]

Defenders of the ideology of self-interest respond that they speak of "**enlightened self-interest**," that is, self-interest taken over the long term that considers one's own needs in relation to the needs of others around us. They maintain that it is in the long-term self-interest of a manager and a firm to produce high-quality goods in order to maintain the loyalty of customers. The same can be said about healthy and open working conditions that help to hold able workers. Financial contributions to universities and community groups are justified because they will eventually provide a benefit to the firm and the firm's community. Indeed, evidence shows that a firm that obeys the law, is more socially responsible, and contributes more to charities does have better financial performance.[67]

Money and wealth are instruments to help people live a happier life. Business is the mechanism that brings jobs, goods, and services to people. Therefore, money and business are not ends in themselves. When money and wealth become ends in themselves, ethics and values are bent to serve those goals. We will discuss the strengths and weaknesses of free enterprise in greater detail in Chapter 6.

Free Market Fundamentalism

George Soros, who made billions on hedge funds (more than $2.7 billion in 2007 alone), is convinced that the problems discussed in this chapter stem largely from the elevation of self-interest to a moral principle, and that this has corrupted business, politics, and personal decisions. Self-interest as a guiding principle—an ideology—for personal and group activities has become dominant, especially in the United States. This ideology Soros calls "**market fundamentalism**." He

---

[66] Laurence Shames, *The Big Time: Harvard Business School's Most Successful Class and How It Shaped America* (New York: Mentor, 1986), pp. 181–182.

[67] Michelle Conlin, Lauren Gard, and Jessi Hempel, "America's Top Philanthropists," *BusinessWeek*, November 29, 2004, pp. 86–94; Richard E. Wokuch and Barbara A. Spence, "Corporate Saints and Sinners: Philanthropy, Crime and Organizational Performance," *California Management Review* 29 (Winter 1987): 62–77.

defines market fundamentalism as follows: All social activities and human interactions are viewed as transactional, contract-based relationships and valued in terms of a single common denominator, money. All economic and social activities should be regulated only by the invisible hand of profit-maximizing competition, and by government as little as possible. Market fundamentalists are convinced that markets are self-correcting and that any attempt to ensure the common good or the collective interest of the community distorts the market mechanism, reduces efficiency, and is ultimately ruinous.

Soros is convinced that the spread of market ideology into fields outside business is destructive. As an example, he makes a distinction between "making the rules" and "playing by the rules." Making the rules in the form of laws and regulations attempts to determine what is best for the public interest or the common good of the group; in a democracy this is done through the political process. Market behavior is guided by playing by the rules or observing the laws and regulations. But Soros says that

> Unfortunately the distinction is rarely observed. People seem largely to vote their pocketbooks and they lobby for legislation that serves their personal interests. What is worse, elected representatives also frequently put their personal interests ahead of the common interest. Instead of standing for certain intrinsic values, political leaders want to be elected at all costs—and under the prevailing ideology of market fundamentalism, or untrammeled individualism, this is regarded as natural, rational and even perhaps desirable way for politicians to behave.[68]

This results in the corruption of the political process, which in turn lessens respect for government. This then paradoxically becomes a strong argument in favor of giving markets even freer reign. Soros acknowledges that markets are more efficient than the political process. Or, in his words, the failure of politics "is much more pervasive and debilitating than the failure of the market mechanism"; yet one of the principal reasons for the failure of the political process is self-centered individualism. Soros's principal concern is that global markets and global capitalism are not working well. He is convinced that the failures he describes have rendered global capitalism unstable, and he has devoted much of his effort and great fortune to encouraging the establishment of a more open society that is available to all.[69] We will discuss his critique as it applies to global free markets in Chapter 9. Let us now turn to how we might restore trust in business.

RESTORING TRUST TO BUSINESS

Concentrating on freedom and personal self-interest makes cooperation, commitment, and community more difficult. One of the most basic human needs is to share joys, hopes, and problems with others. Our deep-rooted values of individualism and

---

[68] George Soros, *The Crisis of Global Capitalism* (New York: Public Affairs, 1998), p. xxvi.

[69] George Soros, *Open Society: Reforming Global Capitalism* (New York: Public Affairs, 2000).

self-interest, which support a free enterprise system, can nevertheless fracture community and turn the individual in on oneself.[70] The business firm values the person who is mobile, energetic, creative, and ambitious. People such as these were attracted to the New World and thrived here in succeeding generations. However, we rarely acknowledge the negative qualities of such people. Granted, the New World gained the energetic and the daring, but it also drew more than its share of the rootless, the unscrupulous, those who value money over people, and those who put self-interest before love and loyalty. These people, when faced with a difficult situation, abandon it all and flee to a new environment. The qualities that we value so highly—mobility and willingness to take risks—encourage us to flee the difficult situation in the hope of leaving our problems behind when we begin again. We have seen lives and careers shattered when a person walks out, whether it be on a firm, friends, or family. Note the biological fathers who are delinquent in their child support payments. It is easier to escape long-term responsibility in the tolerant, freedom-loving United States, if one has a mind to do so.

Integrity or Sanctions

Returning to the corporate financial scandals and frauds: how is it that so many businesses and executives fail so grievously? The Enron and WorldCom bankruptcies were the result of attempts to obscure the truth—so that the firm looked more profitable and healthy than it actually was. There is a powerful incentive in the free market to look profitable, even if one is losing money. As long as analysts and investors can be convinced that profits are steadily increasing, share price also increases. Increasing share price means that the firm can borrow more in order to acquire more firms, and thus increase revenue. What values were present that brought about these failures?

A root cause of the above financial and ethical failures was a **lack of honesty**. CFOs at each firm found themselves with a conflict of interest. They were willing to hide expenses and invent or exaggerate revenues. There was a short-term incentive for them to make the firm look more profitable. A second motivation was greed. In most of the above instances, the executives had lucrative stock options, which made their lying also profitable to them personally. It also increased their performance bonuses, because the "results" looked so good. Arthur Andersen audited both Enron and WorldCom. Moreover, Andersen had large consulting contracts with both firms, and Andersen determined it could not afford to lose them; this provided a powerful incentive for the auditor to overlook accounting misdeeds, again a conflict of interest.[71]

Another root cause of the failures is Wall Street's **obsession with quarterly earnings**. Daily and even hourly TV and radio report stock movements. These reports often are given at the same time as announcements of the daily lottery winners, and both are examples of people trying to make money on speculation. Some maintain

---

[70] Paul Krugman, *The Great Unraveling: Losing Our Way in the New Century* (New York: W. W. Norton, 2003).

[71] Marianne M. Jennings, "Preventing Organizational Ethical Collapse," *Journal of Government Financial Management* 53 (Spring 2004): 12–19.

that the American obsession with short-term earnings and the lottery has turned us into a "casino society"—that is, it is easier to make money by speculation than by working.

The purpose of the free enterprise system is to provide goods, services, and jobs. Profit is an essential measure of the success of a firm, but it is not the only measure of success. If a firm is not profitable, it will fail and will cease providing jobs and goods. However, placing exclusive emphasis on profits ensnares a firm in the difficulties that destroyed Enron and WorldCom. Such emphasis also leads a firm like Wal-Mart to pressure its suppliers to use low-wage, sweatshop manufacturers for its goods, and to pay low wages, along with poor health and retirement benefits to its workers.

Governments step in to provide rules for systems where trust is missing. For example, legislation passed in the wake of the U.S. scandals, the Sarbanes-Oxley (SOX) bill, is designed to lessen some of the conflicts of interest discussed above. It restricts an auditing firm from also consulting with the same company, and the auditing firm must rotate its lead auditor every five years. The audit committee of the company being audited must be composed of all outside directors. The company's lawyers must report evidence of securities fraud to the CEO and the Board. And the CEO and the CFO must each personally certify the quarterly financial reports. Likewise, the U.S. SEC has written new regulations on conflict of interest between investment bankers and analysts, and has set up a Board to oversee the accounting firms. Predictably, many government agencies began considering new regulations as a result of the housing and credit crisis that started in the United States in 2007. For example, U.S. federal regulators have already proposed new rules that would require mortgage lenders to base their loan decisions on a borrower's ability to repay an adjustable rate mortgage at the full interest rate instead of the borrower's ability to pay the low introductory rate, and industry trade publications have already warned their constituents that new regulations are an almost inevitable outcome of the crisis.[72]

Two current trends in political life accelerate the loss of a sense of the common good in the United States: Narrow special interests are now stronger and more vocal, and there is a paralyzing lack of consensus regarding national priorities. In many arenas, the confrontational mode of dealing with others is a part of the American way. Not only do we use the adversary system in the law courts, but we have institutionalized much conflict (e.g., labor versus management, business versus government, and environmentalists versus growth). The rhetoric is one of "battle" and "struggle," "win or lose," as if a win for one group is always a loss for another. Special interest groups gather in Washington, D.C., to push for their narrow objectives. These include the American Medical Association (physicians), National Rifle Association, National Education Association (public school teachers), auto dealers, pro-choice feminists, and the Religious Right. Some special interest groups even work to defeat members of Congress who are not to their liking. The media then give unwarranted attention to protests, scandals, and conflicts; viewers love a good fight! Negotiation and building a consensus are hard work, not glamorous, and thus do not make headlines.

---

[72] Vikas Bajaj, "Senate Questioning on Mortgages Puts Regulators on the Defensive," *The New York Times*, March 23, 2007, p. c4. "Politically-driven post-crisis legislation must be avoided," *The Banker*, April 7, 2007, http://www.thebanker.com/news/fullstory.php/aid/5663/.

Therefore, poor communication, distrust, and cynicism grow at a time when listening, cooperation, and compromise are badly needed.

When Americans agree on an issue, the agreement is often about being against something: taxes, bureaucrats, censorship, and big government. But we Americans find it harder to tell others what we stand *for*—what kind of a society we favor. We find it difficult to express **social ideals** and we lack the vocabulary to do so. We are not helped by our political discussions, which appeal to simplistic ideologies and do not help us to sort out priorities and balance the resulting tradeoffs. Yet it is essential to discuss our priorities, both personal and national, if we are to determine what kind of society we want. These failures in the political forum encourage Americans to be distrustful and not listen to those with differing views. Finding a common bond and developing a sense of community are both more important and more difficult.

However, as we will see in later chapters, many managers around the world are developing a new sense of **global ethical responsibility**. These executives seek to (1) align their firm with its proclaimed values and also encourage commitment and trust within the organization (organizational functioning), (2) establish a good reputation with customers and suppliers (market positioning), (3) avoid legal and financial problems (risk management), and (4) be regarded as good corporate citizens in their community (civic positioning).[73] Moreover, a firm is not penalized financially if it is more responsible. In fact, firms that are ethically and socially responsible tend to be more successful financially, also.[74] This is a value shift for many executives as they broaden the measures of firm performance beyond financial to also include social and environmental criteria. The remaining chapters of this book will expand on these issues and help us to clarify our personal and business goals, better understand our successes and failures, and aid us in planning our future.

Summary and Conclusions

During the last generation, the U.S. economy has been successful in providing jobs and a multitude of low-price goods and services for people. This sparks pride because the successes are built on traditional values of free markets, competition, self-interest, and innovation. On the other hand, recent business scandals—financial fraud; "managing the numbers" to suit the analysts and shareholders; preferential treatment given by banks, mutual funds, and insurance companies to their largest customers; and executives using company funds to purchase personal homes or furniture—are often justified by the same values of competition and self-interest.

Self-interest motivates business and many people. Advertising and the media encourage self-interest. Yet excessive self-interest undermines loyalty, family, community, and helping others. If competition and self-interest are not constrained by integrity, trust, and moral values, free enterprise is at risk of collapsing, because

---

[73] The categories are those of Lynn Sharp Paine. See her *Value Shift: Why Companies Must Merge Social and Financial Imperatives to Achieve Superior Performance* (New York: McGraw-Hill, 2003).
[74] M. Orlitzky, F. L. Schmidt, and S. L. Rynes, "Corporate Social and Financial Performance: A Meta-Analysis," *Organization Studies* 24, no. 3 (2003): 403–441. The researchers analyzed more than 50 published studies and found the positive correlation.

business requires trust. Moreover, it will be impossible for Americans to achieve a fulfilling and happy life if most of us are self-centered. If self-interest becomes a moral norm in all decisions, government, health care, and schools will deteriorate even further. For government to operate effectively and to have adequate education and health care for all requires that we determine our goals as individuals and as a society. The hardest part of democracy is dialogue, negotiation, and compromise.

The following chapters will examine personal moral development (Chapter 2), ethical behavior (Chapter 3), the historical roots of American business values (Chapters 4 and 5), and the effect of those values on society (Chapter 6), on the person (Chapter 7), and in the global marketplace (Chapters 8 and 9), and finally emerging future business values (Chapter 10). As we will see in Chapter 2, we are born self-centered and become more concerned about others as we mature.

Discussion Questions

1. Are the benefits of Wal-Mart's "everyday low price" worth the cost of so many "associates" receiving low wages with poor, if any, health or retirement benefits? Does Wal-Mart take unfair advantage of its workers and suppliers?
2. How much does Wal-Mart's involvement in environmental causes offset criticisms about its other actions? Does it matter if Wal-Mart is undertaking these actions because "they are right" or to "quiet critics"?
3. List the principal benefits of a healthy free enterprise business system.
4. What is a conflict of interest? Describe a conflict of interest for a purchasing agent, a government official, an auditing firm, an investment banker, a mutual fund, and businesses paying taxes.
5. How would you evaluate Dennis Kozlowski's ethics? His moral maturity? Were the actions of Kozlowski and his executive team in the best interest of Tyco and its shareholders?
6. List the (a) strengths and (b) weaknesses of viewing the purpose of the firm as increasing shareholder value. When this results in a short-term view, what are the results for the firm?
7. Do you think that business scandals are at an end, or is the current mortgage and credit crisis the beginning of a new era marked by a lack of ethics and values in business?
8. When U.S. jobs are "outsourced" to increase profitability, what are the advantages and disadvantages to U.S. citizens?
9. List the negative effect of layoffs. When a firm finds it necessary to "downsize," what are its responsibilities to the affected people?
10. How do we judge the impact of jobs that are being created in developing countries against the loss of jobs for Americans? Are Americans able to sustain themselves more easily than people in poor countries?
11. Why do Americans save so little of their income? What are the individual consequences of a lack of savings? What impact does a lack of savings have on business?
12. Cite the evidence for the loss of confidence in business and in business executives. How might this affect the efficiency of business operations?
13. Is it fair to target young children in advertising? Why do we see so many sexually explicit advertisements? Is this an example of a "race to the bottom" in order to grab the attention of the potential purchaser? Do such actions hurt moral standards and the common good?
14. Do many ads promote self-obsession and contempt for rules, and fracture the sense of connectedness that any society needs to cohere and to care about its common problems and least fortunate members?

15. In what way do advertising and the media influence values? Do you think each presents honest or deceptive images of people and what brings them happiness?
16. Is it shallow and dehumanizing to judge a person by the style of clothes or the car he or she drives?
17. Is self-interest the primary motivation of most businesspeople, as you experience them?
18. Is self-interest an adequate motivation for businesspeople? When is it effective? When is it not adequate?
19. What analogy does Kenneth Mason, former president of Quaker Oats, use in rejecting the position that the purpose of the corporation is to maximize returns to shareholders?
20. Does self-interest as a goal for businesspeople necessarily cast government into the role of a regulator? Explain.
21. Describe market fundamentalism. According to Soros, why is self-interested behavior appropriate when purchasing but not when voting? Is self-interest already a moral norm?
22. What values brought about the failures of Tyco, Enron, and WorldCom?
23. Is anything else needed beyond the new legislation and regulation to restore trust to business? If so, what?

Selected Additional Readings

Peter F. Drucker, *Concept of the Corporation* (New Brunswick, NJ: Transaction Publishers, 1993).

Marjorie Kelly, *The Divine Right of Capital: Dethroning the Corporate Aristocracy* (San Francisco: Berrett-Koehler, 2003).

Allan A. Kennedy, *The End of Shareholder Value: Corporations at the Crossroads* (Cambridge, MA: Perseus, 2000).

Ted Nace, *Gangs of America: The Rise of Corporate Power and the Disabling of Democracy* (San Francisco: Berrett-Koehler, 2003).

Wade Rowland, *Greed, Inc.: Why Corporations Rule Our World* (New York: Arcade Publishing, 2006).

CASES

Case 1-1   College Test

Kathy Blankenship and Joe Fontana are juniors at Lincoln University's business school. Both are taking their first course in finance taught by Dr. Hugh Sikora. Kathy is in the Honors Program. Joe is an outgoing young man, and is a "C" student. On the first exam, Kathy scored the second highest grade in the class and Joe failed. The next exam, more heavily weighted, was three weeks later. During the exam Sikora noticed Joe glancing in the direction of Kathy's paper several times. When grading the papers, Sikora noted all 15 multiple choice answers were identical on both Joe's and Kathy's papers, including two responses that were incorrect.

1. You are a student sitting behind Joe, and you see what he is doing. Do you have any responsibility to speak to Joe? To the instructor?
2. As the instructor, you notice Joe's activities during the exam. What should you do? Why?

3. As you grade the papers, you note the identical answers on the exam. What should (or would) you do?

4. What ethical issues are involved here?

■ ■ ■

Case 1-2   Confidentiality of E-Mail

Alana Shoars, an e-mail administrator for Epson America in Los Angeles, arrived at work one morning to find her supervisor reading e-mail messages sent between employees. She protested, and was fired. Although Epson had no stated policy on the privacy of messages, they argued that the network was their property and was for company business only.

CSBP found one employee using e-mail to bet on the horses, and another was running an Amway business from office e-mail.

1. Does a firm have a right to monitor employees' e-mail?

2. Does a firm have an obligation to inform employees of their policies on e-mail?

3. Comment on the ethics involved in the situation at Epson and CSBP.

■ ■ ■

Case 1-3   Global Climate Change and ExxonMobil

Data show that the earth is gradually warming, and scientists agree that the burning of fossil fuels, forming "greenhouse gases," is a cause. Global climate change is breaking up the world's ice packs, which threatens to raise ocean levels perhaps by as much as three feet in 50 years, thus swamping many coastal areas and islands around the world. Climate change also threatens to cause increased storm damage because of warmer oceans. ExxonMobil, one of the largest firms in the world, sponsored the Global Climate Coalition, an industry group that was formed to lobby for U.S. rejection of the Kyoto Treaty; Kyoto was negotiated among the nations of the world to limit greenhouse gases. BP, Shell, Ford, and GM quit the Coalition, once the data on global climate change became clear. ExxonMobil still took the position that there is not enough certainty to make policy decisions. ExxonMobil is also the owner of the ExxonValdez, which ran aground in Prince William Sound in Alaska in 1989, and spilled 11 million gallons of crude oil that covered fish, fowl, mammals, and 1,200 miles of coast. ExxonMobil is still held responsible by citizens and the state of Alaska for the accident, for not doing a thorough cleanup job, and for not paying appropriate damages for the spill.

1. Does ExxonMobil have any responsibility for the production of greenhouse gases? What would lead them to be the last to support the now defunct Global Climate Coalition?

2. What responsibility did ExxonMobil have for the cleanup of Prince William Sound? Did the firm take responsible action on these two issues?

3. What ethical values and norms help you decide these two cases?

Exercises

Exercise 1-1: Personal Goals and Values Inventory

This exercise is intended to help you clarify your own personal goals and values, and to see how your life goals support or conflict with your values and personal experiences.

1. Procedure:
   a. Rank order the values on the value survey below (16 long-range values).
   b. Complete the life goal inventory. Reflect on and record your major goals for the next one to two years in each of the areas indicated.
   c. Write a paper (maximum of six double-spaced typed pages) examining and comparing your life goals, your most important values, and your experiences.
2. **Suggestions** for writing the paper:
   a. Write in the first person, not the third person. It may help to think of this as a letter to a very close friend, to you, or as diary entries.
   b. Describe the origin of your goals and your personal history in a paragraph or two. What specific events in your life affected your goals and values?
   c. Discuss briefly each of the seven goals but describe only your most important values or clusters of values.
      1. Compare your present life, activities, and job with your goals and values.
      2. Is there any particular satisfaction in your life that is explained by support from your goals and values?
      3. Is there any frustration that might be explained by conflict among them?
      4. Clarify the points you make with specific personal experiences and examples.
      5. Do your values support your goals? Or do some conflict?
      6. To what extent has your life been guided or influenced by your goals and/or your values?
   d. Your listing of your life goals and personal values are intended to help you with your analysis. They are merely an aid to help you write your paper. It is not necessary to turn in your personal values or life goal inventory. If you do, include as an appendix.
   e. Write reflections honestly and straightforwardly. No one but the instructor will see your paper. It is confidential, and will be returned quickly.
   f. Use clear language and good grammar. Choose directness and clarity over elaboration.
3. **Criteria** for evaluating the paper are the demonstration of your ability to analyze and articulate your own goals, values, and experiences:
   a. Clarity of analysis of goals, values, and experiences.
   b. Ability to recognize and deal with the meaning of support and conflict among goals, values, and experiences, and their significance for future life and career decisions.
   c. Quality of your paper, including life experiences, correct writing, and examples.
4. Apologies for intruding into your personal goals. However, experience indicates that most of us do not take time to reflect on our goals and values unless (1) a crisis arises in our lives, or (2) we are asked to do so. This exercise and paper will enable you to gain a better understanding of your goals before a crisis arises.

Life Goal Inventory

This inventory[75] is designed to help you examine your life goals. Describe as fully as you can your aims and goals in all areas of your life. List all goals that are important to you, whether they are fairly easy or difficult to attain. Be honest in this assessment; only then will the inventory be useful to you. For example, if your major goal is to enjoy leisure

---

[75] Adapted from: Joyce S. Osland, David Kolb, and Irwin Rubin, *Organizational Behavior: An Experiential Approach*, 7th ed. (Upper Saddle River: Prentice-Hall, 2001).

satisfactions, indicate this, so as to better understand yourself. Describe two to five goals in each of the following spheres over the next year or two. The categories are a guide; feel free to change them to suit your own goals.

Career (goals in employment or career; situation aimed for).

 1.

 2.

 3.

Relationships with People (goals with family, friends, colleagues, others).

 1.

 2.

 3.

Status and Respect (goals in your social circles; people from whom you seek esteem).

 1.

 2.

 3.

Leisure (Vacations, sports, hobbies, other interests).

 1.

 2.

 3.

Learning and Education (knowledge, skills, experiences to learn, areas to study).

1.

2.

3.

Spiritual Growth and Religion (goals: peace of mind, prayer, meaning, giving self to others).

1.

2.

3.

Material Rewards and Possessions (goals in income, wealth, possessions).

1.

2.

3.

Rank Ordering of Personal Values

Rank the following 16 long-range personal values[76] in the order of importance to you, that is, insofar as they are guiding principles in your life. Place 1 in front of the value that is most important in your life, 2 in front of the next most important, and so on. The least important value for you should be ranked 16. If you change your mind, feel free to change the ranking. When you are finished, the list should roughly indicate the importance of the various values in your life.

_____ Achievement (promotions at work)
_____ Beauty (natural and artistic beauty)
_____ Cooperation
_____ Dollar rewards (money and salary)

---

[76] Adapted from Milton Rokeach, *The Nature of Human Values* (New York: Free Press, 1973).

_____ Family security (taking care of and being with family)
_____ Freedom (independence)
_____ Justice (equal opportunity for all; concern for disadvantaged)
_____ Love, friendship, and intimacy
_____ Physical health and well-being
_____ Pleasure (sensually and sexually enjoyable personal life)
_____ Possessions (good car, clothes, home, many material goods)
_____ Recognition (respect, admiration from others)
_____ Self-respect (a good self-image, self-esteem)
_____ Sense of accomplishment (making a lasting contribution)
_____ Spirituality (prayer, meditation, striving to be a good person)
_____ World at peace (lessening of war and conflict)

Exercise 1-2: Prevalence of Advertising in Our Daily Lives

Take a moment to guess how many corporation names or corporate product logos, symbols, and slogans are present within your classroom. Write your estimate down on a piece of paper. Then, spend exactly one minute looking around your classroom and count every instance where you see a corporation name or corporate/product logo/symbol/slogan. If you see a name or logo/symbol/slogan in more than one location, count it each time you see it.

1. How many names and logos/symbols/slogans did you count in one minute?
2. Was your actual count higher or lower than your pre-count estimate?
3. How many items total did each of your classmates count?
4. Where their actual counts higher or lower than their pre-count estimates?
5. Based on the observations of you and your classmates, how prevalent is advertising in our daily lives?
6. Based on the observations of you and your classmates, how much of an impact does this advertising have on our values and decisions?

2

■ ■ ■

Moral Maturity

You have the most powerful weapons on earth—love and prayer.

JOHN MARX TEMPLETON, FOUNDER, TEMPLETON FUNDS

No one can be poor that has enough; nor rich,
who desires more than he has.

LUCIUS ANNAEUS SENECA (4 BC–65 AD),
ROMAN PHILOSOPHER AND PLAYWRIGHT

Universities . . . are producing throngs of narrow-minded specialists
who may be wizards at making money, but who are unfinished
as people. These specialists have been taught how to do, but
they have not learned how to be.

WARREN BENNIS, FOUNDER, LEADERSHIP INSTITUTE,
UNIVERSITY OF SOUTHERN CALIFORNIA

We are not born with moral maturity. We learn a sense of right and wrong from parents, friends, churches, and schools—and from experiences like those we reviewed in Chapter 1. In this chapter we will examine (1) the stress that stems from clouded personal values and goals, (2) the moral development of the individual person, (3) methods of making personal values explicit, and finally (4) the reasons for considering ethics when making important business decisions. To be successful today, it is essential to understand our personal goals, to stay mentally alert and engaged during a 50-year working life, to know in which sort of organization we can work best, and to constantly try to improve our own competency.[1] But first let us examine some examples of people, including executives, who found themselves under stress.

> Katy Spivak, a student at Emory University, yielded to ads and the gifts that were offered to sign up for 14 credit cards. Within three years she had a debt of $9,000. She now works two jobs and has paid down her debt to $7,500. However, 118,000 other young people under 25 have filed for bankruptcy. The adult credit card market has matured, and firms find college students to be easy targets as new customers.[2]
>
> Lee Iacocca was president of Ford and later chairman of Chrysler, but he reported that he flunked retirement. He says his life was so structured and isolated as CEO, that he was not able to handle the flexibility of retirement. His third wife of three and one-half years maneuvered him to move to California, and then fought him in a nasty divorce six months later.[3]
>
> James E. Olson was chairman and chief executive officer (CEO) of AT&T. He oversaw the largest corporate restructuring in American history: the breakup of AT&T into numerous operating systems. In the process, he cut one billion dollars from AT&T's costs, largely through layoffs. One year later at age 63 he died suddenly.[4]
>
> Eli Black, CEO of United Brands, broke the window of his forty-fourth floor office in Manhattan and jumped to his death. Two months later the Securities and Exchange Commission revealed that United Brands had paid a $1,250,000 bribe to a government official in Honduras for a reduction in the export tax on bananas. Black knew about the bribe.

Each of these people faced stress, anxiety, and a conflict in values. They are examples of the strains and anxieties that face businesspeople every day. This chapter will examine the sources of these conflicts, the anxiety and stress that accompany them, and some strategies that will aid in avoiding conflicts and stress.

LACK OF MATURITY BRINGS STRESS

People who are mature and **morally developed** (for definitions, see Figure 2-1) are generally are able to more fully utilize their talents, are more relaxed, enjoy life more, and are generally more liked and respected by their families and peers. Moreover, they are also considered wise and are more often consulted by others. Even in a difficult situation, a mature person—for example, an honest accountant in a firm that is misstating income or a pacifist in a time of war—possesses a basic stability and composure. On the other hand, anxiety, stress, and illness often plague the person who is not mature and morally developed.

---

[1] Peter F. Drucker, "Managing Oneself," *Harvard Business Review,* March–April 1999, pp. 67–74.
[2] "Congratulations, Grads—You're Bankrupt: A Marketing Blitz Buries Kids in Plastic and Debt," *BusinessWeek,* May 21, 2001, p. 48.
[3] "How I Flunked Retirement," Lee Iacocca interviewed, *Fortune,* June 24, 1996, pp. 50–61.
[4] *BusinessWeek,* May 2, 1988, p. 34.

Character: A stable organized personality with a composite of good and bad moral habits within a person.

Common Good: Good of the group as a whole; general welfare

Community: Any group sharing goals, interests, work, etc.

Maturity: State of being fully developed as a person.

Moral Development: Increased ability of a person to distinguish right and wrong and to engage in good behavior.

FIGURE 2-1   **Moral Development Terms**

Midlife Crisis

An individual who has not internalized his own values makes life and career decisions without clear goals and the ability to examine alternatives. This often leads to a midlife crisis.

> Adrienne Glasgow was manager of international finance at Borden at the age of 35. However, she quit her job, because she was not fulfilled. She is now consulting.[5] Two-thirds of women engage in a mid-course correction. Some who fall short of their career goals are more likely to be depressed.[6]
>
> John Miner quit his job as president of Intel Capital, the venture arm of the chip maker. "People think I'm nuts for leaving." But "as I turned 50, I decided there were not too many chances to explore new options."[7]
>
> The *Wall Street Journal*, *BusinessWeek*, and *Fortune* regularly run articles on people who leave well-paid corporate jobs to do something quite different at a fraction of their former pay. These men and women found their work in the corporation to be too confining, and many turned to a simpler and less-structured life. Typical is Ross Drever, age fifty-two, who quit as director of Amsted Industries' research division at a $140,000 salary. He now works a cranberry bog in Three Lakes, Wisconsin. He says, "I have a lot of suits and shoes I'll never use again."

These managers felt they were giving too much time to a job that gave them little satisfaction. They made a radical change; they left comfortable jobs, homes,

---

[5] Betsy Morris, "Executive Women Confront Midlife Crisis," *Fortune,* September 18, 1995, pp. 60–86. This article chronicles a dozen such cases. See also Abigail J. Stewart and Joan M. Ostrove, "Women's Personality in Middle Age: Gender, History, and Midcourse Corrections," *American Psychologist,* 53 (November 1998): 1185–1194.

[6] Deborah Carr, "The Fulfillment of Career Dreams at Midlife: Does it Matter for Women's Mental Health?" *Journal of Health and Social Behavior,* 38 (December 1997): 331–344.

[7] "John Miner's Midlife Crisis at Intel," *Institutional Investor,* May 2006, p. 1.

and friends to carve out a new life. These women and men show us how some at midlife examine their new values and goals and act on what they find. They find that one cannot have it all at once; it is necessary to make choices. The challenge is to make choices that enable both oneself and one's loved ones to grow.

This reassessment often occurs around the age of 40. One looks around and asks if this is the way one would choose to lead the rest of one's life. Time is running out; there may be only two decades of healthy work life left—maybe more, maybe less.

A midlife crisis can be traumatic—to family, to fellow workers, and to the person experiencing it. On some occasions, the person experiencing the midlife transition panics and seeks a dramatic change. The individual sometimes breaks all connections to the past, leaves spouse and children behind, and goes off accompanied by different friends. This sort of radical break causes fractures and hurts families, neighbors, and coworkers. Such a reaction to the midlife journey is desperate and immature. However, the frequency of these sharp midlife breaks shows that many of us have not sufficiently probed our own goals in order to take charge of our lives. Rather than setting our own goals, we often choose the job that has the best compensation and allow these criteria to determine our career and goals for us.

In an effort to help his own professional school graduates set priorities that will give them long-term satisfaction, the dean of Harvard Business School gave them the following advice:

There is no success in business that can compensate for failure at home. Invest first at home, and think of that as your most important investment in your lives. The most important work you do in your whole lives will be inside the walls of your home.[8]

Businesspeople sometimes spend too many hours at work, and thus neglect their family. Moreover, an ideology of personal freedom can encourage a person to leave home, job, city, marriage, and friends to find personal fulfillment, but ironically those relationships are probably their best hope for personal fulfillment.[9]

The **midlife journey** can be a gradual, life-giving reassessment, especially if the person has made her goals and values her own. The journey can become a crisis if one's goals and values have not been examined and if one's life has been determined by salaries and status, instead of by enlightened choices.[10] The objective is to consciously take possession of your own goals and values. The more clearly you recognize what your heartfelt goals are and what brings you real happiness, the greater the chance that your midlife reassessment will be gradual, peaceful, and life giving.

---

[8] *BusinessWeek,* June 26, 2000, p. 83.

[9] Jonathan Haidt, *The Happiness Hypothesis: Finding Modern Truth in Ancient Wisdom* (New York: Basic Books, 2006), p. 133.

[10] Denise Lyons, "Freer to Be Me: The Development of Executives at Midlife," *Consulting Psychology Journal,* 54 (Winter 2002): 15–27.

Stress at Work

Self-esteem depends on the candid feedback a person receives from others. Those who gain the esteem of their peers consider themselves successful. Such people are typically competent, goal-oriented, conscientious, ambitious, humble, and hard working, qualities which stem from the Protestant ethic, as we will see in Chapters 4 and 5.

The culture, through families, schools, churches, business, and government, communicates its values to the individual. A culture thus gives people direction. Without this socialization process, it is not possible to know what one person may expect of another in everyday dealings. We will examine the socialization process within the firm in Chapter 7.

Job performance, self-esteem, and satisfaction at work and at home are influenced by the values that people share, such as the importance of work and wealth, individualism, self-interest, and time thrift. These same values can also cause conflict and stress. We are stressed by our ideals and the expectations we have for ourselves, and it is this stress that drives us forward. Nevertheless, we must be careful lest our expectations drive us too far and hard in how we treat ourselves, our families, colleagues, and fellow citizens. These values promote competitiveness, self-interest, desire for control, and frequent job changes—which place us in greater stress.[11]

Stress occurs when an individual faces a constraint, demand, or opportunity related to what he or she desires and for which the outcome is both important and uncertain.[12] Stress in the workplace is common. The vast majority of U.S. workers feel stress on the job; 62 percent say their workload has increased and 53 percent say work leaves them "overtired and overwhelmed." In addition, 42 percent say that job pressures are harming their personal relationships, and 35 percent say that their jobs are harming their physical and emotional health. Workplace stress is estimated to cost the United States more than $300 billion each year in health care and missed work. Moreover, this stress seems to be increasing.[13] There are a variety of causes for this stress, among them, pressure to finish a job, fear of losing one's job, and lack of control over outcomes. In addition, Americans are working harder and longer hours as their coworkers are laid off, and those left must do extra work. At present, Americans put in more time on the job than do workers in any other nation. Japanese held first place until 1995, when Americans surpassed them in total hours worked. Workplace demands and stress are not limited to the United States and Japan. Half of the workers in the European Union complain that they must work at very high speed, must face tight deadlines and monotonous tasks, and have no opportunity to rotate tasks.

---

[11] Michael Peterson and John F. Wilson, "Work Stress in America," *International Journal of Stress Management,* 11 (2004): 91–113.

[12] Adapted from R. S. Schuler, "Definitions and Conceptualization of Stress in Organizations," *Organizational Behavior and Human Performance* (April 1980): 189; also Lorne Sulsky and Carlla Smith, *Work Stress* (Belmont, CA: Thomson Wadsworth, 2005).

[13] Bruce Cryer, Rollin McCraty, and Doc Childre, "Pull the Plug on Stress," *Harvard Business Review* (July 2003): 102–107; Arthur Schwartz, "Always on the Job, Employees Pay With Health," *The New York Times,* September 5, 2004, p. B1; "Attitudes in the American Workplace VII," (Harris Poll, 2001).

For most of us, success in business is considered important, and people who are not successful are often judged inferior by others. Such lack of success is a source of stress. Further job-related stress is caused by conflict and confusion over a person's responsibilities, or when the job calls for actions that run counter to a person's ethics.[14] In these cases, either a compromise is reached or something is sacrificed. In either case, the result is stress and frustration.

Those who are judged successful according to the prevailing norms (i.e., wealthy, ambitious, and hardworking) may also suffer anxieties. Successful corporate managers are mobile. They leave their present jobs and homes in order to move on to "better" positions. Psychologists tell us that anxiety is caused by moving from the known to the unknown. Having mastered one environment, it is unsettling to be asked to move to a new one. This is especially true when one has been laid off. Executives now tout workplace flexibility as a desirable quality. But in the process of moving from job to job, firm to firm, and city to city, loyalty to both firm and community is lost.[15] It is true that in order to mature, one must take risks and change. Yet being uprooted every few years—leaving behind not just the confidence built in mastering a job but also friends, relatives, and knowledge of the community—can diminish the willingness to commit oneself to a new job or neighborhood. These mobile managers thus demand their spouse and children undergo the same cyclic trauma of arriving and departing, and the accompanying pain and anxiety it causes. People in such situations may be forced in upon themselves and may come to depend more on their aggressiveness than on the help and cooperation of coworkers, friends, and neighbors. In some cases, destructively narcissistic managers focus on themselves, devalue others, impair an organization's morale and performance, and add to workplace stress. On the whole, stress appears to be increasing, and work is the primary source of stress. Work–family conflict is a principal cause of stress, especially with the increase in the number of families where both spouses work.[16] We will discuss this issue in Chapter 7.

Causes of Stress

The unknown, and even more the uncontrolled, produces anxieties. Ulcers and stress are often manifestations of anxiety; they can result when there are conflicting demands on the individual. Neuroses have been experimentally induced in animals exposed to

---

[14] See Peter J. Frost, *Toxic Emotions at Work: How Compassionate Managers Handle Pain and Conflict* (Boston: Harvard Business School Press, 2003), pp. 36–55, 92–93. See also the comprehensive overview, James Quick, Jonathan Quick, Debra Nelson, and Joseph Hurrell, *Preventive Stress Management in Organizations* (Washington, D.C.: *American Psychological Association*, 1997). For coping with stress, see Salvador R. Maddi and Deborah M. Khoshaba, *Resilience at Work* (New York: American Management Association, 2005).

[15] Richard Sennett, *The Corrosion of Character: The Personal Consequences of Work in the New Capitalism* (New York: W. W. Norton, 1998).

[16] Daniel S. Hamermesh and Jungmin Lee, "Stressed Out on Four Continents: Time Crunch . . . " *Review of Economics & Statistics* (May 2007): p. 374ff; Suzanne M. Bianchi, Lynne M. Casper, and Rosalind Berkowitz King, *Work, Family, Health and Well Being* (Mahwah, NJ: Erlbaum, 2005); Ray Labit, "The Long-term Organizational Impact of Destructively Narcissistic Managers," *Academy of Management Executive,* 16, no. 1 (2002): 127.

ambiguous stimuli. After the same or similar stimuli, the animals were sometimes rewarded and sometimes not (or sometimes punished). Gastriculcers developed in caged laboratory rats that spent one month subjected to ambiguous stimuli. During 47 hours of every 48-hour period, they had to endure an electric shock every time they went to the food box or the water cup. They needed the food, but also feared the shock. Furthermore, because they were not subjected to shock during the remaining hour, they were never sure whether they would get a shock as they ate their food. The conflict of wanting the food and yet being afraid of the pain, plus a lack of control over the situation, produced the ulcers. Control rats, which were simply deprived of food and water for 47 of the 48 hours, did not develop ulcers.[17]

Cats that were first fed and then subjected to shock following the same buzzer exhibited a wide variety of aberrant physical activities, such as restless roving, clawing at wire cages, butting the roof with their heads, and ceaseless vocalizing— all indicating a high degree of anxiety. These cats were then given the opportunity to drink milk that contained alcohol. Half the animals quickly learned that the alcohol relieved the symptoms of their anxiety, and they chose the 5 percent alcohol mixture served in a distinctive cocktail glass. The cats preferred the alcohol as long as their tensions persisted and they remained neurotic. When the animals experienced psychic pain because of lack of control, they sought relief in withdrawal, and their neurotic symptoms disappeared under the influence of the alcohol.[18]

People, too, attempt to escape from the pain that arises from uncertainty and the inability to control their immediate environment. That escape can be healthy or can result in a refusal to face the issues that are causing the problem. The stress that follows can trigger ulcers, high blood pressure, a heart attack, or even cancer.

Job-related stress has become a vital concern for business, because large amounts of stress cause poor job performance.[19] Stress and the illness, absenteeism, and health care costs that result from stress have become immense expenses for business. The hard driving, competitive, harried person is called a **Type A personality**. Anger, irritability, and aggressive competitiveness are some of the factors that cause heart disease. This is manifested in being quick to anger and having a cynical mistrust of other people. Children who do not get unconditional love from parents and much physical contact are more likely to become adults who are cynical and easy to anger. So if the Type A manager is hostile and quick to anger, that person is more likely to suffer from heart disease because of the stress it engenders.

Time off work can lessen stress. However, the United States ties Japan for having the fewest average annual vacation days (10), a possible time of renewal. Most European countries have two to three times as many vacation days.[20] In addition, in a

---

[17] Nancy G. Vogeltanz and Jeffrey E. Hecker, "The Roles of Neuroticism and Controllability/Predictability in Physiological Response to Adverse Stimuli," *Personality and Individual Differences,* 27 (1999): 599–612; Bernard Berelson and Gary A. Steiner, *Human Behavior: An Inventory of Scientific Findings* (New York: Harcourt, Brace & World, 1964), pp. 276–279.

[18] *Ibid.*

[19] Victoria Doby and Robert Caplan, "Organizational Stress as Threat to Reputation: Effects on Anxiety at Work and at Home," *Academy of Management Journal,* 38, no. 4 (1995): 1105–1123.

[20] "Yankees: Nose to the Grindstone," *BusinessWeek,* September 4, 1995, p. 28; Kevin Williams and George Alliger, "Role Stressors, Mood Spillover, and Perceptions of Work-Family Conflict in Employed Parents," *Academy of Management Journal,* 37, no. 4 (1994): 837–868.

few notable court cases, firms have been held responsible for work-related stress. However, not all stress is bad for the individual or for job performance. In fact a moderate amount of stress is linked to better job performance; the "fight or flight" response releases a moderate amount of stimulants and thus enables a person to better achieve the objective. Social support, regular noncompetitive **exercise and relaxation** will reduce stress. Firms such as Bank of America, International Business Machines (IBM), General Motors, Xerox, Johnson & Johnson, and many others provide wellness programs that support physical and mental health for their people.[21]

Stress can also lead people to seek quiet places in order to reflect on themselves and their goals, thus enabling them to emerge from the stressful situation healthier and in better control of their lives. Quiet time, reflection, meditation, and prayer have been rediscovered. They are effective tools for moderating normal stress and in helping people to grow in maturity. We will discuss spirituality in the workplace in Chapter 7. The need for businesspeople to take charge of their own lives and to actively pursue their own moral and emotional development is underscored by the fact that Stephen Covey's books have been best sellers for decades.[22] Stress and anxiety are lessened when people recognize their own values. In the process, they become morally and emotionally mature.

MORAL DEVELOPMENT

We know people who are willing to work unselfishly for the benefit of others, even when it requires personal sacrifice. Some people in every community spend their lives providing food and shelter for the sick and homeless. Some executives habitually take into account the effect of their decisions "on the little guy." Some leaders take the blame for the blunders of subordinates. We consider such people to be morally good; they have a high level of moral development.

On the other hand, we also know others who consider only themselves. Note some colleagues who are polite and helpful to superiors but who are harsh and demeaning to subordinates. Some are well educated, articulate, and skillful in hiding their self-centeredness. Others are straightforward in their greediness.

Let us examine the moral development of some graduate business students. Business students often display conventional thought and lack clear personal goals. At Harvard Business School, an examination of students' values found that

> Many students came in the door, as it were, repeatedly espousing such credos as "The important thing is to act—whether you are right or wrong." or "I must do my personal best." The implications of these credos tend to flow something like this:
>
> INTERVIEWER: When all is said and done, what would you like your life ultimately to be about?

---

[21] Richard Boyatzis and Annie McKee, *Resonant Leadership: Renewing Yourself and Connecting with Others Through Mindfulness, Hope, and Compassion* (Boston: Harvard Business School Press, 2005); and William M. Kizer, *The Healthy Workplace: A Blueprint for Corporate Action* (New York: Wiley, 1987).
[22] Steven Covey, *The 8th Habit: From Effectiveness to Greatness* (New York: Simon & Schuster, 2004); and his classic, *The 7 Habits of Highly Successful People: Powerful Lessons in Personal Change* (New York: Fireside, 1990); also Covey's *Principle-Centered Leadership* (New York: Fireside, 1991).

STUDENT: I would like to achieve my personal goals.

INTERVIEWER: What might some of those be?

STUDENT: I guess that would depend on what company I was with.

INTERVIEWER: What kind of company would you like to work with?

STUDENT: It wouldn't really matter.

The authors concluded that the graduate business students' "primary values are those of **achieving success**; however it is defined by the prevailing culture, and involves little self-reflective choice. And if this is the case, such students are vulnerable to becoming the victims of inadequate and ill-considered goals."[23] Is this troubling judgment too severe?

Moral development is somewhat like physical development. People grow physically, psychologically, and morally. As an infant's body develops, it must physically progress through the stages of creeping, crawling, toddling, walking, and finally running. Similarly, a person progresses morally through certain identifiable phases. As a result of moral development, the person has an increasing ability to recognize moral issues and to distinguish right from wrong. This ability to make moral judgments and to engage in moral behavior increases as one matures. People are not born possessing moral skills; they **must be nurtured**—like skills of other kinds.

Scholars have observed moral development for centuries and have classified the stages of development in various ways.[24] Child psychologist Jean Piaget was the first to collect data from observing and interviewing children. Following Piaget, psychologist Lawrence Kohlberg investigated moral development over the life span, and his work is the starting point for most current research on moral development.[25]

Stages of Moral Growth

Lawrence Kohlberg found that **moral development** proceeded through three levels. Each level consists of two stages, and each stage enables the person to better deal with moral dilemmas than the previous stage. Let us now examine these levels and stages.

LEVEL I: SELF-INTEREST At this level a child is able to respond to rules and social expectations and can apply the labels *good*, *bad*, *right*, and *wrong*. The child sees rules (1) as something imposed from the outside and (2) largely in terms of the pleasant or painful consequences of actions or in terms of the power of those who set the rules. The

---

[23] Sharon Daloz Parks, "Is It Too Late? Young Adults and the Formation of Professional Ethics," in *Can Ethics Be Taught? Perspectives, Challenges and Approaches at Harvard Business School* (Boston: Harvard Business School Press, 1993), pp. 24–25; see also Frederick P. Close, "The Case for Moral Education," *The Responsive Community* (Winter 1993/1994): 23–29.

[24] See, for example, Craig A. Wendorf, "History of American Morality Research, 1894–1932," *History of Psychology*, 4 (August 2001): 272–288.

[25] Lawrence Kohlberg, "The Cognitive-Developmental Approach to Moral Education," in *Readings in Moral Education*, ed. Peter Scharf (Minneapolis: Winston Press, 1978), pp. 36–51; and Jean Piaget, *The Moral Judgment of the Child* (Glencoe, IL: The Free Press, 1948).

child views situations from his or her own point of view. The child does not yet have the ability to identify with others, so the child's point of view is largely one of self-interest.

Stage 1: Punishment —I won't do it, because I *don't want to get punished.*—[26]
The child does the right thing to avoid punishment or to obtain approval. There is little awareness of the needs of others. The physical consequences of an act determine its goodness and badness regardless of the wider consequences.

Stage 2: Instrumental Egoist —I won't do it, because I *want the reward.*—
Right actions are those that satisfy the child's own interests. Right actions are performed to serve one's own needs. The child now thinks "What's in it for me" or "You scratch my back, and I'll scratch yours." And, on the other hand, "If someone hits you, you hit them back." At stage 2 the world is often seen as morally relative.

LEVEL II: APPROVAL This level is typical of adolescents and adults. Maintaining the expectations of one's family, peer group, or nation is viewed as valuable in its own right, regardless of the consequences. The person is now able to understand another's point of view and assumes that everyone has a similar point of view. The person conforms to the group's norms and subordinates the needs of the individual to those of the group. The person at this level is loyal to those groups and attempts to maintain and justify that order.

Stage 3: Social Relations: "Good Boy–Nice Girl"—I won't do it, because I *want people to like me.*—
Good behavior is conduct that pleases or helps close family and friends and is approved by them. Right action is conformity to what is expected within the family. One earns approval by being a good brother, mother, or worker. Being good means keeping mutual relationships, such as loyalty, trust, respect, and gratitude. Behavior is frequently judged by intention: "He means well." The moral behavior of members of adolescent gangs, fraternities, and sororities is often at this stage of moral development. Young men in al-Qaeda may also be at this stage.

Stage 4: Law and Order —I won't do it, because it would *break the law.*—
Laws, conventions, and order are essential because they enable a society to function; loyalty to the nation and its laws is paramount. Right behavior consists in doing one's duty, showing respect for authority, and maintaining the social order. The person now sees other people as individuals yet also as part of the larger social system that gives them their roles and obligations. Order and laws are essential; if someone violates a law, it is morally wrong. The person enters this stage as a result of experiencing the inadequacies of stage 3.

LEVEL III: AUTONOMOUS, PRINCIPLED, OR ABSTRACT IDEALS The person no longer simply accepts the values and norms of the groups to which he belongs. There is an effort to find moral values and principles that impartially take everyone's

---

[26] For this adaptation of Kohlberg's model, thanks to William Damon, "The Moral Development of Children," *Scientific American* (August 1999): 73–78.

interests into account. The person questions the norms and laws that society has adopted and redefines them so that they make sense to any rational individual. Proper laws and values are those to which any reasonable person would be committed whatever the society or the status held within that society.

Stage 5: Social Contract —I won't do it, because *moral law obliges me* not to.—

The individual is aware that people hold a variety of conflicting views, but rules must be upheld in the interest of society and the social contract. Laws are agreed on and must be followed impartially, although they can be changed if need be. Laws are regarded as social contracts rather than absolutes. But absolute values, such as life and freedom, are held regardless of differing individual values or even majority opinion. Utilitarianism ("the greatest good for the greatest number") is the characteristic ethical standard. The morality of this stage is the "official" morality of U.S. democracy and the Constitution.

Stage 6: Conscience and Principle —I won't do it, because it's not right, no matter what others say.—

Right action is determined by decisions of conscience that are based on universal ethical principles which are chosen by the person because of their comprehensiveness, universality, and consistency. These ethical principles are not specific, concrete moral codes like the Ten Commandments. Instead they are based on the belief that all persons have human dignity and are ends in themselves and should not be used merely as means. The motivation for doing right is built upon care for fellow human beings and a belief in the validity of universal moral principles. So action is never a means but always an end in itself; one acts *because* it is right, and not because it is instrumental, legal, or previously agreed upon.

While Kohlberg insisted that stage 6 exists, he had difficulty finding individuals who consistently used it; it appears that people rarely reach stage 6 of Kohlberg's model. Stages 1–5 are supported by research findings.[27]

Modeling Moral Development

Observations of morally mature people show that *all* persons move upward through these stages. Individuals are not able to move to a higher stage until they have passed through the lower stages. An example of one who has moved through the earlier stages to probably Level III is Farooq Kathwari, CEO of furniture retailer Ethan Allen. Born in Kashmir, India, and a Muslim immigrant to the United States, he has made the Ethan Allen chain of stores profitable. In selling goods, Kathwari refuses to give in to pressure from "big box" retailers to provide them discounts, because he judges it would be unfair to the smaller retailers. In addition he takes on responsibilities beyond his business. He has formed a group of experts in an attempt to bring peace to Kashmir. The project is highly respected by the Indian, Pakistani, and U.S. governments. Also, after the September 11, 2001 terrorist attack on the United States, he took out ads in major newspapers calling for "fostering unity among people of all faiths."

---

[27] F. C. Power, A. Higgins, and L. Kohlberg, *Lawrence Kohlberg's Approach to Moral Education* (New York: Colombia University Press, 1989).

Note that Kathwari's motivation goes beyond pleasing others (stage 3), or even obeying the "rules of the game" (stage 4). He pursues the "greatest good of the greatest number" (stage 5), and may even be seeking the welfare of *all the people* (stage 6). His principles lead him to use his talents and energy in order to help all—even those who have less voice.

However, Kohlberg found that few people reach the highest stages of moral development. Most Americans remain stuck at stage 3 or 4 for their entire lives.[28] For example, Kohlberg scores former President Richard M. Nixon as never getting beyond moral stage 3 or 4. According to Kohlberg, Nixon did not understand the U.S. Constitution, which is a document built on a stage 5 foundation. World renowned psychiatrist Karl Menninger agrees with Kohlberg's assessment of Nixon, but goes further and adds him to the list of men that Menninger calls evil, which includes Adolph Hitler, Lyndon Johnson, and President Reagan's antienvironmental Secretary of the Interior, James Watt, who served time in jail.[29]

Some people claim that schools should be **value-free** and not try to encourage moral development. Kohlberg responded that this is nonsense, because all teaching communicates values. Choosing to be value-free is itself taking a value position. So the question becomes: What are the values that *are* communicated? And what values *should be* communicated? Supporting Kohlberg on the importance of moral education is the finding that moral development is positively related to the level of education. On the other hand, business students are more conventional, less reflective, and seem to be less ethical than other students.[30]

The moral development of managers affects their ethics. In one study managers with high cognitive moral development, who expected their organizations to condone unethical activities, became more ethical; low cognitive moral development managers in the same environment became less ethical. Another study found that "managers typically reason at stage 3 or 4" when they consider moral dilemmas. Mid-level business managers, 86 percent of whom were male, were interviewed and asked how they would respond to three moral dilemmas. Managers in smaller organizations (under 250 employees) or self-employed, were more likely (54%) to reason at stage 4. Managers in larger organizations were more likely (again 54%) to reason at stage 3.[31]

When raising **children**, moral development can be nourished, but it is difficult. In communities where there is a consensus about moral values, such as honesty and

[28] Kohlberg, *op. cit.*, p. 38.

[29] "Famed Psychiatrist Karl Menninger Analyzes the World, Finds It Needs Help," *The Wall Street Journal,* December 23, 1985, p. 8; see also Karl Menninger, *Whatever Became of Sin?* (New York: Hawthorn Books, 1972).

[30] Anthony J. Daboub, Abdul M. A. Rasheed, Richard L. Priem, and David A. Gray, "Top Management Team Characteristics and Corporate Illegal Activity," *Academy of Management Review,* 20 (January 1995): 155.

[31] Neal M. Ashkanasy, Carolyn A. Windsor, and Linda K. Trevino, "Bad Apples in Bad Barrels Revisited: Cognitive Moral Development, Just World Beliefs, Rewards, and Ethical Decision-Making," *Business Ethics Quarterly,* 16, no. 4 (October 2006): 449–473; James Weber, "Managers' Moral Reasoning: Assessing Their Responses to Three Moral Dilemmas," *Human Relations,* 43, no. 7 (1990): 687–702.

integrity, "Teachers did not tolerate cheating on exams, parents did not let their children lie and get away with it, sports coaches did not encourage teams to bend the rules for the sake of a win and people of all ages expected openness from their friends." However, in communities that are divided on these issues, "Coaches espoused winning above all else, and parents protested when teachers reprimanded their children for cheating or shoddy schoolwork. Under such circumstances children learned not to take moral messages seriously." In order to achieve moral development in young people, people should work to achieve shared moral standards in harmonious communities. This is a "youth charter," which is developed for the sake of the children.[32] This is a good suggestion, but it raises a question: Can shared moral values be agreed upon in a pluralistic society that places such a high priority on freedom and individual rights?

In his research several decades ago, Kohlberg used only males as subjects to gather data. Following Kohlberg, **Carol Gilligan** examined the moral development of women. She found that, especially in the later stages, women's moral development differs from that of men. Whereas men tend to judge good and bad on the basis of reasoning and principles, women more often consider relationships, caring, and solidarity. Some women and men at the higher stages of moral development decide right from wrong on the basis of the effect the proposed action would have on **relationships**, love, and caring.[33] With these insights, ethicists have identified caring as an additional norm for making ethical decisions. Caring will be discussed in the next chapter, along with the older ethical norms of rights and duties, justice, and utilitarianism.

Kohlberg studied moral development and has provided a useful model.[34] These theories of moral development have been both supported and challenged, but even most challengers agree that moral development takes place roughly in the way he described.

The stages of moral development described by Kohlberg are similar to those described by Dewey and Piaget. Edward Stevens uses Kohlberg's levels of moral development, and proposes that some popular ethical theories can be explained by the fact that their originators were stuck at one of Kohlberg's lower levels. He finds that both social Darwinism (see Chapter 4) and Ayn Rand's objectivism flow from a primitive, self-interest stage of moral development (see Table 2-1).

---

[32] William Damon, "The Moral Development of Children," *Scientific American,* 281 (August 1999): 72–78. See also Damon's book, *The Youth Charter: How Communities Can Work Together to Raise Standards for All Our Children* (New York: Free Press, 1997).

[33] Carol Gilligan, *In a Different Voice: Psychological Theory and Women's Development* (Cambridge, MA: Harvard University Press, 1982). Robbin Derry found justice and caring moral orientations in both men and women and so did not verify the sex differences; see Robbin Derry, "Moral Reasoning in Work Related Conflicts," in *Research in Corporate Social Performance and Policy,* ed. William C. Frederick, vol. 9 (Greenwich, CT: JAI, 1987), pp. 25–49. See also Susanne M. DeCrane, *Aquinas, Feminism and the Common Good* (Washington, D.C.: Georgetown University Press, 2004).

[34] See, for example, James Rest, Darcia Narvaez, Muriel J. Bebeau, and Stephen J. Thoma, *Postconventional Moral Thinking: A Neo-Kohlbergian Approach* (Mahwah, NJ: Lawrence Erlbaum, 1999); for a detailed description of maturity, including Kohlberg's moral development model, see Robert Kegan, *The Evolving Self: Problem and Process in Human Development* (Cambridge, MA: Harvard University Press, 1982), esp. pp. 50–71.

TABLE 2-1 Moral Development and Ethical Theory: An Overview

Theories of Moral Development and Corresponding Stages[1]			Ethical Theories Corresponding to Stages of Moral Development[2]
Jean Piaget's Theory	John Dewey's Theory	Lawrence Kohlberg's Theory	Edward Stevens's Theory
0. Premoral		0. Premoral	Group A
			1. Social Darwinism
	I. Preconventional	I. Self-interest	
1. Heteronomous (age 4–8)		1. Punishment	2. Machiavellianism
2. Autonomous (age 8–12)		2. Naively egoistic	3. Objectivism (Ayn Rand)
	II. Conventional	II. Approval	Group B
		3. Interpersonal relations: "good boy–nice girl"	4. Conventional morality
			5. Legalistic ethics
		4. Law and order	
			6. Accountability model of ethics
	III. Autonomous	III. Autonomous and principled	Group C
		5. Social contract	7. Pragmatism
			8. Marxism
		6. Conscience and principle	9. "Economic humanism"

[1]*Adapted from Lawrence Kohlberg, "The Cognitive-Development Approach to Moral Education," in* Readings in Moral Education, *ed. Peter Scharf (New York: Winston Press, 1978), pp. 36–37.*

[2]*Adapted from rough congruence presented by Edward Stevens,* Business Ethics *(New York: Paulist Press, 1979).*

Kohlberg found that moral judgment is the single most important factor in moral development. It is impossible to be morally mature without the ability to address various ethical dilemmas and to make intelligent judgments as to the correct ethical action. Moral judgment depends on moral reasoning, and we will discuss both moral judgment and moral reasoning in the next chapter.

Individualism Impedes the Common Good

Moral development and acting ethically presuppose that some acts are morally better than others, and that there is some consensus on what they are. Robert Bellah and his coauthors investigated the American view of a good society.[35] They interviewed a wide variety of Americans from coast to coast and found that society places obstacles in the path of determining the moral good and of achieving a national consensus on important issues. The principal value for most Americans is **freedom**, as we see in Chapter 1 and in later chapters. Hear the authors:

> Freedom is perhaps the most resonant, deeply held American value. In some ways, it defines the good in both personal and political life. Yet freedom turns out to mean being left alone by others, not having other people's values, ideas, or styles of life forced upon one, being free of arbitrary authority in work, family, and political life. What it is that one might do with that freedom is much more difficult for Americans to define. And if the entire social world is made up of individuals, each endowed with the right to be free of others' demands, it becomes hard to forge bonds of attachment to, or cooperation with, other people, since such bonds would imply obligations that necessarily impinge on one's freedom.[36]

Making freedom such an important value has given Americans a respect for other people and has encouraged creativity and innovation. However, it also has its costs:

> It is an ideal freedom that leaves Americans with a stubborn fear of acknowledging structures of power and interdependence in a technologically complex society dominated by giant corporations and an increasingly powerful state. The ideal of freedom makes Americans nostalgic for their past, but provides few resources for talking about their collective future.[37]

Such a sense of freedom leaves both the person and society with little inclination or vocabulary to address common concerns. The traditional term *common good* refers to the good of society as a whole, that is, all people taken together. The fact that now we so rarely use the term speaks volumes about the primary concerns of Americans. The more diverse the United States becomes, the more tolerance is stressed. Yet tolerance is a personal virtue, and it does not contribute to a commitment to improve society.

---

[35] Robert N. Bellah et al., *Habits of the Heart: Individualism and Commitment in American Life* (New York: Harper & Row, 1985).
[36] *Ibid.*, p. 23.
[37] *Ibid.*, p. 25.

This emphasis on freedom is generally hostile to older ideas of the moral order. The center of our current moral order is the individual, who is given freedom to choose careers, commitments, and a life, not on the basis of obligations to others or of truths outside the individual, but on the basis of self-satisfaction as the individual judges it. Commitments—from marriage and work to political and religious involvement—are made as a way to enhance individual well-being rather than out of obedience to moral imperatives. If it is satisfying to me, I will do it; if it is not satisfying, I will withdraw. In a word, what is good is what one finds personally rewarding. If preferences change, so does what is considered good. Even the most fundamental ethical virtues are treated as matters of **personal preference**. Hence, the basic ethical rule is that individuals be able to pursue whatever they find rewarding as long as they do not interfere with the actions and values of others.[38] Note that this is the child-like Level I of moral development.

In extensive surveys of peoples' values in many countries, the United States ranks as first of 53 nations in individualism and the lowest in collectivism.[39] That is, it is difficult for Americans to work in groups and to cooperate. Individuals often elevate their individual, subjective view of themselves and their world and declare it reality. It is true that our personal goals and values are the bedrock and upon them we build our life, friends, conscience, and future. We are responsible before God to the extent we follow our conscience. Nevertheless, personal values are rarely sufficient for society to use as a foundation in order to construct our future together.

An individualistic value system makes it difficult to discuss issues that face groups of people. It provides no "**public philosophy**," no means of addressing public policy issues. If every person is "defined by their preferences, but those preferences are arbitrary, then each self constitutes its own moral universe, and there is no way to reconcile conflicting claims about what is good in itself."[40] We thus turn away from the moral norms of Abraham Lincoln, Martin Luther King, John F. Kennedy, Mahatma Gandhi, Nelson Mandela, and even the Protestant Ethic. Feeling good is more important than being good; self-expression is more important than authority; and utility displaces duty. Not only are our common values few, but often we do not even live out the ideals that we often profess. Our individualistic values make it more difficult to develop a consensus and hence useful public policy on such basic issues as: peace, a clean environment, health care, public transportation, global climate change, or planning cities that are humane for all. Working for the common good would find fewer people saying "I want this" and more saying "This would be good for the community to which we belong."[41]

Americans have lost much of their spirit of cooperation and community—their willingness to do things for each other—what is called *social capital*. Over the past generation two-career families, suburban sprawl, TVs, PCs, and other electronic

---

[38] *Ibid.*, pp. 6, 47; see also the primacy of individualism for Americans compared with 53 other nations of the world in Geert Hofstede, *Culture's Consequences* (Thousand Oaks, CA: Sage, 2001), p. 215.

[39] Geert Hofstede, *Culture's Consequences* (Thousand Oaks, CA: Sage, 2001), pp. 209–278.

[40] Bellah et al., *op. cit.*, pp. 76–77.

[41] David Hollenbach, S.J., *The Common Good and Christian Ethics* (Cambridge: Cambridge University Press, 2002).

gadgets have contributed to the fact that fewer of us are engaged in community groups. "Our growing social capital deficit threatens educational performance, safe neighborhoods, equitable tax collection, democratic responsiveness, everyday honesty, and even our health and happiness."

An activity that increases social capital is **community service**. Well-designed service-learning programs in schools and cities "improve civic knowledge, enhance citizen efficacy, increase social responsibility and self-esteem, teach skills of cooperation and leadership, and may even reduce racism." The popularity of community service-learning programs in schools is explained through a survey which found that 61 percent of 13–25 year-olds say they feel personally responsible to making a difference in the world. More than 75 percent said business firms should help in this effort.[42]

On the other hand, we find that the gap between our moral ideals and what we actually do is often large. In public opinion polls of Americans, 94 percent say that voting is an important obligation, yet only 24 percent of 18–29 year-olds and 53 percent of those over age 30 voted in the 2006 election. Keeping fully informed about news and public affairs is important to 92 percent, yet only 52 percent read a newspaper daily. Three-quarters of working people say that excessive emphasis on money in the United States is an "extremely serious" or "serious" problem, yet 47 percent say that making a lot of money is "absolutely essential" or "very important." Finally, 83 percent say tolerance is an important personal guiding principle, yet 48 percent would not approve of an interracial marriage.[43] Our ideals do not much affect our actions, so our moral development is stunted. Our goals tend to be personal, so we are less likely to take actions for the sake of the community or the common good.

Postmodernism, deconstructionism, and even some aspects of feminism can contribute to confusion over morals in the United States. These intellectual trends, popular in many universities, can also undermine efforts to build character. Some intellectuals challenge the influence of the current power elite (e.g., business, government, religious, and education leaders), because their control bends society to the elite's own benefit.[44] Their critique is worth considering and holds much truth. But their criticism of accepted beliefs can also undermine efforts to agree on common moral principles from which we might develop character in our children and a consensus on public policy.

A lack of accepted moral principles forces each person to decide the moral good for himself, so there is a flimsy foundation for deciding difficult moral issues. A person is thus her own separate judge on the most important questions in life. Our individualistic notion of the moral good is thus isolated from family values, religious values, and the values of the Founding Fathers, the U.S. Constitution, and our history (see Chapters 4 and 5). When these sources no longer provide moral

---

[42] Robert D. Putnam, *Bowling Alone: The Collapse and Revival of American Communities* (New York: Simon & Schuster, 2000), p. 367; and Robert Putnam and Lewis Feldstein, *Better Together: Restoring the American Community* (New York: Simon & Schuster, 2004); see also Felicia L. Wilczenski and Susan M. Coomey, *A Practical Guide to Service Learning* (New York: Springer, 2007). The survey data are from "The Big Picture," *BusinessWeek*, November 6, 2006, p. 13.

[43] "Moral State of the Union," *The Responsive Community* (Winter 1994–1995): 76–77.

[44] Clarence C. Walton, *Archons and Acolytes: The New Power Elite* (New York: Rowman & Littlefield, 1998).

principles, it is more difficult to develop personal or community goals to aid moral development. As a result, three out of four Americans think we are in moral and spiritual decline. However, there have been some efforts to probe our shared values, common goals, and even the common good in U.S. business life.[45]

Wealth and Status as Goals

People planning a career and a college major are faced with a dilemma: Should I choose a college major that will provide the best salary, or should I choose a major that satisfies me? Students and parents debate this issue, and it is not easy to resolve. Some occupations—such as accounting or engineering—offer higher starting salaries. Some young people choose careers that provide higher initial salaries, but which will not satisfy them later in their lives.[46] To what extent should greater wealth be a person's personal goal? Let us provide some background.

Wealth and status are individualistic goals. They are sought out of self-interest: They appear to be good goals for me. However, evidence is accumulating that people who focus on goals of personal financial success or social recognition have no better and generally poorer psychological and physical health than do those who believe that such goals are less important. Except for those living in absolute poverty, increased wealth does not bring greater happiness or satisfaction. A researcher followed 5,000 U.S. adults for nine years. Those that had a large increase in wealth during those nine years did not show a significant increase in happiness or satisfaction.[47] Another study found that 22 individuals who won large lottery prizes had no greater general satisfaction than their poorer neighbors. On the other hand, those focused on material goals preferred to work alone, play alone, and put more physical distance between themselves and other people. They also report more headaches, backaches, sore muscles, and sore throats than individuals less focused on such goals.[48] These findings hold true whether people are wealthy or poor and have been validated in many countries across the globe. Money is like health; its absence can bring misery, but it does not guarantee happiness.

Those who are successful in accumulating more wealth find that this does not satisfy them. There is **more to obtain**, so happiness eludes them. This is illustrated when people were asked whether they are "haves" or "have-nots." Of those in the top third in income of U.S. households (i.e., $75,000 per year and above), 19 percent said they were "have-nots." When increased wealth comes, individuals and even nations of

---

[45] See John W. Houck and Oliver F. Williams, eds., *Is the Good Corporation Dead? Social Responsibility in a Global Economy* (Lanham, MD: Rowman & Littlefield, 1996); also "Where Have Our Values Gone" and "Appealing to the 'Better Angels,' " *U.S. News & World Report,* August 8, 1994, p. 100 and Feburary 7, 1994, p. 88; and Robert B. Dickie and Leroy S. Rouner, *Corporations and the Common Good* (Notre Dame, IN: University of Notre Dame Press, 1986).

[46] David Koeppel, "Choosing a College Major: For Love or for Money?" *The New York Times*, December 5, 2004, p. BU1.

[47] E. Diener, E. Sandvick, L. Seidlitz, and M. Diener, "The Relationship Between Income and Subjective Well Being: Relative or Absolute?" *Social Indicators Research,* 28 (1993): 195–223.

[48] Kathleen D. Vohs, Nichole L. Mead, and Miranda R. Goode, "The Psychological Consequences of Money," *Science,* 414, no. 17 (November 2006): 1154–1156; and Tim Kasser, *The High Price of Materialism* (Cambridge, MA: MIT Press, 2002), p. 11.

people may experience short-term improvement in happiness, but that happiness does not last. The attainment of material goals does not bring happiness for several reasons: (1) We become habituated to what we get, and then want more. (2) We compare what we have to others; a neighbor who has more spurs us to desire more. (3) We fail to address the underlying issues that lead to feelings of emptiness and unhappiness. Pursuing wealth, we spend less time with family and close friends, and thus we receive less support for our needs for competence, esteem, and companionship.[49]

People who possessed a strong materialistic orientation were more likely "to watch a lot of television, compare themselves unfavorably to people they saw on television, be dissatisfied with their standard of living, and have low life satisfaction."[50] Moreover, strong materialistic values are linked to **depression and anxiety**, accompanied by physical problems and personality disorders such as narcissism and antisocial behavior.

People who live in poverty do gain in their sense of general well-being when their incomes rise. But for the advanced market democracies of the world, the spirit of unhappiness and depression haunts them. Even though inflation-adjusted personal income in the United States has more than doubled since 1950, the percentage of people who describe themselves as very happy has not increased during this same period. In developed countries during this period, one can find a doubled divorce rate, more than doubled teen suicide rate, and mushrooming depression. Describing citizens in this period, another researcher summarizes,

> . . . a postwar decline in the United States in people who report themselves happy, a rising tide in all advanced societies of clinical depression, increasing distrust of each other and of political and other institutions, declining belief that the lot of the average man is getting better, a tragic erosion of family solidarity and community integration together with an apparent decline in warm, intimate relations among friends.[51]

Psychological findings help to explain some of the above sobering data and conclusions. Let us now briefly summarize. First, economic growth in affluent countries has provided no apparent boost to human happiness. Second, having fewer rather than more personal material needs is more likely to bring one happiness.[52] Let us now turn to that ever-elusive goal: the quest for happiness.

---

[49] "Down and Out in a Top Bracket," *BusinessWeek*, October 29, 2007, p. 23; Daniel Nettle, *Happiness: The Science Behind Your Smile* (Oxford: Oxford University Press, 2005); and Richard Layard, *Happiness: Lessons from a New Science* (New York: Penguin Press, 2005); summarizing study casting doubt on national economic data is David Leonhardt, "Money Doesn't Buy Happiness, Well, on Second Thought . . . " *The New York Times*, April 16, 2008, pp. C1 & 7.

[50] Kasser, *op. cit.*, p. 55.

[51] Robert E. Lane, *The Loss of Happiness in Market Democracies* (New Haven: Yale University Press, 2000), p. 3; also Jonathan Clements, "Money and Happiness: Here's Why You Won't Laugh All the Way to the Bank," *The Wall Street Journal*, August 16, 2006, p. D1.

[52] David G. Myers, *Exploring Social Psychology* (Boston: McGraw Hill, 2000), p. 319. Also Myers, "The Funds, Friends, and Faith of Happy People," *American Psychologist,* 55 (January 2000): 56–67; and his *The Pursuit of Happiness: Who is Happy and Why?* (New York: William Morrow, 1992), pp. 39–41.

Pursuit of Happiness

Happiness is a goal of most people. Each of us hopes to find happiness in our lives: work, family, leisure, and personal relationships. As we saw above when one pursues wealth in order to be happy, this often hinders relationships and reduces happiness. If we have material goals, we are less likely to spend time and energy on **relationships** and communities. This is reflected in low-quality relationships "characterized by little empathy and generosity, and by objectification, conflict, and feelings of alienation."[53] Behavior that flows from pursuing money and wealth undermines caring, marriage, families, and local communities.

Pause and ask yourself: "What was my most satisfying moment in the past week?" When researchers asked that question of university students, they found that fulfilling self-esteem and belonging needs were the most important contributors to happiness. Very happy students are not distinguished by their wealth, but by their satisfying close relationships.

In parallel research, we find that when more money is available, spending it on others brings greater happiness than spending it on oneself. That is, if one has an increase in income or a bonus, giving money or gifts to other people brings one greater happiness than spending it on oneself. Those who give little or nothing to others say that the reason they do not do so is because they do not have it to give. Yet ironically, other research shows that poor people with income of less than $20,000 spend a larger portion of their income on charity and are thus happier than are wealthy people who do not contribute as much to charity.[54]

On the other hand, no one can be happy all the time. It is important to recognize that everyone has mood swings. In addition, when something does make us happy, such as an increase in salary, being acknowledged for achievement at work, or building a relationship, we quickly adapt to the new situation. Then this can set a new floor for our expectations, so we want more. In individualistic societies such as the United States, we also tend to compare our situation with that of our peers. If they seem to have a better job, more friends, or make more money or seem to be happier, we are not satisfied unless we have what they have or more. These tendencies to adapt to our new situation and to compare ourselves with others affect our expectations.[55] If we are not aware of and do not compensate for this, we will never be as happy as we might be.

A calamity can surely affect one's sense of happiness. However, researchers find that even tragedy is not permanently depressing. People who become blind or paralyzed generally recover near-normal levels of happiness. Kidney dialysis patients report being just as happy as healthy people after a period of adaptation.

---

[53] Kasser, *op. cit.*, p. 72; see also Mihaly Csikszentmihalyi, *Good Business: Leadership, Flow, and the Making of Meaning* (New York: Viking, 2003); and Martin E. P. Seligman, *Authentic Happiness* (New York: Free Press, 2002).

[54] Elizabeth W. Dunn, Lara B. Aknin, and Michael I. Norton, "Spending Money on Others Promotes Happiness," *Science,* 319 (March 21, 2008): 1687–1688; Arthur Brooks, "The Poor Give More: Surprising Findings Show that Low-wage Earners Step Up to the Charity Plate Big-Time," *Conde Nast Portfolio* (March 2008), pp. 94–97.

[55] Daniel Gilbert, *Stumbling on Happiness* (New York: Knopf, 2006).

Psychologist David G. Myers has done much work on and collected other's research findings on happiness. He concludes that psychological researchers have found that people who are happy tend to have high self-esteem, especially in individualistic countries; have work and leisure that engage their abilities; have close friendships or a good marriage; are optimistic, outgoing, and agreeable; get enough exercise and sleep; and have a meaningful religious faith. On the other hand, he finds that happiness does not seem to depend on age, gender, level of education, having children, or physical attractiveness.[56] And, as we noted above, increasing wealth brings only a temporary period of happiness, unless we live in abject poverty. Another researcher offers this seemingly counterintuitive advice:

> [P]eople would be happier and healthier if they took more time off and "spent" it with their family and friends, yet America has been heading in the opposite direction. People would be happier if they reduced their commuting time, even if it meant living in smaller houses, yet American trends are toward larger houses and longer commutes. People would be happier and healthier if they took longer vacations, even if that meant earning less, yet vacation times are shrinking in the U.S.[57]

The well-being of a nation is most often measured by its **gross domestic product** (GDP—the final value in economic terms of all goods and services produced in a country). The king of the Himalayan nation of Bhutan finds this measure is inadequate, and for 30 years has been developing a broader measure of well-being. The new measure is called a nation's **gross national happiness** (GNH). According to the king, the GNH seeks "to insure that prosperity is shared across society and that it is balanced against preserving cultural traditions, protecting the environment and maintaining a responsive government." For example, even though household incomes in Bhutan remain among the lowest in the world, life expectancy from 1984 to 1998 increased by 19 years to 66 years. While the GNH is still a work in progress, it nevertheless offers an alternative to the individualistic pursuit of money and wealth as a means to happiness. We will return to the influence of personal goals on our sense of well-being when we examine these issues within the organization in Chapter 7.

Leader's Vision and Shared Values

Shared values for colleagues who work together are one of the most important characteristics of successful firms. Leaders of organizations, including business firms, have a responsibility to formulate and articulate shared values.

It is essential that leaders understand what they stand for and can articulate it. Their values set the standards and influence the behavior of everyone in the organization. Moreover, greater initiative and energy results when the values of leaders and

---

[56] For an excellent summary of the research on happiness, see David G. Myers, *Psychology* (New York: Worth, 2004).
[57] Haidt, *op. cit.*, p. 99.

those in the organization coincide. The most admired leaders easily and proudly speak of high ethical aspirations. They know that work colleagues want to live up to these aspirations. They do this by means of a vision with carefully chosen language, metaphors, and stories.

Examination of business leadership shows that shared values:

1. Foster strong feelings of personal effectiveness;
2. Promote high levels of company loyalty;
3. Facilitate consensus about key organizational goals and stakeholders;
4. Encourage ethical behavior;
5. Promote strong norms about working hard and caring; and
6. Reduce levels of job stress and tension.[58]

When people do communicate and cooperate in the workplace, it generates "**social capital**" (alongside financial and physical capital), and this constitutes wealth that is created for the organization. Communities that have greater social capital have been found to be more efficient and productive, and their people more motivated and happier.[59] In Chapter 8 we will see examples of successful organizations in which the leaders articulate clear and inspiring values for their colleagues within the organization.

Abraham Lincoln was one of the most effective and inspiring presidents in U.S. history. Lincoln faced the potential end of the United States during its Civil War. Note how he combines his own values and a deep concern for others:

> It is not merely for today, but for all time to come that we should perpetuate for our children's children this great and free government, which we have enjoyed all our lives. I beg you to remember this, not merely for my sake, but for yours. I happen temporarily to occupy this big White House. I am a living witness that any one of your children may look to come here as my father's child has. It is in order that each of you may have through this free government which we have enjoyed, an open field and a fair chance for your industry, enterprise, and intelligence; that you may all have equal privileges in the race of life, with all its desirable human aspirations. It is for this the struggle should be maintained . . . That nation is worth fighting for.[60]

A business leader's vision and values are an inspiration for developing virtue and character for the members of that organization.

---

[58] James M. Kouzes and Barry Z. Posner, *The Leadership Challenge: How to Get Extraordinary Things Done in Organizations* (San Francisco: Jossey Boss, 1987), pp. 192–193.

[59] "The Ties That Lead to Prosperity: The Economic Value of Social Bonds," *BusinessWeek,* December 15, 1997, p. 153.

[60] Donald T. Phillips, *Lincoln on Leadership: Executive Strategies for Tough Times* (New York: Warner, 1992), pp. 164–165.

VALUES OF BUSINESSPEOPLE

In surveys across many nations, Americans rank first in **individualism**. They are motivated by individual responsibility, personal rewards, visibility, and salary; they give less priority to cooperation, consensus, firm, family, and nation than do people in the 53 other countries.[61] For more than a generation, concern for people has been a value of less importance to business managers. And business students have been more pragmatic, materialistic, and self-centered than other students.

The values of managers from five countries—Japan, Korea, India, Australia, and the United States—were measured and compared.[62] The value systems of these managers in widely varying cultures were more similar than different. Among the differences, Japanese were more pragmatic and more homogeneous in their values and Indian managers were more moralistic.

However, there were significant differences between the values of younger and older managers. Compared with their senior peers, **younger managers** in all cultures tended to be more individualistic; they:

1. Place less importance on organizational goals
2. Place less importance on coworkers and more on themselves
3. Place less importance on trust and honor
4. Place more importance on money, ambition, and risk
5. Are slightly more pragmatic.

The picture that emerges is that of the competitive, individualistic gamesman focused on his own life and career and less concerned with the organization, trust, honor, or other people. On the other hand, note the contrast with the results of a study which examined the CEOs of firms that have been highly successful. These leaders tend to be humble. They do not take credit for the accomplishments of their very successful firms, but rather give credit to other people. Their ambition is for their firm, not for themselves.[63]

Measuring Personal Values

Another examination of the values of working people found six distinct clusters of values: conformist, manipulative, sociocentric, existential, tribalistic, and egocentric.[64] The first four of these value sets were most common among managers. The **conformist value** set was common among older, lower-level, and less-educated managers. The **manipulative value** set was found most often among the well-educated, high-income

---

[61] Geert Hofstede, *Culture's Consequences* (Thousand Oaks, CA: Sage, 2001); Gordon Allport, Philip Vernon, and Gardner Lindzey, *Study of Values* (Boston: Houghton Mifflin, 1931); for the values of business managers, see William D. Guth and Renato Tagiuri, "Personal Values and Corporate Strategy," *Harvard Business Review,* 43 (September–October 1965): 126.

[62] George W. England, "Managers and Their Value Systems: A Five-Country Comparative Study," *Columbia Journal of World Business* (Summer 1978): 35.

[63] Jim Collins, *Good to Great* (New York: HarperCollins, 2001), pp. 21–37.

[64] Vincent S. Flowers et al., *Managerial Values for Working* (New York: AMACOM, 1975).

workers in large retail organizations in the northeastern United States. Those who possess **sociocentric values** tended to be well-educated, well-paid company presidents over 60 years of age.[65]

A surprise in these studies is worth our attention. Company presidents are humble and have **cooperative values**: They encourage the development of cooperative, friendly relationships between people. For them, working with people toward a common goal is more important than getting caught up in a materialistic rat race.[66] Ironically, cooperative managers are significantly underrepresented in jobs just two levels below the presidency. Upper level managers focus on long-term goals, while younger managers are more likely to have short-term individualistic goals of being recognized and getting ahead. Therefore, the values that get a person to within sight of the top job are not the same values that will push her or him along further. Those searching the organization for potential successors to the CEO will find *few* candidates among many in the best preparatory slots in the organization: division managers, directors, and parallel positions.

In every examination of values, managers are found to be pragmatic—focused on efficiency and productivity. Interestingly, 61 percent of all managers respond that an improvement in the quality of life in the United States will come by means of a return to basic values, especially commitment and integrity. Overall, 80 percent of managers believe that their company is guided by "highly ethical standards." However, this belief is stronger among top managers, and more cynical views are held by those of lower rank.[67] Clear, strong, engaging values are essential to good leadership. "A leader needs a philosophy, a set of high standards by which the organization is measured, a set of values about how employees, colleagues, and customers ought to be treated, a set of principles that make the organization unique and distinctive."[68] Indeed, where members of a firm share values, the members tend to be more ethical. On the other hand, where values are not shared, managers are more likely to take bribes, falsely report earnings, and steal company secrets.[69]

The above value probes show that young managers are more concerned about themselves and less about the organization. But most firms need and so encourage teamwork, cooperation, and concern for customers and fellow employees; thus, the attitudes of younger managers present a problem for business. Young Americans coming into business are more self-centered and bring the individualism of their culture into the firm. Therefore, it is a challenge to recruit new members who respect their peers and can work in teams, and to socialize them to have even greater

---

[65] For a comprehensive review of research on personal, work, institutional, and group values, see Bradley R. Agle and Craig B. Caldwell, "Understanding Research on Values in Business," *Business and Society*, 38 (September 1999): 326–387.

[66] Collins, *op. cit.*, pp. 36–37.

[67] Warren H. Schmidt and Barry Z. Posner, *Managerial Values in Perspective* (New York: American Management Association, 1983), pp. 29–41.

[68] James M. Kouzes and Barry Z. Posner, *The Leadership Challenge* (San Francisco: Jossey-Bass, 1987), p. 187.

[69] Barry Z. Posner, James M. Kouzes, and Warren H. Schmidt, "Shared Values Make a Difference: An Empirical Test of Corporate Culture," *Human Resources Management*, 24 (Fall 1985): 299.

concern for other people.[70] The exercise at the end of Chapter 1 is designed to help individuals clarify their own goals and values.

Personal Growth and the Media

In earlier generations, children growing up would witness in their family father and mother working in or near home—as a farmer, shoemaker, or baker. They observed the skill and effort required in work and also the joy of accomplishment. Because commercial work is now generally done away from home, children do not often directly witness it and only hear about it through comments, often complaints.

The attitudes of all people, especially the young, are influenced by the media. Consider business as it is presented on TV and films. Most TV and film writers have no direct experience of business. As a result, their portrayal of businesspeople is often a caricature or stereotype. Recall the TV show *The Apprentice*, in which Donald Trump chooses one person from a pool of competing applicants with his signature phrase "you're fired" to those who are "losers." Notice how the businessperson is generally pictured as shallow, grasping, narrow, and petty, focusing only on wealth and status. When did you last see a TV program or film that presented useful achievement or satisfaction at work?

When we try to develop good moral habits, which we will discuss in Chapter 3, TV is a major hindrance. It relentlessly dramatizes materialism, status, sex, and violence. A task force of psychologists reported that the average child each year spends 1,500 hours watching TV versus 900 hours in school; that same child witnesses at least 8,000 murders on TV by the time she leaves *elementary* school. Another group estimates that ABC, CBS, NBC, and Fox displayed more than 10,000 sexual incidents. For every scene depicting sexual intercourse of married partners, the networks showed 14 scenes of sex outside marriage. TV markets materialism and **immediate gratification** by means of its roughly 20,000 commercials a year.[71] The director of the Center for Screen Time Awareness, Robert Kesten, says, "Television is the great enabler. It enables us to be sedentary, to buy unhealthy food products, and our kids to watch bad role models."[72] Thus the shallow, greedy, and biased view of life as shown on TV forms the values of children and others.

The Internet is a major part of the life of most young people. Young people build communities of never seen new friends with whom they form personal and emotional bonds. These bonds are formed with people known only to the imagination: anonymous, sometimes misrepresented, and not accountable. More than 40 percent of Internet users feel that their online friends are as important to them as their real-life friends.[73] When these relationships glue the young person to their PC,

---

[70] Compare the humble CEO that Jim Collins found with the "Gen X" manager, see Jay A. Conger, "How 'Gen X' Managers Manage," *Strategy & Business,* First Quarter 1998, pp. 21–29.

[71] "The War Over 'Family Values,' " *U.S. News & World Report,* June 8, 1992, p. 36.

[72] "Unplug the Television," *BusinessWeek,* January 1, 2007, p. 75.

[73] Bernadine Healy, M.D., "Alone in a Parallel Life," *BusinessWeek,* May 21, 2007, p. 66.

and they substitute their "avatar" (a virtual representation) for themselves and for real friends, it is a cause for concern for parents and citizens. It is a serious concern that child molesters find the Internet a convenient place to recruit victims.

In sum, while the value tests described above support some of the media stereotypes of businesspeople, these same evaluations show that older managers have strong religious and social values and that successful top executives have more cooperative values and are more humble. Yet these latter facts are rarely reflected in the media. Thus, biased stereotypes, film, TV, ads, and the Internet have a powerful influence on all of us, especially the young and impressionable.

Helping Behavior

It is not merely businesspeople and business students who hold cooperative values in relatively low esteem; this reflects the values of much of American culture. As laboratory experiments have shown, people are heavily influenced by the values and activities of others. In any culture, norms of right and wrong are inculcated by the family, media, the neighborhood, and the workplace. But the attitudes of bystanders in the immediate vicinity have a large influence on whether our social values influence our personal values. Several laboratory experiments were prompted by the early morning murder of 28-year-old Kitty Genovese in New York City. She was stabbed to death in full view of many apartment dwellers. Later investigation showed that at least 38 people saw or heard the attack but not one person tried to help; no one even phoned the police. This story shocked the country, and some researchers decided to try to uncover what elements influence helping behavior.

In one experiment, each subject was led to believe that there were other people placed in adjoining rooms connected by an interoffice phone.[74] Sometimes the subject was told there was one other person, sometimes that there were two other people, and sometimes that there were five. In reality, the subject was the only one present and who was being tested. During a discussion over the phone on a topic of current interest, one "participant" suffered what seemed to be an epileptic seizure; that person choked, stuttered, and called out for help. The greater the number of persons the subject thought were present, the less likely the subject would be to help and would be slower to help. The subject felt the problem could be left to others. If the subject thought there was no other person to help, the subject was more likely to feel the responsibility to respond to the participant calling for help.

Similar results were obtained when individuals were placed in a room and asked to fill out a questionnaire. A subject was either alone in the room or accompanied by two other subjects, or two confederates who were instructed to remain impassive. After a few minutes, smoke began to pour into the room through a small wall vent. Results of this experiment again showed that when other individuals are present, a person is less likely to respond in a responsible way. When subjects were alongside passive confederates, they reported the apparent fire only 10 percent of the time.

---

[74] Leonard Berkowitz, *A Survey of Social Psychology* (New York: Holt, Rinehart & Winston, 1980), pp. 374–375.

Individuals will act responsibly when they personally feel the responsibility. When another unknown person is present, they are not as likely to act responsibly. Nevertheless, these and other studies also show that people will help others, even if they don't expect anything in return. Furthermore, people respond more quickly and responsibly if they have been the recipients of help themselves or if they have previously been successful in helping others. These data suggest that people working in small firms and in smaller work groups are more likely to feel responsibility for others in the workgroup.

Helping other people has a significant positive effect on the giver's health. Researchers have found that "doing regular **volunteer work**, more than any other activity, dramatically increased life expectancy (and probably vitality). Men who did no volunteer work were two and a half times as likely to die during the study as men who volunteered at least once a week."[75] The results were not so dramatic for women, perhaps because most women already have close personal, helping relationships. In an attempt to explain the results, researchers point out that when one volunteers to help others there are physiological changes in the brain, which may explain the feeling of warmth when one helps another. Moreover, researchers theorize that people have evolved to depend upon others. They say that evolution has less regard for the individual than the survival of the species, and so sets up an instinct for helping others. An exercise that integrates service work to help the poor into an academic course is included at the end of this chapter. Let us now examine the need for businesspeople to develop their ability to identify ethical issues so to more easily engage in moral behavior.

ETHICS IN BUSINESS

No society can long exist without a level of **trust and concern for others**. Nevertheless, more than three-quarters of Americans (78%) think that the state of moral values in the United States is weak. More Americans worry about moral values (53%) than about the economy (38%). Perhaps more surprising, 60 percent think that the government ought to be involved in promoting moral values.[76] Recent national elections demonstrate that most Americans judge moral values to be important. Managers recognize the need for ethical norms to guide their everyday actions. Actions at every level of the firm are influenced by ethics, such as subordinate and peer interactions, use of company property, quality of work, worker and product safety, truth in advertising, and use and disposal of toxic materials.

Managers understand that without ethics the only restraint is the law. Without ethics, business agreements that are not written in contract form cannot be trusted. Government regulation can limit freedom. However, to avoid regulation managers must exercise better ethics in their everyday business actions. If

---

[75] Eileen Rockefeller Growald and Alan Luks, "Beyond Self: In the Body/Mind Economy, the Benefits of Helping Other People Flow Back to the Helper," *American Health,* March 1988, pp. 51–53; also Susan Steiner and Mary Anne Watson, "The Service Learning Component in Business Education," *Academy of Management Learning and Education,* 5, no. 4 (2006): 422–434.

[76] Data from a Gallup/CNN Poll quoted in *USA Today*, August 6, 1996, p. 4A.

business managers do not act ethically, more regulation is required, as we see in Sarbanes-Oxley legislation enacted after the business scandals of 2001 and 2002. Reasonable regulations protect businesspeople; otherwise corrupt managers lower their costs by marketing unsafe drugs and dumping toxic wastes in our lakes and rivers. Because of unethical managers, business requires detailed contracts, insurance, reports, and more lawyers. We might ask ourselves: Shall we be honest and free or dishonest and policed?

A business manager does **act ethically** under the following conditions: (1) when she believes that a moral principle has a bearing on a situation, and (2) when she perceives herself as having power to affect the situation.[77] And not only top managers but also middle managers act ethically, especially when they understand the ethical issues and see that they have some influence on the outcome. However, as a group, middle managers are almost twice as likely to be unethical as either top managers or lower-level managers.[78]

Fraud is stealing by concealment, and it is the most common unethical business act. Losses to business from fraud may be in the hundreds of billions of dollars annually. Fraud raises costs, lowers profits, and accounts for 30 percent of business failures. Fraud is more likely if a person is under financial pressure, if there is an opportunity for it, and if the person can rationalize the crime as justified, harmless, or temporary.[79]

The fraud and misdeeds of managers at Tyco, Qwest, Computer Associates, HealthSouth, ImClone, Arthur Andersen, and so many other firms at the beginning of this century remind us of the need for ethical managers. Unfortunately, such unethical behavior is not new. Earlier a large number of American firms were involved in unethical and illegal activities. During one 10-year period, 11 percent of the largest U.S. firms were convicted of bribery, criminal fraud, illegal campaign contributions, tax evasion, or price fixing. Firms that had two or more convictions include Allied, American Airlines, Bethlehem Steel, Diamond International, Firestone, Goodyear, International Paper, J. Ray McDermott, National Distillers, Northrop, Occidental Petroleum, PepsiCo, Phillips Petroleum, Rapid-American, R. J. Reynolds, Schlitz, Seagram, Tenneco, and United Brands. Leading the list are firms that had at least four convictions each: Braniff International, Gulf Oil, and Ashland Oil. Both large payoffs to government officials and smaller "facilitating" payments hurt economic development by diverting resources and undermining competition.[80] But crime and immorality are punished when the market price of a

---

[77] See the field research reported in the series of three articles by James A. Waters and Frederick Bird, "Everyday Moral Issues Experienced by Managers," *Journal of Business Ethics,* 5 (October 1986): 373–384; "The Nature of Managerial Moral Standards," *Journal of Business Ethics,* 6 (January 1987): 1–13; "The Moral Dimension of Organizational Culture," *Journal of Business Ethics,* 6 (January 1987): 15–22.
[78] "Middle Managers Most Likely to Be Unethical," *Management Accounting,* December 1987, p. 3.
[79] W. Steve Albrecht, Gerald W. Wernz, and Timothy L. Williams, *Fraud: Bringing Light to the Dark Side of Business* (Burr Ridge, IL: Irwin, 1995).
[80] "The Destructive Cost of Greasing Palms," *BusinessWeek,* December 6, 1993, pp. 133–138; Irwin Ross, "How Lawless Are Big Companies?" *Fortune,* December 1, 1980, pp. 56–64; see also Robert K. Elliott and John J. Willingham, *Management Fraud: Detection and Deterrence* (New York: Petrocelli Books, 1980).

firm's stock collapses when news of the criminal act is made known.[81] The ultimate punishment met the worse offenders as Braniff went bankrupt and Gulf and Ashland Oil were taken over. Management fraud in the early twenty-first century ended in bankruptcy for Enron, Adelphia, WorldCom, and Arthur Andersen.

Most of the large U.S. petroleum firms illegally contributed to presidential election campaigns: Exxon, Sun, Chevron, Ashland, Phillips, Gulf, and Getty. The chairman of Phillips personally handed Richard Nixon $50,000 in Nixon's own apartment. Managers in many firms also made multimillion-dollar foreign bribery payments: Exxon, Lockheed, Mobil, McDonnell Douglas, United Brands, Gulf, and Phillips. When Congress learned of this, they passed the U.S. Foreign Corrupt Practices Act (see Chapter 8). The chief executives of Gulf, American Airlines, and Lockheed lost their jobs because of the unethical payments. On the other hand, the CEOs of Exxon, Northrop, and Phillips, who were just as guilty, were excused by their respective boards of directors. U.S. firms are not alone in engaging in bribery and other unethical behavior. Executives from the Japanese electronic firm Hitachi stole trade secrets from IBM. After being caught, the firm and executives pleaded guilty and agreed to pay damages to IBM.[82] Chinese, German, and French firms have also been guilty of bribery and stealing trade secrets.

Personal Greed or Corporate Pressure

Embezzlement and fraud are committed to benefit the individual and are motivated by personal greed. Bribery, price fixing, and compromising product and worker safety are often responses to pressure for bottom-line results. The perpetrators say they do it "for the sake of the firm." When questioned, 59–70 percent of managers felt "pressured to compromise personal ethics to achieve corporate goals."[83] This pressure for results increased among lower-level managers. A majority felt that most managers would not refuse to market below-standard and possibly dangerous products. However, more encouraging, 90 percent supported a code of ethics for business and the teaching of ethics in business schools. They presumably sought agreed upon ethical standards so they would be less pressured into unethical acts. Pressures to act unethically occur in many firms, but especially in large firms that are operating in a changing and competitive environment.[84]

Pressure and organizational culture can dull the ethical judgment of managers. Behavior that the manager finds unethical at home or before taking a job is often considered acceptable on the job. Laboratory research shows that unethical behavior increases as the culture becomes more **competitive** and that it increases even more if such behavior is rewarded. Conversely, a threat of **punishment** tends

---

[81] Wallace Davidson and Dan Worrell, "The Impact of Announcements of Corporate Illegalities on Shareholder Returns," *Academy of Management Journal,* 31 (March 1988): 195–200.

[82] "IBM Data Plot Tied to Hitachi and Mitsubishi," *The Wall Street Journal,* June 23, 1982, p. 4; David B. Tinnin, "How IBM Stung Hitachi: Espionage," *Fortune,* March 7, 1983, pp. 50–56.

[83] Archie Carroll, "Managerial Ethics," *Business Horizons,* April 1975, pp. 75–80.

[84] Melissa S. Baucus and Janet P. Near, "Can Illegal Corporate Behavior Be Predicted? An Event History Analysis," *Academy of Management Journal,* 34 (February 1991): 9–36.

to deter unethical behavior. Whether a person acts ethically or unethically is also very strongly influenced by the individual's personal ethical values and by informal organizational policy.

Instances of unethical behavior by managers point to the need for

1. good character, nourished by a sensitive and informed conscience;
2. the ability to make ethical judgments;
3. a firm's culture that rewards ethical behavior and punishes unethical behavior.

In simpler societies, people daily deal with others whom they might be tempted to cheat, and their regular relationship provides a built-in sanction against cheating. In complex societies, in large organizations, and when people contact one another by telephone or E-mail, developing ethical sensitivities and good character is essential in preventing wrongful acts.

Enlightened Self-Interest and Ethics

Advocates of free markets claim that if managers pursue enlightened self-interest (for definition, see Figure 2-2), it results in greater honesty and better ethics among businesspeople. They argue that high ethical standards are in the long-term best interest of the firm. Such a simple, straightforward position is attractive. However, it does not always work.[85]

One problem with this view is that *enlightened* is an elastic term and does not mean the same thing for everyone. However, even if there were agreement on the meaning of *enlightened*, self-interest in action easily slips into selfishness. Our normal human selfish desires (many call it original sin) distort our view of what is in our long-term interest. Making the situation even worse, the selfish manager, such as "chainsaw" Al Dunlap (who laid off tens of thousands, ruined several firms and took tens of millions of dollars in compensation, and wrote a book on his "triumphs"), is sometimes excused by free enterprise advocates.

Altruism: Concern for the welfare of others and less concern for self.

Enlightened self-interest: Self-interest as used by a mature, enlightened person, viewing the long-term.

Individualism: A view that all values, rights, and duties originate in the individual and that the community has no value not derived from the individual constituents.

Self-interest: Norm for thinking and acting that focuses on the advantages accruing to oneself and/or one's own personal interests.

Selfishness: Concern for one's self without regard for others.

FIGURE 2-2   Self-interest Terms

---

[85] For an imaginative account of how humans tend to be self centered and short term oriented, see V. Barry Dauphin, *Tantalizing Times: Excitements, Disconnects, & Discontents in Contemporary American Society* (New York: Peter Lang, 2006).

Experience shows that for a mature person to operate effectively in any environment, some altruism is necessary. Contrary to the self-interest endorsed by Ayn Rand, one must also consider the benefits and harms that others will experience, and one must even be willing on occasion to sacrifice one's own personal benefits for the sake of others. **Altruism** encourages personal virtue and good character; it supports the individual and society as a whole. On the other hand, in many instances, enlightened self-interest can provide a shortcut method of efficiently solving problems, but it cannot handle all cases. Furthermore, when one chooses enlightened self-interest as a governing ideology, one feels compelled to justify every action by pointing out how it will increase the profitability of the firm. Financial analysts and shareholders may be happy, but this makes people and ethics second to money, and places managers in a simplistic, narrow-minded mind-set.

Instances arise when ethical treatment of others, perhaps people outside the firm, will be at a cost to an individual or firm. Because many popular forms of free market ideology do not permit consideration of others for their own sake, business-people who hold such a position are close to falling over the cliff into immorality. In fact, many do fall, and they are more likely to fall if they hold that enlightened self-interest should always be the motivation for one's actions. Examples of ethically good and selfish behavior among managers will be presented in Chapter 8. In sum, **enlightened self-interest** will take one a long way toward being more efficient and even more ethical, but it falls short of taking one the entire distance.

When considering the ethics of a situation, each of us takes a basic stance toward other people. There are five possible ways one can consider oneself in relation to others:[86]

1. self alone
2. self first
3. self equally as others
4. others first
5. others alone

People who consider only themselves alone are **selfish egoists.** People who consider themselves first but also consider others are more enlightened.[87] Equitable consideration of oneself and others is suggested by the **Golden Rule** ("Do unto others as you would have them do unto you"). Considering others first or others alone are generous forms of altruism.[88] Good parents consider their children first. When such selfless action is not co-dependency, but is done in a mentally healthy way, it is morally mature. Consideration only of others is the attitude of an unselfish, generous, saintly person (e.g., Mother Theresa). Such saintly people are rare, and are models of behavior and heroes for many people.

---

[86] Adapted from Garth Hallett, *Reason and Right* (Notre Dame, IN: Notre Dame Press, 1984).

[87] Al Gini provides a comprehensive case that the principal barrier to ethical behavior is selfishness in his *Why It's Hard to Be Good* (New York: Routledge, 2006).

[88] For an argument that altruism is not common, see George Loewenstein, "Behavioral Decision Theory and Business Ethics: Skewed Trade-offs Between Self and Other," in *Codes of Conduct: Behavioral Research into the Firm*, eds. David M. Messick and Ann E. Tenbrunsel (New York: Russell Sage Foundation, 1996), pp. 214–227.

Customs and Culture

Even though managers recognize the importance of ethics, in the uneducated mind ethics is hard to distinguish from culturally determined attitudes and taste. When ethics is seen as merely culturally determined attitudes, there are no objective norms that can be used to evaluate the situation; ethical dilemmas are then resolved arbitrarily. We noted the predominant American values of individualism and freedom earlier. If each person uses his own unique ethical norms, it is impossible to decide that one action is ethical and another is not. Moreover, even experts in ethics differ among themselves, thus encouraging the notion that ethics is not an objective discipline and no common norms exist.

Most people recognize the need for common ethical norms, yet it is also clear that developing these norms is not easy. We must deal with different value systems, various perceptions of facts, and different judgments on tradeoffs. Moreover, even if we are able to develop adequate ethical decision-making norms, this would not necessarily make decisions easy. Ethical issues are not easily presented in measurable data, unlike financial (return on investment) or marketing (share of market) issues. Nevertheless, a developed sensitivity to other people's concerns and an understanding of ethical principles provides a foundation for making good ethical judgments. In addition, it is insurance against serious ethical blunders, such as Enron and WorldCom lying about income, ITT helping to overthrow the elected democratic government of Chile, and Lockheed bribing top Japanese and Dutch government leaders. Promoting better ethical behavior of managers can also enable a firm to be a better producer, employer, and citizen and thus a more valued and trusted member of society.

The moral growth of organizations can be compared to the moral growth of a person. The moral growth of organizations is one aspect of corporate culture, and it is the responsibility of the leaders of the organization.[89] A multitude of personal ethical decisions provides the foundation for both. Speaking of the growth of an organization in general and its moral growth in particular, Moses Pava says,

> This growth is hardly natural. When it does occur, it is the outcome of literally thousands of large and small decisions on the part of the organizational members and other stakeholders who can impact the organization. When the decision outcomes are more or less correct, organizational growth follows, otherwise, organizations are stymied, corporate decline sets in, and organizational survival is put in jeopardy.[90]

From the above, we can conclude the following:

1. A sense of what is right and wrong, plus ethical norms for making judgments, is essential for a business manager—and indeed for any person.
2. However, ethical norms are not easily derived.

---

[89] For some suggestions, see Helen J. Alford, O. P. and Michael J. Naughton, *Managing as if Faith Mattered* (Notre Dame, IN: Notre Dame University Press, 2001).
[90] Moses L. Pava, "The Path of Moral Growth," *Journal of Business Ethics,* 38 (June 2002): 43–54.

3. When the relevant norms are recognized, there is still sometimes disagreement on the facts of a particular case and the various tradeoffs.

We thus recognize both the importance of the task and the difficulty in accomplishing it.

Morals and Young People

Commentators such as Rousseau and Emerson (see Chapters 4 and 5) believed that human beings are by nature good until tarnished by modern civilization. The data indicate otherwise. The earlier section of this chapter on moral development presents evidence that infants are born self-centered and that individuals must mature in their ethical skills.

Moreover, studies show that many young people are involved in unethical acts. A large-scale study of more than 3,000 Illinois teenagers done over a six-year period revealed some startling facts. One-third of all 14–18 year-olds had been involved in a serious crime. Thirteen percent admitted taking part in a robbery, 40 percent acknowledged keeping stolen goods, and 50 percent admitted shoplifting. Moreover, many of the conventional "predictors" for criminal behavior did not hold true. Except for the most violent behavior, the delinquent was just as likely to be a girl as a boy, to be white as black, to come from a small town as from an inner city. Peers had more influence on these young people than their parents. In fact, in 80 percent of the cases, parents did not know about the offenses their children had committed. One research team member spent two years alongside youths in a wealthy Chicago suburb and reported a "near vacuum of morality enclosed by the perimeter of the edict to achieve. Anything that jeopardizes their occupational future is bad. The rest really doesn't matter." **Peer pressure** has a strong influence on adolescent attitudes and conduct.[91] In a similar and frightening reminder, the parents of the two Columbine school murderers, Klebold and Harris, had little knowledge of their son's activities leading up to their 1999 shooting of a dozen classmates and a teacher in Colorado.

There is also considerable unethical behavior in colleges and universities. A study of 6,000 students in 31 colleges and universities in the United States showed that over two-thirds acknowledged that they had cheated on a test or major assignment while an undergraduate. The lowest percentage of admitted cheaters were in schools of education (57%), and the highest percentage (76%) were in graduate business schools.[92] Once they got into the business world, 66 percent of all students in another survey said that "they would consider lying to achieve a business objective." Roughly the same proportion would "inflate their business expense report."[93] These attitudes, consistent over several decades, present a problem for business firms, business schools, and society as a whole.

---

[91] Donna R. Clasen and Sue Eicher, "Perceptions of Peer Pressure, Peer Conformity Dispositions, and Self-reported Behavior Among Adolescents," *Developmental Psychology,* 22 (April 1986): 521–530; on earlier data, see "Kid Crime: Host of Juveniles Admit Serious Acts," *Detroit Free Press*, January 24, 1977, pp. 1, 2.

[92] Donald L. McCabe, "The Influence of Situational Ethics on Cheating Among College Students," *Journal of Sociological Inquiry,* 63 (1992): 365–374.

[93] Rushworth M. Kidder, *How Good People Make Tough Choices: Resolving the Dilemmas of Ethical Living* (New York: William Morrow, 1995), pp. 48–50.

Need for Ethics in Business and Business Schools

Business managers and business schools know that moral values and ethics are vital to any business enterprise. The need was underscored when nearly 10 percent (39 students) of the 2008 class at Duke University's Fuqua School of Business were caught cheating; this is particularly troubling because Duke has ethics education and an honor code. Nine of 34 students implicated in the cheating scandal were expelled.[94]

To address such problems when they considered introducing ethics into the curriculum, Harvard Business School studied the ethical needs of graduate business students:

> . . . most do not yet articulate a vision by which they believe they could positively affect our collective life—signaling an absence of worthy myths and dreams. Unless they are effectively initiated into the public purposes and ethical norms of their profession, they will be ill-prepared to provide managerial leadership capable of engaging complex relationships among conflicting loyalties within a vision of the common good. They will not be able to provide ethical leadership in public life.[95]

Note the difficulty in recognizing the public good, and how they could help make our society a better place for all. Harvard has since introduced a first-year required course in ethics, and also offers a course on moral leadership which examines how great leaders in history dealt with moral dilemmas.[96]

On whether to introduce a required course on ethics into the business school curriculum, a veteran business educator says,

> When business schools do consider teaching ethics and social responsibility, they wrestle over whether this should be done in specialized courses or by embedding this topic throughout the curriculum. This is an argument that hangs up the process of initiating programs. The all-too-obvious answer is both.[97]

Yet the majority of business schools still do not require a course in the ethics of business or the social and environmental responsibilities of the firm.

Business schools and some business executives often undermine any attempt to communicate the importance of ethics, social responsibility, and good character. The insistence that the primary purpose of the firm is to maximize financial returns

---

[94] *BusinessWeek*, May 3, 2007.
[95] Sharon Daloz Parks, "Is It Too Late? Young Adults and the Formation of Professional Ethics," in *Can Ethics Be Taught: Perspectives, Challenges, and Approaches at Harvard Business School*, eds. Thomas R. Piper, Mary C. Gentile, and Sharon Daloz Parks (Boston: Harvard Business School Press, 1993), p. 19.
[96] The course is described by Sandra J. Sucher, *The Moral Leader: Challenges, Tools, and Insights* (London: Routledge, 2008); and the accompanying volume by Sucher which is "a guide for teachers."
[97] Leonard R. Sayles and Cynthia J. Smith, *The Rise of the Rouge Executive: How Good Companies Go Bad and How to Stop the Destruction* (Upper Saddle River, NJ: Prentice Hall, 2006), p. 137.

for shareholders fits the needs of financial analysts, but it is also a simplification. Managers know that shareholders are not owners in the ordinary sense of the term. The shareholder (often an investment fund) merely finds that for the present this firm is a profitable location to place its dollars. This ideology puts other **stakeholders**—customers, employees, suppliers, and the community—in second place and it encourages a narrow, short-term perspective. As a senior management educator put it, "By propagating ideologically inspired amoral theories, business schools have actively freed their students from any sense of moral responsibility."[98]

In his pleading for more attention to ethics and character education in colleges and universities, a director at the Templeton Foundation provides a bleak assessment of the current situation. He says that few universities have a comprehensive commitment to character development in all dimensions of college life. This is unfortunate, because business regularly looks for people of good character and ethics.[99] Without character education, there will be little ethics in business.

Recent fraud, jail sentences for business executives, and negative publicity on corruption in business have damaged the reputation of business and increased the need for ethics and ethics education. In opinion polls, nearly 75 percent of Americans say that you cannot be too careful in dealing with CEOs of large corporations, and almost 80 percent believe that top managers will take "improper actions" to help themselves at the expense of their firms. Only 23 percent of Americans believe that CEOs of large corporations can be trusted, and 39 percent see Big Business as a threat to the nation's future.[100]

On the other hand, many business executives and their firms demonstrate the importance of ethics. Almost two-thirds of executives are convinced that high ethical standards strengthen a firm's competitive position. Almost all U.S. firms and a vast majority of non-U.S. firms have a code of ethics.[101] More than 100 boards of directors of large firms have established an ethics or social responsibility committee of the board. Annual reports, special social and environmental responsibility reports, and CEO speeches confirm the importance of ethics in business decisions. Groups such as the Aspen Institute and the World Business Council for Sustainable Development are devoted to encouraging ethics and social responsibility in business school curricula.[102]

Colleagues in business firms support this emphasis on ethics when a Deloitte & Touche survey found that 40 percent of workers said that the behavior of management was the most important factor influencing ethics on the job. In a separate survey, the

---

[98] Sumantra Ghoshal, "Bad Management Theories Are Destroying Good Management Practices," *Academy of Management Learning and Education,* 4, no. 1 (2005): 75–91; also David Callahan, *The Cheating Culture: Why More Americans are Doing Wrong to Get Ahead* (Orlando: Harcourt, 2004).

[99] Arthur J. Schwartz, "It's Not Too Late to Teach College Students About Values," *The Chronicle of Higher Education,* June 9, 2000.

[100] Gallup/CNN/USA Today Poll, July 16, 2002. Additional data are available on both the Gallup and the *USA Today* Web sites.

[101] Ronald E. Berenbeim, "Corporate Ethics Practices: Corporate Ethics Codes," (New York: Conference Board Report, 1992); see also Marianne M. Jennings, *The Seven Signs of Ethical Collapse* (New York: St. Martin's Press, 2006).

[102] See *Beyond Grey Pinstripes—2001: Preparing MBAs for Social and Environmental Stewardship* (Washington, D.C.: Aspin Institute, 2001).

same firm found that two-thirds of workers aged 18–26 prefer to work for firms that allow them to volunteer at nonprofit organizations; but only 40 percent said that their current employers offered them a chance to volunteer their skills. We will examine ethical corporate governance in Chapter 8.

In sum, the need for ethics in business is clear. The news stories of unethical business activities remind us of the need for ethical managers. Most executives and managers desire to be ethical. However, we find that many business students and businesspeople have shallow personal goals and are ill-equipped to recognize and decide ethical dilemmas. They do not possess the sensitivity, the concepts, or a method for effectively solving ethical predicaments. The next chapter will provide concepts, norms, and methods to aid managers in solving ethical dilemmas and building character.

Summary and Conclusions

Our individualistic American culture with its emphasis on success and winning can be the cause of stress and serious physical ailments. Particularly prone to heart disease, stroke, cancer, and other illnesses are the irritable, cynical, and aggressively competitive Type A managers. The ambition of aggressively competitive managers pushes them ahead rapidly in the organization. But their insensitive aggression is ultimately a barrier to getting to the top. Most chief executives are patient, humble, and are able to listen, weigh alternatives, and work cooperatively.

Maturity and moral development go hand in hand. In the same way as people grow emotionally and psychologically, so do they also grow morally. Without maturity and moral development, people risk disruptive changes in middle age. On the other hand, people who have reflected on and owned their goals and values do not face the same anxiety, stress, and debilitating diseases that stem from stress; rather they confidently confront the changes that come during the midlife reassessment. Being aware of their own personal goals and values and how they relate to others, they are better able to live, love, and enjoy life and work.

The morally developed person is better equipped to face personal and ethical dilemmas. That person has the maturity and skills necessary to gather the facts, search for the most appropriate ethical norms, and make a reasoned ethical judgment. We will present that process in Chapter 3.

Business fraud, corporate crime, unethical and greedy acts by individuals, and the lack of ethical skills among Americans call for developing our ethical sensitivities and our ability to make ethical judgments. The next chapter presents methods that have proven to aid ethical decision making and character development.

Discussion Questions

1. What happened to the people mentioned at the beginning of the chapter: Katy Spivak, Lee Iacocca, James Olson, and Eli Black? What lessons do they hold for us?
2. What are the symptoms of a midlife crisis? Under what conditions, will the effects of the midlife transition be less traumatic?

3. Why do you think that the Dean of Harvard Business School advised his graduates about the importance of their home lives? Was that advice appropriate and wise?

4. What causes anxieties and stress? What physical ailments do these lead to? What do the above described experiments using rats and cats tell us? What role does alcohol play?

5. What is the relation of moral development and maturity? How does moral development relate to ethics?

6. What did Harvard Business School find regarding the goals and moral vision among its students? Do you think these attitudes and values are typical of all graduate business students?

7. Describe the differences between a person at Kohlberg's Level I and another at Level II. Describe the differences between one at Level II and another at Level III. At what level of moral development are most people?

8. What are the strengths and the weaknesses of the American view that freedom is the most important value? In what way is freedom a moral good?

9. How is this view of freedom an obstacle to discovering the "common good" or encouraging community values?

10. Why does the pursuit of wealth and status generally not bring happiness to people who have already met their basic needs? What physical and psychological illnesses does such pursuit often bring? Why is this so?

11. In order to help children develop moral maturity, a consensus is required in a community (parents, school, coaches), according to William Damon. Does this present a conflict with the American view of individualism and freedom? Is there a solution to this conflict? Explain.

12. Business executives tend to have less social concern than others. What processes tend to perpetuate this lack of concern?

13. Under what circumstances is an individual more likely to come to the aid of another person? Describe the results of the experiments on coming to the aid of another.

14. How does service work for those in need affect the vision and values of most persons?

15. What events of the last decade underscore the need for business ethics? List the ways that firms have responded positively to this need.

16. What are the principal limitations of free enterprise and self-interest ideology? How do the limitations differ for self-interest that is "enlightened"? Does enlightened self-interest ensure that a person will act ethically? Why? Give an example.

17. Is inflating costs or selling poor-quality goods less bad if the individual responsible does not profit?

18. What do the surveys show about the ethics of young people compared with the ethics of their elders? What accounts for the difference?

Selected Additional Readings

Robert N. Bellah et al., *Habits of the Heart: Individualism and Commitment in American Life* (New York: Harper & Row, 1985).

William Damon, *The Youth Charter: How Communities Can Work Together to Raise Standards for All Our Children* (New York: Free Press, 1997).

Tim Kasser, *The High Price of Materialism* (Cambridge, MA: MIT Press, 2002).

Robert E. Lane, *The Loss of Happiness in Market Democracies* (New Haven: Yale University Press, 2000).

Robert D. Putnam, *Bowling Alone: The Collapse and Revival of American Communities* (New York: Simon & Schuster, 2000).

Leonard R. Sayles and Cynthia J. Smith, *The Rise of the Rouge Executive: How Good Companies Go Bad and How to Stop the Destruction* (Upper Saddle River, NJ: Prentice Hall, 2006).

CASES

Case 2-1   Mayor's Infidelity and TV

Los Angeles NBC–Telemundo anchorwoman Mirthala Salinas, 35, broke the news that L.A. mayor Antonio Villaraigosa, 54, was separating from his wife. His spouse of 20 years then sued for divorce. A month later the media learned that Villaraigosa had been having a romantic affair with Salinas. The mayor contends that his private life has no relevance to his public life. Villaraigosa, the first Latino mayor of LA in 133 years, aspires to be governor of California in 2010. Salinas was placed on leave, while her supervisors decide her future.

1. Is Villaraigosa correct that a politician's private life has no relevance to his public life?
2. Does the relationship compromise the objectivity of Salinas when she does news stories on the mayor and city?
3. Is it possible to comment on the ethical maturity of Villaraigosa? If so, what would you say? How would you judge the ethical maturity of Salinas?
4. What ethical norms help you decide this case?

Case 2-2   Inflated Resume

Alex Albertson has performed well as a manager for four years at Sentel Systems. He has applied for promotion to director of product development, so Human Resources checks his resume. His resume says he has an MBA from Santa Clara University. However, HR finds out that he dropped out of the program within two courses of finishing when he accepted his current job.

1. Would you continue to consider Alex for the promotion?
2. Would you fire him?
3. Would you discipline him? Explain.
4. What ethical norms help you in your decision?

Case 2-3   Radar Detector

Louis Dwyer sells dashboard radar detectors to auto supply shops. He works for the largest firm that manufactures the devices in the United States. He is a bit troubled by the fact that the sole purpose of the "fuzz buster" is to evade the law on speed limits. He is a talented salesperson, and has other options for jobs.

1. What ethical norms help most to come to an ethical conclusion?
2. Is selling fuzz busters ethical?
3. Dwyer comes to you for advice. What would you tell him?

■ ■ ■

Case 2-4   SPAM King Arrested

Robert Soloway made more than $1 million over four years by sending spam. In one case, he sent 120 million pieces of spam using software that allowed him to use zombie computers. Computers belonging to unknowing others were commandeered to send the emails. This gave Soloway virtual anonymity. He was arrested in Seattle.

1. Is sending spam ethical or is spam merely an annoyance?
2. Why did Soloway use zombie computers?
3. Is it ethical to use others' computers to send spam?
4. What ethical norm helps you to make the ethical decision?

■ ■ ■

Case 2-5   Bank Deposit Insurance

In an economic downturn, investors worry about the safety and security of financial institutions. Perceptions that banks are unstable could cause investors to withdraw their money, and thus cause the bank's failure. Hence, bank deposits up to $100,000 are insured by the Federal Deposit Insurance Corporation (FDIC).

Branch managers are responsible for maintaining deposit totals in their branch offices. You are an assistant branch manager and you have just heard your manager explaining the FDIC coverage to a customer who maintains over $300,000 in your bank. The customer was obviously very concerned about the safety of her funds. The bank manager incorrectly reassured the customer that her life savings are properly insured when they are not.

The manager's annual performance review and salary increase are partially based on the dollar amount of total deposits in that office. The manager knows that the customer will withdraw the funds that are not insured by the FDIC and that the branch will lose the deposits. You tell the manager that her assurance to the customer was in error. The manager tells you not to be concerned, because the customer does not understand the financial soundness of the bank and is worried only because of a mistaken fear that banks will close as they did during the Great Depression.

1. Since the customer does not understand the intricate workings of the banking system, is the manager justified in allowing the customer to believe her funds are safe?
2. Is the bank manager's explanation acceptable?

Exercises

Exercise 2-1: Your Happiness

Take a moment to briefly describe the three things that make you most happy on a daily basis. It is best to respond quickly and with the first answers that come to mind.

1. _____

2. _____

3. _____

Next, take another moment to briefly describe the three happiest moments of your entire life. Again, it is best to respond quickly and with the first answers that come to mind.

1. _____

2. _____

3. _____

1. What are the common themes/elements in the above two lists? What are the major differences?
2. In the above lists, how many items were primarily based on having or using material possessions? How many were primarily based on being with people? How many were based on other factors?
3. What insights do you have about your own happiness based on the above exercise?

Exercise 2-2: Service Learning in Community

Doing service work for needy people with agencies in the city is experiential learning. Because of what we are able to learn in this fashion, service learning has a place in hundreds of U.S. business programs. Service learning enables you to gain insights into issues that you are studying in this course, such as moral development, personal values, work place diversity, poverty, ecology, responsibilities of management, and corporate social policy. In addition, helping people become satisfied and productive citizens is in the best interest of all, including business. Healthy persons and families are good employees and customers.

In order to participate in the service-learning project, please:

1. Form a *team of 4 or 5 diverse (gender, race) students* who will do service at the same agency.
2. *Do service* in an agency that you and your instructor agree upon for at least 10 hours early during the term. This agency should be one that serves the poor, such as a homeless shelter, soup kitchen, tutoring inner city youth, or delivering food to disabled and elderly in the inner city. The service should be done with team members as much as possible, so that you are able to reflect together on your experience.
3. *Take notes and/or write a journal* on your reflections after each session of service work.
4. *Participate in a reflection session* with the entire class that will help you to assess and articulate your experience. Some questions to consider for the reflection session:
   a. Describe your experience of service learning (agency, setting). For example, describe a person or group that you got to know who is significantly "other" from you.
   b. What about the service experience was most troubling?
   c. What was most encouraging or inspiring?

    d. What in society has caused this problem? What are the social and political roots of the problem (e.g., homelessness, inability to get a decent meal, lack of affordable housing, lack of good education)? What might be done to address the problem? What actions would make this agency unnecessary?

    e. What are the most important things you will take with you from the experience?

    f. What did you learn? Were you affected or changed in any way? How so?

5. Finally, your team will plan and deliver a 15–20 minute oral presentation at one of the final sessions of the course. Your oral presentation will cover the above questions, and will also answer the following additional questions:

    g. Describe at least two concepts from the course that are illustrated in your service.

    h. What are the social problems that this agency seeks to address? Propose at least two policy initiatives that would lessen the underlying problems of the people with which you worked. What would it take to eliminate the need for this agency?

    i. Has this service learning increased your awareness of responsible leadership in our communities? How? Over the next two years, is there an issue about which you would like to learn more?

Your *presentation will be evaluated* on how well you respond to the above questions, plus the quality of the presentation itself (clear, well organized, visuals, engage the audience, each team member is involved).

ALTERNATE PLAN FOR SERVICE LEARNING (in place of teams and oral presentation): *Each student writes a six-page reflection paper* on their service-learning experiences, following the above questions. The reflection paper is due on the second last class.

3

■ ■ ■

Ethics in Business

*When looking for managers, I basically look for three things—
integrity, intelligence and energy. The truth is that if you don't have
the first, the other two will kill you because if you have someone who
doesn't have integrity, you really want them to be dumb and lazy. It is
only if they have the first that the second two count.*

WARREN BUFFET (1930–), CEO, BERKSHIRE HATHWAY

A billion dollars doesn't go as far as it used to.

J. PAUL GETTY (1892–1976), FOUNDER, GETTY OIL COMPANY

*No one was ever honored for what he received. Honor has
been the reward for what he gives.*

CALVIN COOLIDGE (1872–1933), PRESIDENT OF THE
UNITED STATES, 1923–1929

It is better to love than be loved.

ST. FRANCIS ASSISI (1181–1226)

The ethical failures of managers at Enron, Arthur Andersen, WorldCom, and Tyco
underscore the need for ethics. An ethical adult needs moral maturity, the ability to
make ethical judgments, and a developed habit of doing so. We examined moral
development in the last chapter. In this chapter, we will (1) provide the tools for

making ethical judgments and (2) describe how the individual person develops good moral habits, virtue, and character. In the first portion of the chapter we will ask: How does one make a judgment about what is morally right and wrong? What norms, models, and techniques are available for helping us to make ethical decisions?

Ethics can be defined as the principles of conduct governing an individual or a group, and the methods for applying them. Ethics provides the tools to make moral judgments. Let us provide a few examples of situations that call for ethical judgments:

> Jason Stacy, a California graduate student, downloads copyrighted music from the Internet for his own use. He gives some of that music to friends, and also sells it to fellow students.
>
> A Canadian woman visiting San Francisco mistakenly left her purse with jewelry and cash worth about a million dollars in a park. John Suhrhoff found the purse and returned it, saying "Every person I know would have done the same thing." But a San Francisco police sergeant said that Suhrhoff is unusual, and most people would have kept the find.
>
> Andrew S. Fastow, MBA from Northwestern and former Chief Financial Officer of Enron, pled guilty to fraud and is in jail. He admitted setting up false accounts to hide losing transactions of billions of dollars from investors and employees and enriching himself.[1]
>
> In a study of managers' ethics, 47% of top executives, 41% of controllers and 76% of graduate business students were willing to commit fraud by understating write-offs that cut into their company's profits. In addition, 29% of teenagers say that one has to "bend the rules to succeed" in business.[2]
>
> More than 4/5 (82%) of young people admitted that they lied to their parents about something significant at least once in the past year; 60% admitted that they cheated on an exam at least once in the past year; 28% acknowledged stealing something from a store during this same period. Yet, in contrast, 98% said that it was important for them to be a person of good character, and 74% rated their character higher than their peers.[3]
>
> A Pennsylvania man advertised "Blank receipts, 100 restaurant receipts, 50 styles, $5.98. Satisfaction guaranteed." The blank receipts are attractively designed to look like the receipts of restaurants anywhere in America: Captain's Table, Trophy Room, Village Green, P.J.'s, and so on. The purchaser, after filling in the dates, number of diners, and total bill, can use them in reporting expenses. An IRS spokesperson says that selling blank receipts is not illegal.

What are the ethical issues in each of the above cases? How would you go about judging the ethics of each case? Almost all important business decisions

---

[1] Jack Hitt, "American Kabucki: The Ritual of Scandal," *The New York Times,* July 18, 2004, Sec. 4, pp. 1, 3.

[2] "For Many Executives, Ethics Appear to Be a Write-Off," *The Wall Street Journal*, March 26, 1996, pp. C1, C13; for teenagers, *BusinessWeek,* September 20, 2004, p. 16.

[3] "2006 Josephson Institute Report Card on the Ethics of American Youth," Polling done by and reported by the Josephson Institute of Ethics, at http://www.josephsoninstitute.org/reportcard/, accessed July 19, 2007.

contain an ethical component. One purpose of this chapter is to better equip us to make effective ethical judgments.

FACTS, VALUES, AND ACTS

Ethics provides the tools for making **ethical judgments**, and helps develop the habits that result in morally good behavior. Good behavior requires the ability to make moral decisions. So in this chapter we offer a model to help a person make ethically good decisions. Making ethical judgments involves three steps: (1) gathering relevant factual information, (2) selecting the moral norm(s) that most help to make the decision, and (3) making the ethical judgment on the rightness or wrongness of the act or policy (see Figure 3-1).

Ethical judgments are not always easy to make. The facts of the case are often not clear, and the ethical norms to be used are not always agreed on, even by the experts. Hence, to many people, ethics seems ill-defined, subjective, and so not very useful. Just as is true with politics and religion, there is often more heat than light generated by ethical discussions. This lack of knowledge of ethics is unfortunate, because without ethical behavior, it is everyone for him or herself. In such a situation, trust, which is essential to any business transaction, is lost.[4]

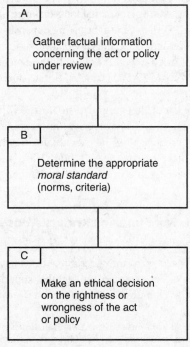

FIGURE 3-1   Steps in Ethical Decision Making

[4] For an overview of the importance of trust in organizations, see LaRue Tone Hosmer, "Trust: The Connecting Link Between Organizational Theory and Philosophical Ethics," *Academy of Management Review,* 20 (April 1995): 379–403; see also Roger C. Mayer, James H. Davis, and F. David Schoorman, "An Integrative Model of Organizational Trust," *Academy of Management Review,* 20 (July 1995): 709–734.

Dilemmas to Decisions

Let us begin our examination of ethical decision making by assessing a case that was first judged by 1,700 business executive readers of the *Harvard Business Review*. This case was part of an early large-scale study of business ethics by Raymond C. Baumhart, S.J.[5]

> An executive earning $150,000 a year has been padding her expense account by about $7,500 a year.

Is it ethical to pad one's expense account? On numerous occasions over the decades, hundreds of other managers have been asked to judge this case, and the results have been substantially the same. Replying to an anonymous questionnaire, 85 percent of executives both in the United States and in Japan think that this sort of behavior is simply unacceptable. Perhaps more important, almost two-thirds of them think their business colleagues would also see such behavior as unacceptable under any circumstances.

Why would padding an expense account be considered wrong by these executives? An expense account is not a simple addition to one's salary. It is intended to pay for expenses incurred in doing one's work.

Pocketing a pencil or making a personal long-distance phone call from the office may seem relatively trivial. Perhaps, but fabricating expenses up to 5 percent of one's salary is not trivial; it is substantial, and thus a violation of justice. The executive in the case is stealing money not owed to her. Presumably the executive's salary is fair compensation for her work; the extra $7,500 is not legitimate salary, nor is it recognized by law as such.

Circumstances are cited that might mitigate the injustice. Some may say, "Many others are also doing it" or "My superior knows about it and says nothing." In the cited study, only about a quarter of the executives thought that their peers would justify such actions for these reasons. Few (about 10%) said that they themselves thought that it would be acceptable in such circumstances. Let us further examine these circumstances.

Others Are Doing It; My Superior Knows About It and Says Nothing

The fact that many people are performing certain actions never in itself makes those actions ethically acceptable. For example, the fact that superiors ordered actions was not accepted as a defense for the unethical managers at Enron. It is not a defense for

---

[5] Raymond C. Baumhart, S.J., *Ethics in Business* (New York: Holt, Rinehart & Winston, 1968), p. 21. For later assessments using the same instrument, see Steven Brenner and Earl Molander, "Is the Ethics of Business Changing?" *Harvard Business Review,* 55 (January–February 1977): 57–71; the dollar figures have been adjusted for inflation. Also, S. T. Vitell and T. A. Festervand, "Business Ethics: Conflicts, Practices, and Beliefs of Industrial Executives," *Journal of Business Ethics,* 5 (1987): 111–122; and Chiake Nakano, "A Survey Study on Japanese Managers' Views of Business Ethics," Society for Business Ethics, Vancouver, B.C., 1995. An expense account is available for expenses that are incurred in the course of one's work. It is not fair to ask an employee to use personal funds, without reimbursement, for legitimate business expenses.

the military guards who tortured Iraqi prisoners at Abu Ghraib prison outside Baghdad. Nor was it a defense for concentration camp officers at the post–World War II Nuremberg war crime trials. Although ethics is influenced by conditions, a moral principle is not established by majority vote.

Let us go back to the case of the expense account. It would benefit the executive if she could increase her salary by $7,500; it would be in her self-interest. Focusing primarily on her own benefit could lead her to be less objective in her search for the right action and would make her more prone to look for excuses to take the money.

Justice calls for a fair distribution of the benefits and burdens of society. In this case, we are concerned with benefits. Is it ever ethical to claim funds from an expense account that were not true expenses? The executive's family is not starving because she has an abnormally low salary, so justice tells us that the expense account should not be used as a salary supplement. Ignorance and coercion can lessen responsibility. However, in this case, the executive can hardly claim that she did not know what an expense account was or that she was forced into taking the money.

But if it is not likely that she would be caught, why shouldn't she pad her expense account? Practically all businesspeople agree that a businessperson should be ethical. That is, individuals should try to do good and avoid evil, not only on the job but in all aspects of life. An essential foundation for business transactions is confidence that most businesspeople are trustworthy and truthful. If one could not trust businesspeople, it would be difficult to purchase goods, sell property or securities, or do most of the exchange that we are accustomed to in modern society.

Admittedly there can be a short-term financial benefit for an embezzler or a supplier who charges $10 million and delivers defective goods. It is because of individuals like this that we have laws, courts, and jails. Yet not all activities can be regulated, nor can all unethical acts be fully punished (in this life, anyway). However, if most businesspeople did not pay their bills and cheated their partners, the market system would collapse.[6]

ETHICAL PRINCIPLES FOR BUSINESS ACTIONS

How to make better ethical decisions has been deliberated for centuries. The norm of **rights and duties** is based on the human dignity of each individual person and results in personal entitlements. Immanuel Kant[7] (personal rights) and John Locke[8] (property rights) developed the theory of rights and duties. The norm of **justice** is also based on the dignity of each person and has a longer tradition, going back to Plato and Aristotle in the fourth century BC.[9]

---

[6] See Nobel prize winning economist Amartya Sen, "Economics, Business Principles and Moral Sentiments," *Business Ethics Quarterly,* 7 (July 1997): 5–15; also James H. Davis and John A. Ruhe, "Perceptions of Corruption: Antecedents and Outcomes," *Journal of Business Ethics,* 43 (April 2003): 275–288.
[7] Immanuel Kant, *The Metaphysical Elements of Justice,* trans. J. Ladd (New York: Library of Liberal Arts, 1965).
[8] John Locke, *The Second Treatise of Government* (New York: Liberal Arts Press, 1952).
[9] Aristotle, *Ethics,* trans. J. A. K. Thomson (London: Penguin, 1953); for influence of firm's culture, see Thomas M. Jones, Will Felps, and Gregory A. Bigley, "Ethical Theory and Stakeholder-Related Decisions: The Role of Stakeholder Culture," *Academy of Management Review,* 32, no. 1 (2007): 137–155.

Businesspeople are most familiar using the ethical norm of **utilitarianism**. This is because the norm examines consequences of actions, and traces its origins to Adam Smith, the father of modern economics. The main proponents of utilitarianism are Jeremy Bentham[10] and John Stuart Mill,[11] who both helped to formulate the theory. Utilitarianism evaluates actions on the basis of their outcomes. In any given situation, the action that would result in the greatest net gain for all concerned parties is considered to be the right, or morally obligatory, action.

The ethical norm of caring was developed more recently from feminist ethics.[12] Work on each of these ethical norms continues to the present.[13] For an overview of these four ethical norms—their history, strengths, weaknesses, and areas of application—see Table 3-1.

Individual Rights and Duties

A moral right is an important, justifiable claim or entitlement to something. Moral rights and duties flow from each person's human dignity and ultimately from the Creator, and are often supported by law; our rights of freedom of conscience and freedom of speech are written into the U.S. Constitution. Moral rights enable individuals to pursue their own interests, and they also impose duties or correlative requirements or prohibitions on others.[14]

Legal rights are stated in laws, rules, or a constitutional system. The U.S. Bill of Rights and the United Nations Universal Declaration of Human Rights spell out individual rights in detail. Most legal rights stem from moral rights; but not all moral rights are enacted into law, and some bad law even attempts to deny human rights (e.g., rights of women in Saudi Arabia, blacks in pre-1960s in the United States, and Jews in Nazi Germany).

Every right has a corresponding obligation or duty. Your right to freedom of speech places an obligation on others to respect that right; moreover, your right to freedom of conscience demands that you may not unnecessarily limit that freedom for others. In business my right to be paid for my work corresponds to the duty of my employer to provide that compensation. In the latter case, both the right and duty stem from the right to private property, which is a traditional pillar of American life and law. However, the right to private property is not absolute. A factory owner may be forced by morality and by law to install pollution control or safety equipment, even though it is expensive. For a listing of selected rights and other ethical norms, see Figure 3-2.

---

[10] Jeremy Bentham, *An Introduction to the Principles of Morals and Legislation* (New York: Hafner, 1948).

[11] John Stuart Mill, *Utilitarianism* (Indianapolis: Bobbs-Merrill, 1957).

[12] See Carol Gilligan, *In a Different Voice* (Cambridge: Harvard University Press, 1982); and Nel Noddings, *Caring* (Berkeley: University of California Press, 1984).

[13] For example, see Thomas Donaldson, Patricia Werhane, Patricia Hogue; Joseph Van Zandt, *Ethical Issues in Business: A Philosophical Approach,* 8th ed. (Upper Saddle River, NJ: Prentice-Hall, 2007); and John Rawls, *A Theory of Justice* (Cambridge, MA: Harvard University Press, 1971).

[14] Velasquez Manuel, *Business Ethics: Concepts and Cases,* 6th ed. (Upper Saddle River, NJ: Prentice Hall, 2006), pp. 71–84; also Richard T. De George, *Business Ethics,* 6th ed. (Upper Saddle River, NJ: Prentice Hall, 2006), pp. 77–84. For a comprehensive European view, see Andrew Crane and Dirk Matten, *Business Ethics,* 2nd ed. (Oxford: Oxford University Press, 2007).

TABLE 3-1 Models for Business Decisions

Definition and Origin	Strengths	Weaknesses	Example	When Used — Summary
1. *Norm of Rights and Duties* Individual's freedom is not to be violated: Locke (1635–1701)—property Kant (1724–1804)—personal rights	1. Ensures respect for individual's personal freedom and property 2. Parallels political Bill of Rights	1. Emphasis on rights can encourage individualistic, selfish behavior	1. Unsafe workplace 2. Flammable children's toys 3. Lying to superior or subordinate	1. Where individual's personal rights or property are in question 2. Use with, for example, employee privacy, job tenure, work dangerous to person's health
2. *Norm of Justice* Equitable distribution of society's benefits and burdens: Aristotle (384–322 BC) Rawls (1921–2002)	1. The "democratic" principle 2. Does not allow a society to become status- or class-dominated 3. Ensures that minorities, poor, handicapped receive opportunities and a fair share of the output	1. Can result in less risk, incentive, and innovation 2. Encourages sense of entitlement	1. Bribes, kickbacks, fraud 2. Delivery of shoddy goods 3. Low wages to Hispanic, African, American, or women workers 4. Sweatshops	1. Fairness, equal opportunity for poor and unemployed 2. Setting salaries for workers vs. executives 3. Public policy decisions: to maintain a floor of living standards for all 4. Use with, for example, performance appraisal, due process, distribution of rewards and punishment

(continued)

TABLE 3-1 (*continued*)

Definition and Origin	Strengths	Weaknesses	When Used		Summary
			Example		
3. *Utilitarianism* "The greatest good for the greatest number": Bentham (1748–1832) Adam Smith (1723–1790) David Ricardo (1772–1823)	1. Concepts, terminology, methods are easiest for business people to use 2. Promotes view of entire system of exchange beyond "this firm" 3. Encourages entrepreneurship, innovation, productivity	1. Impossible to measure or quantify all important elements 2. "Greatest good" can degenerate into self-interest 3. Can result in abridging another's rights 4. Can result in neglecting less powerful segments of society	1. Plant closing 2. Pollution 3. Condemnation of land or buildings for "development"		1. Use in all business decisions, and will be dominant criteria in most 2. Version of model is implicitly used already, although scope is generally limited to "this firm"
4. *Caring* Responsibility to a person because of relationship: Gilligan (1936–) Noddings (1929–)	1. Emphasizes care and responsibility for people 2. Builds trust, healthy communications, and teamwork 3. Supports community and good for group	1. Poor at discriminating various responsibilities and equities 2. Without personal relationship there are no obligations	1. Mentoring colleagues and subordinates 2. Flexible hours and flexible leave policy or sake of family duties 3. At time of delivery of poor performance report or layoffs		1. Emphasizes interpersonal relationships 2. Care for employees and members of work group 3. Concern for those with personal or family needs

Rights and Duties

1.*Life and Safety:* Each person has the right not to have her or his life or safety unknowingly and unnecessarily endangered.
2.*Truthfulness:* The individual has the right not to be intentionally deceived by another, especially on matters about which the individual has the right to know.
3.*Privacy:* The individual has the right to do whatever he or she chooses to do outside working hours and to control information about his or her private life.
4.*Freedom of conscience:* The individual has the right to refrain from carrying out any order that violates those commonly accepted moral or religious norms to which the person adheres.
5.*Free speech:* The individual has the right to criticize conscientiously and truthfully the ethics or legality of corporate actions so long as the criticism does not violate the rights of other individuals within the organization.
6.*Private property:* The individual has the right to hold private property, especially far as this right enables the individual and his or her family to be sheltered have the basic necessities of life.insoand to

Justice

1.*Fair treatment:* People who are similar to each other in the relevant respects should be treated similarly; people who differ in some respect relevant to the job they perform should be treated differently in proportion to the difference between them.
2.*Fair administration of rules:* Rules should be administered consistently,fairly, and impartially.
3.*Fair compensation:* A person should be compensated for the cost of their injuries by the party that is responsible for those injuries.
4.*Fair blame:* Individuals should not be held responsible for matters over which they have no control.
5.*Due process:* A person has a right to a fair and impartial hearing when he or she believes that personal rights are being violated.

Utilitarianism

1.*Organizational Goals* should aim at *maximizing the satisfactions* of the organizations constituencies.
2.The members of an organization should attempt to attain its goals as *efficiently* as possible by consuming as few inputs as possible and minimizing external costs which organizational activities impose on others.
3.The employee should use *every effective means*to achieve the goals of the organization and should neither jeopardize those goals nor enter situations in which personal interests conflict significantly with the goals.

Caring

1.Each person has responsibility for the well-being of those people with whom one has a relation.
2.The responsibility to care increases as the dependency of the other person increases.
3.One cannot be obligated to provide care that one is incapable of providing.

FIGURE 3-2   Selected Ethical Norms

People also have the right not to be lied to or deceived, especially on matters about which they have a right to know. Hence, a supervisor has a duty to give helpful feedback on work performance even if it is time consuming and difficult for the supervisor to do so. Each of us has the right not to be lied to by salespeople or advertisements, even though this right is often violated. Perjury under oath is a serious crime; lying on matters where another has a right to accurate information is seriously unethical. Truthfulness is a basic ethical norm, and it is essential for business.

Rights and duties are moral requirements that protect the individual person, including protection from the encroachment and demands of society or the state. Utilitarian standards promote the group's interests and are relatively insensitive regarding a single individual except insofar as the individual's welfare affects the good of the group.

A business contract establishes rights and duties that did not exist before: the right of the purchaser to receive what was agreed and the right of the seller to be paid what was agreed. Formal written contracts and informal verbal agreements establish new rights and duties and are essential to business transactions.

Americans are more individualistic than any other culture,[15] and so emphasize personal rights more than others. German Philosopher **Immanuel Kant** (1724–1804) recognized that such an emphasis on rights can lead people to focus excessively on what is due them. Kant sought to broaden this perspective, so he emphasized what he called the "categorical imperative." The first formulation is: *I ought never to act except in such a way that I can also will that my principle should become a universal law.* An equivalent statement is: *An action is morally right for a person in a certain situation if and only if the person's reason for carrying out the action is a reason that he or she would be willing to have every person act on, in any similar situation.*[16]

Kant's second formulation of the categorical imperative cautions us against using other people as a means to our own ends: *Never treat another person simply as a means, but always also as an end.* An action is morally right for a person if and only if in performing the action the person does not use others merely as a means for advancing his or her own interests, but also both respects and develops their capacity to choose for themselves. The **Golden Rule**, "Do unto others as you would have them do unto you," mirrors Leviticus (19:18) and Jesus, "Love your neighbor as yourself'" (Matthew 22:19).

Capital, networks, and business firms are means, and are to be used to serve the purposes of people. On the other hand, a person is not to be used merely as a means to achieve my goals. Thus, respect for human dignity places a duty on me that I not deceive, manipulate, or exploit other people.

Norm of Justice

Justice requires that all persons be guided by fairness, equity, and impartiality. Justice calls for evenhanded treatment of groups and individuals (1) in the distribution of

---

[15] Hofstede Geert, *Culture's Consequences: Comparing Values, Behaviors, Institutions, and Organizations Across Nations,* 2nd ed. (Thousand Oaks: Sage, 2001), p. 215.

[16] Immanuel Kant, *Groundwork of the Metaphysics of Morals,* trans. H. J. Paton (New York: Harper & Row, 1964), pp. 62–90.

the benefits and burdens of society, (2) in the administration of laws and regulations, and (3) in the imposition of sanctions and the awarding of compensation for wrongs suffered.

Standards of justice are generally considered to be more important than the utilitarian consideration of consequences. If a society is unjust to a group (e.g., segregation, job discrimination), we consider that society to be unjust and we condemn it, even if the injustices bring about greater productivity. On the other hand, we are willing to trade off some equality if the results will bring about greater benefits for all. For example, differences in income and wealth are justified when they bring greater prosperity *for all.*

Standards of justice are not as often in conflict with individual rights as are utilitarian norms. Both justice and moral rights are based on the recognition of the **dignity of human beings**. The moral right to be treated as a free and equal person, for example, undergirds the notion that benefits and burdens should be distributed equitably. Personal moral rights (e.g., right to life, freedom of conscience, the right to free consent) are so basic that generally they may not be taken away to bring about a better distribution of benefits within a society. On the other hand, property rights may be sacrificed for the sake of a fairer distribution of benefits and burdens (e.g., graduated income tax, limits on pollution).

Distributive justice becomes important when a society has sufficient goods but everyone's basic needs are not satisfied. The question then becomes, what is a just distribution? The fundamental principle is that equals should be treated equally and that unequals should be treated according to their inequality. For example, few would argue that a new person hired for a job should receive the same pay as a senior worker who has 20 years of experience. People who perform work of greater responsibility or who work longer hours should also receive greater pay. Hence, pay differentials should be based on the work itself, not on some arbitrary bias of the employer. Even knowing all of the above, we still wouldn't be able to determine a fair distribution of society's benefits and burdens. In fact, quite different notions of equity are proposed. For example, the capitalist model (benefits based on contribution) is radically different from the socialist (from each according to abilities, to each according to needs).

John Rawls (1921–2003) contributed important ideas to the theory of justice.[17] Rawls would have us construct a system of rules and laws for society as if we did not know what roles we were to play in that society. We do not know if we would be rich or poor, female or male, African or European, manager or slave, physically and mentally fit or handicapped. Rawls calls this the "**veil of ignorance**." Constructing a system of rules under the veil of ignorance allows us to rid ourselves of the biases we have as a result of our own status. Rawls proposes that in such circumstances, each of us would try to construct a system that would be to the greatest benefit to all and that would not undermine the position of any group. According to Rawls, people under the veil of ignorance would agree to two principles:

1. Each person would have an equal right to the most extensive liberty compatible with similar liberty for others.

---

[17] Rawls, *op. cit.*

2. Social and economic inequalities would be arranged so that they are reasonably expected to be to everyone's advantage and attached to positions and offices open to all.

The first principle is parallel to the American sense of liberty and thus is not controversial in the United States. The second principle is more egalitarian and also more controversial. However, Rawls maintains that if people honestly choose as if they were under the veil of ignorance, they would opt for a system of justice that is most fair to all members of society.[18] We now turn to a norm that observes the *consequences* of actions on the entire group.

Norm of Utilitarianism

Utilitarianism examines the **consequences** of an act. It judges that an action is right if it produces the greatest utility, "the greatest good for the greatest number." The calculation is similar to a cost–benefit analysis applied to all parties who would be affected by the decision. That action is ethical which produces the **greatest net benefit** when all benefits to all the affected parties are added and the costs to parties are subtracted. Although it would be convenient if these costs and benefits could be measured in some comparable unit, this is rarely possible. Many important values (e.g., human life and liberty) cannot be quantified. Thus, the best we can do is to list the effects and estimate the magnitude of their costs and benefits as accurately as possible.

The utilitarian norm says that the ethical action is that which produces the greatest net benefit over any other possible action. This does not mean that the right action produces the greatest good for the person performing the action. Rather, it is the action that produces the greatest net good for all those who are affected by the action. The utilitarian norm is most useful for complex cases that affect many parties. Although the methodology is clear in theory, carrying out the calculations is often difficult. Taking into account so many affected parties, and the extent to which the action affects them, can be a tallying nightmare.

Hence several shortcuts have been proposed that can reduce the complexity of utilitarian calculations. Each shortcut involves a sacrifice of accuracy for ease of decision. Among these shortcuts are (1) calculation of costs and benefits in dollar terms for ease of comparison; (2) restriction of consideration to those directly affected by the action, putting aside indirect effects. In using these shortcuts, an individual should be aware that they result in simplification and that some interests may not be sufficiently taken into consideration.

In the popular mind, the term *utilitarianism* sometimes suggests exploitation. We do not intend this meaning. However, a noteworthy weakness of the ethical norm of utilitarianism is that it can advocate, for example, abridging an individual's right to a job or even life for the sake of the greater good of a large number of people. This

---

[18] An organization that treats its employees justly reaps many rewards, see Blair H. Shepard, Roy J. Lewicki, and John W. Minton, *Organizational Justice: The Search for Fairness in the Workplace* (New York: Lexington, 1992).

and other difficulties are discussed elsewhere.[19] There is an additional rule in using utilitarianism: It is considered unethical to choose narrower benefits (e.g., personal goals of career or money) at the expense of the good of a larger number, such as a firm, neighborhood, or a nation. Utilitarian norms emphasize the **good of the** *group*. However, as a result an individual and what is due to that individual may be overlooked. Hence the norm of utilitarianism must be balanced by the use of the norms of justice, rights and duties, and, the norm we will discuss next, caring.

Norm of Caring

Over the centuries ethicists, who were almost all male, developed the norms of rights and duties, justice, and utilitarianism. These norms highlight impartiality and abstract principles. A norm of *caring* has been recognized in the last few decades.[20] Caring is built upon relations between people and is an extension of family life. Rather than autonomous individuals making objective, impartial ethical judgments, we instead experience numerous **relationships**, and these relationships influence our ethical obligations. We care for each other, and we have responsibilities to each other.

Ethicists who advocate caring as a norm demonstrate how women's moral experience has been neglected. When facing moral dilemmas, women tend to focus on the relationships of people rather than on impartial, theoretical principles. As we saw in Chapter 2, Gilligan amended the levels of moral development in light of the experience of women. The male matures by developing autonomy and sees himself in opposition to the other. Thus he insists on personal rights. However, if a businessperson is unduly influenced by rights and competition, it can result in paranoid tendencies that can cause difficulty relating to others or relating to others only by contract.

The female matures by developing relationship-based morality. Although feminist ethicists are reluctant to analyze caring too exactly, we can note some qualifications of the norm of caring. First, the obligation to care is proportional to one's relationship. In extended relationships, caring does not require action if that action is very costly. Second, one's roles and obligations influence the responsibility to care. Caring for one's child has greater priority than caring for someone in one's work group. Third, one cannot be obligated to provide care that one is incapable of providing. For the manager, caring is a relevant norm for many current business challenges. Trust, teamwork, good personal relationships, and communications build upon caring, and must be achieved, if the firm is to be successful.[21]

---

[19] Robert Audi, "Can Utilitarianism Be Distributive? Maximization and Distribution as Criteria in Managerial Decisions," *Business Ethics Quarterly,* 17 (October 2007): 593–611; Gerald F. Cavanagh, Dennis J. Moberg, and Manuel Velasquez, "The Ethics of Organizational Politics," *Academy of Management Review,* 6 (July 1981): 363–374; Manuel Velasquez, *Business Ethics: Concepts and Cases,* 6th ed. (Upper Saddle River, NJ: Prentice-Hall, 2006), pp. 60–71.

[20] See Rosemarie Tong, *Feminine and Feminist Ethics* (Belmont, CA: Wadsworth, 1993), esp. chapters 3 and 4; Gilligan, *op. cit.*

[21] Jeanne M. Liedtka, "Feminist Morality and Competitive Reality: A Role for the Ethic of Care?" *Business Ethics Quarterly,* 6 (April 1996): 179–200; Gerald F. Cavanagh, Dennis J. Moberg, and Manuel Velasquez, "Making Business Ethics Practical," *Business Ethics Quarterly,* 5 (July 1995): 399–418.

Caring engages our emotions, but in order to do *any* ethical reasoning, our emotions must be involved. While ethics is not feeling, it is a sterile intellectual exercise if one's feelings are not engaged in ethical decision making. In making ethical judgments it is essential to consider the interests of others. In order to incorporate the interests of others into one's decision-making processes, one must be able to feel and to empathize with those that are affected by one's decisions. In Kohlberg's terms, one must at least have achieved Level 2 moral development (see Chapter 2). In order to be an ethical decision maker, one must learn how to habitually put oneself in the position of other persons. One must learn how others perceive a situation and sense what others feel and suffer. Without this ability to care for others on a sensible level, it is impossible to examine the moral dimensions of life in any significant way.

Ethical Norms for Global Business

Some claim that the varying business customs and practices in countries around the world demand new norms for international business ethics. They propose a variety of different models, based upon rights, social contract, and negative and modified utilitarianism.[22] Other scholars, however, have found common basic ethical values in business in different cultures. While global business norms do not yet exist, the various attempts to achieve norms and the codes of ethics that we will examine in Chapter 9 are developing an international policy regime.[23] This is gradually providing a consensus of moral expectations for the global firm.

Manuel Velasquez applied the new proposed models to several cases in global business ethics.[24] He demonstrates the limitations of each of those new proposals. On the other hand, he found that the comprehensive model containing the norms of rights and duties, justice, utilitarianism, and caring as presented in this chapter is more flexible and effective for the global business manager. Let us now use these norms to solve some ethical problems.

SOLVING ETHICAL PROBLEMS

A good judgment is preceded by four steps: gather the facts, articulate accurately the issue, select the appropriate norm to use, and make an ethical judgment (see Figure 3-3). Before any ethical dilemma can be assessed, it is essential that all the **relevant facts** be considered. Omissions can result in a faulty judgment: failure to

---

[22] Thomas Donaldson and Thomas W. Dunfee, *Ties That Bind: A Social Contracts Approach to Business Ethics* (Boston: Harvard Business School Press, 1999); also Andrew Spicer, Thomas Dunfee, and Wendy J. Bailey, "Does National Context Matter in Ethical Decision Making? An Empirical Test of Integrative Social Contracts Theory," *Academy of Management Journal,* 47 (August 2004): 610–620.
[23] Duane Windsor, "The Development of International Business Norms," *Business Ethics Quarterly,* 14 (October 2004): 729–754; see the business ethics text in both Chinese and English, Stephan Rothlin, *Eighteen Rules of International Business Ethics* (Beijing, 2004); Japanese business managers have roughly the same values as do American, according to Chaiki Nakano, "A Survey on Japanese Managers' Views of Business Ethics," *op. cit.*
[24] Manuel Velasquez, "International Business Ethics: The Aluminum Companies in Jamaica," *Business Ethics Quarterly,* 5 (October 1995): 865–882; Hans Kung, "A Global Ethic in an Age of Globalization," *Business Ethics Quarterly,* 7 (July 1997): 17–31.

gather all the data, an inadequate understanding of ethical norms, and making an important decision too quickly.[25] To help select the most **appropriate ethical norm**, we have described rights and duties, justice, utility, and caring. Figure 3-3 is a schematic diagram of how ethical decision making can best proceed. Although it contains greater detail than Figure 3-1, it includes the same three steps, data gathering, analysis, and judgment. Even Figure 3-3 is simplified, but nevertheless it can aid in solving ethical dilemmas.

Note that each of the four ethical norms is listed in Figure 3-3. In order to make an ethical decision, we decide which norm is best able to assess the particular case. Basic moral rights, such as the right to life, may not be negated by others, even if doing so would effect greater benefits. The norm of caring may outweigh impartiality when the situation involves close relationships and privately held resources.

To summarize, one can come to an ethical decision when one follows the steps:

1. Gather the **relevant facts** of the case;
2. What is the principal **ethical issue**? [i.e., "Is it ethical to . . . "];
3. Choose the most appropriate **ethical norm**(s);
4. Apply the norm(s) and make an ethical **judgment**.

Let us apply this process and our norms to the case presented earlier of the executive who padded her expense account. We will accept the limited data provided in the case. The ethical issue: Is it ethical for an executive to obtain an additional $7,500 per year by padding her expense account? The rights norm is not so useful here: The executive has no right to the extra money, although we might argue that the shareholders' and customers' right to goods due them is being violated. Using the justice norm, we note that salary and commissions constitute ordinary compensation for individuals. Expense accounts have a different purpose. Most managers responding to the case held that it was unethical for the executive to pad her expense account. John Rawls would maintain that all of us would set the rules to prohibit such padding of expenses if we did not know what roles we ourselves would have in society. Using the utility criterion, we judge that padding her expense account benefits the executive but not others. Her actions hurt shareholders, customers, and honest executives; padding one's expense account adds to the cost of business and in this way also violates utility. Claiming nonexistent expenses does not indicate care for others in the firm. Hence, we conclude that padding one's expense account is unethical on all four ethical norms, and is therefore morally wrong. Note that 73 percent of the executives who were asked came to the same judgment.

Let us consider a case from the beginning of the chapter. Are our ethical norms violated when a student cheats on an exam? If a student looks at another student's paper or takes a "cheat sheet" into an exam, that student's finished exam does not represent what she actually knows. She has "stolen" answers that are not hers, and thus violates justice; she seeks to obtain credit for material that she does not know. Other students, who are playing by the rules, do not have access to

---

[25] Paul C. Nutt, *Why Decisions Fail: Avoiding the Blunders and Traps That Lead to Debacles* (San Francisco: Berrett-Koehler, 2002).

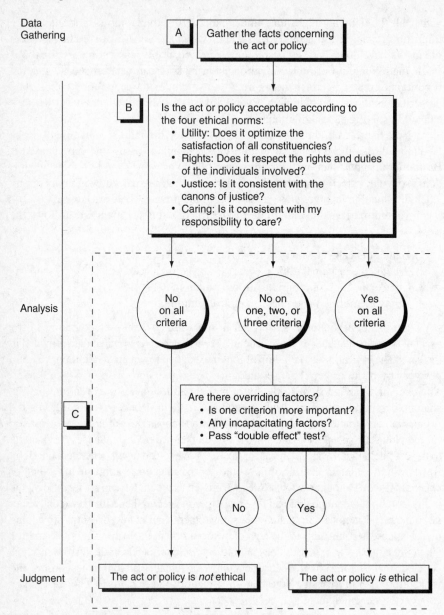

FIGURE 3-3   Flow Diagram of Ethical Decision Making

Source: Adapted from Gerald F. Cavanagh, Dennis J. Moberg, and Manuel Velasquez,
"Making Business Ethics Practical," Business Ethics Quarterly *(July 1995); Manuel*
Velasquez, Gerald F. Cavanagh, and Dennis Moberg, "Organizational Statesmenship and
Dirty Politics," Organizational Dynamics *(Fall 1983).*

answers. So the cheating student is taking unfair advantage of her fellow students. From the utilitarian perspective, the only person who benefits is the cheater. The other students all suffer because their performance is considered to be relatively poorer than the one who cheated. Cheating may hurt even the cheater, because she will not have the knowledge that a future employer may expect her to have. Moreover, cheating can easily become a habit, and that could cause one to be fired for cheating on the job. So, while cheating may benefit one in the short term, in the long term it is not a benefit even to the cheater.

What about the entrepreneur who advertised official-looking blank receipts of fictitious restaurants? Salespeople and managers could fill out the receipts and submit them for reimbursement. The receipts would document meals that never were purchased. Using our norms, how do we judge the ethics of the person selling such receipts? Or of the person buying them and using them? Respond to this case using the flow chart in Figure 3-3. Examine Andrew Fastow's case using the same norms.

When deciding on what is ethical behavior, two short-cut tests may help. First, could my conduct bear the scrutiny of a probing reporter? Would I do it if I knew that my actions were going to be featured in tomorrow's news? Second, could I acknowledge what I did to my mother or another for whom I have respect?

Decision Making Using the Model

Let us examine another case:

> Brian Curry, financial vice president of Digital Robotics Corporation, is about to retire and has been asked to recommend one of his two associates for promotion to vice president. Curry knows that his recommendation will be acted on. He also realizes that since both associates are about the same age, the one not chosen will have difficulty getting future promotions. Debra Butler is bright, outgoing and has better leadership skills. She is the most qualified for the position. Moreover, her father is president of the largest customer of Digital, and Curry reasons that Digital will more likely keep this business if his daughter is made an officer. On the other hand, John McNichols has been with the company longer, has worked seventy-hour weeks, and has pulled the company through some very difficult situations. He has continued putting in extra effort because he was told some time ago that he was in line for the vice presidency. Nevertheless, Curry recommends Butler for the job.

Let us again use our norms and Figure 3-3 to decide this case. Neither Butler nor McNichols has a right to the position. Is it ethical to promote Butler? As for justice, we conclude that because the promotional decision was made on the basis of relevant abilities, it did constitute fair treatment. On the other hand, McNichols worked extra hours because of the promised promotion. Much of his extra work was based on a false promise. McNichols had a right to know the truth and to be treated fairly. Utility tells us that the selection of Debra Butler optimally benefits shareholders, customers, management, and most of the workers, because she is a better leader.[26] Caring is not a primary norm to use in such a case.

Thus, according to the norms of justice and utility, the appointment of Butler is morally acceptable. However, because of the promise earlier made to McNichols, which resulted in extended work weeks, he is being treated wrongly. We can then ask if there are any "overriding factors" that ought to be taken into consideration.

Overriding Factors

Overriding factors are factors that may, in a given case, justify overriding one or perhaps two of the four ethical norms: rights and duties, justice, utility, or caring (see Figure 3-3). Overriding factors can be examined when there is a conflict in the conclusions drawn from the ethical norms. For example, there might be **incapacitating factors**, such as a *lack of information* or *coercion.* If there are any elements that *coerce* an individual into doing a certain action, then that individual is not fully responsible. Let us take the example of Bausch and Lomb. CEO Daniel Gill expected division managers to show double-digit earnings each quarter. Under this unrelenting pressure, the managers faked sales of sunglasses and forced distributors to accept unneeded products. This eventually resulted in a collapse of revenues and an SEC investigation. What the managers did was unethical, but to the extent that they were coerced their guilt is less because they were pressured by their CEO.[27] Also, a *lack of information* may be an incapacitating factor that might prevent someone might from utilizing a norm. A manager might suspect that another manager is embezzling from the firm. However, to report him to superiors could ruin his reputation. Therefore, even though stealing is a violation of justice, in this instance there is not yet sufficient information to act. In addition, a manager may be sincerely uncertain of the norm or its applicability in a particular case.[28]

Consider again our case of appointing a financial vice president. Utility calls for recommending Debra Butler for the position. The right to full information and perhaps justice support McNichols' claim. McNichols has worked more hours and harder because of a promised reward. Because the position was promised to him, fair treatment requires giving him special consideration. On the basis of the importance of a verbal promise and of justice, we might conclude that McNichols should get the position.

There is now a conflict between these two norms. Is one norm more important? The effective operation of the firm is an important ethical goal, because many jobs and family incomes depend upon it. How much better a manager is Butler and how would her selection affect the firm's performance and the jobs of others at Digital?

In examining incapacitating factors, coercion does not seem to be involved. That Debra Butler's father is president of Digital's largest customer might constitute psychological pressure. However, Curry seems to have made his decision freely.

---

[26] A manager can score him- or herself as being predominantly a user of the utility, justice, or rights norm by using a set of questions developed by Marshall Sashkin. See his *Managerial Values Profile* (Bryn Mawr, PA: Organizational Design and Development, 1986).

[27] "Blind Ambition: How Pursuit of Results Got Out of Hand at Bausch and Lomb," *BusinessWeek,* October 23, 1995, pp. 78–92, 146.

[28] For how incapacitating factors lessen a moral agent's responsibility, see Oswald A. J. Mascarenhas, "Exonerating Unethical Marketing Executive Behaviors: A Diagnostic Framework," *Journal of Marketing,* 59 (April 1995): 43–57.

Another factor to consider is exactly what promise was made to McNichols? Was it clear and unequivocal? If the "promise" was in fact a mere statement that McNichols had a good chance at the promotion and if Butler's performance in the VP job is expected to be significantly better than McNichols', then Curry could ethically recommend Butler. However, some compensation should then be made to McNichols.

Selling Cigarettes Globally

Let us assess the ethics of the following case:

> U.S. based Altria spun off Philip Morris International (PMI) and moved its headquarters to Switzerland in 2008. This made the tobacco firm's international operations beyond the reach of U.S. regulations, and the legal and public relations headaches that have stood in the way of its growth. With sales of $22 billion PMI is the third most profitable consumer goods firm in the world after Procter & Gamble (P&G) and Nestle. Smoking rates in developed countries have declined, but have increased dramatically in developing countries (for example, since 2001, up 42% in Pakistan; 36% in Ukraine and 18% in Argentina). China's 350 million smokers annually generate about $30 billion in tax revenue for the country.[29]
>
> Roughly 430,000 Americans and globally almost 5,000,000 people die prematurely each year of tobacco related illness. Medical scientists estimate that 30 to 40 percent of all who smoke will die of cancer, cardiovascular disease, or chronic obstructive lung disease caused by their smoking. Including medical costs and lost productivity, smoking costs the U.S. $167 million per year, according to the American Cancer Society.
>
> Tobacco executives have initiated strategies to market cigarettes to teenagers, minorities, women and people in developing countries. They employ advertising and widespread distribution of free samples. Advertising shows members of the dominant social or racial group smoking cigarettes in attractive surroundings. The market share for U.S. firms in four Asian countries rose 600%, and cigarette smoking was found to be about 10% higher than it would be if it were not for the U.S. cigarettes and advertising. Experts predict the death rate due to tobacco world-wide will reach 10,000,000 annually by the year 2020.[30]

Is it ethical to sell cigarettes? Let us apply our ethical norms to the case. Cigarette executives claim that they are not violating anyone's right to life by selling cigarettes, because information is available on the health hazards. However, some people, especially youth and the poor, may not be aware of the likelihood of serious

---

[29] Vanessa O'Connell, "Philip Morris Readies Aggressive Global Push: Division Spinoff Enables Blitz of New Products; High-Tar Smokes in Asia," *The Wall Street Journal,* January 29, 2008, p. AI.

[30] David Kessler, *A Question of Intent: A Great American Battle with a Deadly Industry* (New York: Public Affairs, 2001); see also Philip Hilts, *Smokescreen: The Truth Behind the Tobacco Industry Cover-up* (Reading, MA: Addison Wesley, 1996); and Richard Kluber, *Ashes to Ashes: America's Hundred-Year Cigarette War, the Public Health, and the Unabashed Triumph of Philip Morris* (New York: Knopf, 1996).

disease and death that follow the use of tobacco. Both justice and rights demand that cigarette sellers be truthful in advertising products with such deadly consequences.

Utilitarians calculate that those who benefit are the cigarette companies, their employees, and the user who is able to feed his nicotine addiction. On the other hand, the user's health is often seriously impaired. This can result in large health and dollar costs to the smoker, their dependents, and employers. Society as a whole pays, because income is lost and insurance costs rise because of the many serious tobacco-related illnesses. Justice calls for tobacco firms, which reap large profits from cigarette sales, to share the burden of paying the additional health costs.

Health concerns and caring might lead tobacco executives to stop attracting new smokers and possibly even to withdraw tobacco products from the market altogether. There do not seem to be any overriding factors in this case, or any incapacitating factors such as coercion. Have we been too harsh on the executives of cigarette firms? How would you analyze the case?

The ethical model and principles described in this chapter are widely used. The model enables the manager to use ethical analysis in business decisions, and to thus balance financial and marketing analyses. Yet problems of conscience can still sometimes face a member of an organization.

Loyalty and Whistle-Blowing

In addition to making ethical decisions, a member of an organization sometimes faces a situation where superiors seem to ignore or be blind to unethical acts. Sherron Watkins of Enron, Cynthia Cooper of WorldCom, and Coleen Rowley of the FBI were named *Time Magazine*'s "persons of the year" for blowing the whistle internally at their organizations.[31] At Enron, WorldCom, and the FBI, they found that information was being falsified, thus misleading important stakeholders of their organization. Whether to blow the whistle is a difficult dilemma and ultimately demands courage. Let us examine the following case, where the stakes are high:

> An engineer in the design section of an airplane manufacturing firm is convinced that the latch mechanism on a plane's cargo door does not provide sufficient security. She is convinced that the door could blow out, causing decompression and a crash; the door should be redesigned to make it more secure. She goes to her supervisor and presents the information, and is told that the U.S. Federal Aviation Administration (FAA) has given the required approval and that she should not "rock the boat." She goes to the president of the firm and gets the same answer.

Would that engineer be justified in making this information public, and perhaps taking it to the news media? The answer to this question is extremely important. The danger to the lives of hundreds of passengers might argue for going public.[32] On the other hand, the reputation and perhaps the financial viability of the aircraft

---

[31] Richard Lacayo and Amanda Ripley, "Persons of the Year," *Time,* January 6, 2003, pp. 30–60.
[32] Janet P. Near, Michael Rehg, James Van Scotter, and Marcia Miceli, "Does the Type of Wrongdoing Affect the Whistle-Blowing Process?" *Business Ethics Quarterly,* 14, no. 2 (2004): 219–242.

manufacturing firm are also to be weighed. A mistake on either side could cause disaster. So it is important to do the ethical analysis very carefully.

The right to life and safety is at issue. If the engineer is correct that the faulty latch mechanism puts the plane in danger of a crash, then the lives of the passengers would be of primary importance in the calculations. While the engineer owes loyalty to her employer, nevertheless justice requires that future passengers should not unknowingly be in danger of their lives due to the faulty design.

Utilitarians would total up the costs and benefits to all parties affected. Redesigning the aircraft and recalling planes already in service would cost the firm hundreds of millions of dollars. More immediately, taking the issue to the scandal-oriented media people would undermine the reputation of the firm. On the other hand, assuming that 300 people are aboard a plane that might crash, how much are 300 lives worth? Utilitarians, too, would conclude that the designer would be justified in taking the issue outside the firm. Caring would cause the engineer to opt for the safety of the passengers also. Even 69 percent of the corporate executives who examined the case thought that the designer was justified in breaching loyalty and taking the issue to the media.[33]

When to Blow the Whistle

Because opportunities for whistle-blowing are more common and the stakes are high, it is important to examine the conditions that would allow and sometimes require whistle-blowing. Whistle-blowing has been defined as "the disclosure by organization members (former or current) of illegal, immoral, or illegitimate practices under the control of their employers, to persons or organizations that may be able to effect action."[34] This definition covers both blowing the whistle internally to upper management (as the three *Time* Women-of-the-Year did) and also to external parties (e.g., government agencies or the media). To be ethical, one should meet several criteria for whistle-blowing:[35]

1. The purpose should be moral: to benefit the public interest.
2. What is protested should be of major importance and should be specific.
3. The facts of the case must be certain; they should be checked and rechecked.
4. In the case of external whistle-blowing, all other avenues for change within the organization must already be exhausted.

Let us examine these criteria. The first demands that the purpose of whistle-blowing should not be to attract attention, to seek revenge, or to achieve some personal goal. Whistle-blowers sometimes are seeking vengeance on a supervisor or a company that they believe has been unfair to them. Perceptions regarding one's grievances can be biased and do not provide a solid basis for whistle-blowing. Instead, the revelation of wrongdoing should be for the **common good**.

---

[33] "Business Executives and Moral Dilemmas," *Business and Society Review,* Spring, 1975, p. 52.
[34] Marcia P. Miceli and Janet P. Near, "Understanding Whistle-Blowing Effectiveness: How Can One Person Make a Difference," in *The Accountable Corporation,* ed. Marc J. Epstein and Kirk O. Hanson, vol. 4 (Westport, CT: Praeger, 2006), p. 203.
[35] Sissela Bok, "Whistleblowing and Professional Responsibilities," in *Ethics Teaching in Higher Education,* ed. Daniel Callahan and Sissela Bok (New York: Plenum Press, 1980).

Second, whistle-blowing requires that the wrongdoing be a serious breach of ethics. Much is at stake, and the action should not be taken lightly. The unethical act protested should be a specific act, not a vague attitude that is hard to document.

Third, the facts of the case must be ascertained, and the **evidence** must be double-checked. The fourth criterion demands that higher officials in the organization who could rectify the situation have been **informed** and that they still refuse to do anything. This requires going to the president and the board before going to an outside party. If a federal regulatory agency could be involved, then, assuming all internal avenues have been tried, the agency is to be preferred to the news media.

U.S. law provides financial rewards to whistle-blowers who find fraud with regard to federal contracts. These rewards have been successful in reducing such fraud, and thus rewards seem to be justified.[36] However, to compensate for possible personal bias, one should seek competent objective advice so as not to blow the whistle on the basis of partial or misleading information. Ideally, the whistle-blower should be willing to accept responsibility for providing the information. This takes courage, since the person's job may be on the line. It is also a test of one's motives. Moreover, anonymous informers are not as trusted.

Let us apply the criteria to the case of the aircraft designer. Her purpose in blowing the whistle is to serve the public interest by preventing an airplane crash and saving hundreds of lives. The facts of the situation should be checked. In this case, let us presume that the engineer is mentally stable, has checked her data with competent peers, and has nothing to gain from the revelations. The whistle-blower has already gone to her supervisor and to the president. The FAA does not seem to recognize the design problem. However, before going to the media, the designer should check to see if the FAA is aware of it. If not, telling the FAA of the design flaw could achieve the safety goal without a public splash, and thus prevent severe loss to the manufacturer and to the airlines that use the plane. Because the whistle-blower has not yet acted, we do not know whether she will identify herself. We also know nothing of her character, but let us presume that no personal advantage will be gained by the whistle-blowing.

In conclusion, the whistle-blower, assuming she has the correct facts, would be justified in going to an external agency. This case is not fictitious. Had someone recognized and protested the cargo door latch problem on the DC-10, a Turkish airliner taking off from Paris would not have crashed and taken more than 300 lives.[37]

Wrongdoing within the firm can damage a company's profitability, hurt its reputation, demoralize its employees, and result in costly fines or lawsuits. Hence, in order for management to obtain information on such potentially damaging actions or products, it should provide a vehicle for an employee to report wrongdoing internally.[38]

---

[36] Thomas L. Carson, Mary Ellen Verdu, and Richard E. Wokutch, "Whistle-Blowing for Profit: An Ethical Analysis of the Federal False Claims Act," *Journal of Business Ethics,* 77 (2008): 361–376.

[37] Paul Eddy, Elaine Potter, and Bruce Page, *Destination Disaster* (New York: New York Times Book Co., 1976), esp. pp. 33–63.

[38] Roberta Ann Johnson, *Whistleblowing: When It Works and Why* (Boulder, CO: Lynne Rienner, 2002); and Michael Gundlach, Scott Douglas, and Mark Martinko, "The Decision to Blow the Whistle: A Social Information Processing Framework," *Academy of Management Review,* 28 (January 2003): 107–123; Marcia P. Miceli and Janet P. Near, "Whistleblowing: Reaping the Benefits," *Academy of Management Executive,* 8 (August 1994): 65–72.

A serious deterrent to whistle-blowing is the fact that many whistle-blowers are penalized by being demoted, frozen out, or fired. They are labeled as "stool pigeons" and "squealers." Legislation has provided some protection for whistle-blowers. People cannot be fired for whistle-blowing, at least under restricted circumstances.

Only when a firm has bad management, poor communications, and managers who do not want to hear bad news, does whistle-blowing occur. Ethical problems do not arise when a firm has, for example, accurate and honest financial reporting, good design of the product, and open communications. Whistle-blowing occurs when supervisors do not listen to subordinates and their concerns. Sometimes these concerns are not well founded, but it is essential that they be heard. An ambitious manager can encourage cheaper, substandard practices and pretend he does not see them as he tries to show higher quarterly profits. In short, blowing the whistle is more likely to occur when an organization has poor management, is not performing well, or both.

GOOD HABITS BUILD VIRTUE AND CHARACTER

Given recent and too common business scandals, executives ask how good character can be developed within the organization. Character development includes the good habits of trust, loyalty, and integrity.[39] Recall CEO Warren Buffet's words in his annual letter to shareholders, "When looking for managers, I basically look for three things—integrity, intelligence and energy. The truth is that if you don't have the first, the other two will kill you; because if you have someone who doesn't have integrity, you really want them to be dumb and lazy. It is only if they have the first that the second two count." Without integrity and good character, intelligence and energy destroy value rather than increase it. The global marketplace makes the need for integrity and character even more important; far-flung operations demand greater cooperation and honesty. Executives cannot build trust, commitment, and effort among the stakeholders of the firm without giving attention to integrity and character development. Moreover, an organization that is virtuous has been shown to be more effective and more profitable.[40] With fewer middle managers today, greater personal responsibility is demanded of members of organizations in order to perform their ordinary tasks. This has been described and measured, and is called "organizational citizenship."[41]

---

[39] See Edwin M. Hartman, "Can We Teach Character: An Aristotelian Answer," *Academy of Management Learning and Education,* 5, no. 1 (2006): 68–81; and Alan Wolfe, *Moral Freedom: The Search for Virtue in a World of* Choice (New York: W. W. Norton, 2002).

[40] Kim S. Cameron, "Good or Not Bad: Standards and Ethics in Managing Change," *Academy of Management Learning and Education,* 5, no. 3 (2006): 317–323; also Kim S. Cameron, Jane E. Dutton, and Robert E. Quinn, eds., *Positive Organizational Scholarship: Foundations of a New Discipline* (San Francisco: Berrett-Koehler, 2003).

[41] Robert H. Moorman, Gerald Blakely, and Brian Niehoff, "Does Perceived Organizational Support Mediate the Relationship Between Procedural Justice and Organizational Citizenship Behavior?" *Academy of Management Journal,* 41, no. 3 (1998): 351–357; also Linn Van Dyne, Jill Graham, and Richard Dienesch, "Organizational Citizenship Behavior: Construct Redefinition, Measurement, and Validation," *Academy of Management Journal,* 37 (1994): 765–802.

Altruism: Unselfish concern for the welfare of others.

Character: A stable organized personality with a composite of good and bad moral habits within a person.

Ethics: The principles of conduct governing an individual or a group, and the methods for applying them.

Habit: An acquired behavior pattern followed until it becomes almost automatic.

Moral: Dealing with or capable of distinguishing right from wrong.

Moral habit: A morally good or bad behavior pattern.

Value: A lasting belief that a certain goal or mode of conduct is better than the opposite goal or conduct.

Vice: A bad moral habit.

Virtue: A good moral habit that has been acquired by choosing the good.

FIGURE 3-4   Moral Habits Terms

Trust and a healthy community life is a foundation for prosperity. Francis Fukuyama maintains that some cultures have low trust (China, Italy, and France), while others possess high trust (Germany, the United States, and Japan). And some nonrational factors, such as religion, tradition, honor, and loyalty, are essential in building trust. But he warns that the predominant American value of individualism is a threat to trust.[42]

Character and virtue (for definitions, see Figure 3-4) are essential for a good manager. But high intelligence does not bring character. The example of intelligent people who supported Hitler (Martin Heidegger, Carl Jung, Ezra Pound), or the straight "A" student who sexually exploits others, demonstrates that intelligence and a good education do not result in good character.[43] Moreover, we often speak of honesty, trust, and integrity as if people are born with those virtues. This is not the case. Virtue is achieved by effort. For centuries, the philosopher **Aristotle** (384–322 BC) has helped us understand virtue. Aristotle shows how the virtuous person avoids extremes, and "what we call selfishness is guaranteed to be self-destructive as well."[44]

A **morally mature** person will develop good moral habits or virtues; "the ultimate aim of the Aristotelian approach to business is to cultivate whole human beings, not jungle fighters, efficiency automatons, or 'good soldiers.'" Certain virtues are important for business: honesty, fairness, trust, and toughness; friendliness, honor, loyalty, caring (developed from using ethical norm of caring), compassion, and justice (developed from using ethical norm). Each of these virtues is strengthened by repeated

---

[42] Francis Fukuyama, *Trust: The Social Virtues and the Creation of Prosperity* (New York: Free Press, 1995).
[43] Robert Coles, "The Disparity Between Intellect and Character," *Chronicle of Higher Education,* September 22, 1995, p. A68.
[44] Robert C. Solomon, "Victims of Circumstances: A Defense of Virtue Ethics in Business," *Business Ethics Quarterly,* 13, no. 1 (2003): 46–62.

actions. Envy and resentment are vices for the businessperson; they poison the firm. Vices are bad habits that develop through repeated acts.

A person is able to develop a good habit by consciously and repeatedly performing that act.[45] As Aristotle put it, "We are what we repeatedly do." Developing a good habit takes effort, but once a habit is established, later similar actions come easily and naturally. Thus a person who intentionally develops good habits through good acts makes additional similar good acts easier to perform. The development of good moral habits is also a test of the basic spiritual values of the individual person.[46] Moreover, people who possess virtue will be more reliable colleagues and will build a more effective firm in the long term.

Ethical decisions are the foundation of moral acts, and these good acts then provide the building blocks for good habits. Once a person has developed a good moral habit, say courage or prudence, that person is able to act with courage or prudence more easily in each new instance. This ability we identify as *virtue*. Before we proceed further, let us provide two examples of good and bad moral habits:

> A demented person placed cyanide in Tylenol capsules, and seven people in Chicago died. Consultants and the FBI advised against a recall of Tylenol, since they thought it would encourage other unstable people to do the same thing. Moreover, a recall of all existing capsules would cost manufacturer Johnson & Johnson hundreds of millions of dollars. However, James Burke, CEO at J&J, quickly decided on a recall rather than endanger additional lives. By Burke's account, this was because he and other managers based their decision on the mission and basic values of J&J (see Figure 8-3) and the good moral habits that thus developed among J&J people over the years.[47]
>
> The New York Stock Exchange (NYSE) is a non-profit, self-regulatory body that oversees the exchange of equity stock in the largest U.S. firms. NYSE's chairman, Richard Grasso, was voted $188 million in pay in 2003. The CEO's of some of the Wall Street firms that he regulated, Goldman Sachs, Lehman Brothers, and Bear Stearns, were on the compensation committee of NYSE that awarded the pay. These and other executives are criticized by shareholders for their own excessive pay. Grasso was fired as head of the NYSE after his pay was revealed.[48]

---

[45] Rushworth M. Kidder makes this same point with examples in his chapter "Ethical Fitness," in *How Good People Make Tough Choices* (New York: William Morrow, 1995); see also George P. Klubertanz, S.J., *Habits and Virtues,* "How is Virtue Acquired," (New York: Appleton-Century-Crofts, 1965), pp. 171–177; For references, see Klubertanz and Alasdair MacIntyre, *After Virtue* (Notre Dame: University of Notre Dame Press, 1981).

[46] Gerald F. Cavanagh and Mark R. Bandsuch, "Virtue as a Benchmark for Spirituality in Business," *Journal of Business Ethics,* 38 (June 2002): 109–117.

[47] See Laura L. Nash, "Johnson & Johnson's Credo," in *Corporate Ethics: A Prime Business Asset* (New York: The Business Roundtable, 1988), pp. 80–82.

[48] Michael Useem, "Behind Closed Doors," *The Wall Street Journal,* September 23, 2003, p. B2; Landon Thomas, "Big Board Said to Want Legal Action in Grasso Pay Case," *The New York Times,* January 8, 2004, pp. 1, 11.

Why did the above two men act so differently? Why did Burke of J&J almost instinctively look to the welfare of customers, while Grasso of NYSE ignored his conflict of interest and seemed to be more concerned with his own compensation? Grasso and executives at Bausch and Lomb sought primarily their own self-interest at the expense of those for whom they have responsibilities, the firm's stakeholders. We will show that moral habits, virtue or vice, account for most of the difference. Virtue inclines a person (Burke) toward doing the right thing, while vice disposes one toward selfishness (Grasso). Moreover, the presence or absence of such moral habits is an accurate predictor of good or bad future behavior. Let us examine moral habits in greater detail.

Courage, Self-Discipline, and Prudence

A virtue is a development of character, and it shows personal excellence in that area of human activity. Virtue is a stable, good moral habit that moves one toward the middle ground or between extremes in acting. Four basic moral virtues were identified by Aristotle and examined in detail by **Thomas Aquinas**. These four virtues are often called the **principal or chief virtues**: self-discipline (temperance), courage (fortitude), justice (fairness), and prudence.[49]

Self-discipline is the developed habit of not pursuing a good excessively. In our appetites (e.g., eating, drinking, sex) or in wanting to possess or control things, we often experience a temptation to have or consume too much of these goods. A temperate person is not greedy. Our senses in themselves are not disciplined, yet we understand that there is a need to stop at a suitable, harmonious mean before we destroy ourselves from gluttony, sclerosis of the liver, or sexually transmitted diseases. Richard Grasso appears to have lacked the virtue of self-discipline when he arranged for his $188 million compensation. Rather he displayed greed. The vice of greed is common today. Many businesspeople rationalize their greed by explaining that the market system encourages them to make as much money as possible. Providing the necessary capital for business is important and generally demands virtue to achieve it. However, Aristotle maintains that to own significantly more than is required for one's family or more than is ultimately a benefit to others is a vice. This assessment on the role of wealth runs counter to the view that the amount of a person's money shows the value of that person.

Courage enables one to overcome obstacles to do what is necessary to achieve a good goal. An entrepreneur must have courage to risk time and resources to begin a new business. Courage enables one to overcome temptations to both cowardliness and rashness, but it also requires the virtues of patience and perseverance. For example, James Burke of J&J had courage to order the $100 million recall of Tylenol. On the other hand, given its nonprofit status of NYSE and the conflict of interest, the members of its board of directors lacked courage when they agreed to the large compensation for

---

[49] Thomas Aquinas, *Summa Theologia,* I-II, Questions 49–67; Aristotle, *Ethics, op. cit.* See Edwin M. Hartman's discussion of virtue, "The Good Life and the Good Community," in his *Organizational Ethics and the Good Life* (New York: Oxford University Press, 1996), pp. 182–185.

Grasso. In our everyday work, it is easy to dodge difficult issues; we need courage to deal with troublesome problems.[50]

The virtue of *Justice* is the regular and constant habit to give another person her or his due. The virtue of justice is related to the ethical norm of justice, which we discussed earlier. The norm enables one to make an ethical judgment. The virtue disposes one to behave justly *because it is just*. The virtue of justice would dispose a manager to pay an equitable wage and to avoid race and gender discrimination—even before having to make a particular ethical judgment. When Bausch and Lomb CEO Daniel Gill forced unrealistic sales goals on his division executives and distributors, he violated the virtue of justice. Rather than foster a corporate culture that promoted justice, Gill's policies pressed subordinates into vicious behavior.

Prudence is the concrete judgment that a person makes to determine the means or strategy to be used to obtain a good goal. The other virtues require prudent judgment in order to be exercised. While the virtues can be assessed independently, they are nevertheless intertwined in each person. For example, without self-discipline greed will lead us to unjust actions. In classes business students often learn the techniques of marketing *any* product, or financing *any* endeavor, and some might call this prudence. However, developing strategies to obtain goals that are not good is not prudence. For example, to develop strategies to sell a product that kills, such as tobacco, or to take over a firm, loot its retirement plan, and fire its employees, is an act of shrewdness, but not the virtue of prudence.[51]

A manager cannot develop virtue in people by forcing them do things. It is harder to develop virtue in a control environment: in China, Saudi Arabia, Iran, or a jail. The motivation must come from within; a person must *intend* the good act. So developing virtue requires a good intention and perseverance, and this is often difficult because of our instinctive self-interest. As one expert puts it, "If people cared as much about the rights of others as they care about their own rights no virtue of justice would be needed . . . and rules about such things as contracts and promises would only need to be made public, like the rules of a game that everyone was eager to play."[52]

Good moral behavior is nurtured by mentoring, modeling, executive vision, and the corporate culture that this creates. Just as individuals choose to be virtuous and repeatedly act to bring that about, so, too, managers must choose a specific style of managing if they seek to encourage a moral corporate culture. However, the contrary is also true. Managers who engage in morally selfish acts thus foster bad behavior and vicious habits in their colleagues and subordinates.[53]

---

[50] See Gerald F. Cavanagh and Dennis J. Moberg, "The Virtue of Courage Within the Organization," in *Research in Ethical Issues in Organizations,* vol. 1 (Stamford, CT: JAI Press, 1999): 1–25.

[51] George P. Klubertanz, *Habits and Virtues.* See also, Charles M. Horvath, "Excellence v. Effectiveness: MacIntyre's Critique of Business," *Business Ethics Quarterly,* 5 (July 1995): 499–532.

[52] Philippa Foot, *Virtues and Vices and Other Essays in Moral Philosophy* (Berkeley: University of California Press, 1978), p. 9. The virtue of loyalty was featured in several articles in a special issue of *Business Ethics Quarterly,* 11, no. 1 (2001). See, for example, Daniel R. Gilbert, Jr., "An extraordinary Concept in the Ordinary Service of Management."

[53] See Rushworth M. Kidder, *Moral Courage* (New York: William Morrow, 2005); and Valerie Folkes and Ykun-Oh Whang, "Account-Giving For a Corporate Transgression Influences Moral Judgment: When Those Who 'Spin' Condone Harm-Doing," *Journal of Applied Psychology,* 88, no. 1 (2003): 79–86.

Leaders of organizations want their organizations to be successful over the long term. To accomplish long-term results requires good moral habits of honesty, fairness, and courage. Good moral habits, like moral principles, enable one to achieve moral goals. There is evidence that a manager's religious belief in God as a person makes a manager more likely to be ethical and socially responsible.[54] Most managers also would like to foster ethical behavior and good moral habits in their colleagues and subordinates. Traits such as honesty, trust, respect for other people, and an ability to cooperate and work with others help make an organization effective.

A good moral habit grows when one repeats morally good actions. Hence, when a person regularly makes ethical decisions and performs ethical acts, it will develop that person's good moral habits or virtues. Good moral acts performed by the members of the work group will also encourage good moral habits in other members of the work group.[55]

The Virtuous Organization

To develop a habit of a particular good moral act requires that the individual **choose** that moral act. Virtue will grow to the extent that the person performs the act because she chooses the behavior for its own sake. However, good moral acts that are motivated largely by fear, peer pressure, a control-oriented supervisor, or extrinsic rewards like compensation will not develop virtue. Nevertheless, motives are seldom pure.

Virtue in organizations is of concern to both managers and scholars.[56] Leaders attempt to select people appropriate for the job and the firm, and to communicate the values of the organization to these new hires and to those who are already colleagues; they socialize them so that they will work better within that organization. We will discuss formal and informal socialization in Chapter 7. Nevertheless here we mention the importance of leaders performing acts of, for example, trust, honesty, justice, and courage, because they are morally *good* acts. When the modeling behavior of leaders support virtue, it can be effective in developing good moral habits, which then change behavior and form a person's character.

A leader must have a vision of how she wishes to operate and must be proactive, if she wishes to affect the behavior of members.[57] Stories of managers who are models of the values of the firm's mission statement support that vision. The compensation system of the organization must also support the kind of behavior that is to be encouraged. A reward system that relies on narrowly defined and easily measurable financial returns may encourage vice rather than virtue. Bausch and Lomb managers inflated profits, coerced distributors, and engaged in other vicious activities. We often build reward systems around measurable standards of performance, but trust, honesty, and courage are not easily measured. A "colleague-of-the-week"

---

[54] Johan Graafland, Muel Kaptein, and Corrie Mazereeuw, "Conceptions of God, Normative Convictions, and Socially Responsible Business Conduct," *Business and Society,* 46, no. 3 (September 2007): 331–369.
[55] Helen J. Alford, O.P. and Michael J. Naughton, *Managing as if Faith Mattered* (Notre Dame: University of Notre Dame Press, 2002), pp. 70–96; and Alasdair MacIntyre, *After Virtue.*
[56] See Dennis J. Moberg, "Practical Wisdom and Business Ethics," *Business Ethics Quarterly,* 71, no. 1 (2007): 535–561; and Cameron, Dutton, and Quinn, *op. cit.;* H. M. Trice and J. M. Beyer, *The Cultures of Work Organizations* (Englewood Cliffs, NJ: Prentice Hall, 1993).
[57] Linda Klebe Trevino and Michael E. Brown, "Managing to Be Ethical: Debunking Five Business Ethics Myths," *Academy of Management Executive,* 18 (May 2004): 69–80; Bruno Dyck and Rob Kleysen, "Aristotle's Virtues and Management Thought," *Business Ethics Quarterly,* 11, no. 4 (2002): 561–74.

program, bonuses, and other rewards can identify people who have generously done something of benefit for others and for the firm.

The development of good moral habits is diagramed in Figure 3-5. Each person has his or her own unique package of good moral habits. Practice in making ethical decisions and performing good acts develop those moral habits. Examining the diagram, Jessica possesses better developed moral habits or virtue, so for her the ethical issues that require judgment and action are easier to identify and decide. So each new act of that virtue will come more easily. That is, each individual act strengthens the virtue, so that the act is easier to perform the next time. Lauren has lesser developed good habits, so it will be harder for her to identify the issues, and more difficult (i.e., a greater stretch) to make an ethical judgment. But notice that for both women, the level of virtue is increased after each individual good moral act.

A person's **character** is formed by the aggregate of that person's moral habits. Every group or organization of which a person is a part influences that person's attitudes, builds good and bad habits, and ultimately forms a person's character. Moreover, an organization made up of people with mostly good habits, and hence good character, will possess a better climate and thus a better corporate culture.

The *goal* of a business, as with any organization, is to increase the well-being of women and men; this includes the development of virtue in colleagues in the working group. Virtue will not develop if a business focuses exclusively on its goals of profit and growth. Profit, return on investment, and increasing market share are important measurable *means* to achieve the *ultimate goals* of the firm.

In the process of becoming a manager, a good manager generally develops many good habits, many virtues. For example, a manager who regularly trusts subordinates develops the virtue of trust and eventually trusts almost instinctively, and encourages the trust of others. A manager who does not trust will spread distrust throughout his unit. That manager finds that it takes far more time and energy for him to be a good manager—if indeed he ever becomes a good manager.

One method of developing virtue is to help the disadvantaged. Ford Motor Company, even in the midst of its financial difficulties, encourages its people to help in

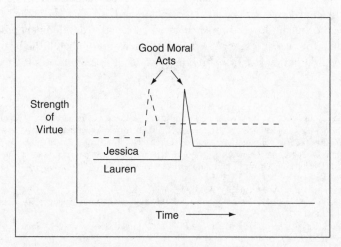

FIGURE 3-5 Development of Good Moral Habits

soup kitchens and homeless shelters, tutor inner-city youth, and engage in other projects for those in need. Ford will provide time off from work for up to 20 hours a year for these service projects. Other firms encourage their people to volunteer to help the poor overseas. Service projects are also common in colleges and universities; a person's horizons are generally broadened by personal contact with disadvantaged people: "If not for the good luck of birth, that homeless man might be me." The virtue and good character that is thus shaped also builds trust, cooperation, and honesty—the social capital of the firm. Moreover, research by health care professionals shows that helping other people is good for one's heart, immune system, and longevity.[58]

For those interested in character education, the organization *Character Education Partnership* provides a Web site that offers resources, conferences, and news.[59] Unfortunately, building character is not a priority in most U.S. colleges and universities. Arthur Schwartz, director of character education programs at the John Templeton Foundation, says:

> Only relatively few institutions—usually small liberal arts colleges or those that are religiously affiliated or faith-inspired—have a comprehensive commitment to character development in all dimensions of college life.[60]

This leads us into the next subject: how ethics and character education are taught in business schools.

ETHICS IN BUSINESS EDUCATION

After the financial and ethical bankruptcies of Enron and Arthur Andersen, the ethical debacles at NASDAQ, Solomon Brothers, Merrill Lynch, and Bear Stearns, and the subprime loan failures, many claim that business education is at the root of the problem. A veteran faculty member of Columbia University Graduate School of business places the responsibility squarely on business schools when he says, "Many business programs still don't even require any course work on ethics or social responsibility"; he then points out how business school faculty have little incentive to expose unethical practices, because their status and extra income come from being paid well as consultants or lecturers in corporate executive development programs.[61]

A study of business school students' attitudes found that at the beginning of their MBA program most felt that the purpose of business was to produce quality

---

[58] S. D. Papamarcos, "The Next Wave in Service-learning: Integrative, Team-based Engagements with Structural Objectives," *Review of Business*, 23, no. 2 (2002); Bruce Speck and Sherry Hoppe, *Service-Learning: History, Theory, and Issues* (Westport, CT: Praeger, 2004); Paul S. Adler and Seok-Woo Kwon, "Social Capital: Prospects for a New Concept," *The Academy of Management Review*, 27, no. 1 (2002): 17–40; Eileen Rockefeller Growald and Allan Luks, "Beyond Self: The Immunity of Samaritans," *American Health*, March 1988, pp. 51–53.

[59] See: www.character.org, accessed July 26, 2007.

[60] Arthur J. Schwartz, "It's Not Too Late to Teach College Students about Values," *Chronicle of Higher Education*, 46 (June 9, 2000).

[61] Leonard R. Sayles and Cynthia J. Smith, *The Rise of the Rogue Executive: How Good Companies Go Bad and How to Stop the Destruction* (Upper Saddle River: Pearson, 2006).

goods and services. But by the end of their MBA education, only one-third continued to see producing goods and services as the purpose, and more than two-thirds said that the purpose of business was to increase shareholder value. Often finance and economics professors give excessive respect for anything that is a result of the free market. In that model a person is expected to be selfish, and not to consider others except as competing economic agents. So it is not surprising that business students become more self-centered during their studies and that business graduate students cheat more than non-business graduate students.[62]

Another empirical study of ethics teaching in business schools found that ethics was not taken seriously at the majority of business schools, and this was especially true at large state universities. As an illustration, the author related how students tried for many decades unsuccessfully to have a required business ethics course in the undergraduate and MBA curriculum. He found that ethics at his own "big 10" university is treated by his peers somewhere between "ambivalence and disdain." Surprisingly, in the last few years and even since the public scandals, many business schools have dropped or downgraded their business ethics courses.[63]

Most agree that the ethical debacles at Tyco, ImClone, Qwest, and Computer Associates were the result of an "overemphasis American corporations have been forced to give in recent years to maximizing shareholder value without regard for the effects of their actions on other stakeholders." Yet most business school faculty teach "running the numbers" and take little account of the effect that these decisions have on employees, customers, or the local community. Ethics and corporate responsibility courses "are considered 'soft' subjects . . . and are given short shrift in favor of applied analytical tools and techniques, conceptual models, and measures of profitability."[64] A quality business education requires a consideration of the ethical consequences of any major decision and policy. Supporting this effort are 85 percent of firm recruiters who say that personal ethics and integrity is "very important" in any person that they seek to hire for their firm.[65]

Recognizing that ethics is as important as finance and marketing, hundreds of business faculty asked the business school accrediting association (AACSB) to require an ethics course in the business curriculum. The accrediting body refused

[62] Donald McCabe, Kenneth Butterfield, and Linda Klebe Trevino, "Academic Dishonesty in Graduate Business Programs: Prevalence, Causes, and Proposed Action," *Academy of Management Learning and Education,* 5, no. 3 (2006): 294–305; also Robert J. Shiller, "How Wall Street Learns to Look the Other Way," *The New York Times,* February 8, 2005, p. 15.

[63] LaRue T. Hosmer, "Somebody Out There Doesn't Like Us," *Journal of Business Ethics,* 22 (November 1999): 91–106; and Marjorie Kelly, "It's a Heckuva Time to Be Dropping Business Ethics Courses: MBA Programs are Downsizing Ethics Requirements at Precisely the Wrong Time," *Business Ethics,* Fall 2002, pp. 17–18.

[64] Sandra Waddock, "Hollow Men at the Helm: Until Business Schools Teach Future Managers How Deep the Connections are Between Business, Society, Nature, and the World, Corporations Will Continue to be Run by Hollow Leaders with No Sense of Ethics or Responsibility," *BusEd,* July/August 2004, pp. 24–29. *BusEd* is published by AACSB, the international business school accrediting Agency.

[65] Ronald Alsop, "Business Schools Recruiters' Top Picks," *The Wall Street Journal,* September 22, 2004, p. R8.

to require ethics, but urged that ethics be an integral part of any graduate or under-graduate program and has provided materials for teaching ethics.[66] Will integrity, ethics, social responsibility, and character be learned at most business schools? Probably not.

The concern for ethics in business education is not new. Executives and citizens have agreed for many years that there was a need for ethics in business and in schools. In a survey two decades ago of corporate CEOs, business school deans, and members of Congress, 94 percent said that the business community is troubled by ethical problems. Further, 63 percent of these leaders believe that a business firm strengthens its competitive position by maintaining high ethical standards. These leaders also said that there was an observable difference in the quality of ethics in various parts of the United States. Areas of the country they ranked from most ethical to least are as follows: Midwest, Northwest, New England, South, Southwest, West, and East.[67]

Difficulties in arriving at an ethical judgment often stem from our lack of knowledge of ethical norms. Most managers are not immoral, but rather amoral. They simply fail to adequately consider the morality of their actions.[68] They are hampered by the fact that ethics and good character generally are not learned in American schools, from grade schools to universities. Competitive and individualistic methods of learning and grading hinder the development of a sense of community and obligations to others. In this way, schools often impede the development of moral maturity and ethics. Managers are constrained by their own lack of moral imagination; that is, their options are narrowed because they often fail to consider the more ethical act.[69]

Ethics was not always so unknown. Ethics, or **moral philosophy**, was the center of the curriculum of American colleges and universities throughout the nineteenth century. An ethics course was required of all seniors and, because of its importance, it was often taught by the college president.[70] This course was designed as an integration of all that students had learned, and prepared them for the working world. It sharpened their ethical sensitivity and enabled them to better address the ethical problems they were about to face.

Educators during this period judged that no nation could prosper without common social and moral values. For a society such as the United States, which is fragmented because of differences in ethnic backgrounds, allegiances, and interests, it was even more important to provide a structure whereby students could unify their

---

[66] *Ethics Education in Business Schools,* Report of the Ethics Education Task Force to AACSB International's Board of Governors (St. Louis: AACSB International, 2004); also available at http://www.aacsb.edu/metf.

[67] *Ethics in American Business: An Opinion Survey of Key Business Leaders on Ethical Standards and Behavior* (New York: Touche Ross, 1988), pp. 1, 10; see also "Why Ethics is Also B-School Business," *BusinessWeek,* January 27, 2003, p. 105.

[68] Archie B. Carroll, "In Search of the Moral Manager," *Business Horizons,* March–April 1987, pp. 7–15.

[69] Patricia C. Werhane, *Moral Imagination and Management Decision Making* (New York: Oxford University Press, 1999).

[70] Douglas Sloan, "The Teaching of Ethics in American Undergraduate Curriculum, 1876–1976," in *Ethics Teaching in Higher Education,* ed. Daniel Callahan and Sissela Bok (New York: Plenum Press, 1980), p. 2.

learning: "The entire college experience was meant above all to be an experience in character development and the moral life, as epitomized, secured, and brought to focus in the moral philosophy course."[71] Is this need still present today?

Business education has long been criticized for being too narrow, analytic, and technical by businesspeople and also by a committee set up by the business school accrediting association (AACSB).[72] This authoritative report concluded that MBA curricula lacked vision and integration. Among other omissions, there was insufficient attention given to ethics and the social and political environment of business.

There are practical reasons for including ethics in the business program. Making ethical judgments before one is exposed to real business pressures to act unethically can result in behavior that is more ethical. In an experiment, college students were given a case involving an ethical dilemma and asked to judge a course of action. The experimenters then presented the actual situation to these same students two weeks later. The students acted more ethically than did a control group that had not earlier discussed the case. On the job, the pressures of time and potential short-term cost savings push one to compromise.[73]

When considering a dilemma away from the pressures of the actual situation, one is more inclined to consider the ethical issues in an objective and balanced way. Moral reasoning ability is also improved when ethics is taught in courses.[74] The conclusion is that an informed discussion of ethical cases and making ethical judgments will have a positive effect on ethical behavior, and it can provide the foundation for developing good moral habits.

Executives and firms have policies and training to help workers understand ethical issues. A survey of firms showed that ethics policies and codes are distributed to almost all workers. Moreover, more than 85 percent of firms require that people verify in writing that they have received the ethics policy and are in compliance with it. In addition, 55 percent of workers say that their employers provide ethics training; this number goes to 68 percent if restricted to firms of 500 or more workers. Ethics training programs are more effective when they are integrated into other training at the firm. The goals of ethics programs are, on the one hand, to provide information and policies on what is and what is not acceptable, and on the other hand, to lessen penalties on the firm if an errant worker is charged with a crime. General Electric, IBM, Johnson & Johnson, Boeing, Merck, and many other firms all provide ethics training and have done so for many decades.[75] We will discuss ethics codes and training in greater detail in Chapters 8 and 9.

---

[71] *Ibid.*, p. 7.

[72] Lyman Porter and Lawrence McKibbin, *Management Education and Development: Drift or Thrust into the 21st Century?* (New York: McGraw-Hill, 1988).

[73] Steven J. Sherman, "On the Self-Erasing Nature of Errors of Prediction," *Journal of Personality and Social Psychology,* 39 (March 1980): 211–219.

[74] Elinar Marnburg, "Educational Impacts on Academic Business Practitioner's Moral Reasoning and Behavior: Effects of Short Courses in Ethics or Philosophy," *Business Ethics: A European Review,* 12 (October 2003): 403–413.

[75] Linda Klebe Trevino and Gary Weaver, *Managing Ethics in Business Organizations* (Stanford: Stanford University Press, 2003), pp. 79–80; also Susan J. Harrington, "What Corporate America is Teaching About Ethics," *Academy of Management Executive,* 5 (February 1991): 21–30.

Summary and Conclusions

We examined moral development in the last chapter and found that selfish (Kohlberg's Level I) behavior is more typical of adolescents and the immature than of mature women and men. Most businesspeople want to be ethical; they have many good moral habits. Nevertheless, fraud, bribery, overstating revenues, hiding expenses and important information from customers, and stealing trade secrets remain major ethical problems for business. In many cases, managers say that they could not distinguish the right action from the wrong action. Generations now growing up have fewer moral skills. Many people have not learned how to recognize ethical problems and how to make ethical judgments. Furthermore, the media and advertising tell us that ethics is relative.

The ethical principles, models, and cases in this chapter are intended to aid the development of ethical skills and character. The decision norms and models are not perfect; they will not solve all ethical problems easily. But these ethical norms and models can be learned and used, and thus be an aid to businesspeople. Making ethical judgments in the classroom brings about more ethical behavior in business. Moreover, ethical acts affect behavior, enabling people to be more honest, trustworthy, and ultimately possess greater integrity and virtue.

Business leaders lament the lack of ethical skills among new workers and the lack of formal ethics in college curricula. In earlier centuries, ethics had a central place in the education of college students. It is a paradox that businesspeople learn precise decision rules for inventory, finance, and brand marketing, but have few models for moral decisions and actions. If businesspeople are not moral, business will become a wasteful, inefficient jungle that is hostile to people.

The intentional repetition of good moral acts develops good habits or virtues. Superior moral habits among colleagues can make a working environment more productive and humane. Few business schools are thorough in presenting ethics and ethical tools for future businesspeople. Yet graduates who have learned ethics and developed character are more trusted and mature, will not cost their firm its reputation, and will more likely achieve executive responsibilities.

Discussion Questions

1. What is the principal difference between rights and duties and utilitarian norms? Do an individual's intentions have any role in utilitarianism? Do intentions have a role in the theory of rights? Explain.
2. What does John Rawls add to the traditional theory of justice? Compare Rawls' theory and the traditional theory of justice with utilitarianism.
3. Upon what is the norm of caring built? How does it compare with rights and duties, justice, and utilitarianism?
4. Indicate the strengths and weaknesses of using the norms of (a) utility, (b) justice, (c) rights, and (d) caring.
5. Is anything always morally right or always morally wrong (e.g., murder)? Is lying or stealing always or generally wrong, or is it relative, a matter of social expectations, and the law?

6. Outline the criteria for whistle-blowing. If you knew of payments by a manager in your firm to a manager in a competing firm for insider information, should you blow the whistle? Apply the criteria in deciding this question.

7. How can the four principle virtues—self-discipline, courage, justice, and prudence—help an individual succeed?

8. Do many college students take a course in ethics? What is the advantage of such a course? What is the disadvantage of ethics not being learned? Have you had such a course?

9. Is the purpose of studying ethics to develop ethical decision-making skills or to influence good behavior? Does the former affect the latter? How?

10. Describe how a person can develop good habits. What is the relation of virtue and character?

11. Give an example of when you have exercised a virtue. What virtues do you see in others?

12. As a manager would you prefer that the members of your work group have good character? As a peer in a firm, would you prefer colleagues have good character? Why?

13. What is the purpose of business, according to graduate business students at the beginning of their program? How does that attitude shift by the end of their program?

14. In a fragmented, pluralistic society of the nineteenth and twentieth centuries, colleges and universities saw the need for integration of education with a capstone ethics course for all students. Is this need still present today?

15. Do business schools have a responsibility to help student learn ethics and develop good character? Why or why not? Do most business schools offer a required ethics course?

Selected Additional Readings

Daniel Callahan and Sissela Bok, eds., *Ethics Teaching in Higher Education* (New York: Plenum Press, 1980).

David Callahan, *The Cheating Culture: Why More Americans are Doing Wrong to Get Ahead* (New York: Harcourt, 2004).

Richard T. De George, *Business Ethics,* 6th ed. (Upper Saddle River: Prentice Hall, 2006).

Thomas Donaldson and Thomas W. Dunfee, *Ties That Bind: A Social Contracts Approach to Business Ethics* (Boston: Harvard Business School Press, 1999).

Rushworth M. Kidder, *Moral Courage* (New York: William Morrow, 2005).

Stephan Rothlin, *Eighteen Rules of International Business Ethics* (Beijing, 2004).

Manuel Velasquez, *Business Ethics: Concepts and Cases,* 6th ed. (Upper Saddle River, NJ: Prentice Hall, 2006).

CASES

Case 3-1 Encyclopedia of Ethical Failure

Government workers found misbehaving are generally fined, suspended, fired, and/or prosecuted. In addition, Stephen Epstein, director of the Pentagon Standards of Conduct Office, enters them and their actions on an Internet list with others who have been caught; he calls it the *Encyclopedia of Ethical Failure.* While names are not listed, it is not difficult to find out to who the culprit is. With huge amounts of money in the defense budget, the temptation is great to cheat; in five years Epstein has listed more than 250 people. It is a community punishment for wrongdoing, and thus is a deterrent; Epstein says, "It is like public executions."

1. Is this a wise procedure? Would such a list be a deterrent to people?
2. Is it acceptable to publicly list the names of people who have misbehaved or broken the law?
3. What ethical norm is most helpful in this case?

■ ■ ■

Case 3-2 PepsiCo and Bottled Water

PepsiCo uses a mountain top design on the label of its popular Aquafina brand of bottled water, but it has agreed to notify consumers that Aquafina actually comes from ordinary tap water. Meanwhile, environmentalists argue that producing plastic bottles needlessly uses energy, and the used bottles pollute the environment. Others point out that if a consumer drank eight glasses of water a day from plastic bottles, it would cost them up to $1,400 a year.

1. What are the ethical issues in this case?
2. Is it deceptive to sell bottled water that is no more pure than tap water? Should water bottlers notify consumers of the source of their bottled water?
3. Is there any ethical problem in producing the plastic bottles?
4. What ethical norms help in deciding this case?

■ ■ ■

Case 3-3 Double Expense Account

Frank Waldron is a second-year MBA student at Eastern State University. Although he has had many job offers, he continues to have the university placement office arrange interviews. He reasons that the interview experience is good for him and he may receive a better job offer. Frank has also discovered a way to make money from job interviews.

Two firms invited Waldron to Los Angeles for visits to their home offices. He scheduled both visits on the same day and billed each for his full travel expenses. In this way he was able to pocket $1,000. When a friend objected that this was dishonest, Frank replied that each firm had told him to submit his expenses and that therefore he was not taking something to which he had no right. One firm had not asked for receipts, so he determined it was making him a gift of the money.

1. What are the ethical issues in this case? Is what Frank doing unethical?
2. Which norms help most in deciding the question?
3. What advice would you give Frank?

■ ■ ■

Case 3-4 PETA vs. Pfizer

People for the Ethical Treatment of Animals (PETA) want all drug companies to stop or do less testing on animals. PETA filed a shareholder resolution with Pfizer, asking the firm to reduce the amount of animal testing that it does. The occasion of the resolution was that Pfizer lost a dog which was left in a cage that was sent through scalding water to be cleaned. The U.S. Department of Agriculture's investigation labeled the death as an accident. Nevertheless, PETA pressed its case against Pfizer with a shareholder resolution. Pfizer's Board voted unanimously against the resolution. In Britain animal rights activists have slashed researcher's tires and have placed pipe bombs at laboratories. Additional security costs British pharmaceutical firms $128 million per year, and some estimate that Britain with more stringent regulations on animal testing than the United States is losing $2 billion a year in new investment.[76]

1. What are the ethical issues involved in Pfizer's use of animals when testing pharmaceuticals?
2. Should Pfizer curtail or stop its use of animals in its testing?
3. What are the ethics of the protesters tactics?
4. What ethical norm (s) are most helpful here?

■ ■ ■

Case 3-5 Tax Assessment Kickback

You own a large building in a major city. The real estate assessor offers, for a fee, to underestimate the value of your property and save you a substantial amount in real estate taxes. Assume that this is a common practice in the city.

1. What are the ethical issues in this case?
2. Do you pay the fee?
3. Which ethical norm is most helpful here?

Exercises

Exercise 3-1: Memo to the Chief Executive

You are a manager in a firm in a very competitive industry. A competitor has made an important scientific discovery that could give it an advantage that would substantially reduce, but not eliminate, the profits of your company for about a year. A scientist who knows the details of the discovery applies for a job at your firm. There are no legal barriers to hiring the scientist.

The CEO knows that you studied ethics in your MBA program and so asks you to give her your advice. In a single-page memo to the CEO, indicate the major issues and ethical norms to be used, and make a recommendation.

---

[76] "Animal-Rights Activism Turns Rabid: Attacks on Drug Companies and University Labs are Chilling Research," *BusinessWeek,* August 30, 2004, p. 54.

Exercise[77] 3-2: What are Your Values?

In class answer each of the following questions as either T = True or F = False

1. _____ Ethics and religion are the same thing.

2. _____ Males, more than females, will "dump" friends when opportunities for career advancement come.

3. _____ Insurance companies are justified in charging higher auto insurance premiums for young males because their accident rate is higher.

4. _____ When a manager's personal value system conflicts with the organization's value system, the organization is the first priority.

5. _____ It is just to deny the vote to people on welfare because they are not contributing to society.

6. _____ Few people reach the stage of moral development at which they are willing to challenge either authority or generally agreed belief systems.

7. _____ There is a widening gap in the United States between the values held by the wealthy and powerful and those values held by common people.

8. _____ When a conflict develops between liberty and justice, liberty should come first.

9. _____ Given globalization, the best guide to ethical behavior when in other cultures is to follow the rule "When in Rome, do as the Romans do."

10. _____ People who possess great power in an organization and who violate the law showed be punished more severely than people with little power who commit the same illegal act.

11. _____ The American belief that "big is better" is the best organizational philosophy, because not to grow is to shrink.

12. _____ Capitalism rests on the value of self-interest—a value that, by its very nature, should worry church leaders who stress sacrifice.

Exercise 3-3: Ethical Climate of a Firm Compared to Caux Round Table

Principles for Business

This exercise will show how the Caux Round Table's (CRT) *Principles for Business* might be used as a benchmark for evaluating a firm's code. Compare one firm's (if possible, the one for which you work) *Mission, Vision,* and *Code of Conduct* with the CRT's *Principles for Business* (see http://www.cauxroundtable.org/principles.html).

Specifically, the assignment is to:

1. Obtain a copy of the firm's Mission, Vision, and Code of Ethics.
2. Compare the (a) firm's statements with (b) CRT's *Principles for Business.* In your comparison, note the major issues that are covered by both documents. Compare the content of both codes and evaluate the adequacy and comprehensiveness of your firm's code.
3. Write a paper to summarize your comparison of the firm's *Mission, Vision,* and *Code of Conduct* with the CRT's *Principles for Business.*

The following questions may help you to examine and compare:

General Principles

Does your firm's *Code, Mission, or Vision* have any statements like Caux's "General Principles?"

Briefly describe them. Does the firm's code cover the material of the seven *Principles?* Answer for each. If so, briefly describe how it is covered.

---

[77] Thanks to the late Clarence C. Walton for these questions.

Stakeholder Principles

Does your firm's Code have a section on responsibilities to customers?

If so, briefly compare the two codes.

Does it have a section on responsibilities to employees? If so, briefly compare the two codes.

Does it . . . on responsibilities to owners/investors? If so, briefly compare the two codes.

Does it . . . on responsibilities to suppliers? If so, briefly compare the two codes.

Does it . . . on responsibilities to competitors? If so, briefly compare the two codes.

Does it . . . on responsibilities to the community? If so, briefly compare the two codes.

Finally and most importantly, is your firm's Code designed to protect only the company? Or is it designed to protect customers, employees, and outside stakeholders, also? Does it give proportionate coverage to both the firm and the various stakeholders?

Summarize your comparison of the firm's *Mission, Vision,* and *Code of Conduct* with the CRT's *Principles for Business.* The paper should be no more than 10 double-spaced pages. Use any format that is useful for your comparison. Include a copy of the relevant *Mission, Values,* and *Code of Conduct* of the firm you use in an Appendix. Organization, spelling, punctuation, and grammar will be included in the evaluation.

4

■ ■ ■

History of Business Values

Probe the earth and see where your main roots are.

HENRY DAVID THOREAU (1817–1862), AMERICAN PHILOSOPHER

Whatever you have, you must use it or lose it.

HENRY FORD (1863–1947), FOUNDER OF FORD MOTOR CO.

Those who do not study history are doomed to repeat it.

GEORGES SANTAYANA (1863–1952), PHILOSOPHER, POET

The businessperson and the business student enjoy an advantage, if they know history. The manager who knows history is able to recognize problems that were solved earlier by others, and is better able to recognize situations that are new and demand new solutions. History demonstrates to us what stimulates the growth of business, cities, and the entrepreneurial attitudes of earlier generations.[1]

We are products of our past. No matter how rapidly society changes, current attitudes have their roots in history. What we do and how we think are much influenced by **past values** and attitudes.[2] Whether we view the present as part of an organic development from earlier events or as breaking new ground, the past has great influence. For example, a historical **faith in progress** undergirds the conviction of many

---

[1] "Why History Matters to Managers," a roundtable discussion with Alfred D. Chandler et al., ed. Alan M. Kantrow, *Harvard Business Review,* January–February 1986, pp. 81–88; and the importance of history, ethics, and social responsibility in business, see Steven P. Feldman, *Memory As a Moral Decision: The Role of Ethics in Organizational Culture* (New Brunswick, NJ: Transaction Press, 2002).

[2] *Ibid.*, p. 84.

that global markets are good for all. On the other hand, concern for work satisfaction and a sustainable environment stems partly from disenchantment with attitudes of earlier generations that were short-sighted and wasteful. It is impossible to fully understand our current values and what the future will bring without understanding the path that has led us to where we are.

QUESTIONING OUR ROOTS

People in contemporary societies assess their goals and values for several reasons. First, the many choices that we face—choosing a career, a lifestyle, whether or not to marry, and when to have children—require that we know our goals and values in order to make useful decisions.

Second, change now takes place so rapidly that we need a firm foundation for our goals and activities. Some goals are basic, provide a **sense of stability**, and endure through major changes; other goals become obsolete. It is essential to examine our values so as to determine which remain relevant.

Third, as we have more education, we become more questioning and reflective.

Fourth, an examination of basic goals and values is necessary because rights, actions, and even goals often conflict. For example, the goal of producing at lowest cost conflicts with the goal of avoiding sweatshops and pollution. The goal of loyalty to a firm conflicts with downsizing. The resolution of these conflicts requires clarification of personal and group goals.

Some ask the fundamental question: Why work? What is the value of work? Further, what is the value of business? If I want a car or a PC, someone must design and manufacture it and I must have money to obtain it. But if I can obtain it in a lawful fashion without working, why not? If I can get rich speculating or gambling, why not do so? Does work have any value to a person or to society beyond the dollar rewards?

These questions are not new; however, now they are asked by more people. In earlier centuries, they were asked only by the few educated people, not by ordinary citizens. The ordinary worker's life was largely determined at birth. If a man's father was a shoemaker or a baker, he would become one also, and would use the workshop, tools, and home that had belonged to the family for generations. Rarely was there any question of whether a person *would* work, or at what occupation. There was little choice. Heredity, geography, and custom determined most of a person's life. To ask a poor person why they work is like asking them why they try to stay alive. They have little reason to question the value of work. Attitudes toward work are the foundation blocks for business success. Let us examine that foundation.

LEARNING FROM OUR FOREBEARS

Change took place rapidly in the United States from its beginning. Most of its people emigrated from other lands, initially from Europe. The Founding Fathers were influenced by European thinkers, such as John Locke, Jean-Jacques Rousseau, and Adam Smith, on the value of work, business, and private property. Although there were alternate strands of thought in the East, those values had less impact on American business values. Hence we will focus largely on how Western history and philosophies affect business.

Throughout history, **work** has been an **integrating** activity for most people. It was a binding cord for the fabric of the family, the city, and the social system. It gave stability and meaning to people and their relationships. However, industrialization brought changes: mass production, division of labor, and "scientific management." From the individual's standpoint, the worker had more choice as to the type and location of the work he or she performed. But it is ironic that just when individuals were able to choose their work and thus hope for greater satisfaction from their jobs, more people worked in large organizations and work became more fragmented, repetitive, and less able to provide pride of workmanship.

The Ancient Greek Attitude Toward Business and Work

The ancient Greeks thought of work and commerce as **demeaning** to a citizen. It was a burden required for survival—a necessary evil. However, what we know about ancient attitudes toward work is colored by two limitations. First, most of our information comes from written sources whose authors were generally citizens and hence persons of leisure, a minority. The writers were not from the working class. Second, most of the work was done by slaves under dirty, grueling, and often unsafe conditions. These slaves were uneducated and often prisoners of war from conquered nations.

Plato speaks of work as if it were a temptation to be avoided because it hinders a person's ability to live, to think, and to contemplate. In his *Laws*, Plato speaks also for his fellow citizens when he urges, "If a native stray from the pursuit of goodness into some trade or craft, they shall correct him by reproach and degradation until he be brought back again into the straight course."[3] Citizens of ancient Athens thought of work as something not worthy of a citizen. Plato, however, reveals the extent to which his contemporaries' attitudes were based on the conditions under which work was done, as he cuts to the heart of their disenchantment and even revulsion with work:

> Suppose the very best of men could be compelled—the fancy will sound ludicrous, I know, but I must give it utterance—suppose they could be compelled to take for a time to inn-keeping, or retail trade or some such calling; or suppose, for that matter, that some unavoidable destiny were to drive the best women into such professions: then we should discover that all are humane and beneficent occupations; if they were only conducted on the principles of strict integrity, we should respect them as we do the vocation of mother and nurse.[4]

Thus, Plato recognizes that most of the objections to work are not inherent in work itself. In fact, these occupations are in themselves "humane and beneficent."

---

[3] Plato, *The Laws of Plato*, trans. A. E. Taylor (London: Dent, 1934), p. 847B.
[4] *Ibid.*, pp. 918B–E.

Plato's pupil Aristotle is more severe in his condemnation of the life of the worker or tradesperson. To him, such a life is irksome and beneath the dignity of a citizen:

> Citizens must not lead the life of mechanics or tradesmen, for such a life is ignoble, and inimical to virtue. Neither must they be a farmer, since leisure is necessary both for the development of virtue and the performance of political duties.[5]

From his observations, Aristotle found crafts, trade, and business detrimental to health and character. Much of the work was done in cramped and unhealthy surroundings, and it was necessary to have daily dealings with unprincipled, unethical, and rude people. So industrial and commercial life was thought to rob a body of its health and to degrade character. This work was generally done by slaves, and many contemporary states did not admit the skilled worker and laborer to citizenship. "Even in states which admitted the industrial and commercial classes to power, popular sentiment held trade and industry cheap."[6]

Aristotle speaks of two types of business and trade activity, and his distinction goes to the root of a difficulty that perplexes many to the present day: the difference between the careful **management** of goods and a selfish **profit** orientation. He approves of the first but disapproves of the second. *Oeconomia*, from which our word economics derives, is literally "household management." It includes careful, prudent use not only of the household but of all one's property and resources. On the other hand, *chrematistike* means the use of skill and goods to achieve a profit. This term described the city traders, who were few in number compared with the farmers and skilled workers. These traders often resorted to deceptive practices; and it seemed to Aristotle, and generations that followed him, that they contributed little or nothing to society. Aristotle's objections are similar to those of Karl Marx: The trader's service as a middleman adds no value to the good. Hence, Aristotle approved of *oeconomia* but disapproved of *chrematistike*.

Plato and Aristotle generally agree in their objections to the pursuit of a career in trade or a craft, although Aristotle raises these objections more strongly: (1) The practice of business or a craft deprives a person of the leisure necessary to contemplate the good, the true, and the beautiful. (2) It hinders proper physical, intellectual, and moral development. (3) It is "illiberal" because it is done for pay. (4) It is less good because it is not valued for its own sake.

Work in Biblical Times

Unlike the Greeks, who had slaves, the ancient Hebrews, who at times in their history were slaves themselves, could not avoid work. They saw **work** as an **essential** part of their lives but also a hardship. The painful aspect of work had its self-inflicted cause in original sin. Stemming from their strong sense of God and

---

[5] Aristotle, "Politics," in *Basic Works of Aristotle*, ed. Richard McKeon (New York: Random House, 1941), p. 1141.
[6] W. L. Newman, *Politics of Aristotle*, vol. 1 (Oxford: Clarendon Press, 1887), p. 98.

community, the Jews pointed to the commands of God in Genesis that men and women were to cultivate the world and subdue it (Gen. 2:15).[7] This gave reason, integrity, and even vitality to what for most other cultures was only something to be endured. Craftsmen like Bezalel, who built the Ark of the Covenant, were honored in the Jewish tradition (Exodus, 35:30–33).[8] Thus work was **integrated** into the lives of the Hebrew people and had meaning for them. Yahweh, the God of the Hebrews, is close to them. Yahweh is often pictured as one who labors: a vine dresser (Ezek. 15:6), a pottery maker (Gen. 2:7), a soldier (Is. 27:1). Contributions to the ethics of commerce continue to come from Jewish scholars and the Jewish tradition.[9]

Christianity built on the Jewish tradition regarding work, trade, and commerce. Early Christians were from the **working class**. Jesus was a carpenter (Mark 6:3) and Paul, a tentmaker (Acts 18:2). The apostles were all working people; many were fishermen. They were not from the priestly class. Jesus in the Gospels cautions against an excessive concern about work and the things of this world (Matt. 6:24–34), but he also makes clear that work is a serious responsibility for the Christian (Luke 12:41–49). Furthermore, in the often-quoted parable of the talents (Matt. 25:14–30), the servant who has intelligently and profitably invested his money and his efforts is the one who is given additional rewards.

But the unique contribution of Christianity on the value of work is its view that work is done also out of **love and concern** for one's brothers and sisters. Work is necessary not only to earn one's living, asking alms of no one, but above all so that the goods of fortune may be shared with one's needy sisters and brothers. The foundations of industrial civilization rest on a new concept of love preached by Jesus Christ and presented in the New Testament. It is "a peculiarly generous concept of charity, of the opportunity we have to give ourselves to others here and now, insofar as we love our neighbors for God."[10] Throughout the ages, including our own time, Christians most often have fallen short of these ideals. Nevertheless, as a foundation for work and business values, especially in its emphasis on love of neighbor, Christianity was an important step forward.

In the early centuries of the Christian era, the most important commentator was Augustine. He approved of handicraft, farming, and commerce on a small scale. But when selling, no more than a *just price* can be asked; charging interest on the use of money is immoral. Those who have wealth should prize it as a trust from God. After their own modest needs are met, they should give the rest to the poor.[11] Let us now examine the spirituality of several other great world religions, Islam, Hinduism, and Buddhism, and how they have influenced work and business values.

---

[7] Moses L. Pava, *Business Ethics: A Jewish Perspective* (Hoboken, NJ: KTAV Publishing, 1997), p. 84.

[8] Thanks to Daniel H. Kruger for this insight; and Rabbi Jeffery Salkin, *Being God's Partner: How To Find the Hidden Link Between Spirituality and Your Work* (Woodstock, VT: Jewish Lights Publishing, 1994).

[9] Edwin Epstein, "Contemporary Jewish Perspectives On Business Ethics: The Contributions of Meir Tamari and Moses L. Pava," *Business Ethics Quarterly,* 10, no. 2 (2000): 523–541; see also three additional articles on Jewish contributions in *Business Ethics Quarterly,* 7 (March 1997).

[10] John U. Nef, *Cultural Foundations of Industrial Civilization* (Cambridge: Cambridge University Press, 1958), p. 89; see also Parker J. Palmer, *The Company of Strangers: Christians and the Renewal of America's Public Life* (New York: Crossroads, 1981).

[11] John M. Rist, *Augustine: Ancient Thought Baptized* (New York: Cambridge University Press, 1996).

Work in Islam, Hinduism, and Buddhism

Muslims take the Qur'an as the verbatim word of Allah, as revealed to the prophet Mohammad and dictated by the Archangel Gabriel in the period 610–632. The Muslim view of **life is holistic**. All aspects of life are determined by the Qur'an, including family, worship, politics, and work. Although 1.3 billion Muslims live in varying cultures and hence have different views, there is consensus that the teaching of the prophet in the **Qur'an defines Islam**.[12]

According to the Qur'an, labor has the potential of worship, and so is sacred. Hence all forms of exploitation of labor are forbidden. Moreover, methods of production should not cause undue and excessive harm to Allah-given resources. Any buying and selling must be done honestly (Qur'an 83:1–3). However, some products and activities are forbidden, such as wines or other intoxicants, gambling, prostitution, or other indecent occupations.[13] The Qur'an supports private property, commercial honesty, and competition tempered by concern for the disadvantaged. It rejects the free market doctrine that "personal actions, motivated by selfishness can produce socially desirable outcomes." Taking the same position as Aristotle, if guided by Islamic Law, "people will be consistently altruistic, principled, and avoid waste and extravagance."[14]

Unlike Medieval Western Europe, the Islamic world at that time was remarkably **unified**—sharing the same language and many of the same religious and secular customs:

> In the high Middle Ages the commerce of the Islamic Middle East was in every way ahead of that of Europe—richer, larger, better organized, and more commodities to sell and more money to buy, and a vastly more sophisticated network of trading relations. By the end of the middle Ages, these roles were reversed.[15]

In most Muslim countries, **commerce and trade** are more highly valued than is agriculture. While Muslim societies excelled in irrigation techniques, they developed few innovations in farming. Industrial innovations were and remain rudimentary.

Muslim business attitudes differ from those of Western peoples on several major points. First, for Muslims money must not be lent at interest (Qur'an 2:275). Second, in conservative Muslim societies, such as those in the Middle East, women are not allowed in business. Third, the belief that all laws come directly from Allah and are inviolable causes rigidity and retards innovation. Deviants are often branded as

---

[12] Jamal A. Badawi, "Islamic Teaching and Business," in *Business, Religion and Spirituality*, ed. Oliver F. Williams, CSC (Notre Dame: University of Notre Dame Press, 2003), pp. 139–167; see also Tanri Abeng, "Business Ethics in Islamic Context: Perspectives of a Muslim Business Leader," *Business Ethics Quarterly,* 7 (July 1997): 47–54.

[13] *Ibid.*, p. 151.

[14] John L. Esposito, ed., *The Oxford Encyclopedia of the Modern Islamic World.* See articles "Capitalism and Islam" and "Economic Theory" (New York: Oxford University Press, 1995).

[15] Bernard Lewis, *The Middle East: A Brief History of the Last 2000 Years* (New York: Scribner, 1995), p. 169.

"apostates" or "infidels." This belief also causes divisiveness in nations where not all people are Muslim. Muslim nations such as Indonesia attempt to provide basic rights for people of all faiths. However, in conservative Arab states of the Middle East, such as Saudi Arabia, strict Muslim rules ("Shariah") are imposed on non-Muslims also.[16] Some in these states see Islam and Western business conflicting, and they act on this in a violent way.

Muslim terrorists destroyed the New York World Trade Center in 2001 (9/11) and have killed thousands of people in suicide bombings in many Muslim and Western countries. After a series of terrorist attacks on innocents, Abdel Rahman al-Rashed, manager of the al-Arabiya news channel, wrote,

> Self-cure starts with self-realization and confession. We should then run after our terrorist sons, in full knowledge that they are the sour grapes of a deformed culture . . . The mosque used to be a haven, and the voice of religion used to be that of peace and reconciliation. Religious sermons were warm behests for a moral order and an ethical life. Then came the neo-Muslims. An innocent and benevolent religion, whose verses prohibit the felling trees in the absence of urgent necessity, that calls murder the most heinous of crimes, that says explicitly that if you kill one person you have killed humanity as a whole, has been turned into a global message of hate and a universal war cry . . . We cannot clear our names unless we own up to the shameful fact that terrorism has become an Islamic enterprise; an almost exclusive monopoly, implemented by Muslim men and women. We cannot redeem our extremist youth, who commit all these heinous crimes, without confronting the Sheikhs who thought it ennobling to reinvent themselves as revolutionary ideologues, sending other people's sons and daughters to certain death, while sending their own children to European and American schools and colleges.[17]

Fundamentalist clerics and terrorists violently misinterpret the Qur'an.

Hindu and Buddhist spirituality and religion are not as cohesive or coercive as is Muslim spirituality; they are more open and tolerant. Hinduism focuses on the **interior peace** of the individual, according to the Vedic scriptures. The notion of *dharma*, one of four major goals of human life, includes the virtue and good character of the individual.[18] Good *dharma* brings peace, emancipation, and liberation to the person. For Hinduism, among the differences from Western attitudes that pertain to business is that women must be subject to men. Although the caste system is outlawed in India, the largest Hindu nation, the effects of **caste** are still present. Depending upon

---

[16] Sayyid Abul A'la Maududi, *Toward Understanding Islam* (Lahore: Idara Tarjumank-ul-Quran, 2000).

[17] *Al-Sharq Al-Awsat*, September 6, 2004, as quoted in Thomas Friedman, *The World is Flat*, p. 406.

[18] Krishna S. Dhir, "The Corporate Executive's *Dharma*: Insights from the Indian Epic Mahabharata," in *Business, Religion and Spirituality, op. cit*, pp. 122–138; also see Arvind Sharma, "A Hindu Perspective on Spirituality and Management," in *Spiritual Intelligence at Work: Meaning, Metaphor, and Morals*, eds. Moses L. Pava and Patrick Primeau (Amsterdam: Elsevier, 2004).

heredity, the caste system requires the placing of a person in a work role of their "lower" or "higher" caste. This causes discrimination at work.

Buddhism gives prominence to practices, and does not include the worship of a creator God. It seeks to bring about personal **serenity**, largely through the practice of **meditation**. Among the Buddhist basic elements is "right livelihood"—to be achieved by one who transforms their experience so as to be fully responsible for their lives, and thus develop wisdom and compassion. Buddhism is characterized by nonviolence, tolerance of differences, the practice of meditation, and a lack of dogma. Among the hindrances to the wise life are selfishness and laziness. Buddhist values are counter to the individualism, selfishness, and deception sometimes found in Western business managers.[19]

The above is a brief overview of some of the elements and differences in Muslim, Hindu, and Buddhist attitudes that affect work.[20] Let us now return to the early Christian era, and examine the Benedictine monasteries where new work values developed.

Monks as Capitalists

Christian Benedictine monasteries (founded by St. Benedict of Nursia, 480–549) are credited as being "perhaps the original **founders of capitalism**."[21] The Benedictine Rule, as embodied in tens of thousands of monasteries throughout Europe, brought a more positive attitude toward work. For the monks, manual work was not a curse and a degradation. They looked on work as an opportunity to build, grow, and develop personally and as a **community**. They choose to work together, and they were among the first to cooperate voluntarily in all tasks. Because the monks often worked in groups and varied their occupations, they found it useful to schedule their work. They standardized tasks so that anyone could handle the job, and they began and ended their work together.

Living and working as a cooperative community promoted the use of **labor-saving devices**. When, in 1115, Bernard of Clairvaux led a band of monks to found a new monastery, one of his prime requisites for a new site was that it be next to a rapidly moving stream that could be harnessed by the monks to help them do their work. Bernard himself gives us a description of his famous abbey at Clairvaux, and he tells of the mechanical devices that are geared to water wheels to make the work of the monks easier.[22]

[19] For additional insights on Buddhism, Hinduism, the other faith traditions, and their influence on business life, see Edward D. Zinbarg, *Faith, Morals and Money: What the World's Religions Teach us about Money in the Marketplace* (New York: Continuum, 2001).

[20] For additional material on Islam, and Judaism, Buddhism, and Christianity, see Steward W. Herman, ed., *Spiritual Goods: Faith Traditions and the Practice of Business* (Bowling Green: Philosophy Documentation Center, 2001); also Edward D. Zinbarg, *Faith, Morals and Money: What the World's Religions tell us about Money in the Marketplace* (New York: Continuum, 2001).

[21] Lewis Mumford, *Techniques and Civilizations* (New York: Harcourt, Brace, 1934), p. 14.

[22] Bernard of Clairvaux, *Patrologiae Latinae*, ed. Migne, vol. 185 (Paris: Garnier, 1879), pp. 570–574. A translation of much of this is in Samuel J. Eales, *Life and Works of St. Bernard*, vol. 2 (London: Burns & Oakes, n.d.), pp. 460–467. The quoted words that follow are those of Bernard himself.

The monastery is built at the base of a mountain and extends over a fast-moving stream to make best use of the waterpower. The river is guided by "works laboriously constructed" by the monks so that the water may be of the greatest help to their efforts. The water thus "passes and repasses the many workshops of the abbey"; it is channeled so that it drives the wheels of a mill. In moving these wheels, "it grinds the meal under the weight of the mill-stones, and separates the fine from the coarse by a sieve." The river's waters are also harnessed to raise and drop hammers for the fulling of cloth and to help the shoemaker in his chores. The waters are then split into smaller streams where they help "to cook the food, sift the grain, to drive the wheels and hammers, to damp, wash, soak and so to soften, objects; everywhere it stands ready to offer its help." The monks also constructed an elaborate irrigation apparatus to water the fields. Recall that all this happened in the twelfth century, six centuries before the Industrial Revolution.

A century later the great Christian theologian of the Middle Ages, Thomas Aquinas (1225–1279), provided a **rationale for work**. He spelled out clearly the reasons why it seemed to him that manual labor was necessary for all: to obtain food, to remove idleness, to curb concupiscence, and to help the poor.[23] Although Aquinas saw that work was not only necessary but also of great value, there was still a remnant of the view that work was a burden, something to endure for the sake of later leisure.

Work, however, was not a burden for the monks; it was a means of **love and service**. When setting up a new monastery, the monks would deliberately choose a site far from existing towns. They did this both because it would be a better locale for prayer and because they deliberately set out to communicate their new view of the value of work as rooted in charity. Benedict and Bernard expected their monks to work in the fields and the shops, whether they were sons of aristocrats or of serfs. According to Lynn White, Jr., historian of technology and industry, this provision

> marks a revolutionary reversal of the traditional attitude toward labor; it is a high peak along the watershed separating the modern from the ancient world. The Benedictine monks regarded manual labor not as a mere regrettable necessity of their corporate life but rather as an integral and spiritually valuable part of their discipline. During the Middle Ages the general reverence for the laboring monks did much to increase the prestige of labor and the self-respect of the laborer. Moreover, since the days of St. Benedict every major form of Western asceticism has held that "to labor is to pray," until in its final development under the Puritans, work in one's "calling" became not only the prime moral necessity but also the chief means of serving and praising God.[24]

---

[23] Thomas Aquinas, *Summa Theologica*, II-II, qu. 87, art. 3.
[24] Lynn White, Jr., "Dynamo and Virgin Reconsidered," *American Scholar*, 27 (Spring 1958): 188. Quoted by permission. See also Rodney Stark, *The Victory of Reason: How Christianity Led to Freedom, Capitalism and Western Success* (New York: Random House, 2006).

The monks lived together thriftily, and that enabled them to invest in productive machinery like that described above to aid them in their work. This is why some call the monks the first capitalists. Their cooperation and inventiveness resulted in division of labor, interchangeable work, a clock-regulated workday, and ingenious labor-saving equipment—all of which contributed to greater productivity. They used the additional time that was then available for their prayer and life together. A few hundred years later, this same love-centered ethic was brought to the cities and marketplaces of seventeenth-century France by an eminent group of artists, poets, theologians, and saints. Some maintain that it was this unique emphasis on the centrality of love for one's sisters and brothers, especially as embodied in women, along with its requirement of cooperation and hard work, which made industrial society possible.[25]

By 1700, Christianity, and its central love ethic, had helped to provide many of the elements necessary for the development of business and commerce. Work was valued—it provided self-discipline and an integrating force in a person's life. Christianity helped that person to focus on the value of the product of work; if the same thing could be produced more easily, this was good—especially when it enabled one to help one's family and neighbors. The importance of producing a greater quantity of goods and a new awareness of time developed first in the monasteries and then spread to the larger society. Furthermore, the Catholic Church urged all to attend mass side by side: rich and poor, worker and artisan, peasant, scholar, and duke. This fostered communication and cooperation.

In its otherworldly theology, however, Catholicism thwarted the coming of capitalism. Material goods, wealth, and success were not the measures of holiness. According to Jesus, the purpose of life on earth was not merely to build up material goods. This attitude led to suspicion of those who would lend money to others and charge them for the use of it. Even as late as the sixteenth century, theologians condemned the opening of state banks. Lending money at interest was the sin of usury in both the Christian and Muslim traditions.

In Christian society, work and industry were more respected than they had been in aristocratic Greece or Rome. The average citizen had many reasons to do tasks well, and there were no slaves to do them instead. In addition, a person's trade or craft gave meaning and integrity to life. But it was the Protestant Reformation that provided the impetus for the development of attitudes that would propel Western society toward rapid economic growth.

From Luther and Calvin to the Protestant Ethic

It was Protestantism that eventually established hard work and the making of profits as central to a Christian life. Ironically, Martin Luther (1483–1546), who began this new movement, disapproved of the commerce and economic individualism of his day. Luther was appalled at the regal high living of merchants, princes, and popes. The contrast between the ideals of Christianity and what Luther actually found around him motivated him to push for reform. He called for a return to a simple,

---

[25] See Nef, *op. cit.*; see also his briefer *Civilization, Industrial Society and Love* (Santa Barbara, CA: Fund for the Republic, 1961).

hardworking **peasant life**; this would bring sufficient prosperity for all. A person should earn a living and not make an excessive profit.

Luther thought a number of Christian customs encouraged idleness: the many religious holidays, the mendicant friars glorifying begging, and the monasteries' support of some who did not work. Idleness is unnatural, according to Luther, and charity should be given only to those who cannot work. His original contribution was in emphasizing the importance of one's profession. The best way to serve God was to do the work of one's profession as well as one could. Thus Luther healed what had been a breach between worship and work. As long as work was done in obedience to God and in service to one's sisters and brothers, every type of work had equal value in God's eyes.

Luther held that a person's salvation is achieved solely through faith in God; good works do not affect salvation. Moreover, all legitimate human activities are acts of worship. Because formal prayer, and especially the monastic life of prayer, is no more valuable than tilling the fields, Protestantism released all human energies for the world of work. The farmer, the smith, and the baker all do work that is as honorable as that of the monk or priest. Although the life of the simple worker is better, Luther concedes that

> trade is permissible, provided that it is confined to the exchange of necessaries, and that the seller demands no more than will compensate him for his labor and risk. The unforgivable sins are idleness and covetousness, for they destroy the unity of the body of which Christians are members.[26]

Luther was vehement in preaching against lending at interest, yet paradoxically his denial of religious authority eventually set economic life free from strictures on usury. This denial left business and commerce to develop their own life and laws independent of existing moral authorities. Capitalism thus set up its **own norms of right and wrong**, and capitalist activity was carried on beyond the influence of the church.

Luther's insistence on giving everyday life the same value as worship and on breaking the system of religious authority eventually resulted in profound changes in economic and social life. The prescribed relationships with neighbor, family, and church were swept away. Although they were encumbering and limiting, they also provided roots, personal relationships, and meaning for life. Work, business, and secular interests now formed a separate world removed from the religious and moral values that had until this time governed all aspects of life.

The most important influence on what we now call the Protestant ethic was the theology of John Calvin (1509–1564), who followed Luther as a reformer of Christianity. Calvin and his followers did not idealize the peasant, as did Luther, but accepted urban life as they found it. "Like early Christianity and modern socialism, Calvinism was largely an **urban movement**."[27] Calvin's central theological notion, which distinguishes his position from that of Luther and of Catholicism, is

---

[26] R. H. Tawney, *Religion and the Rise of Capitalism* (New York: Mentor, 1947), p. 83.
[27] *Ibid.*, p. 92.

predestination. According to Calvin, God is infinite, absolute, supreme, and totally above and beyond human beings. It is impossible for us to fully understand God and God's ways. Moreover, God because of infinite wisdom knows all people who were and *will be* saved in the world. In God's power and wisdom, God has determined that it is fitting for his glory if only a small number of men and women are saved. Moreover, Calvin maintains that there is absolutely nothing a person can do to influence his or her own salvation; from all eternity God has freely predetermined it. A person lives to glorify God, and the major way a person glorifies God is in his or her life. If a person bends every talent and expends every energy in work and achieves success, this may be an indication that he or she is one of the saved. Although these individual efforts cannot directly effect salvation, if successful they do glorify God and may thus be a sign that the person is counted among the elect. Perhaps even more motivating was the conviction that if a person was idle, disliked work, or was not successful, these were most likely signs that person was not among the saved.

Calvin taught that **all must work** and must never cease working. Profits earned must not be hoarded but must be invested in new works. Investment and the resulting profit and wealth were thus encouraged. These religious convictions bred a new man: active, austere, and strong-willed. Luxury, waste, and idleness are condemned as sin. Calvin proposed a unique paradox: Deny the world; live as an ascetic in the world, because it cannot guarantee your salvation. Yet remember that your one duty is to glorify God, and the best way of doing that is by being a success at your chosen work, your calling. It is a precarious balance, difficult to achieve and even more difficult to maintain.

The Protestant ethic, therefore, stems from Calvin's teachings. He stressed the importance of hard work and the necessity to reinvest one's earnings in new works. Moreover, Calvin did not condemn interest and urban trade, as did Luther and Catholic leaders. Calvin urged working hard at one's occupation, and held that successful trade and commerce was another way of glorifying God.

Weber's Analysis of the Protestant Ethic

Before leaving the influence of the Reformation on business ideology, let us look at the analysis of that influence more than 300 years later by the sociologist Max Weber in *The Protestant Ethic and the Spirit of Capitalism*. It is ironic that Weber, a German, cites no other person more often as an example of the Protestant ethic than Benjamin Franklin, an American. We will examine Franklin's contributions later in this chapter.

Weber began his analysis by noting that "business leaders and owners of Capital, as well as higher grades of skilled labor, and even more the higher technically and commercially trained personnel of modern enterprises, are overwhelmingly Protestant." He went on to compare the Catholic and the Protestant: "The Catholic is quieter, having less of the acquisitive impulse; he prefers a life of the greatest possible security, even with a smaller income, to a life of risk and excitement, even though it may bring the chance of gaining honor and riches."[28]

---

[28] Max Weber, *The Protestant Ethic and the Spirit of Capitalism*, trans. Talcott Parsons (New York: Scribner, 1958), pp. 35–41. Quoted with permission.

In trying to determine the reason why Protestants seem to be more successful in business, Weber examined the roots of the theology of Luther and Calvin, as we have done above. He noted that Reformation theology encouraged individuals to look on their **life and work more seriously**. Life demanded sobriety, self-discipline, diligence, and, above all, planning ahead and saving. In addition to having its own rewards, success was a reflection of God's glory and hence a hint as to whether that person was saved or not. It was therefore incumbent on all to be successful. Moreover, the individual had the means to achieve that success: "In practice this means that God helps those who help themselves. Thus the Calvinist himself creates his own salvation, or, as would be more correct, the conviction of it."[29]

An asceticism flowed from the Calvinistic ethic: "Waste of time is thus the first and in principle the deadliest of sins." On the same theme, the Calvinist asceticism "turned with all its force against one thing: the spontaneous enjoyment of life and all it had to offer." On the positive side, in the Calvinist and Puritan churches Weber found "the continually repeated, often almost passionate preaching of hard, continuous bodily or mental labor." But Weber observed that "the people filled with the spirit of capitalism today tend to be indifferent, if not hostile, to the Church." When that happens, the pursuit of business and a career often take on the all-embracing aspects of active religion. But this is what is "so irrational about this sort of life, where a man exists for the sake of his business, instead of the reverse." The Protestant ethic changed history. Contrary to the ethical convictions of centuries, "money-making became an end in itself to which people were bound, as a calling."[30]

Weber quoted founding Protestants John Wesley and John Calvin when they point out a paradox. It is religion that makes people careful, hardworking, and frugal; and this, in turn, enables them to build up wealth. "But as riches increase, so will pride, anger, and love of the world," in Wesley's words. Speaking of those on the lower end of that same economic ladder, Weber quoted Calvin: "Only when the people, i.e., the mass of laborers and craftsmen, were poor did they remain obedient to God."[31] Therein lies a paradox; the men who themselves are most responsible for the Protestant ethic foresee its collapse. Their religion demands hard work and saving, and this provides wealth. But wealth brings pride, luxury, and lack of will. It is therefore an unstable ethic, in part because its religious foundations dissolve. The "Protestant ethic" is a descriptive term and is often called the "Puritan ethic." As we will see when we examine Benjamin Franklin, this ethic will take on a secular life of its own.

The Protestant ethic, also called the Puritan ethic (see Figure 4-1) derives from the Calvinist vision of how people should act in order to be successful in this

---

[29] *Ibid.*, p. 145.

[30] *Ibid.*, pp. 70–73, 157–66.

[31] *Ibid.*, pp. 175–77. Some reject the attempt to show a relationship between economic success and religious faith. They maintain that there are more plausible explanations for commercial success, such as "special education, family relationships and alien status." See Kurt Samuelson, *Religion and Economic Action*, trans. E. G. French (New York: Basic Books, 1961), p. 154. Nevertheless, the fact that Weber's theses are so widely accepted makes it a theory to be taken seriously. Whatever the causal relationships, religious values and economic development are there to be observed, and they have had a marked influence on one another.

THE PROTESTANT ETHIC URGES:
Hard work
Self-control and sobriety (that is, humorlessness)
Self-reliance
Perseverance
Saving and planning ahead
Honesty and "observing the rules of the game"

FIGURE 4-1   **The Protestant Ethic**

life and also in the next. Following its tenets, many have achieved success and developed the values that we describe in the next chapter in the section "Values in Modern Life."

The Protestant ethic urges planning ahead, sobriety, diligence, and self-control for the individual. It promises a material reward and, in its religious strand, a good chance of salvation. Moreover, the Protestant ethic serves an additional purpose. It assures the successful and wealthy that their wealth is deserved. They have property because they have worked for it and so have a right to it. As Weber observed, the wealthy man is not satisfied in knowing that he is fortunate:

> Beyond this, he needs to know that he has a right to his good fortune. He wants to be convinced that he "deserves" it, and above all, that he deserves it in comparison with others. He wishes to be allowed the belief that the less fortunate also merely experience their due.[32]

Thus the Protestant ethic not only provided a set of directions on how to succeed and a motivation for doing so but also attempted to legitimate the wealth that was acquired. The successful person can say, "Anyone who was willing to work as hard as I did could have done as well, so it is clear that I deserve the wealth I have." This attitude laid the foundation for social Darwinism and the survival of the fittest, which we will examine later in this chapter.

John Locke and the Right to Private Property

John Locke (1632–1704) had a considerable influence on the American Founding Fathers and through them on the American Constitution. He and Jean-Jacques Rousseau also influenced the French Revolution and most of the subsequent efforts to move toward more democratic governments. The Oxford-educated

---

[32] Max Weber, "The Social Psychology of World Religions," in *Max Weber: Essays in Sociology*, eds. H. H. Gerth and C. Wright Mills (New York: Oxford University Press, 1946), p. 271.

Locke was both a philosopher and a politician. He was a practical man, having served various government figures of his day, so he wrote about political and social questions.

Locke focused on natural rights, but the right to which he devoted most of his energy was the right to **private property**.[33] Locke held that an individual has a right to self-preservation and so has a right to those things that are required for this purpose. Individuals require property so that they may feed and clothe their families and themselves. A person's labor is what confers primary title to property. If individuals settle on land and work it, they therefore deserve title to it. Locke's ideal was America, where there was unlimited land available for anyone who was willing to clear and work it.

Locke has been criticized for overemphasizing the rights of private property and thus catering to the interests of his landowning patrons. However, he disapproved of a person who amassed wealth without limit. Whatever is beyond what the individual can use is not by right his or hers.[34] It belongs to others and should be allotted to them.

Rousseau's Social Contract

Jean-Jacques Rousseau (1712–1778) distrusted contemporary society and its institutions, as did other members of the French Enlightenment. He believed that society, and even Enlightenment ideals such as reason, culture, and progress, had created unhealthy competition, self-interest, pseudo sophistication, and a destruction of the "simple society" he valued. He believed society was unjust, effete, and dominated by the rich and by civil and church authorities. According to Rousseau, "Man was born free and everywhere he is in chains." Men and woman's original state in nature is free, and although society is necessary, the ordinary person, family life, reverence, and freedom must be central to it.

The **Social Contract** was an attempt to achieve the necessary activities, associations, and governments required in a civilized society without losing basic individual rights. A citizen's duty of obedience must be founded on more than the possession of power by those in authority. To be legitimate, it must rest on some sort of freely given consensus.[35] Rousseau's distrust of society's institutions also included private property. According to him, when private property was introduced into a society, equality disappeared. Private property marks a departure from primitive simplicity and leads to numerous injustices and evils such as selfishness, domination, and servitude. In the state he proposes, Rousseau supports a sharply increased tax on any property that is not necessary for people to modestly support

---

[33] John Locke, *An Essay Concerning the True Original Extent and End of Civil Government*, especially chap. 5, "Of Property," and chap. 9, "Of the Ends of Political Society and Government." See also the summary in Frederick Copleston, *A History of Philosophy*, vol. 5 (London: Burns and Oates, 1964), pp. 129–131.

[34] Matthew Kramer, *John Locke and the Origins of Private Property: Philosophical Explorations of Individualism, Community, and Equality* (Cambridge: Cambridge University Press, 1997).

[35] Jean-Jacques Rousseau, *The Social Contract and Discourse on the Origin and Foundation of Inequality Among Mankind* (New York: Washington Square Press, 1967). See also the summary of Rousseau in Copleston, *History of Philosophy*, vol. 6, especially pp. 68–69 and 80–100.

themselves and their family. For property that is necessary for support, there should be no tax at all. Rousseau and Locke agreed that excessive wealth was not legitimate.

Adam Smith and Free Enterprise

The Scot Adam Smith (1723–1790) is the grandfather of capitalism and of free enterprise economics. As a political economist and moral philosopher, he was among the first to emphasize free exchange and to present economics as an independent branch of knowledge. He is best known for his classic work, *The Wealth of Nations*, which in 1776 supported independence for economics and business—the same year that the American colonies declared their political independence from England. In an earlier book that is often ignored, Smith provided a humane foundation for the economic system with his emphasis on virtue, sympathy, and justice.[36]

In explaining **economics** Smith said, "Nobody ever saw a dog make a fair and deliberate exchange of one bone for another with another dog." Later he spelled out the implications of this inability to exchange by showing that each animal was obliged "to support and defend itself, separately and independently, and derives no sort of advantage from that variety of talents with which nature has distinguished its fellows." Human beings, said Smith, are quite different in that they can take advantage of one another's unique genius. What one is good at he does in abundance, sells to others, and thus "may purchase whatever part of the produce of other men's talents he has occasion for." Smith's most familiar example is of the division of labor in making pins. One man, working alone and forming the entire pin, might "make one pin in a day, and certainly not make twenty." But when the operation is divided up into a number of separate operations so that "one man draws out the wire, another straights it, a third cuts it, a fourth points it, a fifth grinds it at the top for receiving the head," and so on, a group of pin makers are able to make pins at a daily average of 4,800 pins per pin maker.[37]

In addition to the value of exchange and the division of labor, Smith also examined the value of the free market, competition, and profit maximization. Smith was among the first to make a clear and plausible case that when morally conscientious individuals follow their own self-interest, it works to the benefit of society as a whole. As individual competitors pursue their own maximum profit, they are all thus forced to be more efficient. This results in cheaper goods in the long run. Free competition in all markets and for all goods and services is thus to be encouraged; government intervention serves only to make operations less efficient and is thus to be avoided. The same principles apply to international trade. There should be a

---

[36] Adam Smith, *The Wealth of Nations*, ed. J. C. Bullock (New York: Collier, 1909), pp. 19–23. His earlier book is, *The Theory of Moral Sentiments* (New York: A. M. Kelly, 1966, 1853). For a comparison of the two works, see James Buchan, *The Authentic Adam Smith: His Life and Ideas* (New York: Atlas/Norton, 2006); Samuel Fleischacker, *On Adam Smith's Wealth of Nations: A Philosophical Companion* (Princeton, NJ: Princeton University Press, 2004); and Patricia Werhane, *Adam Smith and His Legacy for Modern Capitalism* (New York: Oxford University Press, 1991).
[37] *Ibid.*, pp. 9–10.

minimum of government interference in the form of duties, quotas, and tariffs. Smith's is the classical argument in support of free trade.

· Smith took some of his insights from the English philosopher Thomas Hobbes (1588–1679). Hobbes maintained that individuals act simply to gain that which gives them pleasure or to avoid that which causes displeasure. Because this may differ for each individual, there is no objective good or value in reality itself. Hobbes's view of human motivation is that of *egoistic hedonism*. Because Hobbes's view was that human nature is largely self-seeking and that there is no objective morality, it is not surprising that he held that might makes right. It is important to have power to protect one's person and goods. Whatever a person has the power to take, belongs to that person. Hobbes acknowledged that this leads to insecurity and even war but maintained that they are an inescapable part of the human condition. On the theme of trade and economic activity, Smith quoted Hobbes's claim that "wealth is power." Wealth enables its possessor to purchase what he or she wants, and this in itself gives that person considerable control over others. So it is in the self-interest of individuals to increase their wealth.

To explain profit maximization, Smith used the example of rent. Even though the owner of the land contributes nothing to production beyond the fact of ownership, nevertheless the owner will strive for a contract stipulating the highest rent the tenant can possibly afford to pay. Contrary to the earlier principle of a "just price," the landlord will try to leave the tenant as little as possible of what he or she earns. Smith contends that this is as it should be. On some occasions, the landlord may leave the tenant a bit more for him- or herself, but this is and should be exceptional; it is due to "the liberality, more frequently the ignorance, of the landlord."[38]

As the grandfather of modern economics, Smith spelled out clearly and graphically most of the current major principles operating in economic and business theory. He illustrated the advantages of the division of labor, the free competitive market, and profit maximization, and how they contribute to more efficient production. As individuals pursue self-interested goals, Smith's famous *invisible hand* guides economic and business activities so that they are more productive and cheaper and thus benefit society as a whole.

Industry and commerce in the two centuries following Adam Smith have been extraordinarily successful. Moreover, business activities closely followed the model Smith described. The free market encouraged rapid economic growth. Economic motivation for most people up to Smith's time had been based more on obligations to a lord, proprietor, or one's family and on threats, fears, and sanctions. The free market and potentially unlimited monetary rewards shifted the motivation for economic activity.

The free market and the possibility of unlimited profits are at the heart of the system's greatest strength: It taps positive motivation and rewards. It draws a person into greater activity and creativity and rewards those efforts. Furthermore, the rewards are tangible and measurable; there is little doubt as to who is a success. On

---

[38] *Ibid.*, pp. 153–171. See also William Keep, "Adam Smith's Imperfect Invisible Hand: Motivations to Mislead," *Business Ethics: A European Review,* 12 (October 2003): 343–353.

the other hand, this new model for economic activity also includes its greatest weakness. It can insulate a person from obligations to friends, family, fellow citizens, and the larger community, and replace these obligations with an easily broken contract whose purpose is to obtain individual profit. Hence, individuals can much more readily come to feel that they are alone, isolated, and easily replaceable. Literature on the attitudes of managers and blue-collar workers alike show that most have experienced this feeling of isolation and alienation.[39] Adam Smith recognized that free markets can encourage selfishness and isolation. As a moral philosopher himself, he emphasized that a free market required a moral and ethical foundation for it to be efficient. He pointed out that the free market system could only work effectively when its participants understood and practiced moral principles, also.

Using an analogy, Adam Smith and the Industrial Revolution that followed shifted people's view such that they tended to **compare society to a machine instead of an organism**, as they had formerly. In earlier times, men and women knew they were part of something larger than themselves. Families worked together, and they cared for their neighbors. They were dependent upon one another—like parts of an organism. They had a stake in their community and they belonged. This was replaced by a market in which one's own work was sold. One no longer belonged, and one's very self became just another commodity in the market. Every individual can and will be replaced when he or she becomes obsolete, old, and inefficient, just as is true for a machine.[40]

Adam Smith provided an accurate and integrated picture of developing business activities. He detailed the advantages of free exchange. As such, he is the father of free market economics. Smith is widely quoted and remains today a principal spokesperson for capitalism and free enterprise. European thinkers and leaders formed many of the foundation values for the "New World." Let us now turn our attention to the activities of that new people across the Atlantic Ocean.

ENTERPRISE VALUES IN THE NEW WORLD

The Europeans who crossed the ocean to this "New World" came as immigrants to a land they thought of as open and free. Yet Native Americans had been on the continent for scores of centuries before the Europeans arrived. Because natives were few, they were ignored unless they got in the way. Often the settlers made peace with them. As more immigrants arrived, conflict arose between the new farmers, the miners, and the hunter-gatherers who reverenced the mountains. The newcomers took the land and minerals that they wanted, and treated the native peoples in a self-centered, entrepreneurial fashion.

Like immigrants today, these earlier settlers came to the New World risking their lives and their fortunes in the hope of finding freedom and new opportunities. They

---

[39] See evidence of this dissatisfaction, for example, in Theodore V. Purcell and Gerald F. Cavanagh, *Blacks in the Industrial World* (New York: Free Press, 1972), pp. 72–75, 236–238.
[40] For this and other insights, I thank Otto Bremmer. Concerning Smith anticipating and providing suggestions on the major moral failures of capitalism, see James Q. Wilson, "Adam Smith on Business Ethics," *California Management Review*, Fall 1989, pp. 59–72.

came to a land that seemed to them to have **limitless natural resources**—timber, coal, minerals, and much good farming land. Clearing the land was backbreaking, but the result was good, fertile acreage that could be handed on to one's children. The changing climate encouraged work—it was brisk and invigorating—and the winters, when there would be no fruits or crops, demanded that settlers plan ahead and save something from the harvest. Two wide oceans provided natural defenses that allowed the New World to focus on its own needs and development without much fear of foreign intrusions.

These natural characteristics affected the values and ideology of the people. But when the settlers came, they also brought their own values and ideals which also influenced their attitudes. Many of the early American immigrants came to the colonies for religious reasons—some because of religious persecution in their native countries. They sought a land where they could live and pray as conscience dictated. The men and women who settled the new continent came from Europe and so also brought the religion that predominated there—Christianity. The Catholic Spanish came first to Mexico and Peru, and founded cities, colleges, and businesses. But the English Puritans, who came a century later to the northern new world, had a more lasting influence on business values and ideology.

The **Puritans** fled Europe so that they might freely follow their antihierar-chical religious faith and practices. To these men and women, who came before the American Revolution, their work or their "calling" was an essential part of their total world view. To us today, the Puritan ideal is a delicate, even mysterious, paradox. Puritan preacher John Cotton (1584–1652) described it thus:

> There is another combination of virtues strangely mixed in every lively, holy Christian: and that is, diligence in worldly business, and yet deadness to the world. Such a mystery as none can read but they that know it.[41]

Puritans plunged into their work with a dedication that could come only because it was their calling. Worship of God was not shown in hymn singing, colorful religious services, or sterile monasticism; worship was a simple, reverent prayer. Moreover, the Puritans' prayer was not separated from work, for work was their means of giving glory to God. So work was disciplined and clear-eyed, because "when he serves man, he serves the Lord; he doth the work set before him and he doth it sincerely and faithfully so as he may give account for it."[42] This early Puritan ideology strengthened the emerging social order by giving importance to every type of work. Again, in John Cotton's words, "[faith] encourageth a man in his calling to the most homeliest and difficultest and most dangerous things his calling can lead and expose himself to."[43] Self-discipline was also important. They were ascetics in the world; although in it, they were detached from it.

---

[41] Perry Miller, *The American Puritans* (Garden City, NY: Doubleday, 1956), p. 171.
[42] *Ibid.*, p. 173.
[43] John Cotton, quoted in Miller, *op. cit.*, pp. 176–177.

Two generations later, Cotton Mather (1663–1728) was born into the same family of learning and clerical leadership. Like his grandfather, Mather held that

> A Christian has **two callings**: (1) a general calling to serve the Lord Jesus Christ, and (2) a particular calling which was his work or his business. Both of these callings are essential if the Christian is to achieve salvation. Contemplation of the good means nothing without accomplishment of the good. A man must not only be pious; he must be useful.[44]

The Puritan businessman fully integrated his work and his worship. Often he would mention God in his invoices, thanking God for a profit or accepting losses for God's greater glory. Moreover, each individual determined his or her calling, and work was generally done individually. In the same fashion, people achieved salvation individually.

American Puritans did not invent this position; they took the theology of John Calvin and spelled out in detail the implications for the businessperson. The businessperson in turn, eager for some justification of the efforts to which he devoted most of his day, happily received the Puritan preacher's words. So there began a mutual understanding and support between preacher and businessperson that became a hallmark of New World society.

Benjamin Franklin's Way to Wealth

In the period before the American Revolution, Benjamin Franklin (1706–1790) accepted the work values of the Puritans, shifted them from a religious to a **secular foundation**, and restated them for Americans. Franklin, especially in *Poor Richard's Almanac*, was incisive, mundane, prolific, and influential. Many of his homely bits of advice have become common sayings in our language. Franklin brought together 25 years of his *Almanac* writings on work and business and published them in 1758 as the essay "The Way to Wealth."

> God helps them that help themselves. Diligence is the mother of good luck, as Poor Richard says, and God gives all things to industry. Then plough deep, while sluggards sleep, and you shall have corn to sell and to keep, says Poor Dick. Work while it is called today, for you know not how much you may be hindered tomorrow. Be ashamed to catch yourself idle. When there is so much to be done for yourself, your family, your country, and your gracious king, be up at peep of day; 'Tis true that much is to be done, and perhaps you are weak handed, but stick to it steadily, and you will see great effects, for constant dropping wears away stones and little strokes fell great Oaks.[45]

---

[44] A. Whitney Griswold, "Two Puritans on Prosperity," in *Benjamin Franklin and the American Character*, ed. Charles L. Sanford (Boston: D. C. Heath, 1955), p. 41.

[45] Benjamin Franklin, *The Autobiography and Other Writings* (New York: New American Library, 1961), p. 190. For an overview an assessment of Franklin's writings, J. A. Leo Lemay, *The Life of Benjamin Franklin Vol II: Printer and Publisher, 1730–1747*, pp. 170–213.

In his own graphic way, Franklin focuses on the importance of saving and the need for capital when he notes that "a man may, if he knows not how to save as he gets, keep his nose all his life to the grindstone. If you would be wealthy, think of saving as well as of getting."[46] It was satisfying to Franklin's early American contemporaries to see him supporting the same values and justification for their work as did their Puritan ministers. He provided a rationale for work and a purpose for life; at the same time, he buttressed the existing social order.

Franklin's writings were best sellers in his day and have exerted a significant influence up to the present. In his *Almanac*, his *Autobiography*, and his own life, Franklin embodied the Puritan virtues. He was successful as an inventor, printer, statesman, diplomat, and businessman. Although John Adams resented Franklin's popular wisdom, he was held in esteem by the people. Harvard-educated John Adams, second president of the United States, was brilliant and courageous but also haughty and contentious. Adams conceded that Franklin was a genius, a wit, a politician, and a humorist, but he questioned his greatness as a philosopher, a moralist, or a statesman.[47] Despite Adams's petty quarrels with Franklin, history shows Franklin to have had a greater influence on values. Even today Franklin is cited in calling for restraint in the pursuit of work and money because of moral commitments ingrained by character. Otherwise chasing the American dream will bring more discontent than happiness.[48]

Thomas Jefferson (1743–1826) agreed with the hard-working, individualistic ideals of Franklin, although Jefferson, who wrote the *Declaration of Independence*, was convinced that these virtues could best be fostered in, and the new nation grow best as, an agricultural society.[49] Jefferson felt that as long as one had one's own land to till and crops to care for, the economy would thrive and people would be happier. At this time more than 80 percent of American workers were farmers, and if Jefferson had his way, that is how it would have remained. Jefferson was opposed to the industrialization he had seen in England. He would rather import finished manufactured goods than undergo the undesirable changes manufacturing brings: urbanization, landless workers, and banking. In an agricultural society, where work and initiative immediately pay off for the individual and for the society as a whole, government intervention could be kept to an absolute minimum. Government would only retard the natural forces of growth through regulations and bureaucracy. In Jefferson's own oft-quoted words, "That government is best which governs least." The ambivalent feelings toward and even fear of business appear early, for business spawns cities. An agrarian society is simpler; duties and rewards are more easily seen and measured. So early Americans were not always favorably disposed toward business or cities, or the increasing government that both require.

---

[46] *Ibid.*, p. 192.

[47] For this essay, see John Adams, "An Exaggerated Reputation," in Sanford, *Benjamin Franklin*, pp. 22–26; see also David McCullough, John Adams (New York: Simon & Schuster, 2001).

[48] Robert Wuthnow, *Poor Richard's Principle: Recovering the American Dream through the Moral Dimension of Work, Business and Money* (Princeton, NJ: Princeton University Press, 1996).

[49] Arthur M. Schlesinger, "Ideas and Economic Development," in *Paths of American Thought*, ed. Arthur M. Schlesinger, Jr., and Morton White (Boston: Houghton Mifflin, 1963), pp. 108–109.

Slavery and Productivity

Slavery was early practiced in the United States; four of the five first presidents were slave holders.[50] Slaves constituted one-fifth of the new nation's population in 1776, and slavery continued in the Southern states until the U.S. Civil War. Slavery gave the slave holder an **economic advantage** over his competitors. The work of slaves cost their master only food and shelter for the slave, and thus slavery increased productivity in the southern slave states by an estimated 9 percent over the free states.[51] U.S. businesses, such as JPMorgan Chase and several large insurance firms have acknowledged that they profited from the slave trade.

Forced labor continues to exist in various forms in many countries—especially in Asia, Africa, and Latin America. Slavery goes under many names: forced labor, debt bondage, forced prostitution, abusive treatment of migrant workers, and organ harvesting. Because slavery is part of the illicit economy, there are no exact figures on its extent. But researchers estimate that today there are 27 million people worldwide living in slavery. Traditional forms of slavery, such as absolute ownership of a person and debt bondage are still widespread.[52] Trafficking in human beings is today's fastest growing form of forced labor, and it affects four million people. Slavery or bonded labor is known to exist in many nations, such as Sudan, Brazil, Liberia, India, Pakistan, and Bangladesh. For centuries slaves were the reward of victory in war, because slaves bring lower labor costs for the winners. In Sudan, a civil war raged for decades between the northern Arabic Muslim rulers and the poor southern black Christians and animists. Tens of thousands of men have been killed, and perhaps 90,000 women and children were abducted and put into slavery. In another current case, there are probably 90,000 young Indian women from villages who were forced into prostitution in the single city of Mumbai (formerly Bombay), India.[53]

Virtually all people in all cultures agree that slavery is both unethical and illegal. Slavery denies the human dignity and the most basic personal rights of the person enslaved. In addition, it is unjust because the slave master obtains the economic benefit of the slave's work, and slaves receive little or no wage for their work. In the United States, slavery supported and helped develop the U.S. economy, especially southern agriculture. Even today millions of poor and defenseless people are enslaved in many nations. Let us bring this issue closer to each of us. In wealthy nations we benefit from low price apparel, shoes, sports gear, jewelry, and toys. Their costs are kept low because of people working at slave-like wages and working conditions in mines and manufacturing facilities.

---

[50] See Henry Wienek, *An Imperfect God: George Washington, His Slaves, and the Creation of America* (New York: Farrar, Straus & Giroux, 2003); and Gary Wills, *Negro President: Jefferson and the Slave Power* (Boston: Houghton Mifflin, 2003).

[51] Robert Fogel, "Three Phases of Cliometric Research on Slavery and its Aftermath," *American Economic Review,* 65, no. 2 (May 1975): 37–46. See also Robert Fogel and Stanley Engerman, *Time on the Cross: The Economics of American Negro Slavery* (New York: Norton, 1989).

[52] For an informed presentation of these issues, see Kevin Bales, *Understanding Global Slavery* (Berkeley: University of California Press, 2005), p. 58; and Matthias Busse and Sebastian Braun, "Trade and Investment Effects of Forced Labor: An Empirical Assessment," *International Labour Review,* 142, no. 1 (2003): 49–71.

[53] Richard Re, "A Persisting Evil: The Global Problem of Slavery," *Harvard International Review,* 23, no. 4 (Winter 2002): pp. 32–35.

The American Frontier

The westward expansion on the "new" continent kept alive the simpler, measurable agrarian values, and this frontier had its effect on the American character. For successive waves of hunters, traders, ranchers, and finally farmers, there were always new lands to conquer. It seemed to be a **world without limits**. Most of the Native Americans were nomadic, and there were fewer of them to offer resistance. For the brave and hearty immigrant, it was worth taking great risks, whether in moving or in building. Success brought wealth; failure allowed one to try again somewhere else.

The new territories demanded the strenuous labor of clearing the land. The first farmers faced the difficult task of pulling out trees and building their homes and barns. Nevertheless, the rewards were great: They would have homes and farms, and could pass them on to their children. The rewards were clear, tangible, and permanent, and they gave settlers incentive and zest. The land was open to human effort; if one worked harder, one would be able to produce more.

Frederick Jackson Turner summed up how the frontier has affected the American character:

> That coarseness and strength combined with acuteness and inquisitiveness; that practical, inventive turn of mind, quick to find expedients; that masterful grasp of material things, lacking in the artistic but powerful to effect great ends; that restless, nervous energy; that dominant individualism, working for good and for evil, and withal that buoyancy and exuberance which comes with freedom—these are traits of the frontier or traits called out elsewhere because of the existence of the frontier.[54]

Turner's thesis is widely quoted and has had a great influence on thinkers and leaders. Do current challenges demand the same kind of creativity, decisiveness, energy, risk taking, and sense of purpose?

Tocqueville's View of Americans

As anyone who has lived in another culture knows, the characteristics of that culture stand out in bold relief to the foreigner. In that same process, one is also better able to recognize the unique qualities of one's own culture. A people's values and ideology can be understood more readily when comparing them with the values and ideology of another culture. Thus a perceptive foreign visitor often is able to describe the values and characteristics of the host people with penetrating insight. Alexis de Tocqueville was such a person, and he became one of the most incisive commentators on the American character.

A young French lawyer, Alexis de Tocqueville came to the United States in 1831 to observe and learn from the people. His reflections, in his book *Democracy in America*, attained instant success not only in France but in England and the United States, as well. Published in English translation in 1838, the book was immediately

---

[54] Frederick Jackson Turner, *The Frontier in American History* (New York: Holt, 1920), p. 37.

praised for its insight and lack of bias, and 170 years later it is still regarded as one of the finest commentaries on American life. Tocqueville tried to understand Americans on their own terms.

On arriving, Tocqueville noted the physical expanse of the new country: "The inhabitants of the U.S. constitute a great civilized people, which fortune has placed in the midst of an uncivilized country."[55] This was to help give rise to the independence, resourcefulness, and frontier spirit of which Frederick Jackson Turner was later to write. Tocqueville noted that, preoccupied by the great task to be accomplished, Americans tended to value facts more than consistent ideals, that which works more than the beauty of a comprehensive ideological system. He characterized the American "philosophical method," the American method of reflection and learning, as "to evade the bondage of system and habit, of family maxims, class opinions, and, in some degree, of national prejudices." Americans accepted tradition only as a starting point, the existing situation only "as a lesson to be used in doing otherwise and in doing better." Each person seeks to understand for one's self. All these characteristics Tocqueville summed up as an individualism of thought: "Each American appeals only to the individual effort of his own understanding." This mentality shows that a generation gap is not new: "Every man there readily loses all traces of the ideas of his forefathers or takes no care about them."[56]

Tocqueville saw Americans as hardworking and **individualistic**. The only rationale they might have for their actions and attitudes is **enlightened self-interest**. They are not inclined to reverence tradition, to philosophize, or even to engage in much reflection. He focused on the same favorable attitude toward work that the Puritans, the immigrant, and the frontier settler possessed. Americans see work "as the necessary, natural, and honest condition of human existence." Labor is not only not dishonorable, it is held in honor among the people. Even the rich person feels the obligation to take up some sort of worthwhile work, whether this work is private or public.

When Americans were asked why they work, act, and think as they do, Tocqueville reported that they gave a rather consistent response:

> Americans are fond of explaining almost all the actions of their lives by the principle of self-interest rightly understood; they show with complacency how an enlightened regard for themselves constantly prompts them to assist one another and inclines them willingly to sacrifice a portion of their time and property to the welfare of the state.[57]

Although not unique to America, by the time of Tocqueville's visit, enlightened self-interest had taken firm root in the United States.

Tocqueville underscored both the strengths and the weaknesses of this philosophy. The principle of self-interest does not entail lofty goals, but it is clear

---

[55] Alexis de Tocqueville, *Democracy in America*, trans. Henry Reeve, vol. 1 (New York: Knopf, 1946), p. 422.
[56] *Ibid.*, vol. 2, pp. 3–4. For a commentary, see Sheldon S. Wolin, *Tocqueville Between Two Worlds: The Making of a Political and Theoretical Life* (Princeton, NJ: Princeton University Press, 2001).
[57] *Ibid.*, vol. 2, pp. 152, 122.

and certain. It does not demand much of a person, yet acting according to it does produce results. It is not difficult to understand for all classes of people. As a principle of human life, self-interest builds on people's infirmities:

> By its admirable conformity to human weaknesses it easily obtains great dominion; nor is that dominion precarious, since the principle checks one personal interest by another, and uses, to direct the passions, the very same instrument that excites them.[58]

The principle of enlightened self-interest produces no great acts of self-sacrifice, but it encourages a daily discipline of self-denial. Self-interest cannot make people good and virtuous, and hence can hardly serve as a cornerstone of morality. Nevertheless, said Tocqueville, "it disciplines large numbers of people in habits of regularity, temperance, moderation, foresight, self-command."

Enlightened self-interest is closely related to **individualism** (for definitions, see Figure 2-2). Tocqueville was the first person to discuss individualism and, in fact, he brought the word into the English language. It is characteristic of Americans that individualism was not a common word among them, even though it so well described some of their salient attitudes and values. People develop a vocabulary for those things of concern to them and what they want to discuss. Tocqueville suggested that there was probably no other civilized country in which less attention was paid to reflection and philosophy than the United States. Americans were not then, nor are they now, a very reflective people.

Tocqueville described individualism as a mature and calm feeling which disposes each member of the community "to sever himself from the mass of his fellows and to draw apart with his family and his friends." Each individual retreats to his or her own familiar turf and thus "leaves society at large to itself." The Frenchman compared individualism and selfishness, and he found both deficient:

> **Selfishness** (emphasis added) originates in blind instinct; individualism proceeds from erroneous judgment more than from depraved feelings; it originates as much in deficiencies of the mind as in perversity of heart.
>
> Selfishness blights the germ of all virtue; individualism, at first, only saps the virtues of public life; but in the long run it attacks and destroys all others and is at length absorbed in downright selfishness.[59]

Tocqueville pinpointed probably the most serious weakness of the American character. Enlightened self-interest and individualism narrow one's perspective. They encourage one to think less of public responsibilities, and they lead eventually to selfishness. When we read Tocqueville now, he sounds like a contemporary critic

---

[58] *Ibid.*, vol. 2, pp. 122–123.

[59] *Ibid.*, vol. 2, p. 98. For a comparison of contemporary U.S. individualistic and more collective cultures, see Harry C. Triandis, "The Many Dimensions of Culture," *Academy of Management Executive*, 18, no.1 (2004): 88–93.

reflecting on the sins of the unethical corporate executive or politician. Tocqueville's sensitive assessment of the American character—task-orientation and individualism; impatience with tradition, reflection, and abstract ideals; self-interest leading to selfishness—still stands among the great social commentaries. Later observers often use Tocqueville as a starting point, but few have done a better overall appraisal than he.[60] In the generation following the publication of *Democracy in America*, social Darwinism was to make even more popular the doctrine that acting in one's own self-interest contributes to the common good, as we will now see.

Social Darwinism and Herbert Spencer

Events of the latter half of the nineteenth century had a profound impact on attitudes and values. The Industrial Revolution, the growth of cities, and the concept of evolution shook the foundations of life and thought. Herbert Spencer's theories of "social Darwinism" were based on the newly discovered theories of evolution.

Spencer (1820–1903) proposed a grim **survival of the fittest** philosophy. His thesis was that the bright and able contribute most to society and so are to be encouraged and rewarded. The poor, the weak, and the handicapped require more than they contribute and so should not be supported but rather should be allowed to die a natural death. Harsh and demanding reality provides a maturing experience that should not be diluted by well-intentioned but actually destructive charities and handouts. If "natural" principles are followed, evolution and the survival of the fittest in the competition of human life would be the result.

Spencer did not set out to examine any particular society and its values; rather, his critique was proposed as "culture-free." According to Spencer, it applied to all people, for it was derived from basic, organic principles of growth and development. Spencer applied to society the same principles that Charles Darwin saw in biological life—hence the name **social Darwinism**.

Spencer and other proponents of the new evolutionary social ideology were impressed by the suffering of the poor, but they nevertheless felt that progress in an industrial society could come only by means of long hours of work, saving, self-discipline, and even the death of the less able. Rather than considering this a tragedy, they were convinced that through this process of natural selection, those of greater talent, intelligence, and ability would survive and be successful. The physically and mentally handicapped, unable to compete successfully, are less apt to survive. It is a mistake for a government to provide assistance to these handicapped and deficient persons. That would allow them to stay alive, and worse, to reproduce and so transmit their deficiencies to future generations.

Any attempt to minister to the needs of the poor or needy is misguided on several counts. It keeps alive those who are less able. It diverts the attention and abilities of able people who would be better off pursuing more fruitful careers. And, finally, it insulates the less able from a sobering harsh reality and poverty, an opportunity that might jar

---

[60] See, for example, Michael A. Ledeen, *Tocqueville on American Character: Why Tocqueville's Brilliant Exploration of the American Spirit is as Vital and Important Today as it was Nearly Two Hundred Years Ago* (New York: St. Martin's Press, 2000).

them from their complacency and encourage them to work harder to better themselves. Although it is painful to all in the short run, the overall good of society in the long run demands that it not support these less fit individuals. Society improves because of the survival of the fittest:

> The poverty of the incapable, the distresses that come upon the imprudent, the starvation of the idle, and those shoulderings aside of the weak by the strong, which leave so many "in shallows and in miseries," are the decrees of a large, farseeing benevolence. Under the natural order of things society is constantly excreting its unhealthy, imbecile, slow, vacillating, faithless members.[61]

It is especially clear in primitive societies that the strongest and cleverest survive. But this is a natural process, and so it occurs in civilized societies, too. People would be wise to prepare themselves and their children for this struggle.

Society as a whole will benefit from this struggle for survival. Because the most intellectually and physically fit survive, the race will improve. Given a difficult and demanding environment, over several generations the ideal man and woman will develop. There should therefore be little state interference in this natural selection process. The state must not regulate industry, impose tariffs, give subsidies, establish a church, regulate entry into the professions, operate schools, or run the mail service. Most especially, the government must not provide for the poor, improve sanitation, or look to the health needs of the less able.[62]

An example of applying Spencer's views to social issues occurred in 1845–1850. Ireland then experienced a blight of the potato—its staple food, which caused widespread famine, disease, and death. England had invaded and occupied Ireland for several hundred years, and the English took the most fertile land to grow grain to send back to England. At the time of the famine, grain was available from these fields in the Irish midlands. Members of British Parliament were advocates of free markets and they used Spencer's arguments in debating whether to continue to send the grain to England or to allow some grain to go the Irish. Members of Parliament in London argued that the Irish race would be stronger and better if the weaker and less able did not survive. It would be harmful in the long run for the government to intervene. So Parliament voted not to provide grain to those who were starving. More than one million people out of a pre-famine population of eight million in Ireland died.[63]

Herbert Spencer's philosophy was and is more popular in the United States than in his native England. His praise of the strong, clever, and aggressive individual was similar to the American spirit. Further, his theory of inevitable progress was

---

[61] Herbert Spencer, Social Statics: The Man versus the State (London: Appleton, 1850), pp. 323–326, 353.
[62] See Donald Fleming, "Social Darwinism," in Paths of American Thought, ed. Arthur M. Schlesinger, Jr. and Morton White (Boston: Houghton Mifflin, 1963), pp. 124–125.
[63] R. Dudley Edwards and Desmond Williams, The Great Famine (Dublin: Browne and Nolan, 1956), pp. 177–186, 243–246; also, E. R. R. Green, "The Great Famine (1845–1850)," in The Course of Irish History, eds. T. W. Moody and F. X. Martin (New York: Weybright and Talley, 1967), pp. 268–274.

received enthusiastically in a country already marked by general optimism. Spencer's thinking provided both a rational foundation for existing attitudes and a justification for many public and private practices. In the last third of the nineteenth century, Spencer was an influential leader of thought and a hero to many in the United States.

The personal attributes that Spencer extolled are those that many hold to be necessary for a free enterprise system: an intelligent, hearty, adaptable individual in a hostile climate. Survival requires careful planning ahead, hard work, loyalty, and responsibility to family, and individual self-sufficiency. Spencer's theories are conservative; he thought it best to not interfere in the way things were. There was no need to change or to plan ahead on a local or national level. Because natural processes will inevitably produce the best people and thus the best society, any sort of government or private intervention will hurt society in the long run. Citizens must repress their feelings of pity for the poor and allow natural processes to work themselves out. Spencer's theories challenged the mainstream religious views of the time and were opposed by many. But to others his position seemed a natural extension of the traditional Puritan ethic, especially its secularized counterpart as expressed by Benjamin Franklin. It is no surprise that Spencer's theories were so enthusiastically received by the business community of his day.

Struggle for Survival

The businessperson, and especially the entrepreneur, has always found the world to be a struggle for survival. One may want to be humane and conscientious, but cannot afford to be. Herbert Spencer's theories of the survival of the fittest and what has come to be known as social Darwinism had an immense influence on America of the late nineteenth century.

William Graham Sumner (1840–1910), a social science professor at Yale, was an advocate of Spencerism. Sumner's father was an immigrant English workingman who taught his children the Puritan virtues of thrift, self-reliance, hard work, and discipline.[64] His son was convinced that stressing the human dignity and equality of all men and women, made fashionable by the French Revolution and the freeing of slaves, would undermine the initiative and independent spirit that encourage the best people to develop their talents fully. According to Sumner, the less able and adept are jealous of the successes of the more talented and through the political process they will require the latter to support them. This perversion undermines the creativity and motivation of the better and more talented people. Sumner clashed with Yale president Noah Porter when the latter objected to Sumner's assigning Herbert Spencer's book to students. Nevertheless, Sumner won the long-term battle and also thus won probably the first clear statement of academic freedom within the university.

Sumner and Spencer urged a tight-fisted, unemotional aloofness. Both one's self and one's wealth must be saved and not spent without chance of a good return on

---

[64] Fleming, *op. cit.*, p. 128.

investment. Following the Puritans, free emotions and spontaneity were suspect; a person could lose all in a lighthearted or thoughtless moment. In the same vein, Sumner urged that government should not intervene in social and economic affairs. The environment should be kept clear of restrictions, taxes, restraints, and other needless and even harmful laws and regulations.

The opposition to social Darwinism was led by Lester F. Ward (1841–1913). Ward, in his *Dynamic Sociology*, held that people should **control their environment** and not allow it to control them. Evolution and natural selection as outlined by Darwin led to change without direction and without goals. According to Ward, the great value of evolution and natural selection was that they had brought people to the position in which they found themselves now. Moreover, it was precisely in the current era that individuals became able to control their own future and not leave it to blind chance. For Ward, it would be the supreme paradox for men and women, now that they had discovered these natural laws and forces, to retreat and allow themselves to become victims of them. Ward labeled Spencerism a do-nothing philosophy.

Summary and Conclusions

From ancient times to the Middle Ages, Western attitudes toward work became progressively more positive. Biblical injunctions and monastic practices helped to integrate work, labor-saving devices, and a planned day into the average person's life. Then, in the sixteenth century, the Protestant Reformation made the successful performance of an individual's "calling" or occupation one of the primary duties of life. Although a joyless vision, it focused energies that made possible rapid economic growth. The central importance given to private property and the freedom of the individual further supported this growth.

Geography, inherited values, and personal characteristics also contributed to the major values and ideals in American life. The vast expanse of virgin land was a challenge to the righteous, task-oriented Puritans. Their moral theology supported their work ethic: early rising, self-denial, hard work, and thrift. Furthermore, the favorable results of working hard showed that the person was saved. Though not a Puritan, Benjamin Franklin approved of this work ethic, and he presented a secularized version of it.

The values of American Puritans—hard work, saving, regular habits, diligence, self-control, and sobriety—still characterize the American work ethic for some. These values constitute what is known as the Protestant ethic, which will be discussed in greater detail in the next chapter.

Discussion Questions

1. How does knowledge of history help the manager? How does it help in understanding the development of business values?
2. What were the attitudes of Plato and Aristotle toward work? What would be the view of the ancient Greeks about work in the United States today?

3. What influence did Jesus and the Gospels have on peoples' attitudes toward work?
4. What is the "love ethic" that was encouraged by Christianity? How did it affect work values?
5. Describe Muslim, Hindu, and Buddhist views on life and work. Do they differ from Western values? How so?
6. What outlook on life and work did the early Benedictine monasteries contribute? What meaning might these attitudes have for work today?
7. Did Martin Luther have a favorable view of business and commerce?
8. Describe John Calvin's attitude toward work. How did his notion of predestination lead to hard work and the Puritan ethic?
9. What is the Protestant ethic? Is it the same as the Puritan ethic? What are its elements?
10. Describe how John Locke's position on private property influenced the Protestant ethic and early American attitudes? How does it influence current business values?
11. What elements did Weber and Calvin note that would bring the collapse of the Protestant ethic?
12. Did Locke and Rousseau advocate a high tax on property that is not necessary to support a family? Why or why not?
13. Why is Adam Smith called the grandfather of economics? How did Adam Smith's theories shift the model of society from the earlier view of society as an organism to that of a machine?
14. Compare Adam Smith's position on work and efficiency with that of Benjamin Franklin.
15. According to the Puritans, what constitutes a person's calling?
16. How did Benjamin Franklin alter the Puritan ethic?
17. Compare and contrast Benjamin Franklin's attitudes toward work with those of Thomas Jefferson.
18. Does slavery increase productivity? Is slavery still practiced? Where and how? What are the ethical arguments against slavery?
19. Describe the effect of the frontier on American values.
20. Outline Alexis de Tocqueville's appraisal of enlightened self-interest.
21. According to Tocqueville, what are the strengths and weaknesses of enlightened self-interest as a basic motive for people? To what extent are his assessments still valid today?
22. What is social Darwinism? Why does Herbert Spencer maintain that evolution and the "survival of the fittest" are not to be thwarted? Does this ideology exist today?
23. Compare the effect of the frontier and the effect of social Darwinism on American values.
24. Of the various historical business values illustrated in this chapter, which most closely reflect your own views? Explain.

Selected Additional Readings

Frederick Copleston, *A History of Philosophy* (London: Burns and Oates, 1964).

Alexis de Tocqueville, *Democracy in America*, trans. Henry Reeve (New York: Knopf, 1946).

Benjamin Franklin, *The Autobiography and Other Writings* (New York: New American Library, 1961).

Adam Smith, *The Wealth of Nations*, ed. J. C. Bullock (New York: Collier, 1909); and Smith, *The Theory of Moral Sentiments* (New York: A. M. Kelly, 1966, 1853).

Gary Wills, *Negro President: Jefferson and the Slave Power* (Boston: Houghton Mifflin, 2003).

Robert Wuthnow, *Poor Richard's Principle: Recovering the American Dream through the Moral Dimension of Work, Business and Money* (Princeton, NJ: Princeton University Press, 1996).

CASES

Case 4-1   Purchasing Freedom for Slaves

Harvard University freshman Jay Williams heard of the plight of slaves in Sudan, as a participant in the American Anti-Slavery Group (AASG). He then raised money to purchase the freedom of slaves. Before his sophomore year, Williams traveled to Sudan with AASG people and purchased freedom for 4,400 slaves. He went to Sudan again in 2001 and purchased the freedom of another 7,000 slaves. Many of the slaves had been physically abused and 80 percent of the women reported sexual abuse.[65] Some criticized Williams' paying the slave traders, thus providing rewards and encouraging slave trafficking.

1. What ethical norms are violated in taking people into slavery and using their labors?
2. Should Williams pay the slave traders and thus reward them?
3. What ethical norms are in conflict here? Explain your position.

■ ■ ■

Case 4-2   Cell Phone Talking While Driving

We pride ourselves on being able to accomplish several tasks at the same time; teenagers listen to music while doing their homework. Using a cell phone while driving is multitasking, yet evidence is mounting that talking on the phone distracts from driving. Research shows that a person is four times more likely to have an accident if one is on a cell phone. Therefore many states and cities have outlawed talking on a cell phone while driving. Lawmakers are also considering prohibiting drivers from using computers, playing video games, and having a front-seat TV.

1. Is it fair to ban cell phones while one is driving?
2. Should using computers, video games, and front-seat TVs be outlawed?
3. If a person is better at multitasking, should she be exempt from the law?
4. What ethical norm(s) most help to analyze this case?

■ ■ ■

Case 4-3   Insurance Premiums for Smokers and Obese

Lewand Pharmacies began to charge smokers and obese people up to 100 percent more for medical insurance. They argue that it is not fair for nonsmokers and healthy people to subsidize the medical bills of those who expose themselves to cancer and

---

[65] Re, *op. cit.*

diabetes. Moreover, smoking and to a lesser extent being overweight are personal choices. Moreover, Lewand argues that the higher costs will motivate people to live healthier lifestyles.

1. Is Lewand's new medical insurance policy fair? . . . for smokers? . . . for obese?
2. Upon what ethical norm(s) would you base your judgment?

■ ■ ■

Case 4-4   Tax-Free Personal Computer

Eric is about to purchase a new $800 personal computer over the Internet. His state has a sales tax on Internet purchases, and requires the purchaser to declare it. The tax on this purchase would be about $25. Eric also knows that he can undoubtedly get away with not declaring the purchase. Eric's friend, Joan, says, "Nobody declares those purchases. And the state has too much money anyway." Eric agrees and does not declare the PC.

1. What are the ethical issues in this case?
2. What ethical norms help most in coming to an ethical conclusion?
3. Does Joan's statement make ethical sense?
4. What should Eric do? Why?

■ ■ ■

Case 4-5   Drug Test

Karen Matthews, 38, was working in her laboratory when her supervisor handed her a small bottle and told her to produce a urine sample. Karen refused. The next day Karen was fired for her refusal.

1. Was Karen correct to refuse?
2. Does the company have the right to ask for a urine sample?

Exercises

Exercise 4-1: Business Firms and Social Justice

Find evidence of how a particular organization (your own, if possible) acts either well or poorly on each of the following criteria. In each block, "Positive examples . . . " and "Negative examples . . . ," provide specific instances of your organization's policies and/or actions. Information may be obtained from official documents (indicate if mission or goals statements), media reports, outside assessments, or your own knowledge and experience.

You may not be able to fill in all the blocks with the information that you have, but do the best you can. Bring your assessment to the next session of the group.

Name of firm: _____ Your name: _____

Social Justice Teaching	Positive Examples of Company Policies and Procedures	Negative Examples of Company Policies and Procedures
1. The dignity of every person and human rights		
2. Solidarity, common good, and participation		
3. Family life		
4. Subsidiarity and the proper role of government		
5. Property ownership: rights and responsibilities		
6. The dignity of work, rights of workers, and support for labor unions		
7. Economic development and justice		
8. Peace and disarmament		
9. Option for the poor and vulnerable		
10. Stewardship and Sustainability		
11. Transparency*		

*While Transparency is not ordinarily listed as a Principle, we have included it as an aid here. The 10 principles are derived from various documents as a summary of Catholic Social Teaching, presented in "Business Environmental and Workplace Reporting and Activities and Catholic Social Thought," by Gerald F. Cavanagh, S.J. Jeanne M. David, Simon J. Hendry, S.J.

Exercise 4-2: Religious Roots of Business Values[66]

This chapter shows how many of our business values stem from religious roots. There are a variety of religious and spiritual ideologies in the United States, and each contributes to our business ideology. Each faith tradition supports some portion of American values, and each faith probably does not support other elements. Identify a cleric of a faith that is not your own. Call to make an appointment, and then ask that person if you could ask her or him about their faith and business values. Among the questions you might ask are:

1. In what way does your faith support and/or not support the values of American business, as you understand them?
2. Does your faith see greed as an evil? If so, how do you reconcile this for the businessperson?

---

[66] Thanks to Charles Fornaciari for suggesting this exercise.

3. Would your faith maintain that wealth beyond what is necessary should be shared with the needy, either voluntarily or through graduated taxes (as did Carnegie, Buffet, and Bill Gates, Sr.)?

4. In what way does your faith agree or disagree with the tenets of the Puritan ethic (Figure 4-1)? (For this question, it may be necessary to explain the elements of the Protestant ethic.)

5. Would your faith support Spencer's notions of the survival of the fittest? Why or why not?

6. Would your faith agree with John Locke's position on private property?

Write a summary of the results of your interview in a one or two page, double-spaced paper, including name of the interviewee and place of the interview, to be turned in to class.

5

■ ■ ■

Factories, Immigrants, and Wealth

In the past the man has been first; in the future the system must be first.

FREDERICK WINSLOW TAYLOR (1865–1915), FOUNDER
OF SCIENTIFIC MANAGEMENT

To continue much longer overwhelmed by business cares and with most of my thoughts wholly upon the way to make money in the shortest time must degrade me beyond hope of permanent recovery.

ANDREW CARNEGIE (1835–1918), FOUNDER OF U.S.
STEEL, PHILANTHROPIST

Where there is no vision, the people perish.

PROVERBS 20:18

The lives of people are strongly influenced by their history, as we have seen in the last chapter. Our ancestors' experiences in business and in life help us understand current business values. In this chapter we continue to examine the people and events that have affected us. We then investigate the origin and content of business values and ideology.

Values and ideologies are statements of purpose, but they are more than that. They also motivate people to act. A personal ideology gives a rationale for life and action, and answers questions such as: What goals and activities are most important to me? How do I explain my life, my values, and my actions when I am questioned by others?

Both a person and a group can possess an ideology. An ideology embodies the accepted ideals (for terms, see Figures 1-1, 2-1, and 2-2) and ultimate goals possessed by an individual or a society. Thus ideals can significantly influence values. Ideals are sometimes distant, whereas values affect actions. Unless ideals are integrated into an ideology, they do not have much influence on values, choices, and actions. We can better understand our goals and values by examining how history has influenced us. Let us now learn from our forebears.

CAPITALISM AND INDIVIDUALISM STEER BUSINESS PRACTICES

We continue to explore the business values of a new nation. In Chapter 4 we investigated the work values of earlier generations, and considered the writings of the Puritans and Benjamin Franklin. After the United States gained its independence, those values had a unique opportunity to be realized. The new nation provided an ideal testing ground for enterprising farmers, traders, prospectors, and entrepreneurs. Business and commerce grew very rapidly. We now examine that development and the values that provided the foundation for it.

The rapid growth of **American industry**, which was to make the United States the most productive nation in the world, began by the middle of the nineteenth century. In 1849 the United States had 6,000 miles of railroad, but by 1884 its **railroads** operated 202,000 miles of track, or 43 percent of the total mileage in the world. Leland Stanford, Mark Hopkins, Charles Crocker, and Collis Huntington formed the Central Pacific Railroad and met the Union Pacific in Utah in 1869 to build the first transcontinental railroad. Tracks were laid and tunnels bored through the Sierra Nevada Mountains, and probably 1,500 people died in the building. The four bent laws, broke rivals, and bribed governments; each was driven by money and became enormously wealthy.[1] John D. Rockefeller's Standard Oil Company increased production of its refineries during the 1870s from 500 to 2,000 barrels a day, and thus reduced the cost of its principal product, kerosene, from 5 to 2.5 cents per gallon. Standard Oil soon controlled 90 percent of the petroleum market. By 1894 the value of the output of American industry equaled that of the combined output of the United Kingdom, France, and Germany.

In 1914 Henry Ford introduced the assembly line; it reduced the time to build an **automobile** from 12 hours to 1.5 hours. Ford manufactured 1,000 autos a day from his assembly plant in Detroit. This enabled Ford "to sell his cars at far lower prices than any competitor, to pay the highest wages in the industry, and to acquire within a decade an enormous personal fortune."[2] Growth continued to accelerate, until soon the United States was producing more than a third of the industrial goods of the world.

---

[1] Richard Rayner, *The Associates: Four Capitalists Who Created California* (New York: W. W. Norton/Atlas, 2007).
[2] Alfred D. Chandler, Jr., Franco Amatori, and Takashi Hikino, *Big Business and the Wealth of Nations* (Cambridge: Cambridge University Press, 1997), p. 77.

Mining in the mountains of the far West provides a paradigm of the strengths and weaknesses of the American character: energetic, flexible, and **enterprising**, but also **self-centered** and with little concern for long-term consequences. Tales of silver, gold, and other minerals in the mountains thrilled people across the continent. Mining called for strong, resourceful workers. Hundreds of thousands took the challenge, risking their lives, their fortunes, and often their families to search for the ore. Vast amounts of capital and superhuman energies were expended. The "get rich quick" spirit of these prospectors was a prelude to the values of the entrepreneurs who came later. Virginia City, Nevada, was built over the Comstock Lode of silver ore. What had been bare desert and mountains in 1860 became within five years one of the most rapidly growing and thriving cities in the western United States. The energies and genius of thousands sank dozens of shafts into the rock, supported them with timbers, built flumes—and an entire city. Between 1859 and 1880, more than $306 million worth of silver was taken from the mountains. The magnitude of the effort and the accomplishment can be gathered from this description:

> In the winter of 1866 the towns and mills along the Comstock Lode were using two hundred thousand cords of wood for fuel, while the time soon came when eighty million feet of lumber a year went down into the chambers and drifts. Since the mountains were naked rock, flumes (channels for carrying water) had to be built from the forested slopes of the Sierras, and by 1880, there were ten of them with an aggregate length of eighty miles.[3]

Adolph Sutro owned a quartz mill on the opposite side of the mountains on the Carlson River, and he envisioned an easier way to get the ore out of the mountains. He planned a three-mile-long tunnel that would extend through the mountain from the river valley and intersect the Comstock mines 1,600 feet below the surface. The tunnel would drain dozens of mines to that level and also enable the ore to be taken out through the tunnel for processing where fuel and water were plentiful. By 1866, Sutro had obtained contracts from 23 of the largest mining companies to use the tunnel when it was completed:

> After incessant effort, in which any man of less marvelous pluck and energy would have failed, he raised sufficient capital to begin the project. In 1869 he broke ground for the tunnel and set a corps of drillers upon the task that was to occupy them for eight weary years.[4]

Sutro finished his tunnel and put it in use in 1877. But within three years, the boom collapsed. The value of the silver mining stock sank from a high of $393 million in 1875 to less than $7 million in 1880. People began to leave Virginia City, and today

---

[3] Allan Nevins, *The Emergence of Modern America*, vol. 8 (New York: Macmillan, 1927), pp. 136–137. See also Daniel T. Rodgers, *The Work Ethic in Industrial America, 1850–1920* (Chicago: University of Chicago Press, 1978).
[4] Nevins, *op. cit.*, p. 137.

it is a ghost town; only remnants of roads, homes, saloons, and an opera house are left to remind us of its short life.

Virginia City illustrates how the talents and wealth of a people can be quickly channeled to accomplish **enormous tasks**; it also shows how such accomplishments are often **short-lived** and are not designed to provide stability. This sort of activity attracts energetic and fast-moving entrepreneurs; it does not appeal to people who desire family and neighborhood relationships. Virginia City illustrates both the strengths and the weaknesses of the American entrepreneurial spirit. The gold rush a decade earlier in California left a more permanent mark, because the fortune seekers did not leave when the gold ran out. The prospectors and miners converged from all parts of the country, disrupting families and communities. Before their coming, California had a unique style. "To these California imperatives of simple, gracious, and abundant living, Americans had come in disrespect and violence." Exploitation of the land kept people moving, and left problems in their wake:

> Leaving the mountains of the Mother Lode gashed and scarred like a deserted battlefield, Californians sought easy strikes elsewhere. Most noticeably in the areas of hydraulic mining, logging, the destruction of wildlife, and the depletion of the soil Americans continued to rifle California all through the nineteenth century.
>
> The state remained, after all, a land of adventuring strangers, a land characterized by an essential selfishness and an underlying instability, a fixation upon the quick acquisition of wealth, impatience with the more subtle premises of human happiness. These were American traits, to be sure, but the Gold Rush intensified and consolidated them as part of a regional experience.[5]

Throughout these years of rapid economic change, the role of entrepreneurs was central. Their brains, ingenuity, and willingness to risk gave us most of our economic success and growth. At the same time, their narrow desire for short-term gain caused many failures and much personal anguish. Given this background, let us return to the leaders of thought who have had a profound influence on American business values.

American Individualism and Ralph Waldo Emerson

To this day, the American businessperson is characterized as an individualist. One articulate and influential champion of freedom and the importance of the individual was Ralph Waldo Emerson (1803–1882). Coming soon after the French Enlightenment and Rousseau, Emerson is the best-known American proponent of **individualism**. He sees human nature as having natural resources within itself. Societal structures and supports tend only to limit the immense potential of the individual. Given freedom, individuals can act, grow, and benefit themselves and

---

[5] Kevin Starr, *Americans and the California Dream* (New York: Oxford University Press, 1973), pp. 33, 63–66. Starr is the California State Librarian Emeritus.

others. But they require an absence of restraints imposed by people, cultures, and governments. Emerson's friend Henry David Thoreau acted on this ideology and built a hut outside Boston at Walden Pond, where he lived for two years while he reflected and wrote alone in the unimpeded, open atmosphere of trees, grass, and the lake.

In Emerson's book of essays *The Conduct of Life*, there is one entitled "Wealth."[6] Here Emerson applied his philosophy of individualism to economics and the marketplace. A person should contribute and not just receive. If an individual follows his or her own nature, he or she will not only become a producer but will also become wealthy in the process. Individuals contribute little if they only pay their debts and do not add to the wealth available. Meeting only one's own needs is expensive; it is better to be rich and thus be able to meet one's needs and add to wealth as well. And doing both builds upon one's own natural inclinations. Emerson insisted that getting rich is something any person can achieve given a little ingenuity. It depends on factors the person has totally under his or her own control:

> Wealth is in applications of mind to nature, and the art of getting rich consists not in industry, much less in saving, but in a better order, in timeliness, in being at the right spot. One man has stronger arms, or longer legs; another sees by the course of streams, and growth of markets, where land will be wanted, makes a clearing to the river, goes to sleep, and wakes up rich.[7]

Emerson's heroes were the independent Anglo-Saxons. They are a strong race who, by means of their personal independence, became the merchants of the world. They do not look to government "for bread and games." They do not look to clans, relatives, friends, or aristocracy to take care of them or to help them get ahead; they rely on their own initiative and abilities. Emerson's optimistic view of the potential of the free and strong individual released from the fetters of government and custom remains an important support of American values. While many values of the Protestant Ethic have changed, Emerson's view of the individual remains.

Children and Immigrants in Nineteenth Century U.S. Factories

Before 1840, factory workers in the United States labored 12–14 hours a day, six or seven days a week. An 84-hour workweek was common. By 1860, the average workday dropped to 10.6 hours a day, six days a week, but the 12–14 hour workday was still typical in many industries, including the textile mills of New England.[8]

In 1890, steel workers labored 12 hours a day, seven days a week; most made $1.25 a day. Those wages went for rent, and there was little left to buy even food.

---

[6] Ralph W. Emerson, *The Conduct of Life and Other Essays* (London: Dent, 1908), pp. 190–213.
[7] *Ibid.*, p. 192.
[8] Gary M. Walton and Ross Robertson, *History of the American Economy* (New York: Harcourt Brace Jovanovich, 1983), pp. 280, 437.

Even if a steel worker worked 12 hours a day every day of the year, it was still not sufficient to support a family.[9] Therefore, many of these poor immigrants were single, and others left their families in Europe.

When the **immigrants** came, they knew that the work would be **difficult and dangerous**. They were at the bottom of the status ladder and therefore had to accept the hardest and most poorly paid work. A Hungarian churchman examined the conditions in Pittsburgh steel mills and said, "Wherever the heat is most insupportable, the flames most scorching, the smoke and soot most choking, there we are certain to find compatriots bent and wasted with toil."[10]

Many young children also worked under some of these same conditions. In 1910 two million boys and girls, one-fifth of all American children 10–15 years old, worked 10–14 hours a day. In Syracuse, New York, factories would not hire children unless they were at least eight years old.[11] Those who worked were the children of the immigrants and the poor, because their families needed the additional income. **Child labor** was a bargain for employers, because children's wages were less than those for adults. Further underscoring contemporary values and the acceptance of such factory conditions is the fact that before 1920 two laws passed by the U.S. Congress to restrict child labor were declared unconstitutional by the Supreme Court. Child labor still exists in the United States; more children illegally work in the United States than in any other developed country.[12]

Working conditions were often miserable and dangerous. Textile workers suffered brown lung disease, quarry workers breathed stone dust, coal miners suffered black lung disease and many deaths due to cave-ins, and other workers inhaled toxic chemical fumes. The annual toll of those killed or injured in industry was almost one million in 1900.

At U.S. Steel's South Works in the Pittsburgh area in 1910, "almost one-quarter of the recent immigrants in the works each year—3,273 in five years—were injured or killed."[13] Working on the railroads was also very dangerous. In 1890, 2,451 railroad workers were killed, and this does not include many more civilians killed by trains. In the United States, some 30,000 workers were killed and 500,000 injured each year.[14]

Companies often provided housing for their workers. Steel companies built good housing for managers and what the companies called "shanties" for the unskilled. Four men slept, ate, and washed in a 10-by-14-foot shanty. The annual rent charged was more than twice the cost of building the pine board shanty.[15] Steel owners and executives had ready responses to criticisms: The immigrants were eager for work, they made much

---

[9] David Brody, *Steelworkers in America: The Nonunion Era* (Cambridge, MA: Harvard University Press, 1980), p. 98.
[10] *Ibid.*, p. 99.
[11] Walton and Robertson, *op. cit.*, p. 439.
[12] Marvin J. Levine, *Children for Hire: The Perils of Child Labor in the United States* (Westport, CT: Praeger, 2003).
[13] Brody, *op. cit.*, p. 101.
[14] Otto L. Bettmann, *The Good Old Days: They Were Terrible!* (New York: Random House, 1974), p. 70. See also Harold Evans, "The Grim Face of Labor: America's Working Stiffs Included Men, Women and Children," *U.S. News and World Report*, October 12, 1998, p. 32.
[15] Brody, *op. cit.*, p. 110.

more than they would have made in Europe, and their living conditions were poor because they used their salaries on beer and whiskey.

Given such low wages and poor treatment, it is not surprising that in the United States during this period the rich became richer and the poor became poorer. One percent of the population owned as much as the remaining 99 percent combined.[16]

Churches and Their Influence

Churches and preachers have had a great influence on American society. Protestant churchmen in the decades prior to the American Revolution preached the welfare of the community, not merely the benefit of the individual. The supportive church and town influenced this early American religious respect for community.[17] But support for community changed in the following decades as Americans moved to the cities.

Churches have two roles to play in society: (1) to help people worship God and (2) to help them understand and deal with the moral issues of their everyday lives. These roles sometimes are in conflict. The second role involves sensitizing people to the moral problems that exist. Before 1920 this required calling attention to the abuses indicated above: child labor, dangerous working conditions, and working hours so long that decent family life was impossible. But as a church and its leaders become respected in society, they are easily lulled into blindness concerning the evils of the society that gives them support and status; they are thus deterred from acting as prophets who prod the conscience of managers.

A church has a responsibility to help all. Therefore most churches make special attempts to help the poor, because often the poor have desperate needs and lack a voice in society. On the other hand, a church can be so influenced by its affluent members that it becomes part of "The Establishment," and its leaders oppose change, social justice, and what they called "rabble rousers." The leaders and members of the church risk losing too much if change occurs. We can learn a lesson for today by examining the actions of some of the respected churches in the early United States.

The dominant American Protestant churches in the nineteenth century, while preaching charity and concern for the poor, nevertheless defended the economic system that the Protestant Ethic had produced. In this period, churches and schools had more influence over American life and morals than they do today. The prestigious private colleges in the Eastern United States taught the values of private property, free trade, and individualism. These religiously oriented schools (both Harvard and Yale then were still Protestant) generally taught conservative economic and business values along with moral philosophy.

Many clergy believed God had clearly established economic laws, so it would be foolish and dangerous to challenge them. Francis Wayland, president of Brown University and author of the most popular economics text then used, intertwined economics and theology in stating his basic position: "God has made labor necessary

---

[16] Donald T. Phillips, *Lincoln on Leadership: Executive Strategies for Tough Times* (New York: Warner Books, 1992).
[17] Barry Alan Shain, *The Myth of American Individualism: The Protestant Origins of American Political Thought* (Princeton, NJ: Princeton University Press, 1994).

to our well being." We must work both because idleness brings punishment and because work brings great riches; these are two essential, powerful, and immutable motives for work.[18] Wayland concluded from this simple principle that all property should be private and held by individuals. Charity should not be given except to those who absolutely cannot work, and the government should not impose tariffs or quotas or otherwise interfere.

In the last 25 years of the nineteenth century, the major Protestant churches went through an agonizing reexamination. Up to this time, the churches had wholeheartedly accepted Adam Smith's economics and canonized it as part of the "divine plan." They defended private property, business, the need to work, and wealth. Then two severe, bloody **labor disturbances** occurred that forced the churches to reconsider their traditional survival-of-the-fittest theories.

The first of these conflicts followed a severe economic depression in 1877. Wages of train workers were cut by 10 percent, and they protested. They picketed and halted trains. Army troops were called to defend railroad property, and they fought desperate mobs of workers. In the confusion, scores of workers were shot. The churches generally supported the Establishment and self-righteously preached to the workers on the divine wisdom of the American economy. Hear the newspaper *Christian Union*:

> If the trainmen knew a little more of political economy they would not fall so easy a prey to men who never earn a dollar of wages by good solid work. What a sorry set of ignoramuses they must be who imagine that they are fighting for the rights of labor in combining together to prevent other men from working for low wages because, forsooth, they are discontented with them.[19]

The religious press, reflecting the attitudes of its patrons, took a hard line against what it saw as anarchy, riots, and support of weak and lazy men.

A decade later another serious confrontation occurred. On the occasion of a labor meeting at the Haymarket in Chicago, the police shot several in a group of strikers. A few days later, a bomb was thrown at the police. As is often the case in such situations, facts and circumstances were forgotten as near hysteria swept the press. The journal *Protestant Independent* was typical: "A mob should be crushed by knocking down or shooting down the men engaged in it; and the more promptly this is done the better."[20] Only when these strikingly un-Christian outbursts had ended did the clergy have the opportunity to reflect on what had happened and how they themselves had reacted. It then became clear how uncompassionate, biased, and even violent had been their attitude—hardly what one would expect of churchmen. During this period, the clergy had been anxious to accommodate their churches' position to the new industrial

---

[18] Henry F. May, *Protestant Churches and Industrial America* (New York: Harper & Row, 1949), p. 15.
[19] *Ibid.*, p. 93.
[20] *Ibid.*, p. 101; for a detailed account of the Haymarket event, see James Green, *Death in the Haymarket: A Story of Chicago, the First Labor Movement and the Bombing That Divided Gilded Age America* (New York: Paneheon Books, 2006).

movements. They changed no creeds or confessions but "progressively identified [themselves] with competitive individualism at the expense of community."[21] From the rubble of these mistakes and later reflection came the impetus toward a new social consciousness, specifically in the form of the Social Gospel.

Praise of Wealth

Defense of free enterprise and praise of acquisitiveness and riches were not limited to the predominant Congregational and Presbyterian churches. The Baptist preacher Russell Conwell traveled the country giving his famous speech "Acres of Diamonds." He delivered it more than 5,000 times around the turn of the century to enraptured audiences eager to hear that to gather wealth was God's will.

Conwell's speech tells of a man who goes out to seek wealth; in the meantime his successor on the farm finds diamonds in the yard he had left behind. His message: Any man has it within his grasp to make himself wealthy if he is willing to work at it:

> I say that you ought to get rich, and it is your duty to get rich. How many of my pious brethren say to me, "Do you, a Christian minister, spend your time going up and down the country advising young people to get rich, to get money?" "Yes of course I do." They say, "Isn't that awful. Why don't you preach the gospel instead of preaching about man's making money?" Because to make money honestly is to preach the gospel. That is the reason. The men who get rich may be the most honest men you will find in the community.[22]

Conwell here cites what to him were the happy confluence of deeply felt religious convictions and the life of the marketplace. Because of the traditional religious values of poverty and humility, riches often brought qualms of conscience to believers. Conwell tried to wed faith and fortune: There can be no better demonstration of faith in God than to use one's abilities to their fullest, to be a success, and to accumulate the goods of the earth (to be used responsibly, of course). Conwell himself made a fortune from his lectures and, following his own advice on investment, used the money to found Temple University. Conwell is much like preachers in contemporary mega churches who gain thousands of followers by lecturing that Jesus wants them to be successful financially. Critics point out that the message is eagerly received, but that it disregards the essential Christian elements of human suffering, sin, death, redemption, and resurrection.

Andrew Carnegie and John D. Rockefeller

Praise of wealth also came from those who were wealthy. A handful of industrialists—called "the robber barons"—had an immense, enduring influence on America and American industry around the turn of the century. Among them, the immigrant

---

[21] Martin Marty, *Righteous Empire: The Protestant Experience in America* (New York: Dial, 1970), p. 110.
[22] Russell Conwell, *Acres of Diamonds* (New York: Harper, 1915), p. 18. A more carefully made argument is presented by Benjamin M. Friedman, *The Moral Consequences of Economic Growth* (New York: Knopf, 2005).

Scot Andrew Carnegie (1835–1919) enjoyed his role as industrial and "moral" leader. Financier J. P. Morgan helped Carnegie put together U.S. Steel. Carnegie accumulated immense wealth in the process and loved to tell all who would listen why he deserved it. He established 2,509 libraries in cities and towns, most in the United States, each proudly bearing the Carnegie name.

Carnegie amassed a huge personal fortune, even though he was well aware that his own steelworkers were very poorly paid. He maintained that God gave him his wealth. Carnegie made no apology for the inequality and in fact defended it as the survival of the fittest. The rich man's money would do no good if it were paid to the workers:

> Much of this sum, if distributed in small quantities among the people, would have been wasted in the indulgence of appetite, some of it in excess, and it may be doubted whether even the part put to the best use, that of adding to the comforts of the home, would have yielded results for the race at all comparable.[23]

According to Carnegie, it is only the wealthy who are able to endow libraries and universities and who are equipped to look after the long-run good of society. The money is much better spent when the wealthy accumulate it in large amounts so that they can use it to accomplish great things.

For this reason, Carnegie preached that the wealthy person should "set an example of modest, unostentatious living, shunning display or extravagance." He should hold his money in trust for society and be bound by duty to administer it in the way that, in his judgment, is best calculated to produce the most beneficial results for the community. He wrote that the accumulation of great fortunes is good for society, as is the concentration of business in the hands of a few. He believed that this concentration of wealth enables the most able to use the funds for the best interest of society. He also campaigned for disarmament and world peace, and founded the Carnegie Endowment for International Peace, which supports cooperation among nations, redistribution of income, and wealth given to support the needs of society. During his lifetime, Carnegie gave away $350 million or $8 billion in today's dollars.[24]

Carnegie defended his fortune and his right to have it and dispose of it as he saw fit. Thus he was able to overlook the injustices he and his company supported. Of course, he was not entirely objective in his examination of the socioeconomic system; he profited much from it.

During the same period, John D. Rockefeller formed the Standard Oil Company. To build his firm, he sold his product below cost until competitors were forced out of business; then, as the sole seller, he doubled his prices. He also received rebates and kickbacks from the railroads on his large shipments. The Standard Oil Company monopoly was later broken up by new U.S. antitrust legislation.

---

[23] Andrew Carnegie, "Wealth," in *Democracy and the Gospel of Wealth*, ed. Gail Kennedy (Boston: D. C. Heath, 1949), p. 6.

[24] David Nasaw, *Andrew Carnegie* (New York: The Penguin Press, 2006); also Maurey Klein, *The Change Makers: From Carnegie to Gates, How the Great Entrepreneurs Transformed Ideas into Industries* (New York: Henry Holt and Company, 2003).

On the other hand, during his lifetime Rockefeller gave away $530 million, most of it to medical research. As a devout Baptist, Rockefeller believed that God gave him his money. In a "complex amalgam of godliness and greed, passion and fiendish cunning," he lived by the Protestant Ethic.[25] During the Microsoft antitrust trial, many compared the monopoly, business activities, resulting wealth, and civic mindedness of Bill Gates with that of Rockefeller. Both Carnegie and Rockefeller were convinced that a rich man should wisely contribute to society most of their wealth, and they both did so before they died. Carnegie favored a steep inheritance tax, if it was necessary to force the rich to give their money to society rather than leave it to pampered heirs.

Manufacturing and Scientific Management

The growth of manufacturing provided a new and much faster means of attaining economic growth and personal wealth. Moreover, as productivity increased, higher wages could be paid and greater profits obtained for the owner at the same time. This was a major departure from past eras, when fortunes were made by trade, transport, lending, wars, and plunder. Thus, in the past, wealth had been considered more a fixed quantity: What one person gained, another lost. The advent of manufacturing demonstrated that the economy was not a zero-sum game—it was possible for each party in the exchange to benefit financially. Increases in productivity allowed this to take place.

Frederick W. Taylor (1865–1915), founder of scientific management, focused on better methods in manufacturing as a way to increase **productivity**. Productivity is measured as the amount of a product that is produced per input of resource—generally per worker. Mechanization and careful planning enabled workers to produce more than they could without planning. Taylor's insight was that worker and management experience plus intuitive judgment are not enough. To achieve greater productivity, which benefits all, the work setting and the motions of the job itself ought to be carefully planned to utilize the most efficient tools, techniques, and methods.

As factory work became more complex, Taylor gained greater support for his view. No single person, worker, or supervisor could be aware of all the mechanical, psychological, and technological factors involved in planning even one job. Superior efficiency required meticulous planning by a team that possessed various competencies. Intuition, experience, and seat-of-the-pants judgments would no longer do. Scientific management undermined Spencer's notions of survival of the fittest. Taylor pointed out that allowing the "best person" to surface naturally was inefficient. In this new complex world, few people had the ability to achieve maximum productivity by themselves. Greater efficiency and productivity demanded the intervention of planners.[26]

---

[25] Ron Chernow, *Titan: The Life of John D. Rockefeller, Sr.* (New York: Random House, 1998). See also Chernow's "Philanthropy the Smart Way: Today's Rich Can Learn from the Robber Barons," *The New York Times*, September 27, 1999, p. 23.
[26] Frederick Winslow Taylor, *Scientific Management* (New York: Harper & Brothers, 1947), pp. 36, 98, 99; see also Daniel Nelson, *Frederick W. Taylor and the Rise of Scientific Management* (Madison: University of Wisconsin Press, 1980).

Taylor favored higher wages and shorter hours for workers, but he saw no need for unions. If scientific management is implemented and the most efficient means of production is achieved, there will be no grounds for petty quarrels and grievances. Policies and procedures will be set by scientific inquiry into what objectively is most efficient. And that which is most efficient will benefit both workers and managers, because both will share the increased profits that result from greater productivity. In Taylor's scheme, the personal exercise of authority would be eliminated. Managers would be subject to the same policies, rules, and methods as the workers themselves.

Taylor followed the traditional managerial ideology that workers pursued their own self-interest and tried to maximize their own return. But he challenged the notion that each person worked out this struggle in isolation, apart from and competing with other human beings. In an industrial organization, greater productivity can be achieved only when each worker, alongside management, cooperates to find the best means of production. Taylor pointed out how the returns to all were diminished if a single worker is not working at his or her most efficient job and pace. Taylor set out to help both worker and manager achieve maximum efficiency, which can be done only in cooperation. Up to this time, a lazy man or woman had been penalized. Now Taylor proposed to reward workers by enabling them to work to their greatest capacity and receive greater financial return.

Scientific management was not greeted happily by either workers or managers, because it deprived each of some freedom and judgment. Scientific management chronicled the shift from craft to industrial work. In the long run, Taylor's methodology, and perhaps even more his ideology, has had an immense impact on industrial life.[27] In a sharp break from earlier American individualism, Taylor demonstrated that productivity and the system, in this case manufacturing, were more important than the lone individual. The emerging corporation itself bore additional testimony to the new importance of expertise, planning, and cooperation. In subsequent decades, under pressure from labor unions, the business firm provided more benefits to individuals: vacations, retirement, and medical care. Soon most people worked together in larger groups to achieve greater productivity, and this still characterizes American business.

Biased Management

The ideals and values we have discussed in this chapter are those of the business*man*. Historically, business, commerce, and trade were largely "for men only." Women did not even obtain the right to vote in the United States until the twentieth century. Half of the potential technical and managerial talent was lost, although women currently have a better chance of being promoted.[28]

In addition, a glance at any firm's listing of its employees by rank, race, and ethnic group spotlights the results of centuries of racial prejudice. There are few blacks, Hispanics, or women in top management. Moreover, it has been only within

---

[27] See Martha Banta, *Taylored Lives: Narrative Productions in the Age of Taylor, Veblen, and Ford* (Chicago: University of Chicago Press, 1993).

[28] Russell I. Kent and Sherry E. Moss, "Effects of Sex and Gender Role on Leader Emergence," *Academy of Management Journal,* 37, no. 5 (1994): 1335–1346.

the past two generations that religious prejudice in the executive suites of the largest corporations has broken down; the WASP (White Anglo-Saxon Protestant) clique has cracked. Blacks, Jews, Catholics, and women are now climbing the managerial ladder into the executive suites.

Americans as Seen from Abroad

An outsider visiting a culture notices elements of that culture to which natives are often blind, as we noted earlier with Alexis de Tocqueville. Tocqueville had superb insights about America. Other visitors also expressed important insights.

Another French observer, the Jesuit paleontologist **Pierre Teilhard de Chardin** (1881–1955), lived and worked in the United States more than a century later and noted many of the same qualities as did Tocqueville. Teilhard had a sympathetic view of the American character, in spite of his own personal inclination for reflection and asceticism. Working alongside Americans while on an expedition in the Gobi desert, Teilhard said,

> People here are inclined to treat the Americans as a joke, but the more I see of them the more I admire their ability to work and get things done and the kinder and more approachable I find them. In my own branch of science it's the Americans who are showing us how we must set to work on the earth if we are to read its secret and make ourselves its masters.[29]

Granting the ability of Americans to **get a job done**, their orientation to action is also the source of criticism. Many foreign observers see Americans as individualistic, shallow, and materialistic—more wedded to things than to people, more inclined to do than to reflect. Let us examine some comments on Americans made by other foreign observers.

Albert Einstein (1879–1955), the brilliant mathematician and physicist, who came to live in the United States in the 1920s, admired the country. But in a caution that sounds contemporary, he said,

> The cult of individuals is always, in my view, unjustified. To be sure, nature distributes her gifts unevenly among her children . . . It strikes me as unfair, and even in bad taste, to select a few for boundless admiration, attributing superhuman powers of mind and character to them. This has been my fate, and the contrast between the popular estimate of my powers and achievements and the reality is simply grotesque.[30]

Is today's admiration of sports, entertainment, and business celebrities, such as Tiger Woods and Donald Trump, "grotesque"?

---

[29] Pierre Teilhard de Chardin, *Letters from a Traveler*, trans. Rene Hague et al. (New York: Harper & Row, 1962), p. 106.
[30] Albert Einstein, *Ideas and Opinions*, ed. Carl Seelig (New York: Modern Library, 1994), p. 4.

Israeli writer **Amos Oz** adds that the American individualistic view is spreading throughout the world:

> America has promoted and spread all over the world the simple ideal of **individual happiness**. Various religions, civilizations and ideologies throughout history regarded happiness as a collective rather than an individual experience. Almost all of them are losing ground to that triumphant American vision of private happiness. Hundreds of millions of people, from Tokyo to St. Petersburg, from Cairo to Buenos Aires, dream of being happy in the American way. But is the new global America, this international happiness-oriented village, a happy place? The popular American dream of living happily ever after, while dazzling the world, reminds me of the American landscape itself: plentiful, elusive, and forlorn.[31]

Foreign businesspeople are more positive about American values. Hear Akio Morita, the founder and former chairperson of Sony Corporation of Japan,

> What I like about the Americans is their **frankness**, their openness. In America, I feel I can openly express whatever opinion I have, and it is welcomed, even if it conflicts with other opinions. In Japan, even among friends we can't have a difference of opinion—disagreement destroys friendship. But in America, a difference of opinion can make friends, bring people closer together. That open-mindedness and frontier spirit is why I am so comfortable in the US.[32]

Foreign social commentators have noted the strengths and weaknesses of the American character. They underscore the openness, flexibility, pragmatism, and respect for individuals. But they also see parochialism, lack of interest in other languages and cultures, materialism, and self-centeredness. It is essential that each of us be aware of our own national character lest we uncritically be victims of our own biases. Such awareness is even more important if one attempts to influence one's own values and the values of one's nation. We must be more conscious of our values if we are to live and compete in the global marketplace.

Historical events and commentators provide insight into one's origins and character. Examining these foundation values also helps us to get a better grasp of current business values. In the past, the geography of the United States and the attitudes and values of the people who settled there gave the country a unique world position. It had rich and abundant farmland, protected east and west borders, a slowly retreating frontier, and a people who work by the Puritan ethic. The geography and history of a land and the personality of its people contribute to values that are shared by all.

---

[31] Quoted in "To See Ourselves as Others See Us," *Time,* June 16, 1986, pp. 52–53. Quoted by permission.
[32] Quoted in "To See Ourselves."

IDEOLOGY AND VALUES

An **ideology** embraces a person's values and life goals. An ideology is a coherent, systematic, and moving statement of basic values and purpose. It is a **constellation of values** generally held by a group, and members of the group tend to support one another in that ideology. An ideology answers questions such as: What is most important to us? Why are we doing this? How can I explain my life and my society to myself and to others? A corporate or group mission statement attempts to articulate an ideology, as does a personal mission statement (for additional terms, see Figure 1.1).

Without an explicit ideology, a group or nation is left without clearly understood purposes, and hence without a consensus or the drive that comes from purpose. When an ideology is explicit, it can be examined, challenged, and altered as conditions change and new needs arise. It is then open for all to accept or reject as they see fit. When an ideology is not explicit, some then claim that there is no ideology; but this is hardly true. The ideology exists; it is simply implicit, unspoken, and hence unexamined. Having only an implicit ideology destabilizes a group, because difficult questions that arise can cause confusion and chaos.

Ideologies possess certain common features. They are **selective** in the issues they treat and in the supporting evidence and arguments they use. Ideologies are straightforward and uncomplicated, even when the issues are complex. Their content is limited to what is publicly acceptable. Finally, although ideologies are answers to questions and hence address the intellect, they nevertheless do so in a manner that also engages the emotions. They can inspire and **motivate** men and women to cooperate and even undergo great hardship for the sake of a compelling goal.

The positive effect of an ideology is that it gives people direction, coherence, norms, and motivation. It can bring clarity and assurance to the mind and hence vigor and enthusiasm to life and work. These are advantages, especially to people troubled by doubts, inadequate leadership, and little confidence in institutions, as is often the case in contemporary societies. An ideology offers a group meaning, direction, and drive. Nations and peoples have left their mark on history, whether for good or ill, to the extent to which they possessed a comprehensive and compelling ideology—for example, ancient Rome (Pax Romana), Victorian England (Mother England), and Nazi Germany (master race). Currently the ideologies of Islamic and other fundamentalists provide motivation, and those groups are thus having a strong impact on us.

Most of the important things we do stem from an often implicit ideology, from raising children to going to work, from conducting foreign policy to meeting neighbors. Groups within a society, such as the Rotary Club, possess an ideology. Generally the more embracing a group, movement, or state, the more comprehensive will be its ideology.

On the other hand, ideologies have some disadvantages. They can **rigidify**. They may lock persons and societies into classes, roles, and expectations. A doctrinaire ideology can cause fanaticism, intransigence, and uncompromising attitudes (e.g., white supremacist). It can impede progress and cause problems for those who oppose elements of the ideology, often those who are the more creative and talented. The group then may spend much effort defending its position instead of looking to the future.

Leaders of a nation should spell out national values and the ideology in which they are embedded, thus clarifying them for themselves and for their followers. Some maintain that contemporary Western nations have ideologies that are inadequate to current needs.[33] So demands for a development and clarification of one's ideology come from a variety of sources:

1. Many ask themselves, their peers, and their national leaders, what are we about? What are our goals? What is worth living for? Why?
2. Less government regulation requires that individuals and organizations internalize their ideology, goals, ethics, and self-discipline—which respect the public interest and the common good.
3. As population increases and we live closer together, what a person does often touches others. Many actions place burdens on *other* people, for example, building a Wal-Mart on farmland, driving a pollution-producing vehicle, or moving to a water-scarce area. As citizens, managers, or government officials, we need criteria for making such decisions that impinge upon others.
4. Disagreements over public policy, on, for example, taxes, climate change, pollution control, and support for the poor, force us to more basic questions on what kind of society we want, what our priorities are, and what tradeoffs we are willing to make. Special interest groups plead their causes, and care little for the common good. Under such conditions, people find it easier to repeat what they dislike than their more important positive goals and policies.

Each person is challenged to formulate her or his own constellation of values. Moreover, some **consensus** is necessary on these values in order to articulate consistent national policies. Without an agreed upon ideology, major policy decisions are made based upon unexamined and short-term criteria, popular myth, and the most vocal and powerful special interest groups. The agreed-upon values that touch on the issues of public life are an ideology. As such, they provide direction and verve. A firm's ideology provides a clearer psychological contract and potentially greater satisfaction in the work place for the individual.[34] And an awareness of the dangers of any ideology—for example, that it may mask privilege or that it may rigidify—should better enable us to avoid those dangers. There is a parallel need for a mission statement for business firms, and this will be discussed in Chapter 8.

Origin and Impact of Ideology

An ideology that is a rationalization of the existing order defends the status quo. An ideology based on ideals that aim to change that status quo into something that is viewed as better is called **utopian**.[35] To Americans, utopian has an idealistic,

---

[33] Sigurd N. Skirbekk, *Dysfunctional Culture: The Inadequacy of Cultural Liberalism as a Guide to Major Challenges of the 21st Century* (Lanham, MD: University Press of America, 2005).

[34] A critical examination of changing managerial ideologies over the past century is presented in Ernesto R. Gantman, *Capitalism, Social Privilege and Managerial Ideologies* (Burlington, VT: Ashgate, 2005); Jeffery A. Thompson and J. Stuart Bunderson, "Violations of Principle: Ideological Currency in the Psychological Contract," *Academy of Management Review*, 28, no. 4 (March 2003), pp. 571–586.

[35] For a critique of management ideologies, see Ernesto R.Gantman, *Capitalism, Social Privilege and Managerial Ideologies* (Hampshire, England: Ashgate, 2005).

pejorative connotation; here we use it as a descriptive term only. An ideology is utopian if it has ideals that transcend reality. Utopian ideologies provide the motivation for groups to act and challenge the existing order. Such utopian ideals "tend to shatter, either partially or wholly, the order of things prevailing at the time."[36]

Many utopias of today become the realities of tomorrow. The principles of freedom and democracy were utopian in the minds of Jefferson, Adams, Washington, and the others who founded the United States. Their notions of individual rights and representation were ideals that, when they were written into the *Declaration of Independence* and *The U.S. Constitution* and acted upon, shattered the status quo and the existing order, and caused a revolution. A utopian ideology of freedom for all races in the United States became the civil rights movement of the 1960s. Looking back over the history of rising aspirations, the ideology of freedom was a utopia. Freedom of thought and political freedom were unheard of in earlier societies.[37]

Any nation or group that wants to translate its ideals into reality must formulate an ideology that builds on the existing needs, values, and aspirations of the people. This utopian ideology may then catch the imagination and be the inspiration for change. The "New Deal" (unemployment insurance, minimum wage, etc.), woman's rights, and the environmental movement all possess an ideology; and each left a positive imprint on society. However, for every utopian ideology that becomes reality, there are many others that never get beyond the ideals. But they may cause discord in society, and their adherents may be considered fanatical.

There are dangers inherent in any ideology in addition to those pointed out earlier. The dangers of fanaticism and of being closed to facts: Nothing is more removed from actual events than the closed rational system. Under certain circumstances, nothing contains more irrational drive than a fully self-contained intellectual world view. Al-Qaeda, Nazis, skinheads, survivalists, and the rural militia are examples of groups that get their direction and enthusiasm from an ideology. The lack of real goals and ideology among the majority of people in a society encourages such fringe groups. Moreover, an absence of a consensus ideology results among the majority because many feel they are well adjusted to the current state of affairs, and thus have little incentive to reflect. These people are comfortable, and so they defend the status quo.

As long as people are content, they reflect little about situations in which they find themselves. They then tend to regard their current situation as "This is the way things ought to be." They then focus on practical "how to do it" concerns—the means of coping within existing structures. It is only in the face of challenges to the status quo that most people reflect. So the reflection and therefore the ideology of

---

[36] Karl Mannheim, *Ideology and Utopia*, trans. Louis Wirth and Edward Shils (New York: Harcourt, Brace & World, 1936), p. 192. Quoted by permission; for an overview of various world ideologies and religions, see Ninian Smart, *Worldviews: Crosscultural Explorations of Human Beliefs* (Englewood cliffs, NJ: Prentice Hall, 1995).

[37] *Ibid.*, p. 203. A presentation of empirical work on ideologies and some synthesis is chapter 2 of Harrison M. Trice and Janice M. Beyer, *The Cultures of Work Organizations* (Englewood Cliffs, NJ: Prentice Hall, 1993), pp. 35–76. However, Trice and Beyer neglected the empirical work on these subjects from the social issues in management literature.

the majority of people are generally not as profound or comprehensive as that of the challengers. Thus the "most recent antagonist dictates the tempo and the form of the battle."[38]

Self-Examination and Fundamentalism

A valuable by-product of challenge to goals and ideologies is that people are compelled to examine themselves. Making ideology explicit can clarify goals for individuals and society as a whole. A society that has a weak ideology, or one in which ideology seems unimportant, is generally stable, complacent, and at ease in its inherited laws, customs, and ideals. Karl Mannheim paints a sad, even desperate, picture of a society or a people without a utopian ideology:

> The disappearance of utopia brings about a static state of affairs in which man himself becomes no more than a thing. We would be faced then with the greatest paradox imaginable, namely, that man, who has achieved the highest degree of rational mastery of existence, left without any ideals, becomes a mere creature of impulses. Thus, after a long, tortuous, but heroic development, just at the highest stage of awareness, when history is ceasing to be blind fate, and is becoming more and more man's own creation, with the relinquishment of utopias, man would lose his will to shape history and therewith his ability to understand it.[39]

Mannheim presents an alienating prospect of a nation or group without ideals or motivating goals.

On the other hand, injustices can be perpetrated in the name of an irrational but compelling ideology. Any strong, moving ideology risks being gross, oversimplified, and unjust. Mannheim's own Germany a few years later was to undergo a tragic revolution in the name of "Aryan superiority" and the "master race." "Ethnic cleansers" in Iraq, Bosnia, Rwanda, and Sudan; neo-fascists; and armed citizen militias are confident, closed, paranoid, and often not well-educated people. Each of these ideologies fills a vacuum. In Middle Eastern countries, both Islamist and secular ideologies contend for supremacy. There is a dominant ideology in the United States, and in numerous other countries. Many hold the ideology that if each person or group uses their talents, intelligence, and resources to pursue their own long-term self-interest, it will work out best for all. However, this ideology does not address the needs of the group: local, national, and global.

In sum, without an ideology people lose direction and enthusiasm for life. People cease questioning themselves and their goals. So little new is accomplished and society does not improve. Some ideology is required for a healthy, stable society. Such an ideology has ideals that are as yet not attained and questions the status quo. Some **utopian** ideology is needed for a society to improve itself.

---

[38] Mannheim, *op. cit.*, pp. 219, 229, 231.
[39] *Ibid.*, pp. 262–263.

Power, Economic, and Ecological Values

We will now outline some basic human values, and then give attention to the values that characterize industrial societies. Focusing on business and the society it serves, veteran business scholar William C. Frederick has identified two basic values of business, **economizing values** and **power aggrandizing values**. He finds that these values are in tension with the third and more important value of society, which he calls **ecologizing values**. Ecologizing is preserving life and what is necessary for life, and it is thus more basic than the other two.

The efficient use of resources and the profit orientation stem from **economizing values**. **Power-aggrandizing** is also common in organizations; it operates when executives, managers, or others act to accumulate power and status. Power aggrandizing often frustrates efforts to economize. While economizing and power aggrandizing are found to varying extent in all business organizations, these values are not sufficient. Often ecologizing goals are undermined by those pursuing economizing and power aggrandizing values. Nevertheless, ecologizing values must be supported by business leaders if business is to aid, and not injure, people in the long term.[40]

Individualism and enlightened self-interest are dominant American values, but we will now outline additional specific values. These values are a part of our direct experience and hence our vocabulary; they affect work attitudes and entire life styles. Note that when predominant American values are listed how many of them support work attitudes and flow from individualism. Challenges to some of these values will be discussed in later chapters. Let us attempt to sketch these values.[41]

ACHIEVEMENT AND SUCCESS American culture has been and still is characterized by a stress on individual achievement. Sam Walton, who rose from poor boy to riches, is a legend. The American myth says that anyone who works hard enough can succeed in what he or she sets out to do. Moreover, when we meet a successful person, we are more impressed if he or she did not inherit wealth. William H. Gates, Sr. maintains that everyone should be able to earn their own money, and not inherit millions. Someone who was born poor and then worked hard to obtain what she has is a model. For some, it is embarrassing to be reminded that many recent U.S. presidents had the advantage of being born into a wealthy family.

Money and wealth are valued for the comforts they bring, but even more because they are symbols of success. Income is a signal to the owner and to others of one's personal worth. People want growing businesses, large homes, and luxury automobiles; these indicate success. The values of achievement and success ideal are most manifest in business. The drive to achieve is strong among business managers, and this will be discussed further in Chapter 7.

---

[40] William C. Frederick, *Values, Nature and Culture in the American Corporation* (New York: Oxford University Press, 1995).

[41] For a basic work to which the author is indebted, see the chapter "Values in American Life," in Robin M. Williams, Jr., *American Society: A Sociological Interpretation*, 3rd. ed. (New York: Knopf, 1970), pp. 438–504; see also Deirdre N. McCloskey, *The Bourgeois Virtues: Ethics for an Age of Commerce* (Chicago: University of Chicago Press, 2006).

ACTIVITY AND WORK A devotion to work on the part of both the unskilled worker and the executive has provided most of the wealth we now enjoy in the United States. Work is respected not only because it results in wealth but also for its own sake—"The devil finds idle hands." A person's self-respect is damaged when he or she is without work. Americans have traditionally not valued leisure for its own sake; it is valued if afterward a person can work better. Leisure has a purpose. Task orientation has become a compulsion for which Americans are frequently criticized.[42]

Workers know that even though they are ahead of schedule on their job, they had better appear busy. To call a person lazy is a serious criticism, especially because the amount of activity is something over which a person has control. Americans set out to shape and control their own lives and their world. They heed the injunction in Genesis 1:28 "to subdue the earth."

EFFICIENCY AND PRACTICALITY Closely related to the above cultural values are efficiency and practicality, which describe methods of working and acting. Tocqueville was much impressed by American ingenuity and ability to "get the job done." Americans are criticized for overemphasizing technique, and having less concern for goals. Critics say that engineers, accountants, and lawyers run American society. They know how to accomplish a specific task but rarely consider whether it is good to do so. A practical person, focusing on efficiency, assumes the basic worth of the task and of the economic and social order itself. A practical orientation requires only short-range adjustments to immediate situations.

Americans are known as people who can quickly and effectively find the best way to accomplish the task. They are active in the search for solutions and are rarely reflective or contemplative. To call an American a "dreamer" or "impractical" is a criticism. Characteristically, the best-known American philosophers, such as Dewey, Peirce, and William James, are not idealists but rather pragmatists.

EQUALITY American emphasis on equality is found in early ideals and the Constitution: All people are created equal. Citizens of the New World witnessed the eventual elimination of indentured servitude, imprisonment for debt, primogeniture, slavery, and property requirements for voting and public office. New immigrants were able to acquire land and a free public education, and minorities and women gained important civil rights.

Observers remark on the unusual informality, frankness, and lack of status consciousness in American interpersonal relations. Such open and direct relations can endure only if they are supported by the values of recognizing the human dignity of each person and equality among all. But the value of equality can run counter to that of freedom. When people pursue freedom in the rugged individualist climate in which the fittest survive, it results in a few becoming very rich and many remaining poor. Varying opportunities, talents, and effort will influence what a person can achieve.

---

[42] Edward C. Stewart and Milton J. Bennett, *American Cultural Patterns* (Yarmouth, ME: Intercultural Press, 1991), pp. 69–76.

Of all the government and corporate policies to bring about equality of opportunity in the workplace, none meets more opposition than "affirmative action." In order to compensate for past discrimination, those who support affirmative action hold that when an equally qualified minority or woman is a candidate for a position, the minority person or woman should be chosen. Ironically, both the reason for the practice (to compensate for discrimination) and the major objection to it (reverse discrimination) stem from the American ideal of equality of opportunity—and more basically, justice.[43]

EXTERNAL CONFORMITY Visitors find uniformity in speech, housing, dress, recreation, and attitudes in the United States. Observers point to a certain flatness, homogeneity, a lack of serious challenge, and dissent. Witness the same styles on young people, the desire to own a fashionable car, and books written on dressing for success. To individualists, these comments may seem unfair. Yet for many, American individualism consists largely in the rejection of government restrictions on personal and business activity.

FREEDOM Freedom is a primary value in American life. The individual has freedom to operate in the social Darwinian world in which the fittest survive. He or she may freely choose a marriage partner, friends, a home; change jobs; or move. Freedom is the bedrock value not only of our laissez-faire, free enterprise economic system but for most of the rest of American life. Freedom has been touted alike by the Founding Fathers and the members of the local neighborhood group. American individualism is possible only when freedom is the foundation value.

The ideal of freedom inspired the women's and civil rights movements. Cultural norms that bind persons to expected roles can be oppressive. Freedom urges the elimination of these one-sided and unjust bonds. American foreign policy is based on a defense of freedom, and freedom is the cornerstone of the business system—*free* enterprise. Freedom so permeates business ideology that it is discussed in almost every chapter of this book.

INDIVIDUALISM Closely related to freedom is individualism. This value is very strong in the history of the United States (Chapters 4 and 5), and we will see its influence in the remaining chapters. In the United States individuals are expected to look after themselves, and this has a higher priority than does concern for firm, extended family, neighbors, or other groups. In numerous empirical tests of people across many nations, the United States came out as the most individualistic people out of 53 countries in the world. Note how many of the values in this list, such as achievement and success, activity and work, efficiency and practicality, along with freedom, stem from individualism.[44]

---

[43] See Theodore V. Purcell and Gerald F. Cavanagh, *Blacks in the Industrial World: Issues for the Manager* (New York: Free Press, 1972), especially chap. 10, "Equal Versus Preferential Treatment," pp. 275–293.
[44] Geert Hofstede, *Culture's Consequences*, 2nd ed. (Thousand Oaks, CA: Sage, 2001), pp. 209–216.

MATERIAL COMFORT Americans place a high value on possessing a cell phone, a microwave, a spacious home in the suburbs, and a good meal. For each item, the underlying reason that they are highly valued may range from its being a symbol of achievement to its providing hedonistic gratification in its own right. Americans are more likely to spend their income on items that bring them comfort than to save for future needs.

The rise in popularity of computer games, television, rock concerts, professional sports, packaged tours, iTunes, and alcohol indicates peoples' greater passivity. There is less personal activity and more passive desire to be entertained. The drug culture and chemically induced pleasure take this tendency to its limit. Seeking pleasure follows a decline in the Puritan values of self-denial and asceticism.

MORAL ORIENTATION AND HUMANITARIANISM Although Americans are practical, they still see the world in moral terms. Conduct of others is constantly judged. Someone may be gauged as honest, trustworthy, "a winner," or lazy. Basic honesty and frankness are also part of our moral and humanitarian value orientation. The effectiveness of President Bill Clinton's presidency was limited by his personal moral failings and lack of honesty. Foreign commentators are often surprised at how open and straightforward they find Americans to be. American charities and social legislation are evidence of humanitarian attitudes. Social security, the minimum wage, and medical care for the poor are examples of our attempt to take care of the less fortunate. However, a moral person can become cynical if that person finds his or her moral code to be superficial, inapplicable, or too idealistic.

PATRIOTISM Every society claims its own people are of greater value. In tribal societies, the rules of respect for another's person and property do not apply to "outsiders." They apply only to the members of one's own tribe. Racism and sexism stem from these same parochial values. In the early United States, loyalties were more to local cities (Boston, Philadelphia) than to the states. In time of war, our loyalties go to the nation. Individual patriotism is often considered a moral issue.

RATIONALITY AND MEASUREMENT This value is probably best exemplified when approaching a problem. A person is expected to be objective, to gather the facts first, and not to be unduly influenced by bias or emotions. The scientific method, which embodies this approach, is the model for problem solving. If data for a solution can be measured, that makes the solution more objective and therefore acceptable. The value of science is demonstrated by its intelligent use in mastering our external environment. This orientation is compatible with a culture that does not value emotion, and looks on the world as open to eventual control.

OPTIMISM AND THE INEVITABILITY OF PROGRESS The combination of an immigrant people willing to work hard, the existence of the frontier, and what seemed like unlimited natural resources created an optimistic atmosphere in the United States during the nineteenth and much of the twentieth centuries. Anything could be accomplished if only one put one's mind to it. The result was a growth of jobs, products, and cities. We define progress largely in economic terms. As long as revenues and gross national product are increasing, progress is occurring.

	Increase or Decrease* 1945–2008
Achievement and success	+ −
Activity and work	−
Efficiency and practicality	+ −
Equality	+ −
External conformity	+ −
Freedom	+ −
Individualism	+
Material comfort	+
Moral orientation and humanitarianism	−
Patriotism	+ −
Rationality and measurement	+ −
Optimism and the inevitability of progress	−

+ = increase   − = decrease

+ − = indicates evidence of both.

FIGURE 5-1 **Changing Importance of Basic American Values**

*Adapted from Robin M. Williams, *American Society,* Geert Hofstede, *Culture's Consequences,* and Harrison Trice and Janice Beyer, *The Cultures of Work Organizations.*

Figure 5-1 charts the growth or decrease of each of the values we have discussed here. The problems that stem from global competition, low worker wages, wasteful use of finite resources, the necessity of reconsidering what we mean by "progress," and the impact these issues are having on business and business values will be discussed in the following chapters.

THE NECESSITY OF AN IDEOLOGY FOR BUSINESS

An ideology is essential for business, as it is for any social system. For people in a business firm, an ideology (or a mission statement) supports shared values, decisions, operations, and cooperation.[45] A mission statement aids global business, because it provides a useful foundation for solving problems:

1. Global operations require a firm to be clear about its goals and objectives, because managers operate in different cultures. Yet markets demand that a firm be flexible and able to quickly meet new needs. A mission provides goals but not a "book of rules."

---

[45] Janice M. Beyer, "Ideologies, Values, and Decision Making in Organizations," in *Handbook of Organizational Design,* eds. Paul C. Nystrom and William H. Starbuck, vol. 2 (New York: Oxford University Press, 1981), pp. 166–202; this provides an overview of social science research on values and ideologies in organizations. See also Richard M. Weiss and Lynn E. Miller, "The Concept of Ideology in Organizational Analysis," *The Academy of Management Review,* 12 (January 1987): 104–116.

2. Executives sometimes manage for short-term results and neglect long-term planning and needed investment for the firm. An ideology and mission statement help a manager to focus on the long-range goals of the firm.
3. Some have long questioned the legitimacy of the corporation. Because the corporation was originally chartered to serve a public purpose, is its present form legitimate? A clear and inspiring ideology can provide legitimacy.

Managers and scholars alike know the importance of organizational legitimacy.[46] Without a mission statement, it is difficult for businesspeople to move swiftly to make decisions, establish new policies, rectify abuses, and defend themselves against unfair attacks. Without an ideology, the corporation risks losing its privileged position in the United States, perhaps even its legitimacy. Adolph A. Berle expressed his classic position on the corporation,

> Whenever there is a question of power there is also a question of legitimacy. These instrumentalities of tremendous power have the slenderest claim of legitimacy. . . . Legitimacy, responsibility and accountability are essential to any power system if it is to endure.[47]

Notice how Berle links legitimacy, responsibility, and accountability. In responding to these basic issues, the corporation is on weak ground. Without reviewing the classic position of Berle and Means,[48] suffice it to say that the corporation is responsible to no one. Management often has little ownership, yet makes decisions. Shareholders generally have little input into major corporate decisions. Although various fund managers have recently exercised influence, it is often not in the best long-term interests of other stakeholders. The board of directors is elected from a slate chosen by the board itself.[49] If there are three directors to be elected, only three candidates are on the ballot. This is hardly a democratic process.

The role and responsibilities of the chief executive officer and the board of directors will be discussed in more detail in Chapter 8. As we will see, assessment of these issues requires understanding the purpose and responsibilities of the corporation, its very reason for existence—its ideology.

A mission for the individual firm and for business in general will enable executives and others to answer the questions of purpose and legitimacy. A firm's statement of purpose must be understandable to its many stakeholders and the firm must be held accountable to act according to it. If this does not occur, business risks losing its respected position in American society. The following chapters are intended to help build trust in the business firm.

---

[46] See Mark C. Suchman, "Managing Legitimacy: Strategic and Institutional Approaches," *Academy of Management Review,* 20 (July 1995): 571–610.

[47] Adolph A. Berle, *Economic Power and the Free Society* (New York: Fund for the Republic, 1958), p. 16.

[48] Adolf A. Berle and Gardiner C. Means, *The Modern Corporation and Private Property* (New York: Macmillan, 1932). David Cowan Bayne, a disciple of Berle, maintains that trust is the essential controlling element of corporate power. See his *Philosophy of Corporate Control* (Chicago: Loyola University Press, 1986).

[49] Harold S. Geneen, "Why Directors Can't Protect the Shareholders," *Fortune,* September 17, 1984, pp. 28–32.

Summary and Conclusions

The business values described in this chapter supported a period of expansion, rapid growth, and exploitation of land and resources. A new nation built its railroads, mines, banks, manufacturing firms, and cities. Businesspeople exploited the immigrant's eagerness for work and gave the poor an opportunity to advance.

Visitors to America note an honesty, frankness, and directness. They find a pragmatic people who do not spend time on unproductive theorizing. Freedom is a bedrock value that has been institutionalized in the U.S. Constitution, laws, and attitudes.

Several elements contributed to this new American business ideology:

1. The **frontier** provided opportunities for the immigrants who had come to the New World looking for new opportunities in farming, mining, or manufacturing, where potential rewards were immense.
2. The **Protestant Ethic** was carried to the New World by the Puritans and translated into a secular vision by people like Benjamin Franklin. These values—hard work, competition, regular habits, diligence, self-control, sobriety, saving, and planning ahead were preached in church, school, and town meeting.
3. Faith in **free enterprise** gave a person motivation and confidence. Free enterprise encouraged economic growth, and classical economists showed it to be intellectually and practically sound.
4. **Competition** became more explicit because of the theory of evolution, the principles of natural selection, and the survival of the fittest. Natural forces, operating without constraint, would identify the best people and the efficient firm.
5. The **role of government** was to protect the private property of its citizens and constrain business as little as possible. Thomas Jefferson is often quoted: "That government is best which governs least."

It is an irony of history that emphasis on the rugged individualist peaked during the latter half of the nineteenth century, just at the time the business scene was dominated by trusts and oligopolies. One or a few firms in each industry (e.g., U.S. Steel and Standard Oil) virtually controlled production, prices, and wages. It was difficult for even a talented individual to raise the capital necessary to compete. Since that time, it became apparent that this American business ideology, although it provides a motivation and a vision for the entrepreneur, is not an entirely accurate description of the marketplace. For the market is not totally free.

Given this historical background, we assessed the major values and ideology of Americans. Business and business values exist in society, yet there remains considerable suspicion of big business. An adequate response to this lack of trust is possible only by spelling out an ideology for business firms that better meets the expectations of businesspeople and citizens alike.

The goal of the traditional American business ideology is expansion, growth, and material reward for the individual. But the assumption that an individual always seeks more material goods leads to further questions. Is the prospect of more material goods sufficient to motivate the morally mature person to give so much of her physical and psychic energy to the business enterprise? Are there other personal values that must be tapped if we are to continue to be economically successful and a healthy society? To what extent will one's "calling" continue to be central in one's life? Is a goal of material growth necessary for a business creed for the future? If so, what sort of growth? These and other, similar questions will be addressed in the following chapters.

Discussion Questions

1. Citing historic events and attitudes, indicate what characteristic American values were illustrated during the silver-mining days at Virginia City, Nevada. How does the Sutro Tunnel demonstrate both the positive and negative values?
2. According to Ralph Waldo Emerson, how does one achieve success and wealth?
3. Describe the wages, hours, and working conditions of immigrants, the poor, and children before 1920.
4. Describe the attitudes of the dominant Protestant church leaders to the immigrant U.S. laborers in the late 1800s. Compare their attitudes with those of the factory owners during the same period.
5. What are the two conflicting responsibilities of churches? How does your church meet each of these responsibilities?
6. How did the Protestant Ethic aid the economic development of the New World? Compare the similarities and differences of the Protestant ethic and American individualism.
7. Outline the arguments of Conwell on the goodness of acquisitiveness and wealth.
8. What was Andrew Carnegie's position on wages? What was his justification for the wealth of the rich? Is this position held today? If so, by whom?
9. According to Carnegie, how should a wealthy person use one's wealth? For self? Or for society? Why? How were Rockefeller's business activities and attitudes the same or different?
10. Compare Carnegie's attitudes on work with those of Frederick W. Taylor (scientific management). What do they have in common? How do they differ?
11. What are the insights of Pierre Teilhard de Chardin, Albert Einstein, Amos Oz, and Akio Morita on the American character? Describe common themes that run through their observations.
12. Distinguish among values, goals, ideals, and ideologies.
13. What is an ideology? What does a utopian ideology do for a society? What sort of an ideology do people in the U.S. possess? Is it utopian?
14. What are the advantages to a society of having a well-articulated ideology? What happens to a society without such an ideology? What are the potential dangers in an ideology? How do values relate to an ideology?
15. Are the American values outlined in this chapter predominant for the average American? For people in your life? For you?
16. Do businesses today possess a consistent and motivating ideology? What are the advantages of having such a business ideology?
17. What is the ultimate purpose of a business? Is it to make a profit? Or is it to provide quality goods and/or service at a low price, while also providing jobs and family income? What is the difference?
18. Does your firm have a mission and goal statement? Is it comprehensive and motivating?
19. To repeat the questions in the summary of the chapter: Are there other personal values in our society that must be tapped if we are to continue to be an economically successful and healthy people?
20. To what extent will one's "calling" continue to be central in a person's life? Is a goal of material growth necessary for a business creed for the future? If so, what sort of growth?

Selected Additional Readings

Alfred D. Chandler, Jr., Franco Amatori, and Takashi Hikino, *Big Business and the Wealth of Nations* (Cambridge: Cambridge University Press, 1997), p. 77.

James Green, *Death in the Haymarket: A Story of Chicago, the First Labor Movement and the Bombing That Divided Gilded Age America* (New York: Paneheon Books, 2006).

Geert Hofstede, *Culture's Consequences*, 2nd ed. (Thousand Oaks, CA: Sage, 2001).

David Nasaw, *Andrew Carnegie* (New York: The Penguin Press, 2006).

Richard Rayner, *The Associates: Four Capitalists Who Created California* (New York: W. W. Norton/Atlas, 2007).

Frederick Winslow Taylor, *Scientific Management* (New York: Harper & Brothers, 1947).

CASES

Case 5-1   Olympic Gold Medal Winner

Joey Cheek, 26, won a gold medal with a $25,000 bonus in the 500-meter men's speed-skating contest at the 2006 Winter Olympics. He later won a silver medal with a $15,000 bonus. He donated all his prize money to help refugee children forced into camps by violence and genocide in the Darfur region of Sudan. He also asked his sponsors to donate, and many did including Nike, Jet Set Sports, and the Gap. His actions received much TV and newspaper attention, and his U.S. teammates elected him to carry the flag in the Olympic Parade.

1. What ethical norm might have prompted Cheek's actions?
2. Is it appropriate for him to call for his sponsors to also donate?
3. Why would the media give his action such publicity? Is this sort of action that unusual?

■ ■ ■

Case 5-2   Credit Card Safety and Truthfulness

Alex takes orders for an auto supply firm. Jeff phones in an order to avoid the risk of entering his credit card number on the Internet. However, when a customer calls in an order, Alex routinely enters the order on the firm's Internet system. Alex's boss tells him that if a customer ever asks if he is entering information on the Internet to tell them "no." Jeff hears keyboard clicking and asks if Alex will enter his card number on the Internet.

1. What should Alex do? If he uses a noiseless keyboard, and Jeff asks, what should Alex do?
2. What ethical norm helps us come to a decision here?

■ ■ ■

Case 5-3   Damaged Goods and Beer

Joan works in a small clothing store where the owner is often not present. The owner tells employees to throw into the dumpster some slightly damaged jackets. Two of Joan's fellow workers keep the jackets, and when the owner is not present, sell the jackets to customers and keep the money. They then use the money to buy beer.[50]

1. Are the actions of Joan's coworkers acceptable? What should Joan do?
2. Would it make a difference if the coworkers used the money for food? . . . if they gave it to needy families?
3. What ethical norm(s) help us to decide this case?

■ ■ ■

Case 5-4   Safe Drug

Your firm has developed a prescription drug that cures the flu. The Food and Drug Administration has delayed giving it clearance. Your own scientists think that the drug is safe, and that the FDA is overly cautious. Other governments, which also have high standards for safety, have approved the drug for sale in their countries.

1. Should your firm market the drug overseas? Or should you wait for U.S. approval?
2. What ethical norms help to make this decision?

Exercises

Exercise 5-1: International Management Consultant

Business today is global. To be successful, businesspeople must understand other cultures and other peoples. A fellow student from another country is a resource for learning about that person's country and its people. The purpose of this project is to learn about the climate for living and doing business in a country that has different customs, expectations, laws, and language. Consult someone from another country who has been in her/his home country within the last six months for information and help.

Procedure
1. Find a student from another country whom you can interview. Try not to overburden the same consultant.
2. Examine a single social issue that faces business in that country, for example:
   a. Sustainability practices
   b. Equal employment opportunity (minorities or women)
   c. Air or water pollution
   d. Marketing or advertising practices
   e. Safety of products or workplace
   f. Corruption: bribery, kickbacks, tax evasion, or other practices

---

[50] Thanks to Dr. Denis Collins for this case and the previous one.

  g. Operation of foreign firms within the country
  h. Host government regulations
  i. Other (consult instructor)
3. Prepare a summary report on a single sheet of paper outlining the following:
  a. Country chosen
  b. Name of international student consultant
  c. The issue or problem examined, and provide some background
  d. Any special industry or firm involved

Exercise 5-2: An American Ideology

A utopian vision or ideology that is intelligent, consistent, and inspiring is necessary for any society to advance. The *Declaration of Independence* was such an ideology which motivated early citizens to risk their lives and fortunes for the country. Commentators have noted that in recent federal election campaigns little utopian vision of society is presented to citizens by candidates of either party. Sound bites, 30-second TV ads, negative attacks, and appealing to special interests, crowd out and make it difficult to outline a vision that will appeal to most U.S. citizens.

For this exercise, outline in a few paragraphs (maximum one page) an ideology for U.S. citizens that is cohesive, motivating, and inspiring. You might choose to use as a beginning some of the values outlined in this chapter. Moreover, you may include any additional values or ideals that you think appropriate.

6

■ ■ ■

Critics of Capitalism

In a country well governed, poverty is something to be ashamed of. In a country badly governed, wealth is something to be ashamed of.

CONFUCIUS (CHINESE PHILOSOPHER, 551–479 BC)

Seven blunders of the world that lead to violence:
politics without principle,
wealth without work,
commerce without morality,
pleasure without conscience,
education without character,
science without humanity,
worship without sacrifice,

MAHATMA GANDHI (1869–1948)

Where did this idea come from that everybody deserves free education? Free medical care? Free whatever? It comes from Moscow. From Russia. It comes straight out of the pit of Hell.

TEXAS STATE REPRESENTATIVE DEBBIE RIDDLE[1]

---

[1] Quoted in Henry A. Giroux, *The Terror of Neoliberalism* (Boulder, CO: Paradigm, 2004), p. 82.

Free enterprise, or capitalism, is the economic system of most of the countries of the world. Free enterprise is taken for granted almost as much as the air we breathe. But we have seen in earlier chapters the strengths and also the weaknesses of free markets. So free enterprise has many critics; and no critique is as perceptive and comprehensive as that of **Karl Marx**. Marx raises penetrating questions about the **moral and social consequences of capitalism**.[2] He had an extraordinary ability to pinpoint and articulate the deficiencies of the free market system.

On the other hand, Marx and his followers were not as successful in providing a workable alternative to capitalism. For much of the twentieth century, Russia, China, and Eastern Europe had collectivist, Marxist governments. These nations equitably improved their economies and provided jobs. In fact the status of the average citizen in Russia has deteriorated since the fall of Communism. The expected life span of a Russian dropped from 70 years in 1985 to 59 in 2002 due to a rise in poverty; spread of diseases such as TB, diphtheria, and HIV/AIDS; and an increase in alcoholism. In former Communist countries, from 1990 to 2001 the rate of extreme poverty jumped from 0.4 to 5.3 percent.[3] Because of its earlier success, Marxism became the banner around the world for many who supported the plight of the poor. Nevertheless, because of inefficiencies, favoritism, trampling on individual rights, and persecution of critics, these governments collapsed in the early 1990s.

The Marxist critique of Capitalism deserves our attention. Marxist ideology is in contrast to the ideology of free markets and self-interest. There is much that is admirable in Marxist ideals of shared living and working. Moreover, we can still learn from their valid criticisms of free enterprise, and the **cooperative values** that they espouse.[4]

Throughout history most communities worldwide and many still today are built on cooperative, rather than competitive, ideals. Medieval European communities were more cooperative than their contemporary counterparts. Extended families, stable populations, and guilds all lived within walking distance and gave cohesion to communities. On the other hand, these communities also had a rigid and hierarchical social system. If your father was a carpenter, so too were you. This remains true today of many communities in Africa, Asia, and among Native Americans. We will discuss examples of successful cooperative economic communities later in this chapter.

We must also remember that the United States has only one version of a free market economy. The European Union (EU) is close to this model, although European governments provide greater guidance for their economies. For example, EU countries provide health care for all.[5] China now has a free market economy, although it still has a repressive Communist government. Russia and Eastern

---

[2] Arthur F. McGovern (1929–2000) authored this chapter in the first three editions of this book. I remain indebted for his competence, wisdom, insights, and friendship.

[3] Linda Starke, ed., *Vital Signs 2006–2007: Trends That Are Shaping Our Future* (New York: W. W. Norton & Company, 2006), p. 110.

[4] Jerry Z. Muller, *The Mind and the Market: Capitalism in Modern European Thought* (New York: Knopf, 2002); and "Marx After Communism: As a System of Government, Communism is Dead or Dying; As a System of Ideas, its Future Looks Secure," *The Economist,* December 21, 2002, pp. 17–19.

[5] Monica Prasad, *The Politics of Free Markets: The Rise of Neoliberal Economic Policies in Britain, France, Germany, and the United States* (Chicago: University of Chicago Press, 2006).

Europe also have "free" markets, although the state has a strong role. After the fall of Communism, some countries, including Russia, became dominated by unscrupulous captains of the market system: a few huge fortunes and many unemployed; products, contracts, and advertisements that cannot be trusted; pollution, bribery, favoritism, and organized crime. Some of these problems characterize China today, also.

Before examining the criticisms of capitalism, let us step back for a moment to probe some of our *own beliefs* (see also Exercise 1-1). To obtain additional clarity on your own goals, beliefs, and value system, reflect on these questions. What do *you* believe regarding the following:

1. Does each person have equal rights? Do all people have a right to life? Does this include a right to water? To food? To medical care? To education? Or do you agree with Texas Representative Debbie Riddle, who is quoted at the beginning of the chapter?
2. Is competition the most effective motivator for you? Is cooperation more effective, or do you respond to some combination?
3. Are human beings essentially good, needing only support and encouragement for their development, or are they essentially self-seeking, such that an economic system is wise to build on this selfishness and make best use of it?
4. Are human beings headed for progress and a better life or will we see overcrowded cities, depleted resources, and a decline of civilization?
5. If neither progress nor decline is inevitable, are we able to influence our society and the world 10 years hence? If so, in what way?
6. Does life end at death? Is there an afterlife? How does your response influence your life, work, and attitudes?
7. Have you ever thought about the above questions or do you put them aside— either because you do not understand their relevance or because you do not have time?

Your answers to these questions can expose the framework you use to make daily and long-term decisions. On the other hand, you may not have thought much about these questions. Perhaps your goals, values, and ethics are taken from other people: parents, peers, neighbors, media, or superiors at work. In that case you are making decisions, some everyday and others having broad impact, without examining the assumptions beneath your decisions. Problems that stem from not being aware of our assumptions, and how people cope or fail to cope, will be discussed in Chapter 7.

Each of the above questions could be asked of any of the leaders we have examined in this book. If we asked Bernard of Clairvaux, John Calvin, Benjamin Franklin, Adam Smith, Karl Marx, or Mahatma Gandhi, how would they respond? But let us now continue our examination of Marx's critique of capitalism.

THE MARXIST CRITIQUE

Karl Marx's (1818–1883) criticisms of capitalism were incisive and based on actual data. His language was intentionally polemic; he and his followers used terms like *exploitation*, *imperialism*, and *alienation*. The criticisms come from a viewpoint that is foreign to most Americans. But despite the differences in language, values, and attitudes, the Marxist critique helps us to examine our own values. The Marxist critique also helps us to better understand national priorities and the values that govern our economic, political, and social policies. Moreover, if we seek an objective examination of the goals and values of free enterprise, we must consider its critics.

Marx was a real genius who had both analytic skill and an ability to weld his ideas into an overall theory of history. According to his theory, **economic forces** are the primary determinant of history. Economic structures give rise to class differences; class conflicts provoke social and political struggles. Marx thought that the class conflict between workers and owners that he experienced in his lifetime would inevitably erupt in revolution and usher in a new socialist system of production.

Marx said that economists view the **factors of production** (money, raw material, and labor) as things. Marx insisted that economics does not deal only in things; it involves **social relations**. Every commodity produced and sold and every wage paid involves relationships between human beings. In failing to recognize these social relations, capitalist theory ignores the real effects of the system on human beings and society.

The following review is divided into several accusations made by critics of the capitalist system. Some may find these accusations exaggerated and one-sided. But we present them in the conviction that considering intelligent criticism leads to a more effective and just socioeconomic system.

Exploitation of the Worker

Free enterprise, following Adam Smith, is based on the theory that when people work for their own self-interest, they will simultaneously contribute to the welfare of all. Everyone profits from economic growth, and each person receives monetary rewards in proportion to his or her efforts and skill. Marxists challenge these assumptions. For Marx, who knew the Industrial Revolution during its grimmest stage, it was difficult to see how workers benefited proportionate to their labors. As we saw in Chapter 5, factory workers lived in hovels, worked exhausting 12-hour workdays, 6 days a week, and died prematurely. Marx's classic work, *Capital*, describes the price paid in human suffering for industrial growth: workers suffering from pulmonary diseases caused by the dust and heat of factories, small children working 15-hour days, a young girl dying of exhaustion after 26 consecutive hours of work.[6] Workers were forced to live on subsistence wages while owners acquired fortunes and lived in luxury.

In capitalist countries the gap that existed a century ago between the poor and the wealthy remains today. In some countries labor unions and government legislation have brought higher wages and better working conditions. But in order to provide

---

[6] Karl Marx, "The Working Day," *Capital,* vol. 1 (New York: International Publishers, 1967), pp. 244–254; for additional data, see Giovanni Andrea Cornia and Sheldon Danziger, *Child Poverty and Deprivation in the Industrialized Countries 1945–1995* (Oxford: Oxford University Press, 1997); also Donald R. Stabile, *Work and Welfare: The Social Costs of Labor in the History of Economic Thought* (Westport, CN: Greenwood Press, 1996).

low-cost consumer goods, globalization forces slimmer margins on producers, and the "outsourcing" of work takes many formerly well-paid jobs, both skilled and unskilled, to countries where wages are much less. The less skilled jobs left in the United States are low-wage jobs, and most often without medical or retirement benefits.[7] Globalization is a result of capitalism and open markets, and we will examine its positive and negative impacts further in Chapter 9.

If one looks at the **distribution of wealth and income**, very large **inequalities** are present, and those gaps are increasing. In a study of incomes of 16 industrialized countries during two recent decades, the **United States had the *greatest inequality*** of all. The income gap between the rich and the poor was wider in the United States than in any other industrialized country. Next in income disparity were Ireland, Italy, Canada, Australia, and Britain, in that order. Finland had the least disparity, followed by Sweden, Belgium, the Netherlands, Norway, and West Germany. By another measure, we find that in the United States the wealthiest 1 percent of all households control 38 percent of national wealth, while the bottom 80 percent control only 17 percent. Note that in an opinion poll, 19 percent of Americans believe they are in that top 1 percent. In yet another measure of inequality, in 1960 the richest 20 percent of the global population received 30 times the income of the poorest 20 percent, but by 2000 this grew to 60 times.[8]

For a Marxist, the reason for this gap is clear. At best, workers can only bargain for higher wages. Managers determine compensation both for workers and for themselves. The manager controls the system, and inequalities are a result. Workers are not paid the full value of their work contribution. The difference between the value workers add to the product, and their actual wage is the source of profit, according to Marx.

Marx argues that profit is the surplus after all costs have been paid. Marxists recognize the need for investment in new equipment and research and development; their only quarrel is when it is privately possessed and controlled. If workers are a prime source of production, then they, not managers and owners, should be prime beneficiaries, and they should also have a significant voice in the production process. The fact that labor unions have reduced the inequities for workers does not alter the basic fact of exploitation for a Marxist. Managers still seek to pay as little as possible for workers' services. The resulting profits are not the rewards of the capitalist's hard work or enterprising spirit, but simply result from ownership of property and control over the work of others.

Sweatshops are common in Asia and Latin America, and exist even in the United States. Workers labor 12 hours a day, 6 days a week for less than local minimum wage, and are often kept in virtual slavery. Adolescent girls sew and assemble shoes, sportswear, toys, and name brand garments. The purchasing policies of firms

---

[7] Aaron Bernstein, "Waking Up from the American Dream: Dead-End Jobs and the High Cost of College Could Be Choking Off Upward Mobility," *BusinessWeek,* December 1, 2003, pp. 54–58.

[8] Richard J. Ward, "Worsening Income Gaps and a Sustainable Future," *International Journal of Social Economics,* 29, no. 6 (2002), pp. 480–490. "Inequality: Would you Like Your Class War Shaken or Stirred," *The Economist,* September 5, 2003, p. 28; Edward N. Wolff, *Top Heavy: The Increasing Inequality of Wealth in American and What Can Be Done About It* (New York: The New Press, 2002).

like Wal-Mart and Nike require suppliers to manufacture clothes and shoes under such low-cost conditions. The garments and shoes are often sold at premium prices, and the profit goes to owners.

Marx challenges the contention that wealth has been the product of "free" enterprise. Can the wealthy claim to have "earned" their income in the past without acknowledging the takeover of native lands, slavery, or the minimal wages paid immigrant workers, as we saw in the last chapter? Or today, do low-paid service workers receive a wage proportionate to their work when top executives of the same company earn a salary 450 times greater? The poor are now falling even further behind, because well-paying careers require a college education and often knowing the right people. For young people growing up in a poor, single-parent family and attending an inner-city school, the odds are against them.

The income gap between top managers and others in the same firm continues to increase. Excessive CEO pay in the United States is of concern to shareholders, workers, and the public. The pay of CEOs has risen to 369 times that of the average employee in the United States. Compare this with those of other countries: Brazil, 57; Mexico, 46; United Kingdom, 25; Canada, 21; France, 16; Germany, 11; and Japan, 10; J. P. Morgan said that CEOs should receive no more than 20 times the average salary in their firm. Because of excessive CEO compensation, shareholders are rebelling and are threatening to replace company directors if they do not exercise more effective oversight.[9]

. These large salary increases were granted at a time when many of these same executives were cutting jobs and asking others to accept pay reductions. Two examples illustrate different approaches. Ronald Allen, CEO of Delta Airlines, announced the reduction of 15,000 jobs, about 20 percent of the workforce; Allen did not take a bonus and actually took a pay reduction himself. He said that if flight attendants, reservation clerks, and others were taking pay cuts, he should do the same. Allen has worked for Delta all his life, and he wants to maintain solidarity with the rest of the workforce and support their loyalty. On the other hand, Donald Carty, CEO of American Airlines, negotiated sweeping wage concessions from the major unions, because the airline was facing serious financial difficulties—even bankruptcy. However, just weeks earlier a $41 million pension fund was set up for 45 top executives, and they were granted bonuses worth twice their salaries. When this became public, the bonuses were canceled and Carty was forced to resign. Carty was more concerned with the welfare of the executives than the loyalty of the workers.

In another case, Albert J. "chainsaw Al" Dunlap, CEO of Scott Paper, announced cuts in the Scott workforce of about one-third or 11,200 jobs. He then received $3,500,000 in salary and bonus, while his predecessor the previous year had received but $618,000. He argues that he added much to shareholder value. Loyalty and solidarity of the workforce were not important for Dunlap. He left Scott shortly

---

[9] Jane Sasseen, "A Better Look at the Boss's Pay: New SEC Rules Require Greater Disclosure, but Don't Expect CEOs to Take a Hit," *BusinessWeek,* February 26, 2007, pp. 44–46. Also, Leonard R. Sayles and Cynthia J. Smith, *The Rise of the Rouge Executive* (Upper Saddle River: Prentice Hall, 2006), pp. 179–198. For current data on the pay of hundreds of CEO's, see http://www.aflcio.org/corporatewatch/paywatch/; this site is maintained by AFL-CIO, accessed July 18, 2007.

thereafter and again cut thousands of jobs and gave himself immense pay at Sunbeam. The SEC later charged Dunlap with accounting fraud of $60 million during his tenure at Sunbeam. Edward Brennan of Sears Roebuck announced job cuts of 50,000 and then received a 198 percent increase in compensation the following year to $3,000,000. George David, CEO of United Technologies, cut 10,600 jobs, and then received a 115 percent increase in pay. Most CEOs take pay increases despite cutting jobs and asking for sacrifice on the part of others in order to cut costs. As a result of the above, 68 percent of Americans think that the top executives of large U.S. companies make too much money.[10]

Critics of free enterprise argue that investments produce more income than work itself. Of people who reported incomes of $1 million or more, 4 percent of their income came from salaries; the rest came from dividends and capital gains.[11] Estate or inheritance taxes can provide a more even playing field for those beginning a career and life. For this reason, William H. Gates, Sr., the father of Microsoft founder Bill Gates, despite both his and his son's considerable wealth, advocates a steep inheritance tax. Gates, Sr. cites U.S. Supreme Court Justice Oliver Wendell Holmes, "Taxes are the price we pay for civilization."[12] Andrew Carnegie argued that wealthy people ought to give their entire fortune away to worthy causes while they were still living; both Carnegie and John D. Rockefeller used their wealth to fund libraries and education. As important as these issues are, Marx was concerned about more than the distribution of wealth and a fair wage for work done. Let us now turn to the worker's attitude toward their work.

Alienation of the Worker

Job dissatisfaction and a lack of commitment and loyalty are common among working people today. Marx saw the roots of this when he charged that work was forced and dehumanizing. The work is forced because jobs are scarce and the average worker, though theoretically free to accept a job or not, has little choice but to take the job. Nor do workers have much freedom in the way they do their work. Most do their job in the way and at the pace designated. The work is thus **dehumanizing** because it does not enable workers to make decisions, to be inventive, or to develop different skills. Few jobs challenge one's real skills, imagination, or spirit. The worker is often simply an appendage to a machine.

Free enterprise stresses efficiency and increasing shareholder value more than humanizing work. In most traditional societies one's work is one's life. Work, play, and social life flowed into each other. Work meant simply tasks to be done, and there was no division of life into work and nonwork. For most moderns work is not pleasant.

---

[10] Hugh M. O'Neill and D. Jeffery Lenn, "Voices of Survivors: Words that Downsizing CEOs Should Hear," *Academy of Management Executive,* 9 (November 1995): 23–34; and "Too Much Corporate Power?" *BusinessWeek,* September 11, 2000, p. 149.
[11] Richard C. Edwards, Michael Reich, and Thomas E. Weisskopf, eds., *The Capitalist System* (Englewood Cliffs, NJ: Prentice Hall, 1986), pp. 223–224; and Ferdinand Lundberg, *The Rich and the Super-Rich* (New York: Bantam Books, 1968), pp. 43, 935–936.
[12] William H. Gates, Sr. and Chuck Collins, *Wealth and Our Commonwealth: Why America Should Tax Accumulated Fortunes* (Boston: Beacon Press, 2003).

Note the number of people who take early retirement. Because of specialization, a worker is assigned to a small portion of a task. The work is finished by another: out of sight and out of mind. Thus there is little satisfaction from the completion of a job. Many occupations require one to simply follow exact routines in an orderly way, such as fast-food work. As a result, work does not mean much to most of those people and they do not enjoy it.[13]

Workers are not asked to use their mind or to be creative. Frederick Taylor proposed Scientific Management in the late nineteenth century as we saw in Chapter 5, and it influenced the U.S. workplace by deliberately divorcing mental and physical labor. Taylor wrote,

> The managers assume the burden of gathering together all of the traditional knowledge which in the past has been possessed by the workmen and then of classifying, tabulating, and reducing this knowledge to rules, laws, and formula. All possible brain work should be removed from the shop and centered in the planning or laying-out department.[14]

Assembly lines carried this concept of mechanized labor to its fullest expression. Henry Ford's decision in 1914 to raise workers' pay to five dollars a day was hailed as an enlightened, progressive move done to enable workers to become better customers. Critics maintain that this view overlooks the fact that Ford faced an angry revolt by workers against his new assembly lines. The turnover rate in 1913 at Ford Motor Company was 963 percent.[15] Clerical work as well as manual work often does not allow for creativity. The need for speed and efficiency reduces work to simplified, routinized, and measured tasks.

Although work is sometimes inhumane, unemployment proves still far more degrading. To speak of *only* 6 percent unemployed does little to describe the frustration, powerlessness, and anxiety of millions of unemployed people. Unemployment benefits may permit an income on which to live for a short time, but it is dehumanizing. From a Marxist perspective, worker exploitation and alienation are among the most serious failures of the free enterprise system. Chapter 7 will present more on the effect of the work environment on workers.

Big Business Dominates National Goals

Americans take pride in their **democracy**: "Whatever its faults, it's the best in the world." Every citizen has a voice in the government. All can vote; all can aspire to political office. The two-party system offers choices in policies and candidates. The division of executive, legislative, and judicial is a model of balance of power.

---

[13] Kenneth Keniston, "The Alienating Consequences of Capitalist Technology," in Richard C. Edwards, Michael Reich, and Thomas E. Weisskopf, *The Capitalist System* (Englewood Cliffs, NJ: Prentice Hall, 1996), pp. 269–273; see also Herbert Gintis's essay on alienation, which follows Keniston's.

[14] Harry Braverman, *Labor and Monopoly Capital: The Degradation of Work in the Twentieth Century* (New York: Monthly Review, 1974), pp. 31–39, 112–118.

[15] Braverman, *Ibid.*, p. 149.

Critics challenge this faith in U.S. democracy. These critics do not question the ideals of democracy but rather the claims that they have been realized in the United States or other free market nations. Marx argued that political freedoms create only an "illusion" of true human freedom, because political power reflects economic power. When John Locke, the seventeenth-century English philosopher, stated that the chief end of persons uniting to form a government was "the preservation of property," he reflected the goals of his social class of wealthy people. The democratic state in market societies claims to represent the common good of all its citizens, and indeed sometimes it will pass legislation to legitimize that claim. But it serves primarily to further the interests of the wealthy and powerful.[16]

The government provides benefits to business and to the wealthy in many ways. While some wealthy complain of excessive taxes and government regulation, they receive more than their fair share from government: a reduction of taxes on the wealthy, tax breaks for large firms, and subsidy of many industries and products. A study showed that 82 of the largest firms in the United States, including General Electric, Citigroup, SBC Communications, and IBM, paid no federal income tax for at least one of the first three years of the George W. Bush administration. General Electric had the largest saving and a $9.5 billion tax break for the three-year period. The official U.S. corporate tax rate is 35 percent of profits, but in 2003 the actual corporate tax rate was 1.2 percent, the second lowest rate recorded since 1946.[17] The **state also assists business** by setting up structures that aid commerce (e.g., subsidizing exports, antitrust and bankruptcy legislation, and Federal Reserve Bank) and by bearing much of the burden of social expenses (e.g., education, social security, and some health care). Government subsidy of business is illustrated in the automobile industry. Cars need roads, but business does not bear the cost of building them. The federal government pays 90 percent of the cost of interstate freeways and 50 percent of the cost of all other primary roads.

The state subsidizes business, and hence profits, in a variety of ways: subsidizing exports, helping to finance new commercial building, providing tax abatements, funding research, and providing tax exemptions for building depreciation and oil exploration. U.S. Government policies have long subsidized "family farms." Yet over the last two generations, the number of small- and medium-sized farms has declined dramatically; farming is now dominated by huge agribusinesses such ADM, Tyson, Perdue, Swift, and Cargill which receive most of the benefits of these subsidies. For example, the United States spends $1.7 billion to subsidize the purchase of U.S. cotton, while another $10 billion over seven years was also given to U.S. cotton farmers.[18] It pays for much of the cost of cleaning up pollution caused by businesses. Moreover, government picks up most of the responsibility that business escapes through bankruptcy and negligence.

---

[16] "The Communist Manifesto," in *The Marx-Engels Reader,* ed. Robert C. Tucker (New York: Norton, 1972), p. 337.

[17] "Some Top Companies Avoided Federal Income Tax Under Bush," *The Wall Street Journal,* September 23, 2004, p. 2.

[18] Elizabeth Becker, "U.S. Subsidizes Companies to Buy Subsidized Cotton," *The New York Times,* November 4, 2003, p. C1.

In addition, corporations know how to **avoid paying taxes**, as we saw above. As a result, the average American today pays a larger portion of federal taxes than they did two generations ago. At that time, roughly half of federal taxes were paid by individuals and half by corporations. However, individuals now pay 86.3 percent of federal taxes collected, and businesses pay only 13.7 percent. KPMG and other major accounting firms set up lucrative tax divisions which advertised that they could eliminate a firm's tax burden by exploiting provisions of the Internal Revenue Service Code.[19]

Because the role of government is to protect the **common good of** *all citizens*, how does big business obtain such favorable policies? The short answer is **lobbying**, money, and influence on government. Lobbying by deep-pocketed organizations worries many, because it generally includes large contributions of money to a candidate running for public office. Moreover, it is expensive to run for public office because of the cost of ads, staff, and polls, so politicians are always seeking more money. Sen. John McCain (R, Ariz.) said that the federal campaign finance system is "an elaborate influence peddling scheme in which both parties conspire to stay in office by selling the country to the highest bidder." Others say that we now have "the best Congress that money can buy." In the 1920s, U.S. Congress made it illegal for a corporation to contribute to an American candidate or party, and in 1977 made it illegal for a U.S. corporation to contribute to (to bribe) a foreign political leader. Yet legislation to restrict corporate contributions is sidestepped, because business executives who gather enough $2,000 personal contributions (the legal limit) are rewarded by the GOP by being called "pioneers" or "rangers." And donors expect something in return for their "contributions." The 2008 U.S. federal elections will cost $3 billion, more than five times the 2000 campaign.[20]

Charles Lindbloom, in his classic *Politics and Markets*, examines the influence of big business on the state. Lindbloom defends the market economy, but he believes that giant corporations are not consistent with democracy. Business executives and not government officials, he argues, make most of the public policy decisions that affect the life of the nation. Their decisions, in turn, affect almost every aspect of life—jobs, homes, consumer goods, leisure. Executives influence tax and trade policy, and government regulations, and also determine outsourcing, salaries paid, plant locations, technologies used, and executive compensation.[21] These major decisions that affect all citizens are made by or heavily influenced by business leaders. Thus citizens have little control of policies that touch every sphere of their lives.

The influence of business leaders on government and public policy is much greater than that of any other group in society. Jobs, prices, production, outsourcing, the standard of living, and the economic security of everyone are under their influence.

---

[19] Nanette Byrnes and Louis Lavelle, "The Corporate Tax Game," *BusinessWeek,* March 32, 2003, pp. 79–87.

[20] Nina Easton, "Electionomics '08: Get Ready for the $3 Billion Campaign," *Fortune,* March 5, 2007, p. 16.

[21] Charles Lindbloom, *Politics and Markets: The World's Political-Economic Systems* (New York: Basic Books, 1977), p. 171; see also his *The Market System: What It Is, and What To Make of It* (New Haven, CT: Yale University Press, 2001); Harold J. Leavitt goes further in his "Big Organizations Are Unhealthy Environments for Human Beings," *Academy of Management Learning and Education,* 62, no. 2 (2007): 253–263.

Business leaders are not just managers; the welfare of all people in a society depends on what they do. When business leaders ask for tax reductions to stimulate investment; subsidies for research, transportation, and overseas exports; for troops to protect investments in foreign countries; or for similar advantages, the government often responds favorably.

All citizen groups can compete in politics, but they must use their members' volunteer resources and energies. Business corporations can spend corporate funds, work on company time, and can hire paid lobbyists to influence legislation. Business executives have many avenues by which to present their point of view. Through lobbying, gifts, entertainment, and real or threatened litigation, business uses its resources to obtain what it desires. More than $250 billion a year is spent on advertising and other sales promotion.[22] This promotes a firm and a brand, and some corporate advertising has an overtly political content. This is equal to all the funds spent on education or health in the country. Dissenting voices do not have similar resources to compete with dominant business views. It is for these reasons that Lindbloom concludes that the large private corporation is not consistent with a democracy.[23] Critics point out that this same influence of business today extends to the entire world.

Corporations Exploit Other Countries

Critics of free enterprise often focus on the influence of capitalism in poor countries. When people praise the achievements of free enterprise, they point to the affluence of Europe, Japan, and the United States, along with the new jobs being created in India, China, and developing countries. But in much of Latin America, the Middle East, Africa, and Asia, free enterprise generally leaves desperate poverty for the majority, corruption, right-wing rule, and exploitation by foreign companies.

Four-fifths of the world's peoples subsist on one-fifth of the world's income, and one-fifth live in abject poverty on less than $1 a day. Direct private investment in poor countries dwarfs foreign aid. But the least developed countries receive but 0.5 percent of that investment, and that investment often does little to help the poor country and often damages the people. Wealthy countries (the United States, Japan, France, and Germany) subsidize their own agriculture, thus making it difficult for poor countries to export their agricultural products. Moreover, aid is often given as surplus corn, wheat, rice, and other agricultural products, which undermines the ability of poor local farmers to sell their produce. Intellectual property rights make access to life-saving drugs and electronic services difficult. And immigration rules are stacked against the poor and uneducated. And despite international bans, toxic waste from developed countries is still dumped in less developed countries.[24]

---

[22] *Statistical Abstract of the United States—2006* (Washington, D.C.: U.S. Department of Commerce, 2006).

[23] Lindbloom, *op. cit.*, pp. 172ff, 195, 214; see also the more recent criticism of the corporation's power in society, Ted Nace, *Gangs of America: The Rise of Corporate Power and the Disabling of Democracy* (San Francisco: Berrett-Koehler, 2003).

[24] Robert Picciotto and Rachel Weaving, eds., *Impact of Rich Countries' Policies on Poor Countries: Towards a Level Playing Field in Development Cooperation* (New Brunswick, NJ: Transaction, 2004); Jennifer Clapp, *Toxic Exports: The Transfer of Hazardous Wastes from Rich to Poor Countries* (Ithaca: Cornell University Press, 2001).

In El Salvador free enterprise means 2 percent of the population owns 60 percent of the land and 8 percent receive half of all personal income. The remaining 92 percent of the population live in poverty and three-fourths of the children suffer from malnutrition. Yet for decades efforts at reform have been crushed by right-wing death squads, often trained in the United States and by the U.S. Army at what was called the "School of the Americas" at Fort Benning, Georgia.[25]

Critics argue that capitalist countries want to maintain the status quo in developing countries in order to exploit them. **Exploitation is profitable**. Less developed countries of the world provide natural resources and cheap labor which make investment lucrative, if the political regimes are stable and favorable. Economic development has brought jobs and income for some poor, and also huge financial rewards to the wealthy elite in Brazil, Colombia, Indonesia, India, and China.

The beginnings of capitalism in Europe, many contend, were made possible by the plunder of gold, silver, and other minerals from the American "colonies." Then specialized economies that are less flexible were developed by foreign investors. Today certain products bring to mind specific countries—coffee in Brazil, tin in Bolivia, copper in Chile, sugar in Cuba. But the specialization in such commodities did not result from initiatives within those countries. The economies of these countries were focused by European and U.S. firms to meet the needs of developed countries. The concentration on one or two products generally upset a natural balance of production and created **"one-crop" economies** dependent on the fluctuating prices in the world market for that one crop. For example, Brazil's northeast was once that country's richest area; now it is its poorest. Portugal granted lands to Brazil's first wealthy landlords, and sugar production flourished for a few generations. When the soil was depleted and eroded, the landlords then took their profits and left.[26] Barbados, in the West Indies, suffered the same fate. It once produced a variety of crops and livestock on small holdings: cotton, tobacco, oranges, cows, and pigs. Cane fields devoured all this; the soil was then exhausted and unable to feed the population. The story is similar in Africa. Gambia once grew its own rice on land now used to grow peanuts. Northern Ghana grew yams and other foodstuffs on land now devoted to cocoa. Much of Liberia and Vietnam were turned over to rubber plantations. Seizures of land, taxation, undercutting of domestic prices, and forced migrations were all employed by colonizers to gain control of the land. Even today if a country elects a government that seeks to protect its workers and enact regulations to protect its environment, multinational corporations will invest less in that country.[27]

This has left a world divided between a very few who live in opulent affluence and the majority who live in "dehumanizing poverty, servitude, and economic insecurity." While American CEOs, entertainers, athletes, investment bankers, and

---

[25] For further documentation, see Gilbert Joseph, Catherine LeGrand, and Richardo Salvatore, eds., *Close Encounters of Empire: Writing the Cultural History of U.S.—Latin American Relations* (Durham, NC: Duke University Press, 1998).
[26] Eduardo Galeano, *Open Veins of Latin America: Five Centuries of the Pillage of a Continent*, trans. Cedric Belfrage (New York: Monthly Review, 1973), pp. 72–75.
[27] Paul M. Vaaler, "How Do MNCs Vote in Developing Country Elections?" *Academy of Management Journal*, 51 (February 2008): 21–44; Frances Moore Lappe and Joseph Collins, *Food First: Beyond the Myth of Scarcity* (Boston: Houghton Mifflin, 1977), p. 78ff.

financial speculators bring in incomes of many millions of dollars each year, about one billion of the world's people "struggle in desperation to live on less than $1 dollar a day."[28]

The countries and the people who are already wealthy control the priorities and determine what is to be financed, made, and traded. They have the power to make the rules to suit their own interests. Consider the following data:

> El Salvador and Costa Rica . . . grow export crops such as bananas, coffee and sugar on more than one fifth of their crop land. Export cattle ranches in Latin America and southern Africa have replaced rain forest and wildlife range. At the consumer end of the production line, Japan imports 70% of its corn, wheat, and barley, 95% of its soybeans, and more than 50% of its wood, much of it from the rapidly vanishing rain forests of Borneo . . . (meanwhile) millions of pigs and cows are fattened on palm-kernel cake from deforested lands in Malaysia, cassava from deforested regions of Thailand, and soybeans from pesticide-doused expanses in the south of Brazil in order to provide European consumers with their high-fat diet of meat and milk.[29]

Foreign mining firms, manufacturers, fruit growers, and banks do bring some needed capital, technology, and know-how to poor countries. However, the income that comes back to the richer country from private investment in poor countries exceeds that going into initial investment by more than 80 percent. In a typical year, only 30 percent of the earnings generated in developing countries is reinvested in those countries. The remainder is sent back to the wealthy country. Compare this with 63 percent of similar earnings reinvested in developed countries. Putting the situation graphically, if a box of bananas retails at $13.45 in the United States, producers in Honduras receive roughly $1.49; this covers tending the bananas and cutting and packing them. Chain supermarkets in the United States gross $4.23 on that same box.[30]

The global economy has created a market in which competition among communities is as real as competition among firms. Moore Country, South Carolina won a bid in the 1970s to bring a Proctor Silex plant to their community. They then floated a $5.5 million bond to finance sewer and water for the firm. Then in 1990, the business moved to Mexico, leaving behind 800 unemployed Moore County residents.[31] Similar competition exists among cities, when they compete with one another to subsidize stadiums for professional athletic teams, subsidizing players who are annually paid an average of $1.5 million dollars each.

---

[28] *World Development Report*—2004 (Washington, D.C.: World Bank and Oxford University Press, 2003). See also David C. Korten, *When Corporations Rule the World* (San Francisco: Berrett-Koehler, 1995), p. 20. Korten provides a well-documented and reasoned critique of current global economic policies.

[29] Alan Durning, *How Much Is Enough? The Consumer Society and the Future of the Earth* (New York: W. W. Norton, 1992), p. 56. Quoted in Korten, p. 30.

[30] "U.S. Direct Investment Abroad," *Survey of Current Business* (August 1986), pp. 42, 70; Lappe and Collins, *op. cit.*, pp. 194–198. The dollar figures have been adjusted for the rise in prices.

[31] Korten, *op. cit.*, pp. 128–129.

"The market will decide" and **"consumer sovereignty"** are bywords justifying such free enterprise and global markets. But the consumer who decides is the consumer who has money. The poor and hungry cannot pay enough for food to match the profits that can be made on exports. Therefore, Central America sends its vegetables to the United States, where large quantities are dumped or used as animal feed because their quality is not good enough or markets are oversupplied. Mexico grows strawberries, cantaloupes, and asparagus for Del Monte and other firms to sell in the United States. Colombian private owners grow flowers for export because one hectare of flowers brings nine times the profit that wheat or corn could. Now, because "customers" in the United States and Europe demand it, cocaine now brings far greater profits to farmers in Colombia and Afghanistan.[32]

When poor peoples attempted to achieve a fairer democratic society, the United States often intervened and supported a **military takeover**. The United States sent Marines into Guatemala in 1954, supported the military overthrow of Goulart in Brazil in 1964, used the CIA to undermine and overthrow the elected Allende government in Chile in 1973, and supported the extreme right-wing dictatorship in El Salvador until 1988. In Cuba, before Castro's revolution, U.S. companies controlled 80 percent of Cuba's utilities, 90 percent of its mines, and almost 100 percent of its oil refineries. U.S. firms received 40 percent of the profits on sugar, a crop that represented 89 percent of all Cuban exports. Castro made this argument and it garnered him the support of Cuba's people. The U.S. invasion of Panama was to protect the Panama Canal, and the wars in Iraq protect our supply of petroleum. The reason for many military interventions is the protection of U.S. business investments. John Perkins writes how he was recruited by consulting firms working for the U.S. Government to encourage poor nations to build immense projects, like power plants, airports, and industrial parks. It required an immense debt to pay for the projects, and the debt made them dependent on the United States.[33]

Finally, because foreign policy supported by military intervention is used to protect overseas business, the U.S. defense industry is essential to free enterprise. It also sells planes, missiles, tanks, and guns to friendly poor countries, which can barely afford them. Defense contracts, in turn, provide U.S. business, jobs, and reelection for politicians. Hence we see that exploitation of other countries, military support of business interests, and a large arms industry are important elements of American "free markets."

Social Consequences of Capitalism

Social problems abound around the world that are the consequence of placing profits above social concerns. These problems are familiar. The United States has destroyed 85 percent of its wildlife and 80 percent of its forests; millions of acres of farmland have been misused, paved over, and lost. **Pollution** is rampant. U.S. carbon emissions

---

[32] *Ibid.*, pp. 255–256.
[33] John Perkins, *Confessions of an Economic Hit Man* (San Francisco: Berrett-Koehler, 2004).

and **global temperatures** are increasing dangerously.[34] **High infant mortality** rates reflect the lack of medical care poor people receive. Crime, violence, and poor public schools undermine urban life. Armed robbery in Washington, D.C., is 20 times that of London. Unemployment, inadequate housing, broken families, racial prejudice, drugs, and great disparities in income are problems in most market economies.

The United States, Western and Eastern Europe, and Japan pride themselves on enjoying a high standard of living, but are now plagued by these serious **social problems**. Their citizens enjoy more material benefits than any other people in history. But many question even this achievement. How much of what we consume is a response to real needs? Our consumer-propelled economy demands the creation of new, artificial "needs." Advertising and fashions lead us to be dissatisfied with what we have and to buy what we do not need: the latest shirts, shoes, PCs, iTunes players, and more luxurious clothes and autos. Vacation advertisements try to convince us to go to ever more exotic and expensive places. Meanwhile, in Mexico, India, and Indonesia, the poor flock to the cities seeking work. Unable to find work, they subsist in shanty towns that have no water, electricity, or roads—places that are not good places to raise children.

The critics' charges about our economic and political systems are many. A greater share of a firm's profit goes to executives and shareholders than to workers. Investment returns increases the disproportionate distribution of wealth. Factory work often stunts the capacities of workers. Workers are seldom tapped for their initiative, self-determination, and voice in decision making. Competition, "survival of the fittest," and self-interest characterize work at every level. Poverty and unemployment are considered to be one's own fault. A wealthy, powerful elite controls the highest public offices. Minorities and women are often still subservient. Laws favor the wealthy and protect their incomes by tax loopholes; large companies use their political influence to insulate themselves from competition. As a result, 74 percent of Americans say big companies have too much political influence.[35] Pollution, crime, drugs, racial discrimination, and false needs are by-products of an economy focused on more and more production and profits.

The corporation has been granted the **status of a person** under U.S. law. This has given the corporation privilege and freedom. But if we consider the corporation as a person, it manifests many of the signs of a pathological person. Arthur Andersen and Enron were not unique; they and most other firms are characterized by an obsession with profits, greed, a lack of concern for others, and an inclination to push the limits of or break legal restrictions. The corporation is thus acting as a **psychopath**: irresponsible, grandiose, lacking empathy, manipulating people and data to serve its own purposes, refusing to accept responsibility for its actions, and unable to feel remorse. From this perspective, we see that business scandals are less the result of unethical executives than they are the result of a legal and economic

---

[34] For data, see Lester R. Brown, *Plan B 3.0: Rescuing a Planet Under Stress and a Civilization in Trouble* (New York: W. W. Norton, 2008); and *Vital Signs—2006* (New York: W. W. Norton, 2007). Also United Nations Intergovernmental Panel on Climate Change, June 2007.

[35] See Raghuram G. Rajan and Luigi Zingales, *Saving Capitalism from the Capitalists* (New York: Crown, 2003); also Charles Perrow, *Organizing America: Wealth, Power and the Origins of Corporate Capitalism* (Princeton, NJ: Princeton University Press, 2002); and *BusinessWeek*, September 11, 2000, p. 149.

system that encourages this selfish behavior. An award-winning documentary film, *The Corporation*, makes these points with video and interviews with well-known CEOs, economists, and critics, and thus is a surprisingly rational and coherent attack on capitalism's most important institution.[36]

Critics then ask why we have allowed ourselves to be fooled into thinking that the corporation and the unneeded growth that it pursues present the best plan for the future. Why not instead "concentrate on ending poverty, improving our **quality of life**, and achieving a balance with the earth. We can achieve these goals—if we can free ourselves from the illusion that *any* kind of growth is *the* path to better living."[37] The Social Issues Division of the Academy of Management consists of business faculty in universities from around the world, and is pursuing these questions.

Critics are often perceptive and eloquent in portraying the flaws in the free market system, and they tell us much. If we ignore the critics, our weaknesses will not disappear, but will likely become worse. This could bring distress, instability, and potential breakdown of the system itself. We are wise to hear the critics, and try to repair the flaws in the system while they can still be repaired.[38] Giving priority to developing a **sustainable economy** that meets all peoples' needs, including the poor at home and in developing countries, is an important goal. There are tradeoff costs, but the costs are less than the potential disruption and chaos.

Cooperative or Competitive Market System

Programs designed to bring about a more just distribution of wealth and income generally result in a loss of efficiency and productivity. Government programs require planning and administrators. They are expensive, are influenced by political interests, and do not always achieve their intended goals. Moreover, such programs can have a negative effect on the incentive to work for both low- and high-income people. On the other hand, critics accuse capitalism not only of exploitation and alienation of the worker but also of encouraging selfishness. Excessive competition and selfishness among individuals can damage not only the health of a society, but also the efficiency of a firm.

Two ideals of a democratic society, **justice and efficiency**, are thus placed in opposition to one another. That is, in the minds of many people, increasing one requires sacrificing some of the other.[39] The ideal of *justice* (or equity or fairness) is basic to any society, especially to a free, democratic one: All men and women have a right to life and the basics of food, shelter, and some education; all men and women should have an opportunity to work and should be treated fairly at work; all people

---

[36] See the review of the film, "Face Value: The Lunatic You Work for," *The Economist,* May 8, 2004, p. 64. The film is based on the book by Joel Bakam, *The Corporation: The Pathological Pursuit of Profit and Power* (New York: Free Press, 2004).

[37] Korten, *op. cit.*, p. 38. See also Roger Terry, *Economic Insanity: How Growth-Driven Capitalism Is Devouring the American Dream* (San Francisco: Berrett-Koehler, 1995).

[38] See for example the caution in Paul Hawken, "WTO Showdown," *Yes!: A Journal of Positive Futures,* Spring 2000, pp. 45–53.

[39] See Arthur Okun, *Equality and Efficiency: The Big Tradeoff* (Washington, D.C.: Brookings Institution, 1975).

should be treated equally before the law; and there should not be a huge unnecessary disparity among families in income and wealth.

The ideal of *efficiency* is a pragmatic goal of industrialized societies. It includes the following convictions: A more efficient and productive society yields more jobs and income for all; all individuals should work hard according to their abilities; rewards should be in proportion to an individual's work and merits; and people, material, and capital should be able to move freely.

These two goals of justice and efficiency are basic. Although we periodically fail in one or the other, it is also true that both remain real, explicit goals for Americans and people in other countries, also. Often achievement of one occurs at the expense of the other, yet we also know that it is unwise significantly to undermine either justice or efficiency. Both are essential to any society. A person at Kohlberg's Level III values would reach this conclusion, as we saw in Chapter 2.

Increasing **productivity** is a standard measure of efficiency. We commonly define productivity as output per person-hour. That is, productivity increases as the amount of labor expended to produce a given good or service decreases. Less often do we define productivity as a function of energy or raw materials used. Energy and materials are essential to a sustainable economy, but are becoming scarce and valuable. We should encourage the effort to use less energy and materials, and generate less pollution, while providing more people with jobs. Perhaps we need new terminology to describe this, perhaps *energy productivity* and *materials productivity*, and describe labor productivity more broadly as the productivity of *all available* workers.

A modern economy needs to be regulated. **Government regulation** provides protections which are necessary for business to operate. Regulation prohibits monopolies; limits toxic pollution; and ensures, for example, truthful advertising, accurate information on pharmaceuticals, and financial disclosure of publicly held firms. Bankruptcy legislation protects owners from going to debtor's prison. Government legislation "levels the playing field" to assure fair business dealings for consumers, producers, and investors. Without such government regulation and monitoring, the business environment would be a jungle. Business planning and growth would be impossible. We need only to witness pollution in China, insider deals and corruption in Russia, or the few rich versus the vast majority of the poor in Latin America.

Every economy operates following selected priorities and a resulting set of rules. Thus, the important question is, on what priorities are the rules set? For example, ideally a nation provides services and assesses taxes in order to be of the greatest benefit to its people as a whole. That is, legislation, taxes, and other government activities are directed to the **common good**.

Rules or legislation generally require that some must sacrifice some short-term benefits. For example, taxes to pay for fire protection and parks are levied on those who may never use the fire department or the park. Thus, this demands a political decision that fire protection and parks are benefits for which all people should pay whether or not they use these services.

Good governmental decisions require an objective and far-sighted approach when assessing the common good. Some laws are not popular among certain citizens, because they may cost them in the short term. Making long-term decisions is becoming harder, due to lobbyists, special interest groups, and contributors to a candidate's election campaign. It is difficult for a senator or representative to support legislation that would result in long-term benefits for most people, if that law results in a short-term cost for a wealthy and powerful supporter. Good government is thus subverted by rich and influential special interests which slant government policy to their own benefit.

For example, it would benefit people in the United States if we could simultaneously reduce both pollution and our excessive purchases of goods overseas. An **energy plan** that would reward consumers for using less petroleum would accomplish this. Such an energy plan could reduce pollution and the amount of petroleum we import, slow global climate change, aid city planning, slow urban sprawl, and preserve farmlands. The more than $80 billion that the United States spends annually for imported petroleum is a principal cause of its balance of payments deficit. Japan and the European nations have enacted a $4 to $5 per gallon gasoline tax for the above reasons. Such a tax would enable the United States to lower income taxes and balance its budget at the same time. But the U.S. Congress does not have the will to encourage efficient consumption by taxing the use of petroleum.[40] Americans thus transfer tens of billions of dollars to ExxonMobil and Saudi Arabia, rather than devote them to building schools, libraries, and national parks. In addition, the United States has earned the disapproval of other nations because of our voracious use of petroleum and our refusal to acknowledge these long-term common interests.

Enlightened self-interest motivates the businessperson to provide the products and services that people want—and to do so efficiently. But enlightened self-interest also can encourage persons to be more selfish. An infant is born self-oriented, but as it matures it begins to recognize the importance of other people (see Chapter 2). Excessive stress on self-interest can stunt a person so that he remains at an early stage of development with a focus on "me and mine." The common good can only be achieved when individuals look beyond merely what is good for them. This is especially true in contemporary society, where so many of our actions impact others (e.g., pollution, noise, use of scarce resources). These conflicts are also discussed in Chapters 1, 5, and 7.

Private ownership of large firms is justified primarily in the name of efficiency. The large disparities in income and wealth that we witness in the United States and Europe are also defended on the basis of efficiency: Money motivates people to work and to work harder. The private sector is generally more efficient than the public sector. However, it is difficult to prove that large disparities in income and wealth bring greater efficiency. In fact, there is opposing evidence that such disparities within a firm (or a community) bring discontent, jealously, and a lack of loyalty. We will discuss executive compensation in Chapter 8. Here we find one of the most

---

[40] For the same reasons, several national journals for decades have advocated a gradual but substantial tax increase on gasoline. See *BusinessWeek,* March 1, 2004, p. 44; May 27, 2002, p. 28; August 23, 1993, p. 14; November 23, 1981, p. 152; *U.S. News and World Report,* April 12, 2004, p. 80; August 27–September 3, 1990, p. 88; November 5, 1979, p. 92; *The New York Times,* June 28, 1988, p. 29.

clear-cut conflicts among our basic values: justice versus efficiency. In this regard recall that, in the name of justice, John Rawls requires that we must demonstrate that disparities in income, wealth, and power must in some fashion contribute to the advantage of all (see Chapter 3). Do you agree with Rawls' assessment?

FREE ENTERPRISE QUESTIONED FROM WITHIN

Rising median family income and increasing gross domestic product are generally considered indicators of a successful society. The United States has been successful in the production and consumption of material goods, so many would like to make that the measure of success for all nations. Frederick Winslow Taylor, the founder of scientific management, put it succinctly when he said, "In my judgment the best possible measure of the height in the scale of civilization to which any people has arisen is its productivity."[41]

An opposing point of view was presented a generation before Taylor, when England was at its height as an industrial and world power. Matthew Arnold objected to those who said that England's greatness was based on its railroads and steel. He went on:

> If England were swallowed up by the sea tomorrow, which, a hundred years hence, would most excite the love, interest, and admiration of mankind—and which would most, therefore, show the evidences of having possessed greatness?

Arnold asked whether it would be the England of the preceding two decades, a period of industrial triumph, or would it be an earlier period when culture was more valued? Arnold answered for his contemporaries:

> Never did people believe anything more firmly than nine Englishmen out of ten at the present day believe that our greatness and welfare are proved by our being so very rich.

And then he goes on to give his own response:

> The use of culture is that it helps us, by means of its spiritual standard of perfection, to regard wealth as but machinery, and not only to say as a matter of words that we regard wealth as but machinery, but really to perceive and feel that it is so.[42]

---

[41] Frederick W. Taylor, *Hearings Before the Special Committee of the House of Representatives to Investigate the Taylor and Other Systems of Shop Management,* vol. 3 (Washington, D.C.: Government Printing Office, 1912), p. 1471.

[42] Matthew Arnold, *Victorian Prose,* ed. Frederick William Roe (New York: Ronald Press, 1947), p. 399. A similar argument on the economic priority of people over dollars is made by Rebecca M. Blank and William McGurn, *Is the Market Moral? A Dialogue on Religion, Economics, and Justice* (Washington, D.C.: Brookings, 2004).

This same issue faces all of us as we live through the twenty-first century. How are we to judge the success of our civilization? What is our goal and what are our criteria for judging whether or not we are successful? Frederick Taylor says it is productivity; Matthew Arnold says productivity and wealth are merely tools to achieve something more. In this lasting debate, on which side do you stand? Or must we fashion some middle ground? A purpose of this book is to help each of us answer these questions.

Prediction of the Decay of Capitalism

Fears of the decay of free enterprise and capitalism were voiced as long ago as the sixteenth century by religious reformers John Calvin and John Wesley. These men who fashioned the ideals underlying the Protestant Ethic foresaw its ultimate breakdown (see Chapter 4). They predicted the collapse of the system once the goals of more material goods, greater financial rewards, and better efficiency in production would be attained. An economist, Joseph Schumpeter, also predicted such a collapse.

Schumpeter provides a detailed description of this decay of capitalism. He points out that the very success of the capitalist economic system in providing goods and income paradoxically lessens dependence on the system. As free enterprise is successful, human needs are satisfied and opportunities for investment are fewer. That same success undermines the need for, and so the prestige of, the entrepreneur, who is no longer dominant or highly respected in society.[43]

Intellectuals contribute to the growing hostility to capitalism. Academics and intellectuals are quick to see inequities and evils in any system.[44] The problems are there, and it is the work of the intellectual to point them out. Intellectuals and idealistic youth are the principal critics of totalitarian regimes worldwide. However, Schumpeter says that most intellectuals have had no experience in trying to manage an organization, so they do not possess the practical wisdom of those who have gotten their hands dirty.

Another difficulty, according to Schumpeter, is that the professional manager does not have the same long-term goals as the owner she replaces.[45] A hired manager is likely to move on to another job that offers greater financial reward, and will not stay and fight for the integrity of a firm. Schumpeter's indictment is broad-gauged: He even goes into some detail as to how capitalism and the materialistic attitudes it encourages tend to undermine family life and child rearing.

Schumpeter identifies yet another weakness of capitalism: It has no compelling, motivating, all-embracing ideology and set of values. It is a pragmatic system, designed and pursued for a narrowly conceived end—economic growth. He then contrasts capitalism and Marxism. Marxism has a vision of the world that **benefits all workers** and a systematic ideology; it calls on its followers to sacrifice for the sake of

---

[43] Joseph A. Schumpeter, *Capitalism, Socialism and Democracy* (London: Allen & Unwin, 1943), pp. 131–139.

[44] See also Ernest van den Haag, "The Hostility of Intellectuals to Capitalism," *The Intercollegiate Review* (Fall/Spring 2000–2001): 56–63.

[45] Schumpeter, *op. cit.,* pp. 143ff, 156.

the poor and for a more just distribution of goods. This vision inspires people. As much as we dislike it, al-Qaeda attracts idealistic young Muslim men who are willing to sacrifice for the vision of a better world. In contrast, capitalism promises only a higher standard of living and is not directly concerned for the poor and disadvantaged. Capitalism is effective in production but crass and narrow in its view of people and their environment. Schumpeter's critique has been widely quoted and many contemporary business leaders agree with his criticisms.

John C. Bogle, founder and CEO of Vangard Investments for two decades, criticizes the capitalism he sees today:

> By the latter years of the twentieth Century, our business values had eroded to a remarkable extent. Yes, we are a nation of prodigious energy, marvelous entrepreneurship, brilliant technology, creativity beyond imagination, and, at least in some corners of the business world, the idealism to make our nation and our world a better place. But I also see far too much greed, egoism, materialism, and waste to please my critical eye. I see an economy overly focused on the "haves" and not focused enough on the "have-nots", failing to allocate our nation's resources where they are most needed—to solve the problems of poverty and to provide quality education for all. I see our shocking misuse of the world's natural resources . . . [46]

Is Bogel accurate in his assessment of the limitations of contemporary capitalism?

Argument for Free Markets

An intelligent **defense of capitalism** and free markets provides a counter argument to critics. The most respected, articulate, and spirited spokesperson for free market ideology is Nobel Prize–winning economist Milton Friedman. He considers freedom the most important value in any economic or political system, and he sees economic freedom as absolutely essential to political freedom.

Friedman's position supports the free market and opposes government intervention. His is the familiar position that allowing every person the opportunity to buy and sell openly and without restriction will ensure that people will obtain the goods and services they need at the lowest possible price. Free competition in the marketplace will lead to the greatest efficiency in producing the goods people wish to purchase. The corporation, as the predominant economic institution, is a focus of Friedman's concern. He sees a corporation as solely economic, responsible primarily to its stockholders. Management has no right to dispose of stockholders' money in any manner that does not directly benefit the corporation. Management cannot make the workplace safer, install pollution-control equipment, or give money to universities, unless in some way these actions benefit the corporation itself, at least in the long term.

---

[46] John C. Bogle, *The Battle for the Soul of Capitalism* (New Haven: Yale University Press, 2005), p. xvi.

Friedman also argues that government has no role in economic planning. He speaks disparagingly of the government exercising control over the market in the "public interest." In addition, he finds that citizen public interest groups generally have a negative influence:

> All of the movements . . .—the consumer movement, the ecology movement, the protect-the-wilderness movement, the zero-population-growth movement, the "small is beautiful" movement, the antinuclear movement—have had one thing in common. All have been **antigrowth** (emphasis added). They have been opposed to new developments, to industrial innovation, to the increased use of natural resources.[47]

Friedman believes these public interest movements have hurt rather than helped the operation of the market.

Nevertheless, problems such as worker safety, product reliability, and industrial pollution must be addressed. If government legislation and regulation are to be kept to a minimum and if public interest groups do more harm than good, then the only alternative for solving such problems is management initiative. Yet Friedman argues that management has no right to take the initiative on such issues. Friedman vehemently denies that corporations do have, or even *can* have, social responsibilities: "The only entities who can have responsibilities are individuals; a business cannot have responsibilities."[48] To presume that a corporation has social responsibilities

> shows a fundamental misconception of the character and nature of a free economy. In such an economy, there is one and only one social responsibility of business—to use its resources and engage in activities designed to increase its profits so long as it stays within the rules of the game, which is to say, engages in open and free competition, without deception or fraud.[49]

He is convinced that the growing sense of corporate social responsibility undermines basic freedoms:

> Few trends could so thoroughly undermine the very foundations of our free society as the acceptance by corporate officials of a social responsibility other than to make as much money for their stockholders as possible. This is a fundamentally **subversive doctrine** (emphasis added). If businessmen do have a social responsibility other than making maximum profits for stockholders, how are they to know what it is?[50]

[47] Milton Friedman and Rose Friedman, *Freedom to Choose: A Personal Statement* (New York: Harcourt, Brace, Jovanovich, 1980), pp. 54–56, 95, 191.

[48] Milton Friedman, "Milton Friedman Responds," *Business and Society Review,* 1 (Spring 1972), p. 6.

[49] Milton Friedman, *Capitalism and Freedom* (Chicago: University of Chicago Press, 1962), p. 133.

[50] *Ibid.*

He points out that some German business executives contributed to the Nazi party in the 1930s.

Friedman argues for the **abolition of all corporate taxes** and for returning corporate profits to the stockholders, who can then decide how they will spend their money. Because it is their money, it should be their decision whether or not to use it for community purposes. His position is simple, straightforward, and consistent: The interests of stockholders, consumers, and citizens as a whole are best served if the corporation sticks to its traditional role of producing goods and services and does that as efficiently as possible. This is the best long-run service that a business firm can provide for society. He does, however, recognize the problem of unemployment and disability, and proposes a **guaranteed minimum income** (or "negative income tax") for all those of wage-earning age in the economy. He would substitute a minimum income for the variety of welfare, disability, and unemployment programs that have proliferated, all of which now require separate, expensive, and inefficient administrative apparatuses.

The same principles also apply to schools and medical care. Friedman does not think the government should operate schools, for government-funded public education is a bureaucratic monopoly insulated from the challenges to efficiency and excellence that come from competition. Rather, the government should provide redeemable tuition certificates for parents and children to use at the school of their choice. As is true in the production of goods and services, he is convinced that better and more effective education will result when there is free competition.[51] He has a similar position with regard to medical doctors and the monopoly that certification gives to the American Medical Association. Better, more efficient, and cheaper medical service would result if there were no monopoly. If anyone who has some medical knowledge could hang out a sign, the public would eventually find out who was giving better service and who should not be patronized. Friedman says this would better enable us to find the most effective and efficient treatment. But let us now examine cooperative methods of organizing an economy, which have been popular for centuries and continue to the present.

ALTERNATIVES TO CAPITALISM: COOPERATIVES

Some immigrants who came to the United States organized their economic life cooperatively rather than competitively. After experiencing dangerous work, exploitative bosses, and child labor, many came to the New World precisely to pioneer cooperative living. Hundreds of cooperative communities were formed in the United States during the last two centuries.[52] Most were inspired by a Christian vision of members sharing work and income equally. They opposed the divisive competition encouraged by capitalism and felt that only through

---

[51] Friedman and Friedman, *op. cit.*, pp. 150–188.
[52] Rosabeth Moss Kanter, *Commitment and Community* (Cambridge, MA: Harvard University Press, 1972); see also David French and Elena French, *Working Communally* (New York: Russell Sage Foundation, 1975); and William A. Hinds, *American Communities* (Chicago: Charles Kerr, 1902).

cooperation could a truly human and Christian community develop. Each of the communities we describe here counted their members in the hundreds and often thousands.

One example of such a community was **Brook Farm**, which was located in West Roxbury, within the present-day city of Boston. Another is a still existing communal group called the Shakers. They are a religious group that began in the United States in 1774 and by the early 1800s had grown to 19 separate communities scattered throughout New England and the Midwest; their land holdings totaled nearly 100,000 acres. The suburb of Cleveland called Shaker Heights takes its name from the **Shaker community** that was there; its Shaker Lakes were built as millponds. Shaker men and women lived in separate communities; there was little contact between them at work or socially. There was no marriage; new members had to be converted. In the early days there were many converts, and the number of Shakers reached 6,000. They called themselves the *Millennial Church.* It was outsiders who, observing the long, loud, shaking movements in their prayer services, dubbed them *Shakers.* The Shakers were innovative: They invented the flat brooms we use today, washing machines, packaged seeds, rotary harrow, wrinkle-resistant fabric, and a machine for coring apples. They were also among the earliest to use photography, electricity, and automobiles.[53]

Most of the community members were farmers, but there were other skills present also. Notable among communities where manufacturing began is the **Oneida** community in New York State, which was founded by the minister John Humphrey Noyes in 1848. Although it is no longer a commune, it has paradoxically developed into a multimillion-dollar international company and is now the largest maker of stainless steel tableware in the United States.[54]

The communal experiment at **New Harmony**, Indiana, a community started by Robert Owen, was famous during its time. Owen, a wealthy British factory owner, initiated work and social reforms; he was the first in England to limit the workday to 10 hours. Owen's dream was a community in which all work, life, and leisure would be shared. Unlike most other early commune organizers, Owen's vision was not religious in origin. In 1825, Owen purchased land and buildings from a religious community called the Rappites in southern Indiana and renamed it New Harmony. He advertised for members and accepted almost all comers; more than 900 arrived, among them some talented and well-known professional people. However, because of his other obligations, Owen himself found little time to be at New Harmony. Farming and other basic skills were scarce among the community members, and lack of a common vision and subsequent discord brought the community to an end after only two years. It was an expensive and highly publicized experiment, but it was shorter lived than most cooperative communities.

---

[53] Richard and Joyce Wolkomir, "Living a Tradition: At a Handful of Sites Shaker Communities Transport the Past into the Present," *Smithsonian,* April 2001, pp. 98–108; and Marguerite F. Melcher, *The Shaker Adventure* (Princeton, NJ: Princeton University Press, 1941), p. 302.
[54] Hinds, *op. cit.,* pp. 173–214.

Religious Communities that Aid Others

A much older example of cooperative life is the **Benedictine monks**, whom we described in Chapter 4. From the beginning, Christians were called to share their goods (Acts 2:44–47). Monastic living is a lasting model of sharing, living, and working together. However, Protestant and Catholic religious orders of women and men were not intended for everyone; they are voluntary associations which depend on shared Gospel values and a lifelong commitment.

In this spirit, there are today within the **Christian and Buddhist communities** tens of thousands of women and men in almost every country of the world who choose to live a life together in religious community. They choose to sacrifice some personal liberty in order to be of greater service to people and God. The Christian ideal is generally a life-time commitment, while the Buddhist tradition calls for men and women to spend a year of their life in a monastery living with monks.

Members of these communities seek to serve God, to try to make the world a better place, and to help other women and men especially those who are poor and in need. They work in hospitals, schools, colleges, and social service agencies throughout the world. They live together and choose to hold income and property in common, such as salaries, savings, houses, autos, TV, and PCs. Thus, they seek to be a witness that one can live without being caught up in the vices of self-centeredness, materialism, and an overemphasis on sexuality.[55]

In summary, effective leadership characterized all of the successful cooperative communities, and most were religious in origin. For a community to survive, it must continue to attract vigorous and talented people, not those who are looking for a refuge from the problems of the world. Self-discipline and order are necessary to solve the multitude of differences that arise in a community, yet these are impossible to sustain without a shared vision. Many of the early American communes failed after the original leader was gone and the early goals and inspiration for the community faded. The older religious communities lasted longer. Living together and sharing ones life with others is not a new social phenomenon.[56] It is a manifestation of a deep-rooted desire that people have for humane relationships, cooperation, and communication based on shared values, and it brings satisfaction and joy to its members.

Working in Community

Encouraging cooperation is healthy in free market societies, where enlightened self-interest pushes people toward individualism and selfishness. Religion is an aid in all societies in giving purpose to life, forming character, bringing people together,

---

[55] For additional information, see Patricia Wittberg, S. C., *Creating a Future for Religious Live: A Sociological Perspective* (New York: Paulist Press, 1989); Wade Clark Roof, *A Generation of Seekers: The Spiritual Journeys of the Baby Boom Generation* (San Francisco: Harper, 1993).

[56] For an account of advanced social system communes for thousands of Native Americans, see Larry Rohter, "Missions of a Lost Utopia: Where Paraguay, Brazil and Argentina Meet, Tourists are Discovering the Haunting Remains of a Jesuit Social Experiment," *The New York Times,* December 3, 2006, Sec. 5, pp. 1–13.

and helping them formulate long-range personal and group goals. However, because of fear of intolerance, many Western countries keep religion at the periphery of society and public policy. However, in recent years religion is a newly respected force in shaping public and political values. We will discuss the growing interest in religion and spirituality in the workplace in Chapter 7.

Excessive individualism in Western countries has spawned problems of crime, the breakdown of the family, and deserted central cities, according to group called *communitarians*. This group calls us to build shared values and mutual understanding in order to address our problems.[57] Communitarians hold that any society must limit a portion of what some people claim as "rights," in order to achieve the common good. For example, allowing everyone to claim as a right to do whatever they choose undermines both character formation for children and long-term public policy.

There are additional cooperative models for organizing free markets. Three of these are (1) European **social democracy**, (2) the Mondragon model of cooperative work, and (3) The Economy of Sharing. The social democracy model is best known and practiced in Sweden, Norway, Holland, Germany, and Austria. People there see government as the conscience of the free market. Jobs are considered as an essential of a society, so Sweden keeps unemployment at less than 2 percent. The Swedes choose to pay 50 percent of their income for taxes that support education, health, housing, and other social security–type programs. They and other Europeans see taxes as a necessary price of civilization.

Mondragon Cooperative Corporation is a group of 150 manufacturing, retailing, and banking businesses in northeastern Spain. The firms are worker owned and managed, and have been financially and socially successful for 70 years. Mondragon includes firms making household appliances, machine tools, automotive parts, engineering capital goods, as well as banks, schools, universities, stores, and hospitals, and has 78,000 worker/members. Each worker has an ownership stake in the firm. Annual sales of the group in 2006 were 11.9 billion Euros ($16.0 billion), and profits were up over the previous year 8.6 percent. Every major management decision has input from the worker/members, and the salary of each position is decided by a Committee which consists of representatives of both management and worker/members. Most of each firm's profits go back to the cooperative, but some is set aside for social projects in the community. When layoffs are necessary, the cooperative provides 80 percent of salary until that person returns to work. The Mondragon model requires that people have job skills, and it provides a world-renowned example of cooperative prosperity for both individuals and the community. Mondragon and the next example are both based on Gospel values.[58]

The **Economy of Sharing**, also called the Economy of Communion (EOC), is an international cooperative business initiative that began in Brazil in 1991. This

---

[57] Amitai Etzioni, *The Spirit of Community* (New York: Touchstone Books, 1994). See also Bill Shaw and Frances E. Zollers, "Managers in the Moral Dimension: What Etzioni Might Mean to Corporate Managers," *Business Ethics Quarterly* (July 1993): 153–168.

[58] Charles M. A. Clark, "The Mondragon Cooporacion Cooperativa," *Review of Business,* 25 (Winter 2004): 4–5; and Francisco Javier Forcadell, "Democracy, Cooperation and Business Success: The Case of Mondragon Corporación Cooperativa," *Journal of Business Ethics,* 56 (February 2005): 255. Also see MCC's Web site: http://www.mcc.es/ing/empresas/websdemcc.html, accessed July 17, 2007.

group of more than 700 businesses voluntarily pledge to divide their profits in three ways: helping the poor (especially by providing jobs), investing to grow their own business, and educating people in the Economy of Sharing. According to founder Chiara Lubich (1920–2008), "Unlike the consumer economy which is based on the culture of having, the economy of communion is the economy of giving . . ." One EOC economist says they hope "to transform the field of economics from a place where apparently irreconcilable individual interests clash, into a place of encounter, of personal fulfillment." The EOC has spread to Italy, the United States, France, Israel, Cameroon, Germany, and Serbia, and they meet regularly.[59]

Cooperation in the Workplace

Many current programs that encourage greater cooperation and commitment among members of business firms are attempts to attain better product quality, create a more humane workplace, and achieve greater profitability. A producer cooperative, such as Mondragon, is an entire group of businesses built on cooperative ideals. More limited plans, such as participative management, **employee stock ownership plans** (ESOPs), flexible work schedules, and profit sharing, are designed to build greater cooperation and commitment among workers in firms.[60]

ESOPs have a long history around the world. The largest 100 ESOPs in the United States range from 359,000 associates (United Parcel Service) to 200 people. They include firms in manufacturing, financial services, fast food, construction, and almost every other industry. Springfield Remanufacturing Corp. (SRC) in Missouri places decision responsibility on the individual worker, and annual bonuses are often 18 percent of salary. The firm encourages new ideas and entrepreneurship by funding dozens of new ESOP enterprises; one of these is a spin-off that teaches other executives and firms how to operate a participative ESOP. Some of these new enterprises thrive, and this enables SRC to keep its number of employees at its intended size of about 450. An organization that supports ESOPs boasts 1,200 firms and 750,000 employee-owners in the United States. Among the ESOP firms are Procter & Gamble, Anheuser-Busch, Amsted, and W. L. Gore Associates.[61]

Another example of cooperation at work is Linux software, which is cooperatively owned, and constantly improved by volunteers. The conviction that

---

[59] Luigino Bruni and Amelia J. Uelmen, "Essays: Religious Values and Corporate Decision Making: The Economy of Communion Project," *Fordham Journal of Corporate & Financial Law*, 11, no. 3 (2006): 645–681; Michele Zanzucchi, "Economy of Communion: 10 Years from the Beginning," *Living City*, July 2001, pp. 6–10. See also the Web site: http://www.focolare.org/, accessed July 17, 2007.

[60] Richard Marens, Andrew Wicks, and Vandra Huber, "Cooperating with the Disempowered: Using ESOPs to Forge a Stakeholder Relationship by Anchoring Employee Trust in Workplace Participation Programs," *Business and Society* 38 (March 1999): 51–82. For a summary of participation programs, see Chap. 3, "Work and Job Satisfaction," in *Ethical Dilemmas in the Modern Corporation*, eds. Gerald F. Cavanagh and Arthur F. McGovern (Englewood Cliffs, NJ: Prentice Hall, 1988).

[61] Information from http://www.esopassociation.org/, accessed June 4, 2007; for the list of the 100 ESOPs, see Marjorie Kelly, "A Tale of Two Employee-Owned Companies: Moving Beyond Ownership to Governance," *Business Ethics*, September/October 2001, pp. 12–17.

operating system software should be available to all, and to provide competition for Microsoft's Windows monopoly, encourages Linux scientists to contribute to its success. Microsoft has tried to thwart its success. Nevertheless Linux has been adopted by several large corporations, is used on a growing number of Web sites, and by computer hardware manufacturers IBM and Dell.[62]

An award-winning example of an ESOP is Chroma Technology Corp. of Rockingham, Vermont. It is 100 percent employee owned, and makes optical fibers for microscopes. With 68 workers and sales of $16 million, it is the major supplier for microscope manufacturers in Germany, Japan, and China. Most major decisions are made on the shop floor by the people doing the work. No person at Chroma makes less than $37,500 and no one makes more than $75,000. A disadvantage of the flat pay structure is that it is more difficult to attract people with executive experience or graduate degrees; nevertheless Chroma has three PhDs in biology. Chroma associates prefer the "the cooperative atmosphere, the self-direction, and the lack of a managerial class."[63]

The stakeholder theory of the firm provides a rationale for worker cooperation and partnering with all who depend on the firm: employees, creditors, suppliers, customers, local communities, and government. Some stakeholders then share in the decisions that affect them. Doing this successfully demands that executives possess listening and negotiating skills, but it also gives that firm a new legitimacy in society.[64]

Some people perform better when they work cooperatively, while others do better given individual incentives. Individualists are happier and work more efficiently when they have specific, personal tasks to perform and are rewarded by individual incentives. On the other hand, others are more satisfied and operate more effectively when they cooperate in a group and are rewarded by group incentives. Thus it is important to know what motivates oneself and those one manages. These differences influence managing and building incentive systems, and one's success in various global cultures. Participation is appropriate in certain industries and with certain people.[65] Why people work, how work can be more satisfying, and the effect of the organization on motivation will be discussed in the next chapter.

---

[62] "The Wild and Woolly World of Linux," *BusinessWeek,* November 15, 1999, pp. 130–134; see also http://www.linux.org/, accessed June 4, 2007.

[63] Peter Asmus, "Chroma Technology Corp.: Living Economy Award," *Business Ethics,* Fall 2004, pp. 9–10; also Robert Hutchinson, "Knowledge and Control: A Marxian Perspective on the Productivity Paradox of Information Technology," *Rethinking Marxism,* 20, no. 2 (April 2008): 288–304.

[64] See R. Edward Freeman, "A Stakeholder Theory of Modern Corporation," in *Ethical Issues in Business,* eds. Thomas Donaldson, Patricia Werhane, and Margaret Cording (Upper Saddle River: Prentice Hall, 2002), pp. 38–48; see also Freeman's earlier, *Strategic Management: A Stakeholder Approach* (Marshfield, MA: Pitman, 1984).

[65] Jeffrey S. Harrison and R. Edward Freeman, "Is Organizational Democracy Worth the Effort?" *The Academy of Management Executive,* 18 (August 2004): 49–53; See also the articles on organizational democracy which follow in this special issue. See also, R. Christopher Early, "East Meets West Meets Midwest: Further Explorations of Collectivistic and Individualistic Work Groups," *Academy of Management Journal* (April 1993): 319–348. This research was done using Chinese, Israeli, and American subjects.

Summary and Conclusions

Karl Marx pinpointed the weaknesses of capitalism and free markets. He and his followers have shown that free enterprise has undesirable consequences which often result in:

1. Exploitation of the worker,
2. Alienation of the worker,
3. Big business dominating national policy, and
4. Corporations exploiting other countries.

Marxists are at their sharpest when criticizing capitalism. But defenders of free enterprise do not advocate unemployment, poverty, and corruption. A critique of capitalism and the market system raises the vital question of how priorities are formulated. Who decides the primary goals of an economy or society? At best priorities are discussed by citizens in the political forum. Government can regulate and tax, but does not set economic goals. Free enterprise advocates defend this nonintervention as more efficient. Free enterprise recognizes one priority: "Will a given product, service or action return a profit?" The system does not ask how important the want is that is being met; it has no method of rating products or services on any scale other than dollars. Moreover, there are many goods, such as streetlights, police, parks, and public transportation, whose market value does not reflect their long-term value to society as a whole.

Who sets national priorities and implements them in free market countries? Do purchasers have the vision to ensure the long-term good of society and future generations? For example, how did we decide that private automobile travel was better than public rapid transit? How did we decide that we should spend more on advertising than on education, or on dog food and cosmetics than on helping hungry peoples feed themselves? As we will see in Chapter 8, in a market economy it is not clear where the responsibility for such decisions lies. Those advocating greater business responsibility point to the negative moral and social consequences of some business practices, such as toxic waste disposal, unsafe products, plant closings, and wastage of energy and resources. But the issue of national priorities goes beyond these policies. Both efficiency and justice are vital goals for any society. Competition encourages efficiency. However, selfishness and competition often bring a decline in efficiency, and almost always lead to a decline in justice.

Some of the values that we cultivate to be more efficient and successful make us less efficient and less successful. Moreover, in the process we can become blind to the importance of cooperation and justice. Considering critiques of free enterprise enables us to examine our own priorities. It helps us to see the limitations of our own values, so that we may amend them and thus improve our ability to live a happy and fulfilled life.

Discussion Questions

1. What does Mahatma Gandhi mean by each of the "seven blunders . . . that lead to violence." According to Confucius, in a country well governed, why should we be ashamed of poverty? What are the basic values of Texas Rep. Debbie Riddle?
2. How do you respond to each of the seven questions posed at the beginning of the chapter?

3. What evidence does Karl Marx provide that capitalism exploits the worker? Is his argument valid? How does a graduated income tax affect the inequality?
4. What evidence does Marx use to support his claim that capitalism alienates the worker? Evaluate this claim for the contemporary working person.
5. How does big business dominate the formulation of national goals? Is this true today? Provide evidence for your answer.
6. Why does Charles Lindbloom say that giant corporations and democracy cannot successfully coexist? What evidence does he cite?
7. How do large corporations exploit poor countries? Cite evidence and explain.
8. Do the four major problems of capitalism cited by Marx stem primarily from capitalism or industrialization? Why?
9. Do you agree that a society that is wholly directed to efficiency is likely to be unjust and that a society that is wholly directed to equality is likely to be inefficient? Why?
10. How does one measure the success of a society? By its gross national product? By the average per capita income of its members? By its literature or art? By its care for the poor and disadvantaged? Which criteria would you use?
11. Why did Joseph Schumpeter say that capitalism would decay? How are his views on this subject the same or different from those of John Calvin?
12. Does Milton Friedman think that a corporation has social responsibilities? Why? What are Friedman's free market prescriptions for education? For medical doctors? Do you agree?
13. Should profits and shareholder value be the sole goal of a business firm? Why?
14. Who has the responsibility to look to the long-term welfare of all citizens? Do business executives have any responsibility for this?
15. Describe the origins and characteristics of early American communal societies.
16. How do early American communal societies differ from Christian religious communities in their motivation? In their work ethic? . . . in their ability to last? What elements in a communal society support its continued existence?
17. Assess: (a) European social democracies, (b) Mondragon cooperatives, and (c) the Economy of Sharing? Are these free enterprise businesses? Explain. What could we learn from each model?
18. Outline the advantages and disadvantages of (a) cooperative and (b) competitive economic systems.
19. What are the advantages of introducing teamwork and participation in the workplace. Will it undermine competitive free enterprise? What are the advantages and disadvantages of Employee Stock Ownership Plans (ESOP)?

Selected Additional Readings

John C. Bogle, *The Battle for the Soul of Capitalism* (New Haven: Yale University Press, 2005).
Richard C. Edwards, Michael Reich, and Thomas E. Weisskopf, ed., *The Capitalist System* (Englewood Cliffs, NJ: Prentice Hall, 1986).
Milton Friedman and Rose Friedman, *Freedom to Choose: A Personal Statement* (New York: Harcourt, Brace, Jovanovich, 1980).
William H. Gates, Sr., and Chuck Collins, *Wealth and Our Commonwealth: Why America Should Tax Accumulated Fortunes* (Boston: Beacon Press, 2003).
David C. Korten, *When Corporations Rule the World* (San Francisco: Berrett-Koehler, 1995).
Karl Marx, "The Communist Manifesto," in *The Marx-Engels Reader*, ed. Robert C. Tucker (New York: Norton, 1972).
John Perkins, *Confessions of an Economic Hit Man* (San Francisco: Berrett-Koehler, 2004).

CASES

Case 6-1   Death Sentence for a Chinese Official

Zheng Xiaoyu was such a crusader for safe drugs in China that he was appointed as the top food and drug regulator. Nevertheless, several years later in both China and the United States high levels of toxins and other poisons were found in drugs and food which originated in China. A Beijing court found Xiaoyu guilty of approving counterfeit medications, and taking bribes from food and pharmaceutical firms. The court condemned him to death, and he was executed.

    1. How could a crusader for safe drugs approve toxic and counterfeit drugs?
    2. Is the death sentence appropriate? What is a suitable sentence for such a crime?
    3. What ethical norms help in assessing this case?

■ ■ ■

Case 6-2   Nike and Sweatshops

Nike is the largest producer of athletic footwear in the world. Nike's founder Phil Knight cultivates a brash, arrogant style. In the late 1990s Nike faced charges of using 14-year-old girls in Indonesia and Vietnam as workers; they worked 65 hours a week and breathed carcinogens as they assembled Nike shoes, and were often fired when they reached the age of 30. At first Knight and Nike said they had no control; the girls worked for subcontractors. After popular protests and critical articles in the U.S. media, Knight decided to require subcontractors to raise the mandatory minimum hiring age from 14 to 18 and to provide better conditions in the factories.

    1. Is this an example of exploitation of the worker? Why or why not?
    2. What ethical norm is most helpful to us in dealing with these issues?
    3. Do you think that Knight would have changed his position without the negative press reports?
    4. Why is Nike especially vulnerable to such negative publicity?

■ ■ ■

Case 6-3   California Sweatshop

Authorities raided an El Monte, California, sweatshop that employed 72 undocumented immigrants from Thailand. They were often forced to work 17 hours a day, were closely guarded, and held against their will; if they refused to work, they were sent back to Thailand. The Thai workers were making clothing that was sold at retailers like B.U.M. and Mervyn's. Federal authorities had heard about the situation three years earlier, but failed to investigate.

    After their release, lawyers defending the Thai immigrants obtained more than $1 million in back wages, largely because of the abuse they had undergone. Seven years later 71 Thais were granted permanent residency in the United States. Some government officials said that they thought that providing back pay and residency would encourage other illegal immigrants to come to the United States.

1. What ethical norms are most helpful in deciding the issues in this case?
2. Discuss the ethical responsibilities of the (a) owners of sweatshop; (b) Thai illegal immigrants; (c) government authorities; (d) clothing retailers.

■ ■ ■

Case 6-4   Superior's Expense Report

Sara McIntyre, a young management accountant at Tuloc, Inc., received a request for reimbursement of expenses from Elmer Cole, vice president of the division. He requests $3,100 for a two-day trip to Boston, and most of the items have no receipts and seem inflated to McIntyre.

1. What ethical norm is most helpful to McIntyre?
2. What should McIntyre do? What are her obligations and to whom?

Exercises

Exercise 6-1: Goals Notebook[66]
This exercise builds on the findings of the *Personal Goals and Values Inventory* from Chapter 1. It will enable you to learn more about your goals, using both your left (logical) and right (creative) brain modes of thinking:

1. Write a personal mission statement in no longer than one page (a single paragraph is even better).
2. Record your goals in order of importance to you. Use the *Personal Goals and Values Inventory* from Chapter 1.
3. List in detail five goal statements. At least two goals should be long term (attained in three to five years) and two should be short term (within six months). Each of the five goal statements should be one or two pages and should include:
   a. A statement of a goal that is specific, measurable, and attainable.
   b. The time frame in which you will attain this goal.
   c. Pictorial representation of the goal (e.g., clip art, photographs, cut-outs, drawings).
4. On the final page list at least three things you learned from this exercise.

Exercise 6-2: Debate Pro and Con of Free Trade
The purpose of a debate is to enable two teams to research an issue (one pro, the other con), prepare and outline an oral presentation, and make their arguments to the class. Each team should be of two to five people, and each member of the team should have something to contribute to the presentation(s). To enable the teams to prepare, the teams and the subject are

---

[66] For this exercise, I thank Dr. Mary Ann Hazen, College of Business Administration, and University of Detroit Mercy.

assigned one week prior to the debate. A subject for debate that is suitable for this chapter is: *Free trade is the best economic system for all countries of the world.*

The order and time schedule of the debate could be:

Pro: Prepared Presentation (7 min. max)
Con: Prepared Presentation (7 min. max)

Preparation of rebuttals (3 min.)
Con: Rebuttal of the previous pro presentation and summary (3 min. max)
Pro: Rebuttal of the previous con presentation and summary (3 min. max)

The same format may be used and additional subjects may be debated, also. Another subject for a debate might be: *The Global Reporting Initiative (GRI) is good for business* (see Chapter 8).

7

■ ■ ■

Personal Values and the Firm

*Try not to become a man of success but rather to
become a man of value.*

ALBERT EINSTEIN (1879–1955), NOBEL PRIZE–WINNING PHYSICIST

Money is my first, last, and only love.

ARMAND HAMMER (1898–1990), CEO, OCCIDENTAL PETROLEUM

*In the medieval system capital was the servant of man, but in the
modern system it became his master.*

ERIC FROMM (1900–1980), GERMAN/AMERICAN PSYCHOANALYST, WRITER

Indra Nooyi became chairman of the board and CEO of PespiCo in October 2006 after
having served as its CFO since early 2000. In ascending to the top spot at Pepsi,
Nooyi assumed one of the highest profile corporate jobs in the world. By all
accounts her entire career had been building toward this very moment. Nooyi was born
in 1955 in Chennai, India. She received her bachelor's degree from Madras Christian
College and a graduate degree from the prestigious Indian Institute of Management.
Shortly thereafter, she moved to the United States to earn her master's degree in
management from Yale University. After graduating from Yale, Nooyi worked for the
Boston Consulting Group, Motorola, and ABB before joining Pepsi in 1994 as a
senior vice president in charge of strategy. Nooyi has been credited with being a
major force behind many of Pepsi's most important moves during the past decade,
including its decision to spin off Pizza Hut, Taco Bell, and KFC, its acquisition of

Tropicana, its merger with Quaker Oats, and its strong moves into healthier foods and beverages. During her tenure as CFO, Pepsi's revenues increased 72 percent and its profits more than doubled, to $5.6 billion in 2006.[1]

Despite her career successes, Nooyi acknowledges the ongoing issues she encounters maintaining a balance between her work and her personal life. She admits that she struggles to maintain her identity as a woman, a mother of two, and as an Indian in an American white male-dominated business world:

> It's very hard. I tell you I often say that first of all I made a choice to be a business executive, mother, a wife. I am not going to sit here and say, "I am a mother. I need balance. I've got to create balance." So how does this work, this balance business? You have got to go out and get everybody into your program.[2]

Even though she became an U.S. citizen in 1990, Nooyi openly maintains many of her Indian cultural traditions, such as wearing a sari for special Pepsi events and dedicating a prayer space in her house as part of her Hindu faith. At work, she is as well-known for walking the halls barefoot, for singing songs from her days as a member of an all-girl rock-and-roll band in college, and for being a passionate New York Yankees fan as she is for being a brilliant, but direct-speaking manager.[3] Over the years Nooyi has brought her children to work to spend time with them when office demands were great, and she speaks of the extensive network of family members who watch her children when she or her husband travels. Finally, Nooyi greatly credits the people and the work environment over the years at PepsiCo that have accepted her dual roles as mother and executive.[4]

Indra Nooyi recognizes the importance of both her work life and her personal life. She is one of a growing number of managers who are unwilling to give unlimited priority to her work. Facing the same issues, but acting differently, in 1998, Brenda Barns, then 43, quit her job as head of PepsiCo North America to spend more time with her three children. In May, 2004 Sara Lee named her president and chief operating officer.[5] Both women have a strong influence on the people with whom they work.

The work environment, in turn, has as strong an influence on Nooyi and Barns as it does on each of us. The groups and organizations of which we are a member—from family to corporation—influence our personal values, goals, and ethics, although we are seldom explicitly aware of this influence. Personal values, which are among the basic components of personality, develop from exposure to others. Values are often received uncritically from parents, peers, teachers, and the media. A loving

---

[1] Diane Brady, "Indra Nooyi: Keeping Cool in Hot Water; The CEO's Smart Moves Have Helped Pepsi Cut Down on Junk Food," *BusinessWeek,* June 17, 2007, p. 49.

[2] Indra Nooyi, "Tuck School of Business at Dartmouth CEO Speaker Series Question & Answer Segment," September 23, 2002, http://mba.tuck.dartmouth.edu/cgl/downloads/indranooyiqa.pdf.

[3] Chad Terhune and Joann Lublin, "Pepsi's New CEO Doesn't Keep Her Opinions Bottled Up," *The Wall Street Journal,* August 15, 2006, p. B1.

[4] Nooyi, *op. cit.*

[5] *BusinessWeek,* May 27, 2004, p. 48.

and listening parent encourages values that are quite different from those engendered by a parent who is annoyed, distracted, or absent—but both convey values. In a parallel fashion, an emotionally healthy executive or manager has a supportive influence on the firm's culture and climate; then it is likely a challenging and enjoyable place to work. On the other hand, an emotionally ill executive can cause untold stress on people for whom he is responsible.[6]

Later, during working years, we often so identify with an organization that success within it becomes a primary measure of personal worth. Performing well at Merrill Lynch or Dow Chemical can influence my self-concept. When I work in a firm that encourages pride in good work, autonomy, creativity, and risk taking, that can give me self-confidence and joy in doing my work. On the other hand, personal values are sometimes compromised by a business climate that condones unethical acts.[7] Moreover, an individual may identify so closely with work that "success" on the job is the total measure of self-worth. Realization of the inadequacy of that measure often does not come until midlife, which then can bring profound anxieties, frustrations, and even serious physical ailments. We discussed stress on the job and the midlife crisis in Chapter 2.[8]

A business firm can and should meet vital individual and social needs. It can enable an individual to achieve a sense of identity and "develop the skills and loyalties that are necessary to sustain the social structure of responsible and ethical organizational life."[9] For this relationship to develop, trust must exist between the firm and the individual. The importance of such trust has received considerable attention.[10] Ford Motor Company encourages each person to develop their own spirituality. Levi Strauss promotes ethics in each worker's actions; it also seeks employee input on all work-related issues. Canon's founder, Ryuzaburo Kaku, encourages a sense of working and living together for the common good in all business decisions. Avis began employee participation groups when it became employee owned, and earnings and stock prices jumped immediately. Domino's Pizza encourages its employees to use the Golden Rule in the workplace. These practices reinforce human values learned in the family and encourage concern for people—whether they are neighbors, coworkers, suppliers, customers, or subordinates. These firms thus help their people to maintain an integrated personality, not separating the values of family life from those of the workplace.

---

[6] James C. Quick, Joanne Gavin, Gary Cooper, and Jonathan Quick, "Executive Health: Building Strength, Managing Risks," *Academy of Management Executive,* 14, no. 2 (2000): 34–44; see also the more comprehensive, James Quick, Jonathan Quick, Debra Nelson, and Joseph Hurrell, *Preventive Stress Management in Organizations* (Washington, D.C.: American Psychological Association, 1997).

[7] William C. Frederick and James Weber, "The Values of Corporate Managers and Their Critics: An Empirical Description and Normative Implications," in *Research in Corporate Social Performance and Policy,* ed. William C. Frederick, vol. 9 (Greenwich, CT: JAI Press, 1987), pp. 131–151.

[8] For a more complete description of work and job satisfaction issues, see Cavanagh and McGovern, *Ethical Dilemmas in the Modern Corporation* (Englewood Cliffs, NJ: Prentice Hall, 1988), pp. 34–63.

[9] Timothy L. Fort, "Business as Mediating Institution," *Business Ethics Quarterly,* 6 (April 1996): 149–163.

[10] See, for example, Bennett J. Tepper and Edward C. Taylor, "Relationships Among Supervisors' and Subordinates' Procedural Justice Perceptions and Organizational Citizenship Behaviors," *Academy of Management Journal,* 46, no. 1 (2003): 97–105, and the entire issue dedicated to trust, "Special Topic Forum on Trust in and Between Organizations" in the *Academy of Management Review,* 23 (July 1998).

Some business firms, and even some universities and hospitals, show little social concern. As we will see later in this chapter, managers of such institutions tend to be more self-centered and show less concern about social conditions and are not willing to help other people when it would require them to make a personal sacrifice. The values of these managers contrast with the self-image most Americans have of themselves as generous. When personal values are held uncritically, they contain the seeds of potential conflict and anxiety. Leaders of organizations who make decisions based on self-centered values often cause severe social disruption. Note some financial analysts who publicly urged a "buy" of Enron and WorldCom, while privately calling the firms "dogs," or the after hours trading at many mutual funds. Managers conceive of themselves as objective, rational, and not led by personal prejudice; they do a careful analysis of all the facts before coming to a judgment. The use of market surveys, outside consultants, product planning groups, and computer analyses indicates the high priority that rational decision making has within firms. Yet these same managers are often unaware of how much their unexamined personal values bias their decisions. They thus hurt both themselves and their organizations.

Managers are often unaware that the decision-making process itself rests on unexamined assumptions. For beneath this rational structure may lay presuppositions about the purpose of the firm—to maximize shareholder value and to increase market share. The ideological assumptions upon which rational decision making is based are often accepted unquestioningly, much as we accept traditional cultural norms.

GENERATIONAL VALUES AND BUSINESS VALUES

Each organization develops a life and norms of its own. Schools provide values to children before they are in the workplace. For example, today's students and recent college graduates are often products of the "self-esteem" movement prevalent in K-12 teaching practices throughout most of the 1980s and 1990s. These students are markedly different than previous generations on a number of emotional and values measures. This newest generation of workers is generally acknowledged to have more self-esteem, be less accepting of criticism, more demanding of continuous praise, more assertive, and less likely to form long-term bonds than their predecessors. These characteristics, which have collectively earned them nicknames ranging from "Generation Me"[11] to the "The Most Praised Generation,"[12] have a huge influence on how educators teach at all educational levels.

While ethical norms and expectations within schools evolve over time to produce new challenges and opportunities, so too is a business affected by the problems it faces. An organization's growth and/or struggle for survival can give apparent

---

[11] Jean Twenge, *Generation Me: Why Today's Young Americans are More Confident, Assertive, Entitled—and More Miserable than Ever Before* (New York: Free Press, 2006).
[12] Jeffrey Zaslow, "The Most Praised Generation Goes to Work," *The Wall Street Journal,* April 20, 2007, p. W1.

legitimacy to many activities that would not be undertaken if subjected to more careful scrutiny. These activities often conflict with the values of honesty, integrity, and concern for others that are possessed by members of the organization. This conflict may then cause members to reflect on the inconsistency of these personal and organizational values. The inadequacy of an exclusive reliance on market values often does not appear until the values of the firm come into conflict with the values of a person or of society; we will discuss this in greater detail in Chapter 8.

This chapter will examine *personal values in business*, including the following topics:

1. The influence of *organizational values*, *climate*, and *expectations* on the values of individuals.
2. *Goals and motives of individuals* and how motives are affected by personal values and ethics.
3. *Workplace pressures*, and how these contribute to personal health or illness.
4. Achieving a *balance between work and the rest of life*.

THE FIRM FORMS WORKERS: SOCIALIZATION

Any group of people working together must share goals and values; otherwise they suffer conflict and confusion. Hence to obtain cooperation, socialization is essential in any human endeavor. **Formal socialization** (see Figure 7-1) is the deliberate attempt by the organization to influence the attitudes of members. Informal socialization takes place among members through ordinary interaction. Many values are introduced in orientation and training programs, but others are formed by exposure to the expectations of superiors and peers during the work week. Socialization takes place through actions, stories, and myth that are passed down through the organization.[13] When coupled with the perceived importance of success in the firm, such socialization brings reinforcement or changes in values. Employee training provides payoffs for the firm; these employees tend to perform better and show more citizenship behavior and more commitment to the firm.[14] For example, Disney Productions, through both formal and informal socialization, ensures that new members know how to make "guests" feel welcome and comfortable.

The organization has its own demands, which arise from actions to maintain the health of the organization. These actions are often guided by the market values of shareholder value, market share, and return on investment. Organizational maturity and stability, without profitability and growth, are not acceptable goals for the long term; CEOs are fired for having such unaggressive goals. Moreover, organizations affect almost every segment of our lives—including our moral lives also. Work climates have a strong influence on the ethical values and thus the actions of

---

[13] For research and theory on organizational culture and socialization, see Geert Hofstede, *Culture's Consequences: Comparing Values, Behaviors, Institutions and Organizations Across Nations,* 2nd. ed. (Thousand Oaks: Sage, 2001); and Joanne Martin, *Organizational Culture: Mapping the Terrain* (Thousand Oaks: Sage, 2002).

[14] Anne S. Tsui, Jone Pearce, Lyman Porter, and Angela Tripoli, "Alternate Approaches to Employee Organization Relationship: Does Investment in Employees Pay Off?" *Academy of Management Journal,* 40, no. 5 (1997): 1089–1121.

TYPES OF SOCIALIZATION	METHODS OF SOCIALIZATION
FORMAL	1. Orientation program
	2. Job descriptions
	3. Training programs
	4. Codes of behavior
	5. Performance appraisal and feedback
INFORMAL	1. Expectations of superiors
	2. Actions of and conversations with peers
	3. Unwritten norms
	4. Organizational culture

FIGURE 7-1 Socialization within the Organization

members of an organization.[15] "Because modern organizations have created and have largely defined the American value system, they must be considered the most important socializing agencies in America."[16]

Organizations are generally effective in selecting individuals and then socializing them into persons who "fit well" into the system. Moreover, people of similar traits to supervisors and peers tend to be picked for promotion in organizations.[17] Each organization has a subtle but potent influence on its members' attitudes, values, and ethics. Sociologist Robert Jackall paints an unflattering picture of American corporate bureaucracy. On the basis of extensive interviews with managers, he points out that managerial decisions are made on a short-term basis. Moreover, most firms reward this short-term perspective, and generally reward on the basis of political considerations rather than performance and merit. The most important thing that is learned in the corporation is mastering expectations and fitting in.[18]

Large organizations offer many examples of such short-sighted and inflexible behavior. New products often come from startups, while Nike and Microsoft become large and inflexible. A large organization develops a life of its own, protecting its own special interests and being jealous of its position, power, and prerogatives. The

---

[15] For an overview of this work, see, James Weber, "Emphasizing the *Ethical* in Ethical Work Climates," Paper presented at National Academy of Management—1993, Atlanta; also Linda K. Trevino and G. Weaver, "Business ETHICS/BUSINESS Ethics," *Business Ethics Quarterly,* 4 (1994): 113–128; Bart Victor and John Cullen, "The Organizational Basis of Ethical Work Climates," *Administrative Science Quarterly* (March 1988): 101–125.

[16] Deborah Vidaver Cohen, "Moral Climate in Business Firms: A Framework for Empirical Research," in *Academy of Management Proceedings—'95,* ed. Dorothy P. Moore (Vancouver, B.C.: Academy of Management, 1995). The original quote is from William G. Scott and David K. Hart, *Organizational America* (Boston: Houghton Mifflin, 1979), p. 36; see also John M. Darley, "How Organizations Socialize Individuals into Evildoing," in *Codes of Conduct: Behavioral Research into Business Ethics* (New York: Russell Sage Foundation, 1996), pp. 13–43.

[17] John Schaubroeck and Simon S. K. Lam, "How Similarity to Peers and Supervisor Influences Organizational Advancement in Different Cultures," *Academy of Management Journal,* 45, no. 6 (2002): 1120–1136.

[18] Robert Jackall, *Moral Mazes: The World of Corporate Managers* (New York: Oxford University Press, 1988).

corporation's procedures, especially when they have been successful in the past, can become rigid and ossified. Each individual is expected to "learn Mitsubishi's way of doing things." Managers select for promotion subordinates who have values like their own. Although these managers pride themselves on making objective and rational decisions, personal likes and values play an important role.

In large organizations, coordination between people and business units is essential. As various responsibilities are spelled out in writing, there is less room for individual judgment. Even in decentralized companies that are trying to be more flexible, standard practices and procedures limit new ideas and initiatives. Deviant values are eliminated, either in the selection process or through socialization.[19] It thus becomes clear which values are accepted and which are not, and whether it is preferred behavior, for example, to come to work early and stay late, or to ask for overtime pay.

Compounding the problem, every organization has **toxic employees**: people who are rude, not civil, and sometimes unethical. These people take a large toll on their colleagues. Their fellow workers try to avoid them and withdrew from groups in which the toxic individual is a member. Because of uncivil and unethical coworkers, some colleagues report that they ceased voluntary efforts, stopped helping newcomers, or stopped offering assistance to colleagues. Often managers do not address the difficulties that the toxic person causes. The toxic person may be judged too valuable or may be protected by regulations that make them impervious to sanctions, including firing. Often the toxic actions are triggered in reaction to the toxic actions of the person's supervisor.[20]

In any organization, the competitive, achievement-oriented manager wants to be noticed quickly as a success. Such a manager then tends to focus on short-run performance, as it is more easily measured and will provide early favorable notice to top management. Market values tend to crowd out personal and social values.

Success at Work

Globalization demands that firms lower their costs. Downsizing, layoffs, outsourcing, and reduced benefits have been the result for decades. These actions have had an immense cost both in human terms and in worker loyalty. As one publication notes,

> It's a vicious cycle. Workers are increasingly feeling that employers aren't looking after their interests, and employers in turn are regarding workers as little more than fair-weather friends, ready to jump ship at the first sign of a more advantageous offer.[21]

Acknowledging that much job security and loyalty have now evaporated, some maintain that if an employer is honest and provides satisfying work, they can expect

---

[19] For a review of the role of deviants in the organization, see Danielle E. Warren, "Constructive and Destructive Deviance in Organizations," *Academy of Management Review,* 28, no. 4 (2003): 622–632.
[20] See Peter J. Frost, *Toxic Emotions at Work: How Compassionate Managers Handle Pain and Conflict* (Boston: Harvard Business School, 2003).
[21] David Lazarus, "Increasingly, Employees Feeling Grumpy about Work," *The Providence Journal,* June 17, 2007, http://www.projo.com/business/content/BZ_lazarus17_06-17-07_3V60ELD.3438600.html.

a new form of commitment from workers.[22] Although a survey shows that 75 percent of workers find satisfaction in their jobs, only 30 percent can be considered truly loyal. Another 34 percent are looking for a job elsewhere and 31 percent feel trapped in their current job because of circumstances.[23] In spite of their insecurity, people still hope that their work will provide satisfaction and fulfillment. Satisfaction generally comes from doing a job well and contributing to the happiness of others. This conviction that one's life is worthwhile gives not only satisfaction but also energy and focus to one's work. Large organizations and efficiency demand specialization of tasks and interchangeability of personnel. As work is divided up and depersonalized, much of the joy of successfully accomplishing tasks is taken away. Whether providing services or manufacturing products, workers rarely produce a finished product by themselves. They perform a portion of the entire job, because specialization of labor lowers costs. A large firm often further divides the labor, creating a greater physical distance between the individual worker and the finished product or service.

As a result, something that is essential for human life is neglected and repressed. Satisfaction, pride in work, and a sense of ownership are often lacking. The goals of a firm—production and growth—take precedence over the goals of individuals. When nonhuman objectives are valued over persons, the result can be isolation, loneliness, and alienation. Even though there may be more wealth and conveniences, life is often less fulfilling.

One reason for a lack of satisfaction is that our work ethic no longer has a foundation. When the Protestant Ethic was the basic value system for Americans (see Chapter 4), personal values supported work values. But for a generation this has not been the case. Daniel Bell wrote,

> What this abandonment of Puritanism and the Protestant Ethic does is to leave capitalism with no moral or transcendental ethic. It also emphasizes an extraordinary contradiction within the social structure itself. On the one hand, the business corporation wants an individual to work hard, pursue a career, accept delayed gratification—to be, in the crude sense, an organization man. And yet, in its products and its advertisements, the corporation promotes pleasure, instant joy, relaxing and letting go. One is to be "straight" by day and a "swinger" by night.[24]

This paradox continues today and is demonstrated in self-seeking individualism and materialism, which can tear apart families, neighborhoods, and business firms.

---

[22] See articles in a special issue of *Business Ethics Quarterly,* 11 (January 2001): 1–68; Domenec Mele, "Loyalty in Business: Subversive Doctrine or Real Need?"; George Randels, "Loyalty, Corporations, and Community"; Brian Schrag, "The Moral Significance of Employee Loyalty"; Daniel R. Gilbert, Jr., "An Extraordinary Concept in the Ordinary Service of Management."

[23] The figures are from "The Walker Loyalty Report for Loyalty in the Workplace—2003." Available from Walker Information at www.walkerinfo.com.

[24] Daniel Bell, *The Cultural Contradictions of Capitalism* (New York: Basic Books, 1976), pp. 71–72.

Money as the Goal

Material values are central for many Americans. These values appear to be even more important as the erosion of corporate loyalty forces workers to reconsider their desire to find happiness and fulfillment through work. To foreign observers, it sometimes appears as if everything Americans do is aimed at acquiring and providing material goods. A few manifestations of this orientation are the centrality of work life, advertising, the latest PC software, and designer clothes. Americans act as if they believed that happiness consists in the latest electronic gadget or a second home for vacations. We conceive of ourselves in terms of the goods we possess. For example, consider the attitudes of today's college students, who mirror our cultural values. More than 70 percent of the entering college freshmen surveyed around the United States believe that being financially well off is a very important goal. This number has remained stable for about two decades, since it rose from 40 percent in 1970. Compare this with another goal. In 1970, 83 percent of college freshmen thought that developing a meaningful philosophy of life was very important; in 2005, the percentage was only 45 percent.[25] Are college students choosing the prospect of wealth over a good education? What does this tell us about our values?

The goals of college freshman reflect the goals of their elders. Consider the well-publicized salaries of entertainers, sports figures, and CEOs; their compensation is huge and disproportionate to their contribution. Derek Bok, former president of Harvard University, is troubled by the immense salaries of corporate CEOs.[26] We will discuss executive compensation further in the next chapter.

Economic goals and business values have a profound influence on our social and political policies as well. Business lobbying often has a decisive influence on legislation and foreign policy. For example, business considerations—to ensure a steady supply of petroleum—were important elements in our decisions to invade Kuwait and Iraq.

In the last chapter, we examined Karl Marx's position that an industrial society separates people from their work and alienates them. Is working an attractive and rewarding activity for most people today? Repetitive work in a fast-food restaurant and menial retail clerical jobs provide little job satisfaction. Lack of satisfaction occurs when work is cut into small segments, supervisors are distant and impersonal, and there is little pride in the final product. In many of these jobs, workers are used like single-purpose tools. Such jobs thus demand little intelligence or imagination, and the workers have little control over their work or work setting. Productivity and efficiency are chosen over pride, responsibility, and the joy that can be gotten from work.

Another factor that has undermined respect for work is its presentation in films and on TV. When did you last see a film or a TV program that showed a

---

[25] Sylvia Hurtado, Linda Sax, Victor Saenz, Casandra Harper, Leticia Oseguera, Jennifer Curley, Lina Lopez, De'Sha Wolf, and Lucy Arellano, *Findings from the 2005 Administration of Your First College Year (YFCY): National Aggregates,* Higher Education Research Institute University of California, Los Angeles, February 2007. Obtained from http://www.gseis.ucla.edu/heri/pdfs/2005_yfcy_report_final.pdf.
[26] Derek Bok, *The Cost of Talent* (New York: Free Press, 1993); and *Fortune,* June 26, 1995, pp. 66–76.

businessperson who worked hard, produced a valuable product, built teamwork among her colleagues, and was satisfied with her work? A PBS documentary entitled "Hollywood's Favorite Heavy: Businessmen on Prime Time TV" was partially underwritten by Mobil Oil. Mobil cites the findings of this documentary, "By the age of 18, the average kid has seen businessmen on TV attempt over 10,000 murders." Businesspeople on TV "seem to make an awful lot of money, without ever having to work hard or produce useful products. To succeed, all they seem to do is lie, steal, cheat, blackmail, even murder." The documentary then shows film clips of popular TV shows in which all of the above take place. These points continue to be made in recent documentaries such as *The Corporation*, *The Smartest Guys in the Room*, and *Who Killed the Electric Car?*, all of which portray corporations and executives as selfish and greedy. Movie critic Roger Ebert says "corporations have replaced Nazis as the politically correct villains of the age,"[27] while law professor Larry E. Ribstein examines both the subtle and the not-so-subtle negative portrayals of capitalists as cold-hearted, criminal, and evil in modern cinema. His subject list includes recent films such as *Erin Brockovich*, *Mission Impossible II*, *Fight Club*, *Boiler Room*, *The Cooler*, *The Perfect Storm*, *Office Space*, *Two Weeks Notice*, and *The Insider*.[28]

Moreover, in most movies and TV shows, school and work are both treated as frustrating, boring, trivial, and/or a joke. One who works in TV and who is also a critic names many specific shows that place work in a poor light. He then asks why we cannot have some TV that shows work as a worthwhile human activity:

> People smart enough to make brilliant shows like "Cheers" or "The Wonder Years" or "Cosby" or "L.A. Law" easily have it in their power to do what Arthur Miller did in *Death of a Salesman*, what Norman Lear did in "All in the Family", and what many other writers have done before them: to show that discipline, work, and all the habits that make people and nations self-sufficient and proud of themselves are not for losers but for winners.[29]

Executives too often show a lack of concern for people. Managers sometimes acknowledge only the short-term, bottom-line goals of better productivity, higher return on investment, and a larger share of the market. The individuals who are attracted and make it to the corporate executive suite have a great need for success. To attain their goals, they must be able to make decisions unencumbered by emotional ties to persons or groups. They must always be ready to move to a new location and leave old friends, associations, and neighborhoods behind. In fact, for

[27] Roger Ebert, "In Good Company," *Chicago Sun-Times,* January 15, 2005, http://rogerebert.suntimes.com/apps/pbcs.dll/article?AID=/20050113/REVIEWS/50103002/1023.

[28] Larry Ribstein, *Wall Street and Vine: Hollywood's View of Business,* Illinois Law & Economics Working Paper LE05-010, http://www.law.uiuc.edu/faculty/directoryresult.asp?Name=Ribstein,+Larry.

[29] Benjamin Stein, "Work Gets No Respect on TV," *The Responsive Community,* Fall 1993, pp. 32–37.

many there is little point in making deep friendships or getting involved in local activities; it would only make parting more difficult. This is not new; it has been true for more than a generation.[30] Those attracted to corporate executive work are often people who do not depend on close personal relationships. They obtain their major satisfaction from completing a task. Their personal values set the tone for the organization; these values are communicated to others in the firm. It is clear to all that those who are promoted are more task-oriented than person-oriented.

Winners and Self-Developers Among Managers

After interviewing managers in large, high-technology companies, **Michael Maccoby** concluded that such people were not primarily interested in skills, power, or loyalty but rather in "organizing winning teams."[31] Hence he characterized successful managers as **gamesmen**. Gamesmen develop many positive intellectual characteristics to aid in "winning the game" (e.g., analysis, problem solving, and policy development), but at the same time they allow their emotional life to atrophy. They are more detached and emotionally inaccessible than others in the corporate hierarchy.

Gamesmen do not have a "developed heart." They lack compassion and appreciation for suffering; they cannot even bear to look at suffering. Maccoby calls them "weak hearted." Many younger managers are weak-hearted gamesmen. For Maccoby, a strong-hearted manager is able to understand and to empathize with the suffering that may come from a particular business decision. The strong hearted make the best executives, in Maccoby's judgment.

Gamesmen also have little sense of social responsibility. Unaware of and hence unconcerned about the social and human effects of their actions on others, they operate on the primitive notion that the success of their organization will automatically benefit all. They refuse to consider undesirable secondary effects.

Although most of the gamesmen that Maccoby interviewed indicated that they wanted friendship and help from their friends, fewer than 10 percent of them said that helping others was a personal goal. Compare this to more than half of a group of factory workers who mentioned helping others as a personal goal. Maccoby found managers in Mexico to be "more aware than Americans that their careers protect them from the poor, but even the Mexican executives are not aware that within their enclaves they are becoming more alienated from themselves." Around their houses they build walls, and on top of those walls they put broken glass or spikes to prevent the intrusion of the poor. In a similar way, many affluent neighborhoods in the United States and in other countries now have walls and guardhouses to separate the wealthy from others.

Gamesmen set out to be "winners." Their intelligent, aggressive behavior makes them successful in focused tasks at work. However, they trade off much of

---

[30] William E. Henry, "Executive Personality and Large-scale Organizations," in *The Emergent American Society,* eds. W. Lloyd Warner et al., vol. 1 (New Haven: Yale University Press, 1967), p. 275.
[31] Michael Maccoby, *The Gamesman: The New Corporate Leaders* (New York: Simon & Schuster, 1976), p. 34.

their affective life. The fatal danger of gamesmen is to be trapped in perpetual adolescence, striving to be a winner at the game throughout adulthood.[32]

Maccoby later identified a growing group among young managers: self-developers.[33] Self-developers value opportunities to learn, grow, and gain a sense of competence and independence in an egalitarian workplace. Wary of being swallowed up by work, they are less likely to become corporate chiefs than are gamesmen. More concerned with learning and cooperation, they are motivated to succeed in family life as well as in their careers and to balance work with play. In the future, with fewer layers of middle management and more moving from one firm to another, it will be important that people be able to manage themselves. The self-developers have those qualities, and seem better adapted to business in the next decades than do gamesmen.

Dissent in the Organization

The importance of independent judgment has always been recognized by Americans. But although we mouth our support of independent judgment, experience and research indicate that it does not hold the high priority we claim for it. On the contrary, attitudes of the group have a profound influence on the individual. Individuals are often willing to deny their own perceptions and judgments because of the stance of their group.[34]

One of the classic experiments in studying the influence of groups on the judgment of members was done by **Solomon E. Asch**.[35] Asch gathered groups of seven to nine engineering students at MIT for "psychological experiments in visual judgment." Members of each group were shown two cards simultaneously; one card bore a standard line and the other bore three lines, one of which was the same length as the one shown on the first card (see Figure 7-2).

They were asked which line is the same length as line X? Is it A, B, or C? In each group, all but one member were "confederates" (i.e., earlier instructed to pick the same incorrect line). The remaining member was "aïve" and was the only real subject of the experiment. The question at issue was: How often would a group member pick the right line even in the face of unanimous agreement by the rest of the group that another was the right one? It was visually quite clear which line was the same length as X, and ordinarily only 1 percent of the subjects would pick the wrong line. The subject was seated near the end of the group so that most of the others had responded by the time it was the subject's turn to do so.

In our reputedly individualistic society, the findings are revealing: Faced with incorrect answers by the majority, 75 percent of real subjects erred as well. Only 25 percent braved conflict with the group and held to their own perceptions. As Asch points out, when a majority of reasonably intelligent and educated young students

---

[32] *Ibid.*, pp. 109, 203.

[33] Michael Maccoby, *Why Work?* (New York: Simon & Schuster, 1988).

[34] Patricia Faison Hewlin, "Facades of Conformity in Organizational Settings," *Academy of Management Review,* 28, no. 4 (2003): 633–642.

[35] Solomon E. Asch, "Opinions and Social Pressure," in *Science, Conflict and Society* (San Francisco: Freeman, 1969), pp. 52–57.

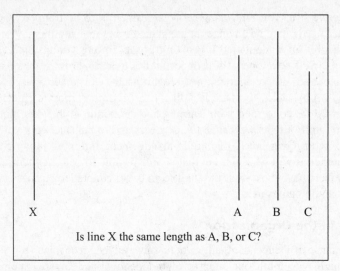

FIGURE 7-2 Line Perception Experiment

will call black "white" when faced with the opinions of the group, it is obvious that we lose much of the benefit of individuals' independent assessments of reality. The opinions and values of the majority can become a tyranny. Americans can easily see this in Cuba, North Korea, or Iran, but we are less able to see it in our own society.

In spite of their positive contributions, persons who exercise independent judgment are not always popular in an organization. This was shown in classic experiments involving problem-solving groups. A **deviant**, a person whose values and attitudes were different from those of the group, was placed in half the groups. In every case, the groups that possessed a deviant had a better solution to the problem they were given than did the homogeneous groups. Each group was then asked to eliminate one member of the group before receiving the next problem. In every case, the deviant was thrown out, although it was clear the deviant had contributed significantly to the work they had done.[36]

Groups generally value harmony and unity more than new information and challenge. This behavior is sometimes called **groupthink**. It describes a deterioration of an individual's mental efficiency, reality testing, and moral judgment as a result of group pressures.[37] The suppression of dissent among those in working groups brings failure, often disastrous failure, as important information and options are not brought forward. Hence it is important to provide a vehicle for the expression of dissent. For example, the Challenger space shuttle accident in 1986 might have been avoided. Morton Thiokol engineers' warnings about the danger of a launch at below freezing temperatures were not heeded by the National Aeronautics and Space

---

[36] Elise Boulding, *Conflict: Management in Organizations* (Ann Arbor, MI: Foundation for Research on Human Behavior, 1964), p. 54.

[37] I. L. Janis, *Groupthink* (Boston: Houghton Mifflin, 1982); see the discussion of groupthink in Stephen P. Robbins, *Organizational Psychology* (Englewood Cliffs, NJ: Prentice Hall, 1993), pp. 348–350.

Administration (NASA). This then resulted in the disaster and deaths of seven crew members.[38] Even then NASA was unable to change, and the Colombia disaster resulted in 2002 for many of the same reasons. Even with human life at risk and in the glare of national publicity, NASA managers failed to take the necessary steps to change the culture and thus to safeguard those lives. NASA has an insular tradition that thought it had all the answers.[39]

Other experiments have shown that in a group, individual competitive behavior (individuals focused exclusively on their own success and satisfaction) often leads to disruption and inefficiency for the group. Competitive behavior may lead to greater efficiency when the job can be done entirely by an individual working alone. Although competitive behavior enhances speed, cooperative behavior enhances accuracy. So, in spite of the American myth, in most settings, including business, cooperative behavior leads to greater efficiency than does overly competitive behavior.[40]

In sum, corporations tend to inculcate and thus perpetuate their own values. Like all organizations, corporations have the goals of survival and growth. These goals, plus the private enterprise goals of profit and shareholder value, have a profound influence on the attitudes and values of a firm's members. Members learn to accept the rules of the game that exist implicitly in their organization. Although creativity is of long-term benefit to the firm, it is not always tolerated. The financial goals of a firm often force individuals to judge the success of their work in numerical terms: numbers of product and dollars of profit. The bias is widespread because it is measurable and "objective." But this bias easily undermines long-range and human values, such as creativity, trust, and cooperation.

WHY PEOPLE WORK: MOTIVATION

Executives regularly ask how to better motivate their associates and workers. There is considerable evidence that there is a direct relationship between a company's financial performance and its commitment to a management style that considers its people as assets, not merely a cost of doing business. Yet much of our recent experience of downsizing, cutting benefits, and increasing responsibilities without increasing compensation does not seem to recognize the importance of people.[41]

---

[38] *Report of the Presidential Commission on the Space Shuttle Accident* (Washington, D.C.: U.S. Government Printing Office, 1986).

[39] William Langewiesche, "Colombia's Last Flight: The Inside Story of the Investigation and the Catastrophe It Laid Bare," *The Atlantic Monthly,* 292 (November 2003): 58.

[40] Bianca Beersma et al., "Cooperation, Competition, and Team Performance: Toward a Contingency Approach," *Academy of Management Journal,* 46, no. 5 (2003): 572–590; and Alfie Kohn, "How to Succeed Without Even Vying," *Psychology Today,* September 1986, pp. 22–28.

[41] For the empirical evidence and the argument, see Frederick Reichheld, *Loyalty Rules!: How Today's Leaders Build Lasting Relationships* (Boston: Harvard University Press, 2001); also Jeffrey Pfeffer and John F. Veiga, "Putting People First for Organizational Success," *Academy of Management Executive,* 13, no. 2 (1999); see also Pfeiffer's *The Human Equation: Building Profits by Putting People First* (Boston: Harvard Business school, 1998).

One of the challenges for an executive is to determine how a firm can pursue its objectives effectively and at the same time encourage the development of its members as persons. From the viewpoint of the person, social scientists have demonstrated that an individual can grow toward full maturity and achieve self-actualization only in an interpersonal atmosphere of complete trust and open communication.[42] Open, trusting interpersonal relationships are essential for a person to mature. Working relationships can seldom attain total openness and trust. However, when managers are able to develop appropriate trust among stakeholders, it will improve firm performance.[43] On the other hand, if the working climate inhibits trust and personal growth, it will result in frustration and a poor working environment. A good manager is therefore concerned about the quality of working relationships within the organization. Management expert Charles Handy summarizes the issue, "The organization which treats people as assets, requiring maintenance, love, and investment, can behave quite differently from the organization which looks upon them as costs, to be reduced wherever and whenever possible."[44]

Many business executives support the personal growth of their employees. At 3M and software designer SAS Institute, for example, executives know that the abilities of their employees can best be tapped by means of such support. It has even been shown that such support can indirectly improve flexibility, innovation, and product quality. The case for shared decision making, which encourages individual initiative and creativity, has been building for decades. One indication of the concern firms have for these issues is the size of their training budgets and the amount of time and effort they spend encouraging shared decision making and cooperation on the job. A variety of **theories of motivation** have been proposed over the years. Here we will examine a few that take account of the role of values and ideologies.

Personal Growth in the Organization

People in firms ask for more communication, participation, and opportunity for individual initiative. Yet executives are not always able to perceive the importance of providing challenging and satisfying work, encouraging a sense of ownership, allowing flexibility, and motivating employees to make their best effort. It is important to note that everyone benefits from the resulting working environment. These policies not only serve the individual need for self-development but also provide the foundation for improved product or service quality, new ideas, and greater efficiencies.[45]

Businesspeople know that there is an intimate relationship between personal values and motivation. Product quality and production efficiencies depend on the

---

[42] Herbert A. Shepard, "Changing Interpersonal and Intergroup Relationships in Organizations," in *Handbook of Organizations,* ed. James G. March (New York: Garland, 1987), pp. 1122–1137. Also see Roger Mayer, James Davis, and David Schoorman, "An Integrative Model of Organizational Trust," *Academy of Management Review,* 20 (July 1995): 709–734.

[43] Andrew C. Wicks, Shawn Berman, and Thomas Jones, "The Structure of Optimal Trust: Moral and Strategic Implications," *Academy of Management Review,* 24, no. 1 (1999): 99–116.

[44] Charles Handy, *The Age of Unreason* (Boston: Harvard Business School Press, 1990), p. 24.

[45] Note the evidence in James E. Post, Lee E. Preston, and Sybille Sacks, *Redefining the Corporation: Stakeholder Management and Organizational Wealth* (Stanford: Stanford University Press, 2002).

values and goals of the firm as articulated by the chief executive. Popular books and lectures of Peter Senge, Jim Collins, and Stephen Covey demonstrate that effective leadership is based on clear values and goals that are apparent in all managers in the firm.[46] These authors find that effective organizations where people are motivated are characterized by clear and articulated vision, values, ethics, and even spirituality. We now turn to several psychologists who have developed widely held and influential theories of motivation.

Self-Actualization

Abraham H. Maslow proposed that motivation arises from a **hierarchy of needs**. Maslow based his theory of motivation on observations of healthy, mature persons. For individuals to develop their own internalized philosophical and religious values, "lower needs" (food, water, safety, and security) must be somewhat satisfied. Maslow found that as lower needs were satisfied, they ceased to be motivators. The person then moved on to "higher needs" (belongingness, love, self-esteem, and self-actualization), so that healthy persons are primarily motivated by their needs to develop their capacities and actualize their potentialities to the fullest.[47]

The higher needs are not dominant, according to Maslow. For all peoples these needs are important for the person, but they often do not emerge in people who do not have enough to eat or a roof over their heads. In Maslow's words, "The human needs for love, for knowledge or for philosophy, are weak and feeble rather than unequivocal and unmistakable; they whisper rather than shout. And the whisper is easily drowned out."

Maslow maintains that as individuals become more mature and accepting, they will establish their own values. He concludes that a firm foundation for a value system is furnished by open acceptance of one's own self, "of human nature, of much of social life, and of nature and physical reality." A society made up largely of self-actualizers is characterized by more free choice and nonintrusiveness. Under these conditions, "the deepest layers of human nature would show themselves with greater ease."[48]

Maslow goes on to describe the personal characteristics of the people he has examined—those whom he calls **self-actualizers**. They tend to be "strongly focused on problems outside themselves"; they are problem-centered rather than ego-centered. Most often these mature, self-actualized individuals have "some mission in life, some task to fulfill," a task outside themselves that enlists most of their energies. Such tasks are generally unselfish; they are directed primarily toward the good of others. Furthermore, self-actualizers have wide horizons; their major concerns are not

---

[46] Peter Senge, *The Fifth Discipline* (New York: Currency, 1995); Stephen R. Covey, *Principle Centered Leadership* (New York: Fireside, 1992); and his *Seven Habits of Highly Effective People* (New York: Fireside, 1990), also James Collins, *Good to Great* (New York: HarperCollins, 2001).
[47] Abraham H. Maslow, *Motivation and Personality* (New York: Harper & Row, 1954), pp. 35–58; also Maslow's, *Eupsychian Management* (Homewood, IL: Irwin-Dorsey, 1965); see also Maslow's work in a larger context in Kathy Lund Dean, Charles J. Fornaciari, and James McGee, "Research in Spirituality, Religion, and Work: Walking the Line Between Relevance and Legitimacy," *Journal of Organizational Change Management,* 16, no. 4 (2003): 378–395.
[48] *Ibid.*, pp. 276–278.

ego-centered, tribal, or petty. They seem to have a stability that enables and encourages them to address large ethical and social issues.

Maslow describes in detail their ethical values. Self-actualizers "are strongly ethical, they have definite moral standards, they do right and do not do wrong." They are less confused about their basic values than others. It is easier for them to distinguish right from wrong, although their judgments do not always coincide with those of the accepted, conventional, surrounding culture.

Maslow holds that as persons grow and mature, they will become less selfish and more concerned with other people and larger problems. Their goals will become clearer, more explicit, and highly ethical. Although Maslow finds that these people are not always theists and some have little loyalty to an institutional church, they are nevertheless the sort who could be described as godly or devout people.[49] We now turn to theories of motivation that explicitly inquire into the effect of the values of businesspeople.

Need for Achievement and for Power

A need for achievement and a need for power are often strong motivations for businesspeople. Entrepreneurs generally have a high need for achievement; corporate executives often have both a high need for achievement and a high need for power. **David C. McClelland** has examined the **need for achievement** and the **need for power**. He finds that the success of an individual or a society is generally positively correlated with a high need for achievement. A person's need for achievement can be measured; it can even be increased, according to McClelland.

McClelland examines the long-range impact of a person's ideology on motivation. Just as we did in Chapter 4, McClelland cites Max Weber on the contribution of the Protestant ethic to attitudes that support modern capitalism.[50] Protestantism encouraged independence and self-reliance. Because the church was no longer the central agency for communicating values, individuals became independent.

Family upbringing has a great influence on an adult's values and motivation, and ultimately her management style. For example, if a child's achievements were never considered to be good enough, the child may become a perfectionist and an approval seeker when it becomes an adult. If parents exaggerate a child's importance, the child may be overconfident and feel it is above the rules and can do no wrong when it becomes an adult. A workaholic more than likely assumed adult responsibilities as a child. A manager who is cowed by a boss, yet treats subordinates like children, likely had a domineering parent.[51] In the present case, McClelland examined attitudes of independence, self-reliance, and the person's need for achievement, and showed how they are influenced by the manner in which

---

[49] *Ibid.*, pp. 168–169. Some empirical verification of Maslow's model is provided by Jean Davis-Sharts, "An Empirical Test of Maslow's Theory of Need Hierarchy Using Hologeistic Comparison by Statistical Sampling," *Advances in Nursing Science* (October 1986): 58–72.

[50] Max Weber, *The Protestant Ethic and the Spirit of Capitalism,* trans. Talcott Parsons (New York: Scribner, 1958).

[51] For a review of recent research, see Michelle Conlin, "I'm a Bad Boss? Blame My Dad," *BusinessWeek,* May 10, 2004, p. 61.

parents bring up their children. From the content of children's stories, dreams, daydreams, and fantasies, McClelland determines whether there is a high or a low need for achievement. Because parents' own values and ideology influence which stories they tell their children and which books they give them, parents thus have a profound effect on their children's motivation. In experimental work, researchers found that boys who showed a high need for achievement had mothers who expected their sons to master a number of activities early in life—to know their way around the city, be active and energetic, and try hard to get things for themselves, do well in competition, and make their own friends.[52] On the other hand, the mothers of boys with a low need for achievement reported that they had restricted their sons more. These mothers did not want their child to make important decisions by themselves or to make friends with children not approved by their parents.

McClelland theorizes that the Protestant Reformation encouraged a new character type possessing a more vigorous and independent spirit. This spirit of self-reliance was then passed on through child-rearing patterns, and McClelland holds that self-reliance forms the foundation for modern capitalism. He cites evidence that the need for achievement increases following an ideological or religious conversion, for example, to Fundamentalism, Marxism, or Catholicism.[53] In the wake of this reflection, a challenge and a need for achievement emerge. According to McClelland, religion, ideology, and values are inextricably intertwined with the need for achievement and motivation in general. The relationship is especially close when a person reassesses and changes his or her values.

McClelland cites Florence in the late Middle Ages as a society where the need for achievement was expressed in art. When one sees the cathedrals of Europe built in the Middle Ages, or the magnificent extant religious temples of the sun and moon built by the ancient civilizations in Mexico, it becomes clear that for many cultures religion was the major means of expressing achievement. However, in modern societies business is the major outlet for the need for achievement. So McClelland's practical criterion for the success (and hence implicit goal) of the achiever today is economic growth. In using this criterion, McClelland accepts traditional business ideology and the prevailing social norms of industrial society—that economic growth is the final goal of a people.

McClelland acknowledges that achievement is measured in money, but he denies that the businessperson with a high need for achievement is motivated by money.[54] Money is a *symbol* of success. An increase in salary is a sign of success and is the reward to one who achieves; it is often demonstrated to friends and neighbors by a more expensive car, an Armani suit, or a home in Aspen. Some observations by Eric Fromm on money as a measure of personal success will be examined later in this chapter.

People who have a high need for achievement are more likely to achieve when they can be their own boss. Someone who begins a business—an entrepreneur—is

---

[52] David C. McClelland, *The Achieving Society* (Princeton, NJ: Van Nostrand, 1961), pp. 46–50.
[53] *Ibid.*, pp. 406–417.
[54] *Ibid.*, pp. 232–237.

motivated by a high need for achievement. Given that most new jobs are created in firms of less than 100 employees, business (and hence society as a whole) depends heavily on individuals who have a high need for achievement.

Most of McClelland's work was done examining males. More recent experimental work shows that males tend to have a high need for achievement and a high need for power, whereas females have a higher need for affiliation (relations with others). Females tend to show achievement through nurturing and support. Women face a greater dilemma than do men in their business careers. Although a woman's career is quite important to her, marriage and having children increase in importance as a woman progresses in her career.[55] This calls for major decisions and often creates stress.

McClelland later turned his attention to the need for power and influence. The need for power is the desire to have an impact, to be strong or influential. McClelland found that top managers in large companies possess a need for power even greater than their need for achievement. This need for power must be "disciplined and controlled so that it is directed toward the benefit of the institution as a whole and not toward the manager's personal aggrandizement."[56] There is evidence that the Tyco, Hollinger, WorldCom, and other recent scandals resulted from the CEO's need for power; our earlier view of "chainsaw Al" Dunlap warned us about that. Recall that most mergers are not profitable and that research shows that a primary motivation for mergers is the desire of the CEO for more power.[57] In addition, the huge salaries of top executives are probably less a reflection of merit and more their need for power. We will discuss executive compensation in the next chapter.

Managers with a high need for power who do not exercise self-control can be very disruptive: "They are rude to other people, they drink too much, they try to exploit others sexually, and they collect symbols of personal prestige such as fancy cars or big offices."[58] People who possess a high need for affiliation are better liked by their subordinates and have a higher level of job performance. The work of the widely respected scholar-manager we examine next distinguishes two fundamental views toward work.

Work as Natural

Douglas McGregor was a business executive for several decades and later taught at MIT. He contrasts two sets of *assumptions* about individuals and their desire to

---

[55] Janet T. Spence, "Achievement American Style," *American Psychologist* (December 1985): 1285–1295. For limitations of McClelland's thesis, see R. Scott Frey, "Need for Achievement, Entrepreneurship, and Economic Growth: A Critique of the McClelland Thesis," *Social Science Journal,* 21 (April 1984): 125–134.

[56] David C. McClelland and David H. Burnham, "Power Is the Great Motivator," *Harvard Business Review,* 54, no. 2 (1976): 101.

[57] Mathew L. Hayward and Donald C. Hambrick of Colombia University Business School are quoted in "An Argument That Big Ego Is Behind a Lot of Mergers," *The New York Times,* September 28, 1995, p. C2.

[58] McClelland and Burnham, *op. cit.*, p. 103.

work.[59] The first, which has heavily influenced management attitudes, he calls
Theory X:

1. People do not like to work and will avoid it if they can do so.
2. People have little ambition, wish to avoid responsibility, prefer to be directed, and want security.
3. Therefore, in order to get them to do their work, they must be coerced, controlled, directed, and threatened by punishment.

In contrast to this older, traditional view, McGregor presents another view, which he calls **Theory Y**:

1. Work is as natural to people as play or rest.
2. Individuals will exercise self-direction and self-control in the service of objectives to which they are committed.
3. Commitment to objectives is a function of the rewards associated with their achievement (especially satisfaction of ego and self-actualization).
4. People learn, under proper conditions, to accept and even ask for responsibility.

Each of these divergent views of the values and goals of people has a profound influence on the organizational culture, climate, and management style of any organization in which it predominates. Theory X leads to a formal, highly structured, control-oriented organization. One disadvantage of such organizations occurs when members turn procedures into goals. Mid-level managers can make adherence to the rules and preservation of their office the goal of their work—often at the expense of the persons or processes they are serving. For example, an official is asked to process 10 people per hour, and dutifully does so—even on a day when the line is five times longer than normal. Strategies to increase motivation are based more on Theory Y. McGregor's approach continues to have a significant influence on managers' thinking and acting.[60]

The above motivation models based on individual orientation, consciously or unconsciously, continue to influence managers and organizations. Meanwhile, other theories of motivation have been developed that take into account a wider variety of personality traits, attitudes, and needs as well as the situation, task, and organizational relationships. As an example, **Equity theory** holds that a worker compares her tasks and compensation with peers. Negative equity is seen when a worker perceives that she is receiving proportionately less than others. Positive equity comes when she perceives that she is receiving more than peers. **Expectancy theory** holds that people's motivation will be determined when they perceive themselves to be receiving either positive or negative equity for their efforts.[61] Lists of salaries—which are now so easy to generate—whether of peers, CEOs, entertainers, or sports figures, enable us to decide that we are not paid enough. This of course results in negative equity (and greater envy) for all except for those at the top of the list.

---

[59] Douglas McGregor, *Human Side of Enterprise* (New York: McGraw-Hill, 1960), p. 33.

[60] See Gary Heil, Warren Bennis, and Deborah Stephens, *Douglas McGregor, Revisited: Managing the Human Side of Enterprise* (New York: Wiley, 2000).

[61] For a summary of these theories, see Henry L. Tosi, John R. Rizzo, and John Schermerhorn, James Hunt, and Richard Osborn, *Managing Organizational Behavior,* 5th ed. (New York: Wiley, 1994), pp. 179–185.

Research shows that a person who is **optimistic** tends to attribute failures to temporary causes that can be overcome. Optimists therefore tend to be more resilient than pessimists. Salespeople who are optimists outsold pessimists by 20–40 percent. Perhaps surprisingly, optimism can be learned; one can change one's own view of one's relation to other people and the world.[62] On a related subject, people ". . . in positive feeling states are more likely to behave generatively, focusing on exploring and obtaining anticipated positive outcomes." People who are "in negative affective states are more likely to focus on . . . preventing negative outcomes, thus exhibiting a defensive behavioral orientation."[63] These attitudes can be influenced, also. Thus each of us can have a notable impact on our own attitudes, values, and motivation.

It is noteworthy that a person's attitudes and values are acknowledged in these theories of motivation. The theories build upon the values of the individual. On the other hand, the values and goals of the organization in which the individual works are not overtly considered. Yet an organizations' goals and values dramatically affect each participant's motivations. If the goals of the organization and the individual are in conflict, it will lead to frustration for the person and inefficiencies for the organization.

Managing with Unexamined Assumptions

After his executive experience and working with Maslow, Douglas McGregor dug into the accepted ideology and the conventional assumptions that lie beneath thinking and literature on management and motivation. He shows that "it is not possible to reach a managerial decision or take a managerial action uninfluenced by assumptions, whether adequate or not." McGregor notes a resulting deficiency from such managerial blindness: "The common practice of proceeding without explicit examination of theoretical assumptions, leads, at times, to remarkable inconsistencies in managerial behavior."[64]

Management training and literature now emphasize the importance of reflection on our actions and goals.[65] It is not easy to cast a cool, clear eye on our own assumptions and values. We all engage in various shortcuts in considering our own and others' values. Rationalization, stereotyping, and other mechanisms hinder our ability to perceive these values. Sometimes these barriers also block our ability to reflect on the goals and the values of the organization. Some convince themselves, for example, that the growth of the organization benefits some people and thus automatically compensates for damage done to others. Some think that businesspeople waste time when they reflect on abstract values and goals.

On the contrary, there is no such thing as value-free management. Carrying out the goals of an organization without knowing what presuppositions undergird those goals is itself choosing to make decisions on the basis of a value. That value is the

---

[62] Edwin A. Locke and Gary P. Latham, "What Should We Do About Motivation Theory: Six Recommendations for the Twenty-First Century," *Academy of Management Review,* 29 (July 2004): 394.
[63] Myeong-Gu Seo, Lisa F. Barrett, and Jean M. Bartunek, "The Role of Affective Experience in Work Motivation," *The Academy of Management Review,* 29 (July 2004): 520. This issue of *AMR* has a special section on the future of work motivation theory.
[64] McGregor, *op. cit.*, p. 7.
[65] See, for example, Jim Collins, *Good to Great: Why Some Companies Make the Leap and Others Don't* (New York: HarperBusiness, 2001); Senge, *op. cit.*; and Stephen R. Covey, *Seven Habits of Highly Effective People* (New York: Fireside, 1990).

unquestioning faith that the goals of the organization are justifiable, and that in a conflict with one's own values, another organization, or with the community, one should pursue the goals of one's firm. The training program for traders at Wall Street's Solomon Brothers taught bullying, deception, and male chauvinist behavior toward customers. General Electric falsified overcharges to the government. Archer Daniels Midland conspired to fix artificially high prices for their products. Many people in each of these organizations were aware of the fraud and even contributed to it. Rationalizations and socialization of newcomers brought on continued corruption in these firms.[66] Each of these scandals encourages a lack of trust in management.

PRESSURE FOR MORE WORK

Pressing for greater productivity, firms are increasing the work hours demanded each week in the United States, and this work week is now longer than in any other developed country. Workers in the United States put in 1,800 hours a year on the job, 350 hours more than the Germans and slightly more than the Japanese, according to the International Labor Office. More than 30 percent of U.S. workers say they are "always" or "often" under stress at work. Perhaps as a result of this, only 49 percent of Americans are satisfied at their jobs; this is a substantial decline from 58 percent in 1995. Motivational consultant Brian Norris bluntly states that "there's a growing disconnect between people loving their job and work being just a paycheck. Increasingly, it's just a paycheck."[67] This growing laissez faire attitude by workers about their jobs and employers is often a way to cope with workplace stress and job satisfaction issues. More disturbing for employers is the extent to which employees seem to be ready to vote with their feet, thus further eroding the loyalty bond that once existed between corporations and their workers. Recent statistics indicate that approximately two-thirds of all American workers were preparing to actively seek new jobs within the next few months, about 50 percent had already posted their resumes online or to recruiters, and three-fourths were actively updating their resumes.[68] What is the cause of this worker grumpiness? A major grievance is the continuing efforts of employers to squeeze more hours from their workers, thus lowering labor costs. In the United States 62 percent of workers say that their job activities and responsibilities have increased during the past six months, and that they had not used all their allotted vacation time. Moreover, 60 percent said that they did not expect any lessening of pressure in the future. In addition, only 20 percent of U.S. workers feel their employer's promotion policies are fair.[69]

Americans not only **work more hours**, but also have less vacation time than people of any other industrialized nation; the American worker takes 10.2 vacation days per year while counterparts in France and Germany enjoy 30 or more vacation days

---

[66] Vikas Anand, Black Ashforth, and Mahendra Joshi, "Business As Usual: The Acceptance and Perpetuation of Corruption in Organizations," *Academy of Management Executive,* 18 (May 2004): 39–53.

[67] Lazurus, *op. cit.*

[68] *Ibid.*

[69] See the figures in John Schwartz, "Sick of Work: Always on the Job: Employees Pay with Health," *The New York Times,* September 5, 2004, pp. 1, C2; and Mark Landler, "Europe Reluctantly Deciding It Has Less Time for Time Off," *The New York Times,* July 7, 2004, pp. 1, C2.

per year.[70] In addition, the globalized economy operates 24 hours a day and 7 days a week, so that 40 percent of all Americans work during the evenings, during the nights, on rotating shifts, or on weekends.[71] Even those with "traditional" nine-to-five jobs are increasingly finding themselves tethered to work during traditional free times— evenings, weekends, travel, lunch, vacations, and so on. The emergence of powerful home computers, high-speed Internet access, virtual private networks, pagers, and integrated phone and e-mail devices such as the Treo and BlackBerry has provided flexibility to many high-value workers. They have also helped to create a culture in many firms where employees are expected to be *always* available to address business needs, lest they be seen as poor performers. The powerfully addictive nature of BlackBerries, often referred to as **Crackberries**, has created strong criticisms for their impact on workers and their families.[72] It is clear that, regardless of one's position on the vices and benefits of these types of devices, their prevalence is a direct result of America's around-the-clock business mentality.

Low-wage workers bear an increasing share of the work burden. Security guards, child-care workers, maids, tellers, cooks, home-health aids, and hairdressers earn less than the federal poverty level (about $9 an hour for a family of four in 2004). Minorities are over-represented in this group, but two-thirds are white; about 60 percent are women.[73]

Some CEOs, such as Steve Ballmer of Microsoft and Andy Grove when CEO of Intel, rule by fear, which further increases stress. Some indict executives and corporations because they have betrayed us through longer hours, reductions in benefits, increased workloads, downsizing for workers, but immense executive compensation for themselves. If people expect meaningful work, most will not find it.[74] This places constant pressure and additional stress on workers and their families. This then results in increased turnover, which is costly in moral, loyalty, and money.[75]

We have examined the increased demands that are placed on people in the workplace for the sake of productivity, and how this results in less satisfaction at one's job and increasing stress in the workplace. Now let us examine the business manager and his impersonal values. A classic empirical study of the business executive characterizes him as a mobile person, able to leave and take up a new job in a new community rather easily: "The mobile [manager] must be able to depart: that is,

---

[70] Lou Dobbs, "The Perils of Productivity," *U.S. News and World Report,* November 10, 2003, p. 58; and "Hate Your Job? Join the Club," *BusinessWeek,* October 6, 2003, p. 40.

[71] "The 24-hour, Seven-Day Global Economy is on Us," *Chemical and Engineering News,* June 28, 1999, p. 88.

[72] Frank Langfitt, "Blackberry or Crackberry? A PDA Culture War," *National Public Radio Morning Edition,* January 12, 2005, http://www.npr.org/templates/story/story.php?storyId=4279486.

[73] Beth Shulman, *The Betrayal of Work: How Low-Wage Jobs Fail 30 Million Americans* (New York: New Press, 2003).

[74] Jill Andresky Fraser, *White Collar Sweatshop: The Deterioration of Work and Its Rewards in Corporate America* (New York: W. W. Norton, 2001); also Joanne B. Ciulla, *The Working Life* (New York: Random House, 2000); and Al Gini, *My Job My Self: Work in the Creation of the Modern Individual* (New York: Routledge, 2001).

[75] Arie C. Glebbeek and Erik H. Bax, "Is High Employee Turnover Really Harmful? An Empirical Test Using Company Records," *Academy of Management Journal,* 47, no. 2 (2004): 277–286. On stress in the workplace, see the two-day series of articles in *The Wall Street Journal,* January 16, B1, B4 and January 17, 2001, B1, B4.

to maintain a substantial emotional distance from people, and not become deeply involved with them or committed to them."[76]

These top managers are thus not always sensitive to the needs of other people. Even though their own success is often built on decisions that result in sometimes substantial loss for others, this does not seem to bother them. They are not "distracted into personal duels, for they do not allow themselves to become so involved with others." When Chevron cut 56,000 jobs and AT&T dropped 100,000 employees, executives could not allow that to overly affect them, even though more than a hundred thousand families were severely hurt. Yet evidence shows that if surviving managers do not understand the rationale for the downsizing effort, it is impossible to do it effectively. It is emotionally wrenching work, and such managers are ". . . often ill-prepared to make a full commitment, especially if they are confused about the reasons for the downsizing and their role in its implementation."[77]

Mobility and lack of concern for others enable these executives to approach managerial decisions dispassionately. This objectivity contributes to their success. But that success does not allow them the satisfaction one might expect. There is rarely time to relax or to look back on their successes, "for an essential part of the system is the need for constant demonstration of one's adequacy, for reiterated proof of one's independence."[78] Also noteworthy is the fact that most chief executives had a master's degree in business administration, and 60 percent did not have a specific career goal in mind when they began in the firm.[79]

Even today most chief executives are still most often white, male, married, and politically conservative. When chief executives were asked what they would look for in their successors, they generally look for people who were much like themselves in background and attitudes. Organizations and their attitudes tend to be self-perpetuating. The ordinary struggle for survival and growth urges people and organizations to seek "their own kind." Although there are now some large black-owned and black-managed firms and women are increasingly in executive positions, African Americans, Hispanics, and women are still under-represented in chief executive positions. In 2006, there were only 12 women and 4 African American CEOs of Fortune 500 companies.[80] In 2005 women held just 16.4 percent of Fortune 500 corporate-officer jobs while women of color—African Americans, Hispanics, and Asian Americans—held just 1.7 percent of corporate-officer positions.[81]

---

[76] W. Lloyd Warner and James Abegglen, *Big Business Leaders in America* (New York: Atheneum, 1963), pp. 81–82.

[77] Hugh M. O'Neill and D. Jeffery Lenn, "Voices of Survivors: Words that Downsizing CEOs Should Hear," *Academy of Management Executive,* 9 (August 1995): 23–34.

[78] Warner and Abegglen, *op. cit.*, p. 83.

[79] "Profile of Leadership Emerges in Study of Top Corporate Executives," *Journal of Accountancy,* March 1987, pp. 36–38.

[80] *Fortune Magazine,* "Women CEOs for FORTUNE 500 Companies," http://money.cnn.com/magazines/fortune/fortune500/2007/womenceos/; *National Public Radio News & Notes,* "Black CEO One of Four on Fortune 500," April 11, 2006, http://www.npr.org/templates/story/story.php?storyId=5336052.

[81] Carol Hymowitz, "Women to Watch (A Special Report); The 50 Women to Watch: 2006: For Women in Business, There are Some New Faces at the Top, but the Overall Numbers Have Barely Budged," *The Wall Street Journal,* November 20, 2006, p. R1.

Consequently, some people who can afford to do so are now retiring early. Eugene Bernosky, 38, sold the semiconductor equipment firm he co-founded, Applied Chemical Solutions, Inc. After putting in 80-hour weeks, he asked himself, "Is this what I really want to be doing?" He says that there are only two things that money cannot buy you—time and friends. Lonnie Fogel, 41, worked as public relations director at Home Depot and had thousands of shares of company stock. He realized he had enough money to quit, if he lived frugally. He is now writing a screen play, bicycling, and doing volunteer work.[82] Another new social phenomenon is spouses deciding to remain behind when the working partner is transferred to another city. The home spouse decides that the move is too disruptive to children's schooling, family, friends, etc. The working spouse then commutes home on weekends to visit the family. One survey indicated that as many as 5 percent remain behind when the transfer is overseas and 7 percent stay behind when the transfer is within the United States.[83]

Following Orders Can Be Destructive

Following orders within an organization is essential to any organization's success. However, to what extent should persons follow orders when those orders seriously violate their own moral values? Evidence of a person's willingness actually to do harm to another individual when instructed by authority to do so was provided by a series of controversial laboratory experiments conducted by **Stanley Milgram**.[84] Subjects were told by an academic authority figure dressed in a white coat that they were to engage in experiments in memory and learning. Each subject was placed at a shock generator with 30 intervals marked, starting with 15 volts (labeled "slight shock") and going up to 450 volts (labeled "danger—severe shock"). Another person (the learner), who was strapped in a chair with electrodes on his or her wrists, could be seen in an adjoining room through a glass partition. The learners were in on the experiment and were not really subjected to shocks. The subject was then instructed to shock the learner, increasing the intensity for every wrong answer the learner gave. As the shock level rose, the learner cried out in seeming increasing pain, yet almost two-thirds of the subjects administered the highest level of shock.

Each subject would become nervous, agonize, and rationalize, but most nevertheless administered the highest level of shock under the auspices of authority. The experiment has been criticized as being unethical. Indeed, it did play on the subject's conscience. However, it also gave us frightening evidence of what one human being is willing to inflict on another when it seems to be called for by some authority.

Obedience in this experiment declines if the subject is in the same room as the learner or if the subject must actually touch the learner to administer the shock. The more impersonal the situation, the more willing the subject is to do harm to another.

[82] "Retire at 40: Some Do, with a Small Fortune and a Dose of Frugality," *The Wall Street Journal,* August 21, 1996, pp. 1, 4.
[83] "To Some Commuters, Going Home Means A Long Plane Ride," *The Wall Street Journal,* March 7, 1996, p. 1.
[84] Stanley Milgram, *Obedience to Authority* (New York: Harper & Row, 1974).

Ancient warfare involved face-to-face contact; some modern warfare is closer to the above experimental situation and easier to wage. A person can push a button and never witness the death and destruction caused by the exploding shell or missile.

Milgram's findings of how willing people are to follow orders have been witnessed over and over again both in other experiments and in the real world. **Philip Zimbardo** was director of the famous **Stanford Prison Experiment** (so named because the study took place in the basement of the university's psychology department) in 1971. His project randomly assigned mentally healthy college students to act as either "prisoners" or "guards" in a mock prison for a period of two weeks. The experiment had to be stopped after six days because the conditions at the "prison" quickly deteriorated into uncontrolled violence and chaos as both sides fully stepped into their assigned roles. Approximately one-third of the "guards" engaged in sadistic behaviors and "prisoners" began a full-fledged riot on the experiment's second day. Perhaps even more frightening as the behavior of the "prisoners" and "guards" in adopting their organizational roles was the fact that of the nearly 50 outside observers of the experiment, only one challenged its morality. Zimbardo calls the phenomenon of good people turning evil as a result of organizational demands the **The Lucifer Effect**. His recently published book of the same title demonstrates how the atrocities of the **Abu Ghraib** prison in Iraq were the result of organizational pressures pushing people into behaviors that they normally would never consider to be morally acceptable.[85] Consider the following words of retired Navy Admiral Harold Gehman, head of the Accident Investigation Board, in describing the problems in the organizational culture at NASA that ultimately led to the death of seven astronauts and the loss of the space shuttle Columbia in 2002:

> If you talk to people, if you really listen to people, all the time you hear "Well, I was afraid to speak up." Boy, it comes across loud and clear. You listen to the meetings: "Anybody got anything to say?" There are thirty people in the room, and slam! There's nothing. We have plenty of witness statements saying, "If I had spoken up, it would have been at the cost of my job."[86]

In the workplace, middle- and lower-level managers are sometimes told to do something that violates their ethics and conscience. The above incidents show that most of us will either perform or allow actions at serious variance to what we know is right if someone in authority instructs us. Yet this sort of obedience has its costs in tension, anxiety, stress, and attendant physical ailments.

Modern organizations are designed to produce results in an impersonal fashion. Downsizings, manipulative advertising, and pollution are all the result of decisions and policies made by executives. Such stressful and often unethical actions occur more often when executives do not see the victims of their actions. The

---

[85] Philip Zimbardo, *The Lucifer Effect: Understanding How Good People Turn Evil* (New York: Random House, 2007).
[86] Langewiesche, *op. cit.*

manager does not have to face his victims; moreover, financial return on investment and preserving the jobs of others demand the downsizing. In the minds of some executives, the system demands that they act impersonally if their firm is to grow.

Selling of Self: Careerism

Although the goals and values of a businessperson are influenced by background, education, and age, they are also influenced by the person's estimate of the profile that will "sell" in the marketplace. The market value of a person, how much that person can obtain in the employment market, has a great influence on notions of self-worth.[87] We call selling oneself **careerism**.

For example, imagine the case of a business woman looking for a new position. She will be concerned about how she appears to prospective employers. Dressing for success and using proper grammar and vocabulary will be important. She might be less concerned about her own goals of achievement, satisfaction, and happiness. In short, her attention will be on pleasing someone else rather than on her own values and goals. The more her self-esteem depends on how much she perceives she is worth in the market, the less control she will have over her own life. She may think that she is not valued for the person she is and that her adequacy is determined by insensitive market forces—the price others put on her. When she receives an increase in salary, it will be less the money itself that delights her than the fact that someone has recognized that she has done a good job. Without a large salary increase, she might sink into depths of poor self-esteem and perhaps depression.

Furthermore, because the market is often the principal determinant of self-worth and because value in the market is subject to many changing, unpredictable forces and fads, she must remain flexible. Her present value may collapse, simply because there are too many with the same talents on the market. She must be able then to shift to a new career. The phenomenon of glutted labor markets demands that businesspeople maintain flexibility and maximum exposure. No matter how much she may like her present work or locale, it is not to her advantage to sink deep roots. If she becomes known as a one-talent person, her value will be severely limited. This situation does not encourage developing loyalty to a firm or becoming involved in a community.[88]

This notion of self-worth makes a businessperson dependent on others for his or her own self-esteem. Self-worth stems not from accomplishments or the affection of others but rather from the impersonal forces of the employment market and from company superiors. The changing work environment makes Americans practical and pragmatic. They consider martyrdom to be folly, and will rarely dispute principles for their own sake. Thomas More's beheading by Henry VIII because he would not betray a principle makes superb drama in *Man for All Seasons*. Americans find the

---

[87] Erich Fromm, "Personality and the Market Place," in Man, Work, and Society: A Reader in the Sociology of Occupations, eds. Sigmund Nosow and William Form (New York: Basic Books, 1962), pp. 446–452.

[88] For more on these stresses, especially those on women in the workplace, see Arlie Russell Hochschild, *The Commercialization of Intimate Life: Notes from Home and Work* (Berkeley, CA: University of California Press, 2003).

episode quaint but difficult to understand and smacking of fanaticism. Indeed, businesspeople find disputes over principles to be unproductive and time-consuming and will rarely allow themselves to be caught up in what seems to be impractical, and hence useless, battles.

BALANCING WORK–LIFE CONFLICT

Being able to balance one's work and the rest of one's life is essential for personal happiness, but very often there is a conflict between them. A challenging job, long work hours, a distant commute, and young children are all conflicting demands. The stress they generate can result in physical and mental illness. Consider the fact that 58 percent of women with children under one year of age work. Also consider the large portion of families in which both spouses work and the number of hours per week that they work. In 2002 dual-career couples with children under age 18 living at home worked approximately 91 hours per week, an increase of 10 hours per week since 1977. The stress of work–family imbalance contributes to depression, hypertension, coronary heart disease, heavy alcohol use, absenteeism, and loss of productivity.[89]

Women bear most of the burden of the work–family conflict. It is more difficult for a woman to be both a successful executive and a successful mother than it is for a man to hold parallel successful roles. Note that of high achieving women, who are 40 years old and making $100,000 or more, only 57 percent are married, compared with 83 percent of men. Moreover, 49 percent of these women are childless compared with 19 percent of men in the same category. Perhaps more troubling, only 14 percent of these women said that they choose to be without children.[90] Promotions go to those who work 40–60 hour weeks and have no other demands on their time. This places working mothers at a disadvantage in the workplace. Over her career, a woman earns only about 44 percent of what a similar man earns.[91] This is because women carry most of the burden of care giving, which requires time and attention; thus women are often not viewed as being "as committed" to their career, so do not receive the promotions.

In poor and lower-middle-income families, children are also the losers. Seventy percent of American children come from homes where both parents work full-time. While some firms provide child care, most do not. Paying for child care

---

[89] J. Bond, C. Thompson, E. Galinsky, and D. Prottas, *Highlights of the National Study of the Changing Workforce* (New York: Families and Work Institute, 2002); Marc Marchese, Gregory Bassham, and Jack Ryan, "Work Family Conflict: A Virtue Ethics Analysis," *Journal of Business Ethics,* 40 (October 2002): 145–154; also Philip Frame and Mary Hartog, "From Rhetoric to Reality: Into the Swamp of Ethical Practice: Implementing Work-Life Balance," *Business Ethics—A European Review,* 12 (October 2003): 358–368.

[90] Sylvia Ann Hewlett, *Creating A Life: Professional Women and the Quest for Children* (New York: Talk Miramax, 2002); also "Mommy is Really Home From Work: More Female High Achievers are 'Stopping Out' to Raise Kids—And Avoiding Corporate American When They Return," *BusinessWeek,* November 25, 2002, pp. 101–104.

[91] Aaron Bernstein, "Women's Pay: Why the Gap Remains a Chasm," *BusinessWeek,* June 14, 2004, pp. 58–59.

costs as much as tuition at a state university, and care is unavailable at night, when many parents must work. The school day is less than two-thirds the length of the work day, the school year is 30 percent shorter than the ordinary work year, and only 20 percent of schools offer after-school programs. The United States is behind 120 other countries in granting paid maternity leaves. France, Belgium, and Finland provide universal school or child care beginning at age two. Global competition pressures firms to cut costs, so business is unlikely to initiate new programs. Unlike other countries, the United States has no national program to aid families with child-care issues that make life for working people so difficult. Moreover, the lack of care and supervision of children now will have a negative effect on the next generation.[92]

Many firms today do recognize the conflict between work and family and provide helpful work options for their people: flextime, telecommuting, a work-week of four 10-hour days, help for child care, and advice and resources for employees on family problems they face. This can help to relieve the conflicting demands of work and home. Firms like Ernest and Young in the accounting industry and Lehman Brothers in the financial services sector are increasingly using flextime to attract and keep the most in demand talent.[93] Motorola, Eli Lilly, Eddie Bauer, Unum Life Insurance, and DuPont also get good marks from their employees for being family friendly firms. While workers at many firms feel that their work has a negative impact on their home life, this is not true in an increasing number of firms. Among other firms credited are American Home Products for child-care programs and Procter & Gamble for new training and internal communication plans for women. These firms and an increasing number of others recognize that work and family have a profound impact on each other. As a result, they encourage supervisors to be sensitive and they allow flexible hours to care for family needs, including children and elders.[94]

However, the benefits described above often are not made available to front-line employees. Wal-Mart, for example, moved away from providing predictable work schedules for its 1.3 million in-store workers. It is adopting a computer-based system that will set individual employee work hours and schedules to match the ebb and flow of customers within each store. Similar systems are already in place in firms like Payless ShoeSource and Radio Shack. Companies hope the new flexible scheduling approach, which often place employees "on call" and can vary the number of hours any employee works from week to week, or even day to day, will lead to greater customer satisfaction and increased profits. Critics, however, worry

---

[92] The data in this section are from Jody Heymann, M. D., *The Widening Gap: Why America's Working Families Are in Jeopardy and What Can Be Done About It* (New York: Basic Books, 2001).

[93] Jaclyne Badal, "Theory & Practice: To Retain Valued Employees, Companies Pitch Flextime as Macho," *The Wall Street Journal*, December 11, 2006, p. B1; Patricia Sellers, "A Kinder, Gentler Lehman Brothers," *Fortune Magazine*, January 17, 2007, http://money.cnn.com/magazines/fortune/fortune_archive/2007/01/22/8397977/index.htm.

[94] "Balancing Work and Family: Big Returns for Companies Willing to Give Family Strategies a Chance," *BusinessWeek*, September 16, 1996, pp. 74–80; and "More Firms Compete to be Named on Lists as 'Family Friendly,' " *The Wall Street Journal*, August 21, 1996, p. B1.

that these systems will further complicate the ability of hourly employees to schedule babysitting services and to create predictable budgets to pay their bills.[95]

Furthermore, increasing numbers of lower level, part-time, and contract workers do not qualify for pensions or medical insurance. The number of employees with job-based medical coverage has steadily eroded, with only 60 percent of U.S. workers having employer-sponsored health care. Out of the 45 million Americans without health insurance in 2003, nearly 80 percent are employed or have family members who are employed. However, they remain uninsured because their employers do not sponsor coverage or they are unable to afford the premiums, which average $282 per month for an individual or $756 per month for a family.[96] This situation places many workers and their families in the position of having to skip routine or minor medical care to prevent the immediate loss of wages, and to gamble against the potentially catastrophic long-term financial and medical harm resulting from inadequate medical treatment.

Laura Nash recommends balancing one's primary spheres of life: happiness, achievement, significance, and legacy, and to recognize that having just enough in each sphere is far better than having too much or being "the best" in one. She maintains that it is more satisfying to maintain balance than to stress oneself over not being "the best."[97] On the individual level, businesspeople often experience a conflict between their personal attributes that are rewarded on the job and those that make for a good spouse and parent. Consider an example. A typical manager is decisive, fact-oriented, and assertive and makes decisions not on the basis of intuition or feelings, but on the basis of data and defensible reasoning. However, this talent of examining only the facts and reasoning does not work so well when the manager is at home in the company of spouse and children. For example, when one's spouse asks to go to a movie, it is not necessarily because she wants to see a particular film; she may simply desire to be alone with her husband for a few hours away from the house and children. In fact, caring, sensitivity, and generosity to others have been found to have a positive value in the work organization, even increasing productivity. In a larger context, cooperation, trust, and good morale build "social capital," which in turn encourages creativity and initiative and increases productivity and profitability—especially in high-growth companies.[98]

The fact-oriented manager may also have difficulty determining what his son or daughter is saying beneath either the quiet or the flurry of words. He has trained himself to look for the facts and so he takes the situation at face value. Furthermore,

---

[95] Kris Maher, "Wal-Mart Seeks New Flexibility in worker shifts," *The Wall Street Journal,* January 3, 2007, p. A1.

[96] Jillian Mintzer, "Living and Working Without Healthcare," *CNN/Money,* December 23, 2004, http://money.cnn.com/2004/12/22/news/economy/poverty_healthcare/index.htm.

[97] Laura Nash and Howard Stevenson, *Just Enough: Tools for Creating Success in Your Work and Life* (New York: John Wiley, 2004).

[98] Juan Florin, Michael Lubatkin, and William Schultz, "A Social Capital Model of High Growth Companies," *Academy of Management Journal,* 46, no. 3 (2003): 374–384; Francis J. Flynn, "How Much Should I Give and How Often? The Effects of Generosity and Frequency of Favor Exchange on Social Status and Productivity," *Academy of Management Journal,* 46, no. 5 (2003): 539–553; also Susan J. Lambert, "Added Benefits: The Link Between Work-Life Benefits and Organizational Citizenship Behavior," *Academy of Management Journal,* 43, no. 5 (2000): 801–815.

he might even loose patience at his wife and children for not saying what they mean. For him, it is not possible to sift through the words to determine what his wife, son, or daughter is really saying—often nonverbally. Moreover, in his impatience he may not be able to be open enough to encourage them to communicate what they really are thinking and feeling. He is sometimes aware of this inability and the resulting conflict, and this causes additional tension and anxiety.

A person like the manager above has what is called a **Type A personality**, which is characterized by impatience, restlessness, aggressiveness, and competitiveness. Type A people also tend to have many irons in the fire and to be under considerable time pressure. Sixty percent of managers in the average organization are Type A. The Type A manager who is angry and cynical is two to five times more likely to have heart disease or a fatal heart attack than other managers. It is the quickness to anger and a habitual hostile outlook that contributes to heart problems. Children who do not get unconditional love from parents and considerable physical contact are more likely to become untrusting, easy-to-anger adults. Interestingly enough, it has been shown that although many Type A managers have the talent and attitude that enable them to rise in the organization, CEOs are generally not Type A; they are more patient and willing to examine the long-term ramifications of decisions.[99]

Spirituality in the Workplace

Interest in spirituality in the workplace has increased dramatically in the last decade.

Spirituality is answering a need for businesspeople; it helps a person to reduce the anxiety and stress that are characteristic of modern society. Spirituality helps to balance some of major negative characteristics of our culture that cause this stress: materialism, depersonalization, the elevation of individual freedom over the community, and the inability to escape the 24/7 demands of the office. It is materialistic to say that the purpose of the market system is merely to create wealth, and not give priority to providing goods, services, and jobs; spirituality helps a manager to see the larger goal of business.

Business managers can depersonalize individuals, and see them largely as workers to be paid or customers to be sold. There is too little opportunity for businesspeople to see themselves as being intimately connected to other people (fellow workers, family, and neighbors), especially when they live in large cities and endure frequent career moves. Finally, the electronic aids for providing information globally link businesspeople. Yet cell phones often ring in restaurants, classrooms, social events, and even in church; this disrupts peoples' lives and leaves little time for quiet, enjoyment, and meditation. The pace and demands of business life often leave little time to connect with the really important elements in one's life.[100] As one

---

[99] Interview with Redford Williams, M.D., "Getting to the Heart of Type A's," *U.S. News & World Report,* May 15, 1989, p. 68.

[100] Gerald Cavanagh, Bradley Hanson, Kirk Hanson, and Juan Hinojoso, "Toward a Spirituality for the Contemporary Organization: Implications for Work, Family and Society," in *Spiritual Intelligence at Work; Research in Ethical Issues in Organizations,* eds. Moses Pava and Patrick Primeaux (Amsterdam: Elsevier, 2003), pp. 111–138; also Gerald F. Cavanagh, "Spirituality for Managers: Context and Critique" in *Work and Spirit,* eds. Jerry Biberman and Michael Whitty (Scranton: University of Scranton Press, 2000), pp. 149–166.

executive put it, "You get to the top of the ladder, and maybe find out that it is leaning against the wrong building."[101]

Spirituality can aid a person in providing a balance and integration for all of one's life, including one's work life. Moreover, spirituality has advantages for the firm as well as for the person. It can help to make the workplace more ethical and humane, where believers and nonbelievers alike can find fulfillment. On the other hand, some fear that spirituality in the workplace can lead to coercion and favoritism, and thus be divisive. This fear is greater when executives or workers bring religion into the workplace. Of course, any religious favoritism in hiring or promotion is unjust, and violates both American ideals and U.S. law.

What do we mean by **spirituality**? A broad definition of spirituality is: *spirituality = a worldview + a path*. According to this definition, anyone who has the ability to reflect on their own life has a spirituality. A spiritual worldview is practical; it engages the person. It can be simple, sophisticated, religious, or even secular. By this broad definition, even materialism or achieving success can be a spirituality if it is the dominant worldview of that person. However, many question the adequacy of a spirituality with a goal of materialism or success. Most spiritualities acknowledge a supreme being or a higher power to whom one is dependant. Spiritualities often are rooted in a religion, and those people pray to that Supreme Being (i.e., God, Allah, Yahweh). Most spiritualities also emphasize our responsibility for each other.

A spirituality also involves a path or a way of proceeding. For example, a Muslim prays and prostrates before Allah four times a day; a Zen Buddhist follows specific meditation practices. For a person who has a secular world view, the path might involve personal appreciation of nature and preserving the environment. The path for many includes gathering in a church of people of similar beliefs where they are able to form community, pray, and do good works for others. There is evidence that religious beliefs, for example, belief in hell and heaven, positively influence economic performance. The authors of a large-scale study think that religious beliefs stimulate economic growth because they support individual values such as honesty, thrift, work ethic, and openness to strangers, which are fundamental to business.[102]

On the other hand, some fear this new interest in spirituality and religion. They note the many acts of cruelty and discrimination that have been done in the name of religion (such as al-Qaeda, Crusades, Inquisition, burning of witches, treatment of women in Muslim countries, and genocide in Sudan and Bosnia). However, the record shows that in most of these cases, religion has been the excuse for longstanding regional or tribal enmities. This raises an important question for contemporary peoples. Is it possible for a group to have strong spiritual and religious beliefs and practices, and yet include among those beliefs a respect and even love for peoples of

---

[101] Marc Gunther, "God and Business: The Surprising Quest for Spiritual Renewal in the American Workplace," *Fortune,* July 9, 2001, pp. 58–80.
[102] Robert J. Barro and Rachel M. McCleary, "Religion and Economic Growth Across Countries," *American Sociological Review,* 58 (October 2003): 760; see also Patrick Primeaux and Gina Vega, "Operationalizing Maslow: Religion and Flow as Business Partners," *Journal of Business Ethics,* 38 (June 2002): 97–108.

other nations, tribes, and religions? The challenge of our modern world is to achieve such global understanding and respect.

Some Americans say they possess a spirituality, but they have little use for religion. Religion generally involves ritual, dogma, and group prayer, which they do not value. Such nonreligious spirituality fits with American individualism. The person is not tied by liturgy, beliefs, or dependence on a congregation. However, such an attitude also bears the negative side of individualism: the reluctance to commit to other people, a group, or a pattern of living one's life.

Some firms have encouraged the formation of employee support groups, based on their common religious faith. Ford Motor Company began the Ford Interfaith Network in 2001, "The Company's global vision for diversity and worklife is to create an inclusive culture that respects the whole person and values all differences . . . since Ford Motor Company is an international, multicultural organization." Ford's objective is to become "a world-wide corporate leader in promoting religious tolerance, corporate integrity, family values, and human dignity."[103] The network links Hindu, Muslim, Catholic, Jewish, Evangelical Christian, and Mormon Ford workers. The Ford Interfaith Network has enabled Ford workers to gather to enrich their personal and shared spiritualities. In another example, Richardo Levy, a Silicon Valley entrepreneur, considered selling a division of Catalytica, his 1,800 employee chemical firm. After doing the financials, Levy had many questions beyond whether the price was right. He was also concerned whether the sale was good for employees and customers. Levy, who is Jewish, ultimately used a Christian discernment process as developed by St. Ignatius Loyola to reach this most important decision to sell the division.

A Career as a Vocation

People expend considerable effort to determine their career; a person's vocation is even more important. A career can be part of a **vocation**, but it is not the same as a vocation. A vocation is larger and more all-embracing. The word vocation is from the Latin word *vocare*, to call. It is my answer to the questions: Who am I? What should I do with my life? Where am I going in my life? Working out one's vocation is not merely an individual task. A vocation is an invitation, and it is generally worked out in prayer accompanied by at least some others of the community. That prayer is most often a careful, disciplined attempt to discern God's will for me in my life. Hearing that call brings me greater freedom. In following the call, I am able to follow my own talents, loves, and intuitions, and help others at the same time. People who do not believe in God consider their vocations in relation to that which transcends the ego, such as a higher power or the world community. Nevertheless, the call is often hard to hear, and sometimes not welcome. In addition, the voice is often drowned out by the busyness that surrounds us every day.

Recognizing that one is "called" to a particular work can give one assurance, courage, and security. When one finds his or her vocation, life is stirred; it engages the emotions. The very process of determining my vocation enables one to be more

---

[103] E-mail to all Ford employees "Ford Interfaith Network," from Martin Inglis, April 12, 2001.

self-reflective and to learn more about oneself. Such reflection also enables one to be more adaptable. Part of a vocation is an invitation to serve communities; it might result in work on behalf of the poor or the environment. Serving the community is an essential part of the Christian tradition, and it is also a part of every other major religious tradition. Finding one's vocation brings a clarity of thought and action, and the inner peace that this provides.[104] Other people generally find that such a person is more centered, compassionate, and understanding. Determining one's calling enables a business executive to follow her own journey, to become a better person and a better executive at the same time.[105]

Meditation is encouraged at many firms, and has also grown among businesspeople—often onsite. People who meditate find that it possesses a number of advantages. New research shows that even short periods of meditation have a profound influence on both the person's mind and body. Stress-related ailments account for 60 percent of doctor visits, according to the Mind/Body Medical Institute. Some find that meditation often alleviates lower back pain, headaches, and arthritis; reduces absenteeism; increases brain wave activity; helps intuitive decision making; and improves concentration.[106] A large-scale and well-publicized research study of Catholic religious sisters in the United States found that, while an active mind and body increased longevity, ". . . profound faith, like a positive outlook, buffers the sorrows and tragedies that all of us experience. Evidence is now starting to accumulate from other studies that prayer and contemplation have a positive influence on long-term health and may even speed the healing process."[107]

However, a caution is in order here. If spirituality, meditation, and even religion are embraced in order to achieve the good health results, that spirituality is likely to be superficial and shallow. Many current books and conferences on spirituality are "limited in scope and avoid the hard issues. Death, suffering, injustice, the nature of the transcendent, worship and awe are mostly overlooked in favor of mental techniques for reducing stress and achieving higher performance."[108]

Ten organizations from around the world were selected as winners of the *International Spirit at Work Awards*. These firms employ over 150,000 people and are headquartered in India, the Philippines, and the United States. Two are chemical manufacturers, two are banks, and six are hospital systems. The largest of the awardees, Ascension Health, has 88,500 full-time employees and was honored for spirituality training programs, a Spirituality Symposium, a Spirituality Scorecard for

---

[104] Joseph Weiss, Michael Skelley, Douglas (Tim) Hall, and John C. Haughey, "Vocational Calling, New Careers and Spirituality," in *Spiritual Intelligence at Work; Research in Ethical Issues in Organizations*, eds. Moses Pava and Patrick Primeaux (Amsterdam: Elsevier, 2003), pp. 175–201.

[105] James J. McGee and Andre L. Delbecq, "Vocation as a Critical Factor in a Spirituality for Executive Leadership in Business," in *Business, Religion and Spirituality*, ed. Oliver F. Williams, C.S.C. (Notre Dame, IN: University of Notre Dame Press, 2003), pp. 94–113; the 16 other articles in this volume are also excellent.

[106] "Meditation: New Research Shows That It Changes the Brain in Ways That Alleviate Stress," *BusinessWeek*, August 30, 2004, pp. 136–137; and "Zen and the Art of Corporate Productivity: More Companies are Battling Employee Stress with Meditation," *BusinessWeek*, July 28, 2003, p. 56.

[107] David Snowdon, *Aging with Grace: What the Nun Study Teaches Us About Leading Longer, Healthier, and More Meaningful Lives* (New York: Bantam Books, 2001).

[108] See Laura Nash, "A Spiritual Audit of Business Firms: From Tipping Point to Tripping Point," in *Business, Religion and Spirituality, op. cit.*

each hospital, and a seven-step ethical discernment process. Medtronic and the *Times of India* are former winners of the International Award.[109]

Yale University has set up a program jointly sponsored by their business and divinity schools to help businesspeople integrate their spirituality and work. Its director, David W. Miller, is also president of The Avodah Institute, which has a mission "to help leaders integrate the claims of their faith with the demands of their work."[110] The Institute sponsors conferences, encourages research, and provides advice for businesspeople.

Executives as Servant Leaders

Executives bear a special responsibility to set the ethical tone of their organizations.[111] They lead their organization such that they provide a sense of integrity, accomplishment, and satisfaction, not stress, to their members. **Robert K. Greenleaf**, a former manager at A&T, coined the term **servant leadership** to describe leaders who view their primary purpose as that of meeting the needs of others and helping others grow and develop. This idea stands in marked contrast to many business leaders whose primary purpose is the self-oriented acquisition of power and/or wealth (the Greenleaf Center for Servant Leadership at http://www.greenleaf.org/index.html provides a comprehensive background of his teachings). Greenleaf's philosophies have had a large impact on the styles of many prominent business leaders. Consider the following two examples.

James Autry a senior vice president of Meredith Publishing, a Fortune 500 firm, offers five guidelines for successful management. Three of these are "Be honest," "Trust your employees," and "If you don't care about people, get out of management before it is too late." He emphasizes his last point by saying "Save yourself a heart attack and save many other people a lot of daily grief." This confirms what we have learned above. He points out that in the work setting, "friends and coworkers are the new extended family." He notes that younger workers are looking for good values in the workplace: This value-quest has produced, for the first time in the history of American publishing, a decade in which business books consistently have been on the bestseller list. And most of those books deal with values and relationships, not high finance. Autry finds that when the sports metaphor is used to describe business it is not helpful.

> By invoking the metaphor of sports teams these days, we imply that we in business are involved in a game in which there must be winners and losers, in which there are stars who play and benchwarmers who watch, in which our personal success is measured only by the numbers on the scoreboard and not by how well we played, and in which our value to society is transitory at best.[112]

---

[109] For further information, see www.spiritatwork.org.
[110] For more information, see www.AvodahInstitute.com or David Miller's book *God at Work: The history and promise of the faith at work movement* (New York: Oxford University Press, 2007).
[111] Terry Thomas, John Schermerhorn, and John Dienhart, "Strategic Leadership of Ethical Behavior," *Academy of Management Executive,* 18 (May 2004): 56–83.
[112] James A. Autry, *Love and Profit: The Art of Caring Leadership* (New York: Avon Books, 1991), pp. 46, 156.

Autry concludes by asking what kind of a CEO Jesus would be.

Max DePree was CEO of Herman Miller, Inc. and he underscores the same points and adds a religious viewpoint. For example, he writes about a business leader forming a "covenant" with the people in the firm. He says, "Covenants bind people together and enable them to meet their corporate needs by meeting the needs of one another." DePree emphasizes that leaders must take a role in developing, expressing, and defending civility and values. As examples, he lists some actions to be avoided:

> To be a part of a throwaway mentality that discards goods and ideas, that discards principles and law, that discards persons and families, is to be at the dying edge. To be at the leading edge of consumption, affluence, and instant gratification is to be at the dying edge. To ignore the dignity of work and the elegance of simplicity, and the essential responsibility of serving each other, is to be at the dying edge.[113]

Autry and DePree are examples of successful business executives who are also servant leaders. As leaders, they are servants of those they lead. They clear the way so that those who report to them are able to do their jobs even better. In the process, those people grow as persons, and also become healthier, wiser, freer, and more autonomous. Research on high-performing business firms found that their leaders were "quiet, humble, modest, reserved, shy, gracious, mind-mannered, self-effacing, understated, did not believe his own clippings. . . ."[114] This style of leadership is now more common, and the servant leadership movement is growing. It will be discussed further in Chapter 10.

Rapid technological change, information richness, and global competition require marshaling the best efforts of all the people in an organization. Executives can bring this about by encouraging teamwork, empowerment of workers, and open and distributed information systems. Such leaders encourage self-leadership—that is, each person takes initiatives and uses their best abilities. The "superleader" listens more, asks more questions, encourages learning, and uses less punishment. In short, organizations can be better workplaces.[115] Clearly indicating the organization's goals, open communications, and development opportunities enable members to understand and thus do their job better, and so enjoy it more. Moreover, such organizations are able to lower turnover, increase productivity, and generally are better financial performers in both the short and long term. For example, national Baldrige winners, such as Federal Express, Cadillac, and IBM Rochester provide a clear mission for all, solicit employee involvement in planning, emphasize teams in employee development and compensation, and communicate constantly with employees via face-to-face meetings, live in-house television, and a variety of other techniques.

---

[113] Max DePree, *Leadership is an Art* (New York: Bantam Doubleday, 1989), pp. 15, 21.
[114] Collins, *op. cit.*, p. 27.
[115] Charles C. Manz and Henry P. Sims, Jr., *The New SuperLeadership: Leading Others to Lead Themselves* (San Francisco: Berrett-Koehler, 2001); see also Linda Klebe Trevino, Kenneth Butterfield, and Donald McCabe, "The Ethical Context in Organizations: Influences on Employee Attitudes and Behaviors," *Business Ethics Quarterly,* 8 (July 1998): 447–476.

Other firms, such as PepsiCo, Silicon Graphics, and AT&T encourage their people to become more reflective and prayerful. Executives in these firms judge that managers and workers alike will be more effective if they take time to reflect on and balance their own goals and activities.[116] Such firm initiatives come from ethical leaders and thus support the moral development of the members of their organization. We examined moral development in Chapter 2.

Recent examinations of organizations focus on "positive organizational scholarship," which recognizes a virtuous organization as one that is characterized by compassion, integrity, forgiveness, trust, and optimism. "Organizations scoring higher in virtuousness were more profitable."[117]

Summary and Conclusions

People's values are heavily influenced by business and the firm. During the working day, supervisors' expectations impact the behavior of employees. In the evening and on weekends, products, corporations, and their values are sold through advertising and television programming.

Successful businesspeople generally are ambitious, achievement- and power-oriented, disciplined, and adaptable. Younger managers are intent on being "winners" and "self-developers," often at the expense of empathy for others. The business manager ingests many of these values when he or she joins the firm. The prevailing values of free market, competition, and opposition to government intervention are learned early, along with the values of the particular firm. Hence many of the goals of managers are determined for them—whatever goals must be accomplished for success within the firm. Moreover, managers' goals include that which must be accomplished for the success of the firm. Further, people often feel compelled to follow orders, even when they suspect those orders may cause harm. Just as early in life the rules of the game were set by others, so now the economic rules of the game come from elsewhere.

People's personal goals are changing. Individuals now desire more than salary and status. People desire challenging work, participation in decision making, the respect and approval of friends, the ability to identify with their community, and a stimulating and fulfilling life. People struggle to balance the demands of work and family, especially as new technologies bring a blurring of the clear distinction between "work" and "personal" time. They find that spirituality, often grounded in

---

[116] Mark A. Huselid, "The Impact of Human Resource Management Practices on Turnover, Productivity, and Corporate Financial Performance," *Academy of Management Journal*, 40 (June 1995): 635–672; Richard Blackburn and Benson Rosen, "Total Quality and Human Resources Management: Lessons Learned from Baldrige Award-Winning Companies," *Academy of Management Executive,* 3 (1993): 49–66; Stratford Sherman, "Leaders Learn to Heed the Voice From Within," *Fortune,* August 22, 1994, pp. 92–100.
[117] Kim S. Cameron, "Organizational Virtuousness and Performance," in *Positive Organizational Scholarship: Foundations of a New Discipline,* eds. Kim S. Cameron, Jane E. Dutton, and Robert E. Quinn (San Francisco: Berrett-Koehler, 2003); also Fred Luthans, "Positive Organizational Behavior: Developing and Managing Psychological Strengths," *Academy of Management Executive,* 16, no. 1 (2002): 57–72.

their faith tradition, brings not only better mental and physical health, but also security, openness, and inner peace. A business firm can help in the achievement of many of these goals if its senior executives are modest and wise in directing it.

Discussion Questions

1. Does rational decision making rest on values and ideological assumptions? What might those assumptions be?
2. Because business managers often claim their actions are "value-free," why inquire about values?
3. What is the relationship between a generation's values system and overall business values?
4. Is it acceptable for a firm to attempt to socialize its members? How does it do so? What are the unexpected costs of socialization?
5. When most college freshmen believe that it is more important to be very well-off financially than to develop a meaningful philosophy of life, what does that tell us? Is the prospect of wealth more important than a good education?
6. Do business managers tend to be more interested in people, power, or tasks? Are executives more conformist or more innovative?
7. Can you name a TV program or a film that pictured a businessperson as one who worked hard, produced a valuable product, built teamwork among her colleagues, and was satisfied with her work? Is this the typical image of the businessperson in the media?
8. What do Solomon Asch's experiments on the influence of groups tell us?
9. What values develop as a person matures and becomes self-actualized? What role does concern for other people play in the set of values of a self-actualized person?
10. How does Maslow's description of the ethical values of the self-actualized person relate to Kohlberg's Level III moral reasoning?
11. What sort of upbringing do people with a high need for achievement tend to have? What in a culture encourages a high need for achievement? Are those elements present in your own culture?
12. If business is the major outlet for a contemporary need for achievement, as opposed to religion and art, does this indicate a poverty of spirit?
13. What special problems in achieving do many women have?
14. Is a high need for power a help or a hindrance to effective leadership? Explain.
15. Do you believe people naturally like or dislike work? What are the managerial implications of this answer?
16. What do expectancy theory and equity theory tell us about how people make value judgments about their work? How do published lists of salaries affect your sense of equity?
17. What role is technology playing in our evolving expectations about work?
18. Describe the family life and values of the mobile manager.
19. What are the effects of authority and organizational pressures on a person's willingness to inflict, allow, or fail to prevent, harm to others? Describe the experiments regarding this subject. Have you seen parallel situations occur in your work career? In your country? Explain.
20. Outline the pros and cons to the individual of having salary and status as goals. Do managers "sell" themselves?
21. Are you concerned with making yourself more "marketable"?
22. What sort of values does this engender in a person?

23. Describe the values that are most valuable to someone in organizational life and the values that are developed in family life. Is there a conflict here? How can it be resolved?
24. Do you find a conflict between your goal of earning a good wage and your own satisfaction within a firm? Does the same firm provide both, or is there a tradeoff?
25. Describe some of the current strains on work–life balance. How does it affect men and women in their careers?
26. How have some firms helped their workers cope with the work–life balance?
27. In your experience, do most people possess a spirituality? What are the varieties of spiritualities that you notice? How do you characterize a spirituality that stems from a religious tradition, and one that does not? What are the advantages of each?
28. Is it possible for a group to have strong spiritual and religious beliefs and practices, and yet include among those beliefs a respect and even love for peoples of other nations, tribes, and religions?
29. In your experience, do many people experience a "calling" in their life and career? What is the benefit of such a calling?
30. Describe some CEOs that have positively affected the humane, spiritual, and ethical tone of their firm for their workers. Is this common? Is it difficult? Does it pay off?

Selected Additional Readings

Max DePree, *Leadership is an Art* (New York: Bantam Doubleday, 1989).

David W. Miller, *God at Work: The History and Promise of the Faith at Work Movement* (New York: Oxford University Press, 2007).

Peter J. Frost, *Toxic Emotions at Work: How Compassionate Managers Handle Pain and Conflict* (Boston: Harvard Business School, 2003).

Frederick Reichheld, *Loyalty Rules!: How Today's Leaders Build Lasting Relationships* (Boston: Harvard University Press, 2001).

Jean Twenge, *Generation Me: Why Today's Young Americans are More Confident, Assertive, Entitled—and More Miserable than Ever Before* (New York: Free Press, 2006).

Philip Zimbardo, *The Lucifer Effect: Understanding How Good People Turn Evil* (New York: Random House, 2007).

CASES

Case 7-1 The Purchasing Manager's Car

Jim Angot is the purchasing manager for Nihco, Inc. He is responsible for buying two $1 million computer workstations. Nihco has a written policy prohibiting any company buyer from receiving a gift in excess of $50 and requiring that all gratuities be reported. A salesperson for a computer manufacturer offers to arrange it so that Angot can purchase a $40,000 auto for $12,000. The auto would be bought through a third party.

1. Should Jim decline the offer?
2. Should he notify his superior? Should he notify the salesperson's superior?
3. What ethical norms help most here?

Case 7-2   The Boss's Work Time

You have a new job as first-level manager in an auto parts store. Your supervisor, the store manager, spends one-third of his work day talking with his friends on the phone.

1. Would you work around your lazy supervisor, or would you inform the district manager?
2. What are the ethical norms that most help in this case?

■ ■ ■

Case 7-3   Shannon and Facebook

Shannon O'Hare is seeking a management training position with Alcorn. Shannon is an honors student, president of the student advisory board of her college, and she impressed her Alcorn executive interviewers at her second on-site meeting. But she loses out for the position, and a friend who works at Alcorn tells her it is because of the content of her entry in Facebook. As a college sophomore, she posted comments calling business executives "greedy and selfish," and told intimate stories about herself and her boyfriend.

1. Is it ethical for Alcorn managers to use Shannon's Facebook entry in their evaluation?
2. What ethical norms help here? From the standpoint of Shannon? From the standpoint of the firm?

■ ■ ■

Case 7-4:   Betty Vinson: Accountant at WorldCom

Betty Vinson, 49, joined the international accounting division of a small long-distance company which became WorldCom, in Jackson, Mississippi at $50,000 per year. A few years later, her supervisor asked her to make false accounting entries to hide expenses to bolster WorldCom profits. She refused at first, but then relented. Each quarter she hoped it would be the last time she was asked to make the false entries. For six quarters she helped to post $3.7 billion in false profits for the firm. When the scam was revealed, she confessed her own role in the hopes of avoiding prosecution. She pled guilty and provided information to prosecutors at the trial of Bernie Ebbers, 63, the former CEO of WorldCom, who was convicted and sentenced to 25 years in prison. At her own trial she said that, because her job was at stake, it was very difficult to say no to her boss. On the contrary, the U.S. prosecutor said that just following orders is not an excuse for breaking the law. Vinson was convicted and sentenced to five months in prison plus three years' probation.[118]

---

[118] Susan Pulliam, "A Staffer Ordered to Commit Fraud Balked, Then Caved: Pushed by WorldCom Bosses, Accountant Betty Vinson Helped Cook the Books," *The Wall Street Journal,* June 23, 2003, pp. 1, A6.

1. Does Vinson's boss bear responsibility for the false accounting entries? Does Vinson bear responsibility herself, even though she was merely following orders?
2. At what point do one's personal values override one's desire to please one's boss?
3. What ethical principles help to understand this case?
4. What lessons does this case have for you?

Exercises

Exercise 7-1: A Life Worth Living
Imagine yourself on your deathbed. You are able to collect your thoughts and memories. How would you complete the following? You may do it in three paragraphs, if you like.
"I wish I had spent more time. . . .

Exercise 7-2: Write Your Own Obituary
Write your own obituary that will appear in your city newspaper. Assume that it is written by your best friend who knows the real you in addition to your accomplishments. After you do a first draft, show it to a good friend for their comments. Write this in a maximum of 300 words.

8

■ ■ ■

Leaders, Trust, and Watchdogs

The only trouble with capitalism is capitalists.
They're too damn greedy.
Excessive fortunes are a menace to true liberty.

HERBERT HOOVER, REPUBLICAN PRESIDENT OF THE
UNITED STATES, 1928–1932

The market economy, if utilized rather than worshiped, is the best
mechanism available for pursuing both economic dynamism and
desirable social goals.

ADAIR TURNER, VICE CHAIRMAN,
MERRILL LYNCH EUROPE

I believe the distinction between a good company and a great one
is this: A good company delivers excellent products and services;
a great one delivers excellent products and services and strives
to make the world a better place.

BILL FORD, CHAIRMAN, FORD MOTOR COMPANY

The ethical and financial failures of so many business firms over the last decade have challenged business managers to rebuild trust in business. The goals and ethics of a person or a firm are best communicated by their actions. Consider these recent events involving well-known firms.

Sprint Nextel is one of the three major cell phone service providers in the United States. One recent national survey ranked it dead last in customer satisfaction among American companies, with over 40 percent of the respondents calling its customer service "poor," while a recent J.D. Power & Associates survey ranked it last in customer service among the major wireless providers for a fourth consecutive time.[1] Unsurprisingly, its "churn," the rate at which old subscribers leaving its service are replaced by new customers, is among the poorest in the industry. Despite its problems, in the summer of 2007 Sprint decided to terminate the cell phone contracts of at least 1,000 customers. Sprint deemed that those subscribers were calling its customer service centers too frequently and thus costing Sprint too much money to support. Ironically, many of these "fired" customers argued that they were repeatedly calling customer service due to Sprint's ongoing inability to produce accurate billing statements and to fix the errors. A short time later Sprint quietly re-instated at least some of its customers after widespread media reports of the "firings."[2]

In 2005 Sony BMG, fearful of mounting losses due to piracy concerns, placed digital rights management (DRM) software on some of its music CDs to restrict their copying onto personal computers. Part of the DRM package was "rootkit" software that attempts to bypass and hide itself from the computer's operating system so it can more effectively do its job. Unfortunately, rootkits can also create potential security risks for the whole computer. Sony BMG's software went unnoticed for months until a security researcher discovered that it was installed on his machine. When confronted, Sony BMG initially denied that the rootkit could create problems, but it eventually provided software to users so they could remove the rootkit from their computers. Sony BMG ultimately had to recall nearly three million copy-protected CDs from its distribution network and offered to exchange nearly two million more CDs that customers had already purchased in order to resolve the issue. As a result, it was also the subject of several lawsuits from angry consumers. The firm wound up agreeing to cash payments to customers and replacements of the affected CDs that could cost it upwards of $50 million.[3]

While the above are two examples that may alter the trust relationships firms have with their own customers, other practices that may impair customer trust are sometimes common across entire industries—what one author calls "Gotcha Capitalism."[4]

---

[1] Christopher Oster, "The Customer Service Hall of Shame," *MSN Money,* April 26, 2007, http://articles.moneycentral.msn.com/SavingandDebt/Advice/TheCustomerServiceHallOfShame.aspx?page=all; Jenna Goudreau, "Sprint Nextel: Last in Customer Service," *BusinessWeek,* July 27, 2007, http://www.businessweek.com/print/technology/content/jul2007/tc20070726.
[2] Marguerite Reardon, "Splitting Up with Your Cell Phone Carrier," *CNET News.com,* July 6, 2007, http://www.news.com/Splitting-up-with-your-cell-phone-carrier/2100-1036_3-6195301.html?tag=item. Reuters, "Sprint Hangs Up on High-Maintenance Customers," *FOXNews.com,* July 9, 2007, http://www.foxnews.com/story/0,2933,288635,00.html.
[3] Tom Zeller, Jr., "Railing at Sony BMG, Disguised as a Review," *The New York Times,* November 21, 2005, p. c3; Ethan Smith, "Entertainment: Sony BMG Pulls Millions of CDs Amid Antipiracy-Software Flap: Recall Could Dent Sales of Artists and Retailers During Key Holiday Season," *The Wall Street Journal,* November 17, 2005, p. D5; Ethan Smith, "Sony BMG Agrees to Settle 15 Suits Over CD Software," *The Wall Street Journal,* December 30, 2005, p. A14.
[4] Bob Sullivan, *Gotcha Capitalism: How Hidden Fees Rip You Off Every Day—and What You Can Do About It* (New York: Ballantine Books, 2007).

For example, credit card companies routinely issue agreements that are several pages in length and written in tiny print. Critics argue that the language of the agreements is made deliberately dense to prevent the consumer from wanting to read the terms of the contract. Elizabeth Warren, a Harvard Law School professor, states, "I've read my credit card agreement, and I can't figure out the terms. I teach contract law, and the underlying premise of contract law is that the two parties to the contract understand what the terms are."[5] Some of the clauses typically found in credit card agreements include ideas like "universal default." Universal default enables a credit card company to unilaterally change the interest rate on a consumer's credit card if the customer has *any* financial problems, for example, being late on a utility bill payment. Another common clause lets the card issuer to unilaterally change the terms of the agreement as long as it provides 15 days' advance notice.[6]

Likewise, the banking industry has adopted several practices in recent years that have impacted the customer trust relationships. For example, some banks now debit funds from customers' accounts at the end of each day from largest check first to smaller check last to improve the chances of creating multiple overdraft charges. Another common practice is to deliberately allow ATM users to overcharge their limits without providing notification that insufficient funds are available to complete the transaction, which again produces overdraft fees for the bank. These practices have resulted in overdraft charges in the banking industry reaching $53 billion in 2006, which represents a total increase of 58 percent in just five years.[7]

A MODEL EXECUTIVE

While the above are short examples of firm or industry practices that often erode trust in business, the actions of individual firm leaders may also contribute to a lack of trust. Let us examine an executive that is often taken as a model of business behavior, Jack Welch of General Electric (GE). Welch was chairman and CEO of GE from 1981 to 2001, and during his tenure shareholders benefitted greatly. When Welch took office, GE was number 11 in the United States in capitalization (total value of outstanding stock); by his retirement, GE was number 1. GE stock price rose 1,500 percent from 1982 to 1997. Reginald Jones, the CEO who chose Welch as his successor, recognized the young man's intellect, energy, intensity, and the absolute determination to get the job done.

Within the first few months on the job Welch presented his norm for success. For each business unit, GE would be either number 1 or number 2 in that market or GE would sell or close the business. The goal was to increase profitability and share price. Welch totally reshaped GE. Prior to his term, most of GE's revenue came from manufactured products, such as appliances and electrical gear; now the principal sources of revenue are entertainment (RCA and NBC) and financial services. When

---

[5] Lowell Bergman and David Rummel, "Secret History of the Credit Card," *Frontline* television series (Boston: WGBH, November 23, 2004), http://www.pbs.org/wgbh/pages/frontline/shows/credit/etc/script.html.

[6] *Ibid.*

[7] Gotcha Capitalism; Gail McGovern and Youngme Moon, "Companies and the Customers Who Hate Them," *Harvard Business Review*, June 2007, pp. 78–84.

Welch purchased NBC, he dropped the notion that a TV network provided a public service, and thus had duties to present the news and other important national events. Welch saw TV news as just another profit center.

There is probably no other executive in the last 50 years about whom more has been written, and who is more admired for his skills as an executive. Veterans of Welch's GE management training are much sought after and have become CEOs of dozens of other firms. Welch became the model for many other CEOs in the United States. Robert Allen was trained and championed by Welch, and became CEO of AT&T. In 1996 Allen eliminated 40,000 jobs, and his personal compensation soared to $16.8 million (another former GE manager, Bob Nardelli, will be discussed later in the chapter).[8] Welch's own compensation during the late 1990s each year ranged from $50 to $90 million.

Welch was made CEO to streamline GE, to shake up the bureaucracy, and to make GE a leader in profits. He accomplished it all. He promised Wall Street analysts continually improved quarterly earnings. GE achieved that, too, "by smoothing the numbers"; that is, they would restate the financials at the end of the year until they achieved the smooth upward swing they wanted in the "final, final, final ledger."[9] In Welch's first few years on the job, he sold scores of businesses, most of them profitable. He shed a total of 100,000 jobs from GE. While cutting off those thousands, he lavishly refurbished an executive office in Manhattan that he used twice a month.

Welch sold the Housewares Division, which included toasters, clocks, coffee makers, and hair dryers. Housewares had been one of the very first GE businesses. Moreover, in each of these markets the product was number 1 in market share and was profitable, but not profitable enough. He fired executives, mid-level managers, and line workers, many of them veterans of GE who felt that their lifetime loyalty deserved more. However, Welch preached that loyalty was an old-fashioned value,[10] along with trust, tradition, and compassion. Loyalty got in the way of efficiency, risk taking, and fast action, and thus it did not contribute to the new, flexible, "lean and mean" GE. Early in his job as CEO, colleagues dubbed Welch "Neutron Jack,"[11] after the neutron atom bomb that would only kill people and leave buildings intact:

> Welch was domineering, immature, abrasive, and competitive to a fault, but, at the same time, likeable in an unvarnished way. One of his charms was that he didn't try to sublimate his personality or his passions; what you saw was what you got. What you saw was a man whose forceful personality made him appear bigger that he was. He talked in machine-gun like bursts, throwing out ideas in a verbal torrent . . . [12]

---

[8] "Gross Compensation? New CEO Pay Figures Make Top Brass Look Positively Piggy," *BusinessWeek,* March 18, 1996, pp. 32–34.

[9] James Martin, S.J., *In Good Company: The Fast Track from the Corporate World to Poverty, Chastity and Obedience* (Franklin, WI: Sheed and Ward, 2000).

[10] Thomas F. O'Boyle, *At Any Cost: Jack Welch, General Electric, and the Pursuit of Profit* (New York: Knoff, 1998).

[11] Jack Welch with John A. Byrne, *Jack: Straight from the Gut* (New York: Warner Books, 2001).

[12] O'Boyle, *op. cit.*, p. 57. See also Phillip M. Thompson, "The Stunted Vocation: An Analysis of Jack Welch's Vision of Business Leadership," *Review of Business,* 25 (Winter 2004): 45–55.

Many managers did not want to work for Welch using his new standards. Even though Welch urged him to stay, one who left GE said, "I didn't respect him as a human being. Jack is a guy who uses and abuses people. That troubled me. I didn't want to be one of Jack's boys." Another executive who also quit because he did not like Welch's style also recognized his personal strengths: "He's funny, charismatic, recalls names, puts his arms around you, the kind of guy other guys like to hang around."

In addition, during Welch's tenure, GE has experienced many ethical lapses:

- GE subsidiary Kidder Peabody was fined by the Securities and Exchange Commission (SEC) for reporting false profits and fabricated record keeping. The division lost $1 billion; what was left was finally sold.
- GE's jet engine division pleaded guilty in 1992 to stealing $42 million from the U.S. Government, and using the money to bribe an Israeli general to purchase GE engines. Two years later that same division paid the U.S. Government $7.2 million in penalties for selling the U.S. Air Force engines that did not meet contract specifications.
- From 1985 to 1992 GE's arms manufacturers were involved in 15 criminal convictions and civil judgments, more than twice as many as the next largest arms manufacturer.
- After Welch said that the nonbiodegradable chemical PCB posed no health risk, the U.S. Environmental Protection Agency ordered GE to clean up the PCBs it had dumped into the Hudson River at a cost to GE of $500 million.
- An NBC *Dateline* news hour rigged a test of GM trucks so that upon impact they would artificially explode. GM sued for libel, and NBC acknowledged their fabrication.[13]

Welch arranged a lucrative retirement package for himself, although his personal assets totaled $450 million. His retirement provides a total *monthly* income of $1.4 million. He maintains that such an income is necessary to meet his retirement expenses. He reports his monthly expenses as $366,000; these include $9,000 for beverages, $5,500 for country club memberships, $1,900 for clothes, and $52,000 for gifts. In addition, his five homes, two in Florida, two in Connecticut, and one on Nantucket Island, cost $51,000 per month to maintain.[14] These figures were revealed during contentious divorce proceedings from his second wife. She filed for divorce after she learned that Welch had become intimately involved with Suzy Wetlaufer. Wetlaufer, as editor of the *Harvard Business Review* (HBR), had been interviewing him. Wetlaufer then lost her job at HBR, but became Mrs. Jack Welch number 3. The two now write a business advice column on the last page of each issue of *BusinessWeek*.

Jack Welch's famously successful career as a CEO of one of America's largest corporations raises many questions. Who benefitted from his tactics of "fix, sell or close" a business, even when it was profitable? Were these tactics, which resulted in

---

[13] O'Boyle, *op. cit.*, pp. 76, 77.
[14] "Here's the Retirement Jack Welch Built: $1.4 million a Month: In Divorce Case, Ex-GE Chief Details a Lavish Lifestyle; Gifts Totaling $52,486," *The Wall Street Journal,* October 31, 2002, pp. 1, 15.

many layoffs and business being sent overseas, good for workers and the United States as a whole? Was his intimidation of subordinates an appropriate way of communicating his and GE's goals and values? What does his immense compensation, both while CEO and in retirement, tell us about Welch, the GE Board which approved it, and the prevailing American culture? What do his living expenses tell us about his values? What does his affair with Suzy Wetlaufer, while married to his second wife (Wetlaufer was also married at the time), tell us? Earlier chapters help us to answer the questions on Welch's goals, ethics, and moral maturity. Executive leadership, compensation, and corporate governance issues will be discussed in this chapter. Welch was not alone in layoffs, his shallow morality, and shady accounting. On the last point, the current GE CEO, Jeff Immelt, said that if quarterly earnings continue on a smooth upward climb, shareholders and the public think they have been manipulated. Immelt acknowledged the earlier slippery practices and now releases more detailed and transparent financial information.[15]

We understand much about a person by watching what that person does and how he or she acts. This is also true of a firm; the policies and the activities of a business firm are the clearest demonstration of its values and ethics. The above actions and the rest of this chapter tell us more about business values than do executive speeches or self-promoting advertisements. Smart managers reward good performance. We will now examine the policies, actions, successes, and failures of some other executives and their firms.

Integrity Slipping

Jack Welch's management style and his goal of increasing shareholder value were the model for many U.S. business executives. However, the business scandals in the first few years of the twenty-first century cast doubt on Welch's style and goals. The financial and moral collapse of Enron and its auditor, the old and revered accounting firm, Arthur Andersen, surprised many.[16] In both cases, tens of thousands of employees lost their jobs and also their pensions. In addition, Global Crossing, WorldCom, Waste Management, Qwest, Computer Associates, and Trump Hotels, among dozens of other firms, deliberately overstated their revenues and understated expenses, so that they could meet the expectations of Wall Street—so that their share price would steadily increase. Meeting "the numbers," that is, share price and earnings per share became the ultimate objective. In contrast, Medtronic is a very successful maker of pacemakers and other medical devices. CEO Bill George regularly told shareholders and analysts that shareholders come third, yet share price increased dramatically. According to George "Medtonic is not in the business of maximizing shareholder value. We *are* in the business of maximizing value to the patients we serve. Shareholder value comes from giving superior service to customers because you have impassioned employees serving them." George points out that the Medtronic

---

[15] "General Electric: Big Game Hunting," *The Economist,* March 16, 2002, p. 64.
[16] Mimi Swartz and Sherron Watkins, *Power Failure: The Inside Story of the Collapse of Enron* (New York: Doubleday, 2003); and Barbara Ley Toffler, *Final Accounting: Ambition, Greed and the Fall of Arthur Andersen* (New York: Broadway Books, 2003).

mission—restoring people to full life—transcends the everyday struggles and provides motivation to Medtronic's 25,000 workers.[17]

Meanwhile, accounting firms and financial analysts were involved in conflicts of interest. The hired overseers of business honesty, the outside auditors, KPMG, Ernst & Young, Delotte & Touche, PriceWaterhouseCoopers, and Arthur Andersen received most of their income from their consulting businesses. They often also had the auditing contract for the same firm. Hence the auditors felt pressure to provide a favorable audit in order to retain the more lucrative consulting business. In a similar conflict of interest, the investment banking firms Merrill Lynch, JPMorgan Chase, and Goldman Sachs generate most of their revenue representing business firms in their merger and acquisition activities. Hence financial analysts at the investment banks felt pressure to give these firms favorable ratings on their share price and any new stock offerings in order to retain the investment banking business. Thus falsely favorable information was given to the public on the financial status of many firms. Those misleading statements led to a collapse of integrity, stained reputations, and the ultimate financial failure of numerous firms.

What was the cause of these failures? One cause was the personal ego and greed of many executives. During the period when so many business scandals were emerging, media headlines told of the excessive compensation and the regal high living of executives. Jack Welch's personal compensation and his management style suggest greed and a need for power. Similarly, Dennis Kozlowski, then the CEO of Tyco, pocketed $170 million in compensation in 1999 yet still charged Tyco for art work for his personal use. The Rigas family charged many of their personal expenses to their firm, Adelphia. Samuel Waksal, while CEO of ImClone, sold his shares in the firm before unfavorable news on ImClone's new cancer drug was available to the public; for this Waksal served jail time. The annual list of the highest paid CEOs featured men such as Michael Eisner at Disney, whose salary dropped from $96 million to $7.3 million in 2003, and Sandford "Sandy" Weil of Citigroup, whose salary dropped from $90 million to $17.9 million in 2003. Both men left their firms under a cloud.

Another cause of this errant behavior is Wall Street's obsessive concern with quarterly earnings per share. We receive daily reports of a stock's movement. Most of the major accounting firms have a tax division. A major role of that tax division is to "sell" tax avoidance by using creative financial structures. Moreover, the auditing firm will show internal auditors how to "manage data" to meet quarterly goals and to avoid taxes. They also recommend relocating outside the United States where there is little or no corporate tax. Tyco rechartered itself in Bermuda, as did Accenture, Arthur Andersen's consulting spin-off.

In this chapter we will examine the effect of values and ethics on a firm's performance. We will note some executives and firms who are excellent models of

---

[17] Bill George now teaches at Harvard Business School and has authored (with Peter Sims) the superb book *True North: Discover Your Authentic Leadership* (San Francisco: Jossey Bass, 2007). See also Ronald Heifetz and Marty Linsky, *Leadership on the Line: Staying Alive through the Dangers of Leading* (Boston: Harvard Business School Press, 2002), p. 211.

concern for people, along with others who seem to show little concern. We will then explore strategies for those managers and firms that seek to improve their performance.

MANAGING FOR SELF OR FIRM

Let us consider different types of managers and management styles. We present good and effective behavior that can be imitated and ineffective management styles that can be avoided. To place this discussion in context, recall from Chapters 4 and 5 the traditional values that have prevailed in the United States. The Protestant ethic (Figure 4-1) urges hard work, self-control, self-reliance, perseverance, saving and planning ahead, honesty, and observing the "rules of the game." These same values also characterize the entrepreneurial middle class in developing countries. The market system encourages and rewards these values. However, for some these values may have shifted toward short-term goals, such as a high salary, high status, self-fulfillment, entitlement, and immediate satisfaction (see Table 8-1). Do you think the traditional values are still predominant, or have a new set of self-fulfillment values been embraced by Americans? We will raise this question later in this chapter and again in Chapter 10.

Executive Pay and Broken Trust

The disproportionately high pay of American CEOs has been criticized for years in the business press. In 2006 the average direct compensation for 350 CEOs of large American firms rose 8.9 percent over the previous year to $6.54 million, while the pay of the average American worker rose only 3.3 percent. The biggest CEO pay winners in 2006 were Lloyd Blankfein of Goldman Sachs ($54.8 million), E. Stanley O'Neal of Merrill Lynch & Company ($48.9 million, who was forced out of the firm the next year due to subprime mortgage losses), Ray Irani of Occidental Petroleum ($48.4 million), John J. Mack of Morgan Stanley ($40.2 million), and Lawrence

TABLE 8-1 Changing Values That Undergird American Business

Protestant Ethic . . . is Shifting to. . . . Entitlement and Self-Fulfillment	
1. Hard work	1. Salary and status
2. Self-control and sobriety	2. Self-fulfillment
3. Self-reliance	3. Entitlement
4. Perseverance	4. Short-term perspective (if not successful here, move on)
5. Saving and planning ahead	5. Immediate satisfaction (buy now, little savings)
6. Honesty and observing the "Rules of the game"	6. Obey the law (in any case, don't get caught)

Ellison of Oracle ($38.5 million).[18] On the other hand, the annual compensation of very successful investor Warren Buffet of Berkshire Hathaway is but $100,000. Also compare the 2003 compensation of Costco CEO James Sinegal of $350,000 with that of Cendant CEO Henry Silverman of more than $17 million; for both firms operating income increased but the market value decreased over the previous five years.[19] Hence CEO pay presents a conflict between the free market that claims to reward talent by compensation and a perception of a lack of justice in such disproportionate pay.

American top management and CEO salaries are higher than those of any other nation. As we have seen above, they are still rising much more rapidly than the wages of other workers. In 1980 the CEO's salary was 42 times that of the ordinary factory worker, but by 2005 it had risen to more than 420 times that of the average worker.[20] How does a CEO's salary become so huge? Many executives do not think their salaries are large; they measure their self-esteem by comparing their salaries with that of other CEOs, and some are making more. Moreover, the chief executive generally chooses the directors who decide his salary. Boards of directors treat CEOs like professional ballplayers or rock stars. What boards and CEOs often seem to forget is that the CEO is leading an organization. And the success of that organization demands the loyalty and team work of the other people, too.

Hedge Fund and Private Equity Salaries

Compensation of some hedge fund managers is even higher than that of CEOs. John Paulson of Paulson & Company earned $3.7 billion in the single year 2007. James Simons of Renaissance Technologies and George Soros received $2.9 billion and $2.8 billion, respectively, that same year.[21] Hedge fund managers do not create new products or wealth; they merely speculate on already existing assets, and the immense rewards go to very few.

Furthermore, recent years have seen increases in acquisitions of public corporations by **private equity** firms. Private equity firms are typically small groups of investors (often including the managers of the target firm) who purchase a public company and then take it private, usually with the intention of selling it back to the public in as short a time as possible. They often use the acquired company's assets as the collateral for the loans they take out to make the purchase, and the size of the acquisitions are often staggering in size. Recent private equity purchases include

---

[18] Joann S. Lublin, "CEO Compensation Survey (A Special Report); The Pace of Pay Gains: A Survey Overview," *The Wall Street Journal,* April 9, 2007, p. R1.

[19] "Executive Pay: A Special Report," *The New York Times,* April 4, 2004, Sec. 3, pp. 1–10; see also "Wall Street's CEOs Still Get Fat Paychecks Despite Woes," *The Wall Street Journal,* March 4, 2003, p. 1; also "Executive Pay: CEO Pay Keeps Soaring—Leaving Everybody Else Further and Further Behind," *The Wall Street Journal,* April 11, 1996, pp. R1–R18.

[20] Phred Dvorak, "Limits on Executive Pay: Easy to Set, Hard to Keep," *The Wall Street Journal,* April 9, 2007, p. B1.

[21] Stephen Taub, "Best-Paid Hedge Fund Managers," *Alpha Magazine,* April 15, 2008, http://www.alphamagazine.com/Article.aspx?ArticleID=1914753.

HCA ($32.7 billion), Equity Office ($38.9 billion), and TXU ($43.8 billion). The deals are structured so that other monies, such as ongoing consulting and acquisition fees, must be paid by the acquired firm to its new private equity owner and various investment banks in addition to the standard dividends demanded by the new private equity owners. The result often is that no matter what, the owners of the private equity group extract enormous amounts of wealth from the acquired company in a short period of time while saddling it with huge debt. For example, Rich Kinder, the CEO and founder of pipeline firm Kinder Morgan, joined with Goldman Sachs to try to take his firm private in 2007 by offering to purchase it from shareholders for $107.50 per share in a transaction valued at $15.2 billion and financed with $7.3 billion in debt. The offer came less than a year after Kinder told his shareholders that the firm would be worth $163 per share by 2010. If the sale is approved by regulators, Kinder's stake in the company will immediately jump from $2.6 billion to $4.5 billion and Goldman Sachs will receive over $240 million in fees for its advising role in the process.[22]

Senior managers at recently privatized firms are typically specialists who excel at making the drastic moves needed to simultaneously service their debts and pay the various fees and dividends to their owners. They are often rewarded more handsomely than their public corporation counterparts. This has resulted in numerous top managers and CEOs leaving well-known companies for the chance at making greater profits in the private sector. Former Gap CEO Millard Drexler joined clothing retailer J. Crew Group. Drexler earned $323 million when J. Crew was taken public four years later.[23] It is estimated that the top 75 managers of Chrysler, which includes numerous executives recently hired from other firms, will receive 5 percent of its equity from Cerberus Capital Management, which bought the automaker for $7.4 billion in 2007 from Daimler.[24] Of course, these generous rewards must be paid for somehow, and it is often at the expense of employees and other firm stakeholders. For example, the Carlyle Group purchased AxleTech, a maker of truck parts, in 2005 for $345 million. One of the first moves its CEO made was to get workers to accept a 33 percent cut in pay and benefits.[25]

Efforts to build trust, cooperation, and better communication are often undermined by such huge compensation packages. When cutting costs, top managers urge hourly and salaried workers to settle for little additional pay. Many CEOs have closed plants, cut wages, urged early retirement for some and fired others. Some of this is necessary, but huge executive compensation does not make the case to others of the need to cut costs. In addition to salaries and stock options, these packages often include perquisites not available to other workers at the firm; this puts additional strain on the relationship between management and employees. These

---

[22] Adam Lashinsky, "Rich Kinder Helped Himself to a Bigger Slice of His Own Company. Do You Have a Problem with That?" *Fortune,* May 28, 2007 (vol. 155:10), p. 64.

[23] Emily Thorton, "Perform or Perish," *BusinessWeek,* November 5, 2007, pp. 38–45.

[24] David Welch, "Why Top Talent is Jumping to Chrysler; Two Big Lures: A Shot at Being Part of a Historic Turnaround, Plus Oodles of Cash," *BusinessWeek,* September 24, 2007, p. 42; Harry Maurer, "Take My Carmaker—Please," *BusinessWeek,* May 28, 2007, p. 28.

[25] Thorton, *op. cit.*

perks can range from interest free loans to supplemental pensions, free financial advising, and free club memberships. Because CEO compensation and benefits are often public knowledge and self-serving, they frequently support selfish attitudes of "everyone for himself" and "I've got to be number 1."

Warren Buffet, one of the most successful investors in the United States, decries the typical immense CEO compensation. In the wake of the business scandals, he says, "What really gets the public is when CEOs get very rich and stay very rich and they get very poor." John Lauer, CEO of Oglebay Norton, thinks that most CEOs are vastly overcompensated. After doing his own careful research, he says that most CEO pay is not linked to performance at all, and in fact it erodes worker loyalty and productivity. The compensation is based on comparison to their peers. If they receive less than others, it injures their self-esteem. Since some short-term costs, such as environmental lawsuits and excessive warranty costs, can be hidden, a portion of CEO compensation could be deferred and paid out after a longer period. So Lauer has tied his own compensation to the long-term performance of his firm, and his bonus is capped at $200,000. His big payoff is a one-time option package that is only redeemable three years into his contract.[26]

There are several **justifications for high executive compensation**. It can be (1) a reward for superior performance, (2) the sum required to attract the talent, and (3) a just return for contributions. Some of the extremely high CEO pay is tied to a rise in the firm's share price. But why should the CEO be the only person in the firm who receives a bonus on the basis of higher share price?[27] Some firms now reward the performance of everyone in the firm who contributed to the successes.

Pay for Performance

While huge compensations may be justified for CEOs of high-performing organizations, corporations have come under fire for the excessive monies paid to CEOs who are fired or resign for poor performance. For example, Hewlett-Packard (H-P) CEO Carleton "Carly" Fiorina led her firm through a contentious acquisition of Compaq Computer that was opposed by many people, including a son of one of its founders. The merger was narrowly approved by H-P's shareholders, largely due to Fiorina's insistence that the acquisition would ultimately improve the company's long-term performance. Less than two years later, in early 2005, Fiorina was removed from her post by her board of directors. The dismissal was largely due to general criticisms about H-P's performance under her leadership—its stock price was down more than 50 percent since she took her position with the firm—but also specifically about her inability to successfully merge the operations of the two companies. Even though Fiorina was removed from her job for performance-related issues, she was still awarded an approximate $21 million severance package.[28]

---

[26] "A Buffett Warning on Executive Pay," *The New York Times*, March 17, 2003, p. C3; see also Mel Perel, "An Ethical Perspective on CEO Compensation," *Journal of Business Ethics*, 43 (December 2003): 381–391; "A CEO Cuts His Own Pay," *Fortune*, October 26, 1998, p. 56.

[27] Nancy B. Kurland, "The Unexplored Territory Linking Rewards and Ethical Behavior," *Business and Society*, 34 (April 1995), pp. 34–50.

[28] Pui-Wing Tam, "Fallen Star: H-P's Board Ousts Fiorina as CEO: Amid Languishing Stock, Computer Chief Resists Pressure to Delegate; A Big Merger's Missed Goals," *The Wall Street Journal*, February 10, 2005, p. A1.

In 2002 Bob Nardelli was hired as the new CEO of Home Depot after he lost out to Jeff Immelt in the competition to succeed Jack Welch as the head of GE. During Nardelli's tenure Home Depot managed to improve its profits substantially through a series of cost-cutting and efficiency-focused actions. However, its profit increase was not nearly as large as those of Lowe's, its main competitor. Further, Nardelli's numbers-oriented management style often pulled employees away from customer-focused tasks to perform administrative duties like report writing. As a result, Home Depot experienced significant customer dissatisfaction and employee morale problems. After nearly five years, Nardelli's actions resulted in virtually no change in Home Depot's share price while Lowes' price enjoyed significant appreciation. Further exacerbating the situation was Nardelli's compensation, which was valued at approximately $38 million in 2006 and over $200 million in total during his tenure. Finally, after increasing pressure from key shareholders, the company's board of directors removed Nardelli from his position and gave him $210 million in severance pay, which had been contractually guaranteed to him when he began at Home Depot. Nardelli's exit package left many Home Depot shareholders wondering if the cure was worse the problem.[29]

Fiorina and Nardelli are particularly well-known, but not uncommon, examples of CEOs that are recipients of **golden parachutes** from their employers. Typically, golden parachutes are contracts given to senor managers assuring them that they will receive large compensation packages if their companies are taken over by another firm and they subsequently lose their jobs. The H-P and Home Depot examples show that managers do not necessarily have to lose their jobs in a merger to receive golden parachutes. For example, Harrah's CEO Gary Loveman's golden parachute lets him receive $94 million dollars if his company's acquisition by Texas Pacific Group and Apollo Management Group is approved by its shareholders. Furthermore, Loveman will get another $18.9 million if he leaves the company within one year of the merger for a number of reasons—including simply quitting his job.[30]

Most of the above examples are notable because of the size of the payout. Perhaps even more troubling is that it is common practice for firms to guarantee their CEOs large exit packages no matter how well or poorly the companies perform under their leadership, or for the simple fact that the CEO leaves the firm. Michael Jensen, a retired Harvard Business School professor, is one of the original advocates of tying CEO compensation directly to the firm's share price, which is commonly called **pay for performance theory**.[31] Jensen's recent research on his theory has produced some surprising results. He discovered that 44 percent of all

---

[29] Alan Murray, "Business: Behind Nardelli's Abrupt Exit; Executive's Fatal Flaw: Failing to Understand New Demands on CEOs," *The Wall Street Journal,* January 4, 2007; Brian Grow with Dean Foust, Emily Thorton, Robert Farzad, and Jena McGregor, "Out at Home Depot," *BusinessWeek,* January 15, 2007, p. 56; Thomas G. Donlan, "The Royal CEO, Part II," *Barron's,* January 15, 2007, p. 55.
[30] Ryan Nakashima, "Golden Parachute Cradles Harrah's CEO," *Washington Post,* February 9, 2007, http://www.washingtonpost.com/wp-dyn/content/article/2007/02/09/AR2007020900067.html?nav=rss_ business/industries.
[31] Michael C. Jensen and Kevin J. Murphy, "CEO Incentives—It's Not How Much You Pay, But How," *Harvard Business Review,* May–June 1990, pp. 138–153.

CEO contracts do not allow for a CEO to be fired without receiving a severance package, even when the CEO is being dismissed due to being convicted of fraud or embezzlement. Further, Jensen found that 94 percent of all contracts do not allow for the CEO to be fired for poor performance without also receiving a severance package.[32] For example, Sprint CEO Gary Forsee led his firm's acquisition of Nextel in 2005. Since the merger, Sprint Nextel has continued to lose customers at a faster rate than most of its cell phone competitors, and its shareholders have lost approximately $20 billion in wealth since the completion of the merger. Despite these grim performance figures, Forsee's last contract, signed in late 2006, guaranteed him a payment of up to $52.7 million if he was fired by Sprint Nextel or $66.2 million if he lost his job as the result of Sprint Nextel being acquired by another company—which is in addition to the $21.3 million in compensation he received in 2006.[33] Unsurprisingly, less than a year later, Forsee resigned as Sprint Nextel's CEO, as its board of directors and some of its major shareholders expressed strong concerns about his ability to lead the company to better times.[34] Similarly, the previously mentioned Merrill Lynch CEO E. Stanley O'Neal received a preplanned $161.5 in retirement and stock benefits when he was forced to retire in October 2007 after his firm reported a surprising $2.24 billion quarterly loss—the largest ever in the company's history. The payout was in addition the compensation of over $70 million that O'Neal had received as CEO during the previous four years. His replacement, John Thain, received a two-year compensation package valued at between $50 million and $120 million depending on the performance of Merrill Lynch's stock.[35]

Derek Bok, retired president of Harvard University, has often spoken, written, and acted on behalf of ethical issues. He notes that in the period since World War I, the only decades in which CEO salaries increased so dramatically, the 1920s and from 1980 on, were "two periods in which America's values moved sharply toward the celebration of material rewards." He also says that this is not inevitable, as in the period from 1940 to 1965, CEO salaries moved up less rapidly than salaries of the average blue-collar worker even though the economy was doing well. Bok's solution is twofold: He urges a change in values away from blatant materialism, and he also urges a graduated income tax on those receiving such large pay.[36]

As long as it is so huge, CEO compensation will continue to receive attention as an example of inequity and greed. Negative reactions from shareholders are causing some boards of directors to examine their executive compensation more carefully to

---

[32] Louis Uchietelle, "Revising a Boardroom Legacy," *The New York Times,* September 28, 2007, p. C1.
[33] Dana Cimilluca, "A $53 Million Golden Parachute for Sprint's Forsee," *The Wall Street Journal Online,* April 10, 2007, http://blogs.wsj.com/deals/2007/04/10/a-53-million-golden-parachute-for-sprints-forsee/.
[34] Joann S. Lublin and Amol Sharma, "Sprint Nextel CEO Steps Down: Forsee's Successor Faces Erosion of Customer Base; Carrier to Miss Forecasts," *The Wall Street Journal,* October 9, 2007, p. A3.
[35] Nancy Moran and Rodney Yap, "O'Neal Ranks No. 5 on Payout List, Group Says: Table (Update1)," *Bloomberg.com,* November 2, 2007,http://www.bloomberg.com/apps/news?pid=20601109&sid=aPxzn5U8zNBo&refer=home; Eric Dash, "Merrill to Pay Chief $50 Million, More if Stock Rises," *The New York Times,* November 17, 2007, p. C5.
[36] Derek Bok, *The Cost of Talent: How Executives and Professionals are Paid and How It Affects America* (New York: The Free Press, 1993); also his "It's Time to Trim Hefty Paychecks," *The New York Times,* December 5, 1993, p. F13.

ensure that it is a reward for the long-term performance of the firm. But let us now examine the ethical aspect of other management issues.

American Supremacy Challenged: A Short-Term Focus

The United States has lost hundreds of thousands of jobs and entire industries in manufacturing and service. Shoes, clothing, toys, cameras, watches, radios, televisions, and video cassette recorders are almost all imported. Even service jobs, such as design of software and call center services, are now carried out in overseas centers. The United States has also lost many middle management and high-wage factory positions. Because of globalization, nations that have lower wages attract these jobs.

Managers are essential for the success of any enterprise, because they provide the vision and leadership for the organization. However, some managers are short-sighted. These executives invest little in worker training and research and development, and spend too much on acquisitions. A group of chief executives and strategy scholars met under the auspices of the Council on Competitiveness and the Harvard Business School to determine why this is the case. Chair of the panel and business strategy expert Michael Porter lays the blame on the way America's financial system allocates capital. In Porter's words, "the money doesn't go to the right companies for the right investments." In the external markets, the system underfunds firms that can deploy capital most productively. Internally, it directs funds to wasteful projects instead of toward research and development, training, and other initiatives that would aid a company's long-term prospects.[37]

Bonus plans are generally based on last year's performance. However, managers often expect to be in their current job just a few years and then to receive a preferable position elsewhere. A newcomer who takes a manager's place would reap the reward of superior long-term performance. Thus there is little financial incentive for a person to plan and budget for even a few years out. A better gage would be to measure performance over a 5- or 10-year term. Substantial growth is best accomplished when managers plan for the long term.

The larger and more diversified a firm is, the more difficult it is for top management to know specific products, markets, and employees. Because of their distance from customers, production, new product ideas, and the public, managers often turn to what it can understand—the only "objective" control mechanism that is available—"the numbers." This encourages short-term thinking, and often results in reducing research, risk taking, and ultimately productivity. Moreover, it also makes managers less likely to examine the ethics of management decisions. The ethical problems of GE under Jack Welch are an example. So we see that pressure to achieve short-term results "by the numbers" also fractures the ability to examine ethical issues.[38]

Perhaps compensation would be more equitable if employees were asked to rate their own supervisors. Many of America's most admired companies do just that; they

---

[37] Judith H. Dobrzynski, "A Sweeping Prescription for Corporate Myopia," *BusinessWeek,* July 6, 1992, p. 36–37.
[38] Alex Berenson, *The Number: How the Drive for Quarterly Earnings Corrupted Wall Street and Corporate America* (New York: Random House, 2003).

call it **upward evaluation** or **360 degree feedback**. Among the firms that ask subordinates to rate their superiors, including the CEO, are Alcoa, BellSouth, DuPont, Eaton, General Mills, H-P, Merck, Herman Miller, Morgan Stanley, Motorola, P&G, and 3M.

In sum, the principal cause of a lack of long-term success is the pressure on managers to achieve short-term results. The same sort of motivation leads to unethical behavior. Managers often publicize measurable, short-term results so that they may appear to be doing their job well. However, other executives are noted for their ethical actions and they lead very profitable firms. Let us examine some of them.

LEADERS SHAPE THE CULTURE AND ETHICS OF A FIRM

Executives have an immense influence on the corporate culture, climate, and ethics of a firm. That influence can be one which makes the firm financially successful, and also successful for its employees and other stakeholders.[39]

James D. Sinegal, founder and CEO of Costco, was listed in a *BusinessWeek* cover story as one of "The Good CEOs."[40] Sinegal opened the first wholesale Costco store in 1983 in Seattle. His strategy is to offer lower prices by stripping away everything judged to be unnecessary. For example, CEO Sinegal answers his own phone and does not have an executive washroom or even an office that has walls, and his office has 20-year-old furniture.

Costco is a retailer that directly competes with Wal-Mart's Sam's Club. But, while Wal-Mart has been criticized for its low wages and poor retirement and health benefits, Costco treats its associates much better. The average hourly wage at Costco is $15.97, while Wal-Mart's Sam's Club is $11.52. Costco's pays annual health costs per worker of $5,735 for 82 percent of the workers, while Sam's Club spends $3,500 each on only 47 percent of its workers. Sinegal is convinced that better treatment of workers pays off. Costco's annual employee turnover is 6 percent, while Sam's Club is 21 percent. More revealing is that Costco's profit per employee is $13,647 while Wal-Mart's Sam's Club is only $11,039. Nevertheless, Wall Street financial analysts object to the higher wage and benefit costs at Costco. Wall Street sees lower labor costs as better for shareholders. However, CEO Sinegal puts it simply, "Paying your employees well is not only the right thing to do but it makes for good business."[41]

Two additional examples illustrate the integrity found at Costco. One of Sinegal's rules is to strictly limit markups to 12 percent on national brands. On one occasion they were selling Calvin Klein jeans for $29.99, when they obtained a batch at $22.99. While they were selling well at the higher price, Sinegal insisted on lowering the price and not taking the possible higher markup. On another occasion Costco was expanding in the United Kingdom, and its bankers recommended

[39] Mark Bolino, William Turnley, and James Bloodgood, "Citizenship Behavior and the Creation of Social Capital in Organizations," *Academy of Management Review,* 27 (October 2002): 505–522; Jacqueline Hood, "The Relationship of Leadership Style and CEO Values to Ethical Practices in Organizations," *Journal of Business Ethics,* 43 (April 2003): 263–273.

[40] *BusinessWeek,* September 23, 2002, pp. 82–83.

[41] Stanley Holmes and Wendy Zellner, "The Costco Way: Higher Wages Mean Higher Profits. But Try Telling Wall Street," *BusinessWeek,* April 12, 2004, pp. 76–77.

structuring a borrowing transaction so that both principal and interest were tax deductible, in place of interest only. It would have given Costco large tax savings. When Sinegal looked more carefully at the proposal, it became clear that it would be exploiting a loophole in the tax code, and Costco refused to do it.[42] With that sort of integrity, do you think Costco will be able to compete with Sam's Club in the marketplace?

Executives as Moral Leaders

We will now spotlight two additional business leaders because of their contributions to business, business values, and business ethics. They are selected because their values and actions can serve as models for all businesspeople.

Ray Anderson, an engineer, began *Interface Carpet* in 1973 and is now Chairman of the Board of the firm. Interface, a billion dollar business, is the largest producer of commercial floor covering in the United States. It sells in 110 countries and manufactures on four continents. In 1994, Andersen, then the firm's CEO, realized that he and his firm were in his words "plunders of the earth."[43] He read Paul Hawkin's book, *Ecology of Commerce: A Declaration of Sustainability*,[44] which changed his view of himself and his firm. Hawkin describes how most manufacturing firms eat through the earth's limited resources without regard for the poisons they leave behind for future generations to clean up. Hawkin argues that business is responsible for most of the damage, but it can also be a part of the solution. Andersen points out that business is the largest, wealthiest, and most pervasive institution on Earth, so business must take the lead in directing the Earth away from collapse and toward restoration.

Andersen says that reading the book "was like a spear in my chest . . . That's the way I had been running my company . . . taking something that wasn't mine." Anderson decided to change. He pledged to work toward not using the earth's natural resources, and to eliminate all waste and harmful emissions by 2020. Anderson runs a firm whose floor tiles are petroleum based, yet he says that "if I can get it right, I will not take another drop of oil from the earth." He has plans for recycling used carpet, and has already contracted with numerous firms to "rent" them carpet. That is, he will provide any new floor covering they require; he will then take back and recycle the old so that it is not thrown into landfills, but rather used for new carpeting. Anderson is on his way to his goals for Interface. He has reduced waste by 80 percent, energy consumption by 31 percent, water intake by 78 percent, and use of petroleum by 28 percent. By doing so he has saved Interface $231 million.

Anderson went beyond making his own firm eco-friendly. He set out to convince other business executives of the importance of not trashing the earth. He has given talks throughout the United States and the world on the importance of sustainability.

---

[42] Interview of John Dienhart, from "Strategic Leadership of Ethical Behavior in Business," *Academy of Management Executive,* 18 (May 2004): 61.

[43] Ray Anderson, "In the Future, People like Me will Go to Jail," *Fortune,* May 24, 1999, pp. 190–200.

[44] Paul Hawken, *The Ecology of Commerce: A Declaration of Sustainability* (New York: Harper Business, 1994).

He defines sustainability as *meeting the needs of today without compromising the ability of future generations to meet their own needs.*[45] In those talks Anderson points out that two-thirds of humanity are starving, unemployed, or living on less than $2 a day, and are thus left out of our current economic system, except perhaps to be exploited. Calling himself a "recovering plunder," Anderson says "as we focus myopically on financial capital through the lens of a misbegotten economic system," human capital (social equity) and natural capital (the environment) are neglected.

Anderson has also made Interface a model for worker, supplier, and customer relations. In 2000 Interface began a "Stakeholder Dialogue" when they ask employees and suppliers for detailed opinions about the company in an anonymous annual survey. The results are compiled by a third party. Interface has also been named as one of the top 100 companies to work for in America by *Fortune*.

Felix Rohatyn is still probably the best-known and best-connected investment banker in the United States. He was senior partner at **Lazard Freres & Co.** and served as U.S. Ambassador to France. For 30 years he was the principal deal maker at Lazard. Rohatyn engineered a deal that enabled New York City to avoid bankruptcy. Lazard Freres reported three times the profit per employee as its closest rival. Rohatyn was one of the earliest and most skillful consultants to firms involved in giant financial deals. He is now stunned by the deliberate falsifications and breakdown of honesty on Wall Street. He points out that "our modern capitalistic system is based on disclosure and veracity." If foreign investors begin to doubt the integrity of the U.S. market, "it could have dramatic repercussions on the dollar, on domestic inflation, on the economy."[46]

Rohatyn is critical of many of his peers in investment banking. He says that the United States has done practically nothing to prevent a recurrence of a stock market bubble and crash. He notes that the primary purpose of the stock and bond markets is to provide investment funds for organizations that need capital. Yet the markets do not accomplish that well:

> The fundamental weakness in the securities markets, world-wide, is the result of excessive speculation, excessive use of credit, and inadequate regulation. This speculative behavior is not driven by individuals, as was the case in the 1920s, but by institutions such as pension funds, banks, savings and loans, and insurance companies. In many cases, these institutions are backed by federal government guarantees. Curbing speculation and promoting investment must be the objective of reform.[47]

Rohatyn points out that it is in the short-term self-interest of investment bankers and lawyers to complete "deals" (mergers or acquisitions); otherwise they do not receive their fee. They are paid even when the merger is not in the best interest of the

---

[45] Ray Anderson, *Mid-Course Correction: Toward a Sustainable Enterprise—The Interface Model* (Atlanta: Peregrinzilla Press, 1998).

[46] "Felix Rohatyn on Wall Street's Corruption," *BusinessWeek*, May 3, 2002; "The Last Emperor of Wall Street," *BusinessWeek*, May 30, 1988, p. 65.

[47] Felix G. Rohatyn, "Institutional 'Investor' or 'Speculator'?" *The Wall Street Journal*, June 24, 1988, pp. 14, 24.

client. Rohatyn also thinks that investment bankers' fees are much too large. Rohatyn feels that he has a "responsibility to save capitalism from itself—that greed, ideological rigidity, or the simple lack of competence outside their narrow arenas of expertise can blind the movers and shakers of the business world to the risks of financial instability they are promoting."

The following are among Rohatyn's suggestions for cooling speculation:

- Impose a 50 percent tax on the profit of securities held for less than a year. This tax would apply to individuals, corporations, partnerships, and currently tax-free institutions. At the same time, reduce capital gains taxes on securities held for more than five years to 15 percent.
- Sharply limit the type and proportion of speculative investments held by federally insured institutions.

With regard to firms in general, being ethical often benefits a firm's sales. Surveys indicate that consumers prefer to purchase from a firm that has a good reputation; 55 percent of consumers say that "they always take a company's ethics and values into account when purchasing a product or service." Forty percent always consider "treatment of employees" and 23 percent always look at the company's environmental record. In a second survey, 78 percent of the respondents said that they would buy a product made by a firm that contributes to education and medical research. Two-thirds said they would switch brands to a manufacturer that supported a cause they deemed worthy. One-third said they were more influenced by a firm's social activism than by its advertising.[48]

There are hundreds of additional cases of firms cooperating with nongovernmental organizations (NGOs) to improve the lives of people in their community. These include Home Depot workers volunteering to build playgrounds for poor children, Microsoft providing funding and computers to set up Internet access in libraries in poor neighborhoods, Denny's helping Save the Children, and Bank of Boston working with the domestic peace corps for minority young people.[49] More than 800 firms that are attempting to be socially responsible belong to a group called *Business for Social Responsibility* (www.bsr.org). The group meets annually, partially to support one another in their efforts to be socially responsible. Among these firms are Shorebank of Chicago, Newman's Own Inc., Tom's of Maine, and Glen Ellen Winery.[50]

Many others could be added to this group of talented and visionary CEOs and firms. On social and environmental measures, European firms are generally ahead of their American counterparts. One account edited by the CEOs of DuPont, Royal Dutch Shell, and Anova Holding lists 67 cases of European, Japanese, and U.S. firms on successful sustainable business operations.[51]

---

[48] The first study is cited in John Adams, "Dissecting Corporate Goodness," *American Advertising,* Spring 1996, pp. 10–15. The second by Roper Starch Worldwide is quoted in "Good Stewardship is Good Business," *Fortune,* March 21, 1994, p. 16.

[49] Shirley Sagawa and Eli Segal, *Common Interest, Common Good: Creating Value through Business and Social Sector Partnerships* (Boston: Harvard Business School Press, 2000).

[50] Mary Scott and Howard Rothman, *Companies with a Conscience* (New York: Citadel, 1994); also Joel Makower, *Beyond the Bottom Line* (New York: Simon & Schuster, 1994), pp. 311–321.

[51] Charles O. Holliday, Jr., Stephan Schmidheiny, and Philip Watt, *Walking the Talk: The Business Case for Sustainable Development* (San Francisco: Berrett-Koehler, 2002).

Executives who have been spotlighted here build an environment that builds organizational wealth. The favorable relationships with suppliers, employees, customers, and the community constitute that wealth, which in turn provides a difficult to copy competitive advantage for the firm in the global marketplace.[52] Moreover, Ray Anderson's vision for the planet and Rohatyn's suggestions for encouraging long-term investments provide a good introduction later in this chapter when we identify business strategies to make ethics and good character integral portions of the fabric of the firm. But in spite of the rewards that integrity and cooperation bring, there are some businesspeople who look to their own self-interest. Let us examine some cases.

Executives Who Destroy Wealth and People

Most executives take their responsibilities to people and the community seriously. On the other hand, there are some executives who focus exclusively on dollar return or personal gain—and that hurts people and ultimately hinders the efficient operation of the firm. Some firms such as Lockheed, Philip Morris, Solomon Brothers, RJR, and General Dynamics have a decades-long reputation for self-interested behavior. Whether you are a customer, employee, or supplier of these firms, it is wise to check your contract closely and leave little to a handshake. Let us now examine some recent examples of selfish behavior.

Conrad Black was CEO of publishing conglomerate *Hollinger International*. The firm published the *Chicago Sun-Times* and dozens of smaller U.S. and Canadian newspapers. When wrongdoing was suspected, the Board set up an internal investigative committee. The committee reported that Black designed the finances of the firm so that he and an associate were able to pocket $400 million, almost all profits for 1997–2003. Moreover, in addition to his regular salary, he charged extraordinary expenses to Hollinger: $1.4 million for a personal chef, maids, and butlers for his four homes; $390,000 for taking care of his RollsRoyce and other cars; $24,950 for "summer drinks"; and $42,870 for a birthday party for his wife.

The report accuses Sir Conrad Black (a Canadian who was knighted and made a member of Britain's House of Lords) of using the firm as a personal "piggy bank." The report goes on, "Behind a constant stream of bombast regarding their accomplishments as self-described 'proprietors,' Black and Radler (former chief operating officer) made it their business to line their pockets at the expense of Hollinger almost every day, in almost every way they could devise." Through an elaborate holding firm scheme, Black paid "management fees" of roughly $218 million to two firms; and almost all of that money went directly to him and his friends. Black was eventually brought to trial for his actions. In 2007 he was convicted of mail fraud and obstruction of justice, but he was acquitted of racketeering and misuse of corporate perks charges.[53]

---

[52] James E. Post, Lee E. Preston, and Sybille Sachs, *Redefining the Corporation: Stakeholder Management and Organizational Wealth* (Stanford: Stanford University Press, 2002).

[53] Associated Press, "Conrad Black Convicted of Fraud," *NPR.org,* July 13, 2007, http://www.npr.org/templates/story/story.php?storyId=11948939.

Fausto Tonna was the CFO of the Italian firm *Parmalat*, a grocery retailer and one of Europe's largest and best-known multinational firms. Parmalat had sales of $9.2 billion and 36,000 employees, but was forced into bankruptcy in December 2003. When Parmalat defaulted on a $185 million loan, investigators found that a claimed $4.9 billion Bank of America account in the Cayman Islands never existed. Vanished assets totaled $8.5 billion to $12 billion. Parmalat used derivatives and other complex financial transactions to make its balance sheet look acceptable. The firm did this via investment banks such as Citigroup and Merrill Lynch. One of these used a Citigroup subsidiary called Buconero LLC, which means "black hole" in Italian. A Citigroup manager later apologized for the name.

The firm had two outside auditing firms during this period, Grant Thornton and Deloitte. Parmalat changed auditors because of an Italian law that seeks to prevent fraud and encourage transparency. Nevertheless, neither firm detected the fraud. Bankruptcy forced Parmalat to lay off thousands and to sell many of its subsidiary businesses. Parmalat's ex-CFO Tonna has now petitioned for $6 million in severance pay from the firm.[54]

Other examples of executive misbehavior are too common. In order to escape U.S. taxes, executives at Tyco, Accenture, and other firms have moved their headquarters to Bermuda; such actions neglect their responsibilities as citizens. Each of the managers in this section had a profound impact on the ethics and the values of the firm he or she led. A manager's influence on peers and subordinates is proportionate to that manager's responsibility in the firm. Let us now consider how a culture of responsible behavior is built and maintained in a firm.

CORPORATION CHARTERED TO SERVE SOCIETY

Corporations were initially chartered by British monarchs to provide a service to society. Founded in 1670, the Hudson Bay Company explored, claimed land, and traded goods; the Massachusetts Turnpike Company was chartered to build toll roads. These were typical of early corporations. For two centuries thereafter the purpose of the corporation was primarily to serve the public good, for example, building and maintaining canals, bridges, roads, water systems, banks, and colleges. Investors were invited to participate and the incentive for that participation was a financial return. But it was clear to all that **the primary purpose of the publicly chartered corporation was to perform a public service**. This changed in the late 1800s when the primary purpose of the corporation shifted from serving the public interest to maximizing the wealth of investors and now also the wealth of hired executives.

The power of the global corporation in the United States and in other constitutional democracies comes from its legal position and its charter. And that power proceeds from the people; the government receives its power from the consent of the governed.

---

[54] "Italy Widens Parmalat Inquiry to Foreign Banks," *The New York Times*, January 8, 2004, pp. C1, 10; and "How Parmalat Went Sour," *BusinessWeek*, January 12, 2004, pp. 46–48.

The modern corporation has vast powers, and great benefits and privileges, legally bestowed by its charter. Very importantly, a corporation has the ability to disguise itself, to run and hide, or to reorganize into a whole new entity. It can sell off divisions and subsidiaries, and rename itself, emerging as, seemingly, a completely different company. Today's corporation wasn't yesterday's and can't be counted on to be tomorrow's.[55]

Because a state charters the corporation, it also has the power to revoke that charter. When a corporation becomes a net liability to society, a state literally could put that firm out of business. Recently a law professor led a court case asking California to revoke the charter of Union Oil Co., and a Circuit Court judge in Alabama sought to revoke the charter of the five major tobacco manufacturers. The criteria upon which a charter could be revoked could be set out very clearly. The mere threat of such action might bring more responsible behavior.[56]

The publicly held corporation now is sometimes thought to be responsible primarily to its investors. The defense of this position is that the investors provide the funds that enable the firm to operate. But this is not true except for **initial public offerings**, when firms initially sell their stock to shareholders and use the proceeds to fund their activities. In daily market operations, stockholders mainly purchase shares from other stockholders, and most capital for the firm's operation is obtained from retained profits and loans. This undermines the legitimacy of the claim that investors should be the primary beneficiaries of a corporation's actions. Nevertheless note how putting investors first has influenced some firms to neglect social responsibilities and brought us the WorldCom, Adelphia, and GE scandals. Pressing for greater profits and "smoothed" earnings was one of the causes of the deceptions at Enron, Computer Associates, Arthur Andersen, and other business tragedies of the last decade. The perceived need to satisfy shareholders pushes managers to focus on profitability and growth. This encourages them to claim false earnings, hide losses, buy tax shelters, and other violations of people and integrity. CEOs also have the ability to set their own compensation, which is often lavish. On the other hand, management is not required to sacrifice themselves, even in difficult times when they are asking for sacrifices from others. Moreover, managers are generally shielded from financial harm by law, insurance, and legal staff.

Shareholders are not the only ones who invest in the corporation. Others invest far more than merely their money. Employees invest their time, talent, and experience; their investment may be decades of their work lives. Customers invest in a firm by purchasing its products. When these are "big ticket" items, this investment is similar to that of stockholders; if they receive a defective product or service, their risk may be more than that of financial investors. Suppliers commit a large portion of their time, equipment, and assets to large corporate customers; this investment and risk are also greater than those of most stockholders. Therefore many propose that requiring corporations to

---

[55] Ralph Estes, "Corporate Accountability: The Tyranny of the Bottom Line," in *The New Business of Business,* ed. W. Harman and M. Porter, (San Francisco: Berrett-Koehler, 1997), pp. 111–120; also Estes', *Tyranny of the Bottom Line: Why Corporations make Good People Do Bad Things* (San Francisco: Berrett-Koehler, 1999).

[56] Russell Mokhiber, "Death Penalty for Corporations Comes of Age," *Business Ethics* (November 1998): 7.

report on their social and environmental impacts, in the same way as they report on their financial results, would provide more information and thus make the market system more efficient and fair. We will discuss these reporting initiatives later in this chapter.

Roles of the CEO and Board of Directors

The **CEO** of a firm is ultimately responsible for the firm's success or failure. The CEO, in consultation with others, sets policy, decides on new products or services, establishes budgets, and sets the vision and mission of the firm. The CEO is the person most responsible for the values, ethics, culture, and climate of the firm.[57]

The **board of directors** represents the organization's owners. The responsibility of the board of directors is to (1) hire, evaluate the performance of, and, when necessary, fire the CEO; and (2) approve major policies and actions recommended by the CEO. This oversight role of the board is essential if the corporation is going to be both effective and ethical. The board's oversight role is effective when board members can exercise independent judgment—that is, if they are **independent directors** (see Figure 8-1). Yet the constitution of corporate boards continues to present problems, because many board members have a conflict of interest. The Disney board was criticized for having too many directors who were not independent. For two years in a row, it topped *BusinessWeek*'s annual list of the worst boards in the United States. The Disney board included the CEO's personal architect, a principal of a school his children attended, and an actor, plus three additional directors with strong financial ties to Disney. Moreover, three directors who were critical of the CEO's policies were not reelected to the board.[58]

There is a potential conflict of interest for an **outside director** (not a full-time employee of the organization), but nonetheless has business relationships with the firm. For example, at one point three directors of Tyson Foods were former Tyson executives who held six-figure Tyson business contracts; another director had a 10-year $4 million consulting contract. Verizon, Bank of America, GE, Nike, and FedEx all have had board members with similar conflicts of interest. It is hard for directors to ask pointed questions of the executives who pay them. Compensation for board members in the largest 200 U.S. firms has increased 13 percent to $176,000 per year for their part-time, albeit

Inside Director:	A director who is in the full-time employ of the firm
Outside Director:	A director who is not in full-time employ of firm
Independent Director:	An outside director, who has no business relationship to firm
Lead Director:	An independent director who acts as chair on regular occasions, when the CEO is the chair

FIGURE 8-1   **Members of Corporate Boards of Directors**

---

[57] For some practical suggestions, see Larry Johnson and Bob Phillips, *Absolute Honesty: Building a Corporate Culture That Values Straight Talk and Rewards Integrity* (New York: American Management Association, 2003).

[58] David Lieberman, "Disney Tries to Work Magic With New Board Lineup," *USA Today,* March 18, 2003, p. 1.

important, job. Furthermore, board members are often setting their own compensation, which raises additional conflict of interest questions.[59] Even after Enron, boards of directors are doling out unearned compensation. For example, Gary Wendt, CEO of Conseco, was given an $8-million bonus although he led his firm to just one profitable quarter in two years.[60]

Another potential conflict of interest exists when the **CEO is also the chair of the board**. Harold M. Williams, a former chair of the Securities & Exchange Commission and CEO himself, said, "The CEO should not be chairman of the board. Control of the agenda and pace of the meeting is a powerful control."[61] Board members are now asked to bear much more responsibility for the integrity of the firm. In response to shareholder and governance concerns GE replaced stock options for directors and in their place provides "deferred stock units" which can be redeemed only one year after they leave the board. This encourages a longer term perspective and greater objectivity. In the United Kingdom, a director is not considered independent if that director has significant stock holdings in the firm or has more than 10 years on a board.[62]

The principal factors that enable boards to be effective are as follows:

- All are "independent" board members;
- The chairperson of the board is an independent director, and not the CEO of that firm;
- Directors are prepared, are sufficiently skeptical, and ask enough questions about proposals presented to board (see Figure 8-2).

When these factors are not present, there are conflicts of interest, which make the board less effective. **Inside directors** are full-time employees of the firm, and this makes it difficult for them objectively to evaluate and criticize company proposals at board meetings. The proposals come from the CEO, the very person who will decide their performance appraisal, promotion, and salary increases. Outsiders, however, also have a limitation, because often they do not have sufficient information to ask good questions. Moreover, some directors sit on too many boards, and thus do not devote the time to do the homework to ask intelligent questions.

A CEO who is also chair of the board thus directs the very body that is charged with evaluating his or her own performance. The chair of the board also determines what is discussed at the meeting, what information is sent to the members, and the order and pace of the board's discussions. A primary role of the board is to assess the performance of the CEO, yet the CEO has vast influence over the very group that sits in judgment. In Japan, very few CEOs chair their own board.[63] Also note the contrast with

---

[59] *BusinessWeek,* October 11, 2004, p. 18; Dan R. Dalton and Catherine M. Daily, "Director Stock Compensation: An Invitation to a Conspicuous Conflict of Interests?" *Business Ethics Quarterly,* 11, no. 1 (2001): 89–108.

[60] "Directors Conflicts of Interest Often Buried Deep in Firms' SEC Filings," *USA Today,* March 5, 2002, pp. 1A–2A; "Look Who's Still at the Trough: Bonuses, Loans, Free BMWs—Boards Are Up to Their Old Games," *BusinessWeek,* September 8, 2002, p. 58.

[61] "Chairman and CEO: One Hat Too Many," *BusinessWeek,* November 18, 1991, p. 124.

[62] "More Work, More Money," and "Where Europe Leads," *The Wall Street Journal,* February 24, 2003, pp. R4, R6.

[63] Dan R. Dalton and Idalene F. Kesner, "Composition and CEO Duality in Boards of Directors: An International Perspective," *Journal of International Business* (Fall 1987): 35, 40.

1. Board members should have top management experience and should represent a variety of perspectives.
2. The optimum number on a board is 8–12.
3. Board members should be independent of the firm, with few exceptions.
4. The audit, nominating, compensation, governance, and ethics committees should consist of *only* independent directors.
5. Board members should be prepared for board meetings, and also be skeptical and willing to challenge management on important issues.
6. Independent directors should meet regularly without the CEO or other management present. (General Motors has a "lead director," who then chairs these meetings.)
7. Directors should not micro manage or interfere with management.
8. A director should not serve on more than three to five boards at the same time.

FIGURE 8-2 **Characteristics of Members of a Business Board of Directors**

university governance. In universities an outsider is the chair, whereas in 80 percent of American business firms the CEO is still the chair. Yet, in business where the profit motive is strong and large sums of money are involved, there is great danger of conflict of interest. Thus most argue that the CEO should not chair the board. Finally, we know that in the Hollinger, Enron, WorldCom, and other debacles, board members did not sufficiently question the CEO and management about their fraudulent actions.

Many boards of directors have attempted to develop the ideal characteristics described above because of increased pressure from the government and institutional investors (see the discussions below). This "Revolt in the Boardroom"[64] has not been without its problems as boards struggle to achieve an appropriate balance between strategic oversight and direct meddling in the activities of senior management, especially when the directors are successful and skilled businesspeople in their own right. Furthermore, outside board members must attempt to balance their need to maintain a good working relationship with senior management and simultaneously fill the role of objective, and sometimes critical, evaluators of management's performance. Perhaps no case is more illustrative of these struggles than the experience of H-P's board of directors over the past several years.[65]

---

[64] Alan Murray, *Revolt in the Boardroom: The New Rules of Power in Corporate America* (New York: Collins, 2007).

[65] The Hewlett-Packard boardroom saga, with its origins in Fiorina's plans to acquire Compaq through its culmination in the pretexting scandal, is one of the most widely reported business stories on a single firm in recent memory. The following chapter section on H-P draws on a wide variety of sources. Readers wishing more information on the story are encouraged to see the following: Carol J. Loomis, "Why Carly's Big Bet Is Failing," *Fortune,* February 7, 2005, p. 50; Pu-Wing Tam, *op. cit.*; Carol J. Loomis, "How the HP Board KO'd Carly," *Fortune,* March 7, 2005, p. 99; Damon Darlin and Matt Richtel, "Hewlett Board in a Shake-Up after Spy Furor," *The New York Times,* September 13, 2006, pp. A1, C5; Peter Burrows, "What Would Hewlett and Packard Say?" *BusinessWeek,* September 18, 2006, p. 35; Rick Newman, "The HP Way? Hardly," *U.S. News and World Report,* September 25, 2006, p. 48; Murray, *op. cit.* (see especially pp. 4–7, 34–62, and 131–154); John Hoak, "Building Ethics from the Ground Up," *Ethisphere,* Q2, 2007, pp. 48–50; Krishna G. Palepu and Jay W. Lorsch, "Hewlett-Packard Company: The War Within," *Harvard Business School Case 9-107-030,* May 8, 2007 (Boston: Harvard Business School Publishing).

Hewlett-Packard: CEO–Board Conflicts and Board Leaks

H-P's problems can be traced to the aforementioned efforts of chair and CEO Carly Fiorina to persuade the board to ratify the purchase of Compaq Computer in 2002. Historically boards, which were often hand-picked by the CEO, were "rubber stamps" on management decisions, and the decision to purchase another company would have readily followed the CEO recommendation. However, H-P's board of directors was a combination of both inside and outside members, including two sons of the company's legendary founders Bill Hewlett and David Packard. While many board members supported the merger, one son openly opposed the deal. A long public fight over the proposed acquisition ensued, both within the board and between the board and senior management. H-P's shareholders barely approved the merger, but at the cost of its board splitting into deeply divided factions. The situation worsened after the merger, as several board members clashed with Fiorina on how to best manage the merged companies.

During the ensuing years, the board experienced a significant turnover in members due to lingering tensions from the merger battle and to personality conflicts with Fiorina. Meanwhile, the merged H-P struggled to achieve the performance that it had promised. At a board meeting in early 2005, some directors took the unusual step of providing Fiorina with specific suggestions on how to manage the firm on a daily basis. Detailed information from this confidential meeting appeared in the business press, and Fiorina and the board suspected that a board member was leaking information to the media. Confidentiality is important because without the assurance of keeping private what is said at board meetings, directors are not likely to speak frankly, especially on controversial issues. Unauthorized leaks can also have the negative effect of publicizing a firm's strategic thinking on issues before they have been finalized by the board. H-P staff and an outside investigating firm failed to find the source of the leaks.

The board held a special meeting a month later to discuss H-P's direction and Fiorina's future. The board forced Fiorina to resign, named independent director Patricia Dunn as nonexecutive chairman, and later it hired Mark Hurd as CEO. When H-P held its annual board meeting almost a year later, once again the press provided extensive details of both the agenda of the meeting and the content of the board's conversations. As a result, Dunn asked H-P's legal, security, and ethics staff to investigate the source of the leaks. H-P then outsourced the investigation. The investigative firms used a variety of techniques to track down the sources of leaks, including pretexting, a practice of pretending to be someone else, to obtain the phone records of its board members' contacts with reporters for the *Wall Street Journal* and *CNET*. Other techniques included attempted installation of e-mail monitoring software on a reporter's computer, physical surveillance of reporters and board members, and background checks. The investigation determined that the leaker was longtime H-P director George Keyworth. Keyworth was a close personal friend of another director, Thomas Perkins, a powerful Silicon Valley venture capitalist whose style was as aggressive as Dunn's was rules-based. Dunn and Perkins often clashed on how the board should be run.

Evidence of Keyworth's leaks was presented to the entire board, several of whom were unaware of the investigations. Keyworth admitted the actions, but denied wrongdoing or providing any information that was harmful to H-P. Board members discussed whether Keyworth should be asked to resign as a director, as he refused to do so. Perkins, however, immediately resigned from the board in protest of the treatment of his friend.

Widespread news stories appeared in late 2006 concerning the tactics of H-P and its contractors in the leak investigation. The spying scandal, as it became known, engulfed the time of both H-P's board of directors and its senior management team. The board decided that Patricia Dunn should resign as chairman but remain as a director; Keyworth also agreed to resign. In addition, H-P apologized to those who it had investigated. The frenzy of the news coverage, however, ultimately caused Dunn to resign from the board, and brought the resignation of H-P's ethics officer and lead attorney.

H-P then reunified the offices of CEO and Chairman of the Board by naming Mark Hurd to both posts. The firm also created a new independent board position which is responsible for reviewing H-P's ethics and compliance programs. It also created a new office of ethics and compliance, with its manager reporting directly to both the CEO and the director overseeing the company's ethics and compliance program.

The H-P scandal illustrates the difficulties of achieving a high-performing board of directors that discharges its duties well. Part of H-P's problems resulted from different philosophies of the duties of the board by its members. When Carly Fiorina was chairman and CEO, board members differed over the optimal mix of strategic oversight and direct operational feedback it should provide to senior management. During the time of Patricia Dunn as chair and Mark Hurd as CEO, questions emerged as to whether oversight should occur observing rules and procedures or whether its operations should be more informal and personality driven. Further, as the spying scandal proceeded, H-P's board found itself in the awkward position of trying to determine how to both govern and investigate itself. The situation put board chair Dunn in the tricky position of overseeing H-P staff on an issue related to board governance. Lastly, the experience indicates the problems outside directors have in not always knowing the right questions to ask, and how or whom to ask.

The H-P story also raises serious questions. Given the need for board confidentiality, was it appropriate for Keyworth, or any board member, to independently talk to the press about board business? Would it be acceptable if he was only providing "nonharmful information"? What are the ethical limits on a firm when it investigates its employees or its board members? Is pretexting an acceptable means of investigation? Finally, what could H-P have done differently to make its board more effective?

Federal Regulation: Sarbanes–Oxley and the SEC

Government regulation of corporations in the United States has been effective in many areas, but was unable to avoid the injurious actions of Computer Associates, Qwest, and so many other firms. The U.S. Congress passed the **Sarbanes–Oxley Act** (SOX, as it is sometimes called), in the wake of these failures. The legislation attempts to correct some of the problems that allowed the deceit to take place.

SOX requires that the CFO and CEO both personally certify quarterly financial reports. This makes it more difficult to claim as did CEO Ken Lay of Enron that he knew nothing of the complex and false Enron accounts. SOX also makes senior management responsible for instituting, evaluating, and routinely reporting on the firm's internal control systems used to generate its financial reports. In addition, all the members of a board audit committee (which receives the outside audit) must be outside board members. The outside auditing firm is not permitted to have both auditing and consulting business for the same firm, in order to avoid being pressured to give a favorable audit in order to retain the more profitable consulting business. The auditing firm must also rotate the lead auditor on an account every five years, lest the lead auditor become too closely tied to the firm being audited.

The U.S. SEC wrote regulations to prevent conflict of interest of investment banks and their own investment analysts. The SEC has also set up a regulatory oversight board for the outside auditing firms. SOX did not address the conflict of interest when the CEO is also chair of the board. Citizens and investors contend that SOX was necessary for business to rebuild its reputation, and SOX has contributed to better board governance procedures. Boards that evaluated themselves jumped from 35 percent to 90 percent. Also boards that provide training for directors went from 14 percent to 80 percent.[66] Yet it is still possible to exaggerate income, hide losses, and avoid corporate income tax. Executives say that while SOX was necessary to rebuild trust, it is also expensive and has not improved ethical standards within their firms.

STRATEGIC PLANNING AND INTEGRITY BUILD TRUST

A business manager, like anyone else, must have a vision and goals to develop a strategic plan. Given that vision, strategic planning and ethics are intimately linked.[67] Moreover, there is a new, strong external argument for encouraging ethical behavior of members of a business firm.

The U.S. Sentencing Commission established the **Federal Sentencing Guidelines for Organizations** (FSGOs) for judges to use when determining the punishment of firms found guilty of violating federal laws. Penalties depend upon the actions that a firm has taken to avoid violations. When a firm is convicted, the guidelines call for more severe penalties if the firm has experienced previous violations, or if firm's managers were aware of the violations. On the other hand, a company that establishes procedures to avoid illegal and unethical acts will receive reduced penalties. So this is a powerful incentive for a business firm to develop an ethical code of conduct, educate members of the organization on ethical questions, appoint an ethics officer, and regularly audit the ethical record of the firm.[68] Following the lead of the SOX, the FSGOs were updated in 2004 to require more active involvement of senior management in the oversight and assessment of their ethics and compliance programs.[69]

[66]"The Big Picture," *BusinessWeek,* October 11, 2004, p. 15; "Companies Complain about Cost of Corporate-Governance Rules," *The Wall Street Journal,* February 10, 2004, p. 1A; also "Governance: Backlash In the Executive Suite," *BusinessWeek,* June 14, 2004, pp. 36–39.

[67] LaRue Tone Hosmer, "Strategic Planning as if Ethics Mattered," *Strategic Planning Journal,* 15 (1994): 17–34; and Daniel R. Gilbert, *The Twilight of Corporate Strategy: Comparative Ethical Critique* (New York: Oxford University Press, 1992).

[68] O.C. Ferrell, Debbie LeClair, and Linda Ferrell, "The Federal Sentencing Guidelines for Organizations," *Journal of Business Ethics,* 17 (1998): 353–363; also U.S. Sentencing Commission, "Sentencing Guidelines for Organizational Defendants," *Federal Register,* 1991, pp. 22786–22797.

[69] Ethics.org, "Federal Sentencing Guidelines," Ethics Resource Center, http://www.ethics.org/erc-publications/federal-sentencing-guidelines.asp.

Successful firms such as Medtronic, 3M, J&J, Sony, H-P, and McDonald's have a clear core mission, a strong set of values, a clear core mission, and employees dedicated to achieving that mission. Values and ethics are important to these firms; executives and managers deal responsibly with ethical issues (e.g., respect for colleagues, honesty in advertising, pollution, relations with the local community). There is greater likelihood that members of that firm will act ethically, and they are less likely to steal or act in other unethical ways, if an ethical work climate is achieved in the firm.[70] Many firms have a high-level officer and staff that plans for and monitors these issues.

Firms integrate ethical and social responsibilities into planning; most financially successful firms are also more ethical. A multitude of studies have shown that a firm that is socially responsible is more likely to have good financial performance.[71] Let us now examine the role of institutions that purchase equity shares in firms.

Institutional Investors

Institutional investors are organizations such as pension funds, mutual funds, insurance companies, trust funds, banks, and university endowments that control large sums of investment funds. These organizations have a significant and increasing influence on publicly held corporations in the United States. This was not true a generation ago. In 1955 pension funds and mutual funds owned less than 5 percent of corporate stock; by 2008 institutional investors owned more than two-thirds of equity stock in U.S. firms, which is valued at more than $24 trillion. Institutional investors have been active in attempting to influence corporate policy and the selection of directors.

Institutional investors have increasing influence on business executives in two ways. First, portfolio managers of these funds, seeking short-term financial gain, can push executives into short-sighted actions. This can include pressuring management for short-term returns and supporting takeover attempts when the expected result will be an increase in share price. Such actions can damage a firm, because a responsible executive must plan for the long term, as we saw in Chapter 1.

A second way of exercising influence is through **voting shares**. Following SEC rules, any shareholder can place an issue on the ballot for vote at the shareholder meeting of any publicly held firm. The proposal initiator generally tries to negotiate with management before placing the issue on a firm's ballot. The trend, which many attribute to shareholder skepticism arising from the Enron-era scandals, is for more proposals to be offered every year. In 2007, shareholders offered 1,164 proposals for

---

[70] James Weber, Lance B. Kurke, and David W. Pentico, "Why Do Employees Steal? Assessing Differences in Ethical and Unethical Employee Behavior Using Ethical Work Climate," *Business and Society,* 42 (September 2003): 359–380; James C. Collins and Jerry I. Porras, *Built to Last: Successful Habits of Visionary Companies* (New York: Harper Business, 1994).

[71] See Marc Orlitzky, Frank L. Schmidt, and Sara L. Rynes, "Corporate Social and Financial Performance: A Meta-Analysis," *Organizational Studies,* 24, no. 3 (2003): 403–444; also Samuel B. Graves and Sandra A. Waddock, "Institutional Owners and Corporate Social Performance," *Academy of Management Journal,* 37 (August 1994): 1034–1046.

consideration. Executive compensation faced a vote at 51 firms, and those resolutions received an average of 43 percent of shareholders approving.[72] Although a majority vote is not binding for shareholder resolutions, a large shareholder vote puts pressure on management to take action. An example was when Walt Disney shareholders expressed a vote of no confidence in the CEO; the board then asked him to resign. A SEC regulation now requires mutual funds to reveal how they vote on shareholder issues; this is causing an increase in voting, so the shareholder proposal is a more effective instrument for reform.

Shareholders place on the ballot and vote on two types of issues, the first being governance (e.g., executive pay, an independent chair, or annual election of board members). The second type encourages a firm to be more socially responsible on issues such as excessive executive compensation, diversity of board members, not advertising tobacco products to teenagers, global climate change, global reporting initiative, HIV/AIDS, and genetically modified organisms. Investors often ask management to provide a report on its progress on the issue. By placing these issues on the ballot, the investors focus top management's attention, inform the general public, and often negotiate an agreement with management that will achieve its ends.

Shareholder resolutions opposed by management often do not receive a majority vote. Nevertheless, even a small percentage of voters can represent thousands of individual and institutional share owners who question management policy. The potential embarrassment of these shareholders voting against management is often pressure enough for management to change policy. The **Investor Responsibility Research Center (IRRC)** helps investors reach a judgment of the merit of the various proposals. The IRRC analyzes the proposal, presents the position of both management and the group that introduced the proposal, and poses the critical questions that merit consideration. The IRRC does not recommend how to vote; that is the investor's decision. At the end of the proxy season, the IRRC publishes a summary of the season's voting. It lists the firms, the issues, and the percentage of shareholders supporting the proposal; it also often indicates which institutional investors supported or opposed individual proposals and why.

Most institutional investors now accept the shareholder resolution as an instrument for raising social policy issues. They recognize that owning stock carries a responsibility to express judgment on major policy questions. The shareholder resolution can also be an aid to management. It alerts management to questions that might be overlooked. It provides a warning that certain issues may become important in the future and deserve attention. Management thus receives important information that it would not otherwise have possessed.

Going a step further, some invest in funds that use a "social screen" to determine the firms in their portfolio; they invest only in firms that have a good

---

[72] John R. Blackwell, "Shareholder Activism on Rise: Here and Nationwide, More Proposals on Table at Firms' Annual Meetings," *McClatchy—Tribune Business News,* April 24, 2008; Tomeoh Murakami Tse, " 'Say-on-Pay' Movement Loses Steam," *The Washington Post,* May 6, 2008, p. D1.

social and/or environmental record. This movement has grown from investments of $40 billion in 1984 to $2 trillion today. Moreover, these socially responsible funds have performed as well and sometimes better than the S&P 500-stock index.[73] Now let us consider a means that a firm has to make explicit its own values and ethics: its code of ethics.

Code of Ethical Conduct

Among large U.S. firms, 80 percent have a **code of ethics** that outlines acceptable and unacceptable business practices. Most of these codes were introduced following the overseas bribery scandals of the 1970s and the introduction of the U.S. Sentencing Commission Guidelines in the 1990s. Two-thirds of managers think a code of ethics raises the ethical level of business practice.[74] These managers want a code of ethics to help them in their own ethical decisions. Cases of overseas bribery (Exxon, Lockheed, ITT, Northrop), of using privileged information for private gain (Wall Street firms, ImClone), and other transgressions have underscored the problem.

The CEO is often the initiator of a firm's ethical code. However, implementation of that code is often delegated to the legal department, which may encourage people to think of the code as rules to obey rather than principles to assimilate. A code is more effective in influencing attitudes and actions when the CEO is actively engaged, and also when those in the organization participate in its development and updating. Firms that have model ethical codes and systems for monitoring them are Johnson & Johnson (see Figure 8-3), Cray, Caterpillar, and Weyerhaeuser.[75] Caterpillar's code is distributed to all managers worldwide, and these managers must report annually to the home office "any events or activities that might cause an impartial observer to conclude that the code hasn't been fully followed." The code's provisions recognize the difference between what is legal and what is ethical.

For Japanese managers, company policy and codes of conduct have a profound effect on their decisions. In Europe the application of justice increases compliance with firm policy, especially for managers operating overseas.[76] Within the United States, however, some codes have had little effect in bringing about ethical conduct in the firm. Recent business debacles show that some firms that possess a code are less ethical than others without. Enron and WorldCom had codes of conduct that

---

[73] Pietra Rivoli, "Making a Difference or Making a Statement? Finance Research and Socially Responsible Investment," *Business Ethics Quarterly,* 13 (July 2003): 271–287; Curt Weeden, *Corporate Social Investing* (San Francisco: Berrett-Koehler, 1998).

[74] Gary R. Weaver, Linda Klebe Trevino, and Philip L. Cochran, "Corporate Ethics Programs as Control Systems: Influences of Executive Commitment and Environmental Factors," *Academy of Management Journal,* 42(February 1999): 41–57; also Raymond C. Baumhart, S.J., *Ethics in Business* (New York: Holt, Rinehart and Winston, 1968).

[75] For additional information on J&J and Cray, see Francis J. Aguilar, *Managing Corporate Ethics* (New York: Oxford University Press, 1994), pp. 61–71.

[76] Chiaki Nakano, "A Survey Study on Japanese Managers Views of Business Ethics," *Journal of Business Ethics,* 16, no. 16 (1997): 1737–1752; The European data are in W. Chan Kim and Renee Mauborgne, "Procedural Justice, Attitudes, and Subsidiary Top Management Compliance with Multinationals' Corporate Strategic Decisions," *Academy of Management Journal,* 36 (June 1993): 502–526.

Our Credo

We believe our first responsibility is to the doctors,nurses and patients,
to mothers and all others who use our products and services.
In meeting their needs everything we do must be of high quality.
We must constantly strive to reduce our costs
in order to maintain reasonable prices.
Customersí orders must be serviced promptly and accurately.
Our suppliers and distributors must have an opportunity
to make a fair profit.

We are responsible to our employees,
the men and women who work with us throughout the world.
Everyone must be considered as an individual.
We must respect their dignity and recognize their merit.
They must have a sense of security in their jobs.
Compensation must be fair and adequate,
and working conditions clean,orderly and safe.
Employees must feel free to make suggestions and complaints.
There must be equal opportunity for employment,development
and advancement for those qualified.
We must provide competent management,
and their actions must be just and ethical.

We are responsible to the communities in which we live and work
and to the world community as well.
We must be good citizens—support good works and charities
and bear our fair share of taxes.
We must encourage civic improvements and better health and education.
We must maintain in good order
the property we are privileged to use,
protecting the environment and natural resources.

Our final responsibility is to our stockholders.
Business must make a sound profit.
We must experiment with new ideas.
Research must be carried on.Innovative programs developed
and mistakes paid for.
New equipment must be purchased,new facilities provided
and new products launched.
Reserves must be created to provide for adverse times.
When we operate according to these principles,
the stockholders should realize a fair return.

Johnson & Johnson

FIGURE 8-3   Johnson & Johnson's Corporate Credo

were highly praised. This is partly explained by the fact that many corporate codes are designed for public relations or are written to protect firms from their own employees. These codes cover kickbacks from suppliers, customer relations, keeping honest financial records, and conflicts of interest. On the other hand, less than one-fourth of the codes cover product safety, product quality, environmental issues, matters of personal character, and civic and community affairs—issues of concern to customers and outside stakeholders.[77] If a firm has only a code and little more, one suspects that the code is established because of the Sentencing Commission Guidelines, and is a cheap means of compliance. However, if the code is part of a program that includes an ethics office, ethics training, and other initiatives, the ethics program is more likely to be effective.

Disclosure and Ethics

In order to communicate the vision of the firm, as well as to make clear the importance of ethics, that firm develops a clear, motivating mission statement and conveys that mission to members of the firm. The mission statement will be discussed further in Chapter 10. However, the development of a mission statement and code is just the beginning of management's job. In addition, managers must hire people who embody those values, and provide rewards to encourage desired actions—perhaps prizes and publicity. The message is reinforced when the CEO sets a good example, gives occasional ethical pep talks, and tells inspirational stories of real people within the firm.[78]

Firms that encourage ethical conduct and discourage misconduct are **transparent in their operations**. Unethical business behavior thrives in secrecy. Disclosure requires the communication of (1) the vision, mission, policies, and models of behavior to members of the firm; and (2) successes and yet-to-be-achieved goals to external stakeholders. We have already discussed internal communication. Let us now focus on external disclosure.[79]

The case for disclosure of social and ethical activities to stakeholders (customers, employees, suppliers, and the community, in addition to stockholders) is that information enables free markets to operate more efficiently. Without accurate information, there is poor allocation of resources and inefficiencies. As Thomas Clausen, former CEO of Bank of America and the World Bank put it, "a company's actions simply cannot be judged efficient, responsive, accountable, or consistent with the public interest, unless sufficient information about its activities is available."

---

[77] Max B. E. Clarkson, "A Stakeholder Framework for Analyzing and Evaluating Corporate Social Performance"; and Thomas Donaldson and Lee E. Preston, "The Stakeholder Theory of the Corporation: Concepts, Evidence, and Implications," *Academy of Management Review,* 20 (January 1995): 65–91, 92–117.

[78] Sandra A. Waddock, Charles Bodwell, and Samuel B. Graves, "Responsibility: The New Business Imperative," *Academy of Management Executive,* 16, no. 2 (2002): 132–147; Bill Fromm and Len Schlesinger, *The Real Heroes of Business* (New York: Currency, 1993); see also Francis J. Aguilar, *Managing Corporate Ethics,* pp. 72–86.

[79] On the importance and means of disclosure, Eliane Ciulla Kamarck and Joseph S. Nye, Jr., eds., *Governance.com: Democracy in the Information Age* (Washington: Brookings, 2002).

He adds that if government regulation becomes burdensome, it will be because business leaders were not sensitive to the needs of their stakeholders.[80] The enactment of SOX regulations, which was triggered by the ethical failures of business, supports Clausen's point.

Cynthia Cooper was head of internal auditing at WorldCom. She and the internal auditing team received word of $400 million taken from a reserve account to boost WorldCom's revenues. They examined accounts more closely and found that the firm had charged expenses as capital costs, which enabled the firm to shift a $660 million loss into a $2.4 billion profit. Cooper confronted WorldCom CFO Scott Sullivan with the data; he was furious with her and told her to back off. Instead she presented her findings to the audit committee of WorldCom's board, and they in turn fired the CFO. The news was out, and WorldCom's stock collapsed. Although she was named a *Time* magazine *Person of the Year—2002*, Cooper refuses to be called a hero. But she is an excellent example of an internal auditor with competence, integrity, and courage—exactly the qualities that one would choose in an internal auditor.[81]

A firm's internal auditor, its external auditor, and the audit committee of the board all have the responsibility to oversee financial reporting and to ensure honest disclosure; this information is communicated in the annual financial report. An internal auditor such as Cynthia Cooper must decide whether information that has been ignored or even hidden by management should be brought to the attention of outside auditors. The willingness of the internal auditor to report fraudulent behavior depends on many variables, especially the ethical climate of the firm. The success of an ethics program depends on the cooperation of the people involved. If the firm is perceived as fair when dealing with its workers, the program is more likely to achieve its goals of establishing an ethical climate. To establish an ethical climate education should come first; punishing a manager for violations of a code should be a last resort. Nevertheless, if it is perceived to be just, punishment can positively influence the behavior of both the person being punished and others in the organization.[82]

Oversight by the board of directors is an important means of implementing socially responsible policies and adequate disclosure. The board's job is easier when it sets up an ethics or social policy committee. Among the firms that have active ethics or social policy board committees are Toyota, PPG, GE, NEC, Levi Strauss, and General Motors. These committees oversee the implementation of the corporate ethics program. The resulting good reputation of a firm is another benefit of good ethics. Given current rapid communications, this is important for building trust with customers, suppliers, and other stakeholders. Planning begins with the firm's vision

[80] Thomas Clausen, "Voluntary Disclosure: An Idea Whose Time Has Come," in *Corporations and Their Critics,* eds. Thornton Bradshaw and David Vogel (New York: McGraw-Hill, 1981), pp. 61–70.

[81] Amanda Ripley, "The Night Detective," *Time,* January 6, 2002, pp. 45–50; Arthur Brief et al., "What's Wrong with the Treadway Commission Report? Experimental Analyses of the Effects of Personal Values and Codes of Conduct on Fraudulent Financial Reporting," *Journal of Business Ethics,* 15 (1996): 183–198. See also, "U.S. Congress Looks at Internal Auditors," *Internal Auditor,* October 1987, pp. 4–7.

[82] Gary R. Weaver, "Ethics and Employees: Making the Connection," *Academy of Management Executive,* 18, no. 2 (2004): 121–125; Linda Klebe Trevino, "The Social Effects of Punishment in Organizations: A Justice Perspective," *Academy of Management Review,* 17 (October 1992): 647–676. See also, Gail Ball, Linda Trevino, and Henry Sims, "Just and Unjust Punishment: Influences on Subordinate Performance and Citizenship," *Academy of Management Journal,* 37 (April 1994): 299–322.

and mission statement, and this mission is then translated into goals. The firm's stakeholders increasingly ask that these goals and the firm's performance on social, environmental, and financial issues be stated, measured, and reported.[83]

Ethics Training, Audits, and Reports

Cummins Engine, Citibank, Boeing, and General Dynamics sponsor ethics training for all managers. Top managers initially spend a day, and middle managers several hours, in ethics training, and there are periodic follow-up programs. About 67 percent of workers in large firms and 41 percent in small firms have some ethics training. Moreover, 77 percent of workers in large firms and 47 percent in smaller firms say that there is a mechanism in place to anonymously report misconduct. In addition, 51 percent of large firms have established an ethics hotline and/or an ombudsman who any employee can speak to anonymously on ethical issues.[84]

A **social report** enables a firm to state its social and environmental goals and to articulate the firm's impact on society. Firms that provided reports on social performance jumped from 7 in 1990 to 487 in a decade. Moreover, 40 percent of these reports now are externally audited.[85] Social reporting is also provided in annual financial reports and on firm Web sites.

A corporate social report discloses corporate activities that have a social impact (e.g., energy saving, environmental actions, diversity in the firm, support of the community, and education) and assesses the success of these activities. Diversity in the firm and environmental issues can be measured and reported. Specific targets can be set and results can be obtained, because it is possible to count the number of people in various jobs and the parts per million of pollutants. A report in these two areas is mandated by the government for many firms. Reporting other issues is often in the form of a description of activities.

Among the hundreds of global firms that now produce a detailed report on their social and environmental activities are H-P, Intel, General Motors, Honda, Philips, McDonald's, NEC, and United Parcel Service (UPS).[86] The reports are prepared internally and provide detail on what the firm is doing on social issues. For example, Ford Motor Company's *Connecting with Society* is published annually and is available in print form and on the Web. It discusses Ford's position on such issues as stakeholder relations, sustainability, global climate change, and corporate citizenship. These environmental and social reports provide information to shareholders and other stakeholders.

However, it is difficult to compare one firm with another, because there is not yet a standard format for reporting, such as the U.S. SEC requires for financial

---

[83] Sandra Waddock, *Leading Corporate Citizens: Vision, Values, Value Added,* 2nd ed. (Boston: McGraw-Hill, 2006); also Kevin T. Jackson, *Building Reputational Capital: Strategies for Integrity and Fair Play That Improve the bottom Line* (Oxford: Oxford University Press, 2004).

[84] *National Business Ethics Survey—2003* (Washington: Ethics Resource Center, 2003); and Gary R. Weaver, Linda Klebe Trevino, and Philip Cochran, "Corporate Ethics Practices in the Mid 1990s: An Empirical Study of the Fortune 1000," *Journal of Business Ethics,* 18, no. 3 (1999): 283–294.

[85] John Ruggie, "Managing Corporate Social Responsibility," *Financial Times,* October 25, 2002; and "The New Accountability: Tracking the Social Costs," *The New York Times,* March 24, 2002, p. 4BU.

[86] These and hundreds of other reports can be accessed at http://www.cswire.com.

reports. There is also no standard repository of reports, although Boston College's **Center for Corporate Citizenship** has a good collection of reports available at their Web site: www.bc.edu/corporatecitizenship. The **Global Reporting Initiative** (GRI) has set standards for reporting, especially in the areas of human rights and the environment; we will discuss GRI in the next chapter. U.K.-based **AccountAbility** (www.accountability.org.uk) annually rates the Fortune-100 companies for their impact on society and the environment. Their 2007 ranking found BP at the top. Among the top 20 were only two U.S. firms, Chevron and GE, while the other 18 firms were European. U.K.-based **SustainAbility** (www.sustainability.com) has also organized conferences and done consulting on social issues for almost 20 years.

A few firms have asked outside auditors to prepare their social performance report. KPMG's Integrity Management Services helped Royal Dutch Shell and Body Shop with their social reports. They also help Home Depot with their sustainable wood sourcing.[87] Toy maker Mattel charged Dr. Prakash Sethi to visit and examine its overseas suppliers, focusing especially on working conditions and child labor, and he independently wrote his report. Ben and Jerry's Homemade Ice Cream published an outside audit of their firm for several years. The Body Shop, a British-based cosmetics firm, chided by criticism of their environmental claims, published an outside audit of their social activities. Because of the U.S. sentencing guidelines and other pressures, some expect such external audits to become more common.[88] When a firm acknowledges its failures and publishes assessments that are critical of its own activities, its reports gain more credibility than when they report only positive accomplishments. The **Dow Jones Sustainability Index (DJSJ)** is produced for investors. It includes more than 300 companies, and is based on each firm's economic, social, and environmental performance. According to DJSJ (www.sustainability-index.com), Japanese firms are in the lead on environmental performance, European firms are best on labor indicators, human capital development, and social and environmental reporting, and U.S. firms lead in codes of conduct and compliance.

Many firms have a corporate **ethics officer** assigned to oversee the firm's ethics initiatives. The ethics officer is asked by the CEO to communicate the firm's code of conduct, and oversee the firm's legal, ethical, and social responsibility issues. Therefore, this person must have intimate knowledge of the firm, and must have good people skills.[89]

In order to provide education and support for corporate ethics officers, the **Ethics and Compliance Officers Association** began in 1992 and now has more than 800 members. Sponsoring members include American Express, BASF, Dow Chemical, EDS, GE, Hershey Foods, Honeywell, Merck, Northrup Grumman,

---

[87] Mary Miller, "In Search of Business Ethics Among the Big Five Accounting Firms," *Business Ethics,* March/April 2002, p. 6.

[88] S. Prakash Sethi, *Setting Global Standards: Guidelines for Creating Codes of Conduct in Multinational Corporations* (Hoboken, NJ: John Wiley, 2003); Meinholf Dierkes, "Corporate Social Reporting and Performance in Germany," in *Research in Corporate Social Performance and Policy,* ed. Lee E. Preston, vol. 2 (Greenwich, CT: JAI Press, 1981). A classic is *The Measurement of Corporate Social Performance* (New York: American Institute of Certified Public Accountants, 1977).

[89] For an excellent overview, see Francis J. Daley, "An Ethics Officer's Perspective," in *The Accountable Corporation,* eds. Marc J. Epstein and Kirk O. Hanson, vol. 2 (Westport, CT: Praeger, 2006), pp. 179–191.

Novartis, Prudential, Sears, Royal Dutch Shell, Siemens, Sony, Texas Instruments, UPS, and Westinghouse. The organization sponsors annual meetings to provide information to the ethics officers, and also publishes a regular newsletter on current issues (see http://www.theeoca.org). But outside stakeholders, especially shareholders, can also have an influence on the values and ethical performance of those in the firm.

Integrity, Humility, and Sacrifice

Indicators provide conflicting signals on the moral health of American society. On the healthy side, we value family, honesty, and integrity. Church attendance is higher in the United States than in other industrialized countries. We have witnessed lying, fraud, and conflict of interest among a few executives, but such actions are the exception and cause scandal and outrage. Yet our society suffers from a high incidence of bribery, alcoholism, drug addiction, street crime, and murders, and there is greater evidence of selfish attitudes among many.

People often become fearful and focus on protecting themselves, when they face such large problems. Special interest lobbying groups in politics have fractured society into competing camps. Witness, for example, the success of gun owners, used car dealers, tobacco farmers, trial lawyers, and petroleum and nuclear power firms in protecting their interests—even when their goals are contrary to the good of the community. Often it is difficult to discuss political issues, because people already have a position and are not open to new evidence and balanced, intelligent discussion. Sometimes political leaders nourish such attitudes by engaging in slogans and negative comments about opponents and this encourages cynicism. Thus among world democracies, the United States has one of the lowest rates of voting. Ronald Reagan, Bill Clinton, and George W. Bush were elected by less than one-third of voters. About half of Americans didn't even bother to vote.

Most of the challenges facing us (e.g., providing sustainable long-term economic growth, confronting terrorism, ending the war, balancing the budget, rebuilding crumbling cities, providing good education and medical care for all, limiting our voracious use of energy, and decreasing the hostility between nations) will require visionary leaders who listen and engage in careful planning; but it will also require an open mind, humility, and sacrifice on the part of all. History tells us that little can be accomplished without sacrifice, but we now hear little discussion of costs. If a politician suggests a need for an increase in taxes, they will most likely not be elected. In order to create a better society we must use our strengths as a people, but few are willing to acknowledge and counterbalance our weaknesses. We will discuss how globalization affects individuals and firms in Chapter 9.

Summary and Conclusions

The goals, values, and ethics of a person and a firm are communicated by actions. Most executives have as a goal the long-term good of the firm and society. Humane, cooperative, and ethical values create a more participative, attractive, and effective culture.

In such a culture, employees are more likely to use their abilities to achieve the goals of the firm. Some executives, however, seek their own personal gain, which harms other people, the firm, and society. Individualism and the Protestant ethic have carried Americans far and fast. But now delayed gratification has given way to the consumer ethic of "buy now, pay later," and individualism encourages "get rich quick" schemes.

American flexibility and openness to change offer some hope. Social concerns are now a part of corporate strategic planning. Pension and mutual funds, endowments, and foundations now exercise more influence, and sometimes bring useful pressure on management through voting on issues at shareholder meetings.

Boards of directors take their responsibilities more seriously, in part because of new legislation, and not all boards of directors are ideal in how they function. Most firms have a code of ethics. Moreover, many firms consider social performance when evaluating managers, and firms provide information to stakeholders about their social and ethical activities.

Executives recognize that stakeholders want more than return on investment from a firm. Quality products, planning for the long term, and working with local communities are some of the expectations citizens have of firms. When firms do not respond to these needs, government is forced to legislate or regulate. Managers maintain flexibility when they voluntarily act to ensure their obligations are met.

Discussion Questions

1. Who benefitted from Jack Welch's tactics of selling or closing a business, even when it was profitable? Were these tactics good for the United States? How do you judge Welch's intimidating management style? What does his personal life style and compensation tell us about his own values and ethics? Use the ethical norms developed in Chapter 3.
2. Is Bill George more correct than Welch when he says that Medtronic is not in the business of maximizing shareholder value?
3. Do you think that American values have shifted as indicated in Table 8-1? How does this affect the values of managers?
4. Is the compensation of corporate executives like Dennis Kozlowski, Michael Eisner, and Sandy Weil reasonable? How about the compensation of hedge fund managers like John Paulson, James Simons, and George Soros? Are CEO salaries a problem in the United States today? Do you agree with Warren Buffet's assessment of CEO compensation? Is such compensation just?
5. Why is U.S. CEO compensation so disproportionate compared to CEOs in other countries?
6. How effective is the pay for performance theory of executive compensation? How can the theory be improved in practice? Is there a more effective way of compensating executives?
7. Should firms award golden parachutes to their senior managers? Why or why not? If yes, are there any conditions where it is inappropriate to award a golden parachute?
8. Do private equity firms ultimately benefit or harm society? Why?
9. Do you agree or disagree with the reasons given why CEOs should receive such large compensation packages? Why or why not?
10. Is there a lack of incentive for managers to plan for the long term? Explain.
11. Given higher labor costs and the integrity of James Sinegal and Costco, do you think they will be able to compete with Sam's Club in the marketplace?

12. How would you characterize the values, ethics, and management style of Ray Andersen of Interface Carpet?
13. Do people consider a firm's ethical reputation when they purchase a product? Do you?
14. How would you characterize the values, ethics, and management style of Conrad Black (Hollinger) and Fausto Tonna (Parmalat)? Examining their overall records, are these executives winners or a losers?
15. Is a corporation a servant of society? Does a corporation receive more benefits than it has responsibilities in society? Does civil society have the ability to withdraw a corporate charter for serious misdeeds? Is such a policy practical?
16. What is the difference between an independent director and an outside director? What is a lead director? What problems arise when a board is made up mostly of insiders? What conflicts of interest arise when the CEO is also chair of the board?
17. Why should board members be skeptical when proposals are brought to board meetings for their approval? Why should independent board members meet periodically without any of the firm's managers present?
18. How much operational and managerial advice should a board of directors give to its CEO? Should its role be primarily limited to setting strategy and evaluating senior management's effectiveness?
19. What obligations do board members have to keep board discussions confidential? Under what conditions, if any, is it acceptable for a board member to speak to the press?
20. What are the limits on how far an organization can go in investigating its employees and its board members?
21. What insights can be gained about board governance from the Hewlett-Packard story?
22. What is the evidence concerning long-term financial performance and an organization's ethical orientation? Do you think the Sarbanes–Oxley Act and the Federal Sentencing Guidelines for Organizations will improve the overall ethical climate of business?
23. Are the vision, mission, goals, values, and ethics of a firm integral to corporate planning? Describe how to make ethics an effective part of planning.
24. Describe what influence institutional investors have on firms in which they hold stock. What are the advantages and disadvantages of this involvement from the standpoint of the firm? From the standpoint of society?
25. Why do firms have a code of ethical conduct? What is the difference between a code that is for public relations and one that is effective?
26. What is the argument for disclosure of financial information? What is the argument for social issue disclosure? Describe the ways in which social issue disclosure is made. What outside groups provide help in assessing social and environmental reports?

Selected Additional Readings

Ray Anderson, *Mid-Course Correction: Toward a Sustainable Enterprise—The Interface Model* (Atlanta: Peregrinzilla Press, 1998).

Bill George and Peter Sims, *True North: Discover Your Authentic Leadership* (San Francisco: Wiley, 2007).

Alex Berenson, *The Number: How the Drive for Quarterly Earnings Corrupted Wall Street and Corporate America* (New York: Random House, 2003).

Alan Murray, *Revolt in the Boardroom: The New Rules of Power in Corporate America* (New York: Collins, 2007).

James E. Post, Lee E. Preston, and Sybille Sachs, *Redefining the Corporation: Stakeholder Management and Organizational Wealth* (Stanford: Stanford University Press, 2002). Bob Sullivan, *Gotcha Capitalism: How Hidden Fees Rip You Off Every Day—and What You Can Do About It* (New York: Ballantine Books, 2007).

CASES

Case 8-1   Ebola Virus and Entertainment

The film *Outbreak* is based on a real-case outbreak of the Ebola virus in Zaire, Africa. The U.S. Center for Disease Control (CDC) sent a team to a "hospital deserted save for a few patients dying the ugly, bloody death of Ebola . . . no running water, no telephones . . ."[90] and contained the disease.

Dustin Hoffman played the movie lead role. C.J. Peters, MD, is Chief of Special Pathogens, Center for Disease Control. Peters is fighting budget cuts for his unit. Note the comparative data.

CDC's Pathogens Branch		Warner Brothers' *Outbreak*	
Salary: Dr. C.J. Peters:	$ 125,000	Dustin Hoffman:	$ 6,000,000
CDC FY 1995 Budget:	$7,200,000	Production:	$54,000,000
Spending on Ebola:	$1,800,000	Gross in 3 months:	$67,000,000

1. What do these comparative expenditures tell us about American values and priorities?
2. Is there an inequity in these figures? Why or why not?
3. What ethical norms help you to deal with the case?

■ ■ ■

Case 8-2   Stock Purchase Deal

Kenneth McGinty is an investment banker working with Maco Corporation on acquisitions. He learns that Maco is about to purchase Digital Optics. Digital is a small publicly held firm that has had an unprofitable year and its stock is undervalued. The price of the stock is certain to rise when the buyout is announced. Set aside legality and look only at the ethical issues.

---

[90] "The Point Man in Germ Warfare," *BusinessWeek,* August 21, 1995, pp. 72–73.

1. Can Ken purchase some stock for himself?
2. May he tell a good friend?
3. What ethical norms are most helpful here? Explain.

■ ■ ■

Case 8-3   Company Controller

Carol Goudreau, company controller, is asked by the CFO to "manage earnings" in such a way as to present more favorable financial results for this quarter. The CFO does Carol's performance appraisal.

1. What should Carol do?
2. Why? What ethical norms would help her decide?

■ ■ ■

Case 8-4   Home Depot and Certified Wood

An independent, not for profit, international organization called the Forest Stewardship Council has been established with input from loggers and environmental groups. It has developed a list of environmentally sound logging practices. The practices include "harvesting lumber at a rate sustainable indefinitely, maintaining old-growth forests and maintaining biodiversity." Timber firms may then request certification and they are inspected to see that they adhere to the practices. Home Depot, the largest buyer and retailer of forest products in the United States, decided that it would eliminate sales of wood products from environmentally sensitive areas, and it would give preference to certified wood.

1. What reasons could you give for this new policy of Home Depot?
2. Will this new policy provide better service to customers? To shareholders?
3. What ethical norms are most helpful here?

9

■ ■ ■

Globalization's Impact on American Values

The central issue of contention is not globalization itself, nor is it the use of the market as an institution, but the inequity in the overall balance of institutional arrangements—which produces very unequal sharing of the benefits of globalization.

AMARTYA SEN (1933–), HARVARD ECONOMIST, NOBEL PRIZE WINNER

Global financial markets are beyond the control of national or international authorities . . . Market fundamentalism has rendered the global capitalist system unsound and unstable.

GEORGE SOROS (1930–), FINANCIAL SPECULATOR, POLITICAL ACTIVIST

Just between you and me, shouldn't the World Bank be encouraging more migration of the dirty industries to the less developed countries? . . . I think the economic logic behind dumping a load of toxic waste in the lowest wage countries is impeccable and we should face up to that . . . I've always thought that under-populated countries in Africa are vastly under-polluted.

LAWRENCE SUMMERS (1954–), CHIEF ECONOMIST, WORLD BANK[1] (1991–1993); PRESIDENT OF HARVARD UNIVERSITY (2001–2006)

---

[1] From a leaked internal memo that was reprinted in *The Economist*, February 8, 1992, p. 66. Summers later apologized for the statement. He was later U.S. Treasury Secretary and then president of Harvard University.

Only large firms operated globally a generation ago. Today every business must be aware of its opportunities to sell overseas, and also defend itself from global competition. **Globalization** thus has a huge influence on American business and American business values. By globalization we mean the integration of communications, markets, and technologies such that individuals, corporations, and nations are able to operate internationally more easily, coupled with a consciousness of world **interdependence**. Let us examine some varying examples of this global marketplace.

China has been growing at a 9.5 percent annual rate for three decades, and has accumulated a world record of $1.2 trillion in foreign reserves. Yet millions of tires, children's toys, cough syrup, shrimp, and toothpaste produced in China and imported into the United States contained poisons, were dangerous, and were recalled. In addition, China has ordered burdensome new safety inspections on U.S.-made medical supplies and not those made in China. U.S. and European officials call this protectionist and unfair.[2]

An eBay technology, ProStores, helps impoverished women in Uganda make jewelry and sell it in developed countries through a Web site, BeadforLife.org. These women have been able to raise their income from less than an average of $1 a day to more than $3 a day. The founders of eBay wanted to enable small producers to be able to transact business easily, and to not allow giant firms to dominate global commerce.[3]

Retailers in Thailand and China sell thousands of pirated DVD movies and music from sophisticated catalogues. Prices are low, and they ship the item the next day. The shop in Bangkok has a catalogue of classic videos from around the world not available in regular stores. Despite some arrests by the local authorities, the business is expanding rapidly. The film industry estimates losses from piracy in 15 Asian countries at $719 million annually.[4]

The global economy promises **low-cost goods**. So there is pressure for lower prices and thus lower wages. There are now stronger links between rich and poor nations and dramatically increased investment in China and India by global corporations. Owners, investors, and speculators have reaped billions of dollars. The two major players on the world stage are global corporations and nations. If we arrange the 100 largest "economies" of the world in rank order, among the nations and corporations we find that 53 are global businesses. For example, ExxonMobil has annual revenues that are greater than the gross domestic product of all but 20 of the world's 220 nations.[5] Because of their economic and political power, global corporations have vast influence on nations. The French, Arabs in the Middle East, and many others complain of Americanization and flattening of local cultural values across the world because of globalization.[6]

---

[2] Steven Weisman, "China Stand on Imports Upsets the U.S.," *The New York Times*, November 16, 2007, pp. C1, 6; and Pete Engardio et al., "Broken China," *BusinessWeek*, July 23, 2007, p. 48.

[3] Catherine Holahan, "Ebay: Going, Going . . . Everywhere," *BusinessWeek*, June 18, 2007, pp. 62–64.

[4] Stan Sesser, "Smooth Operators," *The Wall Street Journal Online*, August 27, 2004.

[5] Archie B. Carroll, "Managing Ethically with Global Stakeholders: A Present and Future Challenge," *Academy of Management Executive*, 18, no. 2, (2004): 114.

[6] Benjamin R. Barber, *Jihad vs. McWorld* (New York: Ballantime Books, 1996); Jeffrey Sachs, "International Economics: Unlocking the Mysteries of Globalization"; and Peter L. Berger, "Four Faces of Global Culture," in *Globalization and the Challenges of a New Century*, eds. Patrick O'Meara et al. (Bloomington: Indian University Press, 2000), pp. 216–217.

The economic health, moral status, and future of the United States are inextricably **intertwined** with the other nations of the world. People in wealthy nations are able to purchase low-priced goods, because of the lower costs of manufacturing in poor countries. Moreover, markets for most goods and services are now global. The Internet has made communication and trade around the world much easier; a housebound sewer of shirts in India can sell her work directly to a purchaser in Chicago. Steel mill pollutants in China and cutting trees in Brazil's Amazon rain forest can shorten lives in Europe and the United States. Let us now examine the extent to which American firms depend on other peoples.

MULTINATIONAL FIRMS AS CORPORATE CITIZENS

Global corporations such as Cisco (the United States), Toyota (Japan), and Royal Dutch Shell (the Netherlands) not only sell their products but also have operations in most of the countries in the world. These firms are like thousands of businesses that affect our lives every day. They are members of the global economy. The North American Free Trade Agreement (NAFTA) tied Canada, Mexico, and the United States together economically. The European Union (EU) goes even further in joining European countries. We are a world without economic borders where capital, products, services, and managers move easily from one country to another. The notion of a major product produced entirely by people of any one country is almost obsolete.

The global corporation provides many **benefits to billions** of people around the world: jobs, goods, and income. Global firms hire local people to manage, and provide them with training and sometimes education. Global firms want stability; terrorism, wars, and revolutions disrupt business as well as bring death and injury to people. The global firm bridges nations, cultures, and peoples. When individual nations and the United Nations are burdened by bureaucracy and nationalism, the global corporation crosses boundaries and deals with people where they live. The global firm requires person-to-person contact and demands that one understand and work with people of other cultures. What we refer to as the global corporation is sometimes also called the **multinational corporation (MNC)** or the **transnational corporation (TNC)**.

If a firm tries to export its own national values and business practices to its overseas operations, it will not be successful; managers must respect local needs and values. Building trust and shared values among people of different cultures is difficult and takes time. Building those shared values in a firm is aided when one understands one's own values and is aware of the processes that reinforce or undermine values, as we have seen in earlier chapters.

Worldwide E-Commerce

Doing business globally demands that one utilize **e-mail** and the **Internet**.[7] The Internet enables businesspeople to communicate globally: selling goods and tracking the global supply chain. It even provides the poor women in Uganda described at the beginning of

---

[7] John Cullen, Praveen Parboteeah, and Martin Hoegl, "Cross-National Differences in Manager's Willingness to Justify Ethically Suspect Behaviors: A Test of Institutional Anomie Theory," *Academy of Management Review,* 47 (June 2004): 411–421.

the chapter the ability to sell their products to first-world purchasers. The Internet offers a powerful ease of communication between peoples and nations. The number of people using Internet went from 1 million in 1988 to more than 1.2 billion in 2007. Internet communication is cheap, accurate, and direct, and can span continents in moments. It is used by firms for billing, ordering from suppliers, planning, and advertising.

At present there is little law that applies to the Internet. Internet purists maintain that there should be no regulation at all. It is true that whatever law there is would probably be easy to circumvent. It is simple to replicate copyrighted work, as we see with pirated DVD movies and music. A person who would never break a car window to steal a radio thinks little of using a key code to copy $300 worth of software, music, or films. And it is hard to detect the theft. Scam artists can obtain credit card numbers from unsuspecting customers, and operate offshore to avoid the law. And pornographic material can be brought into the home by a five-year-old. The Internet is a powerful tool, and we have not yet agreed upon the legal boundaries for its use. Indeed it will be difficult, given the variety of nations involved and the fragility of global codes, to set boundaries. Global business activity has also fostered grave world problems: sweatshops, abusing the earth, safety of imported goods, and speculation.

Sweatshops in Poor Countries

Consumers demand low-cost goods. Consequently, U.S.-based firms such as Wal-Mart, Nike, or GE view themselves less as American firms and more as competitors in a global market, and therefore necessarily free of any one nation's political or social ideology. In this view, people and nations simply provide resources to meet a firm's needs. This strategy results in **outsourcing** manufacturing and service jobs because it is cheaper. Contracting firms will obtain the order if they have lower costs, and these firms then feel compelled to use sweatshops to cut costs. U.S. firms compete with low-priced goods from Asia, and are thus forced to send their labor-intensive operations to low-wage countries. China, for example, has more than a half billion workers who work for very low wages.[8]

People in poor countries welcome any work that provides income. Child labor, long hours, and poor working conditions are secondary concerns. As a result, the International Labor Organization (ILO) estimates that in developing nations 250 million children between the ages of 5 and 14 are working—almost half working full-time. Close to a billion children between the ages of 14 and 18 are fully employed in poorer countries, and "there are upward of 125 million young people who have never had the opportunity to attend school at all."[9] At the other end of their work life, " . . . most manufacturing operations . . . do not keep them beyond the ages of 20 or 21, only to replace them with another wave of 16- to 19-year old workers. The older workers with few skills are then thrown out to join the armies of

---

[8] "The China Price," and "Shaking Up Trade Theory: For Decades Economists Have Insisted that the U.S. Wins From Globalization. Now They're Not So Sure," *BusinessWeek,* December 6, 2004, pp. 100–120.
[9] Frank Vogl, "Forward," in *Rising Above Sweatshops: Innovative Approaches to Global Labor Challenges,* eds. Laura Hartman, Denis Arnold, and Richard Wokutch (Westport, CT: Praeger, 2003), p. xix.

the destitute and unemployed." Some workers who are exploited in China are now protesting official corruption, workplace and social inequities, and the inability to air grievances.[10]

These people labor in manufacturing facilities and often work 10–12 hours a day, 7 days a week, with few toilet and no rest breaks. Moreover, many of these manufacturers demand that people work at machines that can cause physical injury, and they breathe glue that is carcinogenic. A 22-year-old woman from Bangladesh reported that she worked 19-hour shifts for eight cents an hour making caps and garments for U.S. universities and retailers. She said, "We need to keep jobs in Bangladesh, but we also need to improve conditions." Workers can become indentured servants, who fall into debt and have no alternative but to continue working. "For the privilege of working 12 hour shifts seven days a week making plastic bags for Motorola cellphones, Mary, 30, will be in debt for years to come." The promised salary of $460 a month was five times what she could earn in her native Philippines, so she paid $2,400 to a **labor broker** to get her to Taiwan, where the factory was located. Mary did not have the cash as is commonly the case, so she was forced to borrow the money at 10 percent per month to pay that broker. Once she arrived in Taiwan, a second labor broker met her at the airport and demanded an additional $3,900 to deliver her to her new job. In addition, Mary must now pay living and other expenses plus taxes in Taiwan, so it will take her a decade or more to pay off her debts. This practice is legal; the firms in Taiwan need the labor and so encourage the brokers. Mary is at a disadvantage, because firing workers who attempt to organize a union is common in developing countries. The only workers' union in China is a state monopoly, which guarantees worker discipline and output. Protecting the interests of workers is only a secondary function of unions in China.[11]

Students at universities throughout the United States have protested sweatshop conditions, and have pressed their university administrations to make sure that their university garments are manufactured under humane conditions. A labor union was formed at a supplier plant in the Dominican Republic with the help of their pressure. The students and other consumers have had some success in pressing national brands to supply information on the status of working conditions in their supplier plants, and in pressing for better wages and working conditions. Some brands, such as Mattel, Nike, Adidas, Reebok, Phillips-Van Heusen, Levi Strauss, and Liz Claiborne, now publish on their Web sites a report on conditions at their **supplier factories**. Gap goes still further in its candor; its report tells of conditions at 3,000

---

[10] S. Prakash Sethi, *Setting Global Standards: Guidelines for Creating Codes of Conduct in Multinational Corporations* (Hoboken, NJ: John Wiley, 2003), p. 10; for numerous documented cases of abuse and even murder of those protesting substandard conditions, see Vincent A. Gallagher, *The True Cost of Low Prices: The Violence of Globalization* (Maryknoll, NY: Orbis, 2006); Kathy Chen, "China Faces Rash of Protests: Officials' Abuses of Power and Social Inequities Provoke Unrest," *The Wall Street Journal*, November 5, 2004, p. A10.

[11] Jill Murray, "The Global Context: Multinational Enterprises, Labor standards and Regulation," in *Rising Above Sweatshops*, eds. Hartman et al., p. 29; Nicholas Stein, "No Way Out: Competition to Make Products for Western Companies Has Revived an Old Form of Abuse: Debt Bondage," *Fortune*, January 2003, pp. 102–108.

supplier factories around the world. Among the items revealed was that in Mexico 23 percent of the factories paid less than the minimum wage. In Africa over 50 percent of factories did not have adequate safety devices for workers. A majority of the Chinese factories inadequately disposed of toxic materials. The report was a risk for Gap, but it has won praise from analysts and an award for its social report.[12]

However, many other retailers, such as Wal-Mart and Disney, either have not done an audit of their suppliers or refuse to release the results of that audit. Moreover, Chinese factories "continue widespread labor violations, including the hiring of underage workers, mandatory overtime, unsafe working conditions and managers engaged in verbal abuse and sexual harassment."[13] A study of global firms operating in developing countries focused on how to achieve business efficiencies and national growth, as well as decent wages and conditions for workers. The authors concluded that, while government regulations are important, the ultimate responsibility rests with executives of the multinational firms themselves—as they put it "responsibility cannot be outsourced." Retail and brand executives must set standards for suppliers, and then audit those suppliers to ensure that the standards are observed. Nevertheless, it is increasingly important for the global firm to empower and encourage local talent. In spite of all this, some Chinese sweatshops continue to abuse their workers, but have become more sophisticated in concealing their abuses. Chinese suppliers for U.S. firms hire local consultants to help them hide their violations of labor rules during "inspections"; they keep two sets of books to fool auditors, and give scripts to employees on what to say if they are questioned. For a substantial fee, the consultant then guarantees that the supplier will pass the inspection.[14]

The market system seeks the lowest cost. This puts downward pressure on wages, as we have seen throughout the history of capitalism. In Chapter 5 we saw that child labor and inhuman working conditions were common in the United States only a few generations ago. In Chapter 6 Karl Marx demonstrated how the dynamics of the free market system naturally bring about such conditions, unless there is outside pressure or countervailing power.

The Earth as an Exploited Resource

The earth's environment affects everyone. Unlike sweatshops that injure destitute workers in poor countries, environmental degradation affects the lives of rich and poor alike. Therefore, France and the United Kingdom have mandated that business firms report on their use of resources and the amount of pollution they generate. A major current problem is **global climate change**.

---

[12] Amy Merrick, "Gap Offers Unusual Look at Factory Conditions: Fighting Sweatshop Tag, Retailer Details Problems Among Thousands of Plants," *The Wall Street Journal*, May 12, 2004.

[13] David Barboza, "U.S. Group Accuses Chinese Toy Factories of Labor Abuses," *The New York Times*, August 22, 2007, p. C5; David Gonzalez, "Latin Sweatshops Pressed by U.S. Campus Power: Dominican Plant Sings Labor Pact," *The New York Times*, April 4, 2003, p. 5.

[14] Dexter Roberts and Pete Engardio, "Secrets, Lies and Sweatshops: Factories Have Gotten Better at Concealing Abuses," *BusinessWeek*, November 27, 2006, pp. 50–58; see also Engardio, ed., *Chindia: How China and India Are Revolutionizing Global Business* (New York: McGraw-Hill, 2007).

Data show that the earth's average temperature is steadily rising, and scientists agree that the burning of fossil fuels is the major factor behind this warming.[15] It is caused by a "**greenhouse effect**," most of which is formed by carbon dioxide pollution that is emitted from the burning of fossil fuels—coal, oil, and natural gas. Scientists point out that Greenland's glaciers lost more than 53 cubic miles of ice in 2005 alone. They warn that warming is already producing flooding, droughts, crop failures, animal extinctions, and more violent storms, and that these trends will continue and become more pronounced. Moreover, global climate change is proceeding more rapidly than predicted and may bring sudden and catastrophic change.[16]

Delegates from 160 nations met in Kyoto, Japan, in 1997 to write a pact in an effort to reduce the causes of global warming. Europe, Japan, and the United States pledged to reduce carbon dioxide emissions by 6–8 percent. The United States, with less than 5 percent of the world's population, produces almost 25 percent of the greenhouse gases. Even though George W. Bush promised to reduce carbon dioxide emissions when running for office, he withdrew the United States from the **Kyoto Treaty**. He said that the cost of compliance was too high for the United States, and that China, India, and other developing nations were not included in the Treaty. Yet even without the United States, 178 nations hammered out an agreement to implement the Kyoto Treaty in 2001. The developed nations pledged to reduce carbon emissions and pay penalties if goals are not met, establish a system to trade credits for emissions reductions and for investing in energy efficient projects oversees, and set up a fund to help developing nations adapt.

Many American business firms are reducing carbon dioxide emissions on their own; it fits with the firm's goals and values. DuPont has cut its greenhouse gas emissions 65 percent since 1990; Alcoa, Entergy, Pfizer, FPL Group, and International Paper are also among those voluntarily reducing their carbon dioxide emissions. Further, General Motors and Ford are developing renewable energy sources. Even American Electric Power, a principal user of coal, is accumulating worldwide credits for reducing carbon dioxide. Global climate change threatens food sources, livelihoods, and future generations. A firm in California, Hyperion Solutions, offers workers $5,000 each toward the purchase of a "green" car that gets 45 miles per gallon or better. GE is promoting its "Ecomagination," which brings together solar, wind turbines and other green technologies; it has invested in new green enterprises and research.[17] These businesses are doing better long-term planning—for the public good—than is government. There are business opportunities in alternate energy sources, but developing these new sources is expensive. The CEOs of Alcoa, British Petroleum (BP) America, DuPont, Caterpillar, and GE have formed the U.S. Climate Action Partnership, which is lobbying that the United States reduce its greenhouse

---

[15] Intergovernmental Panel on Climate Change, Climate Change—2007, November 2007, Working Group I–III, www.ipcc.ch/.

[16] Jeffrey D. Sachs, "Moving Beyond Kyoto," *Scientific American*, February 2007, p. 30; "Climate Change Impacts Rise," in *Vital Signs, 2006–2007*, eds. Linda Starke et al. (New York: W. W. Norton, 2006), pp. 110–112.

[17] See Ans Kolk and Jonathan Pinkse, "Multinationals' Political Activities on Climate Change," *Business and Society*, 46, no. 2 (June 2007): 201–225; also "Special Report on Business and Climate Change," *The Economist*, June 2, 2007, p. 14; "Drive Green and Get Some Green," *BusinessWeek*, December 13, 2004, p. 14.

gases by 60 percent by the year 2050. Looking to the **common good** of all people is commendable for business; but it is the responsibility of government. However, not all firms are this responsible. ExxonMobil and coal-mining firms spent millions to raise doubts about climate change and have resisted limits on carbon dioxide emissions.[18]

Do you agree with economist Lawrence Summer's comments at the beginning of this chapter that poor countries are a good place to dump **toxic waste**? Because it is illegal, most of the cases go unreported. However, India, Cambodia, Kazakhstan, Slovakia, Estonia, China, Philippines, and Brazil have all been recipients of recorded cases of the illegal shipment of toxic waste. A treaty to control sending toxic waste across national boundaries was signed in 1995; nevertheless, illegal transfer of waste is easy to accomplish, hard to detect, and so continues. The United States, which is the largest producer and a major exporter of toxic waste, has not ratified the treaty. Moreover, every time new rules are agreed to or strengthened, new ways to transfer hazardous waste are devised.[19]

In another case, illustrating the influence of global firms, California firm Unocal built a natural gas pipeline in the military dictatorship nation of Myanmar (Burma). Unocal is accused of cooperating with the Myanmar military to force men from villages to work at no pay to clear jungle and build roads for the pipeline. Villagers said that those who refused to work, or were too weak to continue, were executed by the military. In a similar case ChevronTexaco is being sued on behalf of 30,000 indigenous people in Ecuador for dumping "over four million gallons a day of toxic wastewater, contaminated with oil, heavy metals and carcinogens into open pits, estuaries and rivers" between 1971 and 1992.[20] These cases make clear that government regulation is essential because all firms do not act ethically.

Global Speculation: The Casino Economy

Hedge funds and **private equity** firms hold immense stakes in U.S. business. Their investment in companies is to generate revenue for themselves, and rarely are they interested in actually running a business. Their activity is **speculation** rather than investment. Moreover, United States and overseas markets disproportionately benefit the already wealthy. An entrepreneur and a champion of free markets, Edward Luttwak specifies some dilemmas of the current market:

> They call it the free market, but that is shorthand for much more than freedom to buy and sell. What they celebrate, preach, and demand is private enterprise liberated from government regulation, unchecked by effective trade unions, unfettered by sentimental concerns over the life

---

[18] John Carey, "Climate Wars: With the Skeptics Almost Silenced, Businesses are Fighting over How to Cut Emissions," *BusinessWeek*, April 23, 2007, pp. 90–92.

[19] Jennifer Clapp, *Toxic Exports: The Transfer of Hazardous Wastes from Rich to Poor Countries* (Ithaca: Cornell University Press, 2001), pp. 150–172.

[20] Marianne Lavelle, "The Court of Foreign Affairs: U.S. Corporations Face a Slew of Lawsuits Alleging Human-Rights Abuses," *U.S. News and World Report*, June 23, 2003, p. 31; Abby Ellin, "Suit Says ChevronTexaco Dumped Poisons in Ecuador," *The New York Times*, May 8, 2003, p. C8.

of employees or communities, unrestrained by customs barriers or investment restrictions, and molested as little as possible by taxation. What they insistently demand is the privatization of state-owned businesses of all kinds and the conversion of public institutions from universities and botanic gardens to prisons, from libraries to schools to old-age homes into private enterprises run for profit. What they promise is a more dynamic economy that will generate new wealth—while saying nothing about the distribution of any wealth, old or new . . . they call this the free market, but I call it turbo-capitalism.[21]

An **initial public offering (IPO)** is an investment. Warren Buffett does a careful assessment of any firm into which he places his money; it is as if he were going to purchase the firm. His investment is for the long term. Contrast this with the fund portfolio manager who watches hourly reports on the stock markets. Moreover, if analysts predict that a firm's earnings will increase by 7 percent this quarter, and if they increase by only 6.8 percent, that firm's stock will tumble. That is speculation, not investment for the long term; some call it a "casino economy." George Soros, who made billions speculating, says that such a practice does not bring stability to domestic and world markets, but rather inefficiencies and chaos. To bring more stability to global markets and shield poor countries from financial speculators, Nobel Prize–winning Yale economist James Tobin proposed a small tax on foreign currency trades.[22]

U.S. firms outsource production to countries that do not have adequate **product safety** standards that are enforced, and this exposes U.S. citizens to dangerous toys, paint, tires, food, toothpaste, pharmaceuticals, and many other products. These product failures have received much publicity, yet we do not have a global system for ensuring the safety of products and foods.

Corruption or Transparency

Corruption makes a country less attractive for business; it hinders development when government officials **demand payments** to obtain permits to build or to provide electricity. Bribery and corruption hinder growth for individual firms and also for entire countries. Corruption keeps millions of people mired in poverty and is estimated to cost \$2.5 trillion annually.[23] Not only does this money not go to workers, suppliers, or local investors who deserve it, but business planning becomes

---

[21] Edward Luttwak, *Turbo-Capitalism: Winners and Losers in the Global Economy* (New York: Harper Collins, 1999).

[22] See Barry Eichengreen, "Financial Instability," in *Global Crises, Global Solutions,* ed. Bjorn Lomborg (Cambridge, MA: Cambridge University Press, 2004); George Soros, *The Crisis of Global Capitalism: Open Society Endangered* (New York: Public Affairs, 1998); on the "Tobin tax" see "Economic Forum: A Worldly Philosopher," *The Economist,* March 16, 2002, p. 78.

[23] Raymond Fishman and Jakob Svensson, "Are Corruption and Taxation Really Harmful to Growth? Firm Level Evidence," *Journal of Developmental Economics,* 83 (2007): 63–75; William K. Black, "The *Dango* Tango: Why Corruption Blocks Real Reform in Japan," *Business Ethics Quarterly,* 14 (October 2004): 603–623. The \$2.5 trillion figure is from a *Transparency International* report to executives of the Global Compact in July 2007.

difficult, because one does not know when one will receive a new demand for cash. The person demanding the bribe has a conflict of interest; he turns his back on his primary duty to the country or firm he represents, and uses that power for personal gain.[24] The World Bank calls corruption the single greatest obstacle to economic and social development. It undermines development by weakening local institutions and the rule of law. The poor suffer more than others, because they are more dependent on public services and less capable of paying the extra costs stemming from bribery and fraud.

There is evidence that corruption is increasing in some developing countries. Three of the largest and fastest growing Asian nations, China, India, and Indonesia suffer pervasive corruption. Bribes, kickbacks, and "grease" money are the most noticeable forms of corruption. On the other hand, friendship, sharing information, and gift giving pervade all cultures; such practices support a society's social capital. Such relationships become corrupt when the one seeking favor provides a "gift" that is substantial, and expects a permit or a large contract in return. That gift may be to a government official who has the authority to award a contract or to a business purchasing agent who can purchase the briber's product.

In China *guanxi* is a reliance on relationships, and it can be mistaken for corruption. People depend on people they know, because of a general lack of trust and the inadequacy of the legal system. On the other hand, despite official warnings, corruption is still rampant in China. As a result of corruption and the lack of regulations in China, the world must deal with a giant trading partner that can't control piracy, curb pollution, or guarantee safe products. Chinese made deadly pet food, dangerous tires, toxic jewelry, and poisonous toothpaste and toys that have been sold in the United States and elsewhere.

Children have died in China because of faulty pharmaceuticals. Zheng Xiaoyu was an activist who lobbied for safer drugs. He was then made head of the Chinese version of the U.S. Food and Drug Administration, and held that position for eight years. However, Xiaoyu took bribes worth $850,000 from executives to allow their untested drugs to be marketed. Dozens of people died. He was tried, found guilty, and executed in July 2007. Will this solve the problem? If the head of the government agency is corrupt, one can only imagine how corruption runs through the entire agency. In another case, a county chief's wife was bombed, because of his attempt to get to the bottom of corruption among high government officials.[25] Corruption is often more prevalent as firms begin operations in developing countries. In many countries, corruption reaches the highest levels of government, and is supported by what is called "crony capitalism."

Crony capitalism, rampant in many Asian countries, such as Thailand, Indonesia, China, India, and Malaysia means that who you know and the connections

---

[24] Manuel Velasquez and Kirk O. Hanson, "Managing Conflicts of Interest," in *The Accountable Corporation*, eds. Mark J. Epstein and Kirk O. Hanson, vol. 4 (Westport, CT: Praeger, 2006).

[25] David Barboza, "A Chinese Reformer Betrays His Cause, and Pays," *The New York Times*, July 13, 2007, pp. 1, 10; Pete Engardio et al., "Broken China: Beijing Can't Clean up the Environment, Rein in Stock Speculation, or Police its Companies," *BusinessWeek*, July 23, 2007, pp. 39–48; and John Boatright, "Exporting American Ethics," *Loyola Magazine,* Spring 2004, p. 17.

you have are more important than price or quality. Ruling and military family groups require cash payments for permission to invest. In sum, it is difficult to do business in a nation where there is widespread bribery; costs often are increased by 10–50 percent, and one is never certain that one has seen the end of the demands for money. Moreover, the illegal payoffs do not go to legitimate costs, but to people who already have wealth and power.

Some claim that **bribery** is a part of the culture in certain countries. However, "bribery is illegal and criminal under the laws of virtually every country, even those with cultures that supposedly support corruption."[26] The only people who defend bribery are those who receive the bribe. Ordinary working people are outraged at the injustice of powerful officials taking large sums of money in return for a "favor." Bribery violates Islamic, Buddhist, Judaic, Christian, and Confucian religious norms of how a public official should act. Moreover, developed nations share much of the blame for corruption, because most bribes come from businesspeople in developed countries. U.S. law prohibits overseas bribery, but firms are clever in circumventing the law. Some hire local "consultants" for a large fee to "take care of local arrangements." On the other hand, the U.S. Department of Justice has prosecuted four times the number of bribery cases, since the Sarbanes–Oxley law was passed. In many countries, there is a reaction against corruption. With popular support, Korean courts sentenced to jail for corruption four corporation presidents, including the Chairman of giant Daewoo, and a former president of Korea.[27]

Transparency International (TI) is a **nongovernmental organization (NGO)**, based in Berlin, which for more than a decade has been effective in putting a spotlight on corruption in an attempt to reduce it. TI estimates that the "amount lost due to bribery in government procurement is at least $400 billion per year worldwide." TI's principal vehicle for discouraging corruption is to publish an annual list of countries that are rank ordered from least corrupt to most corrupt. TI used multiple surveys of businesspeople and analysts on a country's corruption, and then averaged those polls to develop the 2007 TI list. For the full Corruption Perception Index, see the TI Web site for the ranking, methodology, and additional information on each of the 179 countries: http://www.transparency.org/policy_research/surveys_indices/cpi.

TI found that corruption is rampant in 49 countries where the public sector is plagued by bribery. These 49 countries scored less than 3 compared with a clean score of 10 on the TI list. A larger number, 105 out of 179 countries, on the index scored less than 5. The chair of TI, Peter Eigen, points out that corruption appears to be most acute in Congo, Guinea, Laos, Afghanistan, Chad, Sudan, Tonga, Uzbekistan, Haiti,

---

[26] Kathleen A. Getz, "International Instruments on Bribery and Corruption," in *Global Codes of Business Conduct: An Idea Whose Time Has Come*, ed. Oliver Williams (Notre Dame, IN: Notre Dame University Press, 2000), p. 143; also Duane Winsor and Kathleen Getz, "Regional Market Integration and the Development of Global Norms for Enterprise Conduct," *Business and Society,* 38 (December 1999): 415–449.

[27] Emma Schwartz, "Hiking the Cost of Bribery: The Justice Department Crackdown on Corrupt Practices Ensnares both U.S. and Foreign Companies," *U.S. News and World Report,* August 13, 2007, p. 31; "Unfinished Business: Kim Sends the Chaebol a Message," *BusinessWeek*, September 9, 1996, pp. 56–57.

Iraq, Myanmar, and Somalia; these countries in descending order have a score of less than 2. Most of the oil-producing countries also have high levels of corruption. Countries that have low rates of perceived corruption with a rating of 9 or higher, Denmark, Finland, New Zealand, Singapore, Sweden, Iceland, the Netherlands, and Switzerland, are wealthy, healthy countries. The United States with a mediocre score of 7.2 is in 20th place, while those with progressively better corruption scores are France, Japan, Ireland, Germany, Australia, Hong Kong, the United Kingdom, Luxembourg, Australia, Norway, and Canada. But poor countries, most of whom are in the bottom half of the list, have the greatest need for help in their fight against corruption. Countries that recorded significant worsening levels of perceived corruption are Brazil, Cuba, Israel, Jordan, Tunisia, and the United States. Countries with a significant improvement are Algeria, Czech Republic, India, Japan, Latvia, Lebanon, Paraguay, and Turkey.

TI also measures the propensity of companies in 30 developed countries to bribe overseas. In this measurement, the United States ranks number 9 out of 30, which is a surprisingly low position for the country that was the first to outlaw overseas bribery in 1977. The mediocre ranking of the United States may be due partially to the U.S. election system. The 2008 national elections are expected to garner over $2 billion from wealthy Americans and firms; they contribute to political campaigns, expecting legislative and regulatory favors in return; most people view this as a form of bribery. Although it is illegal for U.S. firms to directly contribute to political candidates, individuals and firms have found ways around the law to curry favor.

In sum, the World Bank and TI argue that nations must reduce the influence of private money on public decisions; otherwise wealthy people determine public objectives. Corruption is a symptom of such failure; individuals and firms pay government officials to obtain permits and contracts, reduce their taxes, or avoid costly regulations. This results in inefficiencies, loss of confidence in government, and the diversion of taxpayers' money from public projects that benefit all citizens into the hands of wealthy individuals.[28]

Impact of Global Firms

The global business firm produces goods, services, jobs, technology, and wealth. Less widely acknowledged are the values that are communicated. The global firm brings the values of wealthy societies to developing ones. **Values** of discipline, individual responsibility, a regulated workday, and rewards for work under the direction of another come from working in a firm. As modernization proceeds, so do the perceived importance of money, image, possessions, and advertising. These imported values often conflict with local cultural and religious values, and care for extended family, tribe, and village. This causes misunderstanding and resentment in poor countries. Effective global managers understand and build on specific local cultural values.

---

[28] See five articles on corruption in a devoted special section, *Academy of Management Review*, 33, no. 3 (July 2008): 670–770; also Kathleen A. Getz, "The Effectiveness of Global Prohibition Regimes: Corruption and Antibribery Convention," *Business and Society*, 45, no. 3 (2006): 254–281.

People in developing countries seek a better life. For them this means jobs, increased income, and more goods and services. Evidence shows that foreign direct investment often increases in countries with greater respect for human rights. Education, health care, clean water, and sanitary facilities are vital for poor people; and their availability varies widely from country to country. The World Bank has spelled out the strategies that are most effective at making these services available.[29]

In spite of the efforts of the World Bank, the global economy is largely unregulated and thus unstable:

> The global economy with its momentum, inconsistency and amorality, is developing much more rapidly and substantially than the sense of global community with which to moderate, interpret and ground it. Put another way, the global economy unleashes all that is selfish about human nature without a global sensibility necessary for the well being of humans and our natural environment.[30]

One of the problems unbridled competition causes in the global economy is that the **disparity of incomes** between the richest and the poorest peoples increase. Between 1990 and 2003, economic inequality increased in most of the countries of the world—those with 80 percent of the world's population. Moreover, between 1950 and 2000 the worldwide suicide rate among men, a personal measure of happiness, rose from approximately 17 per 100,000 people to about 30.[31] Russia had a dramatic surge in inequality after the fall of communism; the expected life span dropped from 70 to 59. Among the industrialized nations, the United States has the most unequal distribution of income. Over 30 percent of income goes to the richest 10 percent, while the poorest 10 percent receive only 1.8 percent. Three hedge fund managers personally received $3.7 billion, $2.9 billion, and $2.8 billion in 2007.[32] Ironically, one of these three was George Soros, who has often written that the global capitalist system is unsound and unstable and beyond the control of any national or international agency. Moreover, this disparity in incomes has caused envy, anger, terrorism, and wars in many nations, and this could lead to serious instability in the future.

Acknowledging these strengths and weaknesses, an expert on world trade says that globalization will yield better results if it is managed. He then makes specific suggestions, among them encouraging ILO standards, compensating those laid off in poor as well as rich countries, managing trade so it benefits people, and enacting and

---

[29] Shannon L. Blanton and Robert G. Blanton, "Human Rights and Foreign Direct Investment," *Business and Society,* 45 (December 2006): 464–485; *World Development Report—2004: Making Services Work for Poor People* (Washington D.C.: World Bank and Oxford University Press, 2003).

[30] John Della Costa, *The Ethical Imperative: Why Moral Leadership is Good Business* (Reading, MA: Addison-Wesley, 1998), p. 20.

[31] Peter Stair, "Regional Disparities in Quality of Life Persist," *Vital Signs: 2006–2007*, ed. Linda Stark (New York: W. W. Norton, 2006), pp. 110–111.

[32] Jenny Anderson, "Wall Street Winners Hit a New Jackpot: Billion-Dollar Paydays," *The New York Times,* April 16, 2008, pp. 1, 18; Radhika Sarin, "Rich-Poor Divide Growing," in *Vital Signs—2003: The Trends that are Shaping Our World,* ed. Linda Starke (New York: W. W. Norton, 2003), pp. 88–89.

TABLE 9-1 Firms Aid Poor Peoples: Yes and No

Yes	No
1. Provides jobs, income, capital, technology, and managers for local people.	1. Seeks lowest cost and encourages sweatshops—low wages, long hours, unsafe working conditions.
2. Provides training and develops leadership for local people.	2. Closes plants when wage rates rise, workers organize, or regulations become burdensome.
3. Pays taxes and reinvests some of its profits in the local economy.	3. Seeks nations with lenient environmental standards.
4. Provides business for local firms and creates jobs, both through purchasing from suppliers and through workers' purchases.	4. Encourages urbanism and uprooting of rural persons, families, and villages.
5. Provides mechanization, fertilizers, and other aids for farmers.	5. Bribes government officials and retards reform.
6. Produces foreign exchange by exporting goods.	6. Widens the gap between the few very rich and the many poor in the host country.
7. Can aid the host nation's development plans.	7. Sends profits from operations back to richer home nation.
8. Develops technical and professional skills among local people.	8. Often supports more stable authoritarian over democratic government (China, Saudi Arabia, Malaysia, Singapore.)
9. Contributes to local and shared ownership projects.	9. Advertises and sells expensive, unnecessary, and sometimes dangerous consumer goods (e.g., cigarettes, alcohol, weapons.)

enforcing healthy national environmental standards. In sum, the global corporation can be a major factor in assisting the economic development of poorer countries, but it brings problems with it also (see Table 9-1).[33]

GLOBAL POVERTY AND BUSINESS

Our response to global poverty uncovers our personal and business values. Global business will pull people out of poverty in developing nations, according to many. Jobs and opportunities have increased in scores of poorer nations. However, most of

---

[33] Jennifer W. Spencer, "The Impact of Multinational Enterprise Strategy on Indigenous Enterprises: Horizontal Spillovers and Crowding Out in Developing Countries, *Academy of Management Review*, 33 (April 2008): 341–361; Jagdish Bhagwati, *In Defense of Globalization* (New York: Oxford University Press, 2004).

the financial rewards of globalization go to those who already have wealth; investors, owners, and managers are the principal winners in both rich and poor countries. Both within countries and between countries, the gap in incomes between the rich and the poor is growing wider.

Examining the **condition of the poor** may help us understand this gap:

- 1.2 billion people in the world live on less than $1 a day.
- 1.2 billion people do not have clean water; and 2 million children die each year because of this lack of clean water.
- 2.6 billion people do not have basic sanitation.
- Hundreds of millions of poor farmers have difficulty maintaining the fertility of soils from which they eke out a meager living.[34]

As populations grow, people move to cities and add to the polluted environment and thus to the problem. The population of **urban areas** is expected to triple over the next two generations. Of the world's population, the wealthiest 20 percent receive 85 percent of world's income, while 10 percent live on less than 0.5 percent of that income. Note the disparity: "The richest 3 persons on the planet have more wealth than the combined gross domestic product (GDP) of the 47 poorest countries. The richest 15 persons have more wealth than the combined GDP of all of sub-Saharan Africa with its 550 million people."[35]

This disparity is increasing. From 1960 to 1995, the gap in per capita income between the world's 20 richest and 20 poorest countries more than doubled—from 18 to 1 to 37 to 1. In addition, because inequality within countries has also risen, the gap between those at the top and those at the bottom is even more glaring. The president of the World Bank said, "Despite years of relative peace and prosperity in industrialized countries, global poverty is getting worse. More troubling still is the massive and widening gap between rich and poor."[36]

Nobel Prize–winning economist Joseph Stiglitz examines the failures of globalization and offers solutions:

> Globalization was supposed to bring unprecedented benefits to all. Yet, curiously, it has come to be vilified both in the developed and the developing world. America and Europe see the threat of outsourcing, the developing countries see the advanced industrial countries tilting the global economic regime against them. Those in both see corporate interests being advanced at the expense of other values.[37]

Stiglitz, along with other experts, points out that economic globalization has outpaced political globalization. The economic consequences of globalization have come faster than our ability to understand and cope with these consequences through

---

[34] Data from *Human Development Report 2006* (New York: Palgrave-McMillan, 2006), also at http://hdr.undp.org/hdr2006/.

[35] Ismail Serageldin, "World Poverty and Hunger—The Challenge for Science," *Science,* 296 (April 2002): 54–58.

[36] James D. Wolfensohn, "A Call to Global Action," *America,* January 8–15, 2001, pp. 8–12.

[37] Joseph E. Stiglitz, *Making Globalization Work* (New York: W. W. Norton, 2006), p. 269.

the political process. Development assistance (foreign aid) to poorer countries from wealthy countries will be discussed later. However, **private investment is a much greater engine of development**, since aid is only 0.5 percent of direct foreign investment. However, very little investment or aid goes to the poorer countries.[38] Moreover, the International Monetary Fund (IMF) imposed economic policies on poor countries that hindered their development; China and Korea ignored the IMF and so they succeeded, Stiglitz says. On the other hand, Thailand followed the IMF policies, and has not recovered. Even though the IMF was established to aid poor nations, its policies are actually geared to supporting the financial institutions that provide the loans. Just as IMF policies are dominated by financial institutions, the World Trade Organization (WTO) has been dominated by global corporations. The WTO can overrule an individual nation's labor or environmental regulation as a restraint of trade, and it can do this without appeal. Stiglitz's solution is to have appropriate national and international government intervention, so that all people, including the poor, gain the advantages of economic growth.

Entrepreneurs Among the Poor

Muhammad Yunus received his Ph.D. in economics in the United States, and returned to his native Bangladesh to teach. Noting the poverty of people around him, he provided loans of $20–30 that enabled poor illiterate women to purchase raw materials in order to set up their own home-based small businesses. With the **microloans**, women make fabrics and furniture, have photo-developing shops, and rent cell phone time to neighbors. Yunus loans to women because they are more likely to repay the loan, because they consider their families' needs and the need for another loan.

Banks refused to loan to the poor, because they had no credit and were illiterate. So Yunus founded Grameen Bank to provide the microloans, and Grameen now employs 12,000 people and has lent more than $5.1 billion to 5.3 million borrowers. The bank even includes a project called Struggling Members Program that serves 55,000 beggars.[39]

The microcredit movement has become the most popular and successful anti-poverty strategy in the world—so successful financially that hundreds of commercial banks now offer microloans. Microcredit at present provides 100 million poor people small loans through 3,100 institutions in 130 countries. Almost half of the world's three billion poor people may be eligible for microloans. New projects for Yunus are a partnership with Danone to provide nutritious, inexpensive baby formula; he is also planning to set up rural hospitals and low-cost eye care with video conferencing

---

[38] Robert Picciotto and Rachel Weaving, eds., *Impact of Rich Countries' Policies on Poor Countries* (New Brunswick: Transaction, 2004), pp. viii, 8–9.
[39] Muhammad Yunus, "The Micro-Credit Movement: Experiment and Perspectives," in *Improving Globalization*, eds. Maria Cecilia Arruda and George Enderle (Rio de Janeiro: Editora FGV, 2004), pp. 15–34; also Nicholas P. Sullivan, *You Can Hear Me Now: How Microloans and Cell Phones Are Connecting the World's Poor to the Global Economy* (San Francisco: Jossey Bass, 2007); Muhammad Yunus, *Banker to the Poor: The Autobiography of Muhammad Yunus, Founder of Grameen Bank* (Karachi: Oxford University Press, 2001).

between villagers and doctors in the capital, Dhaka.[40] Yunus and Grameen Bank won the Nobel Peace Prize in 2006, and he thinks that gave him and microloans better access to China. The Chinese government now supports 17 organizations within China which provide microloans. In the meantime, microfinance has become so successful worldwide that pension funds, hedge funds, venture capitalists, and major banks are moving in to benefit from its profitability; commercial banks charge 20–30 percent annual interest. With the success of microlending comes exploitation, so some large commercial lending institutions charge poor people up to 80 percent annual interest.[41]

The success of microloans provides a foundation for new economic thinking. Academics, consultants, businesspeople, and politicians now know that people "at the bottom of the pyramid" have both entrepreneurial skills and purchasing power. With examples from Brazil, India, Peru, Venezuela, Kosovo, and Mexico, businesspeople with vision can bring goods and jobs to people who might otherwise be neglected as unskilled, illiterate, and without capital. People who some consider poor and hopeless can have the determination, knowledge, and skills to be successful in business.[42]

Established firms help the poor by better aligning their business with their mission. CEMEX was founded in Mexico in 1906 and is one of the largest building supply firms in the world. CEMEX has dramatically reduced the considerable pollution and greenhouse gas emitted from making cement. It also supports education and health programs.

CEMEX noted that poor families in Mexico find it difficult to obtain a home, so 80 percent build their own. Typical homes are one or two room cinder block structures. When built or expanded by their owners, it is room-by-room as the owner can afford it. Driving through the countryside, one sees homes that remain partially finished for years because the owners cannot afford to do so. Because the principal obstacle was a lack of money, CEMEX developed a program, Patrimonio Hoy ("Property Now"), in which both CEMEX and families contributed to a fund, and the poor could borrow from it to build. The poor were thus able to build at less than one-half the cost, and it took them one-third the time to finish the house. The program helped both the poor and CEMEX's business.[43]

---

[40] Muhammad Yunus, *Creating a World Without Poverty: Social Business and the Future of Capitalism* (New York: Public Affairs, 2007); Celia W. Dugger, "Peace Prize to Pioneer of Loans To Poor No Bank Would Touch," *The New York Times*, October 14, 2006, pp. 1, 6; Jeffrey Gangemi, "Microcredit Missionary," *BusinessWeek*, December 26, 2006, p. 20.

[41] Keith Epstein and Geri Smith, "The Ugly Side of Micro-Lending: How Big Mexican Banks Profit as Many Poor Borrowers Get Trapped in a Maze of Debt," *BusinessWeek*, December 24, 2007, pp. 39–46.

[42] V. Kasturi Rangan et al., eds., *Business Solutions for the Global Poor: Creating Social and Economic Value* (San Francisco: John Wiley, 2007); C. K. Prahalad, *The Fortune at the Bottom of the Pyramid* (Upper Saddle River, NJ: Wharton Publishing, 2005); Christian Seelos and Johanna Mair, "Profitable Business Models and Market Creation in the Context of Deep Poverty: A Strategic View," *Academy of Management Perspectives*, 21 (November 2007): 49–63.

[43] Bradley K. Goggins, Philip H. Mirvis, and Steven A. Rochlin, *Beyond Good Company: Next Generation Corporate Citizenship* (New York: Palgrave Macmillan, 2007), pp. 183–187; see also Mark Wade, "A Commitment to Sustainable Development: The Long Journey Begins," *The Accountable Corporation*, eds. Marc J. Epstein and Kirk O. Hanson, vol. 3 (Westport, CT: Praeger, 2006).

International Stability

The purpose of the World Bank is to alleviate poverty and to stimulate growth in poor nations. To achieve these goals, the World Bank concluded that in addition to sound economic policies, it is also necessary to support education, health, good governance, the fight against corruption, legal and judicial reform, and environmental protection. Fighting poverty is a global concern; the stability of the world depends upon it. Much of the work of reducing poverty must be done by developing nations themselves; they must form suitable civic and legal institutions and rid themselves of corruption. In this effort, experts and resources from wealthier nations can help.[44]

Most developing countries have a large portion of their people working on **small farms**. These developing countries have agreed to open markets, but they find that their best potential export, agricultural products, cannot be sold. Europe, the United States, and Japan together spend $300 billion a year to subsidize their farm products. These subsidies lower production costs for producers in the wealthy countries, and make it difficult for farmers from poor nations to sell their products on the world market. Moreover, much of the U.S. **subsidy** goes to agribusiness, which has access to more money and better equipment, seed, and irrigation. In spite of wealthy nations' call for open markets, their own subsidies crush corn farmers, for example, in Mexico, cotton growers in Pakistan, rice farmers in Indonesia, and sugar producers in Africa. Compare $300 billion spent on agricultural subsidies in developed nations with the $106 billion annually spent by all wealthy nations to financially aid poor countries.[45] While wealthy countries urge open markets on poor countries so that they can purchase finished goods from them, these same rich countries refuse to open their own markets. The globalization of agriculture thus benefits the wealthy nations and penalizes poor nations.

Helping poor nations involves focusing development assistance on poor peoples and their needs for education, health, clean water, and technical skills. Table 9-2 shows the amount of foreign aid that has been provided in 2005 by the primary contributing countries, as measured both in total dollar amount and as a percentage of each country's Gross National Product (GNP). With the exception of aid to Iraq and Afghanistan, most aid contributions have fallen by both measures. Among these nations, the United States contributes the smallest portion of its GNP. Assessing U.S. citizens' perceptions, "The public vastly overestimates the share of government budgets allocated to aid." There is very little awareness that official development assistance as a share of national income has declined from about 0.65 percent in 1967 to 0.22 percent in 2001—despite endorsements by numerous UN conferences of a target of 0.7 percent of national income, or that only five out of 22 aid contributing countries have reached this target (see Table 9-2).[46]

Compare U.S. **foreign aid** of $28 billion with the U.S. **military budget** of $462 billion, which does not include expenditures of $500 billion for the wars in Iraq and Afghanistan. The U.S. military budget is almost as much as the military

---

[44] "Special Report—Global Poverty: There's No Panacea but Here Are Strategies That Work," *BusinessWeek*, October 14, 2002, pp. 107–118.

[45] "Mowing Down Farm Subsidies," *BusinessWeek*, August 16, 2004, p. 108; also "The Rigged Trade Game," *The New York Times*, July 20, 2003, p. 10wk.

[46] Picciotto & Weaving, *Impact of Rich Countries' Policies on Poor Countries*, p. 7.

TABLE 9-2 Development Assistance of Top-15 Contributors, 1992 and 2000

Country	1992 Total (million 2000 dollars)	Share of GNP (percent)	2000 Total (million 2000 dollars)	Share of GNP (percent)
Denmark	1,583	1.02	1,664	1.06
The Netherlands	3,132	0.86	3,075	0.82
Sweden	2,798	1.03	1,813	0.81
Norway	1,448	1.16	1,264	0.80
Belgium	984	0.39	812	0.36
Switzerland	1,296	0.46	888	0.34
France	9,407	0.63	4,221	0.33
United Kingdom	3,659	0.31	4,458	0.31
Japan	12,685	0.30	13,062	0.27
Germany	8,613	0.39	5,034	0.27
Australia	1,107	0.35	995	0.27
Canada	2,861	0.46	1,722	0.25
Spain	1,727	0.26	1,321	0.24
Italy	4,689	0.34	1,368	0.13
United States	13,319	0.20	9,581	0.10
All Countries	68,808	0.33	53,058	0.22

Source: Worldwatch Institute, State of the World, 2001,www.worldwatch.org.

expenditures of all other nations *combined*.[47] U.S. aid to poorer nations is only 4 percent of the U.S. military budget, yet aid is as important as a strong military in keeping the world safe in the future. The U.S. Secretary of Defense, Robert Gates, recommends additional spending for "**soft power**" (diplomacy) and less for "**hard power**" (military). Gates said, "We are miserable at communicating to the rest of the world what we are about as a society and a culture, about freedom and democracy, about our policies and our goals. It is just plain embarrassing that al-Qaeda is better at communicating its message on the Internet than America." He said that it was a mistake to abolish the U.S. Agency for International Development and the U.S. Information Agency. Gates urges "a dramatic increase in spending on civilian instruments of national security—diplomacy, strategic communications, foreign assistance, civic action and economic reconstruction and development."[48]

---

[47] "Military Expenditures Keep Growing," in *Vital Signs 2006–2007*, ed. Linda Starke (New York: W. W. Norton, 2006), pp. 84–85.
[48] Thom Shanker, "Defense Secretary Urges More Spending for U.S. Diplomacy," *The New York Times*, November 27, 2007, p. A6.

Given a limited amount of aid currently available, economists and policy makers, including three Nobel Prize winners, met to discuss how best to help poor nations. The consensus of the panel is for investment in climate change, communicable diseases, civil conflicts, access to education, financial instability, governance and corruption, malnutrition and hunger, migration, subsidies and trade barriers, and sanitation and access to clean water.[49] Would not shifting a portion of the U.S. military budget to civilian aid for clean water, education, health, and combating malnutrition for people in poor nations be a valuable investment in peace?

GLOBAL LAW, CODES, AND REPORTS

The ethical norms described in Chapter 3 are also useful in other cultures. In Chapter 8 we confirmed the importance of a firm having a mission and code of ethical conduct and offered some models of excellent codes. The increasing influence of global business, which is expedited by the NAFTA, the EU, and the organization of Asian nations (ASEAN), makes it clear that individual company codes are not sufficient. Bribery of government leaders for permits and purchases is still common. In many countries workers are paid less than what it takes to live, and their government forbids them to organize to seek better pay and working conditions. Moreover, air, water, and solid waste pollution is daily killing millions in poor countries. Global codes could provide an "even playing field" for business from different nations.

International bodies have attempted to state basic principles of just business transactions that could apply across national boundaries. The United Nations agreed in 1948 on the *Universal Declaration of Human Rights*, and the ILO in 1977 codified the basic rights of working people in the *Tripartite Declaration*.[50] Because of widespread abuse in marketing infant formula, the World Health Organization (WHO) prodded manufacturers such as Nestle, American Home Products, and Abbott Laboratories to agree on international guidelines for marketing infant formula.[51] With regard to the environment, 70 firms, including American Airlines, Bank of America, Coca-Cola, Consolidated Edison, Ford, General Motors, Interface, McDonald's, and Nike, have endorsed the *Coalition for Environmentally Responsible Economies (CERES) Principles*. The endorsing firms pledge to follow the 10 CERES Principles and to preserve and protect the environment at levels beyond what is required by local law. At least once every five years, CERES does an independent audit to certify that the signatory firm is following the 10 principles. For example, CERES did a Performance Review of General Motors and found that "GM made significant progress in cleaning up and reducing factory emissions, conserving resources, and eliminating waste, and

---

[49] See the report, Bjorn Lomborg, ed., *Global Crises, Global Solutions* (Cambridge: Cambridge University press, 2004); also "Putting the World to Rights: What Would Be the Best Way to Spend Additional Resources Helping the Developing Countries?" *The Economist,* June 5, 2002, pp. 63–65; see also Lee A. Tavis, *Power and Responsibility: Multinational Managers and Developing Country Concerns* (Notre Dame,: University of Notre Dame Press, 1997).

[50] For a summary of international compacts, see William C. Frederick, "The Moral Authority of Transnational Corporate Codes," *Journal of Business Ethics,* 10 (1991): 165–177. The United States stands alone in not ratifying the *Universal Declaration of Human Rights*.

[51] The United States is again the only nation that has not agreed to these international guidelines.

has led the way on corporate disclosure and stakeholder engagement." The review of product improvements was less positive, because GM had not increased the fuel economy of its fleet of cars and trucks. The entire report, along with an executive summary, is publicly available. CERES, also founded along with the *UN Environment Program (UNEP)* the *Global Reporting Initiative (GRI)*, will be discussed below.

The United States attempted to make international business conduct more fair through its own legislation. In the 1970s many U.S. firms bribed foreign leaders to obtain permits for doing business in that country or to purchase the firm's products. Executives of Lockheed paid more than $22 million to leaders of Japan, the Netherlands, Saudi Arabia, Korea, and other nations to purchase their aircraft. United Brand's executives paid $2 million to the president of Honduras to reduce taxes on bananas, and Gulf Oil paid the South Korean president $4 million to give it a permit to build an oil refinery. These bribes caused a government to fall in Japan and major embarrassment for the leaders of the other nations. To reduce this bribery of foreign leaders by U.S. executives, the U.S. Congress passed the **Foreign Corrupt Practices Act (FCPA)** in 1977.

The FCPA does not prohibit "expediting" ("grease," or tip—to ensure promptness) payments to customs or other minor officials to cut through red tape. Payments are not illegal in U.S. law if the official has no impact on the final decision, and the payment merely makes the transaction move more quickly. But the FCPA does prohibit a major payment to an official to influence that official's judgment, for example, to obtain a permit or to purchase a product. The firm is also required to keep detailed records and accounts of all payments so that auditors may inspect and judge them. Currently the U.S. Department of Justice is investigating many U.S. firms such as Haliburton, Baker Hughes, Aon, and Willbros Group for violating the law; firms have paid fines for their overseas bribery, and some executives have been jailed.

The *Organization for Economic Cooperation and Development (OECD)* is the major economic policy-making body for the industrialized nations. The OECD finally issued guidelines in 1997 by which member nations were to criminalize bribery in their domestic legislation. The EU is reluctant to prescribe legislation for member states, but agreed to support the OECD guidelines. However, the United States is also investigating and charging foreign firms that have operations in the United States—with the goal to "name and shame" them also into stopping bribery and complying with U.S. and European law.[52]

Firms doing business in China, Myanmar (Burma), Sudan, and other countries with poor records in respecting human rights also have been criticized. In many countries children sometimes labor 80-hour weeks for $2 a day to make goods for wealthy customers. These workers are generally forbidden to organize to ask for better pay or working conditions. Because of this, firms such as Levi Strauss, Reebok, and Nike have developed their own principles of how workers should be treated and they monitor their suppliers.

---

[52] Nelson Schwartz and Lowell Bergman, "Payload: Taking Aim at Corporate Bribery. Inquiry Shows a New Reach for an Old Law," *The New York Times*, November 25, 2007, pp. BU 1, 9–10; see also James Weber and Kathleen Getz, "Buy Bribes or Bye-Bye Bribes: The Future Status of Bribery in International Commerce," *Business Ethics Quarterly*, 14 (October 2004): 695–711.

To reduce world poverty, attention must be given to the fairness of trade, aid, migration, labor standards, investment, and honesty of each country's government. The World Bank and the IMF have given new attention to reducing world poverty. Churches and other NGOs provide aid and lobby for the poor. Even the WTO is now trying to reduce protectionist policies of wealthy countries, so that poorer peoples may sell their corn, cotton, and goods on the world market.[53] To bring some fairness, business executives have fashioned global codes of business conduct. Let us examine two of the most influential.

THE CAUX ROUND TABLE PRINCIPLES FOR BUSINESS

The Caux Round Table (CRT) is an organization of senior executives of firms from Europe, Japan, the United States, Lebanon, Thailand, and many other countries. Their *Principles for Business* were written by top executives from firms such as Siemens, 3M, Canon, Matsushita, Dana, Nissan, Novartis, Philips Electronics, and Sumitomo. The CRT principles are based on two main values. The first, from the Eastern tradition, is "living and working together for the **common good**," enabling cooperation and mutual prosperity to coexist with healthy and fair competition. The second, from the Western tradition, is "**human dignity**"—the sacredness or value of each person as an end, not simply as a means to the fulfillment of other's purposes. The principles include seven "general principles" and specific stakeholder principles, covering customers, employees, owners/investors, suppliers, competitors, and communities.[54] The CRT *Principles* are found in 12 languages at http://www.cauxroundtable.org/principles.html. For the origins of the codes and reporting initiatives discussed here, see Table 9-3.

TABLE 9-3 Origin of Global Codes of Business Conduct and Reporting Mechanisms

Author of Code	Code	Year initiated
Business executives from the European Union, Japan, and the United States	Caux Round Table *Principles for Business*	1996
United Nations and global business executives	United Nations *Global Compact with Business*	2000
Coalition for Environmentally Responsible Economies & UN Environment Programme	*Global Reporting Initiative* (GRI)	2002

[53] A fuller agenda of what can be done is given by Ethan Kapstein, *Economic Justice in an Unfair World: Toward a Level Playing Field* (Princeton, NJ: Princeton University Press, 2006).
[54] Kenneth Goodpaster, "The Caux Round Table Principles: Corporate Moral Reflection in a Global Business Environment"; and Gerald Cavanagh, "Executives' Code of Business Conduct: Prospects for the Caux Principles," in *Global Codes of Business Conduct: An Idea Whose Idea Has Come*, ed. Oliver F. Williams, C.S.C. (Notre Dame, IN: Notre Dame University Press, 2000), pp. 169–195. For more on CRT, see http://www.cauxroundtable.org/.

The CRT *Principles* are offered as a benchmark for a firm to develop or improve its own mission and code of behavior. The Bank of America along with executives from Australia, Malaysia, China, Russia, the Netherlands, Lebanon, and other countries have used the Caux *Principles* as a model for their own firm's code. The CRT meets regularly and they are also concerned with alleviating world poverty and making it possible for poor nations to share in global prosperity. The Caux *Principles* have been taught in dozens of universities worldwide. Members of the International Association of Jesuit Schools of Business, a group of 60 business schools from 20 countries on six continents, at a meeting in Indonesia voted to support and teach the Caux *Principles for Business*.

The CRT has developed a Self-Assessment and Improvement Process (SAIP) to help business address the growing expectations of the public that corporations conduct their activities in a responsible manner. The SAIP "allows senior leaders to 'score' the firm's conduct in relation to an acknowledged global standard for responsible behavior."[55] The scoring is done privately, so executives are able to be more honest with information. At a meeting in Mexico in 2002, the CRT agreed to cooperate with the *UN Global Compact with Business*.

The United Nations Global Compact with Business

World business and political leaders invited the Secretary General of the United Nations to address them at the World Economic Forum. In that presentation, he warned that many people are suspicious of the global economy because "the spread of markets out paces the ability of societies and their political systems to adjust to them, let alone guide the course they take. History teaches that such imbalance between the economic, social and political realms can never be sustained for very long." Until people have confidence in the global economy, it "will be fragile and vulnerable—vulnerable to backlash from all the 'isms' of our post-cold war world—protectionism, populism, nationalism, ethnic chauvinism, fanaticism and terrorism." To avoid a backlash, he invited leaders of large corporations to join with the United Nations in a "global compact" to "support and enact a set of core values in the areas of human rights, labor standards and environmental practices."[56]

As a response corporate leaders fashioned what is now called the *UN Global Compact with Business*. The Compact consists of 10 simple principles that seek to protect human rights, worker rights, and the environment and reduce corruption. The *Compact* is found at http://www.unglobalcompact.org/. If a firm decides to join in the Compact, the firm (1) submits a letter of intent from its CEO, and (2) agrees to publish in its annual report, or a similar report, a description of the ways in which it is supporting the *Global Compact*. The goal is to

---

[55] Kenneth Goodpaster, Dean Maines, and Michelle Rovang, "Stakeholder Thinking Beyond Paradox to Practicality," *Journal of Corporate Citizenship,* no. 7 (2002): 93.

[56] Kofi Annan, "Business and the U.N.," *Vital Speeches,* February 15, 2000, pp. 260–261.

make the principles of the *Global Compact* part of the firm's business strategy, culture, and day-to-day operations.[57]

By 2007 more than 3,000 firms on six continents had joined the *Global Compact*, among them BP, Cisco Systems, Daimler Benz, Deloitte-Touche, DuPont, Hewlett-Packard (H-P), Novartis, Royal Dutch Shell, Unilever, and Volvo. The *Global Compact* helps firms that sign the *Compact* to adhere to the basic principles and to write their annual report through "Learning Forums," which provide an opportunity for firms to share their experiences and successes with each other. A learning forum held in China discussed human and worker rights. The Compact declares that it "does not 'police', enforce or measure the behavior or actions of companies. . . ." Through the Learning Forums, the *Global Compact* encourages collaboration.

On the other hand, the *Compact* has been charged with "**bluewashing**," that is, signing up firms and allowing them to display the blue UN logo although some firms do not file annual reports and do little to implement the *Principles*. They become "free-riders."[58] Some of these firms have been criticized by *CorpWatch*, a U.S. nonprofit organization (NGO), for violating the principles of the Compact. Those criticized include Aventis, Bayer, Nike, Unilever, Norsk Hydro, and Rio Tinto and the International Chamber of Commerce. In 2006 the Compact dropped from membership 300 firms for not filing their annual reports. U.S.-based firms have been more reluctant than European or Asian firms to participate in the *Global Compact*.

Global Reporting Initiative

The *GRI* is a partnership of the CERES and the UNEP. GRI developed globally applicable practical guidelines for reporting on the economic, environmental, and social performance of corporations, governments, and nongovernmental agencies (NGOs). GRI seeks to "elevate sustainability reporting practices worldwide to a level equivalent to financial reporting." The goal is to produce corporate "**triple bottom line**" reports that provide information on environmental and social issues parallel to current financial reports. GRI led stakeholders to develop the guidelines and instruments for measuring progress. GRI's *Sustainability Reporting Guidelines* are widely used by firms.

The GRI guidelines are followed by firms that report their "triple bottom line" results. GRI has about 45 sponsoring organizations worldwide, and many times that number use the guidelines and report their results. Sponsoring organizations include Baxter International, BP, Canon, Ford, GM, Heineken, Nike, and Philips. The firm's reports are posted on GRI's Web site.

Some people and institutions seek such reports. Analysts at socially responsible investment firms, representing $147 billion in assets, have urged firms to do GRI-based

---

[57] *The Global Compact: Corporate Citizenship in the World Economy* (United Nations: Global Compact Office, 2003; see also http://www.unglobalcompact.org/Portal/Default.asp; also Georg Kell, "Do Corporations Threaten Globalization?" *Business Ethics in a Global Economy Conference,* Santa Clara University, February 20, 2003; and Georg Kell and David Levin, "The Evolution of the Global Compact Network: An Historic Experiment in Learning and Action," *Working Draft: UN 8-2002,* Academy of Management Conference, Denver, August 13, 2002.

[58] Oliver F. Williams, "The UN Global Compact: The Challenge and the Promise," *Business Ethics Quarterly,* 14 (October 2004): 755–774; also Pete Engardio, "Global Compact, Little Impact: Four Years in, the UN's Voluntary Corporate Responsibility Plan is Falling Short," *BusinessWeek,* July 12, 2004, pp. 86–87.

reporting; thus funds can make more intelligent buy and sell decisions. They suggest that publicly traded firms annually report on environmental, labor, and other social issues using the GRI guidelines. These analysts seek transparent disclosure from each firm, which provides a view of opportunities and risks associated with environmental and social issues. As one analyst put it, "A company's GRI report should be the first place investors and research institutions consult for information."[59]

Effectiveness of Global Codes and Reporting

The Caux *Principles*, the *Global Compact*, and the *GRI* have each had some success. The CRT *Principles for Business* were written by business executives, have top executives of the Round Table to support it, and are more detailed, covering more stakeholder responsibilities than does the *UN Global Compact*. It was also one of the first global codes, and thus has received favorable attention among some business executives and business school faculty. The *UN Global Compact* has the prestige and the global reach of the United Nations itself. The simplicity and transparency of the reports required by the *Global Compact* make it attractive. The *GRI* was designed to obtain comparable triple bottom line data for firms; it has been successful for reporting firms. Ultimately codes will be effective instruments to bring transparency when firms report on their actions following a common format, and the reports are **audited** by outsiders. The global corporation is such an important player in the twenty-first century that it must be trusted, and in order to be trusted, it must be transparent.[60]

Each of these global instruments is more popular with firms in Europe and Asia than in the United States. The *UN Global Compact* requires CEOs to sign that they will abide by the code. GRI requires reporting. In the litigious U.S. society, corporate lawyers advise executives that to sign a compact or make a report increases exposure to lawsuits. A firm might be sued if someone perceives that it is not acting as it pledges or reports. As a result, some U.S. corporations are reluctant to embrace codes and reporting. To avoid expensive law suits, NAFTA set up an intra-national judicial process outside the U.S. legal system which cannot be appealed, in order to assure that free markets are protected and enforced. Could not similar protections be afforded to firms that follow the CRT *Principles* or the *UN Global Compact*?

A market is efficient and effective when it is open, transparent, and has commonly accepted "rules of the game." These codes and reports attempt to achieve that.[61] Abiding by a global code and reporting economic, environmental, and social

---

[59] See: http://www.globalreporting.org/about/brief.asp.
[60] S. Prakash Sethi, *Setting Global Standards: Guidelines for Creating Codes of Conduct in Multinational Corporations* (Hoboken, NJ: John Wiley, 2003); arguing for voluntary disclosure, not regulation, are Linda C. Rodriguez and Jane LeMaster, "Voluntary Corporate Social Responsibility Disclosure," *Business and Society,* 46, no. 3 (September 2007): 370–385.
[61] Aaron Chatterji and David Levine, "Breaking Down the Wall of Codes: Evaluating Non-Financial Performance Measurement," *California Management Review,* 48 (Winter 2006): 29–51; Gerald F. Cavanagh, "Global Business Ethics: Regulation, Code, or Self-Restraint," *Business Ethics Quarterly,* 14 (October 2004): 625–642; Duane Winsor, "Formulating a Moral Core for International Codes of Conduct," in *Perspectives on International Corporate Responsibility*, vol. 2 (Carnegie Mellon, 2005), pp. 47–63.

results imposes short-term costs. But when firms provide better wages and working conditions and inflict less environmental damage, it is a long-term benefit for them and for all. When firms do not participate in a voluntary code or reporting system, it undermines the best vehicle for encouraging voluntary cooperative action. In that case, there are two other options: (1) individualistic actions that provide short-term rewards to sweatshops and polluters, or (2) global treaties and regulation. Are **global legal restraints** the most practical and desirable solution, given the damage and chaos caused by individualistic actions and the limited success of global codes? For a comparison of the various strategies, see Table 9-4.

Because of problems that are caused by the global reward system, some business executives have concluded that major issues can best be addressed through international agreements. "These subsequently need to be translated into national regulation that is then rigorously and uniformly enforced. Effective self-regulation, in its many forms, is often the first step."[62]

TABLE 9-4 Global Ethical Guidelines for Business: Alternate Strategies

Strategies	Advantages	Disadvantages
Treaties and Regulation	Provides clear guidelines, applicable to all Provides enforcement methods Lessens advantages of "free-rider"	Difficult to negotiate Ineffective without monitors and sanctions Managers' dislike for regulations A nation can remain outside agreement
Codes and Reports	Focuses managers' attention on ethical issues Easier to support because not coercive Encourages cooperation and communication	Many firms do not participate U.S. executives fear costly law suits No mandatory reports or sanctions
Self-Restraint	No limiting restrictions or required reporting Managers able to anticipate regulation Enables stakeholders to identify ethical issues Useful if no regulation or code in place	Inadequate to deal with some issues Provides spotty long-term results Gives financial advantage to unethical firm

Treaties and Regulation: Multilateral treaties and international agreements.

Codes and Reports: Global codes and reporting of business conduct.

Self-restraint: Voluntary self-restraint of individual executives and firms.

---

[62] *Tomorrow's Global Company: Challenges and Choices* (London: Tomorrow's Company, 2007), p. 4. This is at http://www.tomorrowscompany.com/uploads/TGCexcu.pdf, accessed February 22, 2008.

RESPONSIBILITIES OF THE GLOBAL FIRM

Business is the source of products, jobs, and hope for poor people. Yet the pressure to lower costs continues in the global market place. This poses a dilemma for the business manager, because lowering business costs often places a larger cost on others. Earlier we examined working conditions and pollution in developing countries. The challenge for the manager is to provide low-price goods and services and jobs at living wages, and do it in a way that will benefit and not penalize people now and in the future.

Sustainable Development

The last two decades have been sobering for all peoples. In addition to the constant threat of terrorism, citizens in the United States, Japan, and Europe now realize that they will never again possess the supremacy in world markets or the growth rate that they had in the latter part of the twentieth century. In addition, rainforests are being cut down in Latin America, Africa, Indonesia, and India, and we are losing farmland even as world population grows. Housing for millions without electricity or running water plagues Mexico City, Jakarta, Mumbai, and hundreds of other cities. Moreover, we expect up to one billion people in China and India will own autos that require fuel and thus add to greenhouse gas emissions. But this also provides new opportunities for creative entrepreneurs. We realize that our development and growth must be such that **generations following** us also may enjoy a decent standard of living and a livable world.[63] GE with its "Ecomagination" strategy, Philips Electronics, and others focus on new business opportunities that the drive for sustainability brings.

In the United States 15 percent of citizens have family incomes below the poverty level. Earlier we cited the huge compensation of top executives. This gap between the rich and the poor is widening each year, and it is also large and apparent in many Asian, Latin, and African countries.[64] Thus it may be more difficult for business to prosper in the long term, both because potential markets are limited by the poverty of so many, and also because of the danger of social instability. Moreover, many of the new service and some high-tech jobs pay less and are not challenging. They do not provide the opportunity for expanding one's skills or for advancement, as we see at Burger King, McDonald's, and retailing. In addition, **nonrenewable resources**, such as petroleum and metals, are more expensive because we are using them at a nonsustainable rate. Most manufacturing and services now add to pollution, and the cost to clean it up places a burden on others and increases our cost of living. China has double-digit economic growth and many

---

[63] Lester R. Brown, *Plan B 3.0: Mobilizing to Save Civilization* (New York: W. W. Norton, 2008); Linda Starke, ed., 2007 *State of the World: Our Urban Future* (New York: W. W. Norton, 2007); Petra Christmann, "Multinational Companies and the Natural Environment," *Academy of Management Review,* 47 (October 2004): 747–760.

[64] "Rich-Poor Divide Growing," in *Vital Signs–2003: Trends that are Shaping Our Future,* ed. Starke (New York: W. W. Norton & Co., 2003), pp. 88–89.

sweatshops; it is thus trading the cleanliness of its air and water for growth. China is experiencing extreme pollution and environmental degradation. Chinese deaths due to outdoor air pollution are at least 350,000 people annually; indoor air pollution, 300,000; and water pollution, 60,000 people each year. The air in 27 cities in China are up to three times more polluted than in Los Angeles, and 23 percent of the Chinese people do not have access to safe water.[65]

On the other hand, many business firms are now operating sustainably. H-P and IBM collect and **recycle** many of their old computers. Computers contain toxic metals, such as lead, mercury, cadmium, and bromine, which can get into the ground water and poison people; moreover, these materials are valuable and recyclable. Dell, a leading computer manufacturer, announced that it would aggressively recycle. It runs a low-cost pickup service, and its goal is to collect and reuse the materials from 50 percent of the computers it has manufactured.[66] Dell's initiative is aimed at people in the United States and other countries.

A Nation Among Nations

In this world of increasing population, faster transportation and communication, and more choices in life styles, people are more **interdependent**. Each of us depends on others and requires interaction to develop as a person. For example, when people in the United States flee the problems of the city, their suburban affluent children, without parks, libraries, and corner stores within walking distance, find little to do and become bored. Bus service is often not available in these communities, leading to isolation for children, elders, and anyone who does not drive. Many children then turn to alcohol, drugs, drop out of school, and run away from home. On the global scene a war, revolution, or terrorist attack in the Middle East, Latin America, or Asia touches us within hours. Starvation among refugees in Africa enters our living rooms through TV, along with our realization that our use of dog food, lawn fertilizer, and red meat may play a role in depriving poor Africans of life-giving grain. It is no longer possible for any people to assume that what is good for them is good for others. If one faction ignores others, they do so at their peril. Chinese and Indian universities teach business ethics in their business schools, using local religious principles. In this small world, we are linked together. We are interdependent, whether we like it or not.[67]

Most of the problems we have discussed cannot be solved by any nation acting alone. The threat of terrorism, global climate change, malnutrition, toxic waste, dwindling finite resources, and even a balance of trade deficit all demand cooperation.[68] We in the United States and our government are often insensitive to worldwide reaction

---

[65] Joseph Kahn and Jim Yardley, "As China Roars, Pollution Reaches Deadly Extremes," *The New York Times*, August 26, 2007, pp. 1, 6–7.

[66] Peter Asmus, "Dell, Inc.: Environmental Progress Award," *Business Ethics*, Fall 2004, pp. 10–11.

[67] See Henri-Claude de Bettingies and Cheon Kheong Tan, "Values and Management Education in China"; and Priya Rajev, "Wisdom from Ancient Indian Philosophy for the Corporate World," *International Management Review*, 3, no. 1 (2007): 17–37, 72–81; Amitai Etzioni, *From Empire to Community: A New Approach to International Relations* (New York: Palgrave-Macmillan, 2004).

[68] Global climate change is the primary issue that requires a solution, according to the Copenhagen consensus. See William R. Cline, "Climate Change," in *Global Crises, Global Solutions*, ed. Bjorn Lomborg (Cambridge: Cambridge University Press, 2004), pp. 13–38.

to U.S. policies. America's invasion of Iraq, lone vote against the Kyoto Treaty on Global Climate Change, withdrawing from the WHO's code for marketing infant formula, and our repudiation of the Law of the Sea Treaty have lost the United States much international respect and support. Business managers know that nationalistic attitudes that we expected a generation ago are now barriers for the United States and U.S. business. We operate in global markets and must be responsible citizens beyond our home country. As the world gets smaller, all people depend more on each other. Yet, paradoxically, nationalism, provincialism, and fundamentalism are gaining followers around the world. The United States often stands with those few nations that are unwilling to limit their self-interest or their sovereignty. Hence individualism and nationalism clash with the reality of interdependence. This is an unsustainable posture.

Robert Bellah thinks America's failure is in our emphasis on the atomistic self and rational **self-interest** and in our break with the basic understandings of the Founding Fathers. In early America, there was a strong social, collective emphasis: Citizens together were responsible for the state. Bellah demonstrates how this emphasis derived from the biblical covenant between God and God's people and from the gospel notion of a loving community based on membership in the common body of Christ. Bellah shows that the economic system of present-day America is no longer based on the early American view that economic interdependence is the foundation of the political order.[69] Respect for other peoples' position, cooperation, and negotiation are necessary in this interdependent world. The importance and urgency of the problems that the world's peoples face demand that we work together for solutions.

Global Corporate Citizenship

Twenty-first century business managers must see themselves as citizens with multiple responsibilities. The corporation then becomes a constructive player, providing products, services, jobs, and income and leaving behind a healthy globe. A firm must, of course, not lose its competitive edge while it is a good corporate citizen.

Employee ownership of stock in their own firm (**employee stock ownership plan—ESOP**) and socially responsible investing are two growing movements that help a firm and executives to align their own goals with those of citizens. With an ESOP, workers are owners of the firm and are more likely to consider the long-term benefit of fellow workers and customers, as well as the firm's profitability. Socially responsible investment is growing, and both the Domini and Calvert socially responsible funds have outperformed the market during the past 15 years.[70] These issues were discussed in Chapters 6 and 8 of this book.

Becoming a good **corporate citizen** requires vision and humane values, neither of which should be taken for granted in any firm. The vision and values of a firm lay a foundation for the future direction of that firm.[71] For decades executives have financed

---

[69] Robert N. Bellah, *The Broken Covenant: American Civil Religion in Time of Trial* (New York: Seabury, 1975).

[70] William Greider, *Beyond Scarcity: A New Story for American Capitalism* (New York: Simon & Schuster, 2003).

[71] Sandra Waddock, *Leading Corporate Citizens: Vision, Values and Value Added*, 2nd ed. (Boston: McGraw Hill-Irwin, 2006), pp. 77–166.

operations and marketed products globally. A new global structure, a patchwork of institutions, is emerging which will aid the firm. These institutions include treaties, codes, reports, and initiatives to educate and help all peoples, including the poor, to live a decent and better life and even to get a start in business.[72]

Summary and Conclusions

Fast and easy movement of information, goods, services, and people enables business to operate around the globe. To be competitive and grow a firm sells and operates overseas, and must reduce costs. A developing country seeks to attract jobs, investment, and technology. The market urges a firm to choose the country that offers it lower wage rates and one that will allow it to cheaply dump its trash. So we witness sweatshops and environmental pollution in the poorer countries of the world. In addition, if it has fluctuating currency, a country will attract speculators who are able to make millions of dollars in a quick exchange. Bribery and corruption of public officials is also a problem whenever large sums of money are in play. Seeking contracts and permits for operating in poorer countries often leads to payoffs of those officials by agents of global firms.

Business deals in developed countries are regulated by local legislation. Investors have long demanded transparency in financial reporting. European firms lead in also reporting environmental and social impact. TI annually ranks the nations of the world according to the level of perceived corruption in each country. In addition, several voluntary codes and reporting schemes have been developed to bring greater transparency and justice to global business. The CRT *Principles for Business* were written by an international group of business executives. The *UN Global Compact with Business* focuses on workers' and environmental issues. The GRI enables a firm to report on their "triple bottom line" performance: environmental, social, and financial.

The above initiatives are voluntary, so some wonder if they are effective. Voluntary actions place costs on ethical firms, while unethical firms or "free riders" are able to save money in the short term at the expense of the health, safety, and lives of people. In Chapter 5 we saw this in the United States, prior to legislation on wages, hours, safety, and the environment. International standards would provide a level playing field. Would a global minimum wage, global safety regulations, and environmental standards be effective and accepted? Many MNCs have annual sales larger than the gross domestic products of most nations. Thus the global corporation is in a dominant position to influence national and global policies.

Most business executives realize that it is neither just nor wise to place their costs on future generations. This is true in the use of resources, pollution of earth, air, and water, and global climate change. Many Native Americans planned considering

---

[72] Archie B. Carroll, "Managing Ethically With Global Stakeholders: A Present and Future Challenge," *Academy of Management Executive,* 18, no. 2 (2004): 114–120; see the several examples of successful business initiatives from four continents in Maria Cecilia Arruda and Georges Enderle, eds. *Improving Globalization* (Rio de Janiero, Brazil: International Society of Business, Economics and Ethics—ISBEE, 2004).

the seventh generation in the future. A question we might ask: Will my descendants be better off and thank me for having considered them? Or am I leaving them with fewer natural resources and greater pollution than I inherited?

Discussion Questions

1. Describe how communication and transportation have enabled global business to thrive. In what way is this ethically good? What are the ethical problems?
2. In what way are international businesses good corporate citizens? How are some global firms not good citizens?
3. Describe how the free market encourages sweatshops. What are the advantages of sweatshops to purchasers of goods? What are the problems of sweatshops? Are sweatshops just?
4. How have students and other purchasers had influence on the conditions under which products are made in developing countries?
5. Describe how global climate change is a danger to the world. Why do you think that some U.S. firms possess more enlightened policies on carbon dioxide emissions than other firms or the U.S. Government?
6. Do you agree with economist Lawrence Summer's comments at the beginning of this chapter that poor countries are a good place to dump toxic waste? Does this position follow from the economic model?
7. What does Edward Luttwak mean by "turbo-capitalism"? What is the difference between global investment and speculation? What is the danger of speculation?
8. What sort of bribery is outlawed by the U.S. Foreign Corrupt Practices Act and the OECD Guidelines? What is "crony capitalism"? Are bribery and crony capitalism unjust? Why?
9. What is Transparency International (TI)? What is TI's principal method? (see TI's Web site: http://www.transparency.org/). Why do you think some countries are more corrupt than others? Why is the United States only twentieth on the 2007 list? Other things being equal, would you prefer to invest in a country that is less corrupt? Why?
10. Outline the overall contributions and the overall costs of global firms.
11. Roughly how many of the world's people live in poverty? What are the results of living in poverty?
12. What is the significance of the data on the gap in income between the rich and the poor? Could this lead to instability or war—within a nation and in the world? Why?
13. What did Muhammad Yunus and Grameen Bank do to help the poor? Why do they loan largely to women? How does CEMEX's initiative help the poor and the firm?
14. How do U.S. military expenditures compare with the amount of development assistance to poor nations? Could development assistance make the world safer? Would shifting a portion of the U.S. military budget to aid for clean water, education, health, and combating malnutrition for people in poor nations be a good investment in peace?
15. Describe how subsidies to agriculture in the United States, Japan, and Europe are unfair to farmers in poor countries?
16. Where does the United States stand, relative to other developed nations, on the amount of development assistance contributed? Why is this the case? What is the difference between "soft power" and "hard power"?
17. What are the advantages and disadvantages of the Caux Round Table *Principles for Business*?
18. What are the advantages and disadvantages of the *UN Global Compact*? What does it require to join? What sort of annual report does it require?

19. What are the advantages and disadvantages of the *GRI*? Describe the report that the GRI requires.
20. Why is American business more willing to submit to a treaty ensuring fair competition under NAFTA than to ensure global fair working conditions or lowering toxic pollution?
21. Why do you think that the above codes and reports are more popular in Europe than in the United States? What sort of future business environment will the codes and reports bring?
22. How effective are international bodies in developing binding treaties to regulate global business? What are the advantages and disadvantages of voluntary international codes and reports?
23. What are the advantages of international treaties and regulations? Are global binding treaties a feasible way to regulate global business? Would global minimum wage, safety regulations, and environmental standards be effective and accepted?
24. Why is it becoming more difficult for one nation to make decisions for other nations? Are there limits to economic and political power?
25. Describe how the people of the world are now more dependent upon each other. How does American individualism contribute to understanding this interdependence?
26. Will my descendants be better off because of how I have used the earth? Or am I leaving the earth with fewer natural resources and greater pollution than what I inherited?
27. What personal lifestyles will enable us to pass on a more healthy earth to future generations?

Selected Additional Readings

Benjamin R. Barber, *Jihad vs. McWorld* (New York: Ballantime Books, 1996).

Lester R. Brown, *Plan B 3.0: Rescuing a Planet Under Stress and a Civilization in Trouble* (New York: W. W. Norton, 2008).

Vincent A. Gallagher, *The True Cost of Low Prices: The Violence of Globalization* (Maryknoll, NY: Orbis, 2006).

Bradley K. Goggins, Philip H. Mirvis, and Steven A. Rochlin, *Beyond Good Company: Next Generation Corporate Citizenship* (New York: Palgrave Macmillan, 2007), pp. 183–187.

George Soros, *The Crisis of Global Capitalism: Open Society Endangered* (New York: Public Affairs, 1998).

Sandra Waddock, *Leading Corporate Citizens: Vision, Values and Value Added*, 2nd ed. (Boston: McGraw Hill-Irwin, 2006).

Muhammad Yunus, *Creating a World Without Poverty: Social Business and the Future of Capitalism* (New York: Public Affairs, 2007).

CASES

Case 9-1   Employing Untouchables in India

Dalits in India, also known as "untouchables," have historically been condemned to low status, dirty jobs, and little income. Dalits comprise about 16 percent of India's population, but of India's middle class of 300,000,000, they comprise only 100,000 (0.003%). Foreign firms are less concerned about the origins of their workers, so globalization is having a positive effect on the employability of Dalits.

1. Should U.S. firms adapt the customs of India and not employ Dalits? Why or why not?
2. Or, on the other hand, do U.S. firms have a special obligation to seek Dalits to hire? Why?
3. What ethical norm helps most in dealing with this issue?

■ ■ ■

Case 9-2   Selling "Small Lies" in China

A new service is being offered in China. A firm sells small or "white lies" to support interpersonal relations, and charges only about $10.00 each. A man who had just taken a new job hired the firm to call his parents, pretend he was the man's supervisor, and tell his concerned parents that he was doing an excellent job. The firm could also be hired to offer excuses for extramarital affairs. Defenders of the firm say that it is intended to preserve personal and family relations. Others say it is not ethical.

1. What is a "white lie"? Should interpersonal relations be preserved by means of white lies?
2. Should all statements be truthful? Are there any reasons that would lead one to not tell the truth?
3. Is the firm an ethical business? What ethical norm is most helpful here?

■ ■ ■

Case 9-3   Merck and River Blindness

Merck developed a drug for killing parasites in domestic animals. River blindness among people in Equatorial Africa is caused by a larvae deposited by the bite of a fly, and the larvae grows and moves through the human body until it causes blindness. After years of testing, Merck found that a variation of the drug would kill the larvae, if it is taken once a year. The WHO agreed to deliver and administer the drug; however, the people who need the drug have no money to purchase it. Merck was not successful in their efforts to persuade world organizations, foundations, or U.S. foreign aid to purchase it for these poor people. If Merck gave the drug away, it could not recoup its research or even its production costs.[73]

1. What would you recommend to Merck management? Do you think that Merck management should give it away? Would it be fair to shareholders to give it away?
2. What ethical status would you give the poor Africans who suffer from the disease: Do they deserve the drug?
3. What ethical norms are of most help here?

■ ■ ■

---

[73] David Bollier, "Quandaries in Developing a Wonder Drug for the Third World," in *Aiming Higher: 25 Stories of How Companies Prosper by Combining Sound Management and Social Vision* (New York: American Management Association, 1996), pp. 280–293. Merck's $789 million is the second largest of U.S. firm's annual contributions to charities; see "How Companies Hand It Out," *BusinessWeek*, November 29, 2004, pp. 86–104.

Case 9-4   Made in the United States or Asia

Hutchinson Technology makes more than half of the suspension assemblies for computer disk drives. Asian firms purchase 98 percent of its assemblies, but it resists pressure to move manufacturing from Minnesota and Wisconsin to China. Hutchinson requires precision manufacturing and these skills are scarce. It can also more easily introduce labor-saving equipment in the United States. Moreover, Hutchinson also fears that having a facility in China would make it easier for competitors to steal their manufacturing trade secrets.[74]

1. Is Hutchinson recognizing globalization or is it being nationalistic?
2. Is the firm's lack of trust of China a lack of respect for them?
3. What ethical norms are most useful here?

---

[74] Timothy Aeppel, "Still Made in the U.S.A.," *The Wall Street Journal*, July 8, 2004, p. B1.

10

■ ■ ■

Future Business Values and Sustainability

The change is fast and fierce, replete with opportunities and dangers. The issue is: do we shape it or does it shape us? Do we master it, or do we let it overwhelm us?[1]

TONY BLAIR, FORMER PRIME MINISTER, UNITED KINGDOM, 1997–2007

Given existing technology and products, for all six billion people on the planet to live like the average American, we would require the equivalent of three planet Earths to provide the material, create the energy and dispose of the waste.

CHARLES O. HOLLIDAY, JR., CHAIRMAN AND CEO, DUPONT

Failing to plan is planning to fail.

BENJAMIN FRANKLIN (1706–1790), U.S. STATESMAN

We do not see the poor of the world's faces, we do not know their names, we cannot count their number. But they are there. And their lives have been touched by us. And ours by them.

ROBERT S. MCNAMARA, CONCLUSION OF HIS LAST
ADDRESS AS PRESIDENT OF THE WORLD BANK

---

[1] Tony Blair, "Traditional Values for the Digital Age," *The Responsible Community*, Fall 2000, p. 53.

The sobering fact is that globalization without direction will ruin our world for future generations, as the CEO of DuPont indicates above. The complexities of globalization, coupled with the need to leave behind a world in as good shape as the one we found (called **sustainability**), will dominate strategies and actions of business and government leaders in the coming decades. Business leaders may yet help to provide prosperity to billions of people, and still preserve resources and the globe. But the result is by no means certain. Markets and globalization guided only by Adam Smith's "invisible hand" may bring short-term riches to a few, but will be a failure for all in the long term.[2]

The purpose of business is to serve the needs of people by efficiently providing products, services, jobs, and also family income. Increasing profits is a measure of the financial success of the firm. Financial success is necessary, but it is not the exclusive or even the principal goal. The purpose of business, as with most human endeavors, is the welfare of people. Moreover, we share this small planet with many other people (and also animals, plants, and oceans). As intelligent human beings, we would leave the earth's environment and resources intact for future generations. This is the foundation for both successful business and government planning for a healthy society.[3] Nevertheless, many business executives are worried that some business and government leaders do not possess sufficient imagination and innovative skills to deal with vital new issues that will affect future markets, products, services, workers, and society.[4]

Planning for the future is essential for the success of any business. Planning in turn is based on projections of what to expect in the coming years, coupled with the organization's mission and capabilities. Corporate planning seeks markets for new products and requires sensitivity to the expectations of a firm's various stakeholders. But note that both peoples' expectations and demand for products depend upon people's values. Thus, being alert to changing personal values and what is happening on our globe enables a firm to formulate better business plans. This chapter probes current values, examines why having a clear business mission is essential, investigates future scanning, and projects business values over the coming decades.

TODAY'S BUSINESS VALUES

How the values of businesspeople develop and how those values influence business practices have been examined in previous chapters. However, business is not an isolated institution. It operates in a society and is influenced by cultural values,

---

[2] See the report, *Raising Our Game: Can We Sustain Globalization,* by SustainAbility (June 2007). The Report was funded by Shell, Ford, Novo Nordisk, Vodafone, and the Skoll Foundation. See www. GreenBiz.com. The Report is also summarized at the World Business Council for Sustainable Development www.wbcsd.org.

[3] See S. A. Cortright and Michael J. Naughton, eds., *Rethinking the Purpose of Business* (Notre Dame, IN: Notre Dame Press, 2003).

[4] See *Tomorrow's Global Company: A Future for Business which Makes Equal Sense to Staff, Shareholders and Society*, at http://www.tomorrowscompany.com/, accessed June 12, 2008.

government regulation, and global priorities. Government's role is to ensure that all citizens have opportunity and are treated justly. Government regulates business in order to achieve this common good.

Free enterprise is the most productive, efficient, flexible, and innovative economic system ever devised. But free markets do not in themselves provide some goods, such as clean water, safe drugs, and less greenhouse gas emissions—which may be costly to business. How extensive government regulation should be—and when business is not regulated, how much an individual firm should work for the common good when it is costly to do so—is disputed. Some managers of an earlier generation maintain that each firm should exclusively pursue its own profit. These proponents of free enterprise say that efficient markets and lower price goods make people better off, regardless of the costs to others. On the other hand, most managers today hold that a responsible business will explicitly consider the **well-being of others**. This consensus helps us when we examine business and global challenges before us.

Free Markets Rule

Almost all countries today have some form of free market economy. Russia, Eastern Europe, and China now benefit from free market innovation and efficiencies.[5] When asked "How will life be for the next generation?" people in China and Russia say that it will be better. On the other hand, citizens of the United States, United Kingdom, France, and Germany think life will be worse.[6] Global markets provide both benefits and costs to people in every country. If a firm anywhere in the world is able to produce high-quality goods at low cost, that firm can be a success. We also know that efficiencies and loyalty come to firms in which people deal with each other honestly and justly.

Government supplies services that a market does not provide. Free markets do not provide street lights, police protection, and clean air. Without government regulation, free markets encourage firms to lower costs by using cheap minerals and fuels wastefully and dumping toxic trash in local streams. Free markets do provide goods, services, jobs, and wealth. But two opposing models of free enterprise compete as means to achieve the healthiest market. Promoting supply side economics to achieve wealth were U.S. presidents Harding, Coolidge, Hoover, Reagan, and George W. Bush. They urge a free market with few regulations from which they claimed all will benefit, even if it results in great disparity of income, wasteful use of resources, and pollution. This position has been called a *Gospel of Wealth*. The other view is that all people deserve access to the basics of life, including food, housing, and a job, and this view was promoted by U.S. presidents Lincoln, Wilson, Roosevelt, Kennedy, Clinton and Obama and has been called the *American Dream*. But evidence shows that the Gospel of Wealth approach is not as effective in providing overall wealth. That is, the

---

[5] Jared Diamond, "The Wealth of Nations," *Nature*, 429 (June 10, 2004): 616–617.
[6] Figures from Pew Global Attitudes Products, as cited in the online ethics newsletter, *Ethics Newsline*, September 10, 2007; at http://globalethics.Org/newsline/, accessed September 12, 2007.

economy is more prosperous with a demand side approach—providing basic education, health, and security for all people.[7] However, even with the American Dream, free markets are not democratic; some people have more votes than others.

Aristocratic Markets

Some claim that free markets are like a democracy. That is, each of us chooses goods and services with our dollars, and when we spend these dollars it is like voting in a democracy. We thus choose priorities for ourselves and for society. This is called *consumer sovereignty*, because consumers make policies as they make their purchases. However, consumer sovereignty is aristocratic rather than democratic. Wealthy people have more influence on the goods available and thus on a nation's priorities than do others. Some earn 100 times that of another, and as a result possess 100 times the economic "votes." The wealthy may spend their dollars on expensive jewelry, a yacht, a third huge house, or investing in an older city or education for the poor, but more likely the former than the latter. Thus Thomas Friedman says,

> Advocates of compassionate flatism need to educate consumers to the fact that their buying decisions and buying power are political. Every time you as a consumer make a decision, you are supporting a whole set of values. You are voting about the barriers and friction you want to preserve or eliminate."[8]

We say that becoming wealthy is a **reward for hard work**, but we also know that good luck—especially being born in an affluent country or to a well-off family—is more important. A child born to college-educated parents in the United States has many advantages over one born to poor parents in Bangladesh. Many people work harder than those who make 10 times more, yet find it difficult to pay for their rent or food.

Gospel of Wealth proponents urge using consumer sovereignty to set social goals; it distributes responsibility and does not require collective decisions. But then, who is responsible for solving the many problems that we have "voted for" with our dollars in past decades, such as the trade and federal deficit, air, water, and solid waste pollution, and the excessive use of fossil fuels and the greenhouse gases they produce? If we allow consumer sovereignty to set community goals, it leads to pollution, waste of resources, illness, and deaths, along with unplanned, cancerous, damaging growth. Consumer sovereignty is also a handy ideology for those who claim to be value-free, for it enables them to evade important questions about the common good. But consumer sovereignty is not value-free. It fosters short-term thinking, avoids important issues, chooses the individual over the group, and

---

[7] For a fuller discussion and supporting research, see Norton Garfinkle, *The American Dream vs. the Gospel of Wealth: The Fight for a Productive Middle-Class Economy* (New Haven: Yale University Press, 2006).

[8] Thomas L. Friedman, *The World is Flat* (New York: Farrar, Straus and Giroux, 2005), p. 301.

promotes narrow-minded divisiveness and stalemates, as special interest groups determine policy.

Reliance on free enterprise to choose society's priorities enables us to dodge the difficult process of choosing what kind of society we want. That is, we avoid tough questions until crises are upon us, flexibility is gone, and options have been narrowed. For example, decades ago we waited until Lake Erie died before we realized the cost of water pollution. The nuclear power plant disasters at Three Mile Island and Chernobyl had to take place before we acknowledged the dangers and full cost of nuclear power. It took the collapse of Enron and WorldCom and the housing and credit crisis to alert us to the need for new regulations to bring about better financial accountability and corporate governance. We now know about melting glaciers, warming seas, and spreading deserts, yet we wait for disasters to hit us before we take action to cut carbon dioxide emissions to avoid global climate change. We **wait for crises** before we take action.

Free enterprise gives large financial rewards to those who possess capital—that is, those who are already wealthy. We call them investors, but few of their dollars go to innovation and new businesses. They often receive better financial returns through speculation; it generates "income detached from productivity."[9] Furthering the inequity is the imbalance in the distribution of American incomes. The incomes of the 3 million Americans at the top are equal to that of 166 million Americans at the bottom. Or from another angle, the *increase* in income of the wealthy top 1 percent from 2003 to 2005 was greater than the *total* income of the poorest 20 percent of Americans.[10] Free enterprise encourages satisfaction of self and selfishness. Free markets and competition—guided by the "invisible hand"—result in the efficient and profitable use of capital. In addition, it provides an ideology that promotes and blesses self-seeking, self-centered behavior.

Capitalism in the United States was built on self-interest and rugged individualism. In the nineteenth century, huge fortunes were amassed before social legislation was enacted. Thousands of workers and small businesspeople were killed and injured in the businesses of John D. Rockefeller, Andrew Carnegie, and J. P. Morgan. By contrast, later in life these men used their wealth to benefit the public. Andrew Carnegie's defense of large fortunes was based on his claim that rich people can better use the wealth created by industry for public purposes (see Chapter 5). Carnegie funded libraries across the United States, and Collis P. Huntington built a rail-based rapid transit system for Los Angeles (which was torn up in the 1950s by a combine of GM, Firestone, Phillips Petroleum, and Standard Oil of California). John D. Rockefeller built the University of Chicago. Foundations were set up by wealthy men such as Carnegie, Rockefeller, and Ford to serve the public, and these foundations have continued to finance valuable social programs. Bill Hewlett and David Packard used their wealth to fund education and the arts.

---

[9] Marjorie Kelly, *The Divine Right of Capital: Dethroning the Corporate Aristocracy* (San Francisco: Berrett-Koehler, 2003).

[10] David Kay Johnston, "Report Says the Rich Are Getting Richer Faster, Much Faster," *The New York Times*, December 15, 2007, p. B3.

Warren Buffet and Bill Gates' father both endorse a steep **inheritance tax**. Buffet says that his children should not and will not inherit his wealth. Gates, Sr. maintains that the wealthy should pay a larger portion of their income in taxes. According to both men, everyone should have the ability to earn their own million dollars, and we should not establish an inherited moneyed aristocracy. When the wealthy pay a larger portion of their income in tax, it supports American democratic values; progressive taxes protect American democracy against the massing of excessive power by the very wealthy.[11] Buffett and Gates both also argue that inherited wealth establishes an aristocracy whose members oppose many democratic values. Showing that they are true to their convictions, both Buffet and Bill Gates have contributed most of their immense fortunes to support health care and education for the impoverished—especially in poor countries. Will billionaires Larry Ellison, Sandy Weil, Michael Eisner, Donald Trump, and the five Wal-Mart Walton heirs (who are among the wealthiest 11 Americans) use their wealth to help other people?

Special Interests Threaten Democracy

Planning is essential for both business and government. However, during the past three decades we have not planned well for the United States or its citizens. Suburbs sprawl haphazardly, paving over farmland that a generation ago provided food and might have been set aside as parks or rapid transit right-of-ways. Many suburban housing tracts do not have sidewalks for children, elderly, walking, and bicycles. Fewer libraries, museums, or parks are established, and those that exist are poorly maintained. Vision and planning are required to wisely use our resources and to make cities and neighborhoods livable. Such vision is lacking today. Instead we champion gross economic growth: building businesses, offices, and new homes. Meanwhile, older cities lose population and crumble, as do our public transit facilities, railroads, libraries, and parks. We waste our wealth and the community gets poorer, as individuals pursue their own self-interest.

On major public issues Americans are committed to an open system and to consensus. However, it normally takes a catastrophe to alert us to failing national practices. Millions of birds died from pesticides before we learned how we were poisoning them.[12] It took urban riots to force us to deal with racial and job discrimination. Add to this the death of Lake Erie, the nuclear disaster at Chernobyl, the barely averted nuclear disaster at Three Mile Island (PA), and the invasion of Iraq. Many Americans distrust government, and lack of trust makes it difficult to plan and implement national policies for the common good. Moreover, when George W. Bush appointed heads of federal agencies who do not believe that the agency is useful, such as Bush did at Federal Emergency Management, Securities and Exchange Commission, or Environmental Protection Agency, it reinforces the notion that government is inept and useless. Perhaps we must lose our glaciers, submerge

---

[11] William Gates, Sr. and Chuck Collins, *Wealth and Our Commonwealth: Why America Should Tax Accumulated Fortunes* (Boston: Beacon Press, 2003).
[12] Rachel Carson, *Silent Spring* (Boston: Houghton Mifflin, 1962).

coastal areas and pacific islands, and suffer more loss of life from hurricanes and expanding deserts before we reduce greenhouse gas emissions.

A democracy often **requires a crisis** to awaken its citizens to new needs. Moreover, citizens must personally feel that need. Thus long-range planning for a city, a nation, or the globe is difficult. Compounding the problem, legislators feel pressure to please those who contribute money to their election campaigns. Attempts to regulate campaign spending have been thwarted. The 2008 presidential election has doubled in cost over eight years to $1.0 billion. Most of this money comes from people who demand to be heard when legislation that touches them is considered.

A few firms, at some risk to their relations to the incumbent government, refuse to make any political "contributions," because they see them as a form of **bribery**. British Petroleum announced its decision saying that "We'll engage in policy debate, stating our views and encouraging the development of ideas, but we won't fund any political activity or political party."[13] Major contributors expect favors in return. So legislators are pressured to yield to the pet projects of special interests, lobbyists, and felt needs back home, and thus do not to invest in projects that will pay off for the nation a generation from now. Yet policies and actions to support renewable energy, public transportation, or the globe itself are precisely such a tradeoff. Moreover, many of the social problems we face require long-term solutions, for example, broken families, failing public schools, urban decay, pollution, dwindling resources, and distrust among nations. When a crisis erupts before most have grasped the problem, there is little time to find a solution. This may be the most serious flaw of democracy.

Lack of Goals

In a survey some years ago young people were critical of the seeming lack of beliefs and convictions of their elders. Their elders' values, they said, seemed to be absorbed passively from the surrounding culture; they had few thought-out, internalized goals and values. Many of us are victims of mass education, entertainment, and fashion. Mass education affects our thinking, and entertainment influences values through the clothes, food, video games, and TV programs that are cool. Mass education **substitutes fads** for critical thinking. We escape thinking by turning on the iPod, cell phone, or TV. Peoples' character is bent by being pounded for decades by violence and sex, and we expect quick solutions to every problem. We are then surprised when people in other countries dislike American values and culture, based on our TV and films. When traveling abroad, we are often asked, "Are Americans really as violent, sexually deviant and selfish as we see on your TV and film?"

Cynicism, confusion, and apathy can challenge us to probe our own values, goals, and ethics. It is especially important that we know our own goals in a period of rapid change. Otherwise, we have little direction and are tossed by events from one problem to another; then we are not in control of our own lives and careers.

---

[13] "BP Will No Longer Make Any Political Donations," *The Wall Street Journal,* March 1, 2002, p. B4.

Challenges and crises regularly arise, and individuals who do not know who they are, what they do, and why they do it are less able to deal with events. They are more easily confused, frustrated, and hurt.

Democratic capitalism is an alternative to **financial capitalism**, with cooperation in the workplace, worker ownership, and humble, self-effacing executives.[14] If we are concerned about the well-being of the next generation, we will be innovative enough to assemble the imagination and talent to craft solutions. Minds are like parachutes: They only work when they are open. People of all great civilizations are steeped in knowledge of other times and places, but many universities have virtually stopped conveying a tradition. Because we do not learn other cultures and languages, we become a pragmatic, unreflective people, who rarely examine the most important questions in life, such as Where am I going? What kind of person do I want to be?

Core Beliefs

People who know their own values and goals tend to have greater self-esteem, and thus are better able to work with others. Hence both individuals and organizations benefit when we probe our goals and values, and respond to such questions as the following:

- What is my fundamental goal in life?
- Generally are men and women more self-seeking or are they more good and generous?
- Are my own goals focused on myself, my family, or a larger community?
- Do I have a spiritual end, or is this present life with its money, pleasures, and material satisfactions all there is?
- Are there moral goods and evils, such as murder or slavery, or is everything relative?
- Are human beings moving toward long-term progress? Or toward decline and perhaps collapse?

The responses to such questions affect the actions of persons, organizations, and governments.

If you reflect on such questions, and answer them, you will learn about yourself. This complements the findings of the "Personal Goals and Values" paper from Chapter 1. Your answers to these questions may show that you are concerned about others and are sometimes willing to sacrifice for their sake. On the other hand, your responses may show that you are focused on yourself and that you view other people as means to attain your own goals. For another perspective, if you were considering a potential spouse, what **responses would you prefer** from that person? If you were hiring someone, which attitudes would incline you to consider that person as a future employee?

When you are choosing a job, what sort of a firm would you prefer—a firm where workers are more focused on themselves and their own careers, or a firm

---

[14] Ray Carey, who was CEO of ADT, makes a cogent argument in his *Democratic Capitalism: The Way to a World of Peace and* Prosperity (Bloomington, IN: AuthorHouse, 2004).

where people are more sensitive to others? In which sort of firm are you likely to do better work and be happier? In which would you likely be more successful?

A nationwide study of business firms that far outperformed peers in their industry examined their top leadership. They found that they were led by CEOs who were not motivated by compensation. The study "found no systematic pattern linking executive compensation to the process of going from good to great." The best performing firms did not have the highest paid executives. Nevertheless, these executives elicited the best from all the people they worked with. They did not come up with the solutions and give directions, but rather "**led with questions, not answers.**" Moreover, these executives were not motivated by pay, but, in a surprise to the investigators, demonstrated "a compelling **modesty**, shunning public adulation; were never boastful."[15]

Business firms often provide ethics education that stresses practical skills. This helps, but it does not go far enough. A firm's ethics training usually does not stress self-assessment and critical thinking such as we have here, yet this is essential to achieve personal maturity and moral development.

A WORKABLE BUSINESS CREED

The most salient and precious American business value is **freedom**: free markets, free competition, free movement of people and capital, and most especially freedom of the individual. But important as personal freedom is in American society, it is not unlimited. An individual's freedom that is not conscious of other people leads to mistrust, inefficiencies, and ultimately chaos. One does not have the freedom to shout "Fire!" in a crowded theater. Traffic lights are restrictions to which libertarians objected. A business firm does not have the freedom to mislead in its product advertising or to dump its waste in a lake. As people live closer together and are more dependent on one another, **freedom is limited** by both self-control and external checks. It is a paradox that freedom is possible only when people have developed internal constraints; then one may act with freedom knowing that one can trust that others will also act responsibly. Although individualists find it hard to understand, limitations based on a consideration for others (e.g., driving on the right side of the road or truth-in-advertising laws) bring greater freedom for all. People have less fear and greater trust in the safety of driving and in what is claimed for a product, and thus they can act more freely. So freedom is thus undermined if a society's shared values are not strong enough to maintain the moral cohesion on which the discipline of free people rests.

One of the strengths of American business has been its **pragmatism**—getting the job done while avoiding ideological arguments. The ideology of American business is its ability to perform: to provide more goods to more people. A disadvantage of pragmatism is that it leads to actions simply because they work in spite of undesirable by-products and inequities.

---

[15] Jim Collins, *Good to Great: Why Some Companies Make the Leap and Others Don't* (New York: HarperCollins, 2001), pp. 36, 49, 64, 74.

A defense of free enterprise thus cannot rest primarily on the values of freedom and efficiency, because then the questions arise: Freedom for what? Efficiency for what? Freedom, efficiency, and the business system they support are not goals in themselves, but are rather means that allow people to pursue more important goals. Greater freedom and productivity enables us to provide more goods, services, and jobs with less effort, thus allowing people to pursue other goals. Then each person is free to determine what those goals are for themselves and for their society.

Problems for the Future

Some of the problems that now hinder business in the United States have a potential for creating even more trouble in the future. The United States had a trade deficit of $711 billion in 2007; we purchased that many more goods and services than we sold overseas. Compounding the problem, we must borrow from overseas to buy these goods and services. The largest single item we purchase from other countries is petroleum. The United States was once the largest petroleum producer in the world, but we use so much that it was quickly depleted. We now purchase almost two-thirds of our petroleum from overseas at a cost of more than $130 billion annually. Thus, we are on the slippery slope of borrowing foreign money to purchase foreign goods, and so at the same time increasing our foreign debt. We are also placing the immense costs of the Iraq war on future generations. The United States was the largest creditor nation in the world until 1985. We financed many activities beyond our borders and received interest on those loans. Currently we are the largest debtor nation in the world; we now borrow more capital from other nations than any other country. This increases the cost of investment capital for entrepreneurs in the United States. Having a large foreign debt is characteristic of poor nations, who must borrow capital from wealthier nations to pay for their development programs.

In addition to the balance of trade deficit, the United States federal government had a budget deficit in 2006 of $248 billion. That brought the accumulated federal debt to $9.2 trillion.[16] The annual interest on that debt is $500 billion. To get a better idea of what is owed, consider that it amounts to $26,000 for every man, woman, and child in the United States, and that to pay the interest on it costs each person about $1,600 per year. So a family of four pays $6,400 annually for which they have nothing to show. Much of the debt is owed to investors in Arab countries, Europe, and China. Another problem with the huge federal deficit is that soon a large group of boomers will begin to draw on social security and Medicare, and we will not have the dollars to fund what we have promised. Wouldn't it be wise to be **fiscally prudent** and save now so that we are able to meet our obligations? Are we willing to heed a call for sacrifice?

If we are not fiscally prudent now, how will this affect business in the future? To pay for the spending of this generation will require increased taxes on the next generation which will add to their cost of living and business. It thus adds costs when we must be competitive in world markets. Do trade and federal deficits also illustrate

---

[16] See the Congressional budget Office Web site: http://www.cbo.gov/, accessed July 1, 2008.

a current American value: Obtain goods today without paying full price, even if your children must pay later? Ted Turner, founder of CNN and other TV networks, illustrates our spending habits: "In the United States we have 2.5 percent of the children of the world, but we spend 60 percent of all that is spent in the world on toys."[17]

A Clear Mission Brings Success

Firms that have a clear and motivating mission statement tend to outperform their rivals in the marketplace. Put another way, the most successful and profitable firms have a much clearer vision than their competitors. The best companies in a field have a vision that is expressed in their mission statement and acted upon by the people in the organization.[18] The firms examined are well established and highly successful, and they include 3M, American Express, Citigroup, General Electric (GE), Hewlett-Packard (H-P), IBM, Johnson & Johnson, Marriott, Motorola, Nordstrom, Procter & Gamble, Sony, Wal-Mart, and Walt Disney. Each of these companies was founded before 1950, is premier in its industry, is widely admired by businesspeople, and has made an indelible imprint on the world in which we live. Their stock has **outperformed** the market by a factor of more than 12. Moreover, from the standpoint of people who work there, they find more satisfaction with their jobs, *if* they agree with the vision.

Each of these visionary companies "more thoroughly indoctrinate employees into a core ideology than do comparison companies," and more carefully nurture and select senior management. Visionary companies selected their chief executives from inside the company in 96.5 percent of the cases, while comparison companies selected their chief executives from inside in only 78 percent of the cases. An organization's mission statement reflects the core goals and values of those who formulate the statement. The Johnson & Johnson credo (see Figure 8-3) reflects J&J's core values over 50 years. In the CEO's words, it is "the glue that holds the organization together."

The mission statements of the above firms are unique, but they all stress the importance of integrity, respect for the individual employee, service to the customer, and responsibility to the community. It is also likely that the **firm's actions are consistent** with what it claims in its mission statement.[19] They have higher ethical and spiritual ideals, and the resulting culture attracts like-spirited people to the organization. It is essential that all in the organization buy into the mission. Finally, these organizations were able to institutionalize those values so that they remained after the retirement of those who created them.[20]

Excellent business mission statements have been gathered and analyzed along with historical background on the company and the statements. The firms included are General Mills, Georgia-Pacific, Gillette, Hallmark, Honda, IBM, Johnson &

---

[17] Ted Turner's address at the University of Detroit, November 25, 1985.

[18] James C. Collins and Jerry I. Porras, *Built to Last: Successful Habits of Visionary Companies* (New York: Harper Business, 1994).

[19] *Ibid.*, p. 87.

[20] Burt Nanus stresses the importance of discussing the mission statement with the entire group in his "Leading the Vision Team," *The Futurist,* May–June 1996, pp. 21–23.

Johnson, Kellogg, Merck, Motorola, Saturn, Southwest Airlines, and many more. The missions articulate a vision for the firm, and speak of values, a credo, and that customers and employees are treated with respect.[21]

Spirituality and Religion

Problems that we face globally cannot be solved by rational solutions alone. Consider, for example, terrorism, widening gap between the rich and the poor, the dangers of famine, global climate change, and depletion of nonrenewable resources, AIDS, and the shallowness of news and entertainment. To supplement rational insights, some leaders have re-introduced the wisdom of various **religious traditions** to help find solutions to these problems.[22] Historically, religion had much influence in the marketplace, and it remains influential in most cultures today. Medieval Europeans planned their cities with their cathedral on a hill in the center of the city. They expected the church to set standards for fair trade, bring disputants together to resolve disagreements, and finally to ensure that the interests of the poor and the disadvantaged were not forgotten. Such an active role of religion was not limited to medieval Europe. For Native Americans religion was a principal integrating force in the lives of both Mayan and Aztec peoples; their religious temples were the largest and most visible buildings in their cities. Also note the major function of religion in the Middle East, Africa, Latin America, and India.

The Enlightenment at the beginning of the 1800s influenced modern Western countries. The legitimacy of the state and other institutions were reformulated on non-religious principles that all rational individuals could support. This avoids sectarian strife and bias. Thus the U.S. Constitution separated church and state, and religion became a private, personal matter. This separation of religion from business and public life had a profound effect on attitudes.

The civil rights movement in the United States was led by Rev. Martin Luther King, Jr., a Baptist minister. He preached "love for the oppressor" and espoused the nonviolent methods of Mahatma Gandhi (who won independence for India) to gain equal opportunity and social justice for blacks. Many of the most committed social activists are inspired by the Gospels. Gandhi's nonviolent approach to gaining India's independence from England was successful. As a Hindu he was inspired by the life of Christ, and is an inspiration to many around the world.

In Poland and other Eastern European countries, religious convictions moved people to overthrow communism. Many priests and sisters have defended the interests of the poor, and as a result have been murdered in Guatemala, El Salvador, Brazil, Bolivia, Chile, Nepal, and other African and Latin American countries. Their

---

[21] Patrick E. Murphy, *Eighty Exemplary Ethics Statements* (Notre Dame, IN: University of Notre Dame Press, 1997); Jeffrey Abrahams, *The Mission Statement Book: 301 Corporate Mission Statements from America's Top Companies* (Berkeley, CA: Ten Speed Press, 1996).

[22] Dominic Mele, "Religious Foundations of Business Ethics," in *The Accountable Corporation*, eds. Mark J. Epstein and Kirk O. Hanson, vol. 2 (Westport, CT: Praeger, 2006), pp. 11–45; also "In God's Name: Special Report on Religion and Public Life," *The Economist,* November 3, 2007, pp. 3–22; and Steward W. Herman, ed., *Spiritual Goods: Faith Traditions and the Practice of Business* (Bowling Green, OH: Philosophy Documentation Center, 2001).

inspiration comes from Jesus, His love for the poor, and His attempts to bring justice to those at the bottom of the socioeconomic ladder (Matt. 5:3; Luke 6:20). These Gospel-inspired leaders want the poor, ordinary citizen to have sufficient freedom to own land, to vote, and to be a self-respecting citizen, and the freedom to work and earn a fair day's pay. Often they thus oppose the establishment business and military leaders.

There has always been a strong streak of religion and **moralism** in American culture. Witness our condemnation of buying votes in government, the sexual infidelities of Rudy Giuliani and Bill Clinton, and the self-seeking activities of corporate executives such as Conrad Black, Martha Stewart, Dennis Kozlowski, and Michael Eisner. In the nineteenth century, the powerful antislavery (abolition) and antitrust (muckraking) movements were morally motivated and received their inspiration from the Gospels.

Muslim and Hindu fundamentalist groups in Asia, Africa, and the Middle East reject the shallow materialistic Western values that they see in U.S. films and TV. Westerners, influenced by the Enlightenment, have difficulty understanding the appeal of the fundamentalists. However, fundamentalist Muslims and Hindus share many attitudes with many westerners: hospitality, loyalty, family, and sexual modesty.

Spirituality at Work

Spirituality is sometimes now part of the workplace: It can help a person find equilibrium at work. This spirituality in the workplace generally welcomes people of every faith—including Muslims, Jews, and Hindus. In the wake of downsizing, working people feel more pressured and ask "Why do I feel so unfulfilled?" Medtronic, AT&T, Boeing, Ford, and Lotus have programs of prayer and reflection within the firm. Other firms hire "spiritual" consultants such as Thomas Chappell, Tom's of Maine founder; James Autry, former senior vice president of Meridith Magazine Group; poet David Whyte; and Terrance Deal, corporate culture scholar.[23]

Workplace spirituality builds upon traditions that include Thomas Merton and St. Augustine, and also includes New Age followers who find God everywhere. Some business executives gather regularly at prayer breakfasts and sponsor annual religious retreats to pray and discuss their faith, families, and firms. An annual conference on spirituality in business is also held.

The Protestant ethic has had a profound effect on business values; it emphasizes self-reliance and achievement (see Chapter 4). The root of this ideology is the theology of John Calvin, but it has evolved into a secular description of American

---

[23] David Miller, *God at Work: The History and Promise of the Faith at Work Movement* (New York: Oxford University Press, 2007); Jerry Biberman and Michael D. Whitty, eds., *At Work: Spirituality Matters* (Scranton: University of Scranton Press, 2007); Oliver F. Williams, ed., C.S.C., *Business, Religion and Spirituality* (Notre Dame, IN: University of Notre Dame Press, 2003); see also the excellent books by Christian business executives, James A. Autry, *Love and Profit: The Art of Caring Leadership* (New York: Avon Books, 1991); also Max DePree, *Leadership is an Art* (New York: Dell, 1989).

work attitudes. Another spirituality goes back even further in Christianity and provides another perspective; it is called the Catholic ethic:

> The Catholic ethic views the world through the lenses of family and forgiveness. The Protestant ethic views it through lenses of individualism and immutability. In the Catholic ethic, life in this world is a process, a journey, in which forgiveness is always possible. In the Protestant ethic, one's efforts to "succeed" may help in this world but have less influence in the next . . .
>
> The merciful culture of the Catholic ethic has many elements that make the sharing of resources natural and ordinary, and that temper hostility toward the needy, and these elements guide the daily decisions of those who are influenced by this ethic.[24]

By means of **prayerful reflection**, people better understand themselves and their work lives. They break down the walls in their lives, and better integrate their work life, their family life, and their religious faith.

It is no accident that 11 of the *100 Best Companies to Work for in America*[25] are located in two areas of the United States that are heavily influenced by religious values. The 100 firms are rated on pay and benefits, opportunities, pride in work, job security, openness and fairness, and camaraderie and friendliness. Minneapolis–St. Paul is home to Medtronic, General Mills, H.B. Fuller, 3M, and other firms with longstanding excellent records in social responsibility. The area is strongly Lutheran and Catholic and has long been a leader in the United States in business social responsibility. Western Michigan is home to Kellogg, Steelcase, Donnelly, and Herman Miller and is much influenced by the Calvinist Dutch Reformed Church.

PLANNING AND FORECASTING

Vision is essential and must precede **strategic planning** to achieve individual and company goals. This planning builds upon the future needs of people, the values of society, and global developments. So planning can be done only when one has an informed expectation of what will happen in the future. Much information is available from public sources, but also needed are **forecasts** of what public policy issues (see Chapters 1, 6, 8, and 9) will emerge in the future.

Organizing for the Future

A firm may ask in-house staff, a trade association, or a consultant to prepare materials for strategic planning. They obtain, analyze, and report information on **future trends**. Various sources of data, information, and techniques for gathering

---

[24] John E. Tropman, *The Catholic Ethic in American Society* (San Francisco: Jossey Bass, 1995), p. 99.
[25] Robert Levering and Milton Moskowitz, *100 Best Companies to Work for in America* (New York: Penguin, 1994).

information are available. Much information is readily available from public sources on food and agriculture trends, energy and environment, social and economic trends, transportation and communication, production in various industries, availability and price of resources, and perceptions with regard to what constitutes quality of life.[26] The advantages of planning with the required information are that it

1. enables the firm to design a business plan for the future,
2. reduces the possibility of unpleasant surprises,
3. enables the firm to focus on opportunities and get ahead of issues, and
4. enables the firm to engage in consensus building.[27]

Capital-intensive firms in stable industries (e.g., autos, metals) have more need of advance warning of future developments because of their large investment and lack of flexibility.[28] Firms that plan and are adaptable have more opportunity to quickly respond to new trends and opportunities. One way of obtaining educated estimates on forthcoming sociopolitical issues is to use the **Delphi technique**; Delphi is a structured method for arriving at a consensus of opinion among a panel of experts.

Trend Analysis

A second technique used by many firms is called **trend analysis**. Using this technique, certain critical issues are followed (e.g., global climate change, availability of energy, or a trained workforce) in an effort to determine the direction and speed of future developments. The CEO or a group of top managers may initially determine which issues will be followed. Or corporate staff might poll managers or scan media sources to determine which issues are emerging.

The **media** can provide early indications of new trends. Firms can obtain the results of periodic examinations of selected "opinion leaders" from, for example, *The New York Times, The Wall Street Journal*, or online sites. Either corporate staff or a consultant can do a brief summary of articles on the selected public policy issues—for example, instability in the Middle East or potential new government regulations. Over time, interest in a certain issue may increase, as measured by the number of column inches devoted to it in particular print media. This may indicate new opportunities for products, services, or strategies for the firm, new pressures on the firm, or potential government oversight. **Public issues scanning** provides an early warning system that can alert managers to future developments. The life insurance industry has engaged in trend analysis since 1970, and for them it is essential for their planning. GE has also been a leader in such forecasting for decades.[29]

---

[26] See Linda Starke, ed., *Vital Signs—2007–2008* (New York: W. W. Norton & Co., 2007); also *State of the World—2007* (New York: W. W. Norton & Co., 2007). These two reports are issued annually, so previous editions are also valuable.

[27] Burt Naus, "Visionary Leadership," *The Futurist*, September–October, 1992, pp. 20–25. For an excellent presentation of corporate planning in an ethical context, see LaRue T. Hosmer, *Strategic Management* (Englewood Cliffs, NJ: Prentice-Hall, 1982).

[28] John E. Fleming, "Public Issues Scanning," in *Research in Corporate Social Performance: A Research Annual*, ed. Lee E. Preston, vol. 3 (Greenwich, CT: JAI Press, 1981), pp. 155–173.

[29] Ben W. Heineman, Jr., "Avoiding Integrity Land Mines," *Harvard Business Review*, April, 2007; John Stoffels, *Strategic Issues Management: A Comprehensive Guide to Environmental Scanning* (Elmsford, NY: Pergamon, 1994).

Careers with a Future

Globalization, sustainability, electronic communication, and the increasing importance of knowledge and information are having a profound effect on jobs and employment. People can work from a computer workstation anywhere. In addition, more people are hired to do jobs part-time and on contract.

For developed countries to maintain jobs, imagination, innovation, and better productivity will be required. New jobs are in services: accounting, health care, education, hospitality, banking, insurance, transportation, and other services.[30] The need to provide renewable energy and sustainability will bring new jobs in wind and solar energy, fish farming, light rail, and environmental architecture. People must design, manufacture, and maintain the equipment used in manufacturing and services. The new demand for accountants stems largely from the additional financial responsibilities placed on firms following Enron and WorldCom by the Sarbanes–Oxley law. Health care and biotechnology demand skills in nursing, biochemistry, and molecular biology. Skills in energy conservation, laser technology, and hazardous waste disposal are also in demand. Engineering and business skills will continue to be important as work and society become more complex.

The importance of knowledge and innovation skills raises the demand for quality education. There will be less emphasis on rote learning in large groups and more encouragement of creativity and understanding among individuals and small groups. Universities will be more individually oriented, so as to better meet students' needs.

No matter what one's career, it is essential to constantly upgrade one's skills. To be employable in the future, one must learn as much as one can, never stop learning when one leaves school, and be **adaptable**. Business firms will assist this by encouraging lifelong learning and also providing portable health and pension benefits for its workers. The United States should also support more science and engineering research and education for future American innovation, productivity, and employment.[31]

FUTURE BUSINESS VALUES

American business and the values that support it have shifted over the years, as we have seen in earlier chapters. Changes continue at a rapid rate, so it is imperative that we understand the direction and the substance of those shifts.

In this final section of the book, we will review the changes that are taking place and assess their potential impact on American business. We identify emerging values that will significantly affect people and American business. Note that these emerging values stem from traditional American values; there are few sharp breaks (see Table 10-1). We will project by using data and expert opinion.

---

[30] Lindsey Gerdes, "The Best Places to Launch a Career," *BusinessWeek,* September 24, 2007, pp. 49–60.

[31] Thomas L. Friedman, *The World is Flat: A Brief History of the Twenty-first Century* (New York: Farrar, Straus and Giroux, 2005), pp. 239, 275, 284.

TABLE 10-1 Future Business Values

Future Business Values	Traditional American Values
Innovation and Technology	Growth and progress
Sustainable development	Responsible for children (and vulnerable)
Dignity of each person	Personal rights, helping neighbors
Global citizen with local control	Self-sufficiency and frontier
New measures of success	Concern for the community
Mission, vision, and hope	Optimism and openness

Innovation and Technology

New products and new business come from **research and development**, but cost cutting and short-term thinking result in less research. Global outsourcing requires that technology for manufacturing be "transferred" to low-cost countries in exchange for low-cost goods, which, in turn, bring lower prices and increased profits for some firms (Wal-Mart, Sears, and Target). Thus more capital investment is made in developing countries, and less in wealthy, consumer economies. This is a benefit to poor countries, but it results in less research and development in the United States. What does this mean for the cities, and the families living in them, where these investments were located during the last century?

As we transfer technology out, it is essential to increase U.S. innovation and technology capability. However, if we focus on lower priced industries (i.e., bigger firms operating with lower gross margins), the profits to fund research and development will not be available.[32] In addition, if the U.S. Government continues to spend most of its dollars on terrorism and defense, we will not be able to fund research and development programs that could benefit society. Nor will we have the funds to allocate to the education and health of poor children.

Innovation is the principal vehicle to increase business **productivity**. In the future, innovation and technology will continue to be a generator of business "progress."[33] However, the technology that is used reflects the values of those who choose it, and that technology has a profound influence on the values and life-styles of all who use it. The choice of large business firms and electrical power generation grids influences the hours we work and the way we live, even outside of work. Carbon-fueled transportation, asbestos insulation, and chlorofluorocarbon aerosol propellants are examples of choices whose costs we later learned were greater than

---

[32] Henry Mintzberg, *Managers Not MBAs: A Look at the Soft Practice of Managing and Management Development* (San Francisco: Berrett-Koehler, 2004); "Restorative Development: Economic Growth without Destruction" *The Futurist*, July–August, 2003, pp. 23–27.

[33] John Naisbitt, *Mind Set: Reset Your Thinking and See the Future* (New York: Collins, 2006), pp. 233–249; William Halal, Michael Kull, and Ann Leffmann, "Emerging Technologies: 2001–2003," in *Globalization and the Challenges of the New Century,* eds. Patrick O'Meara et al. (Bloomington, IN: Indiana University Press, 2000).

their benefits. The promotion of the automobile with a tax-supported freeway system rather than public rapid transportation is a choice that reflects a "triumph of individualistic over communal values."[34]

Telecommuting—doing work from a computer work station at home—will increase flexibility and freedom, but will decrease teamwork and the sense of community that is found at a central work site. Computers, and their ability to store data, also pose ethical questions of how these data are found and used. TransUnion, Experian, and Equifax hold credit records on each of us that can be obtained for a fee. This record is personal and sometimes wrong, yet it is used to make decisions for hiring and loans. The Internet has extraordinary advantages for swift, global communications. But it also gives marketers information on which Web sites you visit and what you buy, and allows hackers access to your personal, sensitive data. Thus outsiders obtain data that many would prefer remain private. Are there any limits to using this information to sell products? Research and development must be directed to support people over the next century, which leads to our next future value.

Sustainable Development

In the course of meeting people's needs, business firms will operate with greater respect for the **natural environment**. Pollution, scarcity and increasing price of resources, toxic by-products, and global climate change all influence the direction and pace of business growth. These physical constraints are more pressing, and citizens' expectations that firms live within those constraints are clearer.[35] Hazardous industrial waste is a problem; the cost of its transportation and disposal will increase. All of this places large costs on future businesses.[36]

Given the free market, is it surprising that West Africa has been the dumping ground for American and European toxic waste? Responsibly disposing of toxic waste is expensive, so it is cheaper to pay Morocco, Congo, or Niger to bury it on their land. For example, in 1988 American and European private waste disposal firms offered Guinea-Bissau $120 million annually to bury 15 million tons of toxic waste from tanneries and pharmaceutical companies. This is slightly less than the African country's gross national product (GNP) of $150 million. This practice created a furor in West Africa, with many people in these nations demanding that the contracts be repudiated.

We are now more aware of global environmental problems—given better information and communication. In contrast to the ***cowboy economy*** of the 1980s in which gross production and consumption measured success, the ***spaceship economy***

---

[34] John M. Staudenmaier, S.J., "Technology," in *A Companion to American Thought,* eds. Richard W. Fox and James T. Kloppenberg (Oxford: Blackwell, 1995).

[35] See Lester R. Brown, *Plan B 3.0: Mobilizing to Save Civilization* (New York: W. W. Norton, 2008); and "Reaping the Wind: GE's Energy Initiative Is a Case Study in Innovation Without Borders," *BusinessWeek,* October 11, 2004, pp. 201–202; and "How to Market a Groundbreaker: Ford Is Pitching its Gas-electric SUV to Techies, As Well As Greenies," *BusinessWeek,* October 18, 2004, pp. 104–106.

[36] Dennis A. Rondinelli and Ted London, "How Corporation and Environmental Groups Cooperate: Assessing Cross-sector Alliances and Collaborations," *Academy of Management Executive,* 17, no. 1 (2000): 61–71.

of the twenty-first century recognizes that all men and women live together on the same fragile planet. This planet has finite resources and a limited ability to cleanse itself. This raises a fundamental question: If your needs could be met with less use of new resources, less production, and less consumption, would not that economy be superior? To suggest this is economic heresy. However, if we can meet human needs with fewer resources, waste, and pollution, are we not better off? We know that unlimited consumption and production harms people and the environment, so consumption and production are not reasonable goals in themselves.[37]

This recasting of goals and the resulting new criteria for success require that we decide the products we want, the type of growth, and the costs and tradeoffs we are willing to accept. Such decisions require information, shared understandings, and building consensus, which is difficult in a fractured and polarized society. However, more people now purchase sustainably. Most prefer products that are labeled energy efficient; others are vegetarian. Forest products and fish, which are procured in an environmentally sustainable manner, can now receive an eco-sustainable label—by the Forest Stewardship Council and Marine Stewardship Council, respectively. Yet some resist this reformulation of goals and the new criteria for success. It is easier to allow the "free market" to determine which path we take, and this suits some peoples' personal short-term goals. It gives more influence to individual choices and less to community interests. And it also wastes resources, arable land, and human lives. Can it be a responsible policy?

As for work and home life, many prefer a simpler and less stressful day. For example, note transportation. In addition to the work day being longer, today more time is lost in driving to and from work, schools, church, and stores. In older neighborhoods one could walk to each; now many suburbs do not even have sidewalks upon which one could walk. This reliance on the automobile wastes time, petroleum, and minerals and generates pollution. Paradoxically, it ultimately consists in a loss of freedom and thus is not progress. Similarly, time is lost in filling out medical insurance forms and questionnaires and in listening to advertisements. Some urge that wherever there is a choice between making more money and **simplifying life**, the latter road should be taken.

Recall the comments of the Chairman and CEO of DuPont at the beginning of the chapter. A new series of cultural "thou shalt nots" may be required in the future. Humankind may not survive unless we limit our appetites (virtue of self-control), maintain a conscientious concern for others (virtue of justice), and develop a habitual inclination to conserve and preserve (virtue of prudence). These good habits are not easy to develop, but they are essential if we are to lessen terrorism, war, mass starvation, and eventual chaos.[38]

It is essential that we develop human and spiritual values that integrate our everyday life and business decision making. Developing countries, especially China

---

[37] Jared Diamond, *Collapse: How Societies Choose to Fall or Succeed* (New York: Viking, 2004); and John de Graaf, David Wann, and Thomas H. Naylor, *Affluenza: The All-Consuming Epidemic* (San Francisco: Berrett-Koehler, 2001).

[38] See supporting data, *Vital Signs 2007–2008*, ed. Linda Starke (New York: W. W. Norton, 2007); also *State of the World—2007: Our Urban Future*, ed. Linda Starke (New York: W. W. Norton, 2007).

and India, are also experiencing these dilemmas. Fortunately, India and most other nations still have their traditional religions and/or respect for family to support their concern for future generations. On this shrinking planet, economic and political planning must consider the welfare of future generations.[39]

There are numerous success stories—more in Europe and Japan than in the United States—of firms which plan, produce, and profit in a sustainable manner.[40] These new opportunities are having a major impact on business and peoples' lives. The successful manager is aware of these new challenges and will direct the firm's policies and actions to new needs. Future jobs, products, government policy, and personal values will be heavily influenced by the new opportunities in sustainable development.[41]

Dignity of Each Person

Respect for each individual person pervades American attitudes and life. Individualism is also increasing in China, India, Singapore, South Korea, Japan, and other Asian countries. The **dignity of each person provides the foundation** for human rights, democracy, the free market, and a system of just laws. The dignity of each person, coupled with the need for greater productivity, encourages people to learn and upgrade to new skills; it also supports collective bargaining for workers and flexibility in one's workday, workweek, and career. The dignity of the individual also supports the family as the source of social values; the workplace values of hard work, cooperation, and respect for others are bred in the family. Moreover, family values balance individualism.

Each person will develop skills, satisfaction, and maturity in a firm where their talents are challenged, coworkers communicate, and supervisors provide feedback on work. For a business firm to succeed, its workers must be committed to a quality product or service. Products and services will be tailored to individual consumer preferences; this results in more individualized products and smaller product runs.[42] The firm will enlist the efforts of all workers in pursuing its goals by communicating its mission, creating a cooperative climate, and rewarding individuals and groups that contribute to reaching its goals.[43]

---

[39] David Wheeler and Jane Thomson, "Business and Sustainability: Implications for Corporate Governance Theory and Practice," in *The Accountable Corporation: Corporate Governance*, eds. Marc J. Epstein and Kirk O. Hanson, vol. 1 (Westport, CT: Praeger, 2006), pp. 243–270; Mark P. Sharfman, Teresa M. Shaft, and Laszlo Tihanyi, "A Model of the Global and Institutional Antecedents of High-Level Corporate Environmental Performance," *Business and Society*, 43 (March 2004): 6–36.

[40] See dozens of cases involving global firms in Charles O. Holliday, Stephan Schmidheiny, and Phillip Watts, *Walking the Talk: The Business Case for Sustainable Development* (San Francisco: Berrett-Koehler, 2002).

[41] Marc J. Epstein, *Making Sustainability Work: Best Practices in Managing and Measuring Corporate Social, Environmental and Economic Impacts* (San Francisco: Berrett-Koehler, 2008); Dexter Murphy et al., *Organizational Change for Corporate Sustainability*, 2nd ed. (London: Routledge, 2007).

[42] Chris Anderson, *The Long Tail: Why the Future of Business is Selling Less of More* (New York: Hyperion, 2006).

[43] See Donna J. Wood, Jeanne M. Logsdon, Patsy G. Lewellyn, and Kim Davenport, *Global Business Citizenship: A Transformative Framework for Ethics and Sustainable Capitalism* (Armonk, NY: M. E. Sharpe, 2006).

Managers recognize that the way to succeed is to draw on the full talents of all workers. Workers feel that they are part of the team when they provide input on products and processes. Workers then develop a sense of ownership with respect to the job and the firm, and they work better, experience less fatigue, and enjoy greater satisfaction.[44] Most people find that liking their coworkers aids job satisfaction. If coworkers are friendly, cooperative, and interested in each other, one is more likely to look forward to work.

Many American firms have programs designed to increase **employee involvement**. For example, Ford reduced the number of defects in its vehicles by 48 percent in a two-year period by enlisting the insights of workers. Ford engineers took a prototype of a pickup truck to line workers and asked for their suggestions. An assembly-line worker who had worked on a previous model pickup suggested that the design be altered to allow assemblers to bolt the pickup cargo box from above rather than from below. When bolting from below, one had to lift a heavy pneumatic wrench over one's head from a pit beneath the truck. Bolts were not firmly tightened, and customers complained. Engineers used the worker's suggestions to redesign the assembly process, resulting in easier assembly and far fewer consumer complaints.

People who are loved are less self-centered, are more concerned about others, and develop into more mature persons. Self-centeredness and insularity are vices of the immature, as we saw in Chapter 2. Love for others is a human virtue. Expressing love is a matter of giving—often without hope of return. Altruistic love is possible for anyone, although it is more readily achieved by those who have been loved. It is essential for the development of persons, families, and society, yet it is not easy. Economist Kenneth Boulding describes this sort of love:

> It always builds up, it never tears down, and it does not merely establish islands of order in a society at the cost of disorder elsewhere. It is hard for us, however, to learn to love, and the teaching of love is something at which we are still very inept.[45]

Much of the energy of the poor is spent on obtaining the necessities of life. Once a person's basic needs are reasonably satisfied, that person is more inclined to consider the needs of others in society. Thus, material security often comes prior to loving and giving. Having food and shelter enables people to reach beyond themselves and their own problems to other human beings and to realize the interdependence of people, institutions, and nations.

---

[44] See Gerald F. Cavanagh, "Evolution of Corporate Social Responsibility: Educating Stakeholders and Virtuous Entrepreneurs," in *Is the Good Corporation Dead?—Social Responsibility in a Global Economy,* eds. John W. Houck and Oliver F. Williams (Lanham, MD: Rowman & Littlefield, 1996), pp. 169–199.
[45] Kenneth E. Boulding, *The Meaning of the Twentieth Century* (New York: Harper & Row, 1964), p. 146. The importance of the manager's love and caring was reinforced in the 1995 study by Kouzes and Posner, *The Leadership Challenge* (San Francisco: Jossey-Bass, 1995).

Respect for each person requires integrity in the firm, and this begins with the firm's top managers. As a long-time veteran senior vice president at GE puts it,

> There is no more important task for the CEO than demonstrating that the top executives will be held just as accountable for lapses in integrity as they are for missing their numbers—and that the generals will be held to higher standards than the troops . . . Commercial considerations never justify cutting corners.[46]

Concern for others is an important part of the organizational climate at H-P and IBM. Aetna, L.L. Bean, Dow Chemical, Steelcase, and Johnson & Johnson have all established model programs to help their employees improve their health. These programs result in less illness and injury, and thus save money in the long term for the firm.[47]

Global Citizen with Local Control

The **entrepreneur** and the small firm are supported in the United States. The innovative and flexible entrepreneur has an essential role, when there are many changing needs. Pierre Omidyar worried that big corporations would monopolize business done on the Web. So he designed eBay, saying "I wanted to give the power of the market back to individuals." He set up the trading Web site to empower people. Its success in providing an opportunity for every person to be a buyer or seller is demonstrated by the fact that it has 248 million members across the world, and 1.3 million people indicate that selling on eBay is their primary source of income. eBay grossed $7.6 billion in 2007, and is a success as a business.[48]

Small businesses are encouraged in the United States by lower tax rates. Yet large size is often a benefit when competing in large international markets, for example, autos, computers, and some retailing. Nevertheless, encouraging entrepreneurs and limiting the government's role are traditional American values. Even in providing human services, such as education and health, independent institutions can often deliver better services at a lower cost than can government. However, global markets can concentrate wealth in the hands of a few; and seeking their human rights can lead the poor majority to violence as we see in many nations. Destroying the New York World Trade center is viewed by many as triggered by resentment of the poor at extravagance and arrogance in the United States; this sort of violence against the wealthy takes place in nations on every continent.[49]

People increasingly prefer to purchase their food from local farmers' markets, and their clothes at locally run stores. The food is fresher, healthier, and tastier, supports local farmers, and it has a much smaller "carbon footprint" (greenhouse

---

[46] Ben W. Heineman, Jr., "Avoiding Integrity Land Mines," *Harvard Business Review,* April, 2007.

[47] Jeremy Rifkin, *The European Dream: How Europe's Vision of the Future is Quietly Eclipsing the American Dream* (New York: Penguin, 2004); also Shawn Tully, "America's Healthiest Companies," *Fortune*, June 12, 1995, pp. 98–106.

[48] "The Web for The People," *BusinessWeek*, December 6, 2004, p. 18.

[49] Amy Chua, *World On Fire: How Exporting Free Market Democracy Breeds Ethnic Hatred and Global Instability* (New York: Doubleday, 2003).

gases produced in its production and transportation—that is, it is not processed and hauled great distances). These people support local entrepreneurs, and keep their city centers healthy and alive and turn them into community-gathering places. Superior food and a vibrant community are wor th the extra price to this growing group.[50]

Citizens taking responsibility for their own future, and driving responsibility as far down organizational hierarchy as possible, is a longstanding principle that Catholic social teaching calls *subsidiarity*. Each citizen and manager takes responsibility, decides, and acts, rather than expecting a superior to make the decision. Thus consumers realize that every buying decision is also a political act. Every purchase supports a particular firm, which may or may not be operating sustainably. Home Depot sells wood that is certified that it has been harvested in a sustainable manner (perhaps from tree farms, and not from old growth tropical hardwood forests). GE and Shell have invested heavily in renewable energy. Consumers can inquire whether the garments and sportswear that they purchase are manufactured in sweatshops.[51]

As long as the poor have access to the necessary services, **local control** and subsidiarity in both government and business have many advantages:

1. They give people more control over their work and lives, and thus increase personal involvement;
2. They more clearly locate responsibility;
3. They eliminate layers of organizational bureaucracy;
4. They are less costly;
5. They are in the American tradition of self-reliance; and
6. They observe the principle of subsidiarity.

The global economy can give local peoples the opportunity to compete globally. China, India, and other developing countries have innovative and flexible entrepreneurs in the global marketplace, and a few are now amassing immense fortunes.[52]

New Measures of Success

A century ago, Henry Ford broadened the notion of success for the business firm beyond what was generally accepted at the time. Ford said, "I hold that it is better to sell a large number of cars at a reasonably small profit. I hold this because it enables a larger number of people to buy and enjoy the use of a car and because it gives a larger number of men employment at good wages. Those are aims I have in life."[53] Yet today an older view still dominates.

---

[50] For data and discussion of these initiatives, see Bill McKibben, *Deep Economy: The Wealth of Communities and the Durable Future* (New York: Times Books, 2007).

[51] Thomas L. Friedman, *The World is Flat* (New York: Farrar, Strauss and Giroux, 2005), pp. 298–302.

[52] Manjeet Kripalani, "Getting the Best of the Masses: A Wave of Innovation is Yielding High-quality Goods that India's Poor Can Afford," and Bruce Einhorn, "Huawei: More Than a Local Hero: The Telecom Gear Maker Aims to be a Player in Global Innovation," *BusinessWeek,* October 11, 2004, pp. 174–184.

[53] Henry Ford, *My Life and My Work* with Samuel Crowther (London: Heinemann, 1923), pp. 161–162, quoted in *Tomorrow's Global Company: Challenges and Choices* (London: Tomorrow's Company, 2007), p. 12. This can be found at http://www.tomorrowscompany.com/uploads/TGCexcu.pdf, accessed February 22, 2008.

The free market views a person and a business firm as isolated, independent, and competing with others to survive and grow. When a firm shows a growing profit, financial analysts and *Forbes* call it a success. The firm is thus judged successful whether it makes high-quality, energy-efficient necessities with less pollution (e.g., H-P: printers; Novartis: medications) or dangerous, trivial products (Altria-Philip Morris: cigarettes). The firm might be "successful" because it lowered costs through unsafe working conditions (sweatshops) and pollution. Old school economists and business-people urge more profit, production, and consumption; an increase in GNP indicates success. However, making and selling cigarettes and hospital expenses for those with lung cancer or heart disease due to smoking all add to GNP. A serious injury from an auto accident and placing pollutants in the air also lead to an increase in GNP—the cost of repairing the damage to humans, property, and the physical environment. Can we say that the goal of business is to provide for people—whether products, services, jobs, and family income—and also to make peoples' lives healthier, safer, and happier?[54] So financial measuring criteria, that count accidents, pollution, and unnecessary hospital bills as success, have limited usefulness.

Business executives support this view when they wrote a prospectus for the future, *Tomorrow's Global Company: Challenges and Choices*.[55] They say "Tomorrow's global company should expand its view of success and redefine it in terms of lasting positive impacts for business, society and the environment." A goal of people is to obtain **happiness**, and for many this is measured by more compensation and wealth. However, for people who have met their basic needs, evidence shows that personal goals of greater wealth do not lead to happiness. People are happy when they can say "we have enough."[56] We presented the evidence for this in Chapter 2. The success of a business firm can be measured in a parallel fashion.

To be successful, a business firm must be efficient and profitable. However, most business leaders do not claim that profit maximization is the goal of business, or that such a goal automatically benefits society. Chapters 1 and 8 describe many cases where actions and policies that made money for shareholders were not good for most others. New measures of success for business firms are needed, especially when we judge that business firms operate to benefit people.[57] **Businesses are instruments of service to people**—all kinds of people. Customers and shareholders benefit, but so do employees, suppliers, and the local community. Business is not a zero-sum game; benefits to one constituency are most often not at the expense of another group. When Johnson & Johnson acts on its *Credo* (Figure 8-3), which states that its first obligation is to customers and its last to shareholders, the shareholders end up doing better than they would otherwise.

A financial audit is essential for tracking a firm's financial performance. In a similar way, criteria for judging a firm's environmental and social performance are

---

[54] William Greider, *The Soul of Capitalism: Opening Paths to a Moral Economy* (New York: Simon and Schuster, 2003); also "Humanizing Economy is Theme of Conference Held by Bishops," *America*, February 18, 2002, p. 4.

[55] See *Tomorrow's Global Company: Challenges and Choices*, op. cit., p. 4.

[56] See Robert E. Lane, *The Loss of Happiness in Market Democracies* (New Haven: Yale University Press, 2002); and Tim Kasser, *The High Price of Materialism* (Cambridge, MA: MIT Press, 2002); and Richard C. Haas, *We all Have a Share* (Chicago: ACTA Publications, 1995), p. 32.

[57] See the alternate definition of productivity in Hass, *We all Have a Share*, p. 12.

used to measure a firm's success in these areas.[58] Business executives understand the need for these additional performance measures, and many firms prepare annual environmental and social reports. Environmental and social performance thus becomes a goal of managers. We described two methods for such reporting, the **"triple bottom line"** (financial, environmental, social) and the **Global Reporting Initiative** (GRI), in Chapters 8 and 9.

Global economies should operate for the long-term well-being of all people, not just for the financial benefit of a few. If a few benefit and most suffer, it is unjust and fosters envy, instability, and violence. The global economy must be designed so that people have freedom from hunger, illiteracy, premature death from lack of health care, and the tyranny of dictatorships which tend to ignore the poorest. A market economy can accomplish person centered goals, but government regulation is required so the marketplace is a more even playing field for all.[59] Otherwise, firms will pollute and pay less than a living wage to lower their costs and thus are "free riders." They do not do a triple bottom line report and so do not provide this information to stakeholders.

Vision and Hope

Vision and hope have always been American virtues. Immigrants and the frontier inclined Americans to be optimistic about their future. But the problems now before us are immense. Many people today are concerned primarily with their own personal lives and careers, and care little about what they can do to help others who are more in need. Yet we know how to make free markets benefit all people.[60]

In this period of rapid technological change, information overload, and global competition, the best leadership is that which empowers others. A leader is effective when that leader is able to elicit the best efforts from each person. The leader empowers each worker to do their best and thus act as a "servant of the group"; this is called **servant leadership** (see Chapter 7). The Greenleaf Center supports this approach, holds seminars, and publishes books and a newsletter.[61] Another way to develop leadership skills, encourage service of others, and be servant-leaders is to volunteer to help poor people.

The problems that we face—trade and government budget deficits, jobs being outsourced, terrorism, culture divides, failing schools, broken families, pollution, refugees, and corrupt governments—are so immense that many of us find it easier not

---

[58] See S. Prakash Sethi, *Setting Global Standards: Guidelines for Creating Codes of Conduct in Multinational Corporations* (New York: John Wiley, 2003); and James E. Post, Lee E. Preston, and Sybille Sachs, *Redefining the Corporation: Stakeholder Management and Organizational Wealth* (Stanford, CA: Stanford University Press, 2002).

[59] Amartya Sen, *Development as Freedom* (New York: Alfred A. Knopf, 1999). Sen is a Nobel Prize—winning economist.

[60] See, for example, Paul Hawken, Amory Lovins, and L. Hunter Lovins, *Natural Capitalism: Creating the Next Industrial Revolution* (Boston: Little, Brown & Co., 1999).

[61] Larry Spears and Michelle Lawrence, eds., *Practicing Servant Leadership: Succeeding through Trust, Bravery and Forgiveness* (San Francisco: Jossey-Bass, 2004); and the classic Robert K. Greenleaf, *The Servant as Leader* (Newton Center, MA: Greenleaf Center, 1970). *The Servant Leader* and is a newsletter published by The Robert K. Greenleaf Center for Servant-Leadership, 921 E. 86th St., Suite 200, Indianapolis, IN 46240. See http://www.greenleaf.org.

to consider them. These problems often arise when individuals, firms, and nations try to achieve narrow, short-term goals, and disregard how it affects others. Each of us might ask ourselves: Am I willing to be more considerate of other people when I act? Am I willing to seek solutions that might cost more? How can we build the values and institutions necessary for justice and peace at home and throughout the world? As we have seen in earlier chapters, a small group or even a single talented, generous person can have a profound positive impact on the lives of many others.

Summary and Conclusions

The business challenge of the future is to provide products, services, jobs, and a reasonable standard of living for all, and at the same time leave the globe in as good or better shape than what we inherited. Through innovation business firms have achieved unprecedented efficiency, productivity, and growth. Nevertheless, on its own the market does not provide goods such as clean air, water, safe products, or even fair competition. A firm that provides goods and jobs sometimes also trashes the earth and harms people's health, thus destroying real wealth. Indeed a firm's operations may be dangerous and demeaning and use nonrenewable resources.

Providing benefits to people and encouraging cooperation are goals for business and government. Advertising, special interest pressure, apathy, and a lack of clear goals have pushed Americans into many expensive, unfruitful, and frustrating traps. Note, for example, costly and wasteful weapons systems, disappearing farmlands, collapsing railroads and urban public transportation systems, subsidies to lumbering, coal, petroleum, and nuclear power plants, defective and dangerous products, and immense fortunes for a few and no work or health care for many. The problems come from a traditional business ideology that justifies and rewards short-term thinking and selfishness. Compassionate people, who understand the common good, can rectify these costly blunders. Business firms forecast future values so that they can plan products and advertising that meets new needs. For government future planning is even more important.

Business must be innovative and efficient. In addition, citizens now expect that business decisions contribute to the good of society. A business firm is not merely a *private* enterprise; it is chartered by the state to serve the needs of society. If business firms do not act responsibly, legislation or tax incentives encourage such behavior. Surrounded by large bureaucratic corporations and government, Americans want greater independence. Individuals prefer autonomy, personal responsibility, and sharing decisions. Business depends upon and encourages such self-reliance and responsibility.

Spirituality and religion can provide a foundation for business values. Traditional spiritual values encourage love, generosity, and concern for others. Yet in the United States there is little sense of the need to sacrifice for the sake of a more important purpose. Budget deficits, pollution, crime, anxiety, and substance abuse result. Nevertheless, most would sacrifice a third automobile or a vacation in Cancun if it leads to a more satisfying job, a happier life, better relationships, and the knowledge that grandchildren will not inherit a world ravaged by deforestation and cancer-causing pollutants. Spirituality directs people's attention beyond themselves. With this perspective, many will share expertise and resources with poorer peoples of the world so that they, too, may enjoy some of the fruits of business. All major religions urge self-discipline and generosity toward neighbors, especially the stranger, based on a reverence for God and a loving concern for others.

A person who grows to maturity must be aware of one's own values and goals. Especially during times of rapid change, personal goals provide a foundation on which to build a stable, challenging, and satisfying life. The process of articulating a community's or a nation's goals and values requires leadership. Global problems are pressing and complex. Nevertheless, leaders in business, government, education, and religion, and all of us, have an opportunity to set goals that inspire hope and confidence to meet the challenges of tomorrow.

Discussion Questions

1. Outline the current major domestic and international evidence on the success of global free markets.
2. What is the difference between the vision of the "Gospel of Wealth" and the "American Dream"?
3. Describe the difference between "financial capitalism" and "democratic capitalism."
4. What do we mean when we say that free markets are aristocratic? To what extent is this true? Explain. How does an inheritance tax help to solve this problem?
5. What are the strengths and weaknesses of a democratic society in meeting new social needs—for example, public transportation, pollution control, or renewable energy?
6. How do special interests derail the acts of a democracy? Give examples. How does anti-government rhetoric impact the effectiveness of government?
7. Do you think Donald Trump and the hedge and equity fund managers, who made a fortune in this decade, will use their wealth to help other people?
8. How did you answer the questions in the section "An Aid to Core Beliefs and the Work Ethic"?
9. How do some limitations of personal freedom bring greater freedom? Give examples.
10. What are some of the future problems we have created for managers?
11. How would you describe "visionary companies"?
12. What role does spirituality have in the formation of values? What influence do religious values have on business values?
13. Outline the techniques of future forecasting. What is trend analysis through public issues scanning? What career skills will be needed in the future?
14. Which of the "future business values" listed in Table 10–1 do you think are likely to become salient? If they do become dominant, what significance would each have for your organization?
15. If these business values became prevalent, would it increase or decrease the quality of life? Explain.
16. Are "cookies," which track your Internet purchases for Amazon and other firms to use to sell to you, an invasion of your right to privacy?
17. What is the difference between the "cowboy economy" and the "spaceship economy"? Which model is more appropriate for our future? Why?
18. Would people be better or worse off if they could meet their needs with less consumption and less use of resources?

19. The design, making, and selling of which innovative sustainable products hold promise of providing new business opportunities?

20. Does it make any difference whether one's job is to help to produce cell phones, plastic packaging, automobiles, cigarettes, throw-away bottles, nutritious foods, or Coca-cola? Are all goods of equal value to society?

21. Americans need to save more to provide for investment and to reduce foreign borrowing. What portion of your take-home pay do you save? How much does your family save? Why?

22. What does servant leadership mean? Does it encourage an effective or ineffective leadership style? Explain.

23. What examples in your workplace show a particular respect for human dignity? Which do not? What examples of "local control" have you experienced in your firm, your neighborhood, and your life?

24. If we are becoming more globally interdependent, what does this mean for a firm? For you as a citizen?

25. Is an increase in GNP a mark of success for an economy? Why or why not? Can you suggest additional criteria for the success of an economy?

26. Is it possible for us to build the values and institutions necessary for peace and justice at home and throughout the world? Is it important that this take place? Is it likely that this will happen?

27. Are you willing to alter your actions to be more considerate of other people and to bring about greater peace and justice? Are you willing to seek solutions that might cost you something?

Selected Additional Readings

Lester R. Brown, *Plan B 3.0: Rescuing a Planet under Stress and a Civilization in Trouble* (New York: W. W. Norton, 2008).

Amy Chua, *World On Fire: How Exporting Free Market Democracy Breeds Ethnic Hatred and Global Instability* (New York: Doubleday, 2003).

Jared Diamond, *Collapse: How Societies Choose to Fall or Succeed* (New York: Viking, 2004).

Thomas L. Friedman, *The World is Flat* (New York: Farrar, Straus and Giroux, 2005).

William Gates, Sr. and Chuck Collins, *Wealth and Our Commonwealth: Why America Should Tax Accumulated Fortunes* (Boston: Beacon Press, 2003).

Charles O. Holliday, Stephan Schmidheiny, and Phillip Watts, *Walking the Talk: The Business Case for Sustainable Development* (San Francisco: Berrett-Koehler, 2002).

CASES

Case 10-1   Canon Manufactures at Home

Japanese companies have moved manufacturing to Thailand, Malaysia, Taiwan, and China. But Canon decided that it can make its digital cameras faster and more efficiently at home, and will thus keep 60 percent of its manufacturing in Japan. Although monthly wage rates were $3,737 in Japan vs. $126 in China, Canon improves innovation by keeping research close to manufacturing. Canon has also eliminated the traditional assembly line, and replaced conveyer belts with "cells" where workers perform multiple tasks. In these cells, workers feel more responsible for the process and talk about how to improve it. Although Canon knows it cannot compete on price, it feels its customers will pay more for a better quality camera.[62]

1. Is this strategy of Canon realistic?
2. Is it a strategy that could be viable for other firms?
3. What are the advantages and disadvantages of such a policy?
4. What ethical norms would help you judge this case?
5. Does Canon's strategy respect human dignity? Explain.

■ ■ ■

Case 10-2   Local Manager in Trouble

You are the U.S.-based head of overseas operations for Digital Systems. You learn that one of your plant managers has been arrested in Kenya. His alleged "crime" is that goods found in your warehouse lack the proper customs stamps and papers.

But the truth is more complicated. For years, "grease" has been a way of life in Kenya's bureaucracy, and your plant manager has been paying gratuities to the customs officers. A new manager knows that it is against home office policy, so he stops doing so. The price for dropping all charges is $40,000.

1. What would you do? Would you pay the "fine"?
2. Would you let the plant manager be put in jail?
3. What ethical norms are most helpful here?

---

[62] Sebastian Moffett, "Separation Anxiety: Japan's Canon, Inc. Believes the Secret to Innovation is Keeping Most of it at Home," *The Wall Street Journal*, September 27, 2004, p. B11.

INDEX